END-USER LICENSE AGREEMENT FOR ALLYN AND BACON SOFTWARE

You should carefully read the following terms and conditions before opening this Disk package. Opening this Disk package indicates your acceptance of these terms and conditions. If you do not agree with them, you should promptly return the package unopened.

Allyn and Bacon provides this Program and Licenses its use. You assume responsibility for the selection of the Program to achieve your intended results, and for the installation, use, and results obtained from the Program. This License extends only to use of the Program in the United States or countries in which the Program is marketed by duly authorized distributors.

License Grant

You hereby accept a nonexclusive, nontransferable, permanent License to install and use the Program on a single computer at any given time. You may copy the Program solely for backup or archival purposes in support of your use of the Program on the single computer. You may not modify, translate, disassemble, decompile, or reverse engineer the Program, in whole or in part.

Term

This License is effective until terminated. Allyn and Bacon reserves the right to terminate this License automatically if any provision of the License is violated. You may terminate the License at any time. To terminate this License, you must return the Program, including documentation, along with a written warranty stating that all copies of the Program in your possession have been returned or destroyed.

Limited Warranty

The Program is provided "As Is" without warranty of any kind, either express or implied, including, but not limited to, the implied warranties or merchantability and fitness for a particular purpose. The entire risk as to the quality and performance of the Program is with you. Should the Program prove defective, you (and not Allyn and Bacon or any authorized distributor) assume the entire cost of all necessary servicing, repair, or correction. No oral or written information or advice given by Allyn and Bacon, its dealers, distributors, or agents shall create a warranty or increase the scope of its warranty

Some states do not allow the exclusion of implied warranty, so the above exclusion may not apply to you. This warranty gives you specific legal rights and you may also have other rights that vary from state to state.

Allyn and Bacon does not warrant that the functions contained in the Program will meet your requirements or that the operation of the Program will be uninterrupted or error free.

However, Allyn and Bacon warrants the disk(s) on which the Program is furnished to be free from defects in material and workmanship under normal use for a period of ninety (90) days form the date of delivery to you as evidenced by a copy of your receipt.

The Program should not be relied on as the sole basis to solve a problem whose incorrect solution could result in injury to a person or property. IF the Program is employed in such a manner, its is at the user's own risk and Allyn and Bacon explicitly disclaims all liability for such misuse.

Limitation of Remedies

Allyn and Bacon's entire liability and your exclusive remedy shall be:

1. The replacement of any Disk not meeting Allyn and Bacon's "Limited Warranty" and that is returned to Allyn and Bacon or

2. If Allyn and Bacon is unable to deliver a replacement Disk that is free of defects in materials or workmanship, you may terminate this Agreement by returning the Program.

In no event will Allyn and Bacon be liable to you for any damages, including any lost profits, lost savings, or other incidental or consequential damages arising out of the use or inability to use such Program even if Allyn and Bacon or an authorized distributor has been advised of the possibility of such damages or for any claim by any other party.

Some states do not allow the limitation or exclusion of liability for incidental or consequential damages, so the above limitation or exclusion may not apply to you.

General

You may not sublicense, assign, or transfer the License of the Program. Any attempt to sublicense, assign, or transfer any of the rights, duties, or obligations hereunder is void.

This Agreement will be governed by the laws of the State of Massachusetts.

Should you have any questions concerning this Agreement, or any questions concerning technical support, you may contact Allyn and Bacon by writing to:

Allyn and Bacon
Pearson Education, Inc.
75 Arlington Street
Boston, MA 02116

You acknowledge that you have read this Agreement, understand it, and agree to be bound by its terms and conditions. You further agree that it is the complete and exclusive statement of the Agreement between us that supersedes any proposal or prior Agreement, oral or written, and any other communications between us relating to the subject matter of this Agreement.

Notice To Government End Users

The Program is provided with restricted rights. Use, duplication, or disclosure by the Government is subject to restrictions set forth in subdivison (b)(3)(iii) of The Rights in Technical Data and Computer Software Clause 252.227-7013.

Research Methods

A Process of Inquiry
(with Student CD-ROM)

FIFTH EDITION

Anthony M. Graziano

State University of New York at Buffalo

Michael L. Raulin

State University of New York at Buffalo

Boston • New York • San Francisco
Mexico City • Montreal • Toronto • London • Madrid • Munich • Paris
Hong Kong • Singapore • Tokyo • Cape Town • Sydney

Series Editor: *Kelly May*
Editorial Assistant: *Marlana Voerster*
Marketing Manager: *Taryn Wahlquist*
Editorial Production Service: *Raeia Maes*
Manufacturing Buyer: *JoAnne Sweeney*
Cover Administrator: *Linda Knowles*
Electronic Composition: *Omegatype Typography, Inc.*

For related titles and support materials, visit our online catalog at www.ablongman.com.

Between the time Web site information is gathered and then published, it is not unusual for some sites to have closed. Also, the transcription of URLs can result in typographical errors. The publisher would appreciate being notified of any problems with URLs so that they may be corrected in subsequent editions.

Library of Congress Cataloging-in-Publication Data

Graziano, Anthony M.
  Research methods: a process of inquiry / Anthony M. Graziano, Michael L. Raulin.—5th ed.
    p. cm.
  Includes bibliographical references and index.
  ISBN 0-205-36065-3
    1. Research—Methodology.   I. Raulin, Michael L.   II. Title.

Q180.55.M44G7 2004
001.4'2—dc21

2003040313

Printed in the United States of America
10   9   8   7   6   5   4   3   2   08   07   06   05   04   03

To Murray Levine and Joseph Masling, our good friends and colleagues

"Brothers all,

In honor, as in one community,

Scholars and gentlemen."

(William Wordsworth 1770–1850, The Prelude*)*

Contents

4　*Data and the Nature of Measurement*　76

15　*Research Methodology: An Evolving Discipline*　338

Preface

To the Instructor

The fifth edition of *Research Methods: A Process of Inquiry* is a major step in the evolution of this learning package, which now consists of three units: the textbook and two CDs. These units are integrated to enhance their value to students and faculty. This package has evolved over years of teaching research methods, supervising student research, conducting and reporting our own research, and continuously revising earlier editions of the text. The textbook is the anchor for this package. It provides all the necessary content for a research methods course, with supportive elements to aid students' learning. This fifth edition package includes both a free *Student Resource CD* and an optional statistical analysis CD (*SPSS for Windows*). Both will be described later in this preface.

Pedagogical Considerations: Teaching Concepts of Research

The pedagogical needs of undergraduates have guided every phase of the development of all five editions, culminating in this text and CD learning package. Every change for this fifth edition has been designed to enhance content, functioning, readability, and interest level. Research concepts, rather than cookbook-like strategies, are emphasized in order to help students to develop an understanding of scientific research as both an integrated process of thinking and an exciting enterprise. We want students to appreciate that science involves the continuous interplay of rationalism and empiricism, a combination that makes stringent and unique demands on the nature of evidence and of the research methods used. The first two chapters provide a basic foundation of scientific concepts to support the subsequent presentation of research methods.

Programmatic Nature of the Text

We believe that difficult or unfamiliar concepts are best taught programmatically. Thus, complex concepts, for example, validity, operational definitions, and statistical inference, are introduced and defined early in the text, but only to the degree needed for those introductory discussions. Concepts are then systematically reexamined throughout the text, new facets are added, and related concepts are brought together into a coherent model, progressively building more complete and sophisticated conceptualizations. This programmatic development of concepts:

- Provides students with systematic, progressive mastery of ideas, beginning with basic levels and building to more complex and more complete concepts.

- Results in sequential rather than independent chapters, each chapter building on earlier material.
- Requires repetition—the same concepts are discussed several times, but at progressively higher levels of sophistication.
- Requires a coherent theoretical model of research.

The programmatic approach makes complex material more accessible and understandable to students. A complete glossary and a detailed index are included to help students quickly locate specific material and discussions.

Learning Aids Integrated within the Text

Consistent with our pedagogical focus, this fifth edition provides numerous learning aids for students, including:

- A *Student Resource CD* that includes dozens of learning resources, many of them interactive
- Quick-Check Reviews and end-of-chapter summaries
- A list of Key Terms at the end of each chapter and extensive review exercises in the interactive *Study Guide/Lab Manual* on the *Student Resource CD*
- Informational boxes that are set off from the chapter content
- Unique decision-tree flowcharts to teach students how to select appropriate statistical analyses
- A Pre-Data Checklist of items that must be completed before data collection (similar to the preflight checklists used by pilots)
- A Glossary with over 500 terms defined for the student
- Suggested readings for further study
- An expanded treatment of the history of psychology
- Programmatic development of concepts
- Presentation of a coherent model of research
- Extensive use of examples, several of which are repeated to provide continuity to the presentation
- An integrated Web site with additional resources and links to other relevant sites
- Appendices on:
  - Using the *Student Resource CD* and Web site
  - Writing a Research Report in APA Style
  - Conducting Library Research
  - Table of Random Numbers
  - Answers to Quick-Check Review questions

A Coherent Model of the Research Enterprise

This text organizes the research process around a coherent descriptive model. This model integrates inductive and deductive reasoning, empirical observation, concepts of validity, and the phases of research (the basic steps through which each research project progresses). The model also introduces the concept of levels of constraint, which refers to the degree of control that the researcher exercises over the research process. Valuable research can be carried out at any level of constraint, a point on which we differ from some other textbook authors. Experimental research (Chapters 8 to 12) is the most rigorous and allows us to answer questions of causality. But other research questions are also important, such as questions about the strength and direction of the relationships among variables, about differences between already existing groups, and about individuals and their response to treatment. Furthermore, scientific observations can lead to the formation, rather than the testing, of causal hypotheses. All are properly scientific approaches. It is important for students to learn that appropriate scientific research design largely depends on the nature of the questions asked and that research at all levels, whether naturalistic, case study, correlation, differential, quasi-experimental, or experimental, is appropriate and useful. The text builds conceptual foundations leading to experimental research by developing each level of constraint, thereby providing students with a full spectrum of research knowledge and skills. We have devoted three chapters (6, 7, and 13) to nonexperimental research procedures because we believe that nonexperimental designs are valuable tools for the psychologist.

Research Ethics

Ethical considerations are an integral part of the research design process. Because of the importance of ethical issues, this topic has been introduced early in Chapter 3 and, consistent with the text's general organization, is returned to at later points for more detailed discussions. Our intent is to create sensitivity in students for ethical issues in both human and animal research and to teach basic skills in dealing with these issues.

Treatment of Statistics

This is a research design text, not a statistics text. However, because research design and statistics are so closely connected, an appropriate discussion of statistics must be included. Decisions regarding statistical analyses are an integral part of the design process and are not to be added after data collection. Basic statistical concepts are introduced early in the text (Chapters 4 and 5), and their integration into the design process is maintained throughout. Statistical procedures are presented conceptually, with an emphasis on understanding what they can do. Choosing an appropriate statistical procedure often confuses students. We teach that the choice of appropriate statistical analyses follows systematically from the design characteristics of the study. Chapter 14 presents a unique addition to research methods texts—flowcharts that lead the student step by step through the characteristics of any basic research design to the choice of appropriate statistical analysis procedures. We also discuss on the *Student Resource CD* how to use computer analysis packages for data analyses and how to read and interpret the output. In addition, an optional *SPSS for Windows CD* is available. This CD provides a working copy of *SPSS for Windows* for students to use. The bulk of the statistical coverage in the text is conceptual, whereas the *Student Resource CD* includes computational procedures and other statistical resources, such as statistical tables. This organization gives instructors maximum flexibility, allowing them to cover as much or as little statistical material as they wish.

The Student Resource CD

This fifth edition includes a free CD, the *Student Resource CD,* that provides a variety of rich resources for students. Recognizing that most, but not all, students have access to computing resources, we have been careful not to sacrifice anything in the text for the CD. The textbook covers all essential topics, so no student is *required* to use the CD for coverage of core material (unless assigned by the instructor). But for those instructors and students who want to use the CD, there is a wealth of information, pedagogical aids, and other useful resources. This *Student Resource CD* was assembled so that it could be accessed with the student's favorite web browser (Netscape Navigator or Internet Explorer). *Our goal is nothing less than to provide the most comprehensive set of student learning supplements of any research methods textbook on the market.*

Rather than being a supplement to the textbook, the *Student Resource CD* has become an electronic extension of the textbook. Provided free with the textbook, this CD is designed to

- be used interactively with the text;
- clarify conceptual material presented in the textbook;
- present examples of research concepts, procedures, and findings;
- expand concepts to higher levels for those students and instructors who wish to go beyond the usual limits of their immediate research methods course; and
- introduce new material that is not ordinarily presented in methods textbooks.

The *Student Resource CD* provides dozens of specific resources. Instructors and students can select the elements that are most helpful from the following resources:

- An **interactive study guide/lab manual** with chapter summaries; key terms that are hyperlinked to the glossary; sample fill-in-the-blank, true–false, and multiple-choice examination questions with immediate feedback; sample essay questions; laboratory exercises; and suggested readings
- A **library research tutorial** with examples of library searches and exercises to improve the students' library skills
- An **APA style tutorial and reference manual** to provide students with both the basics of the APA style and access to more advanced features, without the necessity of purchasing the *APA Style Manual*
- A **glossary** linked to other resources on the CD
- A **random-number generator program,** with instructions for its use in sampling and assigning subjects to groups
- **Research examples,** organized by both chapter and topic, drawn from both classic and current research
- **Statistical computation instructions** for those faculty who want students to do manual computation of statistical procedures
- **Additional supplementary resources,** such as background information on topics covered in the text, more extensive coverage of topics only introduced in the text, and explanatory examples to help students to understand difficult

concepts. For example, an extensive section on the history of science and psychology provides the equivalent of nearly 100 pages of additional text, with material that is not covered in any other research methods textbook.

Although the CD material is not necessary for the basic usefulness of the textbook, it greatly enhances students' learning experiences. It should also provide students with a valuable reference resource to use throughout their undergraduate career.

The *SPSS for Windows CD* (available at additional cost) provides one of the most comprehensive and easy to use data analysis programs. Instructors can arrange to have the CD bundled with the textbook. This CD includes a working copy of *SPSS for Windows,* Student Edition. This is a powerful and intuitive program that should be able to meet the needs of your students in this course and beyond. The program will run for 13 months after being installed on your student's computer.

Contacting the Authors

Feel free to e-mail either of us at any time with questions, comments, and suggestions. The instructors using this text have been our single best source of ideas for improvement. Our e-mail addresses are

Anthony Graziano: amgraz@acsu.buffalo.edu
Michael Raulin: MikeRaulin@aol.com

Additional Supplements

In addition to the *Student Resource CD,* which is packaged with every copy of the textbook, and the *SPSS for Windows CD,* the adoption package includes an *Instructor's Manual* and a Computerized Test-Item File. The *Instructor's Manual* provides

- a brief outline of the focus of each chapter and the topics covered;
- identification of controversies in the field, with appropriate background reading;
- a selected bibliography; and
- over 2500 multiple-choice test items keyed to text pages on which the material is discussed.

The computerized test-item file utilizes the TestGen-EQ Program, which allows instructors to select from the 2500 plus multiple-choice items, modify or write new items, and construct examinations. This program is available in both Windows and Mac versions.

New in the Fifth Edition

The first four editions of this text were highly successful. The text has been adopted at hundreds of colleges and universities. The approach outlined previously has been continued in this fifth edition. In addition, we have made the following improvements:

- A greatly expanded *Student Resource CD* that provides instructional resources well beyond those available from any other research methods textbook
- An updated final chapter on new directions in research methodology
- A new interactive Laboratory Manual on the *Student Resource CD*
- Additional and expanded informational essays on the *Student Resource CD*
- An extensive new CD section on the history of psychology
- Extensive rewriting and reorganization for improved clarity
- More than 200 content changes within the text, including:

  New informational boxes throughout the text
  Quick-Check Review questions within chapters
  Updated examples and references
  Expanded treatment of research ethics
  Expanded treatment of the history of psychology
  An expanded glossary

- An expanded test-item file

Acknowledgments

A project of this scope would not be possible without the valuable assistance of many people. We want to acknowledge the remarks and suggestions of our many reviewers.

Vincent J. Adesso
University of Wisconsin, Milwaukee

Patricia L. Alexander
Long Beach City College

Jeffrey S. Anastasi
Francis Marion University

Joanne C. Basta
Niagara University

Burt R. Brown
Rutgers—The State University of New Jersey

Steven L. Cohen
Bloomsburg University

Donald A. Czech
Marquette University

Wendy Domjan
University of Texas at Austin

Stephen E. Edgell
University of Louisville

Jeffrey S. Feddon
Florida State University

Mary Beth Gilboy
Immaculata College

Gregory T. Golden
Immaculata College

Timothy E. Goldsmith
The University of New Mexico

Lawrence R. Gordon
University of Vermont

Robert Grissom
San Francisco State University

Richard Hagen
Florida State University

Charles G. Halcomb
Texas Tech University

Madeline Heilman
New York University

John P. Hostetler
Albion College

Sherri L. Jackson
Jacksonville University

James L. Pate
Georgia State University

Linda James
Georgian Court College

Samuel L. Seaman
Baylor University

Cindy J. Lahar
University of Calgary

Jerry I. Shaw
California State University Northridge

Daniel W. Leger
University of Nebraska

Jobie Skaggs
Bradley University

Margaret F. Lynch
San Francisco State University

Patrick D. Slattery
Auburn University at Montgomery

Richard G. Marriott
Lamar University

Robert M. Stern
The Pennsylvania State University

Karen M. McCollam
University of Virginia

David A. Stevens
Clark University

Linda Mealey
College of St. Benedict/St. John's University

Lois E. Tetrick
Wayne State University

Peter Urcuioli
Purdue University

Daniel D. Moriarty, Jr.
University of San Diego

Frank W. Weathers
Auburn University

Robert M. Murphey
University of California, Davis

Several faculty colleagues provided valuable consultation in earlier editions of this text, including Irving Biederman, B. Richard Bugelski, Jennifer Crocker, Jeremy Finn, Edwin Hollander, Elaine Hull, Mark Kristal, Murray Levine, Kenneth Levy, Brenda Major, John Meacham, Dean Pruitt, James Sawusch, and C. James Smith.

To the Student

This fifth edition of *Methods* is a teaching package that consists of the basic textbook plus a *Student Resource CD*. An additional statistics CD is also available. These elements are designed to be used actively by the student. We cannot emphasize too strongly that you should use these CD resources along with the textbook. The CDs are described below.

Many people imagine scientists as white-coated individuals in mysterious laboratories, spending their days squinting at huge assemblies of complicated, flashing, smoking, or data-spewing equipment. But scientific work can be done while sitting under a tree in the woods, thinking through a problem, and using apparatus no more technical than a pad and pencil. This woodsy image emphasizes that the essence of science is its logic. Science is, above all else, *a way of thinking*. The laboratories, equipment, computers, and all the hardware are tools that promote the scientists' central activity—creative, systematic thinking. This intellectual activity is carried out through a *process of inquiry* in which scientists ask and answer questions about nature. This process of inquiry is what we mean by scientific research, and it is the focus of this text.

Our text has two major educational goals. The first is to provide students with the background to become sophisticated consumers of research. We want you to be able to evaluate the many claims for all sorts of products, ideas, and programs that bombard us daily. Too many people in our society, even supposedly educated people, are intellectually hobbled by their lack of knowledge about how to evaluate the validity of such claims. In some ways, adults are as naïve as children and can be easily taken in by pseudoscientific claims and promises. Just look at the number of people who believe in useless health fads, astrology, ESP, alien space abductions, or the superiority of one brand of beer over another.

How do people decide which information is valid? All of us use common ways of doing this, and our everyday methods sometimes lead us down troubled paths. We tend to rely on our hunches, already existing ideas, and respected authorities for answers to our questions. We seldom seek answers in the systematic manner of science. Although thinking scientifically is unfamiliar to most people, it can be learned, and this is the major challenge in this course. We want you to learn to think critically and systematically, to phrase questions clearly, and to demand solid evidence.

Excitement, hunches, vague suspicions, and flashes of insight are very much part of science. So are hard work, rigorous thinking, and procedures that put our ideas to many demanding tests. You will learn to have more confidence in ideas that survive the rigors of scientific scrutiny and to discard those that do not. Knowing how to think scientifically can be a great help, not for all decisions, but for many important ones that are demanded of each of us.

The second educational goal of this text is an elaboration of the first. We want to provide each student with a solid basis for further study in psychology and related disciplines. Our aim is to present basic ideas and to develop your understanding of the processes of scientific research. Learning this material will prepare you for the more sophisticated and complex work required in advanced courses. Some of you may even decide to go on to research careers in psychology.

Organization of the Text

This text has been organized along a definite progression of ideas. You will find that new and complex concepts are introduced to you within familiar contexts and without a great deal of initial elaboration. As you use this text and your sophistication grows, you will see these concepts expanded and progressively linked to other ideas. This progression of ideas has been carefully planned and refined over several editions of this text; it is a programmatic approach designed to maximize your learning and minimize your frustrations.

As you will learn, modern science is a process of gaining knowledge; indeed, the term *science* means "having knowledge." People have used many methods of gaining knowledge about the world, science being only one of them. Chapter 1 provides you with a brief account of the history of science that will help you to appreciate its dynamic nature, growth, and contemporary importance and some of the social and political reasons why today's conflicts between science and some parts of society are the same issues that were debated more than 2000 years ago.

Chapter 2 presents our model of the research process; this model provides the primary organization for the text. Science, as you will learn, is our most sophisticated way of gaining knowledge, but even within science there are different levels of sophistication in the research process. These are *levels of constraint,* and they are defined by the limits and precision of their research methods. Even the lowest level of constraint, *naturalistic observation,* is scientific if it uses the logic and investigative processes that define science. Chapters 3 through 5 present important concepts that underlie all sciences: formulating questions, defining the variables to be studied, resolving ethical issues, measuring the variables, statistically evaluating data, and interpreting and communicating findings. These are core concepts, and they are frequently revisited throughout the text as you learn more about the actual research process.

Starting with Chapter 6, specific research approaches are covered, beginning with the most flexible and informal lower-constraint methods and progressing to the most sophisticated experimental research designs. Chapters 6 and 7 are devoted to the lower-constraint methods, which students often find more intuitive and understandable. With this background established, you will move on to formal discussions of validity (Chapter 8) and methods of enhancing validity (Chapter 9). You will have been introduced to the concept of validity earlier in the text, and by Chapter 10 you will have the understanding needed to expand your understanding of this critical concept as the primary goal of all scientific research. With the concept of validity well established, you will move on to the most sophisticated and precise of scientific methods: experimentation (Chapters 10 to 12). You will then take another look at research in naturalistic settings (Chapter 13) and learn that such research need not be low constraint, but actually may use the sophisticated logic of experimentation.

Chapter 14 presents two important organizational tools to help you to pull everything together, the decisional flowcharts for selecting statistical procedures and a pre-data checklist. Finally, Chapter 15 surveys the new directions of scientific research and how these are changing our research methods.

Several appendices are included as valuable resources for you. These include instructions for using the *Student Resource CD* that is provided free with this text, an outline on how to write a research report, a discussion of library research procedures, a random number table for selecting research participants and assigning participants to groups, and answers to the Quick-Check Review questions. The *Student Resource CD* has expanded versions of many of these appendices.

As the text progresses, you will see how basic concepts are expanded, becoming more inclusive and complex, and how the organizational model unfolds. You will learn how to understand research reports, identify weaknesses in research designs, and design your own research. You will also learn how to plan a research project, conduct a literature search, and prepare an introduction to your project. You will learn how best to phrase research questions and to identify, define, and carefully measure and control the variables to be studied. Finally, you will be introduced to statistical procedures for data analyses and how to interpret and communicate your results.

Study Aids

The best way to learn anything is to process the material *actively.* Therefore, this text has been created for your *active use* and not for just passive reading. A number of important learning aids have been included to help you to study, and you are urged to take advantage of them and be a particularly active participant in your studying.

Information is remembered best if it is organized. A good textbook includes important organizational aids. Unfortunately, many students ignore them or have never learned how to use them. Each chapter opens with an *outline,* which lists the major topics in the chapter. Do not skip this material; it will give you an overview of the concepts and their organization in the chapter and will facilitate your learning. Each chapter includes several *Quick-Check Review questions* and a *Chapter Summary.* Use these review questions and summaries to pause and to integrate what you have read; do not simply read them or, worse yet, skip them. Think about them, reword them in your mind, and relate them to things you already know. Reading is not enough; it is a trap that gives the illusion of learning. You have probably had the experience of spending an evening reading an entire chapter only to realize that you do not remember a thing about what you had just read! You do not learn much by reading; you learn by processing. Process the organization of the chapter by focusing on the chapter outlines at the beginning of the chapter; read the material and then process the content by using the Quick-Check Review questions to force you to think about what you read.

A number of other features have been included to help your active processing of the material. We have already talked about the Quick-Check Review questions. In addition, a list of *Key Terms* for each chapter is provided. Don't just skim the key terms; try to define each of them. This activity will help you to clarify ideas and provide good rehearsal for examinations. You will also find a *Glossary* and an *Index* to help you to track down information. Consult the glossary when needed and, if you want more information on a topic, use the index to direct you to appropriate text pages.

The Student Resource CD

The *Student Resource CD* provides a variety of resources for each chapter. Each chapter lists the relevant *Student Resource CD* material right after the chapter outline. Instructions on how to use this CD are included in Appendix A of the text. You access the material on this CD using your favorite web browser, but because all the material is already on your machine, the material loads much faster than if you were getting it from the Internet.

The *Student Resource CD* includes a *Study Guide/Lab Manual,* which will provide interactive rehearsal for exams and hands-on exercises to develop your research skills. There are also tutorials on statistical analysis, library research, and writing research reports in APA style. There are also extended discussions of peripheral topics, such as how to compute reliability indices and an extended discussion of the history of psychology and science. Many of these resources will be particularly useful in later courses, when you are asked to do independent research or write papers.

SPSS for Windows CD

The *SPSS for Windows CD* can be packaged with the text at your instructor's discretion. You may be able to order the CD through your university bookstore or through the publishers Web site (*www.ablongman.com*). This CD provides a student version of the most popular statistical analysis package in the field at a very reasonable price. It performs virtually all standard statisical analyses and is easy to set up and run. In addition to the tutorials that are included on the *SPSS for Windows* CD, there are also extensive tutorials on the *Student Resource CD* on how to use *SPSS for Windows*. This special student version will run for 13 months after it is installed on your computer.

Authors' Statement

Our goal in writing this text and supplemental package is to provide you with more than just a textbook for one course. We hope it will serve for you as a reference source to aid your research and writing throughout college. The *Student Resource CD* contains material to facilitate your original learning in a research methods course (such as the *Study Guide/Lab Manual*), as well as materials to use in future courses (such as a statistical analysis tutorial, information on writing papers in APA style, and background on advanced topics that are often not covered in research methods texts).

Please send us your comments and evaluations of this text using the evaluation form included on the *Student Resource CD* or available at our Web site. You can also contact us through e-mail (amgraz@acsu.buffalo.edu; MikeRaulin@aol.com).

A. M. G.
M. L. R.

1

Curiosity, Creativity, and Commitment

Among scientists are collectors, classifiers, and compulsive tidiers-up; many are detectives by temperament, and many are explorers; some are artists, and others artisans. There are poet–scientists, philosopher–scientists, and even a few mystics.

—Peter Bryan Medawar, 1967, *The Art of the Soluble*

CD Resource Material[1]

- Extended Discussion of the History of Science
- Extended Discussion of the History of Psychology
- A Primer on Logic

- List of the Divisions of the American Psychological Association
- Student Study Guide/Laboratory Manual

[1]At the beginning of each chapter is a list such as this of resource material available on the *Student Resource CD* and on the Web site for the text. See Appendix A for details on how to access these resources.

Web Resource Material

- History of Science Sites
- History of Psychology Sites
- History of Psychology Organizations
- Pseudoscience Sites
- Home Pages for Psychological Societies

Psychology is a discipline devoted to the scientific study of behavior, especially human behavior. This textbook covers the many research strategies that are used in modern psychology. The text avoids a simple cataloging of these research methods, focusing instead on the rationale behind each approach. As authors, we designed the text with several features to facilitate learning. To benefit from these features, you must understand the best way to use them. We recommend that you read the Preface, especially the section labeled *To the Student* before you read any further.

To understand the science of psychology, we must first understand science. This first chapter begins with a brief discussion of science. It then contrasts the methods of science with other approaches to gaining knowledge. There is a brief review of the history of science, followed by a review of the history of psychology. The chapter closes with a discussion of psychology as a science, which provides the rationale and philosophy for the entire text.

Science

Science is one of several ways of learning about the world. It employs both systematic observation and rational processes to create new knowledge. This section begins by describing how scientists think about the world. It then focuses on how scientists ask questions and concludes with a discussion of the similarities between science and art.

Science Is a Way of Thinking

Scientists seek knowledge through research that is designed to answer their questions. Science is built on highly refined skills in asking and answering questions. Knowing how to ask questions is as critical as knowing how to answer them. **Scientific research** is a process of formulating specific questions and then finding answers in order to understand nature better. Science is a **process of inquiry**—a particular way of thinking.

This process of inquiry generates many tools and useful products, such as laboratory equipment, statistical procedures, computers, space flight, medicines, consumer goods, and powerful weapons. People too often mistake the tools and products of science for its essence, but the essence of science is the scientist's ways of thinking—the logic used in systematically asking and answering questions. A scientist can operate scientifically while sitting under a tree in the woods, thinking through a problem, and using apparatus no more technical than paper and pencil. It is not the bubbling liquids and laboratory equipment that make the discipline of chemistry scientific. Likewise, knowing how to use an electron microscope or run a computer program does not define a scientist. The television image of the white-coated laboratory worker surrounded by complex machines is an effective visual metaphor, but it does not validly portray the essence of science any more than, to use another metaphor, a skyscraper really scrapes the sky. *The essence of modern science is the way of thinking, the disciplined way in which questions are posed and answered. It is the logical processes and demands for evidence, and not the technologies, that lie at the center of science. It is an intellectual process, and its ultimate goal is to understand the natural universe.*

Asking Questions

Asking questions is not new. Socrates and his students asked sophisticated questions over 2400 years ago. A question is one side of an idea; on the other side is an unknown quantity—a potential answer. Every question points to the existence of an unknown, to some area of human ignorance or uncertainty. Socrates knew, apparently to his delight, that posing sharp questions about religion, politics, and morality could spear even the most dignified citizens, revealing their ignorance and uncertainties. Unfortunately for Socrates, the good citizens were made so uncomfortable that they executed him as a subversive and corrupter of youth. It was thus established early in history that asking questions may be hazardous to one's health. But risk taking is part of every scientist's work. Those who raise questions and expose ignorance create social and political strains, and often these people suffer serious reprisals. Leonardo da Vinci and Galileo threatened church dogma concerning the nature of the solar system. Charles Darwin, Alfred Russel Wallace, and a number of 19th-century geologists presented data that questioned the biblical account of creation and the biblically derived age of Earth. But such conflicts did not occur only in the distant historical past. Consider the trial of John T. Scopes (the "monkey trial") in 1925. Scopes was a public school science teacher who was convicted of violating a Tennessee state law that prohibited teaching Darwinian evolution in public schools. Teaching evolution was prohibited because it contradicted the biblical account of creation. The guilty verdict was later voided on a procedural technicality, but the scripture-based law remained intact until 1965. More recently, in 1999, the Kansas State Board of Education effectively removed the teaching of evolution from the state-mandated primary and secondary school curriculum (Gillam, 1999). It was reinstated later upon the election of new state school board members.

Government officials often interfere with the free pursuit and exchange of knowledge. Scientific knowledge has become so important that competing governments impose secrecy on their scientists. For example, U.S. agents canceled 100 scheduled papers at an engineering convention in 1982 because the Department of Defense was concerned that some of the information might be of military value to Russia, whose scientists were in attendance. The tension between scientists' needs to communicate freely and a nation's needs for security continue today (Glanz, 2000).

Another example of state censorship involved the 1989 Exxon Oil spill in Prince William Sound, Alaska. Government scientists and technicians gathered information that was critical for the cleanup efforts. Yet, despite the urgent public need for the information, Alaska's attorney general ordered state scientists not to publish, publicly discuss, or otherwise disclose their data, fearing that such information might be of use to the Exxon Corporation in legal actions (Busch, 1991). Governments have a long history of trying to control scientific information for their own purposes, including governments that profess to value the free expression of ideas.

Scientists resolve questions, not by reasserting old beliefs, but by studying the questions and seeking new answers. Scientists are pervasive **skeptics;** that is, they constantly challenge accepted wisdom in their search for more complete answers. They are willing to tolerate uncertainty and find intellectual excitement in raising questions and seeking answers about nature (Sternberg & Lubart, 1992). Asking a question is a creative endeavor that provides scientists with the personal satisfaction of exercising their curiosity, a major motivator for scientists. "What?" "How?" and "What if?" are basic in the scientist's vocabulary. Curiosity may have killed the cat, according to the old saying, but curiosity sustains the scientist. J. Robert Oppenheimer (1956), whose research team helped to create the atomic bomb, noted that scientific research is "responsive to a primitive, permanent, pervasive human curiosity" (p. 128). According to Linus Pauling (1981), who was awarded two Nobel prizes, satisfying our curiosity is one of life's greatest sources of happiness. B. F. Skinner (1956), who was an enormously influential psychologist, agrees, advising, "When you run onto something interesting, drop everything else and study it" (p. 223).

The scientist's pursuit of curiosity follows unknown paths, sometimes resulting in dramatic and unanticipated discoveries that can appear to be accidental—a matter of luck. But when scientists drop everything to indulge their curiosity, they do so with a "prepared mind," a disciplined curiosity that makes them sharply alert to the possibility of serendipitous, that is, unanticipated, discoveries (see Box 1.1). As the scientist Albert Szent-Gyorgyi noted, a discovery "is said to be an accident meeting a prepared mind" (quoted in Bachrach, 1981, p. 3). Louis Pasteur, while a guest of honor at a large reception, was asked, "Isn't it extraordinary these days how many scientific achievements are arrived at by accident?" Pasteur replied, "It really is remarkable when you think of it and, furthermore, did you ever observe to whom the accidents happen?" (Nelson, 1970, p. 263). Scientists' curiosity is not idle, but active, leading to discoveries, not through blind luck, but because it is embedded within a prepared mind and nurtured by long hours of research. It is a disciplined curiosity, sharpened and focused by labor and frustrations, as well as by successes.

The disciplined approach that scientists use to address questions has a certain predictability. A curious observation, not easily explained by current wisdom, will lead scientists to ask what is happening and why and to try to find answers to these questions. As happens often in science, important discoveries may be made simultaneously and independently by different researchers working from similar theoretical perspectives (see Box 1.2).

Science and Art

The characteristics attributed to scientists—curiosity, creativity, skepticism, tolerance for ambiguity, commitment to hard work, and systematic thinking—are also well developed

BOX 1.1 • *The Three Princes of Serendip*

The term **serendipity** comes from the tale *The Three Princes of Serendip* (Serendip is the former name of Sri Lanka). According to the English novelist Horace Walpole, these princes were very fortunate in making lucky finds. In science, serendipity has come to mean discoveries that are unanticipated, fortuitous, or "lucky." Such finds do not come from systematic applications of existing theory or research, but rather appear to be stumbled on while the scientist is looking for something else. Once discovered, they stimulate new theories and/or research. But these serendipitous findings are not the "happy accidents" that they appear to be. They could easily have been missed had the scientist not been alert to the implication of the observation. Such alertness requires both a prepared mind and a real sense of curiosity.

There are numerous examples in science of such serendipitous findings (Roberts, 1989), including Anton van Leeuwenhoek's (1632–1723) discoveries that microscopic creatures exist. Prior to that time it was believed that cheese mites were the smallest living creatures. Leeuwenhoek's discovery did not come about through his deductions from theory or by following up previous research. Rather, he was enthusiastically turning his new invention, the water-drop microscope, onto just about everything he could, including material scraped from his teeth, thereby discovering that his mouth was alive with what he called "animacules."

A more recent example comes from the neuroscience laboratory of Charles Gross at Princeton University. In the 1970s, Gross and his colleagues were the first to study specific visual processing in the monkey brain. Visual processing in monkeys is thought to be very similar to that in humans. Gross was trying to measure the activity of a single neuron while projecting images on a screen in front of the monkey. However, the neuron did not react to the standard set of visual stimuli (spots, lines, and colored squares). After hours of fruitless testing, the researchers finally gave up. As they were about to shut down the apparatus, Gross waved "good night" to his monkey, and the neuron immediately responded. Gross, being alert, started studying this "accidentally" discovered event. He and his researchers had discovered single neurons sensitive to complex stimuli, such as hands, faces, and even images of food. This discovery stimulated highly significant research into responses of this brain area and helped to create what has become the modern field of cognitive neuroscience.

Another example occurred in the same laboratory about 20 years later. Michael Graziano and Gross (1993, 1998) set out to study visual processing in a small, little understood brain area, the claustrum. They implanted electrodes, measured the activity of individual neurons, and observed some very unexpected results. Not only did the cells activate at the sight of objects as they had expected, but also at the feel of objects touching the body. The researchers soon realized that they were not studying the claustrum at all, but had accidentally implanted the electrodes into a nearby area, the putamen. These neurons allow the monkey to judge the locations of nearby objects and to guide movements toward or away from these objects. Again, an accidental discovery led to development of an important area of neuroscience research.

in poets, sculptors, painters, composers, philosophers, writers, and others. All engage in a mix of artistic and intellectual endeavors, indulge their curiosity, and explore their worlds with skeptical questioning and sharp observations. They attempt to answer their questions and to represent parts of the world through their particular medium, whether it is color, shape, sound, language, or stone. Their representations of ideas become part of

BOX 1.2 • *Charles Darwin and Alfred Russel Wallace*

Charles Darwin (1809–1882) was one of the most important scientists in history. His work *On the Origin of Species* (1859) has had profound effects on science, philosophy, religion, and even political debate. After completing his famous journeys, Darwin spent the next 21 years (1838–1859) in England, refining his ideas for publication. In June 1858, when his book was still far from completion, Darwin received a manuscript in the mail in which his own thesis had already been written. Darwin had been preempted by another naturalist, Alfred Russel Wallace (1823–1913). Wallace traveled in the Amazon and the South Pacific as Darwin had done many years before (Keith, 1954). Wallace was impressed by the diversity of life he found there, and he followed, completely independently, the same line of reasoning as Darwin in making sense out of the observed data. The result was Wallace's manuscript on the biological operation of natural selection in the origins of new species. Wallace mailed his discovery to Darwin for comment.

Who was to be the first to present this momentous discovery to the world? Darwin's associates arranged to have the two men's work presented simultaneously at a meeting of the Linnean Society in London on July 1, 1858. Thus, Wallace and Darwin are credited equally with the discovery. The Greeks had developed a concept of evolution over 2000 years earlier. However, it was Wallace and Darwin who gathered the mass of data and created the concept of natural selection that made their evolutionary theory so important. During the following year, Darwin completed *On the Origin of Species* and soon became the acknowledged originator of the idea of natural selection and the model that derived from it. Wallace, apparently content with this, made no great effort to share in the subsequent acclaim, and the two men remained lifelong friends. Wallace outlived Darwin by 31 years and died in 1913. Wallace made important contributions to science and is recognized by biologists as an eminent naturalist. However, it is Darwin who is remembered for the great biological discovery.

the public domain where they may be viewed, discussed, criticized, accepted, rejected, or, worse, ignored. They are compelled by a combination of curiosity and creativity, and they delight in their discoveries of relationships in nature and in their representations of nature. Their statements are tentative. Symphonies, paintings, and research investigations are presented, not as fixed or complete truths, but as tentative statements of their originators' understanding at a given point in time. This is not to argue that science and art are the same. They are not. Yet each employs variations of the same themes—human curiosity combined with a commitment to ideas, a disciplined process of inquiry, and a product that is a representation of their ideas. Although artists and scientists comprise only a small part of the world's population, they have created an enduring array of ideas and products that have significantly affected the world.

There is a common belief that art and science are so different that artists and scientists must be thoroughly alienated from each other. People may describe someone as the artistic type (poet, musician, or actor), suggesting that the person has no aptitude for science or math. Alternatively, they may assume that a scientist or mathematician cannot appreciate art and literature. These assumptions are false. Consider the 40 national winners of the annual high school Science Talent Search (sponsored by the Intel Corporation). Many of these young people of high achievement in science, mathematics, and technology are also talented in other creative activities, such as music, writing, and the visual arts (see Box 1.3). This should not be surprising. As you will see later in this chapter, art, science, and technology were all generated from the same pool of human skills early in civilization.

BOX 1.3 • *Leonardo da Vinci: A Confluence of Science and Art*

The Renaissance in Western Europe (about 1300 to 1800) was a time of transition from medieval to modern life. It saw upheaval and change and a loosening of the old certainties of the Middle Ages. Humanism flourished, and its values were invested in the physical and moral well-being of human life, rather than on notions of afterlife existence. Life—understanding, improving, and celebrating it—was pursued through momentous developments in art, science, literature, architecture, technology, commerce, politics, and virtually all aspects of human creativity.

Leonardo da Vinci (1452–1519) blended science and art during the Renaissance in remarkable ways, demonstrating clearly the natural affinity of these disciplines. His education was ordinary, but he did manage to get solid training in the natural sciences, mechanics (physics), and music. He even invented a new musical instrument. In adolescence he was apprenticed to a famous painter, Verocchio, and within 10 years was a recognized master himself.

Leonardo studied anatomy to enhance his art, but eventually he became absorbed in the study of anatomy for its own sake. Going far beyond the artistic study of the human body, he developed detailed knowledge and drawings of the major anatomical systems: skeletal, muscular, cardiovascular, respiratory, genitourinary, and embryological. These studies reflect the meticulously detailed observation that is common to the artist and scientist alike.

Leonardo also studied comparative anatomy, dissecting animal bodies and making detailed examinations and drawings. He was the first great medical illustrator (Gross, 1997). In his studies of bird wings we see the artist making observations and recording them in detailed drawings. We also see the scientist and engineer trying to understand the mechanics of the articulation of the bird's wing—which muscles control which actions and what happens to the particular limbs, joints, and feathers in the action of flying. From his study of bird wings came plans for a flying machine (500 years ago!).

Leonardo possessed great skills in science, technology, and art. In Milan and later in Florence, Leonardo's creativity was far-ranging. As a military engineer, he helped develop military fortifications and designed tanklike war machines, an apparatus for troops to breathe underwater, a submarine, and a crop irrigation system. Yet he still found time for other pursuits. For example, he sculpted a huge model for a monumental equestrian statue, which was never completed because bronze was needed to make cannons. He drew plans for buildings and monuments, pursued studies of mathematics and anatomy, and made detailed observations of fossils, river movements, and rock strata. The latter led him to brilliant conclusions that modern paleontologists would not develop for another 300 years (Gould, 1997). As if this were not enough, this monumental scientist also created magnificent works of art, including the *Last Supper* and the *Mona Lisa.*

Leonardo's work wove together science and art using mathematics, anatomy, mechanics, painting, and sculpture. His artistic labor alternated continuously with his scientific inquiry. Although many have been lost, more than 5000 sheets of drawings and notes survive scattered in libraries around the world (Gross, 1997). He exemplified the affinity of art and science in the pursuit of understanding nature. There were no arbitrary divisions between science and art in this Renaissance genius.

Acquiring Knowledge

Science uses systematic thinking to gain knowledge about nature. It places heavy demands on the adequacy of its information and on the processes applied to that information. However, science is only one of many ways of acquiring knowledge. Other ways are tenacity, intuition, authority, rationalism, and empiricism (Helmstadter, 1970). These methods differ in the demands made on the adequacy of the information and on the nature of the processing of the information. Science, which includes rationalism and empiricism, is the most demanding, whereas tenacity, intuition, and authority make few demands on information and require minimal processing. These ways of acquiring knowledge are summarized in Table 1.1.

Tenacity

Tenacity is a willingness to maintain ideas as valid knowledge despite lack of supporting evidence and, sometimes, despite contrary evidence. When ideas have been accepted for so long or have been so often repeated, they may acquire an aura of unquestioned truth. An example from the history of psychology is the powerful belief, held by early 20th-century male psychologists, that women were not as intelligent as

TABLE 1.1 *Ways of Knowing*

Tenacity	A willingness to accept ideas as valid because they have been accepted for so long or repeated so often that they seem true
Intuition	Accepting ideas as valid because they "feel" intuitively true
Authority	Accepting ideas as valid because some respected authority asserts that the ideas are true
Rationalism	Developing valid ideas using existing ideas and principles of logic
Empiricism	Gaining knowledge through observation
Science	A process that combines the principles of rationalism with the process of empiricism, using rationalism to develop theories and empiricism to test the theories

men. Because of this belief, women were excluded from many university programs and professional positions well into the 1930s. Those male psychologists did not question their tenacious beliefs, and they actively ignored and rejected contrary evidence. Tenacity operates also in modern political campaigns in which ideas, often incorrect or distorted, are repeated so incessantly that the voters begin to accept them as true. Advertisers use this method, repeating messages in the hope that consumers will accept them as truth. Television advertising and political campaigning have combined to create some doubtful, but accepted, information based on tenacity. When tenacity operates, there is no demand to check the accuracy of ideas, no serious consideration of alternative ideas, and no subjecting of the ideas to skeptical, critical, and objective review.

In a wonderfully provocative book on how people influence others, Robert Cialdini offers insight into the mechanism behind tenacity (Cialdini, 1993). He suggests that people generally strive to be consistent in their behavior. Inconsistency is viewed as a negative trait, because it suggests that the person has not thought through the issues at hand. Hence, once people act, they have a strong need to continue to act in the same way, even if the initial action was ill-advised or the situation has changed so that the action is no longer appropriate. For many people, it is better to have a strongly held, but wrong, position than to be seen as being inconsistent.

Intuition

Intuition is the supposed direct acquisition of knowledge without intellectual effort or sensory processing. Examples of such supposedly direct access knowledge include extrasensory perception (a contradiction in terms), which self-styled psychics claim to possess, and knowledge received directly from God, claimed by persons who have powerful religious experiences. Mysticism, spiritualism, and even drug-induced altered states of consciousness can lead people to the absolute conviction that they have found truth and knowledge.

Intuition is common in everyday life. For example, people often instantly like or dislike another person within moments of first meeting. They seldom examine their response rationally; they just "feel" it. People commonly have hunches or gut feelings. These serve us well in many situations, but they also lead to errors. Such intuitive responses are rapid assessments based on unexamined experiences, attitudes, and feelings. What makes these experiences intuitive is that people accept this knowledge quickly, without rational thought or examination of facts. Scientists also employ hunches, making conceptual leaps without examining the facts. These hunches, on later careful testing, sometimes prove to have been very productive in advancing research. However, when they are wrong, the process of science weeds them out.

Authority

Authority is the acceptance of an idea as valid knowledge because some respected source, such as the Bible, the Koran, Aristotle, the Supreme Court, the president, the pope, or Sigmund Freud, claims that it is valid.

Tenacity, intuition, and authority make few demands on information and processes. They assert that an idea is true because (1) it has always been accepted as true, (2) it feels true, or (3) an authority says it is true. These methods share an uncritical acceptance of the information and conclusions. Everyone, even scientists, uses these methods in everyday life and is willing to make decisions based on an uncritical acceptance of information. Such methods have value in smoothing personal lives. People might, for example, accept religious teachings intuitively or on authority and experience personal satisfaction in their beliefs. You might accept an urge to have pasta for dinner, without any need for further evaluation. But would you also uncritically agree to saunter across a six-lane highway with your eyes closed because a psychic says he *knows* you will be perfectly safe, despite the 360 cars per minute hurtling by at 75 miles an hour from both directions? Clearly, for some decisions, the information and the process employed to gather it need to be more adequate. Both rationalism and empiricism provide a much firmer basis for accepting information as knowledge.

Rationalism

Rationalism is a way of acquiring knowledge through reasoning. In the rationalistic approach, existing information is carefully stated and logical rules are followed to arrive at acceptable conclusions. Consider this classic deductive syllogism:

> All crows are black. (the major premise)
> This is a crow. (the minor premise)
> Therefore, this crow is black. (the conclusion)

The conclusion is logically derived from the major and minor premises. The same logical processes, however, would lead to the rejection of the following conclusion:

> All crows are black.
> This is black.
> Therefore, this is a crow.

In the rationalistic approach, the conclusion is reached through **logic**—the systematic set of rules that allows us to draw accurate conclusions from a basic set of facts or statements. Logic is a more reliable way to acquire knowledge than tenacity, intuition, or authority. However, rationalism has its limitations. Consider this syllogism:

> All 4-year-old children develop fears of the dark.
> Lisa is a 4-year-old child.
> Therefore, Lisa has developed fears of the dark.

The logic is clear and the conclusion is correct, unless of course Lisa has not developed fears of the dark. What is the limitation? Suppose that it is not true that all 4-year-old children develop fears of the dark, or suppose that Lisa is actually 7 and not 4, or suppose that Lisa is a yacht and not a child. The major limitation of rationalism is that the premises must be true, as determined by some other evidence, to arrive at the correct conclusions. Accurate conclusions depend on both the reasoning process and the accuracy of the premises. There is no provision for assessing their accuracy in the purely rationalistic approach.

Empiricism

Empiricism involves gaining knowledge through observation, that is, *knowing by experiencing through our senses.* It is a method as old as civilization. For the empiricist, it is not enough to know through reason (or tenacity or intuition or authority) alone. It is necessary to experience the world—to see, hear, touch, taste, and smell it. "I won't believe it unless I see it!" is the empiricist's motto. We are good empiricists when we notice a dark sky and distant rumblings of thunder and decide to take an umbrella. Our senses are telling us something. Thales, Hippocrates, Galen, Copernicus, Galileo, and Darwin all based their important conclusions about nature largely on their observations. They rejected the more widely held, nonempirical conceptions provided by mythology, religion, appeal to authority, and rationalism.

Empiricism used alone, however, has limitations. There are two types of empiricism: **naïve empiricism** and **sophisticated empiricism.** The statement "I won't believe it unless I see it!" is an example of the former. If you have never seen Hong Kong, Manchester, Prague, or Nyack, does this mean that these places do not exist? Because you have never seen gravity or the measles virus, should you conclude that you will never fall down or get the measles? If your repeated empirical observations lead you to assert that "I have never been run down while walking along the middle of a highway," does that mean you can continue walking down highways with impunity? And how about when you see something clearly that turns out to be an illusion (see Figure 1.1).

Sophisticated empiricism goes further. People cannot see gravity or heat or, with unaided eyesight, the measles virus. But they can measure the increase in temperature as they turn up a heat source or the rate of fall of a physical body, and they can view a virus through an electron microscope. Empirical observations in science are not limited to direct observations; we can also observe phenomena indirectly through direct observation of their inferred impact on other objects, such as the impact of gravity.

If scientists did nothing but collect facts, all they would have is long lists of facts. They would know nothing about how the facts go together or what the facts mean. Facts are most useful when people can think about them, organize them, draw meaning from them, and use them to make predictions. In other words, empiricism needs to be integrated with rational thinking so that the two bolster each other. You will see in the next section that this is exactly what science does.

Science

Science brings together elements of both rationalism and empiricism, employing rational logic and checking each step with empirical observation. Scientists constantly shuttle between empirical observation and abstract rational thought about general principles and then return to further empirical observation of specific facts. This repeated return to

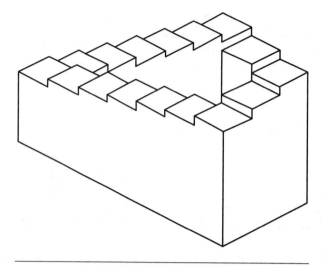

FIGURE 1.1 *Reality or Illusion?* You cannot always trust what you see.

Source: Penrose and Penrose (1958). Impossible objects: A special type of visual. The British Psychological Society. *British Journal of Psychology, 49,* 31–33.

empirical observation in an otherwise rationalistic process characterized the 16th century's apparently sudden surge into science. Much of the progress in science since then has been based on strengthening the empirical component by developing more precise methods of observation.

Science is a way of thinking that involves a continuous and systematic interplay of rational thought and empirical observation. Observed events, whether the movements of planets observed by an astronomer or the behavior of children observed by a psychologist, constitute the major facts of a discipline. But the empirical observation of events and the resulting identification or listing of facts is not sufficient in science. Scientists must go beyond the immediately observable facts to construct general principles and to make new predictions about nature.

Quick-Check Review 2: Acquiring Knowledge

2.1. What are the common methods of acquiring knowledge?

2.2. Which two methods are combined in science?

2.3. What is meant by naïve empiricism? Sophisticated empiricism?

2.4. What are the limitations of rationalism? Of empiricism?

2.5. Explain why science must go beyond the collection of facts.

Emergence of Science

The rapid development of science in the 15th and 16th centuries might suggest that science was suddenly created and that there was no science before Copernicus, Galileo, or Newton. In actuality, science has been one of Western civilization's alternative methods of acquiring knowledge since the Greeks of 2400 years ago, and its antecedents date back 8000 years. Not until the Renaissance in the 17th century did science become independent enough to begin its acceleration into the powerful social movement that it is today. This section reviews some of the historical bases of modern science.

Early Civilization

Civilization developed from primitive hunter–gatherers, through organized nomadic hunting, to settled societies. A broad array of skills evolved over millennia until, in the relatively short period from about 6000 to 4000 B.C., this accumulation of skills enabled a remarkable surge of progress from the late Neolithic period of polished stone tools into the age of metals. Urban settlements grew; technological, social, and intellectual tools accumulated; and societies spread around the eastern Mediterranean. The magnificent civilizations of the Babylonians, Egyptians, and others flourished. The skills passed on to the Greeks included architecture, agriculture, animal husbandry, food preparation, mining, smelting, and tool manufacturing. Commercial enterprises depended on long-distance land and sea navigation, on weighing and numerical calculations, on written records, and on tracking the seasons with accurate calendars. By 4000 B.C., books on astronomy, medicine, surgery, and mathematics were available. All these advances coexisted with imaginative and mystical beliefs about a universe filled with gods, demons, and spirits.

By 1000 B.C., there was a rich legacy of skills, with emphasis on practical information about agriculture, manufacturing, and commerce. The concrete manipulation of the environment led to practical skills and knowledge. From these, more abstract ideas about nature gradually developed (Farrington, 1949a, b). Agriculture and metallurgy are good examples. Using their practical skills, early farmers observed weather phenomena, moon phases, sun positions, and other changes in the sky for clues to help in farming. These observations led to the development of accurate calendars. Farmers also learned about fertilizers and plant growth and developed practical mathematics to measure plots and set boundaries. Artisans learned to recognize types of ores and how to mine them. They knew that heat transforms solids into liquids, could measure by weighing, and understood proportionality so as to reproduce the particular mixtures needed for various alloys. These skills required an abstract understanding of nature gathered and refined through generations of empirical observations and concrete manipulations. Such abstract knowledge was used to carry out practical tasks. The young apprentices of the day did not study abstract astronomy or mathematics, but embedded in the crafts were early elements of these disciplines. Thus, in the early Mediterranean civilizations, the components of modern science were found in the arts and craftsmanship. Science, art, and technology were inseparable in practice.

Science rests on the **orderliness belief** (Whitehead, 1925), the implicit belief that the universe operates in an orderly, lawful manner. If the universe were not orderly and predictable, it would not stay the same long enough to be studied. To apply their skills in a reliable manner, early artisans had to expect orderliness in the physical world. How else could they depend on *this* type of rock, when heated, to release *that* kind of metal, which will always have *these* properties regardless of the different pieces of rock used?

Greek Science

The roots necessary for the emergence of empirical science date back to the pre-Socratic Greek period (from about 600 to 400 B.C.). Thales (625?–547? B.C.) was the first Greek philosopher to combine an empirical–rational view of the universe. Thales lived in Ionia, a Greek colony whose citizens developed impressive commercial skills. The Ionians were pragmatic realists, artisans, farmers, and tradespeople. Empirical knowledge was basic in their culture, and when some, like Thales, turned to philosophy, they developed a clearly empirical view of nature. Thales' philosophy stressed the observation of natural events in a natural universe and rejected mysticism. He speculated about a natural cosmology in which water was the basic substance from which all else developed and to which all will ultimately return. He studied Babylonian astronomy and predicted the solar eclipse that occurred on May 25, 585 B.C. He developed a scientific, albeit primitive, empirical–rational philosophy. His observations were based on empiricism and on what Whitehead (1925) termed "the painstaking attention to observational details." Thales founded abstract geometry and Ionian philosophy and is considered to be the father of science.

Thales' naturalistic speculations were continued by others. Anaximander's (610–547? B.C.) observation that sharks had mammalian characteristics led him to propose that higher-order creatures, including humans, developed from fishes. Xenophanes (560?–478? B.C.) observed rock imprints of fish and seaweed on mountains and in landlocked stone quarries and proposed a theory of geological change over time. Hippocrates (460?–377? B.C.) suggested radical ideas for treating illness. At the time, most people believed that illness was caused by demons invading the body and could be cured by prayers and exorcisms. Hippocrates attributed all illness to natural events. He taught that no demon, spirit, or god played any part in disease, and no prayer or exorcism could make a sick person well. The Hippocratic physician relied on careful observations of patients and on rational thought in trying to understand illness.

The Ionian development of science from Thales through Hippocrates emphasized observation of naturally occurring events. The Ionians were careful observers and systematic thinkers, but not systematic manipulators of events. A later Ionian, Strato, developed the next important step—making the scientist an active observer who manipulates and controls the conditions of observations. Strato (died 270? B.C.), one of the last empirical philosophers, was a successor to Aristotle. He accepted the Ionian cosmology with its emphasis on natural events, its basic belief in the universe as orderly and knowable, and its rejection of mysticism. Strato believed that the best method of acquiring knowledge was empirical manipulation and observation, that is,

experimentation. He performed numerous experiments on air and water, demonstrating many of their properties, and from these experiments he developed some general explanatory principles about nature.

However, by Strato's time, Ionian empirical science was already in decline. Strato's scientific view stood as an alternative to the mystical views propounded earlier by religion and by philosophers such as Socrates and Plato. Then, as now, these views conflicted, leading to the near total suppression of one by the other. The early empirical science was virtually lost for almost 1900 years.

After Socrates, the highest ideals were religion, politics, and rationalistic, mystical philosophy. The pursuit of practical goals was necessary, but was left to slaves, laborers, artisans, farmers, and tradespeople, whereas the upper-class scholars pursued pure reason and abstract ideas. As a result, theology and abstract philosophy were carefully taught and scrupulously preserved in writing. In contrast, empirical skills, not admitted into the realm of scholarship, remained in the oral tradition and were not as fully recorded or preserved. Social stratification was not the only factor contributing to the suppression of empiricism. Religion was gaining social power, promulgating its mystical cosmology. Religious leaders attacked the natural philosophy of the Ionians as atheistic, factually wrong, and subversive.

The genius of the early Greeks had created empirical, rational science that described an orderly universe operating according to a few basic principles. Greek philosophy was one of humanity's major intellectual achievements. The movement away from empiricism and pragmatism after 400 B.C. was led by Socrates and Plato, who focused on the pursuit of pure reason. As Farrington (1949a) noted, "When Plato died (about 347 B.C.) he left behind him a mystical view of the universe set forth in his dialogues in a unique combination of logic and drama. Its weakness was not that it lacked supports in argument, but that it was not open to correction from experience" (p. 13). After 400 B.C., Greek philosophy became increasingly abstract and mystical and eventually joined the attacks on empiricism.

The growing philosophical mysticism produced an affinity for religion and philosophy. The regularity of number relationships discovered by the Pythagoreans and the orderliness observed in astronomy were taken as evidence that nature was controlled by divine intelligence. This led to a shift in the goals of philosophy and science. Earlier investigators were interested in understanding and controlling nature, but later philosophers sought to illustrate divine intelligence through their study of nature. Science was beginning to be used in the service of religion, a role that continued well into the Renaissance.

Medieval Science

By the end of the 4th century, after centuries of persecution, Christianity had become the Roman Empire's sole state religion, and it remained a major social institution and political power in Western Europe for the next 1000 years. Greek reliance on intuition and reason was continued by medieval Christian scholars, who believed that divine intelligence controlled the universe and the scriptures were the ultimate source of truth. **Theology,** the study of God and God's relationship to the universe, dominated; revelation, rationalism, and authority were its major methods of acquiring knowledge. All other methods of study, including empiricism, were secondary to theology. Christian scholars continued empirical studies in astronomy, optics, and zoology, but always secondary to and in the service of religion (Nagel, 1948).

By the 13th century, such theological scholars as Thomas Aquinas and Roger Bacon, influenced by the rediscovery of early classical scholarship, elevated the value of empiricism. Bacon repeated optical experiments performed earlier by Islamic scientists. A Dominican, Dietrich of Frieberg (ca. 1300) used water-filled glass balls to experiment with the visible spectrum, discovering that colors are refracted on the inside of spherical water drops. At about the same time, Jordanus DeNemore experimented with various types of levers and the equilibrium of weights on inclined planes. In 1269, Peter the Stranger of Maricourt published empirical experiments with magnets. His work was "a model of the observational and experimental techniques in physics" (Clagett, 1948, p. 119). Reflecting this increased emphasis on empiricism, Dietrich of Frieberg noted that "one ought never to renounce what had been made manifest by the senses" (cited in Clagett, 1948, p. 119).

The 12th and 13th centuries saw great changes in politics, art, commerce, and exploration. People focused more on the world around them, and a revival of the ancient Greek, Greco-Roman, and Islamic scholarship occurred. Western Europeans expanded their trade around the Mediterranean world. They encountered works of Islamic scholars who had been part of the Moorish high civilization in Spain. These scholars had brought with them Arabic versions of classical works, which they translated into Latin. By the end of the 12th century, medieval scholars knew Hippocratic and Galenic writings in medicine, Euclid's mathematics, Ptolemy's astronomy, Archimedes' physics, and Hindu mathematics. Medical schools, largely based on these traditions, were established across Europe, and the empirically based study of medicine, mathematics, and physics was revived. This rebirth of empirical science remained within the bounds of theology, where, for a while at least, there was room for it to grow. However, science challenged theology and, by the 17th century, began to escape from its constraints.

Two constraints on empirical science were started by the Greeks and strengthened by Christian theologians. The first was that empirical science was not allowed to contradict theological dogma. If a dispute arose between knowledge gained through the senses and knowledge arrived at by revelation or through church authority, the resolution was simple: truth lay with theology, and any contradictory ideas were false. The second constraint was that empiricism was to be used only in the service of religion. Both constraints were challenged by the revival of empirical science. For example, scholars argued that science could be used for the betterment of humanity, such as to combat sickness. The church tolerated this application of science to humanity as long as it did not challenge church dogma. Eventually, however, such challenges did occur.

The Scientific Revolution

By the 13th century, science was established in the new medical centers and scholars recognized the value of science in the service of humanity. This was to become a major theme in science, one that Francis Bacon would stress in the 16th century. However, science remained under the control of religious and political authorities well into the 14th century. Its growth to independent status occurred during a seething 400 years of social change.

During the 13th to 16th centuries, science increasingly conflicted with religious dogma. For example, both Catholics and Protestants condemned René Descartes (1596–1650) for his views. A philosopher and mathematician, Descartes questioned the theological concepts of the soul, arguing for more objective observation and study of consciousness. Two of his ideas became critical in the later development of psychology: his concepts of mind–body dualism and his doctrine of ideas (that ideas arise both innately from processes within the mind and through experience in the external world). Galileo (1564–1642), a brilliant astronomer, physicist, philosopher, and mathematician, also challenged church dogma. In 1633 he was forced by the inquisition to recant his support of the Copernican concept that Earth orbits the sun. However, by then, the scientific revolution, fueled by Copernicus, Bacon, Galileo, Kepler, Newton, and others, had already begun. Established institutions fought what they perceived to be the scientists' attack on religion. But, by the beginning of the 19th century, science had been reestablished and, for the first time since about 400 B.C., had achieved independent status. By the 18th and 19th centuries, scientific centers existed in universities, social resources were available to support science, and scientists were sought after by industries, universities, and governments. By the 20th century, science had become a major social movement.

Science developed rapidly in the latter part of the 20th century. For example, developments in high-energy physics provided insights into the building blocks of matter. In biology, the ability to read and manipulate DNA structure led to new variations of life forms. Neuroscience integrated psychology, biology, neurology, and biochemistry and led to such new technologies as magnetic resonance imaging (MRI). The development of high-temperature superconducting materials and faster computer chips has enormous potential for future applications.

Modern science depends on a heavily endowed social structure that includes research centers, universities, industries, and private agencies. Networks of scientific societies exist, with annual meetings in which scientists communicate their findings and lobby for greater public resources. Scientists also communicate with the general public through newspapers, magazines, radio, television, books, and electronic media. Scientists and laboratories are supported by both the general public and special groups, such as industry.

Scientists have investigated many phenomena and have created specialized disciplines, each with its own content and procedures. The phenomena studied differ from one discipline to another, with methodological procedures differing according to the phenomena being studied, the kinds of questions asked, and the technologies associated with each discipline. Whatever their specialization, all scientists share a strong curiosity about nature and a commitment to the combined use of empiricism and rationalism as a way to understand nature.

Science is not new, but the public often views science as a recent development. One reason for this may be the close association of science and technology. Because technological developments are perceived as new, then so must science be new. The pace of technology has been astounding. Consider the development of mechanical flight. In 1903, after years of research, Orville Wright took off from wooden rails, sailing through the air for 12 seconds in the world's first powered and piloted heavier-than-air flight before losing control and crashing. He survived the crash and lived until 1948, missing by only 13 years seeing the first manned flight into space. Could he have imagined at the turn of the century, when he and Wilbur were experimenting with their wind machines and models of wing surfaces, that a flight into space and back would occur almost within his lifetime? (See Box 1.4.) Although technology advances at a rapid pace and always seems to have the appearance of being new, the science on which it is based has been developing since the time of Thales.

Quick-Check Review 3: Emergence of Science

3.1. How did the early practical skills of artisans contribute to modern science?

3.2. What contribution did Thales make to science?

3.3. What was the relationship of science and theology during the Middle Ages?

3.4. Distinguish between modern technology and modern science.

3.5. What is the orderliness belief, and what does it have to do with modern science?

Psychology

The discussion of psychology will be divided into two sections: the history of psychology and the science of psychology. Psychology has been an independent science for less than 150 years, but was part of philosophy for more than 2000 years. Several texts provide detailed treatment of psychology's history (Benjafield, 1996; Benjamin, 1997; Hergenhahn, 1997; Goodwin, 1999; Fancher, 2000; Schultz & Schultz, 2000). We provide only a brief overview here. An expanded treatment of the history of psychology is presented on the *Student Resource CD*.

The History of Psychology

The context for the emerging discipline of psychology was firmly in place in the early to mid-19th century. This context included 19th-century philosophy and physiology. The philosophical contexts included romanticism, rationalism, and empiricism. Romanticism helped to produce the sweeping 19th-century humanitarian reform movements, while rationalism and empiricism were the major supports of modern science. The earliest psychological research was neurophysiological, including studies of reflex action and localization of brain function.

Early psychology was profoundly influenced by Darwinian evolutionary theory. The concept of evolution suggested continuity of structure and function between

BOX 1.4 • *The Wright Brothers as Scientists*

It is often said that the Wright brothers invented the airplane in a burst of Yankee ingenuity. They have been portrayed as mechanical tinkerers in their bicycle shop whose achievement had little to do with systematic scholarship and research. But in a 1906 interview, the Wrights complained about the way in which they were described in newspapers, noting, "Nearly every writer has characterized us as mechanics, and taken it for granted that our invention has come from mechanical skill. We object to this as neither true nor fair. We are not mechanics; we are scientists" (Oppel, 1987, p. 18). The Wright brothers were referring to their years of study of theoretical principles of flight, their knowledge of the many possible forms of aircraft, and the many attempts and successes of lighter- and heavier-than-air flight by their predecessors. The Wrights used careful development, experimentation, and testing in their Ohio workshop and on the windy sand dunes near Kitty Hawk, North Carolina.

The brothers built on the previous work of scientists and engineers. More than a hundred years earlier, starting in 1797, George Cayley developed mathematical principles of mechanical flight. He built and flew models and full-sized gliders. Cayley established the fixed-wing concept for aircraft, a major departure from the earlier (and later) flapping-wing contraptions. In 1809, he published his important work, *On Aerial Navigation,* and his later writings provided descriptions of a future flying machine, including its lift surfaces, stabilizer, engine, and propellers. In 1889, Otto Lilienthal, a German engineer, published *Bird Flight as the Basis of Aviation.* Lilienthal became the first person to make controlled, heavier-than-air flights, making more than 2000 successful glides in his biplanes and monoplanes. In 1896, with relatively light gasoline-powered engines available, Lilienthal was working on a design for a powered airplane. Unfortunately, he was killed in the crash of one of his gliders before he could develop a powered airplane. Octave Chanute, a civil engineer, followed Lilienthal's work and developed a number of gliders. In 1894 he published an important text, *Progress in Flying Machines.* In 1901 he gave the Wrights his expertise and enthusiastic support.

On hearing of Lilienthal's death, the Wrights increased their own efforts, building on the technical writings of Chanute, Lilienthal, Samuel Langley, and others. The Wrights perfected their gliders, based initially on Lilienthal's designs, and raced to achieve powered flight. They learned that Langley, a physicist at the Smithsonian Institution, was also close to success. Langley, backed by the U.S. government, had successfully flown a small-scale model of a steam-driven airplane in 1896 and a larger gasoline-powered model in 1902, the first unpiloted flights of powered airplanes. All was set in December 1903 for Langley to test his human-piloted, gas-powered airplane. However, his attempt failed, and the press concluded that heavier-than-air flight would not be developed for hundreds of years. But just nine days later the Wright Flyer I, propelled by a 12-horsepower engine and piloted by Orville, flew successfully at Kill Devil Hill.

A long process of scientific and technological advances led to the work of Lilienthal, Chanute, Langley, and the Wrights. This history included the early work of Leonardo da Vinci in the 1500s, the successful balloon flights from France to England in the late 1700s, the improvement of propeller designs by Jean-Pierre Blanchard in 1797, several books on the mathematics and physics of mechanical flight published from 1780 to the 1890s, and the development of the gasoline engine. The Wright brothers developed powered flight within the context of this vast array of scientific and technical development. Building on the work of many others, they added the final developments that made powered flight possible. Their experimentation was neither mere tinkering nor their own solitary invention, but was based on knowledge of all the preceding work. Their achievement is a good example of how science builds on previous discoveries to expand the scientific knowledge base and to create new technologies.

humans and other animals, an idea that ran counter to religion and previous scientific and philosophical thought. Charles Darwin (1809–1882) and Alfred Russel Wallace (1823–1913) suggested that studying animal functioning could help scientists to understand human functioning. Furthermore, the emphasis on adaptation of organisms to their environments highlighted the importance of studying function as well as structure. Darwin's use of data from many sources—geology, paleontology, archeology, demography, naturalistic observations—legitimized the use of diverse data sources and methodologies. The concept of natural selection emphasized individual differences, which helped to set the stage for Galton's work on inheritance of intelligence, psychological testing, and the development of statistical techniques.

Prescientific psychology dates to Aristotle, but the scientific study of psychology did not begin until mid-19th century. Psychology evolved from earlier studies in philosophy, biology, mathematics, physiology, physics, and even astronomy. Ernest Weber (1795–1878) and Gustav Fechner (1801–1887) were among the first researchers to study perceptual processes objectively. They presented carefully measured stimuli to people under controlled conditions and recorded the participants' responses, a method known as **psychophysics.**

The early history of psychology was dominated by a series of schools or movements. Each school of psychology was defined by a central focus, a set of underlying assumptions, accepted research methodologies, and a general philosophy about human functioning and the best ways to study it.

Structuralism.   Wilhelm Wundt (1832–1920) established the world's first psychological laboratory in 1879 in Leipzig, Germany. Wundt's influence was multiplied by his students, who went on to create psychological laboratories in other countries, making him one of the most important psychologists in history. Wundt studied the structure of consciousness using introspection. That is, he tried to infer the basic elements of conscious experience from participants' verbal reports of their mental experiences. Since Wundt was interested in the structure of consciousness, his work was known as **structuralism,** and it dominated psychology during the late 19th and early 20th centuries. Wundt argued that experimentation was not possible in the study of higher mental processes. However, Hermann Ebbinghaus (1850–1909) showed that rigorous experimental procedures could be applied to higher mental processes. His work had a profound influence on the development of psychology as a science.

Functionalism.   By the turn of the 20th century, American psychologists shifted the focus from structuralism to *how* the mind operates, and this new approach was called **functionalism.** Functional psychologists, such as G. Stanley Hall (1844–1924), William James (1842–1910), John Dewey (1859–1952), J. McCattell (1860–1944), and E. L. Witmer (1867–1956), were interested in practical questions of education, training, treatment, and child rearing. Witmer, for example, worked with children with mental retardation or emotional disorders. He created the first psychological clinic and is credited with founding and naming the field of clinical psychology. This new functionalism was shaped by the cultural differences between the United States and Germany. It was heavily influenced by Darwin and by Darwin's cousin, Francis Galton

(1822–1911), and it relied heavily on the study of animal behavior as a way to understand human behavior. Structuralism has disappeared, but the spirit of functionalism continues today in the general orientation of Western psychology toward practical applications and understanding functional processes.

Psychoanalysis. **Pychoanalysis** developed in the late 19th century outside the mainstream of academic psychology, although there were many precursors to psychoanalysis in the early 1800s. Sigmund Freud (1856–1939) popularized them, added his own observations from about 1890 to 1938, and became the acknowledged father of psychoanalysis. While other psychologists were studying human consciousness, Freud focused on unconscious processes. Freud and his followers carried out studies in clinical settings, rather than in laboratories.

Freud was accepted by only a few American psychologists, such as G. Stanley Hall, who arranged for Freud's only visit to the United States. In 1909, Freud presented five lectures in German at Clark University. Despite his support and public acclaim in Europe, Freud was initially ignored and later vigorously criticized by most American psychologists for his lack of scientific rigor. Despite such criticisms, Freud grew in popularity, and the public eventually came to view psychoanalysis as being equivalent to psychology (Fancher, 2000). By the time of his death in 1939, Freud had become world famous.

As Freud was achieving popular acclaim, American psychologists began to subject his ideas to empirical testing. In the 1940s and 1950s, hundreds of articles on psychoanalytic concepts and procedures were published, both supportive and critical (Fancher, 2000). Psychoanalysis became a major clinical model of psychotherapy, reaching its peak in the1940s and influencing psychology, psychiatry, social work, sociology, literature, and history. Although it is no longer a dominant model, psychoanalysis continues to be used clinically by a few small groups of adherents.

Gestalt Psychology and Behaviorism. These two important developments emerged around 1912, and both were critical of structuralism. **Gestalt psychology** originated in Germany, and its founders were Max Wertheimer (1880–1943), Kurt Koffka (1886–1941), and Wolfgang Kohler (1887–1967). They argued that the structuralists' attempts to analyze consciousness into separate parts lost sight of the whole experience. Gestalt psychologists argued that the whole is greater than the sum of its parts.

Behaviorism, which emerged in the United States, criticized psychology as too mentalistic and subjective. John B. Watson (1878–1958) argued for a complete rejection of such mentalistic concepts as mind, consciousness, ego, and id. He maintained that such concepts were meaningless carry-overs from prescientific philosophy. The psychology of consciousness, according to Watson, needed to be replaced by an objective psychology of observed behavior.

Animal psychology was a major factor in modern behavioral psychology. Behaviorists such as Ivan Pavlov (1849–1936), E. L. Thorndike (1874–1949), E. C. Tolman (1886–1959), E. R. Guthrie (1896–1951), C. L. Hull (1884–1952), and B. F. Skinner (1904–1990) believed that studying animal behavior provided clues about such complex events as learning. It had previously been thought that animal behavior was instinctual.

However, animal psychologists found that it was flexible, varied, and systematically modifiable. Even lower animals could learn new and complex behavior.

An applied result of animal behaviorists' research is **behavior modification.** If animal behavior could be modified using behavioral techniques, then similar procedures might modify human behavior, enhancing education and psychological treatment. Behavioral principles could also be used to help to teach people cognitive and behavioral skills. First studied in the 1920s, behavior modification became a major component of education and treatment by the 1960s.

Humanistic Psychology.   Emerging in the mid-20th century and having roots in the early 19th-century romantic philosophies, humanistic psychology was briefly influential, but never developed into a school or movement (Schultz & Schultz, 2000). **Humanistic psychology,** as developed by Abraham Maslow (1908–1970) and Carl Rogers (1902–1987), focused on human conscious experience, human creativity, personal growth, and the assumed natural tendency toward self-actualizing, that is, developing to one's potential. Most of its research was on therapeutic interventions. Its ideas were consistent with an egalitarian American democracy and have been integrated into much of mainstream psychological thought.

Cognitive Psychology.   **Cognitive psychology** is the study of perception, memory, and learning. It grew out of both the early work on human perceptual processes and efforts to study verbal learning in humans. Once almost exclusively an academic discipline, cognitive psychology now routinely addresses applied questions. The design of high-performance aircraft or modern computer software, to name two examples, relies heavily on cognitive psychology research. Cognitive psychologists employ sophisticated experimental methods and logic to infer cognitive processes. However, this approach has had its critics. Skinner (1990) argued from a behaviorist's perspective that cognitive psychologists were speculating too much about what was going on inside a person's head, rather than focusing on the person's observable behavior. Modern cognitive psychology often crosses over into the broader discipline known as cognitive science. **Cognitive science** bridges once separate disciplines, like psychology, behavioral neuroscience, computer science, neurophysiology, and linguistics, providing a unique integrated perspective on brain–behavior relationships.

Women in Psychology

The late 19th century and first years of the 20th century were exciting years for the emerging discipline of psychology. However, women were virtually excluded. In the European tradition, women were not allowed to enroll in colleges. It was not until nearly 1835 that a few colleges admitted a handful of women, but only as undergraduates. The few women who did earn degrees in the early 20th century and who attained important academic and other positions did so against great prejudice and through sheer determination. For example, Christine Ladd Franklin (1847–1930) was refused a doctorate in mathematics by Johns Hopkins University because she was a woman, despite the fact that she had completed all degree requirements (Shultz & Shultz, 2000).

The university finally awarded her the degree 45 years later. Mary Whiton Calkins (1863–1930) completed all requirements at Harvard for the doctorate, but Harvard refused to award it to her. Years later, because of Calkins' outstanding contributions to psychology, Columbia University awarded her an honorary doctorate. She was also elected the first woman president of the American Psychological Association.

Edward B. Tichener, one of the most influential of America's early psychologists, steadfastly barred women from his weekly research meetings at Cornell. Nevertheless, he was an advocate for women's rights to study at universities and to earn degrees. He just did not want them at his male-only, smoke-filled research meetings. Margaret Floy Washburn (1871–1939) was Tichener's first doctoral student and the first woman to earn a doctorate in psychology. She went on to contribute important work in comparative psychology, becoming the first female psychologist elected to the National Academy of Science and the president of the American Psychological Association. But despite Tichener's support of her work, he never allowed her into those research meetings.

Helen Thompson Wooley (1874–1947) studied sex differences for her doctoral dissertation (1903), in which she found that males and females did not differ on intelligence or emotional functioning. Women were slightly higher than men in memory and sensory perception. Thompson was strongly criticized for her alleged bias in failing to find the expected superiority of men.

Leta Stetter Hollingworth (1886–1939), a Phi Beta Kappa graduate of Nebraska University, was forced to resign from high school teaching when she married. The administrators believed that if a married woman was allowed to work outside the home her husband and children would suffer (Schultz & Schultz, 2000). Eight years later Hollingworth earned a doctorate at Columbia and went on to contribute significant research in emotional behavior, childhood education, and the needs of gifted children.

Largely barred from academic positions, women with doctorates in psychology obtained jobs in applied areas such as schools, clinics, and hospitals. Nevertheless, these women succeeded, making dozens of important contributions to applied psychology.

Currently, most doctoral-level psychologists are men; however, this is rapidly changing. Most undergraduate and graduate psychology students are women. Although this field has traditionally been male dominated, the current male–female ratio suggests that there will be a balancing out before too long.

Modern Psychology

World War II catapulted psychology from an academic discipline to an academic and applied discipline. Although some psychologists did testing and counseling, the applied mental health field was dominated by psychiatry prior to World War II, and the major psychotherapeutic model was psychoanalysis. World War II brought academic psychologists into the armed forces to deal with issues of selection, training, rehabilitation, and treatment of military personnel. Many of these psychologists brought with them their objective, laboratory-based procedures and their behavioral orientations. The success of psychology during World War II challenged the dominance of psychiatry and psychoanalysis. Following World War II, the federal government became a major supporter of training programs in clinical psychology.

The clashes between schools of thought that were common in the early history of psychology have given way in the last 50 years to efforts to integrate ideas from different schools. For example, social analysts, such as Karen Horney (1885–1952) and Harry Stack Sullivan (1892–1949), applied sociological theory to psychoanalysis. E. C. Tolman integrated concepts from Gestalt psychology, early cognitive psychology, and behaviorism in his theory of learning. Kurt Lewin (1890–1947) integrated Gestalt concepts with social psychology and child development. Dollard and Miller (1950) modernized psychoanalysis by integrating it with Hull's (1943) behavioral learning theory.

In the last 30 years, **behavioral medicine** and **health psychology** have brought together behavior modification, medicine, nutrition, and health. Since the 1970s, cognitively oriented clinical psychologists have integrated behavioral learning theory and cognitive psychology, essentially bringing consciousness back into behaviorism. The past 20 years have seen the development of integrated disciplines such as **behavioral neuroscience,** which incorporates such diverse disciplines as cognitive and physiological psychology, neurology, and language development.

Psychology continues to build on the gains of the last 100 years, while exploiting new research technologies. For example, there is a growing collaboration between cognitive science and neuroscience as scientists learn to monitor the brain in action using advanced technology. Psychologists are now able to integrate psychological experiences with biological mechanisms, producing a sophisticated understanding of psychological concepts that only a few years ago seemed too complex to unravel (e.g., Sutton & Davidson, 1997). In more applied areas, such as clinical and counseling psychology, this growth in the understanding of psychological and biological mechanisms has led to impressive improvements in the treatment of a variety of psychological disorders (Barlow, 2001). In the past, one psychotherapeutic approach would be applied to virtually any problem. Today, individualized treatments exist for dozens of specific conditions, which have been shown to be effective in controlled research (Chambless & Ollendick, 2001). There has also been a surge of interest by social psychologists in personality development and psychopathology, bringing together aspects of social and clinical psychology. Psychologists today are not strong adherents of any particular school. Rather, most represent **mainstream psychology,** which is integrative in nature.

Throughout its history, psychology has increased the understanding of human and animal behavior. Among the processes studied by psychologists are learning, motivation, memory, personality, physiological influences on behavior, sensation, perception, intelligence, language, problem solving, emotion, development, psychopathology, and social influences on behavior. Today, psychology is an independent scientific discipline that overlaps several other disciplines. For example, biopsychology combines biology and psychology; cognitive psychology overlaps with computer science, linguistics, and neurology; the psychological study of the sensory processes of vision and hearing involves knowledge of the physics of light and sound and the physiology of the brain.

Psychology is a large discipline. More than 159,000 psychologists are members of the American Psychological Association (APA), and another 4900 psychologists are members of the Canadian Psychological Association (Abbondanza, 2000; American Psychological Association, 2000). Many psychologists are members of other associations, such as the American Psychological Society, the Association for the Advancement of Behavior Therapy, the Psychonomic Society, the Society for Neuroscience, and the Society for Research in Child Development. Psychology, like most sciences, is divided into several subdisciplines, each with its own focus. The diversity in psychology is reflected by the fact that there are over 50 divisions within the APA, each devoted to a specific interest area. Although all psychologists receive scientific education, many work professionally in such applied settings as hospitals, clinics, schools, industry, and government service, where their research training helps them to solve practical problems for their clients.

Psychology is often considered to be a social science, but its roots are clearly in the natural sciences. There are many research areas within psychology, each with its own particular content and methods. But in all areas of psychology, the scientific model is used to study the behavior of living organisms. The remainder of this book will focus on the use of scientific research methods in psychological inquiry.

The Science of Psychology

Why is science so critical in psychology? People observe the world, themselves, their actions, the behavior of others, and they try to make sense of it all. Most people are amateur psychologists. But psychology is a field in which amateurs often perform poorly. For example, people think that seeing is believing, but the science of psychology demonstrates that human perceptual systems are limited, biased, and subject to all kinds of distortions. People believe that they remember past experiences, but the science of psychology demonstrates that their memories are fragile at best, almost always biased, and capable of changing a remembered event into something entirely different. People know how their experiences have changed them, shaping their current personalities, but the science of psychology shows that such events seem to have little impact on later behavior and that genes play a powerful role in shaping people. People believe that the more individuals that there are available to help, the more likely that someone will help them when they need it. The science of psychology shows that just the opposite is true: the more people available to help, the less likely that one will get help from anyone. In other words, what most people "know" to be true about the psychological world is often false. The *scientific* study of psychological phenomena often uncovers surprises.

Even more critical, the science of psychology protects us from the pseudoscience of psychology. Most scientific disciplines have some related pseudoscience. Astrologers use the language of astronomers in their claims to foretell the future. Alchemists use the language of chemistry to explain how they turn lead into gold. But psychology is burdened with a plethora of pseudoscience, almost all of it from nonpsychologists. People who would never offer a thought about nuclear physics are perfectly willing to offer theories about personality, psychopathology, social behavior, and child development. Some of these theories are reasonable; others are silly and simplistic. But they are reported in the popular press if they make a good article or story (Lilienfeld, 1998). Much of this pseudopsychology is benign and does little harm, but some of it is far from benign. Often the people behind these theories are well-meaning individuals who are scientifically naïve. The major problem occurs when they put such ideas and theories into action and thus cause harm to largely unsuspecting persons. As the philosopher Goethe (1749–1832) noted, "Nothing is [more] terrible than ignorance in action."

One example involves the theory of recovered memories of childhood sexual abuse (Bass & Davis, 1988; Loftus & Ketcham, 1994). Research suggests that child-hood sexual abuse is more common than most people think and is a major social prob-lem. But some therapists saw sexual abuse, and even satanic ritualistic abuse, in a surprising number of their clients. Parents, grandparents, teachers, and family friends have been accused of such abuse after the patients, with the help of a caring therapist, "recovered" their memories of the abuse. Few doubt that the therapists involved were well meaning and caring, but scientific research shows that the methods that these therapists used to help their clients almost certainly created memories of events that may never have occurred. A few years ago these therapist were telling other people how naïve they were to not realize the extent of sexual abuse. Today, they are more likely telling juries why they should not be found guilty of malpractice for not know-ing the most basic scientific facts about human memory, facts that would certainly have discouraged them from using their techniques (Danitz, 1997).

Another example is the application of a procedure called *facilitated communica-tion* in the education and treatment of nonverbal persons with autism. The method em-ploys a letter keyboard used by the person with some assistance by a facilitator, such as a teacher or therapist. People with autism, who for all their lives had been noncommuni-cative and considered mentally retarded, suddenly began to communicate avidly, typing complex messages with the aid of a facilitator. Professional excitement soared as some 2000 speech therapists and special education teachers rushed to learn this new technique. The whole concept of autism was overturned; hundreds of autistic persons were put into programs of facilitated communication; parents of autistic children were profoundly af-fected because their children were apparently beginning to communicate with them, re-vealing their love and thoughts. Unfortunately, controlled experimentation revealed that the communication had not been produced by the autistic persons at all but by the facili-tators, who were subtly guiding the autistic persons' responses (reviewed by Jacobson, Mulick, & Schwartz, 1995). Why were so many parents and professionals so gullible? Because they fervently wanted to believe that their autistic children and students really did have clear and complex thoughts. But even more critical, they had failed to be skep-tical. They had failed to recognize one of the most elementary ideas in scientific re-search: any phenomenon can have more than one explanation, and good experimental research, as you will learn in later chapters, can eliminate alternative explanations. In this case, there were two explanations: (1) the student is communicating and (2) the fa-cilitator is communicating. Because they wanted to believe, they chose explanation (1) and failed to apply the most basic critical evaluation. (Their problem, perhaps, was that they had not taken a good course in research design.)

Most pseudoscience in psychology is not meant to be malicious, but it can easily end up that way, tearing people's lives apart. Being muddleheaded can be every bit as dangerous as being malicious when you are playing with people's lives. The science of psychology has taught us that people's experiences and impressions are not always

BOX 1.5 · *Science and Pseudoscience*

Pseudoscience uses unscientific methods, theories, assumptions, and conclusions that pretend to be scientific. The ideas are wrapped in distorted, erroneous science, but with enough of the trappings of science to be convincing to many people. The intent is to be convincing.

Among the most common and egregious practitioners of pseudoscience are television advertisers. Their attempts to cloak the supposed benefits of their products with the trappings of science are often blatantly obvious. The scene is a physician's office or a science laboratory, with perhaps a nurse or a lab assistant working in the background. The actor is everybody's idea of the mature and dependable scientist or physician—a well-groomed, professional man (seldom a woman) wearing a white lab coat and possibly with a stethoscope hanging from the pocket. Some colorful, but probably meaningless, charts are on the wall. He holds up a package of the product and in a smooth, professional voice tells us how effective it is. Even if the words *science* or *research* are never voiced, the entire staged set is meant to convey the scientific backing of the product. Unfortunately, many people fall for it.

Pseudoscience is empty or make-believe science, and it is thriving in today's mass communications society. Books, manuals, tapes, and computer programs proclaim new theories and methods to understand our personalities, control our fate, predict our future, and even cure disease.

Pseudoscience can appear convincing, so how do you recognize it? To identify pseudoscience, ask yourself three questions: (1) What is the nature of the evidence for the claims that are made? (2) In what forms is the evidence reported and made public? (3) What are the affiliations of the supposed scientists?

The evidence for pseudoscience is typically a presentation of personal testimonials, use of authority figures (like the fake physician in the TV commercial), and reports of medical or scientific cases. All this is anecdotal evidence, presented in a convincing manner and uncritically accepted by the public. Personal testimony, case reports, and other anecdotal evidence can be starting points for legitimate research, but in pseudoscience they are almost always the primary or only evidence. The major problem with anecdotal evidence is that it is not gathered under controlled conditions. It is highly selective evidence, carefully chosen from many possibilities. In pseudoscience, to prove that a product or idea really works you need only to put forth cases in which it did seem to work and ignore cases in which it clearly did not. Common examples are statements such as "I know that dreams are prophetic because I had a dream about poor Aunt Martha floating in the sky and five weeks later she was dead!" (To the student: Why is this not a convincing example of the prophetic power of dreams?)

Pseudoscience almost never presents its data in mainstream science journals, in which there is quality control through peer review. Rather, it is reported in popular magazines, in newspaper articles, on the Internet, on television, and in radio broadcasts. Unlike scientific journals, these outlets do not provide the details needed to evaluate the validity of the claims and procedures.

Pseudoscientists rarely practice their science in academic or industrial settings. Many are free-lance individuals, or private businesses with impressive-sounding titles, or obscure institutes or colleges. They typically are not affiliated with mainstream universities, colleges, or laboratories, where their work would be subjected to review by other professionals.

Be alert to pseudoscience; be careful about uncritically accepting anecdotal evidence. A good reference is *The Road from Foolishness to Fraud* (Park, 1999).

correct. It has provided real solutions to critical problems, including better teaching methods, more effective treatment for psychological problems, better ways to solve social problems, and ways to help people to deal with the world around them. The pseudoscientific nonsense that masquerades as psychology has provided simplistic explanations for complex phenomena, often giving people confidence in ideas and actions that they should view with skepticism. However, such pseudoscience has never provided a real solution to a real psychological problem. In contrast, the hardheaded scientific research of dedicated psychologists has led to hundreds of improvements in everyday lives. This is why psychological research is so important and is the reason for this course and this textbook (see Box 1.5).

Quick-Check Review 4: Psychology

4.1. What were some of the more influential schools of psychology?

4.2. What is the nature of modern mainstream psychology?

4.3. Why is it critical that psychology be scientific?

4.4. Is psychology a social, physical, or biological science? Explain.

Chapter Summary

Science is a systematic way of asking and answering questions—a disciplined curiosity. There are many ways to gain knowledge, including tenacity, intuition, authority, rationalism, empiricism, and science. Science combines rationalism and empiricism. Scientists order their thinking rationally and seek facts through empirical observations. Empiricism enables scientists to verify their rationally derived theories.

The combination of rationalism and empiricism was first developed in ancient Greece, but was later weakened by a shift to more rational and abstract approaches to knowing the world, particularly as influenced by Plato. Medieval Christian scholars used science but considered it secondary to theology. Scientific thought increased through the Renaissance and emerged by the 17th century largely independent of religion. By the 20th century, science had developed into a widely accepted way of thinking about the universe.

Psychology is a relatively new scientific discipline that studies the behavior of organisms. Over the past century, psychology has grown from a small discipline focused on understanding the mechanisms of human functioning to a vast enterprise studying hundreds of basic and applied issues. The research methods of psychology are drawn primarily from the natural sciences.

Using the sophistication of science in studies of human behavior is critical, because observations and impressions are often deceiving. What people think is true about human behavior often turns out to be false when studied with scientific rigor. Furthermore, many of the simplistic theories that have been offered by people not well grounded in the science of psychology have proved to be less than useless, sometimes causing considerable harm. Psychology is not a field that can tolerate pseudoscientific nonsense, because the application of psychological theories, whether valid or not, will affect the lives of people in significant ways.

Key Terms

Define the following key terms. Be sure that you understand them. They are discussed in the chapter and defined in the glossary.

psychology	empiricism	behaviorism
science	naïve empiricism	behavior modification
scientific research	sophisticated empiricism	humanistic psychology
process of inquiry	orderliness belief	cognitive psychology
skeptic	experimentation	cognitive science
serendipity	theology	behavioral medicine
tenacity	psychophysics	health psychology
intuition	structuralism	behavioral neuroscience
authority	functionalism	mainstream psychology
rationalism	psychoanalysis	pseudoscience
logic	Gestalt psychology	

2

Research Is a Process of Inquiry

Science is built up with facts, as a house is with stones. But a collection of facts is no more a science than a heap of stones is a house.

—Jules Henri Poincare, 1854–1912

CD Resource Material

- Inductive–Deductive Logic Primer
- Discussion of the Importance of Theory in Science
- Examples of the Various Phases of Research
- APA Publication Style Tutorial
- APA Publication Style Manual
- Student Study Guide/Laboratory Manual

Web Resource Material

- Scientific Theory
- B. F. Skinner Background Material
- P. E. Meehl Background Material
- Electronic Communication and Online Journals
- Background Material on Autism

Research is a systematic search for information—a process of inquiry. It can be carried out in libraries, laboratories, schoolrooms, hospitals, factories, in the pages of the Bible, on street corners, or in the wild watching a herd of elephants. Research can be carried out anywhere, on any phenomena in nature, and by anyone. Scientists, rabbis, and head chefs can all carry out systematic inquiry in their own domains. Although all research is a systematic process of inquiry, not all research is scientific. A religious scholar might study and research religious writings. The scholar's research is a serious, systematic process of inquiry, but it is not, and it is not meant to be, scientific. What distinguishes scientific research from other research is the emphasis in science on using integrated empirical and rational processes, that is, gaining knowledge through sensory experiences and through reasoning.

This chapter will introduce you to some of the basic concepts on which science is built. It begins with a discussion of how scientists attack questions and the basic assumptions behind their work. It then describes the single most powerful tool in science—theories. Finally, the chapter closes with a description of a model of the research enterprise; this model provides the organization for this text.

The Scientific Process

In Chapter 1 you learned that science is a way of thinking. In this section you will learn what this means. The section starts with the basic assumption on which all science rests. It then describes the two fundamental processes of science, observation and inference, which represent the empirical and rational elements of science, respectively. It then introduces conceptual models before discussing the use of both inductive and deductive thinking.

Basic Assumptions of Science

Every discipline, including science, is built on **assumptions**—ideas that are tentatively accepted as being true without further examination. Science makes few assumptions, preferring to subject ideas to the rigorous demands of rational and empirical challenges. Nevertheless, the assumptions underlying science provide a strong platform for understanding nature. Whatever their particular discipline, scientists share several basic assumptions about nature and the role of science in understanding nature:

1. A true, physical universe exists.
2. Although there may be randomness and thus unpredictability in the universe, it is primarily an orderly system.
3. The principles of this orderly universe can be discovered, particularly through scientific research.
4. Knowledge of the universe is always incomplete. New knowledge can, and should, alter current ideas and theories. Therefore, all knowledge and theories are tentative.

These assumptions are the cornerstone of science. Scientists assume that there is a real, mostly orderly universe and that the principles by which this universe operates can be discovered. The assumption that theories and knowledge are tentative is as much an admonition to scientists as an assumption. No one has the wisdom to create the perfect theory. In time, the flaws and limitations of every theory will be exposed.

Note what is *not* in this list of scientific assumptions. Scientists do not assume that the entire universe is visible. In fact, scientists would argue that some of the most interesting aspects of the universe may not be detectable through human senses. Scientists routinely hypothesize about such invisible, but presumably real, forces, such as gravity. However, even concepts about unseen factors like gravity must conform to the twin constraints of rationalism and empiricism. As you will see in the next section, science is built partly on concepts that are not directly observable. Yet scientists are confident in using concepts about unseen events because they constantly challenge the accuracy of these concepts. Only concepts that have survived repeated empirical challenges reach the level of "generally accepted scientific theory." Even then, scientists will challenge an accepted theory by either (1) exposing its flaws with well-designed research or (2) proposing a better theory, one that explains current research information and predicts and explains new phenomena that have yet to be studied.

Observation and Inference: Facts and Constructs

At minimum, scientific research involves the following:

1. Posing a question
2. Developing procedures to answer the question
3. Planning for and then making appropriate empirical observations
4. Rationally interpreting the empirical observations

Scientists carefully observe events, reason about why the events occurred, and then make predictions based on the ideas developed during the reasoning process. The elements of empirical observation and rational abstraction are brought together to create a coherent understanding of the phenomenon.

Scientists refer to empirical observations as collecting **data,** which are the facts of research. **Facts** are those events that can be directly, empirically, and repeatedly observed. Each scientific discipline has its particular kinds of facts. In psychology, observed facts include the physiological structures of participants, the physical conditions around them, the behavior of other organisms (including the researcher), and, of course, the participant's own behavior. Most facts observed in psychology are **behaviors:** verbal behavior, nonverbal communication such as gestures, physiological activity, social behavior, and so on. Scientists can observe the behavior of children at play, shoppers in stores, participants in research, clients talking about their feelings, workers at machines, or senators in debate. They can also study animal behaviors in the laboratory and in the natural environment. All these behaviors can be objectively observed and recorded. **Observation** is the empirical process of using one's senses to recognize and record factual events.

In addition to studying behavioral facts, psychologists also study memory, emotion, intelligence, attitudes, values, creativity, thinking, perception, humor, and so on. These are not directly observable behavioral events and thus are not facts. We cannot directly observe intelligence or thinking or perception, but we can observe behavior that we believe to be related to these nonobservable concepts. For example, in some early work with children with autism (Graziano, 1974), we observed that the children frequently exhibited highly disruptive behavior in which they injured themselves and others and caused upheaval in their therapy program. Their behavior was a fact; it was repeatedly observed, measured, and recorded. Initial treatment reduced both the intensity and duration of the disruptive behavior, but not its frequency. That is, the children were "blowing up" just as often as before treatment, but the episodes were shorter and less intense. We had made progress, but still wanted to reduce the frequency of these outbursts. Continued careful observation revealed a subtle but observable change in the child's behavior just prior to the outbursts: activity stopped, facial expressions became contorted and mobile, limbs stiffened, and the severe behavior exploded. We could not find anything external to the child that could cause this observed reaction. We then inferred that just prior to their outbursts the children may have been feeling some intense internal arousal, which may have cued the outbursts. Thus, we reasoned, to reduce the frequency of the outbursts, we would have to control the internal arousal. But how were we to accomplish this? From the behavior therapy research literature, we selected an approach developed by Wolpe (1958, 1990), systematic desensitization, that employs relaxation training as a first step. Although used with adults, it had not to our knowledge ever been applied to children. But in light of our inference that the aroused state of the children led to their outbursts, it seemed a reasonable approach to try. We trained the children in relaxation, and in time the frequency of their outbursts decreased to zero.

What is important in this example is the distinction between our observations of behavior (the outbursts and the facial expressions that preceded the outbursts) and our inferences of an internal condition (arousal). The internal condition is not observable; it is inferred from the observations of behavior. An **inference** is an intellectual process in which conclusions are derived from observed facts or from other ideas.

Scientists often draw inferences from observations of events. Most of the work done by psychologists deals with inferences. When they study anxiety, intelligence, or memory, they are working with inferences. Because inferences are largely drawn from empirical observations (the facts), it is critical that the observations be precise. Otherwise, little confidence can be placed in any inference drawn. For this reason, we should use precisely defined empirical methods in research to develop a solid observational base for drawing inferences about events that cannot be directly observed. Inferences can also be drawn from other inferences, but in science an important starting point for making inferences is careful observation. In general, the better the observational base and the more ties our inferences have to this base, the more confidence scientists have in the inference. When making inferences, we should stay close to the data. As Detective Sergeant Joe Friday used to say to the witness in the old *Dragnet* television series, "Just give us the facts, ma'am." He might have added, "We'll draw our own inferences."

When a researcher draws an inference about a research participant, the inference resides in the researcher and not in the participant. The process involves the researcher's rational activity of accepting the sensory data (the observations) as true and then drawing from them an idea (inference) about nonobservable events. With the autistic children example, the inference was that a state of arousal existed. The inferred state of arousal was not a fact; it was an idea. In other words, the inference of an internal arousal was not in the child; it was an idea created by the researchers, who had no direct observation of what was really going on in the child. The hypothesis of an internal arousal, although plausible, is an explanatory idea, not reality. It helped to explain the observed behavior, and it helped to generate a possible course of action that proved to be effective. This is an important point. Nonobservable inferred events, such as gravity, electricity, intelligence, memory, anxiety, perception, id, and ego, are all rational ideas that have been constructed by researchers. Ideas constructed in this way by the researcher are called **constructs.** Constructs are used analogically, that is, *as if* they exist in fact and *as if* they really have a relationship with observable events. In the example, the researchers never observed the children's internal states of arousal. They operated *as if* the inferred state actually existed and would be reduced if they trained the children to relax. Furthermore, they predicted that if the inferred state were reduced then the frequency of the disruptive behavior would decrease.

The analogical nature of constructs must never be forgotten. A construct may be used so frequently that people begin to think of it as a fact, and they lose sight of its very tentative, analogical nature. For example, some people may believe there really is an id, an ego, and a superego inside each of us. These constructs take on a reality that they were never meant to have. Confusing a construct for a fact is a logical error known as **reification of a construct.** Reification of a construct is just one of several errors that scientists avoid by using logic in their work. Some of the more common errors are described in Box 2.1.

Scientists use both observations and constructs in their day to day work. Note the relationship between the construct of internal arousal and the observed facts in the example of the children with autism. First, the construct was inferred from observed behavior. Then the construct was used as a basis for predicting new behavior that could be observed. The prediction was that reducing the internal arousal would reduce the disruptive behavior. Thus, the construct is related to observed facts in two ways: it was derived from the observations, and it served as a basis for predicting future observations. The construct helped to explain a relationship between two sets of facts. In this instance, the two sets of facts were observations of behavior, one made before relaxation training and the other made after training. Recall that science involves the continual, interactive movement between empirical observation and rational abstractions. Now you can see that this interactive movement is between observations and constructs. The scientist moves from one to the other and back again, at each step refining constructs from observations and predicting observations from constructs. This process provides a description or explanation of relationships among facts and constructs. With the children, the relationship between the observations and the constructs provided a potential explanation of an observed phenomenon, in this case the disruptive

BOX 2.1 • *Logical Interpretation Errors*

Reification of a construct is one of many problems that scientists are trained to recognize and avoid. Listed below are others. You may have used some of these in your everyday thinking. Everyone does. But in science, fuzzy thinking interferes with the challenging work of understanding nature.

Nominal Fallacy

People commit this error when they mistake the naming of phenomena for an explanation of the phenomena. For example, if you recognize that some people consistently behave aggressively, you might appropriately label them as aggressive. But you may also be tempted to explain their aggressive behavior by noting that they are aggressive people. The label, based on their behavior, later becomes the explanation for their behavior—an entirely circular argument.

All-or-None Bias

This is a tendency to see a statement as either true or false, when in most cases in science the statement is probabilistic. Most good theories explain many things and do so with consistency, but they almost never explain everything under every condition. Therefore, they are technically false, although scientists tend to view the theory as true because it is often, although not always, true. It is best to remember that no theory is completely true; rather, it provides accurate explanations for a certain percentage of situations or events.

Similarity–Uniqueness Paradox

This is the tendency to view two things as either similar to one another or different from one another, when in reality they are probably both. For example, two people may be similar in their backgrounds but different in their aspirations. People have a tendency to simplify such comparisons, which can often blind them to important elements.

Barnum Statement

This effect is named after P. T. Barnum of the Barnum and Bailey Circus, who is alleged to have said "there is a sucker born every minute." Barnum statements appear to be insightful comments about an issue, when in fact they are nothing more than statements that are true for almost all issues, situations, or people. For example, telling someone that she "tries to do what is right, but sometimes finds that temptation is strong" will probably be readily accepted by most people as an insightful comment on their personality, but it is not insightful at all. You can say the same thing to 100 different people at random and almost all of them will be impressed by your insight.

Evaluative Biases of Language

Science should be nonjudgmental, but the truth is that language often inserts subtle judgments into the descriptions of objective behaviors. For example, if a person cuts off a telemarketer in the first few seconds of a call by saying, "I do not take unsolicited sales calls," is the person being assertive or aggressive? Labeling the behavior as assertive gives a very different impression than labeling it as aggressive.

behavior. We then used the construct *as if* it adequately represented what was really happening, although we could not observe all the parts.

Inductive and Deductive Thinking

Sherlock Holmes buffs will probably argue that the great detective never said it, but the statement attributed to Holmes, perhaps first voiced in a movie version, has entertained and misled people for some time. You know the scene: at the site of the crime Holmes inspects the room, his keen eyes darting and his nose alert to the lingering tobacco smoke. Suddenly, with an explosive "Aha!" he pounces on a partially burnt matchstick cracked in the middle with a small flake of tobacco stuck to its tip. Holmes examines it closely and then announces, "Our culprit, Watson, is 44 years old, 5 feet 8½ inches tall, 183 pounds. He is right-handed, a veteran of the India conflicts, and still carries a lead ball in his right calf. He is a gentleman, Watson, and had no intention of committing a crime when he entered this room. He left hurriedly by way of that window when he heard us at the door, and, if I am not mistaken, he will return here to confess his crime and will knock on that door precisely…now!"

A tentative knocking is heard at the door. Watson opens it revealing the gentleman so precisely described by Holmes.

"Egads 'Olmes!" says Watson, wide-eyed. "'Ow did you ever know that?"

"Deduction, my dear Watson," says Holmes. "A simple process of deduction."

Actually, it was not deduction alone. Holmes had confused two terms, and what he should have said was "Induction–deduction my dear Watson. A simple process of induction–deduction." Assuming that the great Holmes could in fact have drawn such complete conclusions from such limited evidence, his process was one familiar to everyone. He observed some specific clues and inferred (the induction) something he could not directly observe, specifically, the type of person who would have committed the crime and left those clues. Holmes then made the prediction (the deduction) that the man would return.

When we reason from the particular to the general, we are reasoning inductively; when we use the more abstract and general ideas to return to specifics, that is, to make predictions about future observations, we are reasoning deductively (Copi & Cohen, 2002).[1] Induction and deduction are rational processes and are used constantly by scientists. In terms of the earlier discussion, it is the combination of these two kinds of thinking, induction and deduction, that characterizes science. A researcher who begins with empirical observations and then infers constructs is engaged in **inductive reasoning.** Using the constructs as the basis of making predictions about new, specific observations is **deductive reasoning.** A scientist must use both processes to build and validate conceptual models.

Inductive–deductive reasoning is not unique to science; these processes are used constantly in everyday life. When I return from work on a cold winter day and find the

---

[1]Psychologists tend to use the concepts of induction and deduction as discussed here. However, philosophy students will recognize that this distinction is incomplete, distinguishing only one kind of induction from one kind of deduction (Reese, 1996).

front door left partly open and a single muddy sneaker on the hall rug, I *inductively* infer that "the kids are home from school." Knowing a good deal about these kids, I can also *deductively* predict that "right now Lisa is upstairs talking on the telephone with one of her friends," and I can go upstairs to make observations and check the accuracy of my predictions: from the specific observation to the general idea; from the general idea back to the more specific observation; induction and deduction. People have been thinking inductively and deductively all their lives, although probably not with the precision of the scientist. This last point is important. Although scientists use the same kind of reasoning processes used in everyday life, they must use the process with a precision rarely seen in everyday life. Indeed, the entire scientific research enterprise can be seen as the development of a framework within which scientists can carry out inductive and deductive reasoning under the most precise conditions. Building on a point made in Chapter 1, the essence of science is its process of thinking, a process that entails *systematic inductive–deductive logic.* Science, more than any other way of gaining knowledge, bases its inductive reasoning on carefully observed facts. Making the observations or getting the facts is one of the critical components of scientific research. Thus, the enterprise of scientific research uses facts to fuel the inductive–deductive process and obtains the facts with the greatest precision possible.

Quick-Check Review 1: The Scientific Process

1.1. What is meant by data in research? How are data obtained?

1.2. How do facts and constructs differ? Give examples.

1.3. What is reification of a construct?

1.4. Explain the two ways in which constructs are related to facts.

1.5. What are the basic assumptions that all scientists accept about the nature of the universe?

1.6. What is the difference between inductive and deductive reasoning?

Models and Theories in Science

Scientists study many phenomena, sometimes solving such practical problems as building bridges and curing disease and sometimes making basic discoveries about nature. However, regardless of the phenomena studied or the goals of the research, scientists develop and use theories. It has been said that a major goal of science is to develop good theories, because there is nothing more useful and practical as a good theory. This section begins by defining theories and discussing how they are developed and used by scientists. Then four types of theories are defined. The section ends with a discussion of the importance of judging theories and models on their usefulness, as well as on their accuracy.

A **theory** is a formalized set of concepts that summarizes and organizes observations and inferences, provides tentative explanations for phenomena, and provides the bases for making predictions. To be scientific, a theory must be testable, that is, it must make specific predictions that can be tested empirically, and the predictions have to be such that they can be contradicted by empirical evidence. In other words, a theory that predicts everything and, therefore, can never be contradicted is neither useful nor scientific. Theories, then, must stand the test of disconfirmation or falsifiability (Popper, 1959). A good theory demands a solid empirical base and a set of carefully developed constructs, neither of which can be created easily. Scientific theories are not mere guesses and hunches, nor are they flimsy and ephemeral flights of fancy. They are carefully constructed from empirical observations, constructs, and inductive and deductive logic. In building theories, the scientist brings together and integrates what has been learned about the phenomena under study. Developing adequate theories that organize, predict, and explain natural phenomena is a major goal of scientists.

It is often difficult for a beginning student to appreciate the importance of theory to science. Theory is not required in order to use most of the procedures described in this text to discover new facts, but the facts will be much less useful without the organizing framework of theory. Theory provides a blueprint that organizes facts into ideas and ideas into an understanding of the world. Scientists want their theories to be functional and strong. A functional theory works; it explains how variables are related to one another. A strong theory makes specific predictions that can be confirmed by empirical observation. The strongest theories make unique predictions, that is, predictions that other theories do not make, and these predictions are consistent with subsequent observations. Scientists prefer **parsimony** (literally, the thrifty or economical); a simple, straightforward, *thrifty* theory is preferred over a complex theory if the theories provide equivalent predictive ability. A single theory that explains several different phenomena is preferred over several theories that collectively explain the same phenomena. The principle of parsimony, however, never supersedes the concept that the theory must possess **validity;** that is, it must make specific testable predictions that are confirmed by observation.

All scientific theories involve both induction and deduction, but they often differ in the degree to which they emphasize one or the other. Theories that emphasize induction, called **inductive theories,** stay very close to the empirical data. Inductive theorists follow the data wherever they may lead. Skinner (1972, 1990) epitomized this inductive method of theory construction. He built his theories on extensive observational data, being careful not to extend the theory beyond the data. In an eloquent presentation only days before his death, Skinner (1990) continued to argue that there are serious risks associated with postulating theories that go well beyond the data and that involve processes not directly observable.

The more traditional, formalized theory, the **deductive theory,** emphasizes deductions from constructs. The deductions are stated as hypotheses and are then empirically tested through research. An example is Meehl's (1990) theorizing about the underlying cause(s) of schizophrenia. Meehl postulated a strong theory that made specific deductive predictions. The theory is tested every time a prediction is investigated and is weakened when a prediction is not confirmed. Unlike Skinner, Meehl's deductive theories go well beyond the data, challenging scientists to make new observations. It is worth noting that Skinner and Meehl were colleagues during their early careers at the University of Minnesota. Their discussions on the role of theory in science must have been intense and dynamic.

Most psychological theories are **functional theories** involving about equal emphasis on induction and deduction. All three types of theories have the characteristic functions of organizing knowledge, predicting new observations, and explaining relationships among events.

Another type of theory is the **model.** Any phenomenon can be represented by a model. The word model derives from the Latin *modulus,* meaning a small measure of something. In science, it has come to mean a miniature representation of reality. A model is a description or analogy that helps scientists to understand something usually unseen and/or more complex. A model is somewhat less developed than a formal theory, and consequently models are sometimes referred to as "mini-theories." A model airplane is a good example. It clearly is not equivalent to a real airplane. It has the general form and many of the characteristics of a real airplane, such as wings, rudder, and propellers. Although these characteristics may correspond faithfully to those of a real airplane, the model is not an exact replica of the real airplane. It is smaller, does not have all the working parts, and may be constructed of balsa wood or plastic instead of aluminum.

A model *represents* reality; it does not duplicate it. Models are useful because constructing and examining a model helps scientists to organize knowledge and hypotheses about the reality represented by the model. They can examine a model, observe relationships among its parts, and observe how it operates. They can generate new ideas from the model about how the real world is constructed and how it operates. For example, a model airplane in a wind tunnel can give researchers ideas about how the real airplane might behave and lead them to new ideas or hypotheses about the design and operation of real airplanes. Likewise, our model of the relationship of internal arousal and disruptive behavior in children with autism led us to new applications of behavior therapy.

Models can be constructed to represent any aspect of the universe. We can build models of airplanes or the solar system, of an atom or a bacterium, of wave motions, neurons, memory, thinking processes, or genetic structure. Our knowledge of any phenomenon can be organized into models to represent reality. Furthermore, the models need not be physical in their construction, such as a balsa wood airplane. They can be abstract or conceptual models constructed of ideas and expressed in verbal and/or mathematical language. The classical model of human memory is a good example of an abstract model. It assumes multiple levels of memory, with each level having its own characteristics. The sensory store is assumed to hold extensive information for a very short period of time (about 1 second). The short-term memory holds information longer (about 15 seconds), but has a restricted capacity. The long-term memory provides the long-term, high-capacity storage that people usually think of when they think about memory. Few cognitive psychologists believe such structures exist or that their model is the way information is stored and processed. But a model does not have to be real or true to be useful. It need only make accurate predictions about relationships between observable events. The classical model of memory is a strong one because it is based on hundreds of independent observations. In other words, the model is closely tied to the observational base on which it was first developed. Furthermore, the model proved useful by correctly predicting new observations that were confirmed by careful scientific study. It is not a perfect model of memory and will be replaced by better models as research identifies relationships that the model cannot predict or explain. In fact, this model of memory has already been seriously challenged. Nevertheless, it is convenient and useful and has contributed enormously to our understanding of how things are remembered.

All models share the following characteristics:

1. Models are simplified representations of phenomena and have point to point correspondence with some of the characteristics of the phenomena.
2. Models provide convenient, manageable, and compact representations of the larger, complex, and mostly unknown reality.
3. Models are incomplete, tentative, and analogical.
4. Manipulating models helps to organize information, to illustrate relationships among parts, and to create new ideas and predict new observations.

"This is Gronski's new model of the synaptic transmission mechanism. Nobody understands it, but it won third prize in the campus art competition."

Models and theories are critical in science. Developing models is both an art and a science.

You should not think of a theory only in terms of whether it is *right or wrong,* that is, in terms of its validity. Scientists also judge theories by how *useful* they are in organizing information, explaining phenomena, and generating accurate predictions. For example, the theory of Newtonian mechanics is clearly wrong. When objects move near the speed of light, they do not behave the way Newtonian mechanics predict. Einstein's general theory of relativity describes the movement of objects more accurately regardless of how fast the object is traveling. But Newtonian mechanics survives and is taught extensively in high school and college. Why? The reason is simple. Everyday objects hardly ever travel at speeds approaching the speed of light. Therefore, the theories developed by Newton describe the motion of such ordinary objects accurately. The theory survives because it is useful and accurate in a wide range of situations.

Quick-Check Review 2: Models and Theories in Science

2.1. What is a theory and how is it useful in science?

2.2. What is the difference between inductive and deductive theories?

2.3. What is a model, what are its major characteristics, and how is it used in science?

2.4. Distinguish between observation and inference. Give examples.

2.5. Why are theories judged on the basis of how useful they are in addition to their accuracy?

2.6. What is meant by falsifiability in science?

A Model of the Research Process

Almost any phenomenon can be studied scientifically, and a model can be developed to represent it. One purpose of a model is to help to organize the activities of the person using the model. This section presents a model of psychological research methods to serve as an outline for the text.[2] Like any model, this model is not a complete representation of reality. The model simplifies the complexity of psychological research in order to identify some important aspects of the research process. The model of research presented here has two dimensions: phases of research and levels of constraint.

Phases of Research

Psychological research usually proceeds in an orderly manner through successive phases. This sequencing of phases can vary, but the most general sequence is described in Table 2.1. The concept of **phases of research** provides one dimension of the

---

[2]The model of research presented here is a variation of a model presented by Hyman (1964).

TABLE 2.1   *The Phases of a Research Study*

Idea-generating phase	Identify a topic of interest to study.
Problem-definition phase	Refine the vague and general idea(s) generated in the previous step into a precise question to be studied.
Procedures-design phase	Decide on the specific procedures to be used in the gathering and statistical analysis of the data.
Observation phase	Use the procedures devised in the previous step to collect your observations.
Data-analysis phase	Analyze the data collected using appropriate statistical procedures.
Interpretation phase	Compare your results with the results predicted on the basis of your theory. Do your results support the theory?
Communication phase	Prepare a written or oral report of your study for publication or presentation to colleagues. Your report should include a description of all the preceding steps.

conceptual model on which this text is based. Research begins with ideas and flows through the successive, overlapping phases of the research process. Each phase has its own characteristics, and different work is accomplished in each in preparation for the next phase.

Idea-Generating Phase.   All research begins with an idea. For example, a researcher may have an interest in children's reasoning processes, but no particular idea for a research project. The interest, however, is enough to point the researcher to an area within which more defined ideas can be developed. Being interested in the area to be studied is critical in helping to sustain the hard work to follow. This repeats the point made in Chapter 1 that the scientist's curiosity is critical in research, both in helping to generate ideas and in sustaining the researcher's efforts.

The idea phase can begin with vague thoughts, and initial ideas can emerge in very nonscientific ways. Archimedes is supposed to have had a flash of creative thought while sitting in a bath. Ideas can be generated while in conversation, reading novels, watching television, walking in the woods, buying a hamburger, crossing the street, or even while dreaming. However, getting research ideas is not usually so unsystematic. Most research ideas are generated in a systematic fashion from other research results. Research ideas vary from unsystematic hunches to highly systematic and precise steps in logical thinking. The former are most characteristic of exploratory research, which occurs in the early history of a research area; the latter are characteristic of research at more advanced levels of the research area.

We should not be too critical of initial ideas, because premature criticism might destroy an emerging good idea. The early ideas ought to be taken seriously, nourished, and thought about. Curiosity, interest, and enthusiasm are critical ingredients. Once an area of interest is identified, it is useful to dive right in by reading articles and books and talking with people who work in the area.

Little is known about the processes involved in the creative idea-generating phase of research, although this is beginning to change (McGuire, 1997). Indeed, here is a good area for research: How are creative ideas generated? What seems clear is that productive scientists have many ideas. When asked in a television interview where scientists find their good ideas, the Nobel Prize winner Linus Pauling replied, "Well, you have lots of ideas, and you throw out the bad ones."

Problem-Definition Phase.   The research process begins by identifying an area of interest and generating ideas for study. However, vague ideas are not sufficient. They must be clarified and refined. In this part of the process, the scientist examines the research literature and learns how other researchers have conceptualized, measured, and tested these and related ideas. This careful examination of the literature, usually called *library research,* (see Appendix C and the *Student Resource CD*), is an important part of science. The published research literature provides the detailed information about an issue that is critical in the problem-definition phase. The scientist continues working on the ideas, clarifying, defining, specifying, and refining them based on what is learned in the research literature. The goal is to produce one or more clearly posed questions based on (1) well-developed knowledge of previous research and theory and (2) the scientist's own ideas and speculations.

Carefully conceptualizing and phrasing the research question are critical, because everything the researcher does in the remainder of the research process will be aimed at answering this question. The question might involve a highly specific and precisely drawn hypothesis, or it might be phrased in a much more general manner typical of exploratory research. The research questions largely control the way the rest of the process is carried out.

The activities of the problem-definition phase are rational, abstract processes that manipulate and systematically develop ideas toward the goal of refining them into researchable questions. This rational process is used to prepare for the next phase, in which the procedures for making the observations are designed.

Procedures-Design Phase.   Before any data are collected, the researcher must determine which observations to make and under what conditions, how to record the observations, what statistical methods to use to analyze the data, and so on. The researcher also makes decisions in this phase about what participants to test. Since decisions are being made about using living organisms in research, ethical issues must be considered. The ethics of scientific research includes guidelines for humane treatment of participants. Before the researcher contacts a single participant, the research plan must survive ethical evaluation and must be modified whenever ethical guidelines are not met. Only when the plan can stand up to ethical demands does the investigator proceed with the next phase—making the observations. The ethics of psychological research is a major area that every researcher must know, understand, and apply. The design phase is active, systematic, and complex. Much of the content of research methods courses focuses specifically on this phase.

Observation Phase.   Making the observations (getting the data) is the most familiar phase to beginning students, who often see this as actually "doing the research." This is the empirical phase in which the researcher carries out the procedures that were designed in the previous phase and makes observations of the participants' behavior under the conditions specified. The observation phase is central in all science. Note that the earlier phases serve as preparation for making the empirical observations, and the remaining phases focus on using these observations by processing, interpreting, and communicating them. All scientific research revolves around this most central aspect—making empirical observations.

Data-Analysis Phase.   In the data-analysis phase, the researcher processes and makes sense out of the data. Data-analysis procedures, like the observation procedures, are selected in the design phase. Students are often surprised that data-analysis procedures are selected before the data are gathered. As you will see later in this text, many design decisions, such as sample size, will follow from the choice of data-analysis procedures. In almost all psychological research, the data will be in the form of a numerical record representing the observations made. The numerical data must be organized and analyzed. Statistical procedures are used to describe and evaluate numerical data and to help to determine the significance of the observations. The statistical procedures might be as simple as counting responses and drawing graphs to show response changes over time, or they may be as complex as a two-way analysis of variance (described in Chapter 12). Whatever the statistical procedures, the important point is that the researcher must choose statistical procedures appropriate to the question being asked and to the observational procedures being used. As you will see in Chapter 14, the choice of statistical procedure is determined by the nature of the question and the observational procedures.

Interpretation Phase.   Having statistically analyzed the data, the researcher interprets the statistical results in terms of (1) how they help to answer the research question and (2) how this answer contributes to the knowledge in the field. The interpretation helps to relate the findings not only to the original questions, but also to other concepts and findings in the field. This stage represents the flip side of the problem-definition phase. When defining the research problem, scientists use theories as guides to important questions. Here the scientists use the answers that they have generated to these questions to determine how accurately their theories predict new observations. The problem-definition phase uses deductive reasoning—from the general theory to the specific prediction. The interpretation phase uses inductive reasoning—from the specific results of the study back to the generality of the theory. In many cases, the results of a study suggest ways to expand or modify the theory to increase its usefulness and accuracy.

Communication Phase.   Science is a public enterprise. A critical component of science is the communication of research findings. Scientific communication occurs through presentations at scientific meetings and through publication in journals and books. Scientists communicate not only the results, but also the procedures used and the rationales behind them. Specific guidelines are used to organize concisely all the information needed in a research report. Such guidelines are provided by the *APA Publication Manual* (2001). Writing a research report in APA style is covered in Appendix B and on the *Student Resource CD*.

Scientific publications should describe procedures in detail not only so that other scientists can understand the research, but also to allow them to replicate it. **Replication** means repeating a study to see if the same results are obtained. If a research finding cannot be replicated, then considerable doubt is cast on the genuineness of that finding. By presenting full accounts of research rationales, procedures, findings, and interpretations, the researcher is making the work available for others to evaluate. The writing of a research report should be clear and concise. Avoid the pretentious style illustrated in the Calvin and Hobbes cartoon.

Each finished project can serve as the basis for further questions and further empirical research. Now we have come full circle, back to the beginning phase of generating ideas. In a developing field of research, the ideas for asking new questions and making new observations are mainly ideas that have been generated by previous research. Scientists are stimulated by the work of their colleagues and derive research questions from them. In turn, their own work stimulates others. Figure 2.1 illustrates the circular nature of this process.

Scientists use two major avenues for communicating their work. The most formal is written communication in books and scientific journals. These reports become a permanent record, part of the archives of a scientific discipline. They are preserved and can be retrieved and studied by colleagues soon after publication or many years later. A minor disadvantage of written reports is that the publication process usually takes a year or more after the research has been completed before written reports are available in journals and books.

More immediate and more interactive communications are the researcher's oral and graphic presentations made at scientific meetings and informal communication among colleagues. Scientists visit each other's laboratories, talk on the telephone or during parties or poker games, exchange letters and electronic mail, and so on. This informal,

Calvin and Hobbes   by Bill Watterson

This is not how one should write research reports.

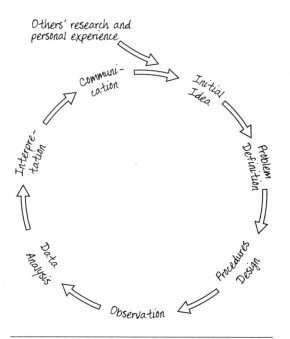

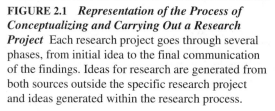

FIGURE 2.1 *Representation of the Process of Conceptualizing and Carrying Out a Research Project* Each research project goes through several phases, from initial idea to the final communication of the findings. Ideas for research are generated from both sources outside the specific research project and ideas generated within the research process.

highly interactive network of communication has been called the "invisible college," and it serves the important function of keeping scientists in communication with each other. Indeed, some believe it is the most critical means of communication among scientists. It is important for the young researcher, if seriously interested in a research career, to become involved actively in this invisible-college network of communications (Osberg & Raulin, 1989). The nature of this invisible college has been changing rapidly in the Information Age, as illustrated in Box 2.2.

The research process just described is common to all sciences. The particular observations may vary from one discipline to another, because each discipline is interested in observing and understanding different phenomena. But the basic processes and the systematic way of studying problems are common elements of science, regardless of each discipline's particular subject matter. The process, and not the content, distinguishes science from other ways of knowing; and the content, the particular phenomena and facts of interest, distinguishes one scientific discipline from another.

Although it is generally true that research proceeds in the sequence described, the sequencing of the phases is not rigid. New ideas might occur while the researcher

BOX 2.2 • *Scientific Communication in the Information Age*

The information superhighway is changing the way that research is conducted, as well as increasing the availability of scientific information. Changes like computerized databases for research articles and books have dramatically reduced the time needed to locate key materials during the planning phase. But more profound changes are also occurring.

Electronic mail (**e-mail**) makes it easy to communicate and collaborate with a colleague across the country (or even around the world). The Internet, the electronic highway that carries these messages all over the world, can be used to transmit a short note or an entire book. The **list server** is a program that receives a message and then sends a copy of it to everyone on the list. It has also changed the way professionals communicate and share ideas. For example, list servers make it possible for hundreds of scientists to carry on extended conversations, literally brainstorming with the best people in the field. In rapidly developing fields, such as the recent work in high-temperature superconductivity and the human genome project, these electronic mail networks virtually took over the process of disseminating information. List servers also provide an opportunity for students to listen in on these high-level discussions by receiving electronic mail almost daily from the best minds in the field. List servers can even be used to generate extended discussion among students on topics raised in classes (Meacham, 1994, 1995; Raulin, 1998), creating a virtual classroom in which ideas can be exchanged at any time of day or night.

The most exciting development of the electronic age is the increasing availability of almost unlimited information in an electronic form, permitting instant location and access to critical material. The World Wide Web provides Internet access to unbelievable amounts of information, and the Web is growing by the hour. A few years ago it was rare to find journals online. Now the major journals in virtually every scientific discipline are both published in the traditional paper format and available online through subscription. The American Psychological Association now offers all its journals online (VandenBos, 1997). In addition, many articles accepted for publication in traditional research journals can now be accessed months before publication through the Internet (Holden, 1995). Soon books may be just as easily accessible. Both books and journals are now available on CD-ROM or on the Web (VandenBos, 1997). You may soon be able to have the equivalent of the Library of Congress at your fingertips in your own living room. The invisible college, not to mention the library, is increasingly electronic in this information age.

This explosion of electronically available information has been a boon for researchers, but it also has its problems. Anyone can publish on the Internet. Just set up a Web site and put whatever you want on it. Some excellent material is available, but there is lots of junk as well. The trick is to be able to tell the difference between quality material and junk. Quality material will have well-designed research to back it up. The junk will usually rest on pseudoscientific backing and sometimes not even that (see Box 1.4).

is involved in the data-analysis phase, and he or she might design and run another study before interpreting and communicating the results of the first. It is also common for some of the phases, such as data-analysis and interpretation, to overlap as the researcher moves back and forth among them.

The empirical observation phase is the center of the research process. Researchers first generate and refine ideas, sharpening them into answerable questions. They then make many decisions about what procedures to use to answer the questions. All this work is in preparation for the central activity—making empirical observations. The remaining phases focus on analyzing the empirical observations and determining and communicating their importance. This central activity, making empirical observations within a systematic rational process, is what characterizes science as a method that is different from other ways of seeking knowledge. Notice that in this process the scientist moves through a systematic, successive cycling of rational thinking, empirical observations, back again to rational thinking, and so on. Research in psychology, as in any other science, revolves around the empirical component. The more systematically and carefully we make the observations, the more solid will be the database on which we can continue to build an understanding of psychological phenomena.

Levels of Constraint

Chapter 1 discussed the various ways that people have used to pursue knowledge: tenacity, intuition, authority, rationalism, empiricism, and science. In the order listed, these approaches range from low to high demands on the adequacy of the information used and on the nature of the processing of the information. Of these approaches, science is the most demanding. Within science itself, already at the high-demand end of this continuum, there are many approaches to gaining knowledge. Some approaches place fewer demands on the adequacy of the information and the nature of processing it; others place more demands. Thus, within scientific research, some methods are more demanding than others, but they all have their useful place in the scientific research scheme. This continuum of demands on the adequacy of the information is called **levels of constraint.**

Within each level of constraint, the researcher must make decisions about how to develop the research plan. The plan may be general, leaving the ideas, questions, and procedures relatively unrefined. This is common in exploratory research undertaken early in the investigation of a phenomenon. On the other hand, the plan might be detailed and refined, with precise hypotheses, procedures, and statistical analyses. In each of these two extremes, the researcher moves through all the phases, but each is obviously at a different level of refinement. Exploratory research is lower constraint and makes relatively few demands for structure or precision on the procedures in each phase. In contrast, highly refined research projects are higher constraint and make many demands on the procedures.

For example, suppose that a psychologist is operating a special training program for exceptional children and has just admitted some children diagnosed with moderate mental retardation. To plan adequately, the psychologist might want to know, among other things, whether children with moderate retardation behave aggressively. Answering this question would not be difficult; the psychologist could ask the parents or could go into a room with several of the children and watch them for a few hours. These observations can generate some tentative ideas about the aggressive behavior of children with moderate retardation. Continuing the research process, these observations and tentative conclusions can then be reported to colleagues in the program, perhaps in a staff meeting. As simple as this procedure seems, it is a complete process of empirical research from original idea to communication of results. It was not highly detailed or structured, but it was research nonetheless.

Note that, because of the noncomplex nature of the question and the observational procedures, there was little demand that the question or procedures be precise, complex, or highly structured. If something interesting and unexpected is noticed, the observation procedure can easily be modified to follow up on this observation. Here, the activities in each phase are flexible. As the research questions become more complex and precise, the activities in each phase of research must become correspondingly more precise and controlled. Increased control is most readily seen in the observation phase of the process. As control over the conditions and methods of observation is increased, more constraints on the researcher's freedom to be flexible are imposed.

In essence, in the search for precision, we must give up flexibility. In almost all research decisions, scientists are required to make trade-offs, and every design decision has a price associated with it. Beginning students often believe that the best way to conduct research is always to be precise and controlled. But precision and control may not always be the ideal, because sometimes the loss of flexibility is too great a price to pay for the increase in precision and control.

The idea of constraint provides a second dimension for our model of the research enterprise. The two dimensions are as follows:

1. **The phases of research.** Each complete research project proceeds along this dimension from original ideas to communication of new ideas.
2. **The levels of constraint.** This dimension is one of precision, structure, and control. Projects of the highest precision demand the greatest constraint on activities in each phase; this constraint is most clearly seen in the controls imposed in the observation phase. By levels of constraint, we mean the degree to which the researcher imposes limits or controls on any part of the research process.

These concepts form a two-dimensional descriptive model of research, which is outlined in Table 2.2. Notice in the table that names have been given to the successive levels of constraint, ranging from the lowest constraint (naturalistic observation) to the highest constraint (experimental research). With the exception of the label differential research, these are all commonly used labels. The term *differential* has been adopted from Hyman (1964) and represents a broad class of research often overlooked in research methods texts. All the constraint levels represent scientific research and combine observation and rational inference. Some researchers hold the view that only high-constraint methods can properly be considered scientific. In our model, all are scientific methods and all can be effective when properly used. The use of a particular constraint level is determined by the nature of the question being asked, the precision of the existing knowledge, and practical and ethical constraints. For example, when Goodall (1971, 1986) was interested in learning about the social behavior of chimpanzees, naturalistic observation was the most appropriate method. Her research resulted in new knowledge about these animals. Her questions were general and flexible, so the

TABLE 2.2   *Two-Dimensional Model of Scientific Research*

	(1) *Idea* *Generating*	*(2)* *Problem* *Definition*	*(3)* *Procedures* *Design*	*(4)* *Observation*	*(5)* *Data* *Analysis*	*(6)* *Interpretation*	*(7)* *Communication*
Levels of *Constraint*							
Naturalistic observation							
Case-study method							
Correlational research							
Differential research							
Experimental research							

This model of the research process includes five levels of constraint; each is defined by the precision and/or flexibility of the observational procedures and/or settings. Regardless of the level of constraint, each research project goes through the same phases from initial idea to final communication.

level of research had to be equally general and flexible. High-constraint research would not have been appropriate and could not have given the information sought. The general nature of Goodall's questions was not a flaw in her work. Any scientist breaking new ground might very well start with just such low-constraint questions. Although all the levels of research in our model are scientific when used appropriately, we should refine our question so it can be answered using the *highest constraint level possible,* given both current knowledge in the field and the practical and ethical constraints on the researcher.

Notice that Table 2.2 is blank except for the labels of the phases of research and the levels of constraint. This table is essentially the outline for the remainder of the text. Later chapters will provide the information that defines each of the implied cells in this two-dimensional model. For now, you should take note of the organization of this model of research activity and recognize that the activities in each phase of the research process may differ depending on the level of constraint of the research.

Like the phases of research, the constraint levels are overlapping, rather than being sharply categorical. This constraint dimension should be understood as forming a continuum and the labels (naturalistic, case study, and so on) as indicating bands or portions of the continuum. The number of levels identified for this model of research is not critical in understanding the research activity that the model seeks to represent. The important concept is that constraint ranges from low to high, and the five labels and their descriptions given next are adequate for describing most psychological research. Later chapters will discuss the levels of constraint in more detail. Here each is briefly defined. Table 2.3 summarizes the levels of constraint.

TABLE 2.3 *Levels of Constraint of Scientific Research*

Naturalistic observation	Observing participants in their natural environment. The researcher should do nothing to limit or change the environment or the behavior of the participants.
Case-study research	Moving the participant into a moderately limiting environment, intervening to a slight degree, and observing the participant's responses.
Correlational research	Quantifying the degree of relationship between two variables. The measurement procedures must be carefully defined and precisely followed.
Differential research	Comparing two or more preexisting groups of participants. The setting is usually highly constrained, and the measurement procedures must be carefully defined and precisely followed.
Experimental research	Similar to differential research, except that the participants are assigned without bias to the various groups or conditions in the study.

Naturalistic Observation.   **Naturalistic observation** requires the researcher to observe the behavior of participants in their natural environment and to make no attempt to change or limit the environment or the behavior of the participants. The only constraints that do exist are those that researchers impose on their observational methods. However, the researchers usually are not bound by strong hypotheses that demand a particular set of observational procedures. Therefore, they are free to shift their attention to any behaviors that seem interesting. This flexible approach is common in the early stages of research on a given topic and is useful in generating hypotheses that can later be tested in higher-constraint research. Such flexible techniques are replaced by higher-constraint procedures as researchers develop familiarity with an area. It is important to make the distinction between naturalistic observation as defined here and higher-constraint research in naturalistic settings. As you will see in Chapters 6 and 13, research in naturalistic settings need not be low constraint; in fact, it often involves detailed and precise procedures.

Case-Study Research.   **Case-study research** is higher constraint because the researcher does intervene somewhat in the participant's functioning, such as asking questions of a participant. Even though slightly more constrained than naturalistic observation, the case-study method still allows the researcher flexibility to shift attention to whatever behaviors seem most interesting and relevant at the time. Case-study research is *not* limited to research on psychopathology or psychotherapy. Rather, these methods can be applied to many issues.

Correlational Research.   **Correlational research** requires greater constraint on the procedures used to measure behavior. The setting can range from a naturalistic one to the highly constrained setting of a scientific laboratory. However, because researchers are interested in quantifying the relationship between two or more variables in the correlational method, they are constrained to use precise and consistent procedures for measuring each variable. As you will see later in the text, knowing the relationship between two variables allows researchers to predict the value of one variable from knowing the value of a related variable.

Differential Research.   **Differential research** involves a comparison of two or more groups of participants. To make the comparison meaningful, the variables must be measured in exactly the same way in each group. That is, the settings and observational procedures must be constrained across groups. When done properly, the only thing that is not identical across the groups is the variable that defines the groups. In differential research, the variable that defines the groups is a **preexisting variable,** which is not under the researcher's control. Such preexisting variables can include clinical diagnoses, age, IQ, sex, socioeconomic class, and so on. For example, research comparing adults born and raised in Canada with adults born and raised in England is differential research utilizing two preexisting groups.

Experimental Research.   In **experimental research,** comparisons are made between participants under different conditions. A major difference between differential and experimental research is the way that participants are assigned to the groups or conditions. In experimental research, participants are usually assigned to conditions randomly. In contrast, in differential research, assignment of participants is based on a preexisting variable that is not within the researcher's control.

The concept of level of constraint does not represent a single, simple dimension. Some levels differ on the basis of the constraint applied to the setting in which the observation takes place, some differ on the basis of the constraint placed on the measurement procedures, and others differ on the basis of the constraint placed on the participant selection and assignment. But as the researcher moves from low-constraint methods to high-constraint methods, more constraint is placed on more aspects of the research. In pure naturalistic observation, the only constraint is that placed on the observer. In pure experimental methods, every aspect of the study is planned in advance, and explicit procedures must be followed throughout the study.

Once the constraint level of the question has been determined, the remainder of the research process must be carried out at this same level of constraint. For example, it would be a mistake to draw high-constraint conclusions from low-constraint data. Also, suppose that we are trying to conduct a field experiment in a school setting. It would be a political mistake to try and force high-constraint laboratory methods onto the classroom. We would not be allowed to randomly remove some children from the classroom and assign others to different experimental conditions. We would not be allowed to alter the seating arrangements in the room or to change the duration of class periods. We would not be allowed to stop all traffic in the hall outside the room to control noise, and so on. It would not work; the principal would probably throw us out for disrupting the school. As the old saying goes, "You can't get apple juice from a tennis ball." You will understand more about levels of constraint as we proceed through this text. For now, just remember that when we mix constraint levels we run the serious risk of distorting or losing important information.

A major function of low-constraint research is the generation of ideas for higher-constraint research. Conclusions drawn from well-executed, low-constraint research can serve as the starting points for high-constraint questions and research methods. For example, when a clinical psychologist observes a consistent pattern of reported childhood trauma in clients with depression, she might ask, "Now that I have observed these consistencies in my clinical sample, do the same consistencies hold in the general population of depressed persons?" This question could lead to research utilizing careful sampling procedures to select participants who adequately represent the general population of depressed people. In this example, it would be unwarranted to conclude that childhood trauma is associated with depression based only on a single clinical sample. The clients of this psychologist might be unusual in some way, thus creating the impression that childhood trauma is typical of clients with depression. Concluding that all depressed individuals have childhood trauma based only on her own clinical sample would be a large leap from her low-constraint data to higher-constraint conclusions. By asking the question as posed above, she could have moved from low- to higher-constraint research.

As we move from low- to high-constraint research, the procedures and findings become more precise. However, we also run the risk that the procedures will become more artificial and more removed from the real world and therefore be less relevant. To help to reduce this **precision** *versus* **relevance problem,** researchers should carry out their research at the highest constraint levels possible and then test their findings in natural settings. For example, there is a growing concern about the possible dangers of using a cell phone while driving. Research has shown that driving is not significantly impaired by listening to a radio or tape. However, manipulating equipment, such as dialing a cell phone or adjusting the radio, does interfere with driving (Briem & Hedman, 2001). But what are the effects of actually holding a conversation on the phone while driving? A high-constraint laboratory experiment can be set up using a driving simulator. Participants might "drive" and be presented with a standard set of road challenges, such as a child suddenly darting in front of the vehicle or a traffic light turning red. The reactions of the participant drivers would be electronically recorded and scored. Participants would be assigned to conditions, such as having a cell-phone conversation while driving and having no cell-phone use while driving, and their scores would be compared.

Strayer and Johnson (2000) carried out a high-constraint, dual-performance laboratory experiment to simulate cell-phone use while driving. The participants manipulated a joy stick to keep a cursor on a constantly moving pattern on a video screen. At unpredicted times a red or green light was flashed. At the red light the participant was to press a "brake button" on the joystick. Participants were randomly assigned to three groups: radio-knob control, hands-free cell phone, hand-held cell phone. They found that response to the red light was not disrupted by adjusting the radio, but was negatively affected by having cell-phone conversations in both the hands-free and hand-held cell phone condition. They concluded that the driving disruption was mediated through interference with attention to driving, regardless of whether the drivers' hands were used on the cell phone.

This high-constraint research provides precise answers to this question: Does cell-phone use disrupt *simulated* driving and increase the chance of driver error? It can serve as a good basis for making public policy about cell-phone use in automobiles. However, as compelling as the research is, we cannot be sure that the laboratory findings would hold in the natural environment. Therefore, it would be useful to design laboratory settings that more closely resemble real driving and to follow up the laboratory findings with research on cell-phone use in actual driving conditions. However, if you think about this research, you will realize that there are both practical and ethical reasons that restrict researchers' choices in situations in which there might be danger to the participants. These and other ethical concerns will be covered in Chapter 3. The rationale for verifying laboratory results in natural settings, that is, seeking *ecological validity,* will be discussed in Chapter 8.

Quick-Check Review 3: A Model of the Research Process

3.1. What are the two main dimensions in the model of research presented in this text?

3.2. Research proceeds in phases. What are they?

3.3. Define levels of constraint.

3.4. What is the major difference between differential and experimental research?

Chapter Summary

Scientists use a combination of empirical observations and rational thinking to study natural phenomena. Based on specific empirical observations, the researcher employs a rational intellectual process of inductive inference to develop more general constructs that represent events that cannot (yet) be observed. Using these more general constructs, the researcher then makes deductive inferences or predictions, which can be tested with observations. The inductive–deductive process (specific to general to specific process) is highly interactive, and it ties together the empiricism and rationalism basic to scientific thinking.

Research is a process of inquiry in which the researcher carefully poses a question and proceeds systematically to gather, analyze, interpret, and communicate the information necessary to answer the question. The central part of this research process is making empirical observations. All activities that take place prior to the observation phase are designed as preparation for the actual gathering of data. All activities following the observation phase focus on analyzing, interpreting, and communicating these observations.

A two-dimensional model of the research enterprise was outlined in this chapter, and it provides the framework for this text. The two dimensions are (1) the phases through which each research project progresses and (2) the levels of constraint.

Key Terms

Define the following key terms. Be sure that you understand them. They are discussed in the chapter and defined in the glossary.

assumptions of science

data

facts

behavior

observation

inference

constructs

reification of a construct

nominal fallacy

all-or-none bias

similarity–uniqueness paradox

Barnum statement

evaluative biases of language

inductive reasoning

deductive reasoning

theory

parsimony

valid

inductive theory

deductive theory

functional theories

model

phases of research

idea-generating phase

problem-definition phase

procedures-design phase

observation phase

data-analysis phase

interpretation phase

communication phase

replication

electronic mail

e-mail

list server

levels of constraint

naturalistic observation

case-study research

correlational research

differential research

preexisting variable

experimental research

precision versus relevance problem

3

The Starting Point

Asking Questions

> *It appears to me that...philosophical...difficulties and disagreements...are mainly due to a very simple cause: namely to the attempt to answer questions without first discovering precisely* what *question it is which you desire to answer.*
>
> —George Edward Moore, *Principia Ethica*, 1903

CD Resource Material

- APA Ethical Guidelines
- Library Research Tutorial

- Student Study Guide/Laboratory Manual

Web Resource Material

- Recovered Memories Controversy
- Learned Helplessness and Depression
- Chaos Theory

- Research Ethics
- Background Material on Autism

Research methodology is concerned with answering specific research questions. However, we must first have a question to answer. Formulating the right question is often one of the most critical elements in good research. This chapter begins by covering the process of formulating and then refining a question for research. It then introduces some of the language that is critical in understanding a research question and communicating about it with other professionals. This includes defining what is meant by a research variable, as well as defining the various types of variables used in research. The concept of validity is also introduced in this chapter, perhaps the most central concept in all research. The majority of this text is devoted to assessing and enhancing the validity of research. Finally, the chapter ends with a discussion of research ethics.

Asking and Refining Questions

Scientists begin research by asking questions. A question is a problem or statement in need of a solution or answer: What are the causes of child abuse? Why are some things so hard to remember? How can we get drunk drivers off the road? Why do some people become depressed? Questions are everywhere; all you have to do is observe and be curious. This section describes several common sources of research questions. It also discusses refining a research question in preparation for a study.

Pursuing Your Personal Interests

Your interests and observations can lead to personally relevant research. For example, you might be interested in emotions, memory, creativity, or social processes, or you might wonder about some aspect of yourself or your family members. You may be puzzled by something you observe and ask yourself, "Why did that happen?" Any of these interests or observations can serve as the starting point for research.

Following Up on the Work of Others

Research often raises more questions than it answers, and these new questions can serve as starting points for more research. Examples of theories and research that have generated considerable study are Freud's (1938a, b) psychoanalytic theory, Skinner's (1938, 1972) research on learning, Miller's (1971) work on physiological influences on motivation, Bandura's (1969) research on modeling, Festingers's (1957) theory of cognitive dissonance, Lovaas's (1973) research with autistic children, Seligman's studies of learned helplessness and depression (Seligman, 1974; Abramson, Seligman, & Teasdale, 1978), Gleick's (1987) discussion of chaos theory, and the controversy around repressed memory (Bass & Davis, 1988, 1994; Loftus & Ketcham, 1994; Loftus & Polage, 1999). To derive ideas from other research, scientists communicate with each other at scientific meetings and over the phone or the Internet, and they study published research. The more you know about a research area, the stronger will be the base for generating new research ideas. For beginning students, it is difficult to read journals and recognize the new questions that are explicitly and implicitly being posed. Therefore, such secondary sources as textbooks or review chapters are more useful. For example, the *Annual Review of Psychology* publishes review chapters on as many as 24 research areas in psychology each year. It is an excellent source of cutting-edge information for both students and professionals. Textbooks typically provide more background information on a given topic, making it easier to understand an area, but textbooks tend to be less comprehensive and less cutting edge than review articles or review chapters. These sources, designed to teach about particular areas, devote considerable space to explaining ideas. In contrast, research journals have severe space restrictions, and most articles are condensed and difficult to understand unless you already have a good background in the area under study. As you gain sophistication in research and in particular areas of research, journal articles become the major source of information.

Libraries have well-organized systems of journal abstracts and cross-referencing systems by topics and authors that allow students and scientists alike to locate quickly most relevant research. In psychology, the *Psychological Abstracts* are the primary source of such data. Its online version, *PsycINFO,* provides abstracts of literature from 1887 to the present and includes more than 1 million records. Other important abstracts include *Index Medicus* (the online version is *Medline*) and the *Social Sciences Citation Index.* In most university and research-center libraries, these abstracts are now computerized. Researchers must become thoroughly familiar with these abstract systems. Reference librarians are very helpful to students seeking to learn how to search abstract systems. Appendix C covers the basics of library research. More detailed coverage is included on the *Student Resource CD.*

Theories and research raise questions for further research in two ways, heuristically and systematically. **Heuristic influence** occurs when a theory or research finding generates interest, including disbelief and outright antagonism, and in this process suggests further study. The works of Darwin and Freud are good examples of this heuristic influence. **Systematic influence** occurs when theories or research provide explicit, testable propositions as the next step for further research. Research in conditioning, for example, has systematically generated considerable research. Both influences, heuristic and systematic, are important in the continued development of science.

Applied and Basic Research

Much of psychology is **applied psychology,** that is, psychology focused on solving real-world problems. Consequently, much of the research in psychology is **applied research,** in which the goal is to find solutions to practical problems. Applied research questions in psychology are fairly easy for the beginning student to generate. Table 3.1 lists some examples. Try generating some of your own.

Research can be categorized as applied or basic research. **Basic research,** also known as **fundamental** or **pure research,** is designed to increase scientific understanding of phenomena, but without any particular practical goals. Basic research findings often become incorporated into applied research. For example, basic research on language development in children might be used to develop training methods for persons with language deficiencies, emotional problems, or developmental disabilities. Unfortunately, it is often more difficult for basic researchers to obtain financial sup-

TABLE 3.1 *Examples of Applied Research Questions*

1. How can we train people to be good drivers?
2. What can department stores do to reduce shoplifting?
3. How can a teacher or parent help an underachieving child to improve academically?
4. What are the best placements of dials and levers on machines so as to reduce worker fatigue and errors?
5. What is an effective approach to calming children before and after surgery?
6. How can nuclear power plant control rooms be designed to minimize operator error?
7. How can psychologists change human behavior on a large scale so as to reduce the incidence of such diseases as lung cancer and AIDS?
8. How can society promote better parenting to reduce child abuse?
9. What can be done to reduce violence in society?
10. What is the most effective treatment for depression?

port than it is for applied researchers, perhaps because those who allocate funds do not realize the importance of basic research as a necessary background for most applied research. Think of it this way: solving practical problems requires a background of knowledge, and much of that information comes from basic research. When that knowledge base grows sufficiently, the practical problems can be solved. It is difficult for even the most creative of individuals to imagine the applications an area of research might have until some basic understanding of the area is achieved. In many cases, research does not break down neatly into either applied or basic research. Instead, the findings of a study contribute to both applications and a basic understanding of a problem. Table 3.2 lists some recent examples of basic research.

TABLE 3.2 *Recent Examples of Basic Research*

1. Exploring how elements of language are processed in both reading and hearing verbal material (McKoon & Ratcliff, 1998)
2. Exploring how the brain codes, organizes, and retrieves memories (Gabrieli, 1998)
3. Studying the processes that control visual attention (Egeth & Yantis, 1997)
4. Studying the neurochemical contributions to thinking (Everitt & Robins, 1997)
5. Identifying the role of specific neurons in basic sensory processing (Parker & Newsome, 1998)
6. Studying the factors that affect the auditory memory of rhesus monkeys (Wright, 1998)
7. Studying the nature of the sleep–wake cycle and the factors that regulate it (Lavie, 2001)
8. Studying bimodal neuron functioning in the parietal lobe (Graziano, Cooke, & Taylor, 2000)
9. Studying the process of associative learning in animals (Pearce & Bouton, 2001)
10. Identifying the factors that influence the development of visual attention in infants (Colombo, 2001)
11. Studying the neural basis of hearing in everyday situations (Feng & Ratnam, 2000)
12. Identifying the mechanisms by which the body regulates food intake (Woods, Schwartz, Baskin, & Seeley, 2000)

Refining Questions for Research

Research begins with a question. The question is gradually refined until it becomes specific enough to give the researcher a clear direction for answering it. Developing the initial question is critical because it determines much of how the research should be conducted. Beginning students may wonder what level of constraint to use, what observational methods are best, or how to select the right statistical tests. Answers to these and similar issues lie partly in the nature of the question asked. Once the initial question is refined, then these other decisions follow.

Suppose that a psychologist is interested in the parenting behavior of elephants in the wild. The psychologist wants to know how long baby elephants depend on their parents or other adults, whether and to what degree male and female elephants engage in parenting, and whether the baby's care is shared by other adult elephants. The psychologist could further refine these questions as follows:

1. In their natural habitat which, if any, adult elephants assist in the birth and early care of the infant elephants and in the primary care of the growing young?
2. At what age do young elephants raised in their natural habitat become independent from the parents and/or caretakers?

Notice two important points about the initial questions. First, the questions themselves have begun to specify the behavior to be observed, specifically, parenting behavior of the adults and independent behavior of the young. Second, the conditions under which the observations are to be made (the elephants' natural habitat) have also been identified in the question. These specific elements are referred to as variables.

A **variable** is any set of events that may have different values. Height is a variable because organisms and inanimate objects exist at different heights. Sex is a variable because there are two sexes. Behavior is a variable because a great number of actions can be performed. Any specific behavior, such as aggression, can be a variable because it can occur in different degrees. Some variables can be easily manipulated, such as the amount of food eaten. Manipulating food intake might change other variables, such as one's weight, at least that's the hope of dieters. In the study of elephants' behavior, two variables are of interest: (1) the setting in which the elephants are observed and (2) the behavior of the elephants. Elephants can be observed in many different settings. This study, however, will focus on the natural habitat of elephants. The researchers will not observe elephants in a zoo or circus. Nevertheless, there will be variability in the observational settings. The elephants' natural behavior is likely to be so variable and complex that the researchers will want to simplify it by establishing broad categories into which it can be classified.

Note that the initial questions have also begun to narrow the choices of just how this research will be designed and conducted. By specifying the natural habitat as one variable, the researchers are committed to observations in low-constraint natural settings. But more is involved. Because the questions are about the normal flow of behavior under natural conditions, the researchers will use naturalistic observations of the animals without manipulating the animals' behavior.

In formulating initial questions, researchers proceed through an often lengthy process of thinking about their area of interest, posing loosely defined questions, studying the research literature, and gradually refining their ideas into initial research questions. This process might take researchers far from their starting point, and their refined questions might be very different from the original questions. They are guided in this process of refining initial ideas into researchable questions by the theories and research of other investigators. Theories are particularly important in this enterprise, because good theories organize and structure vast amounts of information into a few general concepts. Theories often act like maps of research areas, revealing which areas are well understood and which areas could benefit from additional research.

Once refined, the initial question implicitly helps to identify the major variables of interest and to structure the design and conduct of the research. The level of constraint of a research project, and therefore the degree and types of controls, the kinds of observations, and even the kinds of statistical analyses to be used, depend largely on the nature of the question. In general, researchers try to develop the initial question to the highest level of refinement possible given the state of knowledge about the particular area of interest. The more they know about an area, the more refined the question will be and the more likely that high-constraint research methods will be used to answer it. In areas in which little is known about a phenomenon, the initial question will be correspondingly unrefined and less specific, and the procedures will therefore be carried out at lower constraint levels. In the example of elephants' parenting behavior, the question was general, rather than detailed and specific, because little was known about such behavior in elephants. It was not possible to define critical behaviors, because the researchers were not sure what behaviors might be included in the broad category of parenting. They did not want to constrain the observations by trying to be overly specific about what behaviors to observe and how and when to observe them. Doing so might lead to missing something important that had not been expected. In this case, the researchers wanted to maintain maximum flexibility, so no constraints were placed on the behavior of the elephants and few constraints were imposed on the researchers other than to not interfere with the subjects. Had more been known about elephants before beginning the research, the questions would have been more specific and the researchers' behavior would have been more constrained by a specific focus.

Quick-Check Review 1: Asking and Refining Questions

1.1. What are the main sources of research questions?

1.2. How do you distinguish between applied and basic research?

1.3. What is a variable?

1.4. How can basic research be valuable in solving practical problems?

Types of Variables in Research

Several important ways of classifying variables in psychology are summarized in Table 3.3. Variables can be classified on the basis of their nature and/or how they are used in research.

TABLE 3.3   *Classes of Research Variables*

Variables Defined by Their Nature

Behavioral variable	Any observable response of an organism
Stimulus variable	The specific factors that have actual or potential effects on the organism's responses
Organismic variable (or **subject variable**)	A characteristic of the organism that can be used to classify the organism for research purposes

Variables Defined by Their Use in Research

Independent variable	A variable that is actively manipulated by the researcher to see what its impact will be on other variables
Dependent variable	A variable that is hypothesized to be affected by the independent-variable manipulation
Extraneous variable	Any variable, other than the independent variable, that might affect the dependent measure in a study
A constant	Any variable that is prevented from varying (i.e., held constant)

Classifying Variables Based on Their Nature

Three types of variables, behavioral variables, stimulus variables, and organismic variables, are defined by their nature.

Behavioral Variables.   Any observable response of an organism is a **behavioral variable.** This includes a rat running a maze, a chimpanzee opening a puzzle box, a child playing with a toy, a participant pressing keys in an experiment, a person playing the piano, people talking to each other, and so on. Behavioral variables can range from relatively simple behavior, such as a single keypress, to complex responses, such as social and verbal behavior. Because psychology is defined as the study of behavior, behavioral variables are of particular importance and are the type of variable most often observed in psychological research.

Stimulus Variables.   Behavior always occurs in a context, that is, the total situation surrounding the behaving organism and all the factors that make up the situation. The factors that have actual or potential effects on the organism's response are **stimulus variables.** Stimulus variables may be specific and easily measurable or controllable, such as a flashing light as a signal for the participant to respond. They also may be more general, such as the total situation surrounding the participant. Examples of complex stimulus variables are the habitat in which elephants are observed or the condition of a classroom in which a child is observed. Stimulus variables range from simple, such as a light signal, to complex, such as a social situation to which participants are randomly assigned. In psychological research, the researcher typically controls stimulus variables and observes behavioral variables. As research moves from lower to higher levels of constraint, the researcher increases the level of control over stimulus variables.

Some stimulus variables, such as sympathetic nervous system activity, are internal to the participant and are difficult or impossible for the experimenter to manipulate directly. Although some procedures may affect such internal stimuli as mood or anxiety, these variables are difficult to manipulate and are generally not under the direct control of the experimenter. Nevertheless, these variables are still a part of the participant's environment and can affect behavior.

Organismic Variables.   **Organismic variables,** sometimes called **subject variables,** are the characteristics of the participants, such as age, sex, racial attitudes, musical ability, psychiatric diagnosis, and so on. Some of the participants' characteristics, such as sex, can be directly observed and are referred to as **observed organismic variables.** Other participant characteristics, such as racial attitudes, cannot be directly observed, but are inferred from the participant's behavior. These are called **response-inferred organismic variables.** You should recognize that response-inferred organismic variables are also constructs, which were discussed in Chapter 2. Organismic variables can be used to classify participants. For example, researchers might measure the anxiety level of participants and then, based on their scores, divide the participants into three groups: high, moderate, and low anxiety.

Some variables can be classified under more than one of the preceding categories, depending on the way that they fit into the research situation. For example, educational level would normally be thought of as an organismic variable: it is a characteristic of participants. However, educational level could also be a stimulus variable if the researcher provided an educational experience for participants as part of a study. It might also be a behavioral variable if the researcher is interested in the behavior of obtaining more education and what factors might influence this behavior. Thus, it is not just the characteristics of the variable itself that define it as behavioral, stimulus, or organismic, but also how the variable fits into the research project. It can be confusing at times, but do not despair; in a few weeks all these distinctions will be second nature to you.

Classifying Variables Based on Their Use in Research

In addition to classifying variables on the basis of their characteristics, researchers also classify variables based on how they are used in research. This section will define independent variables, dependent variables, extraneous variables, and constants.

Independent and Dependent Variables.   **Independent variables** are manipulated by the experimenter. **Dependent variables** are the participant's response. For example, suppose that a researcher hypothesizes that verbal criticism and aggression escalate as frustration increases. Participants are randomly assigned to simulated work groups of three persons. They are given a series of work-related problems to be solved as a group. The variables in this study are frustration and verbal criticism/aggression. The researcher manipulates the independent variable, frustration. Some groups are given all the information needed to solve the problems readily (the no-frustration condition).

Other groups have some of the information withheld so that the problem is still solvable, but with difficulty (the moderate-frustration condition). Enough information is withheld from still other groups so that the problem appears solvable, but, in reality, cannot be solved (the high-frustration condition). Each group's verbal interactions are recorded and all instances of the dependent variable, verbal criticism/aggression, are counted. In other words, the independent variable of frustration is manipulated, and changes in the dependent variable are observed and measured. The hypothesis is that the dependent variable will be affected by the independent-variable manipulation.

There are two kinds of independent variables: (1) manipulated independent variables and (2) nonmanipulated independent variables.[1] **Manipulated independent variables** are those that the experimenter controls by actively manipulating them, such as the frustration level in the preceding study. With **nonmanipulated independent variables,** also called **classification variables,** participants are assigned to groups on the basis of preexisting characteristics. The largest category of nonmanipulated independent variables in psychology are organismic variables, that is, those variables that are preexisting characteristics of the participants, such as IQ, religious affiliation, age, and political affiliation. The researcher does not actively manipulate such variables, but rather assigns participants to groups based on them. For example, suppose that a researcher wanted to test the hypothesis that moral problem-solving skills are related to religious affiliation. The participants would be assigned to groups based on their identified religious affiliation. They would then take a moral problem-solving test. The test scores of the religious-affiliation groups would be compared to determine whether there were significant group differences.

Researchers often hypothesize a *causal relationship* between independent and dependent variables. A causal relationship between two variables exists when changes in one variable result in a predictable change in the other. However, as you will see in later chapters, it is difficult to draw causal conclusions without the control provided by actively manipulating the independent variable. Thus, conclusions about causal relationships in a study with nonmanipulated independent variables must be tentative. Manipulated and nonmanipulated variables will be discussed more in later chapters. For now, it is important that you be able to make two distinctions: (1) between the independent and the dependent variable and (2) between manipulated and nonmanipulated independent variables.

Extraneous Variables.   **Extraneous variables** are unplanned and uncontrolled factors that can arise in an experiment and affect the outcome. Consequently, extraneous variables must be controlled to avoid their potential effects. For example, suppose that a researcher was studying academic learning and the dependent variable was course grade, which was based on three examinations. Cheating on the examinations would

---

[1]Some would disagree with using the term nonmanipulated independent variable, arguing that an independent variable by definition is manipulated. In general usage, however, the term independent variable is used more broadly to include organismic variables as possible independent variables. We have made the distinction between manipulated and nonmanipulated independent variables explicit to minimize confusion for students, while acknowledging the broad and somewhat inaccurate general use of the term.

be a potential extraneous variable, and the researcher would take steps to discourage cheating. Distractions during the examinations might also constitute extraneous variables. Therefore, it would be wise to give the examinations in a quiet room to remove this potential extraneous variable.

Variables as Constants.　A **constant** is a variable that is prevented from varying. For example, suppose that a researcher is using animals in a study of the effects of hormones on learning. Earlier research has suggested that the response to specific hormones varies depending on the age and sex of the animals. The researcher decides to hold these two variables constant and uses only 4-month-old male rats. Thus, sex and age are constants in this study. By holding these variables constant, they do not affect the outcome of the research. If they were not held constant or were not otherwise controlled, the results of the experiment might be due to uncontrolled variables and not to the variable(s) being manipulated.

Quick-Check Review 2: Types of Variables in Research

2.1. Define each of the various types of variables found in research.

2.2. Define independent and dependent variables. How are they used in research?

2.3. Define manipulated and nonmanipulated independent variables.

2.4. What does it mean to hold a variable constant in research?

Validity and the Control of Extraneous Variables

Validity is one of the most important concepts in research and a central theme throughout this text. **Validity** refers to how well a study, a procedure, or a measure does what it is supposed to do. Validity is a complex idea, and there are many types of validity. Some common questions about validity are: Does this study really answer the question it posed? Does this test measure what it is supposed to measure? What does this laboratory study reveal about the real world? One fundamental task of research is to ensure the validity of research procedures by including appropriate controls. This section provides a conceptual introduction to validity. However, the concept of validity will be revisited repeatedly throughout this text, because it is at the core of the entire research enterprise.

The concept of **control in research** has been mentioned several times. What does it mean? Recall that empirical observation is the central point in the scientific research process. Observations in psychological research are usually observations of behavior, which may be influenced by many factors, some known and others unknown to the researcher. Some of the factors may be of theoretical interest to the researcher, whereas others may be extraneous, distorting the results and making it impossible for the researcher to draw meaningful conclusions. In other words, extraneous variables reduce the methodological soundness, or validity, of the research. Thus, it is important to reduce the influence of extraneous variables on the behavior being observed.

The procedures used to reduce extraneous influences are what is meant by controls in research. Thus, the concept of control in research refers to the *systematic methods employed by the researcher to reduce threats to the validity of the study posed by extraneous influences on the behavior of both the participants and the observer.* Although such controls are most important in higher-constraint research, they are part of the procedures at all levels. For example, in a case-study research project, we might want to observe problem solving in children by testing each child individually. The researcher should prevent the child from being interrupted in the problem-solving tasks by other children, who might make distracting noises or volunteer their own solutions. The researcher can minimize these extraneous factors by testing children individually in a quiet room, separated from the rest of the class. Even in this low-constraint research, controlling the observational setting reduces the effects of these and perhaps other extraneous variables.

The control of extraneous variables is the heart of the research enterprise. Without the control, we cannot be confident of the research findings. Virtually this entire text is devoted to this topic. You will learn that there are several ways to achieve such control. The most powerful is to use research designs that have effective controls built into them. However, there are also control procedures that can be added to any research study regardless of the level of constraint. For now, you need to remember only two things. The first is that uncontrolled extraneous variables threaten the validity of research. The second is that effective controls exist and that it is the responsibility of the researcher to select the necessary controls and include them in the study in order to enhance validity. In later chapters, you will learn what these controls are, how to select them, and how to implement them.

Quick-Check Review 3: Validity and the Control of Extraneous Variables

3.1. What is meant by extraneous variable?

3.2. Why do extraneous variables have to be controlled in research?

3.3. What is meant by validity?

3.4. What does control have to do with validity?

Research Ethics

The researcher makes a series of decisions before observing even a single participant. One of the most important involves research ethics. Researchers make decisions about how they will use living organisms for research purposes. This demands that ethical concerns be included in the decision process.[2]

---

[2]This discussion will focus on research ethics, but ethical concerns also apply to other activities of psychology, such as testing, psychotherapy, and teaching.

Ethical Principles for Human Research

Concern over inhumane treatment of participants was generated by post–World War II revelations of what German researchers did to people, including children, in the name of science. Such organizations as the American Psychological Association and the American Medical Association began to examine their own research practices. Although no inhumanities were found to approximate those of the Germans, concern developed that even in the United States some research participants might be treated badly. In the 1950s and 1960s, there were growing criticisms of biomedical research that placed human participants at risk without informing them of the risks. In some instances, live disease organisms were injected into participants or new surgical techniques were practiced on patients who were undergoing surgery not related to the new techniques. Researchers were careful to provide the best-known medical safeguards; nevertheless, these procedures were carried out without participants' knowledge and consent. To tell participants only that they were to be given a test of biological resistance, while withholding the information that the substance injected into them contained live cancer cells, is at least a serious deception. Many writers maintained that research participants must be protected against deception, dangerous procedures, and invasion of privacy. Participants, they said, have a right to know what is going to be done to them and to be given enough clear information that they can freely consent to or refuse to participate. These issues continue to be debated (Rosenthal, 1994; Reynolds et al. 2001), and these debates have led to increasingly more rigorous safeguards for participants.

Psychological research with human participants is rarely physically intrusive, and the risks to participants are not as great as in some biomedical research. Nevertheless, issues of deception, invasion of privacy, and participants' right to be informed so as to be able to make a free choice still apply to psychological research. Potential **invasions of privacy** occur when researchers examine highly personal and sensitive areas of psychological adjustment, such as sexual behavior, private thoughts and fears, or relationships of a couple. Social scientists often gain access to confidential records of patients in hospitals or of children in schools for research purposes.

Deception involves deliberately misleading participants. Deception is frequently employed in some types of psychological research. Its use rose from 16% of empirical studies reported in a leading psychology journal in 1961 to 47% by 1992 (Bower, 1998). Although deception in psychological research has increased, it is generally more innocuous than in the past (Korn, 1997). However, the use of any deception places the participant at risk. Therefore, if deception is used, safeguards must be employed. The most common safeguards are (1) the researcher's judgment that the deception poses no serious or long-term risks and (2) explaining the true nature of the deception to the participant in a postexperimental **debriefing.** In this debriefing, the participant is informed about the procedures and why they were used, which should counter any lingering misconceptions, possible discomfort, or risk that may have been generated by the deception. Finally, participants have the right to make their own decisions, but they can make reasonable decisions only if they have all the relevant information on which to base their decisions. This principle if referred to as **informed consent.**

At the center of these issues lies a genuine conflict of interests and a moral problem. On the one hand, society demands scientific solutions to a large array of problems. On the other hand, at times searching for such solutions may violate individuals' rights to privacy and to proper treatment. To meet society's demands for new knowledge and treatments for such physical illness such as AIDS and cancer, to solve such social problems as poverty or aggression, or to improve teaching, scientists must be able to carry out scientific research, and this requires the cooperation of participants. It is in the long-term interest of society for individuals to contribute to scientific efforts. One way is by serving as participants in research. Responsible people will consider donating their time, effort, and information as participants to promote scientific knowledge for its potential benefits to society, even when they do not personally benefit. Of course, the decision is up to each individual.

A moral dilemma arises, because research, even with its potential benefits to society, sometimes exposes participants to potential risks. In attempting to solve this dilemma, most research agencies, universities, and professional organizations have adopted the following ideas:

1. Scientific research offers potential benefits to society.
2. It is reasonable to expect that people will behave in a socially responsible manner and contribute to knowledge by participating in research.
3. Participants have basic rights when they elect to participate in a research study, including rights to privacy and to protection from physical and psychological harm. They must also be given clear and sufficient information on which to base their decisions as to whether they will serve as participants in any research project.
4. It is the responsibility of researchers to conduct research in such manner as to respect participants' rights and to protect participants from possible physical and/or psychological harm.

The American Psychological Association (APA) was one of the first professional organizations to develop ethical guidelines for research, recognizing both the need for research and the rights of participants. The APA recognizes that, in order to obtain information, some research uses deception, makes participants uncomfortable, or asks for personal information. These and other aspects of research place participants at risk, which means that the potential exists for the participants to suffer harm as a result of the study. The ethical principles are guides for minimizing risks to participants. Federal policy regarding human participants in research is detailed in several reports (e.g., NIH, 1995, 1998) and it is constantly being updated. Federal granting agencies, such as the National Institutes of Health (NIH), publish current regulations on their Web sites. The American Psychological Association (1998) has recently updated its ethical code for human research. The *Student Resource CD* reviews these ethical guidelines.

The most important safeguard built into the APA guidelines is this: it is the *participant* who decides to participate in research. The participant has the right to refuse or to discontinue the study at any time, even after having agreed to participate. The ethical researcher is bound to honor this right and can neither coerce participants to participate nor prevent participants from withdrawing. Data collection cannot start until participants give their unequivocal consent. Informed consent is an important safeguard. It means that researchers must provide participants with enough information about the research to enable them to make informed decisions about their participation.

Another important safeguard concerns the responsibility of the researcher to maintain strict **confidentiality** of the information gathered about participants. This is particularly important when the research deals with sensitive personal information about participants or information derived from normally confidential personal records, such as hospital or school records. Researchers commonly use code numbers, rather than participants' names, on records that contain sensitive information to protect participants' confidentiality.

When participants are children or have mental or emotional disorders, they may have difficulty in understanding the information or in giving consent. Under these conditions, greater responsibility is placed on both the researcher and designated person, such as a parent, school administrator, or other institutional official, who acts on behalf of the participants to ensure that participants' rights and well-being are protected.

Institutional Review Boards. **Institutional Review Boards (IRBs)** consist of the researchers' peers and members of the community at large. They have been set up in universities, research institutes, hospitals, and school systems to review research proposals to see if they meet ethical guidelines. Every institution that receives federal funding is required to submit all human-participant research proposals to a review board. Members of the board are usually appointed by the president or other administrator of the institution. It is the responsibility of researchers to be sure that their proposals are submitted to and approved by the appropriate IRB before gathering data.

When it functions well, the IRB is a helpful advisory group of colleagues that expedites research, advises researchers, and suggests improvements. The IRB is an additional safeguard, assisting researchers in clarifying and solving potential ethical issues. Even ethical researchers might make self-serving decisions in their research, blinding them to potential ethical problems. The IRB provides an external viewpoint to reduce this problem. However, it does not replace or reduce the researcher's ethical responsibility to design acceptable research. *The final ethical responsibility always rests with the researcher.*

Researchers must judge their research in terms of its value to science, the risk it poses to the participants, whether potential benefits outweigh risks, and whether adequate safeguards have been included to minimize the risks and to protect participants. Should risks to participants outweigh potential benefits, the ethical researcher must redesign or discontinue the project. Thus, if the research is badly designed or carried out so that its results are of little or no scientific value, then (1) the potential informational value will be minimal and (2) participants will have wasted their time and perhaps been exposed to risks in a largely valueless endeavor. The researcher therefore has an ethical responsibility to develop well-designed projects and execute them with care.

Ethical Checks. Assume that you are designing a research project with human participants. You have identified an area of interest and refined the initial question. You have also identified and defined the major variables and determined the nature of the participants, how they will be selected, and how you propose to observe them. The next step is to perform the **ethical checks** listed in Table 3.4. By subjecting the research plan to ethical checks, you identify and correct most ethical problems. The ethical checks are a necessary final test before submitting the proposal to the Institutional Review Board.

Ethical principles in research continue to evolve as psychologists debate larger issues involving social values and scientific research (Kendler, 1993; Prilleltensky, 1994). The American Psychological Association (1998) appointed a task force to update ethical principles in research with human participants. Box 3.1 illustrates with a controversial example how the evolution of scientific technology requires a parallel evolution of ethical principles.

Inevitably, researchers began to study the IRBs themselves. For example, Ferraro, Szigeti, Dawes, and Pan (1999) surveyed over 300 university faculty and graduate students about their experiences with IRBs. A major recommendation of this study is that more needs to be known about the IRB members' qualifications, attitudes, and methods of evaluation. Researchers' concerns about IRB operations and the credentials of IRB members are appropriate. Researchers who are naïve about IRB operations may come to view these boards as adversaries—as impediments to conducting their research. Informed researchers, however, understand the important oversight functions of IRBs. They also recognize that, by maintaining these oversight functions, the IRB helps to bolster public confidence about research, and such confidence is necessary if people are to continue to volunteer to participate in studies.

TABLE 3.4   *Ethical Checks before Beginning the Study*

1. Is the proposed research sufficiently well designed to be of informational value?
2. Does the research pose any risks to participants, such as physical or psychological harm by such means as the use of deception, obtaining sensitive, personal information, or using minors or others who cannot readily give consent?
3. If risks are placed on participants, does the research adequately control these risks by including such procedures as debriefing, removing or reducing risks of physical harm, guaranteeing through the procedures that all information will be obtained anonymously or, if that is not possible, guaranteeing that it will remain confidential, and providing special safeguards for minors and participants who may have impairments?
4. Have I included a provision for obtaining informed consent from every participant or, if participants cannot give it, from responsible people acting for the benefit of the participant? Will sufficient information be provided to potential participants so that they will be able to give their informed consents? Is there a clear agreement in writing (the *informed consent form*) between the researcher and potential participants? The informed consent should also make it clear that the participant is free to withdraw from the experiment at any time.
5. Have I included adequate feedback information, including a debriefing if deception is used, to be given to the participants at the completion of the study?
6. Do I accept *my full responsibility* for the ethical and safe treatment of all participants by myself and *all research assistants*?
7. Has the proposal been reviewed and approved by the appropriate review board?

BOX 3.1 • *Information, Knowledge, and Ethical Questions*

Moral or ethical questions cannot be answered by empirical studies alone. Consider two questions that arise from the application of research on the human genome (Murray, 1996) and fetal development (Graziano, 2001): (1) Should fetuses be aborted when prenatal examination shows the presence of serious chromosomal abnormalities? and (2) Should children or animals be conceived specifically for the purpose of providing fetal tissues, organs, or bone marrow to people with illness? Let's examine one of these questions. The technology exists to conceive and then to abort the embryo or fetus at certain optimal points and then harvest the needed tissues to treat ill persons. But should the technology be used just because it exists? How can this question be answered by science? Science and technology determine if the procedures can be carried out and if they can be successful in medical treatment. But science cannot determine if they *should* be done.

An example is a case in which one reason for conceiving a child was to provide bone marrow transplant for a 16-year-old sister, who was suffering from myelogenous leukemia (Tomlinson, 1990). Because of conflicting blood types, no suitable donors were available, and the girl would live only a few more years if a donor was not found. The parents decided to conceive another child, based on odds of one in four that the child would be a suitable match. A girl was born, the match was successful, and the older daughter received the bone marrow transplant from her infant sister. At this point, both girls are doing well and are enjoying a loving family life. Although this case had a happy ending, should such procedures be done? Are some procedures ethically acceptable and others not? Think about it. How would you answer such questions?

Ethics and Diversity Issues in Research

A research issue that is related both to good research design and to ethical concerns is that of the diversity of participants. In psychological and medical research, there has traditionally been an underrepresentation of women, children, and many ethnic groups. Consequently, information gained from such research may not apply to all members of our increasingly heterogeneous society. For example, the efficacy of some medical treatments were initially tested primarily, or even exclusively, on adult Caucasian males. These treatments might then be applied to women and children on the assumption that they will be effective, but this assumption might be false. Medical treatments developed to be effective with men might not be effective with women or children, thus placing them at a medical disadvantage.

Psychological research has often failed to adequately represent population diversity, thus limiting its value. For example, we never know until the research has been completed whether the same psychological findings apply to different ethnic groups. For this reason, funding agencies, such as the National Institutes of Health, now require that population diversity be included in research proposals through the active recruitment of participants, unless it is scientifically justified not to include them. This means that men, women, children, and members of minority groups must be included. If not included, then a scientifically valid rationale for their exclusion must be presented. Of course, it makes no sense to include children in studies of Alzheimer's disease or men in studies of postpartum depression. However, practical difficulties in recruiting a broad sample of participants are not valid reasons for not having such representation of groups in the study.

Ethical Principles for Animal Research

Concern for the ethical and humane treatment of animals in research is just as important as the concern for human participants. Animal research is conducted in many biomedical disciplines, and large numbers of animals are studied each year. The APA estimates that 7% to 8% of psychological research is carried out with animals.

The major ethical concerns in animal research involve two issues: (1) animals are captive participants and, of course, are not capable of providing informed consent and (2) the nature of the research carried out on animals is generally more invasive than that carried out on humans. Thus, there are often more serious risks to animal participants than human participants. Therefore, more responsibility is placed on the researcher to ensure that animals are treated humanely.

For years, professional and governmental organizations have followed ethical guidelines in the use of animal participants. The APA, for example, has had ongoing professional committees since 1925 to address issues of animal research. This early concern has evolved into a set of standards in animal research that are periodically reviewed. Most scientific societies or government agencies whose members use animals in research have their own policy statements (e.g., American Psychological Association, 1986; American College of Surgeons, 1991; Society for Neuroscience, 1991, 1995; Canadian Council on Animal Care, 1993; National Institutes of Health, 1994, 1996). Anyone who publishes in APA journals and who uses animals as research participants must attest that their research was conducted in accordance with APA guidelines (APA, 1986). All researchers who submit studies to the *Journal of Neuroscience* or to neuroscience meetings must attest that they have complied with animal-use standards and policy as set out by the National Institutes of Health (1991) and the Society for Neuroscience (1991, 1995). The guidelines cover areas such as appropriate selection of animals, adequate and humane housing, preoperative and postoperative care, concerns about inflicting as little pain and discomfort as possible, and the need to have as much confidence as possible that the proposed research is both necessary and well designed.

In addition to the policies demanded by various professional groups, animal research is also constrained by other regulations. Every animal laboratory in the United States, Canada, and Mexico must abide by its respective federal, state, and local laws governing the use and care of animals. In the United States, all laboratories that receive federal funds must have a **Laboratory Animal Care Committee,** which serves the same function as the IRBs for human research. These committees include veterinarians and nonprofessional community representatives, as well as the researcher's professional colleagues. They review for approval all proposed animal care and use procedures, focusing not only on the specifics of humane care for the animals, but also on the relevance of the proposed research for human and animal health, the advancement of knowledge, and the gains to society. Animal researchers must proceed in much the same way as those using human participants. They must thoroughly review the ethical animal-use issues in their planned research, must assume full responsibility for the ethical conduct of the research, and must submit the research plan to their local Laboratory Care Committee for evaluation and approval.

An estimated 22 million animals each year are used in research in the United States, a slight decline over the past two decades. Animal use in research has remained constant in Canada and has declined in the United Kingdom and some European countries (Mukerjee, 1997). There is growing interest in reducing the number of live animals used in experimentation and in training researchers and practitioners. Some centers for this are the Johns Hopkins Center for Alternatives to Animal Testing; the Center for Animal Alternatives, University of California at Davis; the American Veterinary Society; and Psychologists for the Ethical Treatment of Animals. Reductions are being accomplished by sharpening the designs of experiments so that fewer animals are needed, substituting computer simulation for live animals, using cells cultured in laboratories rather than live animals, and substituting realistic models of animals. However, it is difficult to develop alternatives to live animals in behavioral studies because intact, functioning animals are needed to observe behavior and the factors affecting behavior.

Some writers have argued that animal research is unnecessary and contributes little meaningful information. Botting and Morrison (1997) have responded that animal research has been critically important in medicine. It has provided vaccinations against many severe infectious diseases; treatments such as kidney dialysis, organ transplants, open-heart surgery, and heart-valve replacement; and drug treatments for hypertension and diabetes (Morrison, 2001). Neal Miller (1985) pointed out that animal research has also led to successful medical and psychological treatments of disorders, such as enuresis and encopresis, scoliosis (a severe curvature of the spine), anorexia, life-threatening vomiting in infants, and retraining use of limbs following accidents or surgery. Miller and others have noted that animal research has not only contributed to the understanding of disease processes, improved services, and reduced risks for humans, but has also led to more effective and humane care for animals and solutions to problems that animals face in natural environments. For example, behavioral research on taste aversion has led to humane alternatives to shooting or poisoning animals that destroy crops or attack livestock. Behavioral and biological research has led to improved habitat preservation for wildlife, to successful reintroductions of Atlantic salmon and other fish to areas where they had been killed off, and to successful treatment for and vaccination against many diseases of pets, livestock, and zoo animals.

Concern for humane and ethical treatment of animals in research is legitimate, and few researchers deny its importance. A new journal, the *Journal of Applied Animal Welfare Science,* presents issues and developments in the humane care of animals in research, training, and society in general. Discussions of animal research are frequent in psychological journals. For example, the *American Psychologist* published a series of five articles in 1997 addressing important issues in animal research. Even animal researchers have challenged past and current practices. Ulrich (1991), for example, argued that misuse and overuse of animals did occur in research and that scientists, like everyone else, were thoughtlessly guilty of our culture's propensity to consume anything, without regard to ecological issues. Ulrich, an animal researcher for many years, writes thoughtfully about scientists' responsibilities to other life forms and the necessity to consider seriously the ethical issues involved in animal research.

Research with animals has made enormous contributions to the scientific understanding of nature. As with all research, the costs in terms of risks to the participants must be balanced by the potential benefits to society (Carroll & Overmier, 2001).

Quick-Check Review 4: Research Ethics

4.1. What is the moral dilemma in research concerning individuals and society?

4.2. What is informed consent? How is it obtained, and why is it important?

4.3. What are Institutional Review Boards? What do they do?

4.4. What are the major ethical principles in research with animals?

4.5. What is meant by diversity issues in research?

Chapter Summary

The starting point for research is finding an area of interest and generating a researchable question. Research questions can be readily developed from personal experiences and interests, from the published theoretical and empirical work of others, and from attempts to solve practical problems. New research can be generated from current research both heuristically (by stimulating interest or opposition) and systematically (by making precise predictions about the logical next step in the research process).

Psychological research can be categorized as (1) basic research, in which scientists attempt to develop new information without specific practical goals, and (2) applied research, in which scientists attempt to answer questions to help to solve practical problems.

Vague research ideas must be refined and sharpened until they are as precise as possible. The refined question is of considerable importance, because it influences how the research will proceed. Refining the initial question implicitly identifies the major variables of interest and structures the ways in which researchers design and carry out the research. The degree and type of controls, the observational procedures, the methods of measurement, the type of data, and the statistical analyses to be used all depend to a great extent on the nature of the question.

It is necessary to identify not only variables of interest, but also variables in which the researcher has no interest, but which might nevertheless affect the outcome of research. These extraneous variables must be controlled or minimized to avoid threatening the study's validity.

One category of preobservational decisions concerns ethics. The rights of participants must always be balanced against society's need for scientific information. The APA has developed ethical guidelines for psychological research with human participants. The basic focus of the guidelines is to ensure that participants are not coerced into cooperating in research, that they have sufficient information to make an informed decision about participation, that such research is meaningful, and that it poses no undue hazards to participants. It is the responsibility of individual researchers to see that risks to participants are minimized and to have each project reviewed by an appropriate Institutional Review Board.

Ethical concerns in the use of animal participants are equally important. The guidelines for animal research focus on the adequacy of housing, general care of laboratory animals, minimizing pain or other discomfort, and the need for and value of the proposed research. Animal researchers must submit their research plans to their local Laboratory Animal Care Committee for review and approval.

Key Terms

Define the following key terms. Be sure that you understand them. They are discussed in the chapter and defined in the glossary.

heuristic influence
systematic influence
applied psychology
applied research
basic research
fundamental research
pure research
variable
behavioral variable
stimulus variables
organismic variables
subject variables

observed organismic variables
response-inferred organismic
  variables
independent variables
dependent variables
manipulated independent
  variables
nonmanipulated independent
  variables
classification variable
extraneous variables
constant

validity
control in research
invasion of privacy
deception
debriefing
informed consent
confidentiality
Institutional Review Board
  (IRB)
ethical checks
Laboratory Animal Care
  Committee

4

Data and the Nature of Measurement

Since the measuring device has been constructed by the observer...we have to remember that what we observe is not nature in itself but nature exposed to our method of questioning.

—Werner Karl Heisenberg, *Physics and Philosophy,* 1958

CD Resource Material

- Scales of Measurement Examples
- Examples of Operational Definitions Used in Psychological Research
- Measuring Reliability
- Student Study Guide/Laboratory Manual

Web Resource Material

- Scales of Measurement Handouts from Various Courses
- Operational Definitions
- Reliability and Validity
- Background Information on Autism

Chapter 2 introduced the idea that observation is the pivotal phase in the research process. In Chapter 3 you learned that in every research project one or more variables are measured and/or manipulated. The quality of the research depends on how well every variable is measured or manipulated. This chapter takes these ideas a step further by discussing the measurement process. The chapter begins with a description of what measurement is and then introduces the concept of scales of measurement. The chapter then discusses the process of measurement, the best ways to develop suitable measures for a variable, and how to evaluate the quality of measures.

Measurement

Every research project, whatever its level of constraint, includes one or more sets of variables that the researcher manipulates and/or observes and measures. As you learned in Chapter 3, a variable is any characteristic that can take more than one form or value. Because scientific research can study any natural phenomena, any varying event can become a research variable. Variables such as intelligence and memory are complex events that vary from one participant to another and/or from one condition to another. If the events of interest are static with no variation, they cannot serve as research variables. Simply put, *a variable must vary*. The major task in measurement is to represent the research variables numerically.

To measure a variable is to assign numbers that represent values of the variable. The measurements for each participant constitute the data, which are later analyzed and interpreted. The statistical analyses depend on how the dependent variables are measured. Beginning students are often confused about what statistical procedures to use. As you will see in this chapter and again in Chapter 14, choosing appropriate statistical procedures is relatively simple once the observational procedures have been designed and the procedures to measure the dependent variable have been determined.

In assigning numbers to a variable, the researcher works with two sets of information. The first set is the abstract number system, with all its characteristics. The second set is the variable to be measured, with all its characteristics. The task for the researcher is to bring the two systems together, applying one to the other so that the numbers accurately represent the variable. The task becomes complicated because the two systems do not necessarily function according to the same rules. The abstract number system has specific and well-defined rules. However, variables in psychology are not usually so well defined, and they do not necessarily function according to the same clear rules as the abstract number system. Thus, the two systems cannot always be easily matched. It is necessary for the researcher to determine how the characteristics of a measure might fail to match those of the abstract number system so that the appropriate statistical methods can be selected. Serious errors in data analysis and interpretation can occur when the researcher misapplies the number system.

The characteristics or **properties of the abstract number system** are identity, magnitude, equal intervals, and a true zero. **Identity** means that each number has a particular meaning. **Magnitude** means that numbers have an inherent order from smaller to larger; for example, 5 is larger than 3. **Equal intervals** mean that the difference between units is the same anywhere on the scale; for example, the difference between 2 and 3 is the same as the difference between 99 and 100. The zero on the abstract number scale is a **true zero,** which means that zero represents none of the variable.

Because of these properties, numbers can be added, subtracted, multiplied, and divided. However, if the abstract number system is applied to a psychological variable, such as intelligence, the number system and the variable of intelligence do not match exactly. The number system has a true zero point, but the psychological variable of intelligence does not. Zero on an intelligence test is an arbitrary number. There is no living person with zero intelligence. That is, in the unlikely event that a score of zero was obtained, it would not indicate zero intelligence. In this situation, the number system and the psychological variable do not match exactly. In the abstract number system, 100 is twice as much as 50, but because the psychological variable of intelligence has no zero point, we cannot say that an intelligence test score of 100 shows twice as much intelligence as a score of 50.

Suppose that you were doing a study of taste preferences. You give your participants samples of solutions to taste and ask them to rank the drinks according to which one they liked the most, which one second, which third, and so on. You assign numbers to the ranks (1, 2, 3, etc.) and report that number 1 was most preferred, 2 was second, and so on. Would the difference in preference between 1 and 2 be the same as between 2 and 3? Suppose, for example, that you asked your participants to rank Coke, Pepsi, and vinegar from most to least preferred. Now, unless they have strange tastes, their rankings would probably be either 1–2–3 or 2–1–3 for Coke, Pepsi, and vinegar, respectively. Clearly, the difference in preference between Coke and Pepsi is much smaller than that between either of those drinks and vinegar, even though the difference in rank orderings is the same. So the differences between rank orderings will not necessarily be equal at all points on the scale. Similarly, it makes no sense to say that the drink ranked 1 is three times as preferred as the drink ranked 3. In these examples, the characteristics of the variables as they are measured do not match the characteristics of the number system, and so one is limited in the type of mathematical operations that can be performed on the data.

In some cases, however, the variable and the number system can be matched. For example, suppose that an educational psychologist wanted to study how many questions children ask of their teacher. Each question asked by a child was recorded, and the total number of questions asked by each child in each school day was computed.

Table 4.1 shows sample data for 5 days of observation for 10 children and provides considerable information. Because of the nature of the data, all mathematical operations are applicable. We can add the number of daily questions for each child and arrive at each child's total number of questions for the week. If you look across each row in Table 4.1 at the totals for each child, you will see that child 02 asked only 2 questions, whereas child 04 asked 22. This large difference suggests that the children are very different from each other with regard to their willingness to ask questions in class. We can subtract the totals or divide one by the other and report that in this particular week, participant 04 asked 20 more questions or 11 times as many questions as participant 02. We can also can divide the total for the week by the number of children

TABLE 4.1 *Example of Measurement*

Students	Days					
	Mon	*Tues*	*Wed*	*Thurs*	*Fri*	*Total*
01	1	2	1	1	1	6
02	0	0	1	0	1	2
03	4	2	3	3	3	15
04	6	4	5	3	4	22
05	1	3	1	0	2	7
06	2	0	2	1	0	5
07	2	3	1	2	2	10
08	2	0	1	1	0	4
09	1	1	0	2	1	5
10	4	3	5	3	3	18
Totals	23	18	20	16	17	94

In this example, the numbers of questions asked by 10 students in class over 5 days were recorded.

and report the average number of questions per child for the week. Thus, this number-of-questions variable shows a magnitude in the same direction as the number system, so 22 responses are more than 20 responses. It also has equal intervals, so the difference in response between 4 and 6 is the same as the difference between 10 and 12. Finally, it has a true zero point, which means that a child with a score of zero asked no questions during the observation period.

Because of the match of the characteristics of the dependent variable with those of the number system, all mathematical operations on the data are legitimate: addition, subtraction, multiplication, and division. This allows researchers to use powerful statistical tests that cannot properly be used with dependent variables that are not as well matched with the real number system.

Accurate measurement is critical in science and technology. Even an elementary mistake can invalidate an entire project, as illustrated in the infamous case discussed in Box 4.1.

Quick-Check Review 1: Measurement

1.1. What is measurement?

1.2. Why is accurate measurement so critical?

1.3. What are the important characteristics of the abstract number system?

1.4. Why is it important to match the characteristics of the dependent variable with the characteristics of the abstract number system?

BOX 4.1 • *Missing Mars: The Importance of Measurement*

It did not really miss Mars. Indeed, NASA's *Mars Climate Orbiter* most definitely hit the red planet, or at least its atmosphere, with enough force and heat to destroy itself and cost taxpayers more than $125 million. Its mission was to orbit Mars and serve as a radio relay system for a second rocket, the *Mars Polar Lander,* which was scheduled to touch down 3 months later to explore the Martian surface.

What had gone wrong? After all, this was "rocket science," where technological precision is routine. It appears that an elementary mistake had been made in measurement. The two teams working on this Mars mission, the Jet Propulsion Laboratory in Pasadena and Lockheed Martin Astronautics in Denver, *had used two different units of measurement.* The Denver group based its calculations for the propulsion system on pounds of force, while the Pasadena group based its calculations on the metric system. The result was that information based on two different measurement systems conflicted, causing navigational errors and sending the orbiter out of control into the Martian atmosphere, where it burned up.

A most elementary error had been committed. The engineers had failed to convert one measurement system to the other and to use consistent measurements for feeding data into the navigational systems. There is a moral to this sad tale: *Make sure that you have your measurements in order before "launching" your research!*

Scales of Measurement

Some variables used in psychological research closely match the number system, whereas others do not. To help to identify the closeness of match, Stevens (1946, 1957) classified variables into four levels or **scales of measurement.**[1] The scales, arranged from least to most matching with the number system, are nominal, ordinal, interval, and ratio scales. For more complete discussions, see Coombs, Raiffa, and Thrall (1954) and Roberts (1979).

Nominal Scales

Nominal scales are at the lowest level of measurement; they are the scales that least match the number system. Nominal scales are naming scales, and their only property is identity. Such dependent variables as place of birth (Chicago, Toronto, Tokyo, Nyack), brand-name choice (Ford, Honda, Volvo), political affiliation (Democrat, Republican, Green Party, Independent), diagnostic category (panic disorder, schizophrenia, bipolar disorder), and sex of the participant are all nominal scales of measurement. The differences between the categories of nominal scales are qualitative and not quantitative. We can assign numbers to represent different categories. For example, we could label Chicago as 1, Toronto as 2, Tokyo as 3, and Nyack as 4, but the numbers

[1]There are those who disagree with Stevens (Gaito, 1980; Michell, 1986), challenging his distinction between scales of measurement on mathematical grounds. Although we are sympathetic to these arguments, we believe that Stevens's original presentation is still a useful teaching and organizational tool for a textbook at this level.

are only arbitrary labels for the categories. Except for identity, these numbers have none of the properties of the number system and, therefore, we cannot meaningfully add, subtract, multiply, or divide them. Is Chicago, with its assigned number of 1, to be understood as only one-fourth of Nyack, with its assigned number of 4? Nominal scales have no zero point, cannot be ordered low to high, and make no assumption about equal units of measurement. In other words, they are not numbers at all, at least not in the sense that we usually think of numbers. Nominal scales classify or categorize participants, and researchers work with the frequency of participants who fall into each category. The data from nominal scales are called **nominal data** or **categorical data.** Various forms of chi square are the most commonly used statistical tests for nominal data.[2] Some common uses of nominal scales are a number on an athlete's jersey, a social security number, or a telephone number.

Ordinal Scales

Ordinal scales measure a variable in order of magnitude. Thus, ordinal scales have the property of magnitude as well as identity. In ordinal scales, numbers represent an ordering, with some numbers representing more of the variable than others. How much more is unclear in an ordinal scale. For example, using socioeconomic class as a variable, we could categorize participants as belonging to the lower, middle, or upper socioeconomic class. There is a clear underlying concept here of order of magnitude, from low to high. Other examples of ordinal scales are measurements by rankings, such as a student's academic standing in class, or measurements by ranked categories, such as grades of A, B, C, D, or F. Data measured on ordinal scales are called **ordered data.**

Ordinal scales give the relative order of magnitude, but they do not provide information about the differences between categories or ranks. If students are ranked, we can determine from the data which student is first, second, and so on, but we cannot determine how much higher the first ranked student is compared to the second. That is, the numbers provide information about relative position, but not about the intervals between ranks. The difference in academic achievement between students ranked 1 and 2 might be very small (or large) compared with the difference between students ranked 12 and 13. As illustrated in the example of ranking preferred taste for Coke, Pepsi, and vinegar, the intervals in ordinal scaling are not necessarily equal. In fact, it is usually assumed that they are unequal. Therefore, it is inappropriate to analyze ordered data with statistical procedures that implicitly require equal intervals of measurement. The most commonly used statistical tests with ordered data are nonparametric tests, such as the Mann–Whitney *U*-test or the Wilcoxon matched-pairs, signed-rank test.

Interval Scales

When the measurements convey information about both the order and distance between values, then we have interval scaling. **Interval scales** have the properties of ordinal

---

[2]Although we describe the appropriate statistical procedures to use with each scale of measurement, we do not cover these procedures in this text. However, basic computational procedures are included on the *Student Resource CD.*

scales and equal intervals between consecutive values on the scale. Thus, interval scales come close to matching the number system, but still do not have a true zero point. The most commonly used example of an interval scale is the measurement of temperature on either the Fahrenheit or Celsius scale. The units of the thermometer are at equal intervals representing equal volumes of mercury. Therefore, 90° is hotter than 45°, and the difference in temperature between 60° and 70° is the same as the difference between 30° and 40°. However, the zero points on these scales are arbitrary and not true zero points. A temperature of zero degrees does not indicate a total absence of heat. Most variables in psychology are measured in interval scales, including IQ test scores, neuroticism scores, and attitude measures. With an IQ test, for example, we can report that the measured IQ difference between two people with IQs of 60 and 120 is 60 IQ points. However, because there is no true zero point on the IQ scale, it cannot be said that the second person is twice as smart as the other. Data measured on interval or ratio scales are referred to as **score data.**

Ratio Scales

Ratio scales have all the properties of the preceding scales (identity, magnitude, and equal intervals) as well as a true zero point. Thus, ratio scales provide the best match to the number system, which means that all mathematical operations (addition, subtraction, multiplication, and division) are possible on such scales. Such physical dimensions as weight, distance, length, volume, number of responses, or time duration are measured on ratio scales. These scales are called ratio scales because dividing a point on the scale by another point on the scale, that is, taking a ratio of values, gives a legitimate and meaningful value. For example, a person who runs 10 miles is running twice as far as a person who runs 5 miles and five times as far as someone who runs 2 miles. The true zero point and equal intervals give the ratio scale this property. Data measured on a ratio scale are called score data. A variety of statistical techniques are typically used for score data, including t-tests, analysis of variance (ANOVA), and product–moment correlations. Although many variables in psychology can be measured on ratio scales, some can be measured only on ordinal or interval scales of measurement.

The characteristics of the various scales of measurement, along with examples and the statistical procedures most commonly used, are summarized in Table 4.2.

Quick-Check Review 2: Scales of Measurement

2.1. List and define the four scales of measurement.

2.2. What type of data does each scale produce?

2.3. What are the properties of each scale of measurement?

2.4. What is the concept of true zero? What is its importance in measurement?

TABLE 4.2   *Some Aspects of Scales of Measurement*

| | Levels of Measurement | | | |
	Nominal	Ordinal	Interval	Ratio
Examples	Diagnostic categories; brand names; political or religious affiliation	Socioeconomic class; ranks	Test scores; personality and attitude scales	Weight; length; reaction time; number of responses
Properties	Identity	Identity; magnitude	Identity; magnitude; equal intervals	Identity; magnitude; equal intervals; true zero point
Mathematical operations	None	Rank order	Add; subtract	Add; subtract; multiply; divide
Type of data	Nominal	Ordered	Score	Score
Typical statistics used	Chi square	Mann–Whitney U-test	t-test; ANOVA	t-test; ANOVA

Many more examples of the various scales and additional appropriate statistical procedures could be given.

Measuring and Controlling Variables

Now that you have learned about the different types of variables, scales of measurement, and types of data, you can consider how to measure and manipulate variables. A simple example will be used in this section to illustrate several aspects of measurement. The example involves the effects of food intake on weight. Food intake is the independent variable, that is, the variable to be manipulated in the study. The question is this: What effect does a manipulation of food intake have on participants' weight? Therefore, weight is the dependent variable. The hypothesis is that weight fluctuations will be dependent on manipulations of food intake. This example and other examples will help to illustrate the concepts of measurement error and operational definitions.

Measurement Error

Consider the problem of measuring weight. Suppose that you have the participant stand on a standard scale. If the participant leans against the wall, the weight measurement is distorted. If the participant were weighed at one time wearing a heavy coat and boots and the next time in bare feet and no coat, the two weights would not be comparable. Such factors are sources of **measurement error.** Measurement error distorts the scores so that the observations do not accurately reflect reality. Measurement error can also attenuate, that is, reduce, the observed strength of a relationship between variables, giving the impression that two variables are less related than they actually are.

Other sources of measurement error are **response-set biases.** A powerful response-set bias is social desirability. **Social desirability** is the tendency to respond in what participants believe to be the most socially acceptable manner. For example, suppose that you were studying the relationship between level of food intake and weight in a weight-loss program. Have you ever cheated when you were on a diet? If you did, would you always be willing to admit it? There is a good chance that you would not admit it because you would find it embarrassing. In this case, some participants might underreport their food intake because they do not want to admit to the socially undesirable behavior of cheating on a diet. This social desirability response set would affect the validity of the measurement and create measurement error.

Minimizing measurement error is critical. This is best accomplished by developing a well-thought-out operational definition of the measurement procedure and by diligently using the operational definition in the research. This is the next topic.

Operational Definitions

Most people measure their weight periodically by standing on a scale. Measuring your weight is easy because the scales are already developed and readily available. Consider the process of weighing yourself. What you are doing is operationally defining the concept of weight. Think of it this way: concepts like weight, gravity, intelligence, or aggression are *ideas*—abstract, theoretical statements that exist on an intellectual level. To carry out empirical research on such concepts, the researcher must translate them from the abstract level to a concrete level so that they can be manipulated or measured. The process of translating a concept from the abstract level to the concrete level is achieved by developing operational definitions. An **operational definition** is a definition of a variable in terms of the actual procedures used by the researcher to measure and/or manipulate it (Kerlinger, 1992). In this example, the abstract concept of weight is turned into an empirical event by creating an operational definition, specifically, standing on a scale that records pounds and ounces. This is the very core of an operational definition; it brings theoretical abstractions to an empirical level, thus describing exactly how the theoretical abstraction will be measured. An operational definition is like a recipe that specifies exactly how to measure and/or manipulate the variables in a study. This is necessary to carry out the study and to communicate the procedures to other researchers. All research requires operational definitions. Whatever the theoretical concepts under study, to study them empirically, they must be defined operationally. Even for simple measures like weight, every step of the measurement procedure should be carefully planned to avoid confusion and sloppiness in running the study.

Measuring a variable like food intake requires a scale different from the weight scale. Scientists know from past research that food intake is measured in terms of calories and that foods differ in their levels of calories. If you know the calorie level of each type of food and how much of each type of food was consumed, you can compute the total calorie intake. This process of measuring food intake is based on considerable research and theory. We can be reasonably sure that this approach to measuring food intake is effective because it has worked well for researchers in the past, a fact that can be confirmed by reading earlier research.

Researchers often want to create a particular response in participants, such as increasing their motivation, anxiety, or alertness. These factors are within the participants and are therefore difficult to observe. However, such variables can be studied by operationally defining the set of procedures for manipulating them. In a study discussed earlier, the relaxation level of autistic children was manipulated to see whether it would reduce disruptive behavior. The manipulation was defined in terms of the following set of procedures:

> A corner of the room was selected for relaxation training, which was labeled the "quiet spot" and used for no other activity. Lights were dimmed and the children were invited to lie down on a soft blanket. The therapist said in a soft, calm voice, "Close your eyes, just like when you're in bed, nice and comfortable. That's it. Breathe slow and easy, that's it, good job, nice and easy, real relaxed." She continued her soothing quiet instruction and paired the gentle manipulation of arms, legs, and necks, with verbal instructions to relax. Any approximations of relaxed behavior were given immediate verbal reinforcement until the children learned to relax on verbal instructions alone. (Paraphrased from Graziano, 1974, p. 170)

The first training session was about 1 minute in duration and was increased daily until a criterion of 5 consecutive minutes of relaxation had been reached for 12 consecutive training sessions. Relaxation involved the child's being quiet, without talking or squirming and with no perceptible rigidity or muscle tension.

The preceding operational definition gives a clear description of the relaxation procedures. Although wordy, this operational definition served the purpose of giving researchers a clear set of instructions to define the independent variable. Once this independent variable is operationally defined, it is referred to simply as "relaxation training," with the understanding that it refers to the entire set of procedures. A good operational definition defines procedures so precisely that another researcher could replicate them by simply following the description.

In the study of disruptive behavior in autistic children, the dependent variable of disruptive behavior was operationally defined as follows:

> Disruptive behavior is any observed, sudden change in a child's behavior from calm, quiet, cooperative, and appropriate behavior to explosive tantrums, including sudden attacks on people, smashing and throwing objects, throwing oneself into walls or on the floor, self-abuse such as head-banging, biting, scratching, picking sores, and so on, all carried out in a rapid, near "frenzied" manner. Each disruptive behavior incident will be considered to have ended when the child has returned to the previous level of calm, appropriate behavior for at least 3 consecutive minutes.
>
> **Frequency:** Each occurrence of disruptive behavior is recorded as a single event. The frequency score per child is then the total number of events.
>
> **Duration:** Each disruptive event is timed by a stopwatch from the observed beginning to its end.
>
> **Intensity:** Each disruptive event is rated by the observers on a 3-point scale of intensity: low, moderate, high. The rating is made immediately after the event is over and is made for the perceived peak of intensity for the incident.

Developing an operational definition involves drawing on the wisdom reflected in past research, as well as making some arbitrary decisions. The arbitrary decisions are based on an analysis of how best to measure a variable from both a theoretical and a practical sense. For example, the decision to set the relaxation criterion at 5 consecutive minutes for 12 consecutive sessions is somewhat arbitrary. Instructions to use a "soft, gentle, calm, voice" leave room for interpretation by other researchers who may want to replicate the study. Operational definitions used in research vary in constraint. Under some conditions, it is difficult to create precise operational definitions for the variables. Under other conditions, we can operationally define variables very precisely. In any study, the researcher should operationally define the independent and dependent variables as clearly and precisely as possible. The completeness and detail of operational definitions depends on the nature of the issues being investigated, the participants used, and the settings in which the observations are made.

Most concepts can be operationally defined in several ways (see Box 4.2). Each definition can lead to different procedures and thus different research projects. For ex-

BOX 4.2 • *Examples of Operational Definitions*

Independent and dependent variables should be defined in terms of how they are to be measured and/or manipulated. A variable can be operationally defined in different ways, and different operational definitions of the same concept lead to different procedures and thus to different studies. Several examples follow.

Variable	*Operational Definition*
Anxiety	A physiological measure, such as heart rate
	A self-report of anxiety level
	Behavioral observation of avoidance behavior
Aggression in children	Ratings of aggressive behavior made by the child's teacher
	Direct observation during play periods of the number of times a child hits, pushes, or forcibly takes toys from other children
	Child's rate of hitting a punching doll in an experimental situation
	The number of acts of aggression in stories created by participants in response to pictures
Obesity	The pinch test, a measure of fat folds at the waist
	Water immersion, the volume of water displaced by a submerged participant
	Participant's height–weight ratio compared with standard charts
Intelligence	Score on a standardized IQ test
	Judgment by others of person's ability to solve problems
	Grades in school

ample, suppose that a researcher is studying how hunger affects mood. Participants are randomly assigned to three groups (high hunger, moderate hunger, low hunger) and their moods are measured. Here there are two variables to be operationally defined: the independent variable, *hunger,* and the dependent variable, *mood.* Each can be operationally defined in several ways. Hunger can be defined as the number of hours since the previous meal, the number of calories consumed when food is made available, physiological measures associated with hunger, or a score on a questionnaire about how hungry the participant feels. Likewise, mood needs to be operationally defined. (Think about how you might measure mood.)

Over time, many different operational definitions of such concepts as hunger and mood have been developed, and these are available in the research literature. The multiplicity of operational definitions for each concept has several advantages. First, by defining the concept in different ways (e.g., physiologically, behaviorally, cognitively, etc.), different aspects of a complex phenomenon can be studied. Second, when many studies using different operational definitions tend to point to common findings, we have **convergent validity,** that is, multiple lines of evidence converging on the same conclusion. Finally, by knowing the literature, any researcher can select and use operational definitions that have been useful in prior research.

Developing good operational definitions is critical in research. It is essentially a process of taking a broad concept and specifying and narrowing it to a detailed and precise statement of exactly how a variable is to be measured and/or manipulated. It requires knowledge of the relevant literature and experience in the process of specifying operations.

Quick-Check Review 3: Measuring and Controlling Variables

3.1. What is the best way to reduce potential measurement error in research?

3.2. How does an operational definition transform a theoretical concept into a concrete event?

3.3. What is social desirability bias in research? How might it affect research?

3.4. Explain the concept of convergent validity. What is its importance?

Evaluating Measures

Developing measures by operationally defining variables is a critical first step, but researchers are also responsible for evaluating the quality of the measures. Such evaluations should be a routine part of research that uses new operational definitions of variables. By evaluating the quality of measures and publishing these findings, the researcher provides the information necessary to guide other researchers in selecting the best available measures for their research projects. This section will discuss three factors that are relevant to such evaluations: reliability, effective range, and validity.

Reliability

Good measures give consistent results, regardless of who does the measuring. This is referred to as the **reliability** of the measure. In measuring weight, for example, a scale is said to be reliable if it always gives the same reading when measuring the same object, assuming that the object remains constant in weight. There are three types of reliability: interrater reliability, test–retest reliability, and internal consistency reliability.

Interrater Reliability.   If a measure involves behavior ratings made by observers, there should be at least two independent observers to rate the same sample of behavior. To rate independently, both raters must be **blind** to the ratings of the other; that is, they must be unaware of the other observer's ratings. This type of reliability is referred to as **interrater reliability.** It should be used whenever the measure is a rating or judgment. A measure is not wholly reliable or unreliable, but varies in its degree of reliability. If two raters always agree with one another, then the interrater reliability would be perfect. If their ratings are unrelated to one another, then the interrater reliability is zero. However, the actual level of reliability is likely to be somewhere in between. The concept of interrater reliability is illustrated in Figure 4.1. A correlation coefficient (this will be discussed in Chapter 5) can be used to quantify the degree of reliability, although more sophisticated indices are also available (see Nunnally & Bernstein, 1993).

Test–Retest Reliability.   Variables that should remain stable over time should produce similar scores if participants are tested twice with a period of time between testings. This type of reliability is known as **test–retest reliability.** Like interrater reliability, test–retest reliability is not an all or nothing phenomenon and is usually quantified with a correlation coefficient. If you change the labels in Figure 4.1 of rater 1 and rater 2 to time 1 and time 2, you will have a graphical representation of test–retest reliability. In specifying test–retest reliability, it is customary to include both the observed correlation and the length of time between testings. For example, you might report that "The test–retest reliability was .74 over ten weeks."

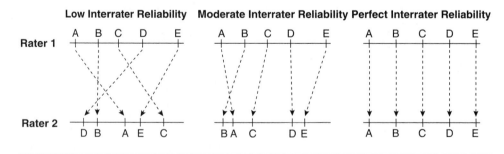

FIGURE 4.1 *Interrater Reliability* This illustration has two raters (1 and 2) and five participants (A, B, C, D, and E). Each horizontal line represents a scale on which the participants were rated by one of the raters. The more disagreement shown in the ratings, the lower the interrater reliability is.

Internal Consistency Reliability.   Another type of reliability is referred to as **internal consistency reliability,** which is relevant when several observations are made to obtain a score for each participant. This might be the case if participants complete a test with several items or if their behavior is observed several times. Internal consistency reliability is high if each item or behavioral observation correlates with the other observations, that is, if all the items are measuring the same thing. A scale that is internally consistent measures one construct with several independent observations or items. Discussing all the ramifications of internal consistency reliability is beyond the scope of this book, but one principle should be mentioned. Generally, *the more observations that are made to obtain a score for a participant, the greater will be the internal consistency reliability of the score.* Take, for example, the typical tests that are used in courses to determine students' grades. The test could be considered an operational definition of the level of knowledge of students in the course. A test with many questions covering all the different topics in the course should give a consistent indication of how much students know. Asking only one or two questions will not provide the same level of consistency, because it is possible that students will misinterpret any given question and answer it incorrectly even though they know the material. This same principle holds for behavioral observations as well. It is better to have several observations of behavior on which to base the measurement of a construct than to rely on only a few.

The concept of reliability of measures is critical in research because, if the measures are not reliable, the study cannot produce useful information. The factors that contribute to reliability include (1) the precision and clarity of the operational definition of the construct, (2) the care with which the researcher follows the operational definition, and (3) the number of independent observations on which the score is based. Discussion of all the potential issues in measuring and improving the reliability of measures is beyond the scope of this book. See Anastasi and Urbina (1997) for further discussion.

Effective Range

Another factor to consider in measuring variables is the **effective range** of the scale. If we are interested in weight changes in people, a normal bathroom scale will usually have sufficient range, because it typically can weigh objects between 0 and 300 pounds. However, weighing very large or very small objects, such as elephants or mice, would require different scales that are capable of accurately measuring weight in whatever range necessary. Although the concept of weight is the same for both mice and elephants, it is unlikely that a scale constructed to measure one can also measure the other. The heavy-duty construction required of a scale to measure an elephant would make the scale insensitive to the relatively light weight of a mouse.

Effective range issues are relevant to most psychological measures. A test of mathematical skill sensitive enough to detect differences among college math majors would be too difficult to detect differences among third graders. A measure of social skills designed for use with children would probably not be appropriate for use with adults. A measure of memory ability challenging enough to detect differences among college students would be too difficult to detect memory differences among brain-injured adults.

Procedures such as inducing anxiety or relaxation designed to affect one group of participants might not be appropriate for other participants. The procedures might lack the range to work with any and all participants. When designing or selecting measures for research, we must keep in mind who the participants will be so as to guide the selection of measures that have an appropriate effective range for that group.

A problem related to the effective range of a measure is **scale attenuation effects.** In this context, attenuation refers to restricting the range of a scale. Using a measure with a restricted range—not ranging high enough or low enough or both—can result in data showing participants bunched up near the top or bottom of the scale. For example, suppose that we are conducting a study on changing college students' attitudes toward tobacco use. For obvious health reasons, we hope to bring about more negative attitudes. We administer our pretest of attitudes, and we find that virtually all participants are already highly negative toward tobacco use. Suppose that we then apply the attitude change intervention and take postintervention measures of attitudes. The posttest results cannot possibly show much change toward greater negative attitudes even if the intervention is effective. The participants, already at the top of the scale before the intervention, have no room to show change toward still higher scores. This direction of scale attenuation is called a **ceiling effect.** Such a restricted scale will have serious effects on the research findings.

A scale can also be attenuated by having a restricted lower range, thus creating a possible **floor effect.** In this situation, participants would tend to score near the bottom of the scale only because the scale does not allow a sufficiently low range. A floor effect would occur if an instructor gave an examination that was too difficult for the class and almost all students scored low. If the scale had a greater lower range, the students' scores might be more spread out, rather than bunched at the bottom of the scale.

Ceiling and floor effects are illustrated in Figure 4.2. The true weights of each of 10 people are illustrated in the first panel by the height of a bar. The second and third panels illustrate what would happen if there were a ceiling or floor effect, respectively. A ceiling effect might occur if the scale read weights up to only 200 pounds. A floor effect might occur if the needle stuck so that it never read below 120 pounds. Notice how the scores are compressed by both floor and ceiling effects and that scores for people outside the effective range are not accurate.

Scale attenuation effects restrict the range of possible scores for participants' responses; that is, they reduce the potential variability of the data. As we will discuss at some length in Chapter 10, restricting variability results in serious errors. Sufficient variability is essential in research.

Validity

The third factor that must be considered is the validity of the measure. To say that a scale to measure weight is valid means that the scale measures what it is supposed to measure—weight. Validity is *not* the same as reliability, which refers to how consistently the weight is measured. A scale for measuring weight, for example, might not be properly adjusted, thereby giving a reading 10 pounds lighter than the object really is. The scale is reliable if it consistently gives the same weight, but it is not valid be-

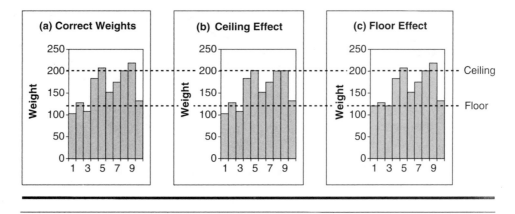

FIGURE 4.2 *Floor and Ceiling Effects* Floor and ceiling effects distort the data by not measuring the full range of a variable. Panel (b) shows the impact of a ceiling effect, in which weights above 200 pounds are read as 200. Similarly, panel (c) shows the impact of a floor effect, in which weight below 120 pounds are read as 120.

cause that weight is not the true weight. *A measure cannot be valid unless it is reliable, but a measure can be reliable without being a valid measure of the variable of interest.* Validity, like reliability, is not an all or nothing concept. There are degrees of validity from none to perfect validity. Once again, a correlation coefficient is typically used to quantify the degree of validity.

We evaluate the validity of a measure by quantifying the ability of the measure to predict other variables. For example, a researcher might want to know if SAT scores predict performance in college. The variable that we want to predict is called the **criterion;** the measure used to predict the criterion is called the **predictor.** When this concept of validity is used, we must always specify the criterion measure. For example, the SAT score may be a valid predictor of freshman college grades. It probably is a less valid predictor of whether a student completes college, because many factors besides ability determine this criterion. Finally, the SAT is probably not a valid predictor of the number of friends a student has or how happy the student is. It makes no sense to say that the SAT test is valid without saying what it is valid for. Validity is a central concept in research. Therefore, we will revisit the concept after you have learned more of the basics of research.

Figure 4.3 illustrates graphically levels of validity. Note the similarity between Figure 4.1, which illustrates reliability, and Figure 4.3, which illustrates validity.

The Need for Objective Measurement

Every science stresses the need for objectivity, or **objective measures,** but often scientists do not make clear why objectivity is so important. Vague references to how objectivity is somehow more accurate than subjectivity are common, but *why* is it more

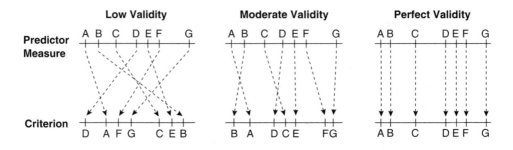

FIGURE 4.3 *Validity* This illustration has two measures (the predictor and the criterion) and seven participants (A, B, C, D, E, F, and G). The top horizontal line represents the predictor measure, and the bottom line represents the criterion measure. The more disagreement shown in the rank ordering of participants on the predictor and criterion measures, the lower the validity is.

accurate? One reason is that subjective measures are person specific; that is, they represent the judgments of only one person. If other people in the same situation make different judgments, the findings will not be reproducible.

A hallmark of science is that the laws of nature should hold no matter who tests them. There may be many reasons why two people disagree on their subjective impressions of a phenomenon. For example, Ellie might judge a room to be hotter than Jenny does because Ellie is accustomed to cooler temperatures and so, by comparison, the room seems hot. Another reason for Ellie and Jenny's disagreement about room temperature might be a differential sensitivity to features other than heat, such as humidity. Yet another reason might be a physiological deficiency in the ability of one or both to sense temperature. Even with something as simple as temperature, subjective impressions pose many problems. If an objective measure of temperature such as the thermometer had not been developed, most of the physical laws relating temperature to other phenomena would have remained undiscovered. The thermometer measures temperature independently of such other variables as humidity. It can measure temperature reliably and across a much greater range than can be accomplished without such an instrument. Finally, the thermometer provides at least an interval scale of measurement of temperature. Although this concept may be difficult to grasp on the basis of this brief discussion, it is important to note that an interval scale greatly simplifies the mathematical description of the relationship of temperature to other phenomena.

If so many problems can emerge with subjective measures of something as simple as temperature, imagine the problems that might arise when trying to measure a complicated construct like self-esteem. Many phenomena that psychologists measure are events that involve human emotions, which can distort perceptions of the phenomena. For example, people who are easily upset by anger might be more sensitive to the presence of anger in an individual who is being frustrated as part of a study on frustration and aggression. Therefore, they might rate the anger as stronger than would people who are less sensitive to anger. Good research, therefore, demands objective measures that can be performed by anyone properly trained to use them and that give the same results regardless of who does the measuring.

Statistical procedures are central in modern research because they provide objective ways of evaluating patterns of events. Insisting on the use of statistical analyses for drawing conclusions is an extension of the argument that objectivity is critical in science. This is the reason that psychology relies so heavily on statistical analyses to evaluate research data.

Quick-Check Review 4: Evaluating Measures

4.1. Define reliability and the different types of reliability.

4.2. Can a measure be reliable but not valid? Can it be valid but not reliable?

4.3. Why must the effective range of a measure be appropriate for the sample under study?

4.4. What are floor and ceiling effects?

4.5. What is the impact of having too limited a range on a research measure?

4.6. How is validity different from reliability?

Chapter Summary

Researchers study relationships between variables. Researchers manipulate and/or measure variables. To assess variables, it is necessary to quantify the observations of the variables. The quantification process, called measurement, involves applying the number system to the variable. The number system has four properties: identity, magnitude, equal intervals, and absolute zero; but the characteristics of variables seldom match all the properties of the number system. Consequently, in applying the number system to variables, we will find that some variables match the number system well, whereas others do not. Four levels of matching in measurement have been described: nominal, ordinal, interval, and ratio measurements. After the observations have been quantified and the level of measurement determined, the selection of an appropriate statistical test is a straightforward decision.

An operational definition details the operations that will be performed to measure a variable. The specifications should be as precise as possible to increase the reliability and validity of the measure and to make replication of the research possible. The reliability of a measure is an index of the measure's consistency. The validity of the measure is its effectiveness in reflecting the characteristic measured. A measure cannot be valid unless it is first reliable, but a measure can be reliable without being valid.

Objectivity is essential in scientific research. Well-conceived operational definitions improve objectivity. Statistical procedures provide objectivity in the analysis of data. Objectivity improves reliability and makes it more likely that researchers can discover valid relationships among variables.

Key Terms

Define the following key terms. Be sure that you understand them. They are discussed in the chapter and defined in the glossary.

properties of the abstract number system	ordered data	interrater reliability
identity	interval scales	test–retest reliability
magnitude	score data	internal consistency reliability
equal intervals	ratio scales	effective range
true zero	measurement error	scale attenuation effects
scales of measurement	response-set biases	ceiling effect
nominal scales	social desirability	floor effect
nominal data	operational definition	criterion
categorical data	convergent validity	predictor
ordinal scales	reliability	objective measures
	blind	

5

Statistical Analysis of Data

The union of the mathematician with the poet, fervor with measure, passion with correctness, this surely is the ideal.

—William James (1842–1910), *Collected Essays,* 1920

CD Resource Material

- SPSS for Windows Tutorial
- SPSS for Windows Inferential Statistical Analyses
- SPSS for Windows Descriptive Statistics
- Pearson Product–Moment Correlation Procedures
- Spearman Rank–Order Correlation Procedures
- Linear Regression
- Reliability Indexes

- The Standard Normal Distribution
- Independent Samples *t*-test Computational Procedures
- Correlated *t*-test Computational Procedures
- ANOVA Computational Procedures
- Effect Size
- Student Study Guide/Laboratory Manual

Web Resource Material _____

- Statistical Resources
- Statistical Power
- Path Analysis
- Statistical Regression

- Analysis of Variance
- Analysis of Covariance
- Multivariate Analysis of Variance

Once a decision on how to measure the research variables is made, the next step is to determine how to analyze the data statistically. **Statistics** are powerful tools for organizing and understanding data. They provide ways to represent and describe groups, summarize results, and evaluate data. Without the use of statistics, little could be learned from most studies.

Statistical procedures and research design are interrelated. The decisions concerning which statistical procedures to use are made in the procedures-design phase as an integral part of the research design and are not something tacked on after data collection. Although this single chapter cannot replace a course in statistics, it will provide an overview of some basic statistical concepts. More advanced statistical concepts and procedures are covered in later chapters and on the *Student Resource CD,* which provides statistical resources, tutorials, and practice exercises. It also presents a hands-on tutorial on how to use the *SPSS for Windows* program for data analysis.

The chapter begins with a discussion of the reason for statistical procedures, specifically, that differences among individuals may mask the impact of research variables. Strategies for organizing and describing the data are then introduced. There is a brief introduction to the logic of statistical decision making before closing with the topic of inferential statistics.

Individual Differences

Statistical procedures depend on variability or differences in responses among participants. No two participants or groups will respond in exactly the same manner. Suppose, for example, that a researcher predicts that participants who are given special memory training will perform better on a memory task than those who are not trained. In this study, participants are assigned to one of two conditions: (1) memory training or (2) no training. The dependent measure is a memory test that yields scores from 0 to 100. Hypothetical data are shown in Table 5.1. You can see in the table that the groups differ in their mean (average) scores. There is also considerable variability of scores within each group. The scores in Group A range from 66 to 98, and those in Group B range from 56 to 94. The variation within each group illustrates that there are **individual differences** in memory skills. Some people, with or without training, remember well; others remember very little; most people fall somewhere in between. All organ-

TABLE 5.1 *Examples of Descriptive Statistics*

	Group A (trained)	Group B (nontrained)
	98	94
	93	88
	90	82
	89	77
	87	75
	87	74
	84	72
	81	72
	78	67
	71	61
	66	56
Median	87	74
Mode	87	72
Mean	84	74.36

These hypothetical data are from 22 participants in a memory study, half of whom received memory training, and the other half did not.

ismic variables studied in psychology show individual differences. Therefore, in the memory study we cannot be sure whether the memory training is the reason for the observed group differences or whether the participants in the training group had better memories to begin with and would have performed better regardless of the training. Most of the variables manipulated in psychology make only small differences in how people perform compared with the individual differences that already exist among people. Statistics help researchers to decide whether group differences on dependent measures are due to the research manipulations or are the result of existing individual differences.

Research studies generate many measures or scores that typically vary from participant to participant. With so many measurements and so much variability, a way is needed to organize and simplify the numbers. **Descriptive statistics** summarize, simplify, and describe a large number of measurements. **Inferential statistics** help researchers to interpret what the data mean. For example, in the study on memory training the means of the two groups (a descriptive statistic) are different. As predicted, the trained group shows a higher mean score than the nontrained group. But the researcher wants to know whether that mean difference is large enough to conclude that it is due to more than chance variation among participants. That is, is the difference found between the groups so large that the difference probably did not occur by chance? Inferential statistics are used to help to answer such questions. These two groups of statistics go together and complement each other. Both descriptive and inferential procedures are applied to the data in virtually every research study.

Organizing Data

This section will introduce two important groups of descriptive procedures: (1) frequency distributions and (2) graphical representations of data. These procedures will be illustrated with the hypothetical data in Table 5.2, which represent responses from 24 participants, aged 18 and above, selected at random from the population of a moderate-

TABLE 5.2   *Sample Data from 24 Participants*

Person	Age	Income	Number of Times Voted in Last 5 Years	Sex	Political Affiliation
1	28	$32,000	6	M	R
2	46	50,000	4	M	D
3	33	44,000	0	F	D
4	40	45,000	5	M	R
5	21	30,000	1	M	R
6	26	35,000	0	F	O
7	39	42,000	6	M	O
8	23	34,000	0	F	D
9	20	27,000	1	M	O
10	26	31,000	2	M	R
11	29	39,000	6	F	R
12	24	34,000	2	M	D
13	34	44,000	2	M	O
14	35	45,000	3	M	O
15	52	46,000	8	M	O
16	31	39,000	4	F	D
17	30	43,000	6	M	R
18	45	47,000	7	F	D
19	18	28,000	0	M	O
20	29	44,000	7	M	R
21	26	38,000	6	F	D
22	23	37,000	3	M	O
23	47	48,000	7	M	D
24	53	51,000	8	M	D

sized city. The researchers are interested in variables that may relate to voting patterns. The information gathered from each participant includes his or her (1) age, (2) income, (3) number of times voted in the last 5 years, (4) sex, and (5) political affiliation (coded as Democrat, Republican, or other). These same data will be used in the next section on descriptive statistics.

What type of data does each of these variables generate? The participant's age, income, and the number of times he or she voted are measured on a ratio scale (score data). Each of these measures has the property of magnitude; for example, 34 is older than 25, $35,000 is more than $28,000, and so on. All three measures have the property of equal intervals; for example, the difference in age between 25 and 20 is the same as the difference between 38 and 33. The variables are measured on ratio scales because they have not only the property of equal intervals, but they each have a true zero point. A person who is zero years old is just being born; a person whose income is zero doesn't earn anything; a person who has voted zero times in the last 5 years has not voted in that time. The other two variables, sex of the participant and political affiliation, are measured on nominal scales. These data are nominal or categorical, and there is no logical way of ordering the categories.

Frequency Distributions

Nominal and Ordinal Data.   For most nominal and ordinal data, statistical simplification involves computing **frequencies,** that is, the number of participants who fall into each category. The frequencies are organized into **frequency distributions,** which show the frequency in each category. Table 5.3 shows the frequency distribution of sex for the data from Table 5.2. In any frequency distribution, when we sum across all categories, the total should equal the total number of participants. It is helpful to convert frequencies to percentages by dividing the frequency in each cell by the total number of participants and multiplying each of these proportions by 100, as was done in Table 5.3.

Sometimes it is useful to categorize participants on the basis of more than one variable at the same time. This is called **cross-tabulation.** For example, participants can be categorized on the basis of each participant's sex and political affiliation. Cross-tabulation can help the researcher to see relationships between nominal measures. In this example, there are two levels of the variable sex (male and female) and three levels of the variable political affiliation (Democrat, Republican, and other), giving a total of six (2 × 3) possible joint categories. The data are arranged in a 2 × 3 matrix in Table 5.4, in which the numbers in the matrix are the frequency of people in

TABLE 5.3   *Frequency of Males and Females in Our Sample*

	Males	*Females*	*Total*
Frequency	17	7	24
Percentage	71	29	100

each of the joint categories. For example, the first cell represents the number of male Democrats. Note that the sum of all the frequencies in the six cells equals the total number of participants. Also note that the row and column totals represent the **univariate** (one-variable) frequency distribution for the political affiliation and sex variables, respectively. For example, the column totals in Table 5.4 of 17 males and 7 females represent the frequency distribution for the single variable of sex and, not surprisingly, are the same numbers that appear in Table 5.3.

Score Data.   Different statistical procedures are used with score data. The simplest way to organize a set of score data is to create a frequency distribution. It is difficult to organize all 24 scores at a glance for the variable "number of times a participant voted in the last 5 years" shown in Table 5.2. Some of the participants have not voted at all during that time, whereas two participants voted eight times, but where do the rest of the participants tend to fall? A frequency distribution organizes the data to answer a question like this at a glance. There may be no participants for some of the scores, in which case the frequency listed for the score would be zero. Table 5.5 shows the frequency distribution for this variable.

If there are many possible scores (25 or more) between the lowest and the highest scores, then the frequency distribution will be long and almost as difficult to read as the original data. In this situation, a **grouped frequency distribution** should be

TABLE 5.4   *Cross-tabulation by Sex and Political Affiliation*

	Males	*Females*	*Total*
Democrats	4	5	**9**
Republicans	6	1	**7**
Other	7	1	**8**
Totals	17	7	24

TABLE 5.5   *Frequency of Voting in Last 5 Years*

Number of Times Voted	*Frequency*
8	2
7	3
6	5
5	1
4	2
3	2
2	3
1	2
0	4

used. This shortens the table to a more manageable size by grouping the scores into 10 to 20 intervals. A grouped frequency distribution is required with a **continuous variable,** in which there are theoretically an infinite number of possible scores between the lowest and the highest score. Table 5.6 shows a grouped frequency distribution for the continuous variable of income, which ranges from $27,000 to $51,000. Grouping the salary range into intervals of $2000 yields 13 intervals.

Graphical Representation of Data

A Chinese proverb states "one picture is worth a thousand words" (Bartlett, 1980), and this is especially true when dealing with statistical information. Graphs often clarify a data set or help to interpret a summary statistic or statistical test. Most people find graphic representations easier to understand than other statistical procedures. **Graphs** and **tables** are excellent supplements to other statistical procedures.

Frequency or grouped frequency distributions can be represented graphically by using either a **histogram** or a **frequency polygon.** Figure 5.1 shows both a histogram and a frequency polygon representing the voting data summarized in Table 5.5. They were generated in just a few seconds using the *SPSS for Windows* data analysis program. These figures are the actual output of the program as it would be seen on the computer screen. Both the histogram and the frequency polygon represent data on a two-dimensional graph, in which the horizontal axis (***x*-axis** or **abscissa**) represents the range of scores for the variable and the vertical axis (***y*-axis** or **ordinate**) represents the frequency of the scores. In a histogram, the frequency of a given score is represented by the height of a bar above that score, as shown in Figure 5.1(a). In the frequency polygon, the frequency is indicated by the height of a point above each score on the abscissa. Connecting the adjacent points, as shown in Figure 5.1(b), completes the frequency polygon. To aid in the interpretation of histograms and frequency polygons, it is important to label both axes carefully.

Two or more frequency distributions can be displayed on the same graph. To compare the distributions, each is graphed independently with different colors or different types of lines, such as solid versus dotted lines, to distinguish one distribution

TABLE 5.6   *Grouped Frequency Distribution for Income*

Annual Income	Frequency	Annual Income	Frequency
$50,000–51,999	2	$36,000–37,999	1
$48,000–49,999	1	$34,000–35,999	3
$46,000–47,999	2	$32,000–33,999	1
$44,000–45,999	5	$30,000–31,999	2
$42,000–43,999	2	$28,000–29,999	1
$40,000–41,999	0	$26,000–27,999	1
$38,000–39,999	3		

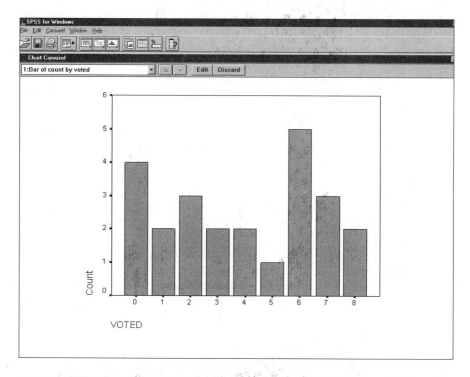

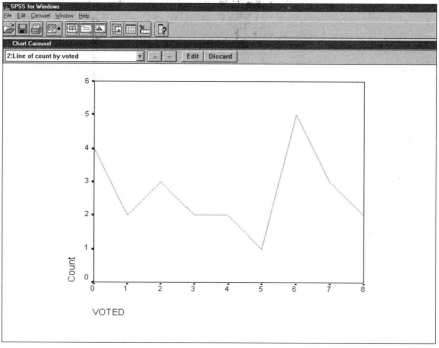

FIGURE 5.1 *Histograms and Frequency Polygons* Graphing the distribution of scores with either a histogram or a frequency polygon helps the researcher to visualize the data.

from the other. Figure 5.2 shows the distribution for the variable "number of times voted in the last 5 years" separately for males and females.

With small group sizes, a frequency polygon is usually jagged. There is an overall shape to the distribution, but the lines connecting the points will go up and down from one interval to another. The distributions graphed in Figures 5.1 and 5.2 have this jagged appearance. As the group size increases, the frequency polygon tends to look more like a smooth curve. Data are often described by drawing smooth curves, even though such curves are seen only when the group sizes are extremely large.

Figure 5.3 represents several smooth-curve drawings of frequency polygons illustrating various distribution shapes. Figure 5.3(a) shows a common shape for a **symmetric distribution,** a bell-shaped curve. In a bell-shaped curve, most of the participants are near the middle of the distribution. Distributions with this shape are referred to as normal curves or **normal distributions.** The normal curve is actually a mathematical curve defined by an equation, but many variables in psychology form distributions similar in shape to a true normal curve. For example, measures of most human characteristics, such as height, weight, and intelligence, are distributed normally. Figures 5.3(b) and 5.3(c) represent **skewed distributions.** In skewed distributions, the scores pile up

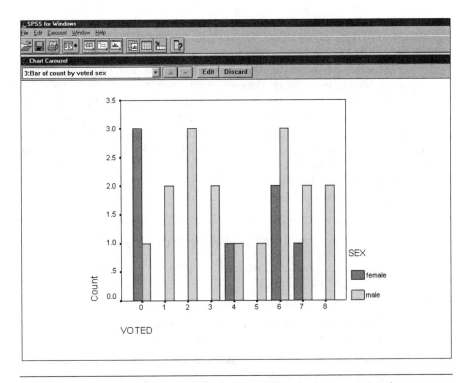

FIGURE 5.2 *Comparing Two Distributions* Graphing the frequency data from two or more groups on the same histogram or frequency polygon gives a visual representation of how the groups compare.

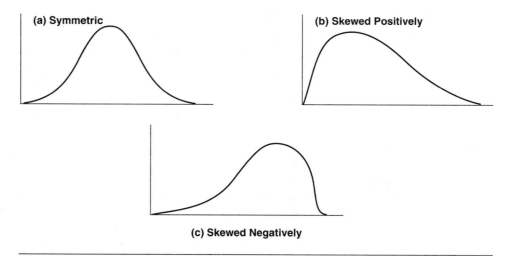

FIGURE 5.3 *Symmetric and Skewed Distributions* Many measures yield the classic bell-shaped distribution. When scores bunch up at either the top or the bottom of the distribution, the distributions are skewed.

on one end of the distribution. The direction of the skewness is indicated by the tail of the curve. In Figure 5.3(b), the curve is **positively skewed,** with most of the scores piled up near the bottom (the tail points toward the high or positive end of the scale). Figure 5.3(c) is **negatively skewed.** Such distributions might be seen on an easy classroom test, on which almost everyone does well and only a few people do poorly. These are the distribution shapes most often seen in psychology. In addition to the shape of the curve, distributions can also be described in terms of the location of the middle of the distribution on the *x*-axis, which is called the **central tendency** of the distribution. The horizontal spread of the distribution, called the **variability** of the distribution, can also be described. An excellent book on graphical presentation of data is Tufte (1997).

Quick-Check Review 2: Organizing Data

2.1. What are frequency distributions? With what kind of data do we use frequency distributions?

2.2. Define cross-tabulation.

2.3. What is the difference between a frequency distribution and a grouped frequency distribution?

2.4. What type of variable requires a grouped frequency distribution?

2.5. What are the basic shapes of distributions found in psychology?

Descriptive Statistics

Descriptive statistics serve two purposes. The first is to describe the data with just one or two numbers, which makes it easier to compare groups. The second is to provide a basis for later analyses in which inferential statistics will be used. This section will cover measures of central tendency, variability, and relationship and introduce you to standard scores.

Measures of Central Tendency

Measures of central tendency describe the typical or average score. They are called measures of central tendency because they provide an indication of the center of the distribution, where most of the scores tend to cluster. There are three measures of central tendency: the mode, the median, and the mean. These are summarized in Table 5.7. The **mode** is the most frequently occurring score in the distribution. In the example shown in Table 5.1, the mode for Group A is 87 and for Group B is 72. If the data are more complicated and a frequency distribution like the one in Table 5.5 has been prepared, the mode can be computed by finding the largest number in the frequency column and noting the score with that frequency. In Table 5.5, the mode is 6. A distribution may have more than one mode. If there are two, then the distribution is **bimodal;** if there are three, it is **trimodal.** The mode has the advantage of being easily computed, but has the disadvantage of being unstable, which means that it can be affected by a change in only one or two scores. The mode can be appropriately used with all scales of measurement.

A second measure of central tendency is the **median.** This is the middle score in a distribution in which the scores have been ordered from lowest to highest. The median is also the 50th percentile, which means that half the scores fall below the median. The median can be easily computed if there are few scores and they have been ordered from lowest to highest. With an odd number of scores, the median is the $(N + 1)/2$ score, in which N is the number of scores. In Table 5.1, there are 11 scores. Therefore, the sixth score $[(11 + 1)/2]$ will be the median. The sixth score in a group of 11 scores will be exactly in the middle, with 5 scores above it and 5 scores below it. In Table 5.1, the median for Group A is 87; in Group B, it is 74. When there is an even number of scores, there will be two middle scores; the median is the average of the two middle scores. The median can be appropriately used with ordered and score data, but not with nominal data. (To the student: Why is the median not appropriate with nominal data?)

TABLE 5.7 *Measures of Central Tendency*

Mode	Most frequently occurring score in a distribution
Median	Middle score in a distribution; the score at the 50th percentile
Mean	Arithmetic average of the scores in a distribution; computed by summing the scores and dividing by the number of scores

The most commonly used measure of central tendency is the **mean,** the arithmetic average of all the scores. The mean is computed by summing the scores and dividing by the number of scores as follows:

$$\text{Mean} = \bar{X} = \frac{\sum X}{N} \tag{5.1}$$

The term $\bar{X}$ (read "X bar") is the notation for the mean. The term $\sum X$ (read "sigma X") is summation notation and simply means to add all the scores. Table 5.8 shows a sample computation of a mean. The mean is appropriately used only with score data. (To the student: Why is this so?)

The mean and the median are frequently used to describe the average score. The median gives a better indication of what the typical score is if there are a few deviant scores in the distribution, that is, unusually high or low scores, as shown in the example given in Table 5.9. The mean, on the other hand, is more useful in other statistical procedures, such as inferential statistics.

Measures of Variability

In addition to measures of central tendency, it is also important to determine the variability of scores. The concept of variability is illustrated in Figure 5.4, which shows

TABLE 5.8   *Sample Computation of a Mean*

Compute the mean for the following ten scores: 12, 7, 8, 5, 10, 8, 9, 13, 9, 6

1. Start by listing the scores in no particular order in a column labeled X at the top.
2. Sum the column.
3. Use the following computational formula to compute the mean.

X
12
7
8
5
10
8
9
13
9
6
$\sum X = 87$

Computing the mean

$$\bar{X} = \frac{\sum X}{N} = \frac{87}{10} = 8.7$$

TABLE 5.9   *Effects of a Single Deviant Score on the Mean and Median*

Assume that there are two companies (Company A and Company B), each with five employees. Listed are the salaries of each employee in each company.

Company A	Company B
$41,000	$41,000
43,000	43,000
45,000	45,000
47,000	47,000
49,000	149,000

The salaries of the employees in both companies have been ordered for ease of comparison between companies. Note that four of the salaries paid out to employees are exactly the same in both companies. Only the top salary is different in the two companies. The top salary is $49,000 in Company A and $149,000 in Company B. The mean salary is $45,000 in Company A and $65,000 in Company B. The median (or middle) salary is the same for both companies ($45,000). Which measure of central tendency gives the most typical salary in each company?

two distributions with identical means. However, curve A is narrower; that is, the scores are bunched closer together. They are less variable than the scores of curve B. For example, if you compared the ages of people who attend county fairs and those who attend pop music concerts, you would probably find that county fairgoers range from infants to people over 90, whereas pop concertgoers are mostly in their teens and early twenties, with few preteens and few people over 30. Clearly, there is far more variability in the age of attendees at a county fair than at a typical pop concert.

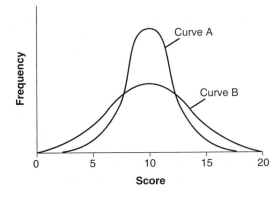

FIGURE 5.4   *Two Distributions with the Same Mean but Different Variances* Although both of these distributions have the same mean, they clearly differ in their variability.

Variability is one of the most important concepts in research. It is also a fact of life. Individuals differ from one another on many factors, and these differences affect their responses to stimuli. This natural variability among participants often masks the effects of the variables under study. Most research designs and statistical procedures were developed to control or minimize the effects of the natural variability of scores.

But as important as the concept of variability is, it is an easy concept to understand. Participants differ from one another, and these differences are reflected in differences in scores for a variable. On some variables, there are large differences among participants; on other variables, the differences are small. There may be many reasons why scores vary among participants, but you need not worry about the reasons at this point. The important ideas to remember are that the scores do vary and that the degree of variability can be quantified.

The measures of variability are summarized in Table 5.10. The simplest measure of variability is the **range,** the distance from the lowest to the highest score. Although the range is easy to compute, it is too unstable because it depends on only two scores, the highest and the lowest. A single deviant score can dramatically affect the range. For example, in Figure 5.4, the scores for curve A range from 4 to 16 (a range of 12), and the scores for curve B range from 1 to 19 (a range of 18). However, if one more score were added to curve A (a score of 22), the ranges for curves A and B would be equal. Nevertheless, even with the addition of this one deviant score, the scores are more tightly clustered or less variable in curve A than in curve B.

A better measure of variability is the variance. The variance utilizes all the scores, instead of just the lowest and highest scores, in quantifying the degree of variability in the data. Furthermore, it has the statistical properties that make it useful in inferential statistics. To begin the discussion of the variance, suppose that you have a set of scores, and you have calculated the mean of this set. Now suppose that you ask a reasonable question about variability: On average, how much do the scores in this set differ from the mean of the set? It is a simple matter to find this value; just subtract the mean from each score (called the deviation), add up these deviations (ignoring the + and − signs), and find their average by dividing the sum of the deviations by the number of scores. This computation is shown in the example in Table 5.11. When you divide this sum by the number of scores, you get the **average deviation.** In Table 5.11

TABLE 5.10 *Measures of Variability*

Range	Distance from the lowest to the highest score in a distribution; may be specified by either giving both the lowest and highest scores or by subtracting the lowest from the highest score and reporting this value
Average deviation	Arithmetic average of the distance that each score is from the mean
Variance	Essentially, the average squared distance from the mean; the variance is computed by summing the squared distances from the mean and dividing by the degrees of freedom (equal to the number of scores minus 1)
Standard deviation	Square root of the variance

TABLE 5.11 *Computing the Average Deviation, Variance, and Standard Deviation*

Compute the average deviation, the variance, and the standard deviation for the data from Table 5.8.

Steps in computing the average deviation
1. Start by listing the scores in no particular order in a column labeled X at the top.
2. Compute the mean as was done in Table 5.8.
3. Label another column $|X - \overline{X}|$.
4. Compute the values of $|X - \overline{X}|$; then add up the numbers in the column. This total is the numerator of the average deviation formula.
5. Divide by the number of scores to get the average deviation.

Steps in computing the variance and standard deviation
1. Start by listing the scores in no particular order in a column labeled X at the top.
2. Compute the mean as was done in Table 5.8.
3. Label another column $(X - \overline{X})^2$.
4. Compute the values of $(X - \overline{X})^2$; then add up the numbers in the column. This total is the numerator for the variance computation.
5. Use Formula 5.2 to compute the variance and Formula 5.3 to compute the standard deviation.

X	$|X - \overline{X}|$	$(X - \overline{X})^2$
12	3.3	10.89
7	1.7	2.89
8	0.7	0.49
5	3.7	13.69
10	1.3	1.69
8	0.7	0.49
9	0.3	0.09
13	4.3	18.49
9	0.3	0.09
6	2.7	7.29
$\Sigma X = 87$	$\Sigma|X - \overline{X}| = 19.0$	$\Sigma(X - \overline{X})^2 = 56.10$

Formulas for computing the mean, average deviation, and variance

$$\overline{X} = \frac{\Sigma X}{N} = \frac{87}{10} = 8.7$$

$$\text{Average deviation} = \frac{\Sigma|X - \overline{X}|}{N} = \frac{19.0}{10} = 1.9$$

$$s^2 = \frac{\Sigma(X - \overline{X})^2}{N - 1} = \frac{56.10}{10 - 1} = \frac{56.10}{9} = 6.23$$

$$s = \sqrt{s^2} = \sqrt{6.23} = 2.50$$

the scores differ from the mean by an average of 1.9 units. The sign is ignored when adding the deviations because, if the sign is not ignored, the average deviation from the mean will always be zero no matter how variable the scores are.

The average deviation is included here only to help to explain the concept of deviation. It is never used in statistical analyses because it lacks the statistical qualities that would make it useful. Instead, the variance and standard deviation are used, both of which are based on the same concept of variability of scores from the mean. The variance is calculated by squaring the deviations of the scores from the mean. That is, the **variance** measures the average squared deviation of each score from the mean. The deviations from the mean are squared to make them all positive. The notation s^2 refers to variance. The formula for variance is

$$s^2 = \frac{\text{SS (sum of squares)}}{\text{df (degrees of freedom)}} = \frac{\sum (X - \bar{X})^2}{N - 1} \tag{5.2}$$

That is, variance equals the sum of the squared differences of each score from the mean (called the **sum of squares**) divided by the number of scores (N) minus 1 (called the degrees of freedom). The **degrees of freedom** is an important concept in statistics, referring to the number of scores that are free to vary (see Box 5.1). To use Formula 5.2, the

BOX 5.1 • *Degrees of Freedom*

Degrees of freedom, a basic statistical concept needed in many computations, refers to the number of scores that are free to vary. Suppose that you are asked to pick any three numbers. There are no restrictions, and the numbers are completely free to vary. In standard terminology, there would be three degrees of freedom; that is, three numbers are free to vary. Now suppose that you are to choose any three numbers, but they must total 15; now there is one restriction on the numbers. Because of the restriction, you will lose some of the freedom to vary the three numbers that you choose. If you choose the numbers 5 and 1 as the first two numbers, you must choose 9 as the third number to arrive at the total of 15. If you choose the numbers 8 and 11 as the first two numbers, the third must be –4 in order to total 15. In both examples, two numbers are free to vary, but one is not. In standard terminology, there are two degrees of freedom; that is, two numbers are free to vary. In comparison to the first example, in which there was no restriction and all the scores could be freely selected, you have lost a degree of freedom.

Now suppose that you are to choose three scores in which (1) the total must be 15 and (2) the first score must be 7. Notice that there are two restrictions placed on these scores. Consequently, two degrees of freedom have been lost, leaving only one degree of freedom. The only score that can vary freely is the second score.

In statistics, the restrictions imposed on data are not arbitrary as they are in this example. Instead, they are determined by the demands of the statistical procedures. Many statistical procedures require that values, such as the population mean, be estimated. These estimates constitute restrictions. The more such restrictions, the more degrees of freedom that are lost. In the computation of the variance, one such restriction is imposed and, consequently, the degrees of freedom are reduced by one. Hence, the denominator is $N - 1$.

mean is first computed. The mean is then subtract from each score and the difference is squared. The squared differences are summed to calculate the sum of squares. The sum of squares is short for "the sum of squared deviations from the mean" and is often abbreviated in formulas as SS. The sum of squares is divided by $N - 1$, the degrees of freedom, to obtain the variance. In Table 5.11, the variance is computed for the data presented in Table 5.8.

The variance is an excellent measure of variability and is used in many inferential statistics. Notice that the variance is expressed in squared units, whereas the mean is expressed in the original units of the variable. A measure called the standard deviation can be computed to transform the variance back into the same units as the original scores. The **standard deviation** (written s) is equal to the square root of the variance. The variance and standard deviation are appropriately used only with score data.

$$s = \sqrt{s^2} = \sqrt{\text{variance}} \tag{5.3}$$

Measures of Relationship

At times we want to quantify the strength of the **relationship** between two or more variables, which indicates the degree to which the two scores tend to vary together. This relationship between variables is best indexed with a **correlation coefficient,** or correlation for short. A **correlation** is a descriptive statistic in that it describes some aspect of the data. However, it is different from the other descriptive statistics in that it always involves at least two variables. There are different correlation coefficients for different types of data. With score data, the Pearson product–moment correlation should be used; with ordered data, the Spearman rank–order correlation should be used.

Pearson Product–Moment Correlation.   The **Pearson product–moment correlation** is the most widely used correlation index. The computational procedures are detailed on the *Student Resource CD.* The product–moment correlation can range from -1.00 to $+1.00$. A correlation of $+1.00$ means that the two variables are perfectly related in a positive direction: as one variable increases, the other variable will increase by a predictable amount. A correlation of -1.00 represents a perfect negative relationship: as one variable increases, the other decreases by a predictable amount. A correlation of zero means that there is no relationship between the variables. The strength of the relationship is indicated by the absolute value of the correlation coefficient. For example, a correlation of .55 indicates a stronger relationship than a correlation of .25, and a correlation of $-.85$ indicates an even stronger relationship. Remember, the sign of the correlation indicates only the direction of the relationship and not its strength. The standard notation for correlation is r. Thus, the correlations above would be noted as $r = 1.00$, $r = -1.00$, $r = .55$, $r = .25$, and $r = -.85$.

The Pearson product–moment correlation is an index of the degree of **linear relationship** between two variables. What this means is best illustrated by examining **scatter plots,** which is a graphic technique used to represent the relationship between two variables. To construct one, standard x- and y-axes are labeled with the names of the two variables. Each axis is divided into a sufficient number of equal intervals to handle the range for the variable represented by the axis. A scatter plot for the relationship between age and income using data from Table 5.2 is graphed in Figure 5.5. As indicated in the figure, participant 1 is 28 years old and earns $32,000 a year. The point representing participant 1 is directly above $32,000 on the x-axis and directly across from 28 on the y-axis. To complete the scatter plot, each person's set of scores is plotted in the same way.

The pattern of scores in the scatter plot is informative. For example, in Figure 5.5 the people with the highest incomes are all older; young people tend to have lower incomes. We could draw a straight line through the middle of the dots from the lower left to upper right of the graph, with most of the dots falling close to that line. This is a good example of a linear relationship; the points in this scatter plot cluster around a straight line. It is a **positive correlation** because incomes are higher for older participants. It is not a perfect correlation. In a **perfect correlation** ($r = 1.00$), all the dots form a straight line, as in Figure 5.6(a). The scatter plots in Figure 5.6 also illustrate other types of relationships. Figure 5.6(b) illustrates a strong **negative correlation** ($r = -.92$). Notice that the points cluster close to a straight line. Figure 5.6(c) illustrates a zero correlation ($r = .00$). Figure 5.6(d) illustrates a **nonlinear relationship,** in which the product–moment correlation coefficient does not represent the data well. In fact, in this case the correlation ($r = -.03$), which is near zero, would be misleading. The near-zero correlation suggests there is no relationship between the variables, but the scatter plot indicates there is a relationship; it is just not a linear relationship. This

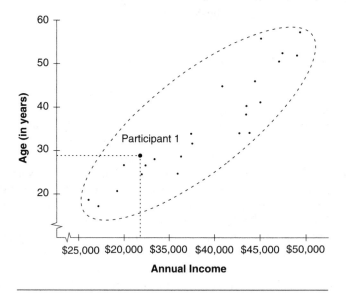

FIGURE 5.5 *Scatter Plot for Age and Income* A scatter plot is constructed by graphing each person's data point. The data point is determined by the two scores for the person.

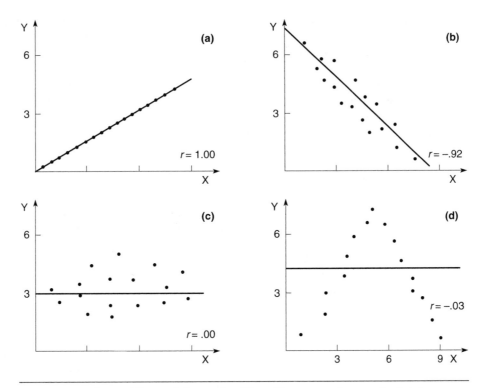

FIGURE 5.6 *Scatter Plots and Regression Lines* You cannot always tell what the relationship between two variables is like from the correlation. The scatter plot allows you to see the relationship, including such complex relationships as the one shown in panel (d).

is one reason why it is advisable to create a scatter plot to see how the scores cluster, instead of relying on a single number like a correlation coefficient to summarize the relationship between variables. With modern computer packages, it takes just a few seconds to create a scatter plot.

Spearman Rank–Order Correlation.   If either or both variables are ordinal (and neither variable is nominal), the appropriate coefficient is the **Spearman rank–order correlation.** The *Student Resource CD* shows the computational procedures. The Spearman rank–order correlation is interpreted like the product–moment correlation: a correlation of –1.00 is a perfect negative relationship; a correlation of +1.00 is a perfect positive relationship; a correlation of zero means that no linear relationship exists. Scatter plots can be drawn using the rank of each participant on each variable.

Note that a correlation coefficient provides a measure of the degree and direction of relationship between variables. Finding such relationships is a major goal of science. Another goal is to make predictions about events. The correlation coefficient is an important part of this, because a strong relationship between two variables provides information that will help to predict one variable by knowing the values of the other. For example, if a correlation is found between test scores and later job performance, then we have information that may help us to predict future job performance.

Regression.   The prediction of the value of one variable from the value of another is called **regression.** We typically assume a linear or straight-line relationship. Nonlinear regression is possible, but the procedures are well beyond the level of this text. (The interested student is referred to Cohen and Cohen, 1983, or Myers and Well, 1995). You may have noticed that a line has been drawn in each of the scatter plots in Figure 5.6. This line is the linear regression line for predicting the variable *Y* from the variable *X*. In Figures 5.6(a) and (b), the points cluster close to the line, suggesting a strong linear relationship. When the correlation is zero, as in Figure 5.6(c), the line is horizontal. When the correlation between *X* and *Y* is zero, the best prediction for *Y* will always be the mean of *Y* regardless of the value of *X*. For Figure 5.6(d), the regression line, like the correlation, is misleading in that it does not reflect the data well. The computational procedures for linear regression are included on the *Student Resource CD*. Statistical analysis packages can compute a regression line easily for any data set. However, you should always request a scatter plot so that you can see how well the data fit a straight-line function.

Reliability Indices.   The concept of reliability was introduced in Chapter 4. Correlation coefficients are used to quantify many types of reliability, including test–retest and interrater reliability. Typically, a product–moment correlation is computed between the two test scores. Since these reliability indices are correlations, they behave like any other correlation. They range from a −1.00 to a +1.00, but for all practical purposes, negative correlations are unlikely when reliability indices are computed unless something is seriously amiss, such as raters using different rating scales. A correlation of +1.00 indicates perfect reliability, and a correlation of 0.00 indicates no reliability.

The internal consistency reliability index, called **coefficient alpha,** is also a correlation coefficient, although a much more complicated one than those covered in this chapter. Coefficient alpha is an index of how intercorrelated the items in a measure are. The more highly correlated the items are with one another, the higher the coefficient alpha. The *Student Resource CD* gives a more detailed description of these reliability indices and computational formulas.

Standard Scores

The **standard score** (written *Z;* also called the **Z-score**) is a useful transformation frequently used in research. The standard score is computed by subtracting the mean from the score and dividing the difference by the standard deviation, as shown in Formula 5.4. This is referred to as a **relative score** because it tells how the participant scored *relative* to the rest of the participants. If the participant scores above the mean, the standard score is positive; if the participant scores below the mean, the standard score is negative. The size of the standard score indicates how far from the mean the participant scored. Many tests convert the standard score to avoid negative numbers and decimals. For example, the standard score on the IQ test is converted into an IQ by multiplying the standard score by 15 and adding 100, producing an IQ distribution with a mean of 100 and a standard deviation of 15. The subtests of the SAT scores have similarly been converted from standard scores to a distribution with a mean of 500 and a standard deviation of 100.

$$Z = \frac{X - \bar{X}}{s} \tag{5.4}$$

The standard score is useful in many situations. Converting several measures taken on each participant to standard scores before summing them gives each measure the same weight in the total. Instructors often use this principle in computing grades: summing the standard scores for each exam, rather than the raw scores. Many statistical procedures use an implicit conversion to standard scores, including most advanced regression procedures. Finally, if the distribution is approximately normal, the standard score can be easily converted into a percentile rank by using a table found in any statistics textbook. A person's **percentile rank** tells what percent of the group scored below the person. The details of this transformation are included on the *Student Resource CD*.

Quick-Check Review 3: Descriptive Statistics

3.1. What are the three measures of central tendency?

3.2. What are the chief measures of variability?

3.3. Define correlation and regression. How are these used?

3.4. What is a standard score and how is it computed?

3.5. Why is the variance a better measure of variability than the range?

3.6. Why is the mean a better measure of central tendency than the mode?

3.7. How does a correlation differ from other descriptive statistics?

Statistical Inference

Using statistics to describe data is only the first step in analyzing the results of a research study. The rest of the analysis is concerned not so much with the specific participants tested, but with what these participants indicate about a larger group of people. This section will cover the logic of this process, and the next section will cover the actual statistical procedures. The section starts by discussing the differences between samples and populations and the processes of drawing inferences about populations based on the samples drawn from these populations. It then introduces the concepts of the null hypothesis and statistical decision making. The section closes with a discussion of the limits of statistical decision making, specifically, judging the error rates in the decision process.

Populations and Samples

It is seldom possible to observe whole populations. Therefore, samples from populations are observed. In human research, a **population** is the larger group of all the people of interest. The **sample** is a subset that is drawn from the population. For example, a researcher might select a sample of high school students from the population of all high school students in the county. A sample is used as if that sample adequately represented the population. In research we want to draw conclusions about the population on the basis of a sample from that population. However, no two samples drawn from the same population will be exactly alike. For example, one sample of participants from the general population may have a mean IQ of 102.2, whereas another sample from the same population might have a mean IQ of 100. Most samples are reasonably representative of the population from which they are drawn, but sometimes samples are unrepresentative of the population, even though the sampling procedure may have been carried out flawlessly. The variation among different samples drawn from the same population is referred to as **sampling error.** This term is misleading in that it does not represent a mistake. Rather, sampling error refers to the variability among samples due to chance. Because samples are not perfectly representative of the population from which they are drawn, we cannot be sure that the conclusions drawn from the samples will generalize to the entire population. In fact, we can never be sure that inferences drawn from a sample are valid for the population; the best we can do is to calculate probabilities about potential inferences. **Probability** provides a numerical indication of how likely it is that a given event will occur. It is a critical concept in inferential statistics.

Suppose that a researcher is interested in sex differences in reaction time and compares men and women. The variable, reaction time, is measured by recording how quickly participants press a button in response to an auditory signal. The samples of men and women would be drawn from the population of men and women. Suppose that it is found that mean reaction time from the samples was 0.278 seconds for the men and 0.254 seconds for the women. Clearly, the sample means are different, but not very different. However, the researcher is actually interested in the population of men and the population of women. That is, the researcher wants to draw conclusions about characteristics of the populations from the results of the samples. Would the observed difference in mean reaction time in the samples lead us to believe that a similar difference exists between the populations, or could the observed difference simply be a result of sampling error? This question, comparing population means, is the type most often raised in such research. Suppose for the moment that the reaction time means for the populations were not different. In this case, samples drawn from the populations should have approximately equal mean reaction times. Are the mean reaction times of 0.278 and 0.254 approximately equal? Are they close enough to infer that the population means, which are unknown, are also approximately equal? This process is referred to as testing the null hypothesis.

The Null Hypothesis

The **null hypothesis** is a general hypothesis that can be applied to many types of comparisons. In the situation just discussed, the means are being compared. Null is from the Latin *nullus,* meaning "not any." Thus, the null hypothesis states that there is no statistical difference between the population means. If the observed sample means were very different, we would reject the null hypothesis and conclude that the population means are not equal. But how different is "very different"? Inferential statistics give a probabilistic answer to this question.

Before proceeding, you need to understand the difference between a population parameter and a sample statistic. If a characteristic of the population, such as the mean, is computed by testing everyone in the population, it is called a **population parameter.** If the same characteristic is computed for a sample drawn from that population, it is called a **sample statistic.** The task in using inferential statistics is to estimate and draw conclusions about population parameters on the basis of sample statistics.

Statistical Decisions and Alpha Levels

Inferential statistics are used to compute the probability of obtaining the observed data *if* the null hypothesis is true. If this probability is small, then it is unlikely that the null hypothesis is true. You would then conclude that the null hypothesis is false. A somewhat arbitrary cutoff point called the **alpha level** (written α) is used for making this decision.[1] Traditionally, researchers set alpha to a small value, such as 0.05 or 0.01. Referring back to the example will help to clarify these difficult but important concepts. The researcher is interested in the reaction time of men and women. The null hypothesis is that the mean reaction times are the same in these two populations. The inferential statistical procedure evaluates the size of the observed mean difference between the samples. If the sample means are so different that it is unlikely that the samples could have come from populations with equal means, we reject the hypothesis that the population means are equal (the null hypothesis).

Type I and Type II Errors

The alpha level that is selected guides the decision about the null hypothesis. When the probability is larger than the alpha level, the null hypothesis is retained; when the probability is at or below the alpha level, the null hypothesis is rejected. Of course, there is always the chance that the researcher's decision will be wrong. For example, the researcher might reject the null hypothesis and conclude that the population means are not equal when, in fact, they are equal. In this case, the researcher has made a **Type I error.** The probability of this error occurring is equal to the alpha level that was set by the researcher. If an alpha of .05 is used, Type I errors will occur 5% of the time. If the alpha is .01, Type I errors will occur 1% of the time. The alpha level is the proportion of Type I errors that we can expect to make if the study is repeated many times.

If alpha is the level of Type I error and the researcher decides what alpha to use, why not set alpha to zero to avoid all Type I errors? The reason is that there is another

---

[1]Alpha, as used here, is entirely different from the reliability index, coefficient alpha. It is a historical accident that the same Greek letter was used for these two statistical concepts.

possible error, known as a Type II error. A **Type II error** occurs when we fail to reject the null hypothesis when it is false. The term **beta** (ß) refers to the probability of making a Type II error. Researchers want to avoid both errors, but because we can never be sure what the real state of nature is, there is always the chance for error in the decision. Decreasing the Type I error rate without doing anything else will automatically increase the Type II error rate. Therefore, these two errors have to be balanced against one another. Table 5.12 summarizes the definitions of Type I and Type II errors.

Quick-Check Review 4: Statistical Inference

4.1. Distinguish populations from samples.

4.2. What is sampling error?

4.3. Define population parameter and sample statistic.

4.4. Define alpha level, Type I error, and Type II error.

4.5. Explain how inferential statistics differ from descriptive statistics.

Inferential Statistics

This section introduces the most common inferential statistics: the *t*-test and the analysis of variance. It also briefly covers several related topics, including statistical power, statistical versus practical significance, effect size, and meta-analysis.

Testing for Mean Differences

Inferential statistics are used most frequently to evaluate mean differences between groups. Such statistical techniques are valuable because research hypotheses can often be specified in terms of mean differences. There are several tests for evaluating mean

TABLE 5.12 *Type I and Type II Errors*

		Researcher's Decision	
		Reject the Null Hypothesis	*Retain the Null Hypothesis*[a]
True State of Nature	**Null hypothesis true:**	Type I error	Correct decision
	Null hypothesis false:	Correct decision	Type II error

[a]Technically, we never actually accept the null hypothesis. Instead, we retain or fail to reject the null hypothesis. The interested student should consult an introductory statistics textbook for the reasoning behind this subtle distinction.

differences between groups, including the *t*-test for independent groups, the correlated *t*-test, and the analysis of variance (ANOVA).

t-Test for Independent Groups. The **t-test for independent groups** is used with score data from two **independent samples.** The samples are independent if different individuals appear in each sample and if the participants in the two samples are not matched in any way. The null hypothesis is that there is no difference in the two population means; that is, the observed difference between the sample means is due only to sampling error. The test statistic is called *t*. Computational procedures for *t* can be found on the *Student Resource CD,* which also shows how to use *SPSS for Windows* to conduct a *t*-test. The general procedure in this and most other inferential statistics is to compute the test statistic and the probability (*p*-value) of obtaining this value of the test statistic if the null hypothesis is true. If the *p*-value is less than the chosen alpha level, we reject the null hypothesis and conclude that the population means are different.

Correlated* t-*Test. Some research designs do not use independent samples. One such design is called a **within-subjects design,** in which the same participants appear in each group. In this design, the groups represent different conditions under which the participants are tested. Another design is the **matched-subjects design,** in which all participants are matched in pairs and then randomly assigned so that one member of the pair goes into one group and the other member goes into another. These designs will be discussed in Chapter 11. In either case, a **correlated *t*-test** is the appropriate statistic to use to analyze the results of the study. The computational procedures and instructions on how to use statistical software to do the computations for the correlated *t*-test are included on the *Student Resource CD.*

Analysis of Variance. When testing for mean differences among more than two groups, an **analysis of variance (ANOVA)** is the appropriate test. The term analysis of variance is confusing because the test actually compares the means of the various groups, but it compares the means by computing and comparing different population variance estimates. Explaining how this is accomplished is beyond the scope of this book. This section will focus on the conceptual basis of ANOVA. Standard terminology and interpretation will be discussed in Chapters 10 through 12. Computational procedures and statistical software instructions are included on the *Student Resource CD.*

   Analysis of variance is a flexible tool for analyzing the results of research. The results of studies that use one independent variable and of studies that use two or more independent variables can be analyzed. When there is more than one independent variable, the independent variables are referred to as **factors,** and the research design is said to be **factorial.** The analysis of a study with only one independent variable is referred to as a **one-way ANOVA;** with two independent variables, as a **two-way ANOVA;** and so forth. Each factor can have many levels or groups. Also, ANOVAs can be used to analyze data from studies in which different participants appear in each condition (a

between-subjects design) or studies in which the same participants appear in all conditions (a within-subjects design). An ANOVA used to analyze data from a within-subjects design is referred to as a **repeated measures ANOVA.** All these concepts will be discussed in more detail in later chapters.

The Power of a Statistical Test

The term **power** or **statistical power** refers to the sensitivity of the statistical procedure to the hypothesized mean differences. Thus, the concept of the power of a statistical procedure refers to the sensitivity of the procedure to provide a basis for correctly rejecting the null hypothesis when it is false. It is equal to $1 - ß$, where $ß$ is the probability of a Type II error. Power is not a function of the statistical procedure alone, but also depends on the precision of the research design. The traditional way of increasing power is to increase the sample size. The size of the sample needed to achieve a specified level of power can be computed on the basis of pilot data as part of the procedures-design phase, a process called **power analysis** (Cohen, 1988, 1992). Increasing sample size is not the only way to increase power. Any improvement in a research design that increases sensitivity will increase power, including sampling more precisely, using more precise measures, using better standardization of procedures, and controlling individual differences through the choice of a research design (see Chapter 11).

Effect Size

In recent years it has become commonplace to go a step beyond significance testing by computing the **effect size** of an experimental manipulation. This is a measure of the size of the difference between the group means (the difference supposedly brought about by the experimental manipulation of the independent variable). The difference is expressed in standard deviation units and is independent of the size of the sample. Cohen (1992) proposed a scale to help to guide researchers in interpreting the calculated effect size (a small, moderate, or large effect), and these scales have become widely used. Effect size and power are related: as effect size increases, power increases. The reason for the increase in power is that it is easier to detect large mean differences than small differences. Effect size is covered more fully in Chapter 15 and on the *Student Resource CD.*

Statistical versus Practical Significance

A statistically significant finding is impressive and usually pleases the researcher, especially if it is in the predicted direction. But the mere fact of finding statistical significance can be misleading, and care is needed so as not to conclude that, because a finding is **statistically significant,** it has **practical significance.**

Suppose, for example, that a researcher compares two large groups of seriously obese adults. The experimental group attends a weight-reduction program and the control group is put on a waiting list. After 6 months, the treated group has lost a mean of 3.4 pounds, whereas the control group has gained a mean of 0.2 pounds, and the difference between the groups is statistically significant. Despite the statistical significance, this question must be asked: Is the loss of just over 3 pounds after 6 months of expensive dieting, exercise, and group meetings of any personal significance to those obese people who wanted to lose weight? Most of the dieters would probably say no. Thus, when evaluating the effectiveness of the weight-reduction program in practical terms, we have to be careful not to let the statistically significant findings blind us to the fact that the program was simply not practically or personally successful for these people.

Meta-analysis

A relatively recent innovation is meta-analysis. **Meta-analysis** is a procedure that allows the statistical averaging of results from independent studies of the same phenomenon, in effect creating the statistical equivalent of a superstudy (Cooper & Lindsay, 1998). Meta-analyses have become increasingly more common in recent years because they provide a more objective way of integrating the findings from several studies on the same general question. Meta-analysis will be discussed more extensively in Chapter 15.

Quick-Check Review 5: Inferential Statistics

5.1. What statistical tests are used to test for mean differences? Under what conditions should each of these statistics be used?

5.2. What is power analysis and why is it important?

5.3. What is the difference between statistical and practical significance?

5.4. What is meta-analysis?

Chapter Summary

Statistics are tools that help researchers to interpret the results of studies. The statistical interpretations are limited by (1) the quality of the data gathered, (2) the appropriateness of the statistic, and (3) the accuracy of the statistical computations. Some statistical procedures (descriptive statistics) describe data from a study. Others (inferential statistics) are designed to help to interpret the data. The appropriate statistic(s) will depend on the nature of the data and the nature of the questions.

This chapter discussed the most commonly used statistics. The *Student Resource CD* outlines procedures for computing statistics manually and with a popular statistical analysis package, *SPSS for Windows*. Chapter 14 presents a flowchart for selecting the appropriate statistical technique based on the research design.

Key Terms

Define the following key terms. Be sure that you understand them. They are discussed in the chapter and defined in the glossary.

statistics
individual differences
descriptive statistics
inferential statistics
frequencies
frequency distributions
cross-tabulation
univariate
grouped frequency
   distribution
continuous variable
graphs
tables
histogram
frequency polygon
x-axis, or abscissa
y-axis, or ordinate
symmetric distribution
normal distribution
skewed distribution
positively skewed
negatively skewed
central tendency
variability
measures of central tendency
mode
bimodal
trimodal
median
mean

range
average deviation
variance
sum of squares
degrees of freedom
standard deviation
relationship
correlation coefficient, or
   correlation
Pearson product–moment
   correlation
linear relationship
scatter plot
positive correlation
perfect correlation
negative correlation
nonlinear relationship
Spearman rank–order
   correlation
regression
coefficient alpha
standard score, or Z-score
relative score
percentile rank
population
sample
sampling error
probability
null hypothesis
population parameter

sample statistic
alpha level
Type I error
Type II error
beta
t-test for independent groups
independent samples
p-value
within-subjects design
matched-subjects design
correlated t-test
analysis of variance
   (ANOVA)
factors
factorial
one-way ANOVA
two-way ANOVA
between-subjects design
repeated measures ANOVA
power, or statistical power
power analysis
effect size
statistical significance
practical significance
meta-analysis
statistical symbols: Σ (sigma);
   X; N; s; s^2; SS; α (alpha);
   β (beta); t; F

6

Field Research

I. Naturalistic and Case-Study Research

(Scientists) must acquire an extensive portfolio of methods…and must apply their skills aided by an immense base of shared knowledge about the domain and the profession.

—David Klahr and Herbert Simon, 2001

CD Resource Material

- Applied Research Strategies
- Making Observation Tutorial
- For What Is a Scientist Remembered? (Sociology of Science)

- Student Study Guide/Laboratory Manual

Web Resource Material _____

- Charles Darwin and the Theory of Evolution
- Jane Goodall
- David Rosenhan

- Sigmund Freud
- Jean Piaget
- Unobtrusive Measures

The term **field research** applies to a variety of research methods, ranging from low to high constraint. They share a focus on observing naturally occurring behavior under largely natural conditions, that is, observing behavior "in the field." Six types of research, described in Table 6.1, are included in the category of field research.

Field research will be covered in two chapters. The lower-constraint field-research methods of naturalistic observation, archival research, and case studies will be discussed in this chapter. After you have learned about higher-constraint research, Chapter 13 will provide a second look at field research, covering the higher-constraint field-research methods of program evaluation, surveys, and field experiments.

Naturalistic and case-study methods are flexible approaches that allow the researcher to take advantage of unexpected occurrences and new ideas developed during the observations. These methods focus on the natural flow of behavior without imposing controls or manipulations by the researcher. Naturalistic research is carried out in the participant's natural environment, such as an animal's habitat, a schoolroom, or a workplace. Case-study research is slightly higher in constraint in that the researcher intervenes to some degree to create situations likely to produce interesting information. This chapter begins by discussing the challenge and the value of low-constraint research. Examples of naturalistic and case-study research, much of it classic research, are provided. The chapter then discusses how such research should be carried out and analyzed and closes by discussing the limitations of these methods.

TABLE 6.1   *Categories of Field Research*

Naturalistic observation	Observation of events as they occur in natural settings
Archival research	Studying information from already existing records made in natural settings
Surveys	Asking direct questions of persons in natural settings
Case studies	Making extensive observations of a single group or a person
Program evaluation	Conducting evaluations of applied procedures in natural settings
Field experiments	Conducting experiments in natural settings in order to understand causal relationships among variables

Note: Surveys, program evaluation, and field experiments will be covered in Chapter 13.

The Challenge of Low-Constraint Research

You might think that, because researchers impose few controls and make observations in a flexible manner, low-constraint methods are easy to carry out. As in all research, however, care and effort are required. Indeed, the very lack of high-constraint procedures adds a burden, because researchers cannot depend on the supports found in laboratory settings.

In naturalistic and case-study research, constraints are primarily on the observer, with little control placed on the behavior of the participant. At higher-constraint levels, more controls are placed on the participants. As you will see in Chapter 13, controlled experiments can be conducted in the field. Martin and Bateson (1993) provide an excellent discussion of field research, from naturalistic observation to field experiments. This section will introduce you to low-constraint methods with several classic examples of naturalistic and case-study research.

Examples of Naturalistic Observation

The defining characteristic of naturalistic observation is that the researcher observes and systematically records naturally occurring events and later develops hypotheses about why they occurred. These characteristics are illustrated by examples in this section drawn from the fields of biology, ethology, sociology, and psychology. Naturalistic observation has a long history in science, predating modern science and the emergence of psychology. Among classic naturalistic research are Darwin's observations of animals and plants, arguably the most important research in all of biology. You learned about his work in Chapter 1. He recorded detailed observations on hundreds of species of plants and animals and then devoted years to trying to understand the processes that might account for the patterns that he observed. From his observations, Darwin developed his concepts of natural selection. Darwin also contributed a pioneering study of child development, recording detailed naturalistic observations of his son's infancy and childhood (Darwin, 1890).

Ethology.   Ethology is the study of organisms in their natural environments. Ethologists, such as Jane Goodall (1971, 1986), have used naturalistic methods to study hundreds of species of animals. In Goodall's case, it was chimpanzees in Tanzania. Goodall persisted for two difficult years in the forests before she was able to make substantial observations. Her naturalistic research presents a remarkable picture of chimpanzees as highly social creatures. She is now applying her knowledge to the conservation of these endangered animals.

Observations by Goodall and others illustrate the range of adaptive behavior in chimpanzees. For example, Boesch and Boesch-Acherman (1991) observed chimpanzees using stones to crack open nuts. The stones were selected according to the type and size of nuts to be opened and were used with great skill. This was the first observation of stone hammer-and-anvil use by nonhuman primates. Goodall (1986) observed that chimps hunt, kill, and eat monkeys, antelopes, and wild pigs. Boesch and Boesch-Acherman (1991) observed chimps hunting cooperatively, a behavior considered by many to be a major step in social evolution. McGrew (1992) identified 19 different kinds of tools used by chimpanzees. Whiten and Boesch (2001), collating naturalistic observations from several research groups in Africa, described distinct cultural differences between groups of chimpanzees. These are behaviors that are unique to one group of chimpanzees and are passed on to the next generation through instruction by the older animals.

Sociology.   Adeline Levine's (1982) sociological study of the Love Canal disaster is an example of naturalistic research with human participants. Around 1950, the city of Niagara Falls, New York, built a grammar school on a toxic dump site, and the adjacent land became a housing development. Unknown to the residents, thousands of metal drums were quietly corroding underground, releasing their toxins into the soil. Over the next two decades, the toxins spread underground and percolated to the surface and into residents' cellars. Small explosions occurred, "brown ooze" clung to the legs of schoolchildren, and odors were so foul after heavy rains that the school playground had to be closed. Pets died and several children were burned by the chemicals. Cancers, miscarriages, and intestinal and respiratory diseases were common in the neighborhood. By 1978, more than 25 years after the toxic dump had been covered up, the residents knew that their neighborhood was contaminated with dangerous toxins, and hundreds of families had to abandon their homes.

Levine (1982) wanted to understand how such a catastrophe could have been allowed to occur, how it affected residents, how community leaders responded, and how everyone coped with it. These questions are not easily studied in the laboratory. Instead, Levine and her students reviewed historical records, met with residents and officials, attended public meetings, and monitored newspaper reports and local news broadcasts. They documented the events and the psychological, social, and financial impacts. Levine's findings had important implications for government policy, and the research could not have been carried out in any way other than through the use of naturalistic research methods.

Another example from sociology is Phillip Davis's research on corporal punishment of children (Davis, 1997). Some forms of corporal punishment, such as hitting, spanking, whipping, and shaking, are routinely used by more than 80% of American parents and may be an important factor in the children's development (Graziano, 1992). Most studies of corporal punishment use surveys asking parents and children for their retrospective reports. But with a sensitive topic such as this, there are obvious problems in simply asking parents, "How often and how severely do you hit your kids?"

Davis used naturalistic observations of parents and children in public places such as shopping malls. His method was classic naturalistic observation. He walked through the malls, watching for adults hitting children and then unobtrusively observed for a few moments. The following is an example of one of the 250 hitting incidents.

> (T)wo men, a woman, and a boy (about six) shop in a department store, one man trying out a treadmill. When the boy gets on (another) treadmill the man snaps "You don't get down I'm gonna whip you in two seconds!" The boy gets astride a bicycle on display and the man on the treadmill tells the others to do something. The other man pulls the boy from the bike

but the bike nearly topples and the man gives the boy a swat on the bottom. He directs a few hushed words at the boy (then) sees the boy making a face at him. He grabs furiously at the boy's jacketed shoulder with a muffled thud and clutches a handful of collar. Twisting the jacket hard in his fist and jerking the boy forward, he leans into the boy's face and angrily snarls something under his breath. Then he spins the boy around, holds him steady, and hits his bottom hard. As the group is about to leave, the man...on the treadmill snaps at the boy "One more time and you're OUT!" They stroll away, but the boy gets on a stair-step machine. The treadmill man tries to take the boy's arm and the boy pulls back slightly. As though offended by the little show of resistance, the man spanks the boy's bottom five times. He says a few angry words and casually walks away. Frozen and mute at first, the boy breaks into a soft cry before bustling after the group.

Davis wanted to know what actually happens to children when they get hit, and he examined the patterns of behavior of the parents, children, and bystanders.

Psychology.   Rosenhan (1973) investigated the use of psychiatric diagnoses and the experiences of mental patients in hospitals. He wanted to understand how psychiatrists handled an ambiguous diagnostic decision in a real-world hospital setting and how they responded later to contradictory information once a diagnosis had been made. He had eight pseudopatients (his research assistants) admit themselves to various mental hospitals with feigned complaints of hearing voices saying "thud, hollow, and empty." The pseudopatients were instructed to display no other signs of mental disorder during their hospital stay. In fact, once admitted, the pseudopatients behaved normally and gave no indication of their supposed hallucinations. Hearing voices is usually a symptom of psychosis, but without additional symptoms, the person would not qualify for any specific diagnosis. Furthermore, the voices that Rosenhan had the pseudopatients report were not typical for patients with psychotic disorders. This should have raised some questions or doubt in the psychiatrists. The eight researchers were admitted to 12 different hospitals, and apparently none of the hospitals' staff discerned that they were not real patients, although some of the other patients did realize it. Most of them were diagnosed with schizophrenia. The pseudopatients observed hospital conditions and the behavior of staff and patients much like an anthropologist might. They were more than neutral observers in that they were an active part of the hospitals' environments. As in the Levine study, naturalistic methods were not only appropriate, but were the best way to investigate the issue.

Scientists use naturalistic methods to study a variety of human behaviors in public places, such as smoking, eating, and drinking in restaurants and bars; drivers' behavior at intersections; children on school grounds or in class; and shoppers in stores. Additional examples of naturalistic studies are given in Box 6.1.

Examples of Case-Study Research

Case-study research imposes mild constraints on the procedures. For example, case studies are not typically carried out in natural environments, but in settings selected by the researcher. In addition, classes of behavior are examined, rather than the total context and natural flow of behavior. By imposing constraints, case studies narrow the

BOX 6.1 • *Examples of Naturalistic Observation Studies*

- **Naturalistic observation of athletic drug-use patterns in professional-caliber body builders.** Participant observation was used to gather data on the use of performance-enhancing drugs by body builders. The data revealed a far greater use of drugs and more extensive communication and support among the athletes than was formerly believed. (Auge, Wayne, & Auge, 1999).
- **Young children doing mathematics: Observations of everyday activities.** The authors observed children in free play and recorded instances in which the children engaged in a variety of mathematical explorations and applications. Many of these instances were advanced well beyond what educators consider to be the children's developmental levels. The authors conclude that these observations can serve as bases for higher-level education in mathematics for young children (Ginsburg, Inoue, & Seo, 1999).
- **Aggression among young adults in the social context of the bar.** Naturalistic observation was used to observe incidents of aggression in bars. The observations, carried out between midnight and 2:30 A.M., revealed that most aggressive incidents had no clear beginning or ending, the participants' roles often shifted during the incident, and most involved five or more persons. Three-fourths of the incidents involved only males (Graham & Wells, 2001).
- **Reactivity effects during naturalistic observation of distressed and nondistressed families.** Audiotaping was used to record families' verbal interactions during dinner times in order to answer the question of whether this type of naturalistic observation is reactive. The data showed that there was no significant reactivity of either the distressed or the nondistressed families to the recording procedure (Jacob, Tennenbaum, Seilhamer, & Bargrel, 1994).
- **Childhood depression and family interaction.** Naturalistic observation was used to compare family interactions of third to fifth grade children diagnosed with depression and a nondepressed control group of children. Family interactions in the children's homes were observed and recorded. The study found that (1) the family environments of the depressed children were less rewarding, more aversive, and more disengaged than those of controls and (2) the depressed children and their parents mutually affected each others' behaviors (Messer & Gross, 1995).
- **Naturalistic observation of adolescent tobacco use.** This naturalistic study was carried out to determine the ecological validity of earlier laboratory findings, and most of its data did validate the earlier reports. However, these data unexpectedly revealed that direct peer pressure to smoke is not as frequent, or apparently as important, as was previously thought. More subtle social control, perhaps through advertising, might be more important (Sussman et al., 1993).
- **Naturalistic observation of children with autism.** Children with autism were observed for their spontaneous verbalizations during social conflict situations and positive social interactions. The data suggested that social conflict might actually be a significant vehicle for the development of social competence, a hypothesis that can be tested in higher-constraint research (Toomey & Adams, 1995).

focus, but retain the essential interest in participants' natural behavior. This section briefly describes the case-study research of Freud, Witmer, Piaget, and Phillips.

Sigmund Freud. In the late 19th century, Sigmund Freud interviewed clients not in their natural environments, but within the mild constraints of his office. He was interested in treating clients who showed puzzling symptoms. Because it was unclear what was wrong with these clients, Freud questioned them about the history of their problems and observed their responses to treatment. His clients talked of their early lives, dreams, fears, and fantasies. Freud noted patterns and drew inferences about their subjective functioning. These inferences eventually were integrated into his psychoanalytic theory and techniques. Freud believed clinical observations were more useful than laboratory observations in studying the subjective events of his clients and uncovering the factors that contributed to their problems. He focused on the psychology of unconscious processes, and his work influenced early psychology, popularizing an alternative to the dominant laboratory-based psychology of consciousness.

E. L. Witmer. At the University of Pennsylvania, Witmer founded the first psychological clinic that treated children with learning and behavioral problems (Brotemarkle, 1966). Like Freud, Witmer was interested in developing treatment for his clients. Unlike Freud, Witmer was part of the functional tradition in the United States. He used medical and psychological examinations of each child to determine whether the child's problems were due to brain pathology or to inadequate teaching and learning. He relied heavily on careful measurement, rather than the clinical observation that was typical of Freud's work, and he focused more on diagnosis as a predictor of what treatments would work. Witmer developed "psychoeducation," a treatment–educational approach to children. He applied psychological procedures, many based on those used in the laboratory, in a case-study method that he called the new clinical psychology.

Jean Piaget. Whereas Freud and Witmer used case-study methods to help persons with psychological problems, Jean Piaget focused on understanding cognitive development in children. He followed a small number of children through several years of development, noting changes in how each child thought about the world and solved practical problems. Rather than passively observing their behavior, Piaget learned about their thought processes by posing specific questions and tasks and observing the children's responses. He used a flexible case-study approach, which allowed him to alter methods and take advantage of ideas or observations that occurred during his studies. Piaget developed hypotheses about children's cognitive development that have held up well under examination by other researchers using higher-constraint research.

Katherine Phillips. A more recent example of case study research is Katherine Phillips's (1996) descriptions of people with body dysmorphic disorder, a psychological disorder in which people have distorted perceptions of their physical bodies. Their intense preoccupation with believing that they are ugly and disfigured, despite contrary evidence, causes severe disruptions of their lives. Only recently have professionals recognized this disorder. Like Freud, Phillips wanted to understand the disorder by carefully documenting the histories of her clients and evaluating how each client responded to treatment. By presenting her clinical case studies, Phillips has helped to describe the phenomenon and to lay the foundation for hypotheses that can be followed up with higher-constraint research.

Quick-Check Review 1: The Challenge of Low-Constraint Research

1.1. What characteristics of the research by Darwin and by Goodall make these examples of naturalistic research?

1.2. Why is the work of Freud, Witmer, Piaget, and Phillips classified as case study?

1.3. Differentiate case study and naturalistic research.

The Value of Low-Constraint Methods

The previous examples illustrate the value of low-constraint research. This section provides a more detailed discussion of its value, when to use it, and what can be learned from it.

Conditions for Using Low-Constraint Research

Low-constraint research is most appropriate when the question concerns the natural flow of behavior in natural settings. For example, if researchers are interested in studying passenger behavior at airports, seating patterns in theaters, responses to environmental disasters, the settings in which people smoke cigarettes, or the first behavioral responses of infants to mothers, then the best research methods involve direct observations of these events as they occur in their natural settings.

Perhaps the most productive use of low-constraint methods is at the early stages of research on topics, that is, in **exploratory research.** For example, adults can organize their behavior with reference to time, but can children do so? The researcher might begin studying this question at a low-constraint level by observing young children at a nursery school. The researcher is seeking evidence in the child's behavior that indicates an awareness of time. Perhaps it will be a child fighting for a toy with the argument "I saw it first!" This suggests that the child has a concept of sequencing of events and thus some idea of time, although it may be that the child is only voicing an argument that he or she saw was successful for another child. Such observations stimulate ideas or hypotheses that can then be tested at higher constraint levels. Thus, low-constraint research is particularly valuable as initial or exploratory research in new research directions.

It would be a mistake for anyone to think that low-constraint research, in its function as an exploratory phase, is only exploratory, only a prelude to the real research. Low-constraint research can be very much the creative and significant starting point in new areas of exploration, facilitating leaps to the next levels of discovery on the very edges of new knowledge. Low-constraint methods are not only useful but necessary in contemporary science. This is a main point in a thought-provoking article by Klahr and Simon (2001), who discuss the importance of low-constraint methods in scientific problem solving. In their model, scientists employ strong methods that are highly constrained in their application. These high-constraint methods, such as experimentation, allow the valid testing of causal hypotheses. But Klahr and Simon argue that the so-called "weak" methods are of equal importance for science. These include thinking by analogy, recognition of patterns, and making conceptual leaps based on our fund of knowledge. In our terminology, these are low-constraint methods that allow the unfettered, wide-ranging search for contingencies. It is this level of methodology that makes important contributions in exploratory research.

Scientists employ both high- and low-constraint methodologies as they pursue their studies. There is growing interest by researchers in studying the scientific problem-solving processes and determining the details of this mix of constrained and unconstrained methods (e.g., Dunbar, 1994; Thagard, 1998).

Naturalistic observation familiarizes researchers with participants or settings that are new to them. Suppose that a researcher has little experience in studying young children, but wants to extend some part of Piaget's work on conservation in children. Conservation refers to the understanding that the properties of an object or substance do not change when its appearance is superficially changed, such as when a fixed volume of liquid is poured into containers of different shapes. It would be useful for the researcher to spend a few hours observing young children in a nursery school. Such direct experience with children would supplement the scientific information gained from the research literature.

Low-constraint procedures can also be used to demonstrate a new research or treatment technique. Here the question is whether the technique is feasible. The researcher is not attempting to test a prediction or develop new hypotheses, but only to see whether some method can be carried out. For example, the researcher who wanted to study conservation will want to be certain that the children are likely to find the tasks interesting enough so that they will cooperate.

Case-study and naturalistic research can enhance the generalizability of research findings, especially in areas in which virtually all the research has been conducted in laboratory settings. In this context, **generalizability** refers to how well laboratory findings predict events in a real-world setting. The advantages of laboratory research are enormous, but we cannot be sure that the behavior observed in the laboratory is representative of behavior in the natural environment. Naturalistic research methods, and to some degree case-study research, can be used to test the generalizability of the theories developed or refined on the basis of laboratory studies. The most useful laws of behavior are those that predict behavior in the real world. Thus, naturalistic observation is not only useful in the early stages of research on a topic, but can also be helpful in establishing the generalizability of findings during the later stages of research.

Case-study research is also appropriate for studying specific individuals. Under such conditions, there is no concern for developing inferences and concepts that can be generalized to a population. This concept is especially relevant for clinical psychologists, who want to understand individual clients and the causes of each client's problems. This issue is discussed in Box 6.2.

Information Gained from Low-Constraint Research

Low-constraint observations can provide descriptive information. For example, Goodall's (1978) observation that a group of chimpanzees in the wild attacked and killed another group was the first observation of behavior that resembled warfare among chimpanzees. These observations could not explain the event or determine what caused it. However, her observations did establish a new fact that had never before been observed and, in the process, raised some very interesting questions. For example, what can trigger both the cooperation with allies and the aggression toward opponents that characterize warfare?

One of the most valuable functions of low-constraint research is that it can negate a general proposition. For example, suppose that prior to Goodall's observation some naturalist had stated the general proposition that "chimpanzees do not engage in group aggression resembling warfare observed in certain insects and in humans." Goodall's observations show that this general proposition is incorrect; she observed at least some chimpanzees engaging in warlike behavior.

Another example of negating a general proposition involves the statement "Man's superiority over other creatures is due to the fact that man is the only tool-

BOX 6.2 • *The Therapist as Scientist*

Case studies can be used in settings other than research. For example, a therapist must gather information and generate hypotheses about the reasons for the client's behavior. The effective use of research methods, especially methods of inference, can greatly improve the therapist's effectiveness. The phases of research presented in Chapter 2 are applicable to the therapy session. The therapist generates ideas about what problems the client has, how they developed, and how they might be corrected. The initial information might be vague, allowing several possible ideas to be developed. The clinician then translates these ideas into specific hypotheses and develops plans for testing them. The observation phase may be no more than asking the client specific questions, or it may involve closely observing how the client responds to specific situations. The analysis phase relies less on statistics and more on rational inferences, and the analysis and interpretation phases are difficult to separate. Therapists record their observations in progress notes so that the information will be available to them or to other clinicians who might work with the client in the future. The important point is that clinicians, in gathering the information necessary for treatment planning, are operating much as research scientists. It is no accident that the most widely accepted model for the training of a clinical psychologist is the **scientist–practitioner model.** Understanding the way scientists gather information and draw conclusions sharpens clinicians' skills in information gathering and treatment planning. Applied research for solving practical problems is discussed more on the *Student Resource CD.*

making and tool-using animal." Again the naturalistic observations of Goodall refute this general proposition. She observed chimpanzees select twigs, strip off the leaves to fashion a flexible rod, insert the twigs into the narrow tunnels of a termite nest, wait a moment, and then withdraw the twig and lick off the termites clinging to it. This was purposeful and sophisticated behavior. The chimpanzees selected and then modified a natural object, preparing it for use as a food-gathering tool.

A final example involves some early research with autistic children. Psychologists who had pioneered the use of relaxation in behavior therapy believed that neither children nor psychotic adults could be taught relaxation. Ignoring the general proposition, Graziano and Kean (1968) succeeded in training four autistic children in relaxation skills, procedures that have since been repeated many times with other children. This case study successfully negated the general proposition that children cannot be taught relaxation skills.

Low-constraint research can negate a general proposition, but cannot establish one. It cannot be concluded from Goodall's observations that all chimps engage in warfare or from the Graziano and Kean study that all children can be taught relaxation skills. We never know if the low-constraint observations are representative. This limitation is related to issues of sampling, which will be discussed in more detail later in this chapter and again in Chapter 9.

Low-constraint research also provides information about relationships among variables. All research seeks to identify and understand relationships among variables. The type of relationship studied varies from one level of constraint to another. In experimental research, the researcher applies systematic controls and manipulates variables to identify causal relationships among variables. In low-constraint research, however, such causal inferences cannot be made, but other useful information about relationships among variables can be obtained. For example, the ethologist Niko Tinbergen (1951, 1963) observed that the parent herring gull provides food for its chick when the young bird pecks a red spot on the adult's bill. When the spot appears, the chick pecks at it; when the chick pecks at the spot, the parent provides food (i.e., when X occurs, then Y will probably occur). Note that this does not state that X causes Y, but only that there is a high probability of one occurring when the other is present. This describes a probabilistic relationship between two variables. When the young bird pecks on the parent's bill, there is a high probability that the parent will provide food. This kind of probabalistic relationship is referred to as a **contingency.** Low-constraint research can identify contingent relationships among variables, and these contingencies can then become the stimulus for higher-constraint research. This is exactly what Tinbergen did once he noticed the contingent relationship between the chick's pecking and the adult's feeding behavior; he followed up this observation by conducting systematic experiments. Contingent relationships observed in low-constraint research can be an important source for hypotheses to be tested with higher-constraint research.

Note that flexibility is an advantage of both naturalistic and case-study research. Unlike the formal, high-constraint experiment, the researcher in low-constraint studies is free to vary procedures during the study by changing the focus on the basis of the obtained data or the changing interests of the researcher. Table 6.2 summarizes the value of low-constraint research.

TABLE 6.2   *The Value of Low-Constraint Research*

Naturalistic and case-study research is useful:

1. As exploratory research at the beginning of a new research area in which little information is available
2. When the researcher wishes to gain familiarity with typical characteristics of settings or participants before planning high-constraint research
3. When the questions specifically focus on the natural flow of behavior and/or on the behavior in natural environment
4. When the study is of a single individual, group, or set of events and the questions are specific to these people, settings, or events
5. For demonstrations or illustrations, such as demonstrating a new procedure
6. As a way of discovering contingencies that can then be used as a basis for higher-constraint questions and research
7. As a way of evaluating the generalizability of findings from laboratory research to natural environments

Furthermore, naturalistic and case-study research can:

1. Describe events, including events never before observed
2. Identify contingent relationships among variables
3. Suggest hypotheses to be tested with higher-constraint research
4. Negate general propositions; although these methods cannot establish general propositions or causal inferences

---

Quick-Check Review 2: The Value of Low-Constraint Methods

2.1. When should naturalistic research be used? Case study research?

2.2. What are contingencies, and how are they used in later research?

2.3. How does naturalistic research allow greater generalization than does laboratory research?

2.4. Explain how naturalistic research can negate a general proposition, but cannot establish a general proposition.

Using Low-Constraint Methods

In higher-constraint research, we can rely on formalized procedures to provide many of the controls that increase the validity of the research. In lower-constraint research, validity depends more on the researcher's clarity of thought.

In recent years, low-constraint research methods, used traditionally in ethological research, have been extended to such disciplines as education, sociology, management, nursing, communications, and psychology (see Box 6.1). Known collectively as

qualitative research methods, their major goal is to describe and analyze functioning in everyday settings ranging from informal conversations among friends to courtroom proceedings. The research methods include naturalistic and participant observation, the use of questionnaires, and analyzing conversations and social networks. The size constraints on this text make it impossible to cover all these low-constraint methods. The interested student should consult books such as Maxwell (1996), Miller and Dingwall (1997), and Weis and Fine (2000).

This section presents the basics of conducting low-constraint research. The section begins by describing the process of formulating problem statements and research hypotheses. It then covers the process of making observations. The section ends by discussing several sampling issues.

Problem Statements and Research Hypotheses

We noted in Chapter 3 the importance of developing a statement of the problem for each research project. Problem statements and research hypotheses are most formalized at the experimental level of constraint, but they are important at all levels of constraint. Problem statements help to organize the researcher's thinking. The inferences that can confidently be drawn differ depending on the constraint level. At the experimental level, the focus is on questions of causality; in differential studies, the focus is on determining differences between groups; at the correlational level, the focus is on the direction and strength of relationships among variables; at the naturalistic and case-study levels, the focus is on contingencies. Causal inferences can be drawn safely only at the experimental level, at which the most complete controls are applied.

Problem statements in low-constraint research are often general because there might be no basis for generating more specific questions. Problem statements also change readily in low-constraint research as the researcher begins to grasp the issues through observation and starts to focus attention on specific behavior. Suppose, for example, that an industrial–organizational psychologist is called in to evaluate a communication problem in a company. The psychologist is knowledgeable about the dynamics of business organizations and strategies that might be applied to specific problems, but the psychologist has no way of knowing what the communication problem really represents. The initial problem statement in this case might be "I wonder what is wrong." Interviewing several key people will likely provide some insight into the problem, but there are likely to be different opinions. Careful observation of interactions between members of the company might suggest an underlying defensiveness. The consultant might narrow the problem statement to focus more on this attitude, suspecting that it may be a key to understanding the problem. But further observation and discussion with employees and managers may suggest that this mentality is more likely an effect of problems in the company, rather than a cause. At this point, the consultant might begin to work with two or three narrower problem statements, which are based in part on the consultant's knowledge of what types of situations could create the scenario observed. Each of these might be independently evaluated through continued observation, fact gathering, and interviewing. All this might occur in just the first day of the consultant's visit, or it might take several days or weeks to get this far.

This example illustrates the strength of low-constraint research—being able to move flexibly from one area to another depending on what is found. Of course, eventually the consultant will need to focus on key elements, gather relevant data, and make specific suggestions. But an early narrow focus can blind us to critical issues and lead to poor recommendations. This example also illustrates how problem statements tend to start out in a more general form and become more focused as the researcher learns more about the issues. Problem statements gradually evolve into specific hypotheses, which guide the researcher in gathering specific information relevant to the hypotheses. However, there is an inherent limitation in this process. Low-constraint research can provide only so much information. If we want to know with confidence what is causing what, then the hypotheses must be translated into higher-constraint research questions. It is often tempting to try to draw causal inferences from low-constraint research, but it would be a serious mistake to do so.

Making Observations

The central phase of any research project is the observation or data-gathering phase. In higher-constraint research, before observations are made, detailed plans of how to gather and analyze the data are prepared. In lower-constraint research, planning is less formal and more fluid. The researcher is free to change hypotheses and modify procedures in the middle of the observations. It is not unusual for the observer conducting naturalistic and case-study research to design a whole new study based on initial observations. While naturalistic and case-study procedures constitute low-constraint research, the observational methods might nevertheless employ highly sophisticated instrumentation. The research is still low constraint; the technological equipment does not define the level of constraint. This section discusses ways of observing behavior, including using measures that have little impact on a person's natural behavior.

How to Observe.   There are two ways to gather data in naturalistic observation: as an unobtrusive observer or as a participant observer. As an **unobtrusive observer,** the researcher tries to avoid responding to or influencing the participant. In fact, the unobtrusive observer tries to blend into the surroundings so as not to be noticed. As a **participant observer,** the researcher becomes a part of the situation and even contributes to it. This may include the normal contributions almost anyone would make in the situation, or it might consist of carefully planned and executed changes in the researcher's behavior as a way of tentatively testing specific hypotheses. Levine's work, discussed earlier, utilized participant observation in parts of her study of the Love Canal crisis. It should be noted that when the observer becomes a participant, then the procedure is no longer naturalistic observation but, rather, has become a case study. One advantage of participant observation is that by manipulating your behavior as an observer, the researcher is able to test hypotheses by creating situations that are unlikely to occur naturally. Case studies often use participant observation. For example, Piaget did not passively observe children. Instead, he asked questions, created test situations, interacted with the children, and observed their responses.

Whether we use unobtrusive observation or participant observation, the goal is to avoid influencing the natural behavior of the participants. The term **measurement re-**

activity refers to the phenomenon of participants behaving differently than they might normally because they know that they are being observed. Some measures, called **reactive measures,** are particularly prone to such distortions, whereas others, called **nonreactive measures,** are not. Measurement reactivity is often a function of what participants believe is the appropriate behavior in the situation. People have a tendency to behave in ways that they think are appropriate when they know that they are being observed. For example, how much more likely is it that you will use a fork and knife to eat your chicken if you are dining in a restaurant than if you are at home alone?

Unobtrusive Measures.   **Unobtrusive measures** are measures of behavior that are not obvious to the person being observed and, consequently, are less likely to influence the person's behavior. Webb, Campbell, Schwartz, and Sechrest (1966) described a number of clever unobtrusive measures. For example, suppose that you want to measure interest level for a museum exhibit. You first need an operational definition of level of interest. One operational definition of interest level is the average of people's interest ratings. You might ask each of the first 200 people who visit an exhibit to rate how interesting it is on a 10-point scale. This measure is not unobtrusive, because each participant is aware that their interest level is being measured, which might make the measure reactive. An alternative operational definition of the level of interest is the number of people who view the exhibit. You could measure this unobtrusively by having an observer count the number of people who approach the exhibit. One advantage of this approach is that the observer can code other information, such as how long people observe the exhibit. However, simpler measures could provide the information you desire. One procedure suggested by Webb et al. (1966) is to note the degree of wear on the tiles of the floor surrounding the exhibit. Tiles around popular exhibits often need to be replaced every few weeks, whereas the tiles around other exhibits will last for years. Another method is the nose-print approach, in which the exhibit is put in a glass display and arranged so that people can get the best view by putting their faces right up to the glass. The glass is cleaned at the start of each day. At day's end, the glass is dusted with fingerprint powder, and the number of nose prints is counted. Of course, not everyone will leave a nose print, and some people will press their nose to the glass in several places, so this method will not give an accurate count of how many people viewed the display. But, remember, you wanted to measure how interesting the exhibit was, and the number of people who viewed the exhibit is an operational definition of interest. The number of nose prints is also a reasonable operational definition of interest level and may, in some ways, be superior to the head-count method.

Using unobtrusive measures raises ethical issues. Normally, participants should be made aware of the procedures in order to make an informed decision. However, this principle is not absolute. If it were, unobtrusive measures could never be used. But to justify unobtrusive measures in a study, the researcher must show that nondeceptive measures would not work and that there is no significant risk of harm from use of the measure. These judgments, often difficult to make, are one reason for having a formal review process for all studies using human participants.

The preceding examples were presented to help you to think more creatively when you develop your own measures. Practice exercises and additional examples are provided on the *Student Resource CD*. There is nothing wrong with asking people to rate the interest level of museum exhibits, but it is valuable to seek some independent data to substantiate the ratings.

Archival Measures. Some measures provide information about phenomena that have already occurred. These **archival records** may include school records, marriage and divorce records, driving records, or census data. Governments gather archival data routinely to identify nationwide problems quickly. Statistics computed from such archival data as the *Index of Leading Economic Indicators* can be accurate predictors of future events. Data gathered from hospitals about diseases under treatment allow officials to identify new diseases and even narrow the range of possible causes of the diseases. Effective use of archival data depends on the quality of the data and their relevance to the question being asked.

It might appear that using archival records is a sloppy way to measure a phenomenon, but this need not be the case. Several sophisticated studies of genetic influences in psychopathology used archival records (e.g., Kety, Rosenthal, Wender, & Schulsinger, 1968; Wender et al., 1986; Baker, 1989; Simonsen & Parnas, 1993). These investigators used records from many sources to track the rates of psychopathology in both the adoptive and biological families of severely disturbed adults who were adopted as infants.

Sampling of Participants

Deciding on the best way to observe participants is critical, but an equally important task is determining which participants to observe. The term **sampling** refers to the selection of participants. In low-constraint research, we need to pay particular attention to the sampling of participants. The more representative the sample, the more confidence we can have in the generalizability of the findings. Although sampling is covered in detail in Chapters 9 and 13, we want to introduce here the concept of representativeness and its relationship to generalizability. **Representativeness** refers to how closely the sample resembles the population to be studied.

In naturalistic and case-study research, sampling may be out of the researcher's control. For example, for psychotherapy researchers, the clients who come for treatment constitute the sample. In a study of the impact of a natural disaster, the people unfortunate enough to be present when the disaster occurs constitute the sample. With these naturally occurring samples, the question must be addressed of how well the samples represent the larger population. For example, people who go to a therapist for help might be different from people in general. They probably have more psychological problems and are more concerned with these problems than is the typical person. They may be wealthier than the typical person, since they can afford the cost of psychotherapy or have insurance that will cover the cost. To the extent that there are differences between the sample and the general population, the sample is said to be unrepresentative of the population. Whenever a sample is not representative of the general population, care is needed in generalizing the findings. *The findings can be generalized when it can be assumed that what was observed in the sample of participants would also be observed in any other group of participants from the population.*

Researchers want to be able to generalize their findings, but can do so only if the sample is representative of the population in which they are interested.

Researchers seldom have the opportunity to select their own samples in naturalistic and case-study research. Therefore, they must judge how well the sample represents the population to which they want to generalize the results. The more representative the sample, the more confident their generalizations can be. However, with low-constraint research, caution is always needed in making generalizations. Such generalizations need to be considered as tentative hypotheses that must be tested with higher-constraint research methods. As you will see later, when researchers control the sampling procedures, they can almost guarantee the representativeness of the sample if the sample is selected properly.

Sampling of Situations

The sampling of situations also affects generalizability. Suppose, for example, that the work habits in factories are to be studied. As part of the study, a television camera is installed to monitor employees' behavior. From the previous section's discussion, you should recognize that the presence of the camera is likely to be reactive: that is, the participants may behave differently because they know that they are being watched. But this same problem can be viewed from another perspective, that of sampling. The sample of behaviors in this example comes from a situation that is different from the situations to which the researcher wants to generalize. Because closed-circuit TV is not used to monitor employees in most factories, this situation is not representative of the population of settings to which the researcher wants to generalize the results, and so the researcher cannot generalize the findings with confidence.

The sample of situations can be distorted in numerous ways. Some variables are beyond the researcher's control, and others can be controlled only at great cost or inconvenience. Suppose that animals in the wild are to be the focus of study. Many animals behave differently during different seasons of the year, being active during some seasons and inactive during others. Most animals show fluctuations in activity on a daily basis. If the observations of the animals were made only during the morning hours of spring and summer, then a distorted picture of the behavior might emerge. An even worse violation of this principle would be studying animals in zoos because they are close and easy to find. The situation in even the best of zoos is dramatically different from the natural environment to which the findings are to be generalized. Therefore, a good rule of thumb in early studies of any population is to sample situations as widely as possible. The broader the sample of situations and the broader the sample of participants, the more confidence that can be had in the generalizability of the findings.

Sampling of Behaviors

Another issue is the importance of adequately sampling behaviors. In any situation, organisms may behave in many different ways. Therefore, a single observation of behavior in a particular situation could lead to an incorrect conclusion about how the organism behaves in this setting. However, by sampling behaviors repeatedly in each situation, it is possible to identify whatever behavioral variability exists.

Evaluating and Interpreting Data

Once observations are made and data are gathered, the next step is to evaluate and interpret the results of the study. This usually involves statistical analyses. In many low-constraint studies, however, statistical analyses are not possible until the data are coded. Low-constraint studies often involve observing and recording everything that happens. For example, in a study of labor contract negotiations, the data set might be the transcripts of all negotiation sessions. In analyzing the data, the interactions can be coded in terms of categories, such as hostile comments, requests for information, and suggested solutions. Dean Pruitt and his colleagues (Rubin, Pruitt, & Kim, 1994; Pruitt, Parker, & Mikolic, 1997) have used similar categories in a series of studies of negotiation and conflict resolution. For lower-constraint studies, the statistical procedures may be no more complicated than descriptive statistics. Some natural comparisons may need to be made, such as between different groups of participants or among the same participants under more than one condition. In the preceding example, the researcher might want to compare the verbal statements of the labor and management negotiators or the negotiation sessions that were fruitful with sessions that were not. If such comparisons are done, inferential statistics can be used. (Procedures for selecting the appropriate statistical test are reviewed in Chapter 14.)

Caution is needed when interpreting the data from low-constraint research studies. By its very nature, low-constraint research employs few controls. Controls help to eliminate alternative explanations for results, making it easier to draw a single strong conclusion. Because such controls are absent from this level of constraint, we seldom are able to draw strong conclusions. Furthermore, these limitations cannot be corrected by applying sophisticated statistical analyses. *No statistical analysis will create controls that were not part of the original study.*

Quick-Check Review 3: Using Low-Constraint Methods

3.1. What are problem statements like in low-constraint research?

3.2. What are the two types of observers in research?

3.3. What are unobtrusive measures, and what are their advantages?

3.4. What are archival records, and how are they used in research?

3.5. What is the researcher's goal in sampling participants?

3.6. Why is it important to sample situations broadly in low-constraint research?

3.7. Explain the concept of measurement reactivity.

Limitations of Low-Constraint Methods

We have focused in this chapter on the value and procedures of low-constraint research. This section discusses the limitations of these techniques, beginning with a discussion of representativeness, which is almost always a problem in low-constraint research. We then discuss the dangers of trying to draw causal conclusions from low-constraint research. The section ends with a discussion of the limitations of observers and the tendency to go beyond the data.

Poor Representativeness

A major weakness in low-constraint research is poor representativeness. Low-constraint research typically studies particular groups of respondents, and there is little basis for generalizing from the studied group to other groups. For example, a clinical psychologist cannot confidently generalize observations of her clients to all other clients. Why not? Her clients might be from a particular socioeconomic class that does not represent all clients or have particular psychological problems that are not found in other client groups. Any clinical sample is biased, because participants select themselves for therapy and not every person in the population is equally likely to seek therapy. Likewise, if a researcher studies a particular group of chimpanzees, the findings cannot confidently be generalized to all groups of chimpanzees. If we want to generalize the findings from our particular sample to the larger population, then we must take care to select a sample that accurately represents the larger population. Such careful selection of a representative sample is a higher-constraint procedure and is not typically found in low-constraint research, particularly that carried out in natural environments for which laboratory controls are not readily available.

Poor Replicability

Another limitation of low-constraint research is related to the very characteristic that gives it its greatest strength—flexibility. Because observations of naturally occurring behavior are made in settings in which the observer has imposed few constraints on participant's behavior, it is often difficult to replicate, or, repeat, such research. Different investigators studying the same phenomenon through low-constraint methods may make different observations and therefore draw different inferences. Replication is possible only if researchers clearly state the details of their procedures. In low-constraint research, the observational methods can shift during a study, and these changes are not necessarily planned at the start of the study. Thus, it can be difficult to document exactly what procedures were followed and why. This makes it difficult for other researchers to replicate what was done.

Causal Inference and Low-Constraint Research

Drawing causal inferences from low-constraint research is risky. **Causal inferences** are conclusions that imply that one or more variables brought about the observed state of another variable. For example, let us suppose that a researcher observes that a teacher in class appears to be angry. Also suppose that the researcher subsequently learns that a child had been misbehaving, although the researcher did not observe the behavior. The researcher might be tempted to draw a causal inference that the teacher was angry because the child had misbehaved. This is an example of ex post facto (after the fact) reasoning.

Ex post facto conclusions are potential problems in low-constraint research. The fact that two variables are related is not sufficient to infer that variable A causes variable B to occur. In the school example just presented, the child's misbehavior might have had nothing to do with the teacher's anger. It is possible that the teacher's anger had more to do with an argument with a colleague than with the child's behavior. Without more information, we cannot rule out this possibility. It is also possible that an angry demeanor by the teacher stimulated the child's misbehavior. It is tempting to conclude that one event has caused the other, but low-constraint research almost never provides enough information to draw such causal inferences accurately.

The identification of contingencies and other relationships among variables is useful in suggesting possible causal relationships. However, it does not provide the controls needed to rule out the possibility that other factors may have been involved. Clinical case studies, for example, are by their nature ex post facto approaches. They lack control over independent variables and are unable to rule out possible effects of other variables. For this reason, we cannot have confidence in any causal inference we might be tempted to draw. Such inferences must be treated as speculative hypotheses for further research. For this purpose, case-study methods can be very useful.

The **ex post facto fallacy** is drawing unwarranted causal conclusions from the observation of a contingent relationship. It is a common and serious error in low-constraint research. It can mislead investigators into severe misinterpretations of the data. Table 6.3 lists several examples of ex post facto fallacies. The logical fallacy is obvious in some of the statements, whereas other, exactly parallel statements seem reasonable. There may even be assertions in the list that you have heard many times and may have accepted without giving them much thought.

The causal statements in Table 6.3 are not supported adequately by the data suggested in the table. However, they are perfectly reasonable hypotheses. They are tentative statements to be tested, rather than already established conclusions. When low-constraint results are interpreted as if they were equivalent to high-constraint research results, the conclusions drawn are likely to be false. These false conclusions can then

---

TABLE 6.3 *Examples of Possible Ex Post Facto Fallacies*

---

1. Hard-drug users all smoked marijuana before turning to hard drugs; therefore, marijuana use leads to hard-drug addiction.
2. Alcoholics started with beer and wine; therefore, drinking beer and wine lead to alcoholism.
3. Child-abusing parents were abused themselves as children; therefore, being abused as a child leads to becoming an abusive parent.
4. Most inmates in U.S. urban jails are black; therefore, being black leads to crime.
5. Many NHL hockey players are Canadian; therefore, being Canadian leads to playing professional hockey.
6. Aggressive children watch a great deal of television; therefore, watching a great deal of television leads to aggressive behavior in children.

Note: The relationships listed might have validity, but this validity can never be established through ex post facto reasoning.

damage the credibility of other research, even well-designed high-constraint research. For example, drinking beer and wine might not lead to alcoholism, but years of research suggest that a combination of heavy drinking and a genetic predisposition to alcoholism increases the risk of alcoholism. If teenagers dismiss the risk of alcoholism because well-meaning people have offered the simplistic and easily refutable argument in Table 6.3, they might choose to drink heavily, believing that there is no risk.

Limitations of the Observer

Another issue in low-constraint research concerns the limitations of the observer. When therapists listen to clients, are the clients giving spontaneous verbalizations or are they saying what they think their therapists want to hear? Does the therapist influence their verbalizing? When anthropologists engage in participant observation, do they influence the behavior of the people that they observe? Likewise, when ethologists observe groups of chimps, does their presence alter the animals' normal behavior? The issue is one of experimenter reactivity or experimenter bias (Rosenthal, 1976).

Experimenter reactivity is any action by researchers that tends to influence the response of participants. For example, if therapists show more interest in their client's statements about feeling angry than about feeling happy, clients are likely to talk more about anger than happiness during sessions. Whereas experimenter reactivity affects participants, experimenter bias affects researchers. **Experimenter bias** is any effect that the researcher's expectations might have on the observations or recording of these observations. For example, if a researcher expects males to be more angry than females, the researcher is likely to interpret ambiguous behavior, such as sarcastic comments, as anger in men, but humor in women. Both experimenter reactivity and experimenter bias distort the measurement process.

To obtain natural behavior, the observer must be uninvolved. In case studies, it is difficult for observers to control their own reactivity and biases—to control the many possible subtle influences that they might have on the participants and/or on themselves. Controls in higher-constraint research minimize the observer's reactivity and bias.

Going beyond the Data

Recall Rosenhan's (1973) naturalistic study of mental hospitals. It created quite a stir. Few of Rosenhan's critics argued with his data; instead, they criticized his interpretation of the data. Other interpretations are possible, and some of these alternatives are more reasonable given other available data. For example, Rosenhan argued that it is unreasonable to make a diagnosis of schizophrenia (11 out of 12 admissions received this diagnosis) on the basis of one symptom (hearing voices). Weiner (1975) notes, however, that by Rosenhan's own admission (1973, pp. 365–366), the pseudopatients showed "concomitant nervousness" and were apparently in serious distress because they had gone to a psychiatric hospital and requested admission. This pattern, plus the fact that the pseudopatients would likely have denied other symptoms and experiences that might have indicated alternative explanations for the hallucinations (Spitzer, 1975), makes schizophrenia the most likely diagnosis. Furthermore, Rosenhan interpreted the discharge diagnoses as indicating that the doctors never detected that the pseudopatients were not psychotic. Spitzer (1975) notes, however, that Rosenhan reported that all the patients were diagnosed as "in remission" at discharge. The qualification "in remission" is almost never used in clinical practice and, therefore, Rosenhan's data clearly indicate that every pseudopatient was seen by the professional staff to be symptom free at discharge.

Rosenhan's research is still widely quoted. His was a powerful study with interesting findings, but there are some who argue that his interpretation of the findings was scientifically unjustified. Rosenhan drew strong conclusions from low-constraint research, conclusions that seem unreasonable when you compare his results with other research data, such as typical discharge diagnoses. His study illustrates both the strengths (i.e., studying a natural phenomenon in its natural setting) and the weaknesses (i.e., the hazards implicit in interpreting naturalistic data) of low-constraint naturalistic research.

Quick-Check Review 4: Limitations of Low-Constraint Methods

4.1. Why is poor representativeness often a problem in low-constraint research?

4.2. What aspect of low-constraint research complicates the process of replication?

4.3. What is the ex post facto fallacy?

4.4. What is the difference between experimenter reactivity and experimenter bias?

Chapter Summary

This chapter covered field research, focusing on the low-constraint methods of naturalistic observation and case studies. These approaches place little constraint on the behavior of participants. Although the behavior of the observer may be tightly constrained by the observational techniques employed, it need not be. In fact, a major advantage of lower-constraint research methods is the flexibility that they allow the researcher.

The most common problem with low-constraint research is the tendency to over-interpret the results, either to generalize the results to a broader population than actually sampled or to draw a causal inference from the data. Even though we cannot easily generalize to other populations or draw causal inferences, low-constraint methods can provide useful information. They can describe events not previously observed, identify contingencies, and negate a general proposition if an appropriate counterexample is observed. Some questions about naturally occurring behavior in natural settings can be answered only with naturalistic research methods. One major function served by low-constraint research is that of exploratory research.

The key issue in low-constraint research is the observation of behavior. Whether the observation is made with only unaided senses or with highly sophisticated equipment, the same general principles apply. Researchers should make observations in ways that will allow generalization to the population of interest. Researchers need to be aware of such processes as experimenter reactivity and experimenter bias. As with any research project, ethical issues in low-constraint research are important and must be considered carefully during every phase of the study.

Key Terms

Define the following key terms. Be sure that you understand them. They are discussed in the chapter and defined in the glossary.

field research	participant observer	representativeness
exploratory research	measurement reactivity	causal inference
generalizability	reactive measures	ex post facto fallacy
scientist–practitioner model	nonreactive measures	experimenter reactivity
contingency	unobtrusive measure	experimenter bias
qualitative research methods	archival records	
unobtrusive observer	sampling	

7

Correlational and Differential Methods of Research

You must be familiar with the very groundwork of science before you try to climb its heights.

—Ivan Pavlov, 1936

CD Resource Material

- Example of Correlational Research
- Computational Procedures for Correlations
- Examples of Differential Research
- Selecting the Appropriate Statistical Analysis Procedure
- Computing Various Statistical Tests
- Student Study Guide/Laboratory Manual

Web Resource Material

- Intelligence
- Schizophrenia

This chapter focuses on the measurement of relationships between variables (correlational research) and assessing the differences among groups defined by preexisting variables (differential research). As you will see, correlational and differential methods, although operationally different, are conceptually similar. The chapter begins with a conceptual discussion of each approach, followed by a comparison of the two. Then, the actual methods are discussed. The chapter closes with a discussion of the limitations of these methods.

Correlational Research Methods

Correlational research assesses the strength of a relationship between two or more variables. For example, the researcher might want to know if adolescents' self-esteem is related to their earlier experiences of having been punished by their parents. She administers to each participant a test of self-esteem and a questionnaire about the amount of past punishment. A correlation quantifies the strength and direction of the relationship between the two measures. As in naturalistic observation, variables in correlational research are not manipulated. However, there are important differences between correlational and naturalistic research. Correlational research always measures at least two variables, and the plans for measuring variables are formalized prior to measurement.

Although a correlation does not imply causality, it does serve two useful functions in science. The first is that any consistent relationship can be used to predict future events. Prediction is possible even if we have no idea why the relationship exists. For example, as early as A.D. 140, Ptolemy developed a complicated system to predict the movements of the planets. Although his predictions were remarkably accurate, he had little understanding of how the planets actually moved. In fact, his model of planetary movement, that all celestial bodies revolve about Earth, was clearly wrong. But the inaccuracy of his assumptions does not diminish the accuracy of the predictions that could be made using his system.

A second valuable function of correlational research is to provide data that are either consistent or inconsistent with some scientific theory. A correlation study cannot prove a theory correct, although it can negate a theory. For example, the question of what intelligence is and how it should be measured has been debated for most of the 20th century. British psychologist Charles Spearman (1904) hypothesized a general intellectual trait, the g (general) factor, that governs performance in all areas of cognitive functioning. Theories are validated by deriving predictions from them that can be tested by gathering appropriate data. One prediction that could be derived from Spearman's g factor theory is that there should be a strong correlation between different cognitive abilities, because each ability is affected by the g factor. Suppose that a randomly selected sample of participants is tested on both math and vocabulary skills, and the two are highly correlated; that is, people who score high on the math skills measure also tend to score high on the vocabulary measure. Do these data *prove* Spearman's theory? No, but they do provide support for it. The data show that one relationship out of thousands of possible predicted relationships exists. To *prove* the theory we would have to test every possible prediction from it, usually an impossible task, because many theories make an almost infinite number of predictions. This is why scientists are so reluctant to use the word prove. However, the data are consistent with the theory and thus increase confidence in the theory.

Suppose that the researcher also tests reading ability, abstract reasoning, short- and long-term memory, and the ability to solve riddles and finds that all possible correlations among the measures are large and positive. Does this prove the theory correct? The answer is still no, because there remain other predicted relationships that have not yet been tested. However, there would be considerably more confidence in the theory because all the tested predictions of the theory are confirmed. But suppose that the researcher finds that memory and math ability are virtually uncorrelated. What do these data mean? If the procedures were done correctly, we would have to conclude that Spearman's g factor theory is incorrect. In other words, just as in naturalistic and case-study research, *correlational research cannot prove a theory, but can negate one.*

Quick-Check Review 1: Correlational Research Methods

1.1. What is the main purpose of correlational research?

1.2. What information can be obtained from correlational research?

1.3. Can correlational research determine causality?

1.4. How can correlational research help to validate or invalidate a theory?

Differential Research Methods

Differential research compares two or more groups that are differentiated on the basis of some preexisting variable. Groups can be determined by either a qualitative dimension, such as sex, political party, or psychiatric diagnosis, or by some quantitative dimension, such as the participant's age or number of years of education. Whether defined qualitatively or quantitatively, the group differences *existed before the study was conducted.* The researcher measures these differences and assigns participants to groups based on them. This classification variable is the independent variable, and the behavior measured in the different groups is the dependent variable. Independent variables in differential research are nonmanipulated independent variables (see Chapter 3). In contrast, the independent variable is manipulated in experimental research. Because differential research involves only measuring and not manipulating variables, it involves studying relationships between variables. Thus, differential research is conceptually similar to correlational research. This conceptual similarity means that the same general principles will be used in interpreting the results from each of these approaches. Drawing causal conclusions from either differential or correlational research studies should be avoided. There is a structural similarity of differential research to experimental research; that is, both have different groups defined by an independent variable, and a dependent measure is taken on all participants in each group. This similarity means that the same statistical procedures are used to evaluate the data from these two approaches (see Table 7.1). Thus, differential research is similar to both correlational and experimental research.

Cross-sectional versus Longitudinal Research

Differential research is used extensively in developmental psychology. In studying developmental processes, psychologists often use a **cross-sectional design,** in which groups of participants at different ages are compared on some set of variables. For example, cognitive development might be explored by giving groups of 3-, 5-, and 7-year-olds a set of problems or puzzles. Differences between the younger and older

TABLE 7.1 *Experimental versus Differential Designs*

A. An Experimental Design

Group 1 Short Time Interval	Group 2 Moderate Time Interval	Group 3 Long Time Interval
Participants	Participants	Participants
1	1	1
2	2	2
•	•	•
•	•	•
•	•	•
N	N	N

B. A Differential Design

Group 1 Caucasian	Group 2 Black	Group 3 Asian
Participants	Participants	Participants
1	1	1
2	2	2
•	•	•
•	•	•
•	•	•
N	N	N

Experimental and differential designs can look the same, but there are critical differences. In the experimental design, participants are randomly assigned to conditions and the experimenter manipulates the conditions. In the differential design, the participants are included in conditions based on their preexisting characteristics, in this case, ethnic identity. Because of this, causality cannot be inferred from the differential design.

children in performance on the task provide insight into cognitive development. This is a differential research design because participants are assigned to groups on the basis of a preexisting characteristic, age.

As with all differential research, caution is needed in drawing conclusions from cross-sectional studies. Suppose that a researcher studies people in their 50s, 60s, 70s, and 80s to understand the aging process better. The researcher must be careful in interpreting the results because some of the observed differences may be due to other variables besides age. For example, participants in their 80s will have lived through the Great Depression, whereas participants in their 50s grew up during relatively prosperous years. If older people were more cautious about going into debt, it should not be assumed that this represented a developmental process, because it could just as easily be explained by differences in life experiences between the groups. The concept that the shared life experiences of people of a given age in a given culture may lead them to behave similarly throughout their lives, but differently from people of other ages, is known as a **cohort effect.** Those who grew up during the Great Depression shared an experience powerful enough that it likely shaped much of their thinking, their expectations, and even their emotional responses.

As you will see later, developmental psychologists have other research designs at their disposal, such as longitudinal designs and time-series designs. **Longitudinal designs,** as opposed to cross-sectional designs, follow the same people over time to observe developmental changes, thus controlling for cohort effects. However, longitudinal designs have the disadvantage of taking a long time to complete. The preceding aging study would take 40 years to complete with a longitudinal design. **Time-series designs** are variations of longitudinal designs that involve multiple measurements both before and after the manipulation. They can be used with individuals or groups of participants. These designs are discussed later in the text.

Artifacts and Confounding Variables

Adding one or more additional groups forces the researcher to add constraint by standardizing the observational methods. In naturalistic research, procedures could easily be changed in order to study any phenomenon that captured the researcher's interest. In differential research, however, observations in one group are compared with observations in one or more other groups. Observations from two or more groups can rightly be compared only if the observations are made in the same way in each group. If different observational methods are used in different groups, then any difference observed between the groups may be real or may be a function of the different observational methods. There would be no way of knowing which of these possibilities is correct. In other words, the two variables are confounded. The two variables in this case are the groups and the different methods of observing in the two groups. Variables are **confounded** if both vary at the same time. In this example, as the group variable changes, the method of observation variable also changes. Because the two variables change together, it is unclear which of them is responsible for observed differences in the dependent variable.

The only way to avoid confounding variables is to make sure that they vary independently of one another, and the simplest way of ensuring this is to hold one of the variables constant. The variable that should be held constant is the variable of *least* interest to the researcher, and the variable of interest should be allowed to vary. In most differential research, the researcher is less interested in the effects of different observational procedures than in how the groups differ from one another. Therefore, the observational method is held constant and the group variable is allowed to vary. To do this, the researcher defines in advance the variables that will be measured and how they are to be measured. Once the study starts, the procedures are constrained by these design decisions, and the same measurement procedures must be used throughout.

Higher-constraint differential research methods are more effective in answering research questions than are lower-constraint naturalistic and case-study observation methods. The increased effectiveness comes from the ability to compare groups of participants who differ on important variables. But a price is paid for this additional effectiveness—a loss of flexibility. When there is only one group, the procedures can be modified easily. But with more than one group, the same observational and measurement procedures must be used in each group in order to make valid comparisons between groups. Failure to constrain the procedures can lead to artifactual findings. An **artifact** is any apparent effect of an independent variable that is actually the effect of some other variable not properly controlled. That is, *an artifact is a result of confounding.* Therefore, if different measurement procedures had been used in the two groups, any observed difference between the groups might actually have been an artifact of changes in the measurement procedure, rather than real group differences.

Higher-constraint research requires precise and consistent observational procedures and detailed planning. How can a researcher make such detailed plans before a study even begins? If the study is the first being conducted on a topic, the researcher usually cannot do so. Detailed planning is usually carried out when the phenomenon under study is already reasonably well understood. High-constraint research is thus seldom used in the early stages of studying a problem. Instead, the flexible low-constraint methods allow the researcher to explore the phenomenon and to gain a sense of what to expect. Such an understanding is necessary if we want to state explicit hypotheses and design appropriate procedures for testing these hypotheses. Research on a particular topic often begins with low-constraint methods and proceeds to higher-constraint research only after a basic understanding of the phenomenon is achieved. Scientists usually study topics that other people have already studied extensively and so may not need to start with low-constraint research. However, most researchers choose to do at least some low-constraint research to gain familiarity with a phenomenon that would be difficult to gain solely from the published accounts of other investigators.

Quick-Check Review 2: Differential Research Methods

2.1. What is the main purpose of differential research?

2.2. What type of independent variable is used in differential research?

2.3. What are artifacts? How do they affect differential research?

2.4. How is differential research structurally similar to experimental research? How is it conceptually similar to correlational research?

Understanding Correlational
and Differential Methods

To understand correlational and differential research methods, it is necessary to understand how they are conceptually similar, what makes one higher constraint than the other, and when to use each method.

Comparing These Methods

Both correlational research and differential research measure relationships among variables, but for several reasons we have listed differential research as higher constraint in our model. One reason is that differential research is structurally similar to experimental research, in which comparisons of two or more groups are made on a dependent measure. However, other, more relevant issues define the level of constraint for differential research.

The researcher conducting differential research is often interested in addressing causal questions. Ideally, experimental research should be used to address a causal question, but often ethical or practical constraints prevent this. For example, it is not possible to assign participants randomly to groups of (1) people with schizophrenia and (2) people without schizophrenia. Randomly assigning participants to groups or conditions tends to equate the groups on potential confounding variables so that the only consistent difference between the groups is the level of the independent variable. Consequently, it is relatively safe to conclude that any observed difference in the dependent variable is the result of the manipulation of the independent variable.

With differential research, participants are assigned to groups on the basis of a preexisting variable, and the groups typically differ on several other variables. For example, people with chronic schizophrenia tend to be from lower social classes, have fewer relationships in adolescence and early adulthood, and spend more time in hospitals than a randomly selected group of people from the general population. These differences are predictable and are well established by past research. Suppose that differences are found between a group of chronic patients with schizophrenia and a general control group on some dependent measure, such as the accuracy of eye tracking. There is no way of knowing whether these differences are due to schizophrenia, to social class differences, to social experiences during adolescence, or to effects of hospitalization or medication. In other words, these group differences, with the exception of the independent variable of diagnosis, are potential confounding variables. **Confounding variables** are uncontrolled variables that might affect the outcome of a study.

Researchers using differential methods are rarely content with this state of affairs. Instead of selecting a general control group, the researcher might select one or more specific control groups using selection criteria that assure that a given control group is comparable to the experimental group on some potential confounding variable. For example, a researcher suspecting that social class might affect the scores on the dependent variable might select a control group that is, on average, of the same social class as the patient group (see Raulin & Lilienfeld, 1999). Thus, social class could not confound the findings. The active control over sampling by the researcher is a form of constraint, which minimizes confounding and therefore strengthens the conclusions drawn from the study. No comparable control is used in correlational research. Hence, differential research has more control procedures available and is higher constraint than correlational research. The more controls that can be applied, the stronger the conclusions that we can draw from the study.

When to Use These Methods

Differential research designs are used most often in situations in which the manipulation of an independent variable is impractical, impossible, or inappropriate. For example, a psychologist might want to compare the effectiveness of two theories of education in creating an effective learning environment. The psychologist could set up two separate schools, institute a different curriculum for each school, randomly assign students, and then evaluate the amount that the students learn. But the expense of setting up such a research program would make the study impractical. An alternative would be to use two existing schools that already have the kinds of curricula that the researcher is interested in evaluating. This would be a differential research design, because these groups are naturally occurring instead of experimentally manipulated.

Differential designs are also used when an experimental manipulation is impossible to carry out, such as in studying the social development of individuals with superior intelligence. Newborns' intelligence levels cannot be experimentally raised or lowered, so random assignment to normal and superior intelligence groups is not possible. However, children of average and high intelligence could be selected and their social development followed.

Finally, some experimental manipulations are technically possible but unethical. For example, it can be hypothesized that prolonged separation from parents during the first 2 years of life might lead to permanently retarded social development in children. However, it is unethical to select infants randomly and separate them from their parents to test the hypothesis experimentally. But some children are separated from their parents for reasons beyond the researcher's control. Such naturally occurring groups might be a suitable population to study to explore this hypothesis.

Another field that uses correlational and differential research designs extensively because of ethical considerations is clinical neuropsychology. A neuropsychologist uses measures of behavior to infer the structural and functional condition of the brain. The neuropsychologist administers tests to people to determine what they can and cannot do. The patterns of such abilities and disabilities can suggest specific neurological problems. Neuropsychologists draw on a wealth of data when they evaluate a person. If a particular pattern of abilities and disabilities is consistently found for people later diagnosed with a specific type of brain problem, then it is reasonable to predict that another person with that pattern might well be suffering from the same neurological dysfunction. The data gathering in this case is correlational, because the researcher is seeking to identify relationships between behavior and brain dysfunction. Some of the relationships observed in neuropsychology are not easily quantifiable in terms of a simple correlation coefficient, but they are relationships nonetheless. By mapping these relationships carefully, an accurate prediction of brain dysfunction can be made on the basis of a person's behavior. Accurate prediction is a principal goal of correlational research.

Quick-Check Review 3: Understanding Correlational and Differential Methods

3.1. What do correlational and differential methods have in common?

3.2. Why is differential research considered higher constraint than correlational research?

3.3. What kinds of things may prevent a researcher from using an experimental research design, thus forcing the compromise of a differential research design?

Conducting Correlational Research

Correlational research seeks to quantify the direction and strength of a relationship among two or more variables. The discussion here focuses on the relationships among two variables only. Correlational designs employing more than two variables (called **multivariate**) will be discussed in Chapter 15. Several examples of correlational research are included on the *Student Resource CD*.

Problem Statements

Unlike the flexible problem statements of naturalistic observation and case studies, the problem statements for correlational research are much more specific. They typically take the following form: What is the strength and direction of the relationship between variable *X* and variable *Y*? Additional questions are often asked, such as this: What is the best equation for predicting variable *Y* from variable *X* (which is called the regression equation)? The most frequent source of correlational research is the secondary statistical analyses commonly done in higher-constraint research to help to explain findings or describe the samples under study. For example, a researcher might be doing a differential research project comparing urban and suburban groups on their fear of being victimized by crime.

A good researcher routinely collects data on **demographic variables.** Demographic variables are characteristics of the sample, such as the average age, education, and social class. It is common to compare groups to see if they are similar on these variables, but it is also common to compute the correlation of each of these variables with the dependent measure(s) in the study. These correlations can give considerable insight into the data and are often highlighted in the research article. The problem statement would likely be this: What is the correlation of each of the demographic variables with the dependent variable(s)? Traditionally, these correlations are computed separately within each group, because the relationship might be different in the groups.

Measuring the Variables

Developing effective operational definitions of the variables is critical in correlational research. Measurement, or the assignment of numbers to variables (see Chapter 4), depends on the adequacy of operational definitions. The operational definition of a variable involves more than just selecting a measure to administer to participants. Researchers must consider every aspect of the measurement process, including how the measurement will be taken. As in any other research, the researcher needs to avoid the possibility of unintentionally influencing participants. This can be accomplished by (1) never allowing the same person to collect both measures on the participant and/or (2) never allowing the researcher to know participants' scores on the first measure until after the second measure has been taken.

Two effects need to be controlled: (1) **experimenter expectancy,** the tendency of investigators to see what they expect to see (Chapman & Chapman, 1969) and (2) **experimenter reactivity,** the tendency of investigators to influence the behavior of participants (defined in Chapter 6). Experimenter expectancy is minimized by using objective measures whenever possible so that little subjective interpretation is necessary. The problem of experimenter reactivity may require the use of two independent researchers. The researcher is most likely to influence participants when participants are being asked to give voluntary responses with the researcher present. Experimenter effects on participants are discussed in more detail in Chapters 8 and 9.

Another potential problem in correlational research is the participant's own influence on the measures. Participants like to be consistent, especially when they believe that they are being observed and evaluated. This is a variation on the measurement reactivity problem discussed in Chapter 6. It can give the impression of a strong relationship between variables when no relationship exists in reality. There are several ways of reducing this effect. One is to disguise self-report measures by including filler items so that participants are unsure of what the investigator is studying. **Filler items** are not meant to measure anything, but rather to draw the participant's attention away from the real purpose of the measure. A second method of controlling the participant's influence on the data is to rely on one or more unobtrusive measures. In this way, participants are unaware that they are being observed and are thus less likely to modify their normal behavior. A third method is to separate the measures from one another, which can be done by taking measurements at different times or by having different researchers take the measurements. Probably the best way to deal with the problem of measurement reactivity is to use measures beyond the control of the participant. For example, anxiety might be measured psychophysiologically, rather than by self-reports or behavior. Most participants have less control over their physiological responses than over what they say or do.

Sampling

A major concern in most research is obtaining a sample that adequately represents the population to which generalizations are to be made. Another sampling issue in correlational research is whether the relationship between the two variables is the same in all segments of the population. If such differences are suspected, samples might be drawn from separate subpopulations. For example, if males and females demonstrate a different relationship between two variables, either in direction or strength, then samples of males and females should be selected separately and separate correlations computed for each group. In this example, sex is a **moderator variable,** that is, a variable that seems to modify the relationship between other variables. Sex is a commonly used moderator variable. If different subpopulations show different relationships between two variables, the relationships can be obscured if the variable that defines the subpopulations is not included in the study as a moderator variable.

For example, if the variables of dependency and hostility are positively correlated in males, but negatively correlated in females, the correlation in a mixed group of males and females will probably be close to zero, suggesting no relationship. The opposite relationships in the two groups cancel each other. In this example, sex is a moderator variable in that sex modifies the relationship between the variables of dependency and hostility. Recognizing potential moderator variables requires a thorough knowledge of the area under study. When in doubt, it is always better to compute correlations for different subgroups. If the same relationship is found in all the groups, you can be more confident that the relationship will hold for the entire population sampled.

Analyzing the Data

Data analysis in correlational research involves computing an index of the degree of relationship between variables. The correlation coefficient computed depends on the level of measurement of both variables. If both variables are measured on at least an interval scale, then a Pearson product–moment correlation coefficient should be computed. If one variable is measured on an ordinal scale and the other variable is at least ordinal, then the appropriate coefficient is a Spearman rank–order correlation. Both correlation coefficients indicate the degree of linear relationship between two variables. Both range from -1.00 to $+1.00$. A -1.00 means a perfect negative relationship exists (as one variable increases, the other decreases in a perfectly predictable fashion). A $+1.00$ means a perfect positive relationship exists. A correlation of 0.00 means there is no linear relationship between the two variables. (See Figures 5.5 and 5.6 for examples of correlation scatter plots.) The computational procedures for these correlation coefficients are presented on the *Student Resource CD*.

The Pearson and Spearman correlations quantify the relationship between two variables. However, some research situations demand more complicated correlational analyses, such as correlating one variable with an entire set of variables (**multiple correlation**) or one set of variables with another set of variables (**canonical correlation**). It is also possible to correlate one variable with another after statistically removing the effects of a third variable (**partial correlation**). Analytical procedures, such as **path analysis,** will test the strength of evidence for a specific causal model using correlational data (Raulin & Graziano, 1995). Detailed discussion of these more sophisticated analytic procedures is beyond the scope of this book (see Nunnally & Bernstein, 1993; Myers & Well, 1995; or Loehlin, 1998). However, it is important to realize that such procedures do exist to meet a variety of research needs.

Interpreting the Correlation

The first step in interpreting the correlation is to note its direction and size. Is the correlation a positive relationship between the variables or a negative relationship? Is the relationship small (close to 0.00) or large (close to +1.00 or −1.00)?

The next step is to test for the statistical significance of the correlation, that is, test to see whether the observed correlation is large enough to convince the researcher that there is a nonzero correlation between the variables in the population from which the current sample was drawn. To state it another way, the researcher is testing the null hypothesis that the variables are not correlated in the population. Computer programs compute the *p*-value for each correlation. This *p*-value is the probability of achieving a correlation this large or larger if the correlation in the population were actually zero. If this probability is low, it means that there is little chance that the population correlation is zero. In other words, the correlation is statistically significant. Traditionally the probability must be quite low (usually .05 or even .01) before researchers declare their findings to be statistically significant. For example, if the correlation between two variables is .67 with a *p*-value of .035, it would be concluded that a significant relationship exists, because the *p*-value is less than the traditional alpha of .05. See Chapter 5 for a more detailed explanation of this terminology.

When using correlation coefficients, we should calculate the coefficient of determination, rather than just rely on the statistical significance of the correlation (Nunnally & Bernstein, 1993). The **coefficient of determination** is computed by squaring the correlation. If the correlation was .50, then $r^2 = .25$. You can convert .25 to a percent by multiplying by 100 ($100 \times .25 = 25\%$). A correlation of .50 indicates that 25% of the variability in the first variable can be accounted for, or predicted, by knowing the scores on the second variable. This statement is shortened by referring to r^2 as the *proportion of variance accounted for.* This procedure allows researchers to estimate how useful the relationship might be in prediction. However, it is appropriate to take r^2 seriously only if there is a good-sized sample (a minimum of 30 participants).

Quick-Check Review 4: Conducting Correlational Research

4.1. What is the difference between experimenter expectancy and experimenter reactivity?

4.2. What are moderator variables? Give examples.

4.3. What are the two most commonly used measures of correlation? Under what conditions is each measure used?

4.4. What is the coefficient of determination? How is it used?

Conducting Differential Research

Differential research is used to compare existing groups on theoretically relevant variables. It is used when experimental procedures are impossible or unethical, but the researcher is still interested in learning as much as possible about the relationship between variables. This section covers the formulation of problem statements, measurement, selecting control groups, sampling, and analyzing and interpreting data.

Problem Statements

Problem statements for differential research are among the most challenging in all of research. At one level they are simple. The problem statement is in this format: Does Group *A* differ from Group *B* on the dependent variable(s)? We could create an infinite number of such problem statements by taking every possible group and comparing it with every other possible group. Why not ask this: Do balding college professors differ from laboratory rats in their preference for music? One reason that you might not ask this question is that it is a dumb question. Although you can compare any group with any other group, it makes little sense to do so unless the comparison tells you something meaningful. In other words, you want to make comparisons that have theoretical significance. Unfortunately, research is done and published using differential designs and making comparisons that make about as much theoretical sense as the balding professor–lab rat example. Picking two groups and comparing them on something is easy; picking the right groups and the right dependent variable in order to advance scientific understanding is much harder, but should always be the goal in differential research.

What makes a comparison in differential research theoretically significant? A useful study will tell the researcher something about factors that affect the dependent variable rather than just reveal differences between two groups. No one would be surprised to find a difference in preference for music between balding college professors and lab rats. In fact, we would expect to find differences on many variables, such as weight, eye color, diurnal cycle, night vision, and social skills. Suppose that differences on all these variables, as well as on music preference, were found. What would it mean? Who knows, or cares for that matter? The problem with this comparison is that the two groups differ on so many variables that there is no way of knowing which are relevant. *The first rule of thumb, therefore, is to develop problem statements that focus on comparing groups that differ on only one variable.* If you are interested in sex differences, do not compare balding professors (presumably male) with a group of fifth-grade girls. These groups differ not only on sex, but also on age, education, social class, and the types and range of experiences that they have had. If you found a difference, you would have no idea what caused it. A better comparison might be fifth-grade girls and fifth-grade boys. However, you still should be cautious in drawing conclusions about the role of sex based on this one comparison.

This leads us to the second rule of thumb: *Use several comparisons when trying to draw a conclusion about the role of a factor from differential research studies.* If you find similar results in comparisons of fifth-grade girls and boys, college males and females, male and female businesspeople, male and female college professors, and male and female truck drivers, you can be more confident in your hypothesis that sex differences account for all these findings. Even with this whole series of findings based on comparing groups that appear to differ only on sex, you have to be careful in drawing a causal conclusion.

Finally, good problem statements focus on group differences in theoretically significant dependent measures. If you were interested in studying self-esteem, you would focus on variables like success, social support, childhood experiences, and internal cognitions. These variables are likely to affect, or be affected by, self-esteem. Variables like hat size, finger-tapping speed, visual acuity, and marital status are less likely to be theoretically relevant, although we could probably dream up some mechanism that could relate one or more of these variables to self-esteem.

In summary, good problem statements for differential research compare two or more theoretically relevant groups on a theoretically significant dependent measure, in which the groups ideally differ on only a single dimension. Since this ideal of the groups differing on only a single dimension is rarely achieved, multiple comparisons are used in drawing conclusions about the role of group differences in influencing the dependent measure.

Measuring the Variables

In differential research, researchers distinguish between the independent variable and the dependent variable. The dependent variable is usually a continuous measure, but it might also be a discrete (categorical) measure. The independent variable is typically a discrete variable. For example, it might be an educational category with two values, such as high school graduate and high school dropout. The independent variable in differential research is measured, rather than manipulated. In the example with educational level, the researcher needs a procedure to measure the education of the people. This seems simple enough, but it can quickly become complicated. For example, in what category would you put someone who obtained a GED (high school equivalency degree)? Where do you get the information? Do you ask the person or check with the school? You need to decide on all these issues before you begin the study. This procedure or set of procedures would be the operational definition of education level. Note that the issues that apply to creating operational definitions for the independent variable are the same that apply in measuring the dependent variable.

Although the nonmanipulated independent variable in differential research is usually a discrete variable, it is always possible to take a continuous variable, such as education level, and break it into discrete intervals, such as high school dropout, high school graduate, college graduate, and so on. This process converts a correlational research design into a differential research design.

Selecting Appropriate Control Groups

The researcher must decide which groups to include in a differential study. In some cases, the decision is simple. If, for example, the study were about sex differences, sex would be the independent variable, and there would be only two possibilities. Because the minimum number of groups required in differential research is two, the researcher would use both a male and a female group. However, such is not the case with other independent variables. If the study is about psychopathology, there are dozens of psychiatric disorders. Choosing which of these disorders to compare must be done within a theoretical framework that guides the researcher in selecting the appropriate comparison groups. The term **control group** is used to refer to any group selected in differential research as a basis of comparison with the primary or **experimental group.**[1]

In some cases, the experimental–control group distinction is irrelevant. With the previous example of exploring sex differences, it makes little sense to say that one sex represents the experimental group and the other sex represents the control group. In other situations, the control group is arbitrarily defined as the group that has none of the characteristics that define the independent variable. For example, if the independent variable is college education and we had three levels (no college, some college, college graduate), it would be customary to refer to the no-college group as the control group.

Recall that control groups are designed to reduce the effects of potential confounding variables. A variable can have a confounding effect in a differential study only if (1) it affects the scores on the dependent variable(s) and (2) there is a difference between the experimental and control groups on the potential confounding variable. For example, suppose that you want to study sex differences in the ability to perceive details in visual scenes. You know that visual acuity affects performance on the task. Therefore, visual acuity is a potential confounding variable. However, if males and females do not differ on visual acuity, then visual acuity cannot differentially affect performance in the two groups. If males and females do differ on visual acuity, then visual acuity would be a confounding variable.

The control group has to be selected with care if it is to be an effective control. *The ideal control group is identical to the experimental group on all variables except the independent variable that defines the groups.* For example, if a researcher was studying the effects of exposure to toxic chemicals on cognitive performance, the experimental group would consist of people who work in industries in which they are exposed to such toxins. An ideal control group would include workers of about the same age, social class, and education level who do similar kinds of work, but work in an industry that does not expose them to these toxins. A group of office workers from the same company as the plant workers in the experimental group might be a convenient control group, but *not* a very good one. The office workers would probably differ from the plant workers on a number of important variables, such as education level, age, and the ratio of males to females. Any of these differences could affect cognitive performance and thus constitute potential confounding variables.

Consider another example of selecting a control group. Suppose that the research is a study of schizophrenia. The experimental group consists of people with schizophrenia. What is a good control group to compare with this experimental group? The choice will depend on the dependent measure and the confounding variables that might affect it. As noted earlier, a variable can have a confounding effect in a differential study only if (1) it affects the scores on the dependent variable(s) and (2) there is a difference between the experimental and control groups on the potential confounding variable. To select an appropriate control group, factors that will affect the dependent

---

[1]Although the term *experimental group* is commonly used, it can be misleading in discussions of differential research. In spite of the common use of the term, differential research is *not* experimental.

measures must first be identified. These represent potential confounding factors, but they will not actually confound the results unless the experimental and control groups differ on these factors. Therefore, it is essential to select a control group that is comparable to the experimental group on these potential confounding factors.

If you are interested in measuring thought processes in people with schizophrenia, you should identify variables known to affect performance on such measures. You can usually find answers to this question in the library. Past research using the same or similar dependent measures often reports correlations with potential confounding variables. Once the potential confounding variables are identified, you can identify a control group that will not differ from the experimental group on these variables. Potential confounding variables might include amount of education, age, and total amount of psychiatric hospitalization. To reduce the threat of these potential confounding variables, you select a control group that is similar to the patients on these variables. If you can accomplish this, the variables will not confound the results.

It is rare to find an ideal control group. Instead, researchers usually try to obtain a control group that controls some of the most important and most powerful confounding variables. A confounding variable is powerful if it is likely to have a large effect on the dependent measure. In the hypothetical study of the thought processes of persons with schizophrenia, a powerful confounding variable might be education. The researcher can identify education as a confounding variable, because the research literature shows that education is highly correlated with measures of cognitive performance.

Another way to deal with the problem of finding an ideal control group is to use multiple control groups. Each control group typically controls for one or more of the major confounding variables, but no group controls for all potential confounding variables. If each of the experimental group–control group comparisons gives essentially the same result and leads to the same conclusion, then the researcher can be reasonably confident that the independent variable and not one of the confounding variables is responsible for the observed effect. Most of the research in medicine and the social sciences relies on such multiple comparisons. It is not always feasible to include all possible comparison groups in one study. Therefore, research often involves multiple studies by different researchers in different laboratories, each using slightly different procedures and control groups. If the phenomenon under study is stronger than the potential confounding variables, each researcher will come to the same conclusion.

In some research, multiple comparison groups are selected because of strong theoretical reasons. For example, anhedonia, the inability to experience pleasure, has been recognized as a central characteristic of schizophrenia for nearly 100 years (Bleuler, 1911/1950). Of course, not experiencing pleasure is also a hallmark of other psychiatric disorders, such as depression. Therefore, it makes theoretical sense to ask if there are differences in the anhedonia experienced by people with schizophrenia and people with severe depression. Blanchard, Horan, and Brown (2001) did just that. Their primary dependent measure was a scale to measure social anhedonia, or failing to experience pleasure from social interactions (Chapman, Chapman, & Raulin, 1976; Eckblad, Chapman, Chapman, & Mishlove, 1982). They speculated that the difference in the anhedonia in schizophrenia and the anhedonia in depression is that the pleasure deficit comes and goes in depression, but remains constant in schizophrenia.

To test this hypothesis, they sampled three groups: people with schizophrenia, people with severe depression, and people with no psychiatric disorder. The group of people with no psychiatric disorder provided a baseline, that is, a measure of normal levels of social anhedonia. These researchers minimized possible confounding by selecting the groups so that they would be approximately the same age, education, and ratio of males to females. They also tried to match as closely as possible on ethnic and marital status, although it was more difficult getting a close match on these variables. They then tested their participants, waited 1 year, and retested them. Depression tends to come and go, so many of the people with severe depression were much less depressed at the retest. The findings, shown in Figure 7.1, were consistent with their hypothesis. Anhedonia remains high in people with schizophrenia and is not affected by the level of the schizophrenic symptoms. In contrast, anhedonia varies in people with depression, and the level of depression affects the level of anhedonia. Interestingly, the level of depression did not affect the level of anhedonia in people with schizophrenia. People with schizophrenia, like other people, are depressed at times and not depressed at other times. These findings suggest that not experiencing pleasure in social relationships may be a different phenomenon in different psychiatric disorders, although to determine the exact nature of the difference will require more research.

We suspect that some students will find this discussion discouraging because it is so difficult to find ideal comparison groups. This is one of the reasons why it is so important to do multiple research studies. Chapter 10 will discuss experimental research designs in which groups are not defined on the basis of preexisting variables, but in-

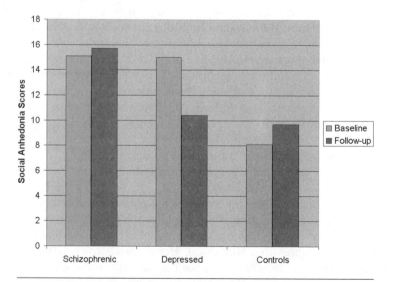

FIGURE 7.1 *Anhedonia in Schizophrenia and Depresison*
Blanchard et al. (2001) found that social anhedonia was a consistent characteritic in people with schizophrenia, but was present in people with depression only during the depressive episode.

stead participants are randomly assigned to the groups. Such random assignment controls most of the problems described in this section. Our advice to students interested in studying areas in which experimentation is unethical or impossible is to realize that drawing strong conclusions is difficult at best.

Sampling

Regardless of the type of research, the same issues of sampling always apply. To be able to generalize to a larger population, researchers must sample randomly from the population. Random sampling is a procedure for selecting participants from a population in which each participant has an equal chance of being selected. To study persons with schizophrenia, researchers should ideally utilize a procedure that samples randomly from all possible persons with this disorder. This ideal is impossible to attain in practice. It would be much too expensive, for example, to obtain a sample of 30 persons with schizophrenia from many different states and hospitals, because the cost of travel alone would be prohibitive. Usually, a sample is selected from all the participants available to the researcher. Unless there is reason to believe that participants from one part of the country are different from participants from another part, the sample need not be from the whole country to be able to generalize to the whole country.

A serious threat to generalizability is the subtle bias that can occur when a researcher has access only to certain groups. For example, if the researcher studying people with schizophrenia obtains all participants from one hospital, the sample might well be unrepresentative of schizophrenia, because most psychiatric hospitals specialize in the kinds of patients that they treat. Some hospitals handle chronic cases that require long-term hospitalization. A sample from such a hospital would underrepresent those who recover quickly. Private hospitals serve more patients from higher socioeconomic levels than state-funded hospitals. In fact, choosing participants from hospitals might result in a biased sample. Many people with schizophrenia who might be cared for at home are in hospitals because they have no family or home to go to. A hospital sample of people with schizophrenia might overrepresent those individuals from unstable homes.

Researchers studying other populations must also be sensitive to these subtle sampling biases. For example, a particular school might not have a representative sample of children. Depending on the location of the school, the children might come from higher or lower socioeconomic backgrounds than children in general. The sample might overrepresent or underrepresent certain ethnic groups. Its students might be of higher or lower intelligence than the average child. Any of these variables can affect the results of a study.

Even when researchers appear to be sampling randomly, it is important to be sensitive to subtle biases. For example, is a random sample of people in a shopping center representative of the population? A shopping center on the west side of town may have very different customers from a similar shopping center on the east side of town. A shopping center in the city is likely to have different customers than one in the suburbs. To obtain a representative sample, it might be best to sample people from several locations. The time of day or day of the week also could affect sample composition. A sample taken on a weekday afternoon would probably overrepresent homemakers, people who work evenings or weekends, the unemployed, kids playing hooky, or people on vacation. Furthermore, people who do not like shopping will be underrepresented. Finally, researchers may make subtle discriminations that could produce a biased sample. Because no one likes to be turned away, researchers might choose to approach people who seem more likely to cooperate and avoid those who seem in a hurry.

The point is that it is easy to obtain an unrepresentative sample that might threaten the generalizability of a study. This is a problem with any research and is particularly relevant in differential research studies. Because the groups in differential research already differ on some preexisting variable, the likelihood is high that they will differ on other variables that might affect the outcome of the research. The investigator must be careful when sampling participants in differential research and must take measures to assure the representativeness of the sample. When a representative sample cannot be obtained, the researcher must use extra caution in interpreting the findings.

In differential research, especially differential research of diagnostic groups, sampling is only one factor affecting the generalizability of the study. The number of participants who drop out can dramatically affect generalizability. Many people with psychiatric disorders might not have the concentration to complete a long study. To the extent that these people are different from those who do perform the task, we cannot generalize to the larger population. Sampling will be discussed in more detail in Chapter 9.

Analyzing the Data

In some respects, the data produced from differential studies resemble data from experimental studies. The researcher typically has scores from each participant in each group. The scores of the experimental group(s) are then compared with the scores of the control group(s). The type of statistical analysis used depends on the number of groups and the scale of measurement of the dependent variable(s). If the dependent measure represents score data and there are two groups, a *t*-test for independent groups is typically used. If there are more than two groups and score data, an analysis of variance (ANOVA) is used. If the data are ordinal or nominal, nonparametric statistics are typically used. With ordinal data, a Mann–Whitney *U*-Test is used; with nominal data, a chi-square test is used. Chapter 14 covers the selection of the appropriate techniques, and the *Student Resource CD* covers computation of the statistics.

Interpreting the Data

Regardless of the statistical test performed, it is interpreted in the same way. The probability value produced by the statistic is always compared with the predetermined alpha level to determine whether the null hypothesis should be rejected. The null hypothesis in differential research is that the population means are equal, and rejecting this hypothesis suggests that at least one population mean is different from at least one other population mean.

Drawing the proper conclusion from the null hypothesis is the easy part of interpreting data in differential research. The difficult part is taking into account possible confounding factors. If it is suspected that the groups might not be representative, then caution in generalizing is critical. If the control groups are inadequate to control for possible confounding, this should be acknowledged in the report of the study.

Confounding variables are so common in differential research that it is difficult to draw solid conclusions on the basis of a single research study. Especially in differential research, results should be interpreted in the context of findings from other studies. Therefore, it is critically important for each investigator to describe the research in detail. Whenever possible, confounding variables should be measured and reported. For example, any study of psychiatric patients should routinely report the diagnoses of the patients and the procedures used to obtain them, as well as such variables as participants' average age, education, social class, amount of hospitalization, and any others relevant to the interpretation of the study. In this way, future investigators will have the information needed to interpret their studies in the context of your study.

Quick-Check Review 5: Conducting Differential Research

5.1. Under what conditions should differential research be used?

5.2. Why is it important to try to develop problem statements that focus on groups that differ on only a single variable?

5.3. What is meant by a nonmanipulated independent variable?

5.4. Why is careful selection of the control groups so critical in differential research?

Limitations of Correlational and Differential Research

Correlational and differential research methods are useful research strategies that can answer many types of questions, but they also have serious limitations. This section covers two limitations: problems in determining causation and problems with confounding variables.

Problems in Determining Causation

Caution is always needed in drawing conclusions from correlational and differential research. Remember, a correlation does not necessarily imply causality. Students might wonder why this point has been so frequently repeated. In the abstract, the point is simple. If *A* and *B* are correlated, then three possibilities exist: (1) *A* causes *B*; (2) *B* causes *A*; or (3) some third factor, *C*, causes both *A* and *B*. These possibilities are illustrated in Figure 7.2. In the abstract, all these are equally plausible. But in real life one

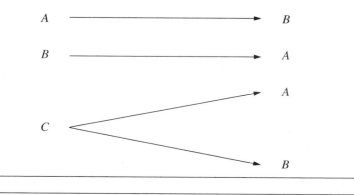

FIGURE 7.2 *Correlation and Causation* When two variables, *A* and *B,* are correlated, there are three possible causal interpretations: (1) *A* causes *B*; (2) *B* causes *A*; and (3) a third variable, *C,* causes both *A* and *B*.

or more of the possibilities might appear implausible, and so the researcher might feel justified in drawing a strong causal conclusion.

Suppose, for example, that a researcher finds that reading and arithmetic abilities are highly correlated. How should that finding be interpreted? It could be interpreted as being consistent with Spearman's theory that some third factor (in this case, the *g* factor) is responsible for both reading ability and arithmetic ability. However, there are other possible interpretations. Can arithmetic ability cause reading ability? It might, but it would be difficult to imagine a mechanism for how arithmetic skills could lead to better reading skills. Therefore, we might be tempted to dismiss such an interpretation as unlikely. Consider the reverse causal chain. Can reading ability cause arithmetic ability? How did you learn about arithmetic? Your teacher in grammar school taught you basic arithmetic, and you read about it and practiced it from your arithmetic textbook. If you had poor reading skills, you might well have been less able to learn other skills, including arithmetic. This is a plausible causal chain that could explain how better reading skills can lead to better arithmetic skills.

Another explanation for a strong correlation between arithmetic and reading abilities should be considered. What does it mean when there is a strong relationship between reading ability and arithmetic ability? We are not asking you to interpret this relationship but, rather, to define what it means in operational terms, that is, how this relationship was quantified. In this case, a sample of people was asked to take tests of reading ability and arithmetic ability. But what do the scores on the tests really mean? Suppose that the arithmetic test includes the following question:

John goes to the market and buys five tomatoes. If tomatoes sell for $6 per dozen, how much change should John receive if he gives the clerk a $5 bill?

Clearly, this question measures the ability to multiply, divide, and subtract. If tomatoes are $6.00 per dozen, they are $0.50 each, and therefore five tomatoes would cost $2.50. The change that John should receive (assuming no sales tax) is $2.50. It seems simple enough. But what other abilities would this question measure? Consider the following example:

> *Jean va au marché et il acheté cinq tomates. Si les tomates se vendent á $6 la douzaine, combien de monnaie Jean doit-il recevoir s'il donne á la vendeuse un billet de $5?*

Unless you read French, you probably found this question considerably harder to answer, yet it is the same arithmetic question. The example illustrates how important reading ability is in tests, regardless of the material being tested. Therefore, a correlation between reading ability and arithmetic ability may actually be an artifact of the phenomenon that reading ability is required to perform well on either test.

Another point is often overlooked when interpreting a correlation. When we say that both *A* and *B* may be caused by some third variable *C*, we are not specifying what the third variable might be. In fact, variable *C* might be anything, so we do not have three interpretations to choose from, but rather hundreds. Suppose that you believe that you can eliminate the possibility that arithmetic skills caused reading skills and the possibility that reading skills caused arithmetic skills. Could you then conclude that the third factor (Spearman's *g* factor) is responsible for both? No, you cannot. Spearman's general intelligence factor is only one of many possible third-factor variables that could account for the observed correlation. General test-taking ability might be a relevant factor. Anxiety level during the testing might be a relevant factor. (Have you ever taken an exam during which you panicked?) The amount of distraction during the testing session might be important, or the level of motivation of participants, or the general quality of their education, or any one of a dozen other variables. Most likely, each variable contributes to the observed correlation. Yet it is tempting to conclude that the one causal relationship being hypothesized is the one that led to the observed relationship.

Now that we have stated that causation cannot be implied by correlations, we want to acknowledge that not all theorists agree with this statement. There are sophisticated correlational designs that are well beyond the scope of this textbook. These designs are often used in such disciplines as medicine and clinical psychology in which direct experimentation is often ethically irresponsible. Some researchers argue that the right combination of correlational studies can so effectively exclude other interpretations of a complex data set that a causal interpretation is reasonable. Even though this may be true, the research literature is littered with hundreds of examples of top scientists drawing incorrect causal interpretations from complex correlational data. Therefore, we believe that the best rule for you to follow is **do not draw causal inferences from correlational data!**

Confounding Variables

As noted earlier, another limitation of differential and correlational research methods is that it is often difficult or impossible to avoid confounding variables. Two variables are said to be confounded when they tend to vary together. Because they vary together, any observed relationships with other variables might be caused by either of the variables or both of them. In differential research in particular, confounding is more the rule than the exception. Some potential confounding variables may be controlled with a carefully selected control group, but rarely will the researcher be able to completely eliminate confounding. Such problems will always make interpretation difficult, although some researchers choose to think of them as simply making the task more challenging.

Quick-Check Review 6: Limitations of Correlational and Differential Research

6.1. What is the major limitation in interpreting correlational and differential research?

6.2. What are the reasons for this major limitation?

6.3. What are confounding variables? Define and explain the concept.

Chapter Summary

Correlational and differential methods of research were covered together because they share the common characteristic that they measure but do not manipulate variables. By surrendering the opportunity to manipulate variables, the researcher surrenders considerable control and thus must be cautious in interpreting the data. It is difficult or impossible to draw causal conclusions from data derived from correlational or differential research.

Correlational and differential research designs are appropriate when the researcher is interested in relationships between variables. Sometimes researchers are interested in a causal relationship, but are unable to conduct experiments because of practical or ethical concerns. In such cases, a differential design is appropriate. Experimental research is generally easier to interpret, and causal conclusions can be drawn more safely from experimental research. However, many questions of interest in psychology and medicine cannot use experimental methods to answer questions posed by researchers. The effective use of correlational and differential research methods, coupled with a thorough knowledge of past research, good theory, and a sophisticated use of logic, can often answer some of these difficult yet critically important questions.

Key Terms

Define the following key terms. Be sure that you understand them. They are discussed in the chapter and defined in the glossary.

cross-sectional design	multivariate correlational designs	multiple correlation
cohort effect		canonical correlation
longitudinal designs	demographic variables	partial correlation
time-series designs	experimenter expectancy	path analysis
confounded	experimenter reactivity	coefficient of determination
artifact	filler items	control group
confounding variable	moderator variable	experimental group

8

Hypothesis Testing, Validity, and Threats to Validity

Nothing is more dangerous than an idea when it is the only one we have.

—Emile Auguste Chartier, 1868–1951; *Libre propos*

CD Resource Material

- Library Research
- Identifying Confounding Variables Exercises
- Student Study Guide/Laboratory Manual

Web Resource Material

- Gender Differences in Learning
- Autism

The main goal of this chapter is to integrate concepts covered earlier in this text and to introduce several new concepts. Some of the material will be review, and several concepts will be expanded. The chapter systematically lays out issues that must be addressed in designing experimental research, which is the focus of Chapters 8 to 13.

Hypothesis Testing

A crucial part of experimentation is developing and testing *research hypotheses* (see Figure 8.1). Developing good research hypotheses involves several steps. First, the researcher refines an initial idea into a *statement of the problem,* drawing on initial observations of the phenomenon and a thorough review of previous research. The statement of the problem is converted into a research hypothesis when the *theoretical concepts* in the problem statement are converted into specific procedures for measurement or manipulation, that is, into *operational definitions* of the concept. Each of these ideas will be discussed at length in this section. The research hypothesis is a specific prediction about the effects of the specific, operationally defined independent variable on the specific, operationally defined dependent variable.

Problem statements, operational definitions, and research hypotheses are important at all levels of research. Research hypotheses take different forms depending on the level of constraint. For example, a research hypothesis at the correlational level of constraint takes this general form: There is a significant (positive, negative) relationship between variables A and B. At the differential level, the general form of the hypothesis is this: There is a significant difference between the groups on the dependent variable. At the experimental level, the research hypothesis might be this: Variable A

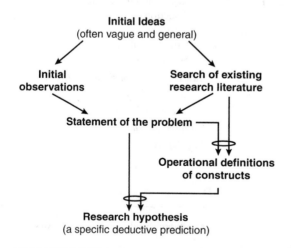

FIGURE 8.1 *Generating Research Hypotheses*
Initial ideas are refined into a statement of the problem, which is then transformed into a research hypothesis by operationally defining the variables.

will significantly affect variable *B*. Note that the hypothesis might be directional (e.g., an increase or decrease in variable *B*) or it might be nondirectional. Hypotheses are tested at all levels of research, but the inferences that can be drawn with confidence vary from one constraint level to another.

Starting the Research with an Initial Idea

A research study begins with initial ideas that are refined and developed into one or more specific questions and predictions. The researcher then designs the procedures to be used to test the predictions and only then proceeds with the observations. Each step is planned carefully, addressing many conceptual and procedural questions. These ideas can come from reading the research literature, from one's own personal interests and observation, and from the general need for solutions to practical problems. The initial ideas focus the research on specific variables. Some examples of initial ideas are listed in Table 8.1. Try to pick out the variables identified in each question in Table 8.1.

Having developed an initial idea, the researcher searches the literature to find research dealing with similar ideas and questions. It is common to find that one's "new idea" has already been studied. The published research provides considerable information, such as how other researchers defined their variables and what procedures they used. Initial ideas are modified, discarded, or retained based on this examination of the literature. In essence, the literature search is the first of many tests of your research ideas.

Statement of the Problem

Initial ideas that survive the literature search are refined into a statement of the problem, which guides the researcher through the remainder of the research. In experimentation, the problem statement makes a causal prediction: Does variable *A* cause a specific change in variable *B*? For example, the initial idea "I wonder if nutrition affects schoolwork" could become the problem statement "Will good breakfasts improve academic achievement?" Table 8.2 lists examples of other problem statements.

Problems are stated in the form of questions, which at the experimental level concern causality. Where possible, the direction of the expected effect is stated; for example,

---

TABLE 8.1 *Initial Research Ideas*

Here are some examples of initial research ideas that may later be translated into specific research studies.

1. Will children do better in school if they are given immediate feedback of examination results?
2. Does cocaine affect learning?
3. I wonder if nutrition affects schoolwork.
4. Is productivity better when employees own stock in their company?
5. Is it true that older people have poor memory?
6. Do men and women have different brain organization?
7. What are the neural bases for locating objects in our visual space?

TABLE 8.2 *Problem Statements*

Here are some examples of problem statements for experimental studies. Each of these problem statements addresses a question of causality.

1. Does the presence of male hormones increase the aggressive behavior of rats?
2. Does the presence of a mediator increase the likelihood of reaching a compromise in a negotiation setting?
3. Are words that are easily visualized more readily learned than words that cannot be easily visualized?
4. Does the presence of a stranger in the room increase an infant's crying?
5. Does the administration of stimulants help hyperactive children to control their behavior?
6. Does the presentation of contingent reinforcement improve the accuracy of maze running in mice?
7. Are people more aggressive when they are frustrated?
8. Will sensory deprivation lead to gross disturbance in thinking and emotional responsivity?
9. Will mandatory arrest and jail time reduce spouse abuse?

immediate feedback is expected to improve arithmetic skill, cocaine administration is expected to reduce learning, and so on. Most experimental research questions are directional, but sometimes a direction cannot be specified. For example, a researcher might suspect that a manipulation will bring about a change in racial attitudes, but cannot predict if it will make the attitudes more positive or more negative. Therefore, the experiment will test whether attitudes change in either direction. The statement of the problem at the experimental level includes (1) a statement about an expected causal effect, (2) identification of at least two variables, and (3) when possible, an indication of the direction of the expected causal effects. Thus, formulating a clear statement of the problem points the researcher toward an effective design.

Developing a clear statement of the problem requires skill and creativity. Consider a deadly social problem, one that does not occur often but, when it does, leaves people bewildered, shaking their heads, and asking, "How can anyone behave like that? How can all of those people just stand there and watch and not do anything to help?" The phenomenon is called the apathetic bystander effect or, as it has sometimes been called, the "Bad Samaritan" phenomenon.

A particularly shocking example occurred on a Detroit bridge late in 1995 (Meredith, 1996). Traffic was stopped and drivers were irritated. It is not clear how it started, but a man began attacking another driver, a young woman. She screamed and ran; he pursued her, beat her, knocked her to the ground, and ripped off her clothes. He laughed and invited other men who were watching to join in. Forty or fifty people, sitting in their cars or standing outside to see better, watched as she screamed and pleaded for help. But no one helped. After what seemed a long time, the beaten, near-naked woman ran frantically from the still-pursuing attacker, jumped onto the railing and fell, or perhaps was thrown, into the water to her death. In all that time, although many had been within touching distance, not a single person had stirred to help the terrified young woman.

Public violence that explodes unexpectedly, like "road rage" (Gryta, 1998), is shocking to witnesses. It is difficult to understand the violence and the lack of response from bystanders. Why won't people help the victim? This question is raised every time but our collective memories always seem to fail us. The best answer was found more than 30 years ago in the classic "bystander effect" research of Darley and Latane (1968). Their research was prompted by the 1964 murder of a young woman, Catherine (Kitty) Genovese, who was repeatedly stabbed by a man during a half-hour period while 38 of her neighbors watched from their apartments. Like the Detroit bridge incident 32 years later, no one came to her aid. No one even called the police until after she was dead. Violent incidents like these raise such questions as "How could this happen?" or "Why didn't anyone help her?" These questions are important, but they are too vague to be tested scientifically. Darley and Latane (1968) refined the questions into something more manageable. How do you do that? Reports of the attack and what the witnesses said about it would need to be studied. You would look for other similar occurrences in police files and in the research literature to see if anyone had studied concepts that might explain what happened to Kitty Genovese. But, in the end, you would need to focus your attention on only one or two factors to create a workable statement of the problem. A major issue in the Genovese case is that none of the 38 people who witnessed the attack or heard the screams came to her aid. Common sense might lead you to believe that the more people that are present, the more likely it is that someone will help. But this incident suggests something contrary to common sense, that is, as the number of people present increases, the likelihood that someone will offer help decreases. This initial idea suggests that one variable (the number of people present) might affect another variable (the likelihood of someone offering aid). You might develop the idea into the following problem statement: Will bystanders be less likely to help a victim when there are many people present than when there are only a few people present? The statement of the problem can lead to specific research studies. When Darley and Latane (1968) studied the problem, they did find that people are less likely to help if other people are present. People apparently assume that, when others are around, someone else will take the responsibility. Darley and Latane could have defined other problems from their initial ideas but chose to start with this particular issue.

The statement of the problem is an important early phase in designing research. Kerlinger (1992) lists several characteristics of a good problem statement:

1. The problem should state the expected relationships between variables (in experimentation, this is a causal relationship).
2. The problem should be stated in the form of a question.
3. The statement of the problem must at least imply the possibility of an empirical test of the problem.

In the research on the treatment of autistic children discussed in earlier chapters (Graziano, 1974), the major question was this: Can relaxation reduce disruption in autistic children? The independent variable was relaxation and the dependent variable was disruption. The expected effect was a decrease in disruption brought about by relaxation training. With the statement of the problem clearly defined, the next step in the development of the research hypothesis is to define operationally the variables suggested by the problem statement.

Operational Definitions

Before the dependent variable can be measured or the independent variable manipulated, they must be defined. At all levels of research, variables are defined both conceptually and operationally. The independent variable in our treatment study of autistic children was relaxation. The concept of relaxation refers to an internal state, a condition in which people function evenly and without stress or anxiety. This internal state cannot be directly observed, but can be inferred; that is, it is not an observed fact, but an inferred construct. The conceptual definition of relaxation provides an idea of what to manipulate. But how can something that is internal to the participant, and thus not directly accessible to the researcher, be manipulated? In other words, how is the manipulation of relaxation to be operationally defined? You learned in Chapter 4 that the children were relaxed by having them lie down while the researcher encouraged them to relax with a soothing voice and muscle massage. The definition was spelled out by describing how the researcher should set up the room as well as what should be said and done to relax the participants. Once the definition is created, the term *relaxation training* should be understood to mean all the procedures. Because the definition provides detailed instructions, other researchers can replicate the procedure.

The dependent variable in this study, disruption, was also operationally defined. It was defined as any behavior that interfered with the activities of others. Numerous examples of specific disruptive behaviors were included in the behavioral description in order to clarify the concept and to simplify the task of recognizing which behaviors are disruptive (see Chapter 4). Operational definitions make it possible for the researcher to proceed a step closer to formulating the research hypothesis.

Research Hypothesis

To evaluate the effects of relaxation on the disruptive behavior of autistic children, we develop the problem statement into a specific, testable prediction. The prediction becomes the research hypothesis. Notice that the problem statement has already suggested one basic way to test it: measure disruptive behavior before and after relaxation training and see whether the predicted difference exists. This approach is called a **pretest–posttest design** (see Figure 8.2). As you will see in later chapters, a pretest–posttest design has several weaknesses, and better designs are available to test the hypothesis. However, this simple design helps to illustrate the use of operational definitions.

Having operationally defined both the dependent variable (disruptive behavior) and the independent variable (relaxation training), we can now combine the operational definitions and the statement of the problem into a specific prediction—the research hypothesis. The research hypothesis in this case is this: Following relaxation training, the frequency, duration, and intensity of disruptive behavior will be significantly less than at the pretraining baseline. A research hypothesis makes a declarative statement about the expected relationship among variables. Even though it is in this form, remember that it is only a tentative statement to be tested. The characteristics of a good research hypothesis are summarized in Table 8.3.

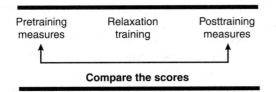

Compare the scores

FIGURE 8.2 *Single-Group, Pretest–Posttest Design* This design follows a single group of participants, testing them both before and after a manipulation.

The Contribution of Theory to the Research Hypothesis

Theory plays a critical role in developing the research hypothesis. Even in a research area that has never been studied before, researchers usually have implicit theories about how things might relate. Most research involves studying constructs that have been studied extensively, and in such situations, explicit theories guide decisions about the research. Often several theories will guide design decisions. Some of these theories will be mature, with hundreds of research studies providing empirical confirmation of the theory's predictions. Some will be new, with only limited validational evidence. Occasionally, a theory is brand new, being tested for the first time in your study, but this situation is rare. Theories are usually interconnected, and the typical study will provide evidence concerning the validity of more than one theory. This network of theories and established empirical relationships provides a foundation for a proposed study. To illustrate this, let's look more closely at the study of relaxation with autistic children. The following are only the most critical of the many theoretical ideas that contributed to the study.

1. Children with autism have severe functional impairments in emotional development, language, personal relationships, and general learning.

TABLE 8.3 *Characteristics of a Research Hypothesis*

A good research hypothesis:

1. Is a declarative sentence.
2. Is brief and clearly stated.
3. Identifies at least two variables.
4. States an expected (predicted) relationship between at least one variable and at least one other variable.
5. States the nature of the relationship. [*Example:* The amount of physical punishment that they experienced as children will be positively correlated with parents' current use of physical punishment on their own children (a correlational hypothesis).]
6. States the direction of the relationship. [*Example:* Participants in Group A will score significantly higher than participants in Group B (a directional prediction).]
7. Implies that the predicted relationship can be tested empirically.

2. Most researchers accept a biological-causation model; that is, the primary condition is a currently unknown brain defect or defects due to genetic factors.
3. Environmental factors are secondary, but still influence functioning.
4. The children's facial grimacing just before each outburst and the nature of the outbursts suggested the presence of strong autonomic arousal.
5. Arousal is a complex construct that relates to many different theories—some physiological, some psychological, and some involving both systems.
6. Some of these theories imply that arousal and relaxation are mutually exclusive constructs.
7. Thus, inducing relaxation might well reduce the inferred state of autonomic arousal in these autistic children.

This brief review only scratches the surface of the role of theory in this relatively simple study. It is unlikely that all the theories that we drew on in developing this one study are perfectly valid (i.e., that they describe accurately all predicted relationships). The study provided an answer to the specific question that we posed and the information that helped us to evaluate the adequacy of some of the ideas that guided the formulation of the question. One idea affected by this study was the notion that autistic psychopathology prevents the learning of new skills. Since these children were able to learn relaxation skills, the validity of this idea was seriously weakened. Subsequent research confirmed that autistic children were able to learn many skills (e.g., Koegel & Koegel, 1995; Lovaas, 1996; Pierce & Schriebman, 1997).

Testing the Research Hypothesis

The research hypothesis is a complex statement, which actually encompasses three hypotheses: the null or statistical hypothesis, the confounding variable hypothesis, and the causal hypothesis. Each will be described in this section.

Suppose that we carry out the study with autistic children as follows: (1) we measure the frequency, intensity, and duration of the children's disruptive behavior during a 4-week pretraining baseline period; (2) we then train the children for 2 months in relaxation to the criteria specified; and (3) after the training, we again measure the frequency, intensity, and duration of their disruptive behavior for a 4-week posttraining period. This is an example of a simple pretest–posttest design. Now suppose that, as predicted, there is less disruption after relaxation training. Can we conclude that the independent variable, relaxation training, reduced the children's disruptive behavior? Not yet, because to answer the research question we must rule out the two other hypotheses, the null or statistical hypothesis and the confounding variable hypothesis. Figure 8.3 illustrates the steps in this process. (To the student: Note in Figure 8.3 that the left and right paths are labeled "Probably" and "Probably not" instead of "yes" and "no." Why was this done?)

Null Hypothesis.   Before we can conclude that relaxation reduces disruptive behavior, we must determine that the posttraining measures of disruption are *significantly* smaller than the pretraining measures of disruption, that is, that the differences observed are not merely due to chance variation. Thus, the first of the three hypotheses to test is the **statistical hypothesis.** The statistical hypothesis is tested with an appropriate inferential statistic (see Chapter 5). The *t*- or *F*-tests for correlated groups are appropriate here because the dependent measure yields score data, and the measures are correlated because the same participants were measured both before and after treatment. This might be confusing right now, but take our word for it. Chapter 14 will present a flowchart system for determining the appropriate statistical procedures in this and most other research.

As you learned in Chapter 5, the null hypothesis states that there is no difference between the two conditions beyond chance differences. If a statistically significant difference is found, the null hypothesis is rejected. If the differences are within chance limits, the null hypothesis is not rejected. Suppose that a *t*- or *F*-test discloses that the posttraining measures are significantly smaller than the pretraining measures; that is, the differences are not due only to chance. The differences are large enough to permit us to reject the null hypothesis. Can we then accept the hypothesis that relaxation training is responsible for the observed reduction in disruptive behavior? Not yet; there is still one other hypothesis to consider.

Confounding Variable Hypothesis.   Although we have found statistically significant differences in the predicted direction in our example, we still cannot be sure that the observed differences are due to the independent variable of relaxation. They might be due to confounding variables. Rejecting the null hypothesis, while necessary, *is not sufficient to draw a causal inference.* We must also rule out the possibility that factors other than the independent variable might have had an effect on the dependent variable. The task here is to rule out confounding variables as explanations of the results. It is best to rule out confounding variables during the design phase, when you anticipate them and design controls to eliminate their effects. This task will be the focus of the next several chapters.

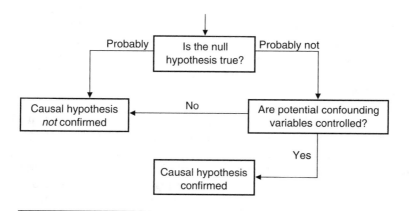

FIGURE 8.3 *Evaluating a Research Study's Results* The causal hypothesis that the independent variable affected the dependent variable cannot be accepted until both the null and confounding variable hypotheses have been rejected.

The **confounding variable hypothesis** suggests that the observed differences might be due to extraneous factors that have systematic effects on the dependent measures. We accept the finding that there is a statistically significant difference, but being systematic scientists, we are not yet convinced that the difference is due to the independent variable. Rather, we consider the possibility that it might be due to the effects of confounding factors. For example, the relaxation training required 2 months, a long time in the life of a growing child. The children could have matured over these 2 months. The observed improvement might have been due to maturational factors and not to the independent variable, relaxation training. Thus, the independent variable is confounded with maturation. Therefore, it is unreasonable to conclude that relaxation training is the variable that brought about the improvement. The confounding variable hypothesis recognizes that relaxation training is only one of several possible explanations for the improvement in disruptive behavior. To have confidence in the conclusions, we must carefully rule out all alternative explanations.

Unlike the statistical hypothesis, the confounding variable hypothesis is not directly tested. Rather, each confounding variable hypothesis is ruled out by first anticipating potential confounding variables, then reducing their likelihood by using appropriate research design and controls, and later inspecting the research design and procedures. This careful inspection shows where the design is weak and where it is strong. The researcher must then judge whether the design is strong enough to rule out the most likely potential confounding variables. As you will see in later chapters, some designs are so powerful that they can rule out most confounding variables. Other designs are less effective in ruling out confounding variables, although careful measurement of possible confounding variables might be sufficient to rule them out. As you learned in Chapter 7, a variable can confound results only if (1) it affects the scores on the dependent variable and (2) the groups or conditions being compared differ on the variable. If you can show that a potential confounding variable is either not correlated with the dependent measure or that the groups or conditions being compared do not differ on this potential confounding variable, you have effectively ruled it out as a source of confounding.

Ruling out alternative explanations is critical in science. Research is conducted not only to find evidence to support research hypotheses, but also to rule out alternative explanations, which are also known as rival hypotheses. Every confounding variable is a threat to the validity of a study. Experimental designs typically rule out most confounding variables.

Causal Hypothesis.   The **causal hypothesis** states that the independent variable had the predicted effect on the dependent variable. Suppose that you tested and rejected the null hypothesis and carefully ruled out confounding variables. (We will discuss how to control or rule out confounding variables in Chapter 9.) You are ready to return to the research hypothesis: Following relaxation training, the frequency, duration, and intensity of disruptive behavior will be significantly less than at the pretraining baseline. Remember that when this research hypothesis was first stated it was a tentative statement to be tested. If we find significantly less disruption after training than before training and can rule out alternative hypotheses, then only one viable hypothesis remains, that the independent variable affected the dependent variable as predicted.

Note, however, that the assertion is not absolute, but rather it is a statement of probability. The first hypothesis was the statistical hypothesis, which was tested in terms of probability. Even though the data were sufficiently persuasive to convince us to reject the null hypothesis of no difference, there is always the possibility of a Type I error (see Chapter 5). It is wise to remember that there are so many complicated steps from initial conceptualization to running the study to interpreting the results that we must always be cautious in our interpretations. We can have confidence, but not certainty, in the results of a well-run study. Every finding in science is considered to be tentative, subject to change due to new observations.

Another important point about developing research hypotheses is that most problem statements can be developed into several different research hypotheses, each of which can then be tested. Recall the problem statement in the research with autistic children: Can relaxation reduce the disruption of autistic children? The essential question being posed here is whether there is a causal relationship between the child's relaxation and the degree of disruption. Relaxation was defined operationally in terms of procedures used to train the child to slow down, and disruption was operationally defined as the frequency, duration, and intensity of each disruptive behavior. These definitions led to this specific research hypothesis: Following relaxation training, the frequency, duration, and intensity of disruptive behavior will be significantly less than at the pretraining baseline.

Now suppose that we study another aspect of the relaxation–disruption hypothesis and operationally define relaxation in terms of the pharmacological effects of a particular drug. Each child is given a drug that is known to relax individuals. The research hypothesis is similar to the original hypothesis, but a different research hypothesis is being tested because relaxation is operationally defined in a different way. This second study uses the same pretest–posttest design, but now drugs, instead of relaxation training, are used to induce relaxation. We are still evaluating the same statement of the problem, but with a different interpretation expressed as a different research hypothesis.

We can make other changes as well in the way that we translate the statement of the problem into a research hypothesis. For example, a different research design could be used. Instead of using the pretest–posttest design, we can randomly assign each autistic child to one of two groups. One group is relaxed with the drug, whereas the other is not given the drug. The disruptive behavior of all participants is then measured and the mean level of disruption in the two groups is compared. This design is called a **two-group posttest-only design** and is illustrated in Figure 8.4. The research hypothesis is stated differently from that of the previous example because the independent variable and the research design have been changed. Here is the new research hypothesis: Autistic children who are given drugs that relax them will show less disruptive behavior than autistic children who do not receive such drugs. Thus, the same problem statement can be combined with different operational definitions of the independent and dependent variables and different research designs. This results in the generation of several different research hypotheses and, consequently, several different studies. In essence, the researcher is able to investigate the same basic problem in different ways by testing different facets of the same issue. This allows researchers to test the hypothesized relationship in several different ways.

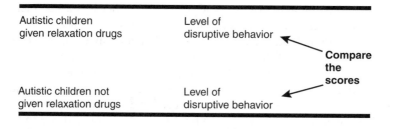

FIGURE 8.4   *Two-Group, Posttest-Only Design* This design used two groups, only one of which received the manipulation.

To summarize: In an experiment, initial ideas are refined into the problem statement, which identifies variables, implies causality, and indicates the direction of the expected causal effect. The variables are operationally defined, and a research hypothesis is constructed by combining these operational definitions with the problem statement. The research hypothesis states a specific testable prediction about the relationship between specific variables.

Testing the research hypothesis involves several hypotheses: the null or statistical hypothesis, the confounding variable hypothesis, which is often a set of hypotheses, and the causal hypothesis. The causal hypothesis is accepted only after rejecting the null and confounding variable hypotheses.

Testing the null hypothesis evaluates the likelihood that the findings were due to chance. It is *equally important* to identify and rule out potential confounding variables in order to draw conclusions about causal relationships between the independent and dependent variables. Statistical tests show only whether there is a significant difference between groups, but not whether the difference is due to the independent variable. To draw that conclusion, competing interpretations must be identified and ruled out.

Finally, one problem statement can be developed into several research hypotheses that lead to several different studies, thus examining different facets of the problem.

Quick-Check Review 1: Hypothesis Testing

1.1. Describe the process of refining initial ideas into a problem statement.

1.2. What concepts are combined to produce the research hypothesis?

1.3. What is the function of the research hypothesis?

1.4. What three hypotheses make up the research hypothesis?

1.5. Why is ruling out potentially confounding variables so important?

1.6. Describe how one problem statement can be developed into several research hypotheses.

Validity and Threats to Validity

A major concern in research is the validity of the procedures and conclusions. The term *validity* has several meanings, the most basic of which refers to methodological soundness or appropriateness. That is, a valid test measures what it is supposed to measure; a valid research design tests what it is supposed to test.

Validity is relevant at any level of constraint, but it is especially important in experimental research, which addresses specific questions about causality. There are many potential threats to the validity of an experiment, and the researcher must (1) anticipate them and (2) create procedures to eliminate or reduce them. This section outlines the broad concept of validity. This presentation follows closely the classic organization of Campbell and Stanley (1966) and Cook and Campbell (1979), who distinguished among four types of validity: statistical validity, construct validity, external validity, and internal validity (summarized in Table 8.4).

Statistical Validity

When statistical procedures are used to test the null hypothesis, the researcher is asking whether the results are due to some systematic factor (ideally, the independent variable) or merely to chance variations? Rejecting the null hypothesis is a necessary first step in testing the effects of the independent variable. **Statistical validity** addresses the question of whether these statistical conclusions are reasonable.

Several possible threats to a study's statistical validity must be controlled. One threat is the possibility that the measures used to assess the dependent variable are unreliable. Another threat to statistical validity is the violation of the assumptions that underlie the statistical tests. Each statistical procedure makes assumptions about the nature of the data. Statistics textbooks normally list the assumptions of each statistic. Violating these statistical assumptions distorts the p-value for your statistical test, and therefore your statistical decision is undependable. Statistical validity addresses the question of whether the basis for your statistical decision is reasonable and dependable. It does not address whether the statistical decision accurately reflects reality. Remember, the statistical decision is based on probability. If alpha is set at .05, it means

TABLE 8.4 *Types of Validity*

Statistical validity	The accuracy of the p-value on which a statistical decision is based
Construct validity	The degree to which the theory or theories behind the research study provide(s) the best explanation for the results observed
External validity	The extent to which the results of a particular study generalize to other people, places, or conditions
Internal validity	The extent to which we can be confident that the observed changes in the dependent variable were due to the effects of the independent variable and not to the effects of extraneous variables

that you will reject the null hypothesis of no difference if there is less than a 5% chance of it being correct. This still means that you will be rejecting the null hypothesis incorrectly 5% of the time. This is not a problem of statistical validity unless the probabilities are in error because of violations of statistical assumptions.

Construct Validity

Every hypothesis tested in research is constructed in a theoretical context of ideas. **Construct validity** refers to how well the study's results support the theory or constructs behind the research and asks whether the theory supported by the findings provides the best available explanation of the results. To help to reduce threats to construct validity, the researcher uses clearly stated definitions and carefully builds hypotheses on solid, well-validated constructs. In brief, the theoretical bases must be clear and well supported, with rival theories carefully ruled out.

An example of a construct validity question is the continuing debate in psychology over the nature–nurture issue. This question has been raised in many different research areas, from questions about the causes of schizophrenia to investigating why males usually score higher than females on math skill measures. On the latter, researchers debate how much of the difference is innate and how much is the result of environmental effects (Lubinski & Benbow, 1992). Environmental variables alone could shape the differences if males receive more training than females in math or are more likely than females to be taught that learning math is important to success. The issue is whether the data on this question support the idea that an innate, genetically determined characteristic is responsible for the observed sex differences (nature) or whether the environment shaped the sex differences (nurture). We are often tempted to interpret data as being consistent with our own preconceptions and ignore other explanations for the data. For example, the finding that men tend to take more math courses than women would seem to be consistent with the nurture hypothesis that males are better at math because they get more training in it. However, we could interpret this finding to mean that men take more math courses because they tend to be good at math and choose courses in which they know they can excel. Therefore, the data are consistent with both a nature and a nurture hypothesis, and the construct validity of any one interpretation would be in doubt.

External Validity

In its strictest sense, the results of an experiment are limited to those participants and conditions used in the particular experiment. But when researchers test college students' memory ability, for example, are they really interested in how well these particular 20 freshmen in Dr. Sawusch's introductory psychology class did on the morning of October 21? No. They are actually interested in memory functions in general. They want to generalize the results beyond the specific conditions and participants to other, similar participants and conditions. **External validity** refers to the degree to which researchers are able to generalize the results of a study to other participants, conditions, times, and places.

To make statements about the overall population based on the findings of a particular sample, the sample must be selected in such a manner that it adequately represents the population. The process of inferring something about a population on the basis of findings from a sample drawn from the population is referred to as **generalization.** Problems of generalization from a sample to a population are best controlled by random selection of participants from the population, as you will learn in Chapter 9. In similar fashion, the researcher must be careful about generalizing across times, places, and conditions; to do so, we *must* sample across those times, places, or conditions. The term **ecological validity** (Neisser, 1976) is often used to refer to the appropriate generalization from the laboratory to real-life situations. The questions of how laboratory-derived information will generalize to the real world and how much it can help scientists to understand real-world issues will depend on how realistically the research captures the critical elements of the real-world scenario.

Internal Validity

Internal validity is of major concern to the researcher because it involves the very heart of experimentation: the demonstration of causality. Internal validity concerns this question: Was the independent variable, and not some extraneous variable, responsible for the observed changes in the dependent variable? An experiment is internally valid when this question can be answered affirmatively. Any factor that weakens confidence that it was the independent variable that accounted for the results is a threat to the internal validity of the study.

In the next section, we will describe several confounding variables, but before we do that, let's look at a couple of examples. Suppose that you are interested in the ability of patients with schizophrenia to judge time duration. You predict that their time estimation will be significantly disrupted by intrusive auditory stimulation. You test patients for their time estimations of short intervals under two conditions: (1) a high-stimulation condition in which loud, rhythmic music is played during testing and (2) a low-stimulation condition in which the testing room is kept quiet. Because of scheduling problems in the hospital, patients are available to you only on Monday and Thursday mornings, when the locked-ward and the open-ward patients, respectively, can be tested. You test the Monday patients under the high-stimulation condition and the Thursday patients under the low-stimulation condition. The research hypothesis is that patients with schizophrenia tested under the high-stimulation condition will make significantly more errors than those tested under the low-stimulation condition. You find, exactly as predicted, that significantly more errors are made under the high-stimulation condition and conclude that external auditory stimulation is a significant factor that affects time estimation by patients with schizophrenia.

The major confounding variable in this study should be obvious: The participants in the two conditions differ not only in terms of the independent variable, high- versus low-auditory stimulation, but also because one group consists of patients from a locked ward and the other group consists of patients from an open ward. Those on locked wards are typically more disturbed than those on open wards, and it is not surprising that they perform more poorly on the time-estimation task. Therefore, it would be unreasonable to attribute the difference between the two groups to the high- and low-stimulation conditions that were manipulated. The fact that the results may be due to severity of illness, rather than amount of auditory stimulation, provides an alternative explanation. Until the alternative explanation is ruled out, you cannot conclude that auditory stimulation affected estimates of time duration. The independent variable in this study (amount of auditory stimulation) is confounded with severity of illness. This confounding provides an alternative explanation of the results. It should have been eliminated in the initial design of the study, long before testing any participants.

Consider also the hypothesis concerning the effects of relaxation training on the disruptive behavior of autistic children and the research procedures used to test it. Can we conclude with confidence that the independent variable, relaxation training, is responsible for the observed reduction in disruptive behavior? In other words, can we be confident about the internal validity of this study? Consider the basic design of the first study, which tested this research hypothesis: Following relaxation training, the frequency, duration, and intensity of disruptive behavior will be significantly less than at the pretraining baseline. To test the hypothesis, we measured the disruptive behavior of the autistic children, then provided relaxation training, and then measured disruption again. It required 2 months for all the children in the study to reach the criterion of successful relaxation. At posttraining, the disruptive behavior was measurably less and the decrease was statistically significant.

It is tempting to conclude that relaxation training was responsible for the decrease in disruptive behavior, but what alternative explanations might there be for the results? That is, what confounding variables might have been operating to produce the results? As suggested earlier, the children might simply have improved over the 2-month period through natural maturational processes, with relaxation having little to do with the observed improvement. This maturation is one potential confounding variable. Another alternative explanation for the observed improvement is that some systematic factor in the research itself, other than relaxation, might have been responsible. After all, the children were in a full-day, 5-day-a-week therapy program. Many procedures were used in addition to relaxation training. Could some other factor that was consistently applied to the children during the 2 months of relaxation training be responsible for the improvement? This is an example of the confounding variable of history; that is, other things that occurred during the course of the research might have been operating.

A phenomenon called *regression to the mean* might also have been operating. Any behavior will naturally vary over time in frequency and intensity, going through ups and downs of severity. Perhaps this research had been started at the peak of severity; perhaps it was even begun because the severity was so great. As time passed, the normal variation of the behavior returned to severity levels closer to the mean. It was then that the posttraining measures were taken. If regression to the mean was operating, then the relaxation manipulation might have had little to do with the observed improvement in behavior.

Yet another possible confounding variable could explain findings of a decrease in disruptive behavior. In the course of the research, the staff making the observations of the children's disruptive behavior might have changed the ways that they observed and measured the behavior. They might have gradually become more accustomed to the children's severe behavior and, in time, tended to record it as less severe. Specifically, the staff's criteria for observations and not the behavior of the children might have changed during the course of the study.

There are many possible confounding variables in research, and there might be several in any given study. Their effects might all be in the same direction, thus compounding the errors, or in opposite directions, countering one another. In any event, if researchers wish to draw valid conclusions about the effects of one variable on another, they must anticipate and control potential confounding variables to eliminate rival hypotheses, thus leaving the causal hypothesis as the most likely explanation for the results.

Quick-Check Review 2: Validity and Threats to Validity

2.1. What is validity?

2.2. Define the various types of validity?

2.3. Which type of validity is concerned about the accuracy of the conclusions about the effects of the independent variable on the dependent variable?

Major Confounding Variables

Cook and Campbell (1979) have summarized the major types of confounding variables. We discuss each of them briefly and summarize them in Table 8.5. The *Student Resource CD* includes exercises designed to help you to spot confounding variables in research.

Maturation

In longitudinal research, especially with children, participants grow older between the pretreatment and posttreatment measures. As they age, they may also become more sophisticated, experienced, bigger, stronger, and so on. Natural **maturational** changes can also occur in participants other than children. Adults placed in a new environment tend to make predictable changes or adjustments over time. Diseases tend to have predictable courses. Thus, observed changes over time may be due to maturational factors, rather than to effects of an independent variable. Researchers must be particularly alert to maturational factors when conducting research with children, for whom change and growth are virtual certainties.

History

During the course of a study, events that are independent of the study can occur, and these events can affect the outcome. In general, threats to internal validity due to **history** are greatest with longer times between pretest and posttest measurements. Historical factors are most important to consider when you are measuring dependent variables

TABLE 8.5 *Major Confounding Variables*

Maturation	Changes in the dependent variable that occur during the course of a study that are due to the normal maturation of the participant
History	Changes in the dependent variable that are due to historical events that occur during the study, but that are unrelated to the study
Testing	Any change in a participant's score on the dependent variable that is a function of having been tested previously
Instrumentation	Any change in the calibration of the measuring instrument over the course of the study that affects the scores on the dependent variable
Regression to the mean	The tendency for participants who are selected because they have extreme scores on a variable to be less extreme in a follow-up testing
Selection	Any factor that creates groups that are not equivalent at the beginning of the study
Attrition	The loss of participants during a study; differential loss is problematic because the participants who drop out are likely to be different from those who continue
Diffusion of treatment	Change in the response of participants in a particular condition because of information that the participants gained about other research conditions from participants in those other conditions
Sequence effects	Effects on a participant's performance in later conditions that result from the experience that the participant had in the previous conditions of the study

that are responsive to environmental events. For example, weight, in contrast to height, is more affected by food intake. Weight also shows more natural variation within a participant over time than height. Therefore, historical factors are more likely to be a confounding variable for weight than for height. Most weight-control procedures would be lucky to hold their own if they are evaluated during holidays, when people are constantly exposed to tempting high-calorie foods.

Testing

The repeated **testing** of participants can threaten internal validity, because participants gain proficiency through repeated practice on the measuring instruments. Testing effects are most pronounced on measures in which the participant is asked to perform some skill-related task, such as tests of memory, IQ, or manual dexterity. Most people do better on the second administration of such tests because of practice.

Instrumentation

Apparent pre-post changes may be due to changes in the measuring **instrument** over time, rather than to independent variable manipulation. This is particularly true when

"OF COURSE I'VE BECOME MORE MATURE SINCE YOU STARTED
TREATING ME. YOU'VE BEEN AT IT SINCE I WAS 14 YEARS OLD."

Any process, including research studies, that takes time can be affected by
maturational and historical factors.

the measuring instrument is a human observer. Observers might become more proficient in making observations or their criteria for judgments might change over time.

Regression to the Mean

The concept of **regression to the mean** suggests that whenever participants are selected *because* their scores on a measure are extreme (either very high or very low),
they will tend to be less extreme on a second testing; that is, their scores will have regressed toward the mean. For example, consider the top 10% of a class based on the
first exam scores. How should the top students perform on the second exam? One
would expect them to do well, but would they all do as well as on the first exam? Probably not. The reason is that some of the students did well on the first exam in part because they studied unusually hard. On the second test, however, some of these students
might not be as diligent. If you took the top 10% of students on the first test and computed their mean score on both the first and second tests, you would probably find that
they scored, on average, closer to the mean on the second test. Similarly, if you took
the bottom 10% of students on the first test and computed their mean score on both the
first and second tests, you would find that they scored, on average, closer to the mean
on the second test. How much regression occurs will depend on how much of the test
performance is due to variable factors, such as amount of study, and how much is due

to consistent factors, such as skill and study habits. The more that these variable factors contribute to the score, the more regression you can expect to see.

Selection

Confounding due to **selection** occurs when the groups being compared are not equivalent before the manipulations begin. Under ideal conditions, participants are randomly selected and then randomly assigned to different groups. When random selection and assignment are not possible, as in most naturalistic, case-study, and differential research, then the possibility of confounding due to selection exists.

Attrition

Sometimes participants drop out of a study; some might go on vacation in the middle of the study, forget their appointments, decide they are not interested, become ill, and so on. If there are no biasing factors, such dropouts will probably be evenly distributed across groups, and they will not differentially affect one group more than others. But confounding due to **attrition** occurs when participants are lost differentially, such as when there are more dropouts from one group than from another or when participants with certain characteristics are lost. Researchers must be careful not to create situations or use procedures that will bias some participants against completing the study, thus differentially affecting the outcome. For example, suppose that a researcher realized too late that nearly all the seniors among the high school participants failed to return for the second half of the experiment because it coincided with school parties, excitement, and general preparation for graduation. Their attrition left primarily underclass participants in the second half of the study, thus biasing the sample and the results.

Sometimes procedures can cause participants with certain characteristics to drop out, leaving a biased sample. For example, in an unpublished study by one of the authors, many sixth-grade boys dropped out because, it was learned later, they thought the procedures were "too girlish." Perhaps, in today's more egalitarian mood, this might be less likely. In any event, care must be taken to avoid confounding studies by allowing attrition of participants to have a differential effect on the outcome.

Diffusion of Treatment

When participants in different experimental conditions are in close proximity and are able to communicate with each other, earlier participants might "give away" the procedures to those scheduled later. Also, experimental participants who receive a treatment may communicate with control participants who are not supposed to receive that treatment or who may not have known that they were in a control group. Such information exchanges, called **diffusion of treatment,** can erode the planned experimental differences between groups. Thus, the groups become more similar because of the information exchange.

Diffusion of treatment can affect studies in many ways. For example, many psychologists use undergraduate participants. Students often hear about studies from other students and many even select the study on the basis of what they hear. When they participate, the knowledge of what their friends experienced might affect how they respond. To compensate for this problem, many researchers try to make their study look the same to participants in all conditions.

Sequence Effects

Much of the research in psychology is designed so that each participant is exposed to more than one of the experimental conditions. These are called within-subjects designs. Although they offer important advantages over other designs, they also introduce another confounding factor, **sequence effects,** in which experiences with earlier conditions of the study affect responses to later conditions. If, in a study with three conditions, the order of presentation of conditions is always condition *A* followed by condition *B* followed by condition *C,* then systematic confounding can occur. For example, performance in conditions *B* and *C* might reflect both the effect of the conditions and the effect of having already experienced condition *A.* Sequence effects are controlled by using more than one order of conditions. Sequence effects and some methods to handle them are discussed in more detail in Chapter 11.

Quick-Check Review 3: Major Confounding Variables

3.1. What is the difference between the confounding variables of history and maturation?

3.2. If your hometown team wins this year's World Series, what prediction would you make for next year based on the concept of regression to the mean?

3.3. Suppose that you are interested in sex differences in second graders, but your procedure is upsetting to girls raised in a single-parent home, and so several such girls drop out of your study before the end. What confounding variable would be operating and what effect might it have?

3.4. What type of design has to contend with the confounding variable of sequencing effects?

Subject and Experimenter Effects

There is a large category of threats to the validity of a study due to subject and experimenter effects. The expectations and biases of both the researcher and the participants can systematically affect the results of a study in subtle ways, thus reducing the study's validity. This section describes subject and experimenter effects, and Chapter 9 discusses controls for these effects.

Subject Effects

Every psychological experiment is a social situation in which both participants and researchers participate in a common undertaking (Orne, 1962). Each behaves according to his or her understanding of how a participant or a researcher should behave. When participants enter an experiment, they are not entirely naïve. They have ideas, understandings, and perhaps misunderstandings about what to expect in the study. People participate for different reasons. Some do so because it is a course requirement. Others participate because of curiosity or because they will be paid for their participation. Some volunteer because they hope to learn something, perhaps about themselves. Participants enter and carry out their role with a variety of motivations, understandings, expectations, and biases, all of which can affect their behavior in the research setting. Furthermore, an experiment is an artificial, contrived situation, far removed from participants' natural environments. When people know they are being observed, they may behave differently than they normally would. This can lead to **subject effects,** which refer to any changes in the behavior of participants that were due to being in the study, rather than to the variables under study.

Most participants do their best to be good subjects. This might lead some participants to try to discern the research hypothesis so that they will know how they are "supposed to behave." Participants are often particularly sensitive to cues from the researcher. Furthermore, researchers, with their own expectations and biases, might inadvertently give such cues. Cues given to the participants on how they are expected to behave are called **demand characteristics.** Demand characteristics usually occur unintentionally. They include not only characteristics of the setting and procedures, but also information and even rumors about the researcher and the nature of the research.

A related phenomenon, the **placebo effect,** can occur when participants expect a specific effect of an experimental manipulation. For example, some participants in a drug study of pain control might enter the study with the clear expectation that the procedures will help, and they actually report feeling better and even show physiological changes, all due to the suggestion that the procedure will work. Participants often report improvement when given a placebo treatment, such as a pill that looks and tastes like the true drug being tested, but lacks the drug's active ingredient.

Experimenter Effects

Experimenter effects are any biasing effects in a study that are due to the actions of the researcher. The researcher attempts to carry out the research plan as objectively and as accurately as possible. But researchers are human and carry their own expectations and motivations into the study. The major expectation of the researcher is that the results will turn out as predicted and the hypothesis will be supported. But how can such expectations bias the results in an objective experimental situation?

Experimenter expectancies refer to the expectations held by the researcher about the outcome of the study. These expectancies might cause researchers to bias results in several ways. These include influencing the participant's behavior toward support of the hypothesis, selecting data that best support the hypothesis, using statistical techniques that best show the particular effects predicted, but not other effects, and interpreting results in a biased manner. The latter occurs, for example, when conclusions are drawn that accept improbable explanations consistent with the research hypothesis, while ignoring more parsimonious explanations that do not support the hypothesis. Common to all these ways of introducing bias is the idea that the researcher will tend to make decisions and choices that favor the hypothesis being tested. This is not to say that researchers deliberately and knowingly falsify data but, rather, behave in ways that tend to support their own expectations and do so without being aware of it.

For example, suppose that a researcher has two groups of participants. The participants have been randomly assigned to the groups to avoid confounding due to selection. Participants in each group are to be tested on a series of arithmetic problems and are timed by the researcher. The prediction is that, because of the difference in instructions to the two groups, the experimental group will take significantly longer than the control group to complete the problems. In this situation, there are several ways that researchers can influence participants. If the researcher knows to which group each participant is assigned and knows the research hypothesis, then it is possible that the researcher might tend to time the experimental participants in a way that would extend their times. The researcher also could influence the results by reading the same set of instructions in a slightly different tone to the two groups, emphasizing speed for the control participants. In either case, the researcher would probably not be aware of this systematic bias and would deny it. However, the bias, accumulated over all the participants in the group, could affect the outcome toward support of the hypothesis.

Much of the scientific understanding of experimenter expectancy effects is due to the research of Rosenthal and his colleagues. Rosenthal and Fode (1963a, b) suggested several ways in which the experimenter might unintentionally affect a participant's responses and thus bias the results to favor the hypothesis. For example, the researcher might unintentionally present cues by variations in tone of voice or by changes in posture or facial expressions, verbally reinforce some responses and not others, or incorrectly record participants' responses. Although such experimenter expectancy effects may occur, it has been difficult to demonstrate clearly that they do occur. Consequently, some question how big a problem this is (Barber & Silver, 1968). But in any research in which experimenter expectancy effects might occur, the effects provide an alternative explanation for the obtained results.

For example, suppose that a journal editor reads a research manuscript that has been submitted for possible publication and determines that such expectancy effects might have occurred. Just raising this possibility is sufficient to cast doubt on the validity of the experiment and lead to the rejection of the manuscript for publication. The editor need not provide data to support the alternative hypothesis that the obtained results were due to experimenter expectancy effects. If the rival hypothesis *could* be true, then we cannot accept the researcher's conclusions about the effects of the independent variable. The researcher would have to repeat the experiment, adding controls to eliminate the rival hypothesis.

Barber and Silver (1968) may be correct in doubting that such effects are as frequent as Rosenthal suggested. However, the simple existence of the rival hypothesis in a study is sufficient to cast doubt on a researcher's findings, and it is therefore important for the researcher to control for potential experimenter expectancy effects.

Quick-Check Review 4: Subject and Experimenter Effects

4.1. What are subject effects?

4.2. How can demand characteristics lead to subject effects?

4.3. How can experimenter expectancies lead to experimenter effects?

Chapter Summary

The focus has been on the development and testing of hypotheses, from initial ideas to specific research hypotheses. The careful construction of the research hypothesis is a critical step in all research, and it is most formalized and most fully developed at the experimental level of constraint. Testing the research hypothesis actually involves three hypotheses: the null or statistical hypothesis, the confounding variable hypothesis, and the causal hypothesis.

Validity and threats to validity should be considered in any research study. The researcher is concerned with four types of validity: statistical, construct, external, and internal validity. Each type can be threatened in a number of ways, and the researcher must anticipate the threats and design appropriate controls. The largest threat to internal validity comes from confounding variables. Researchers need to be alert to these confounding variables so that most can be eliminated in the design stage by the addition of proper controls. The specific controls will vary according to the type of validity being threatened and the nature of the threats. Subject and experimenter expectations and biases can also threaten validity, and these should be routinely controlled in any study.

Key Terms

Define the following key terms. Be sure that you understand them. They are discussed in the chapter and defined in the glossary.

pretest–posttest design	external validity	selection
statistical hypothesis	generalization	attrition
confounding variable hypothesis	ecological validity	diffusion of treatment
	internal validity	sequence effects
causal hypothesis	maturation	subject effects
two-group posttest-only design	history	demand characteristics
	testing	placebo effect
statistical validity	instrumentation	experimenter effects
construct validity	regression to the mean	experimenter expectancies

9

Controls to Reduce Threats to Validity

In the fields of observation, chance favors only the mind that is prepared.

—Louis Pasteur, 1822–1895

CD Resource Material

- Use of the Random Number Program
- Sampling of Participants
- Assignment of Participants to Conditions
- Student Study Guide/Laboratory Manual

Web Resource Material

- Laboratory Automation
- Research Design
- Alcohol and Drug Abuse

Control procedures counteract threats to validity, thus increasing researchers' confidence in drawing conclusions from the study. Threats to validity and control procedures represent two sides of the same conceptual coin. Chapter 8 discussed the many possible threats to validity. This chapter considers the major methods for controlling these threats to validity.

Control is any procedure used by the researcher to counteract potential threats to the validity of the research. Many procedures are available to control threats to validity, but not every threat to validity is likely to occur in every study; thus, not every control measure is needed in every study. Some control procedures are of general value and therefore applicable to nearly all studies. Other controls are relevant only in specific situations and should be carefully chosen to meet specific threats to validity. Controls are necessary at all levels of research, but are most fully developed at the experimental level.

Four types of control are available to the researcher:

1. General control procedures
2. Control over subject and experimenter effects
3. Control through participant selection and assignment
4. Control through specific experimental design

This chapter covers the first three categories. The fourth category, specific experimental design, is introduced here, but covered in Chapters 10 through 13.

General Control Procedures

General control procedures include (1) preparation of the setting, (2) response measurement, and (3) replication.

Preparation of the Setting

The researcher should carefully structure the setting in which the research is conducted. Such preparation of the research setting reduces threats to internal validity. Many studies are conducted in the laboratory to optimize control. The advantage of the laboratory is that many extraneous variables can be eliminated, such as interfering stimuli or the influence of other people. Laboratory studies can eliminate competing variables, simplify the situation, and increase control over independent variables, which increase confidence in the results.

Although laboratory settings have many advantages, they also have potential disadvantages. For example, laboratory settings might reduce external validity if the setting becomes so artificial that it is unlike the natural situation. But external validity need not be compromised if an effort is made to create a natural environment in the laboratory. For example, in a children's fear-reduction study (Graziano & Mooney, 1982), the laboratory was a living room setting in which children were trained in fear-control skills that they would use at home. This setting was similar to their own living rooms to enhance generalization. With modern computer simulation, realistic settings can be created almost anywhere. For example, Bornas, Tortella-Feliu, Llabres, & Fullana (2001) used computer-assisted exposure to flying for training people to control their fear while observing a realistic simulation of flying on a computer screen. Such technology makes realistic exposure possible in the laboratory, making it more likely that treatment will generalize to the real world. Thus, careful preparation of settings in laboratories can enhance both external and internal validity.

Response Measurement

Another general control procedure is the selection and preparation of the instruments used to measure the variables. Using measuring instruments of known reliability and validity improves both statistical and construct validity. We can use measures that have been developed by others or can create new measures, but creating a new measure is not a trivial task. It is the researcher's responsibility to establish the reliability and validity of any new measures that are developed for a study. The quality of measuring instruments can have powerful effects on validity. Unfortunately, in their concern for operationalizing and manipulating the independent variable, researchers sometimes pay less attention to the dependent measures and thereby compromise the validity of the study. Of course, the opposite situation can also occur, in which a researcher might be so involved in creating dependent measures (that's good) that details of the independent variables might be short-changed (that's not good).

Replication

Although not everyone considers replication to be a control procedure, we believe it is. By specifying the laboratory setting, conditions, procedures, and measuring instruments, we make it easier for others to replicate the research. Successful replication provides important information. If phenomena observed in one study can be reliably demonstrated a second or third time, confidence in the original observations increases; if the study cannot be replicated, confidence is shaken. Research in ESP (extrasensory perception) is an example. Some researchers have reported statistically significant ESP phenomena that fail to replicate in later research, thus leaving the earlier reports open to serious question (Milton & Wiseman, 1999). If a finding cannot be replicated, then it might be only a chance event and not an indication of a genuine phenomenon. In statistical terms, the researcher might have made a Type I error. This seems to be borne out by ESP research results. That is, only a handful of studies support ESP, while most fail to support it. If ESP phenomena cannot be reliably replicated, then we must ask if they exist at all.

There are two types of replication, exact replication and systematic replication. **Exact replication,** that is, repeating the experiment as nearly as possible in the way it was carried out originally, is rarely done in psychology. Journals seldom publish exact replication studies, and there are no career benefits to be gained by young researchers spending time repeating other people's research. Although exact replication is rare, researchers often replicate earlier findings by testing some systematic theoretical or procedural modification of the original work, which is known as **systematic replication.**

If, for example, a researcher finds an interesting phenomenon in the alcohol research laboratory, a colleague might reason that a particular systematic modification will bring about a certain specific result. The second researcher uses the initial work, making a systematic modification that, if the initial work was correct, should result in the predicted outcome.

There are still other ways to replicate. Recall that most problem statements can be developed into several different research hypotheses by combining the problem statement with various operational definitions of the research variables or using different research designs (see Chapter 8). Thus, many different studies can be generated from the same problem statement. In essence, the researcher is able to investigate different facets of the same issue. This kind of replication is referred to as **conceptual replication.**

Although replication increases confidence in the validity of findings, it does not guarantee validity. For example, suppose that confounding factors in a study brought about certain results. Then, if the procedures are replicated exactly without recognizing and controlling the confounding factors, the replication might well produce the same invalid results as in the initial study.

Quick-Check Review 1: General Control Procedures

1.1. How can preparation of the research setting improve internal validity? What must be done to the research setting to maximize external validity?

1.2. What characteristics should a research measure possess?

1.3. What is the difference between exact and systematic replication?

Control over Subject and Experimenter Effects

The behavior of both the participants and the researcher may be influenced by factors other than the independent variable, thus threatening the validity of a study. Factors such as motivation, knowledge, expectations, and information or misinformation about the study can powerfully influence behavior. Such factors can significantly bias participants and researchers, affecting not only the experimental procedure, but also the analysis and interpretation of data. Uncontrolled experimenter and/or subject effects are sufficient to cast doubt on research conclusions because they provide alternative hypotheses. Among the available controls for subject and experimenter effects are (1) single-blind and double-blind procedures, (2) automation, (3) use of objective measures, (4) multiple observers, and (5) use of deception.

Single- and Double-Blind Procedures

Experimenter effects arise from the experimenter's knowledge of (1) the hypothesis being tested, (2) the nature of the experimental and control conditions, and (3) the condition to which each participant is assigned. Such knowledge can subtly affect how the researcher interacts with participants. Experimenter effects are controlled by reducing the researcher's contact with, and/or knowledge about, the participants. The researcher might employ an assistant to run the study who does not know the condition to which each participant is assigned. That is, the assistant is **blind** to the assignment of participants to conditions. This is a **single-blind procedure.**

A more powerful control is a **double-blind procedure,** in which both the researcher and participants are blind to the assignment of each participant to a condition. The experiment is designed so that experimental and control procedures are indistinguishable. Double-blind techniques are often used in drug studies. The experimental group typically receives the drug in the form of a pill, whereas the control group receives a pill, called a **placebo,** that is identical in appearance, weight, smell, and taste, but lacks the actual drug. Neither the participants nor the researchers know who is receiving the drug and who is receiving the placebo. This is achieved by having a research assistant who is not involved in collecting the data randomly assign participants to conditions and then prepare the pills for participants. Drug studies often use capsules because it is easier to make the active treatment and the placebo appear identical. After all data are gathered, the information about each participant's experimental condition is used to analyze the results. If researchers are too secretive about this information, they might find themselves in the situation illustrated in the nearby cartoon.

Using placebo control groups in psychological research is more difficult than in drug studies. For example, suppose that a clinical researcher wants to study the effectiveness of exposure therapy for treating adult fears. Participants are randomly assigned to an experimental and a control group. The experimental group is given the exposure therapy and the control group is presented with a placebo treatment. The placebo treatment must be believable so that participants do not know that they are controls. The design problem is to create experimentally adequate, ethically acceptable, and believable placebo manipulations, which is an often difficult task.

In addition to design problems in the use of placebos, ethical issues must be considered. For ethical reasons, participants should be told that they might receive a placebo treatment. But even with such notice, is it ethical to deny treatment to some participants? For both design and ethical reasons, the use of true placebos in medical and psychological research is not recommended when an effective treatment is available. Instead of comparing a new treatment with a placebo, researchers usually compare the new treatment with the best available treatment.

Researchers should be blind to the group or condition that each participant is in during data collection. They should also remain blind during the scoring of data, especially when the scoring involves judgments, because knowledge of the hypotheses and of the conditions under which each participant is tested might affect judgments made during scoring. In some cases, however, it is impossible for researchers to be blind during certain aspects of the study. For example, in a study of sex differences in aggression, the researcher testing participants will know which participants are male and which are female. In these situations, the researcher should attempt to be blind in as many ways as possible, even if it is impossible at every stage. If, for example, the measure of aggression is verbal behavior, someone otherwise not connected with the study should transcribe the tapes of participants' verbal responses so that auditory cues to a participant's sex are not available when the data are scored. Someone other than the

"IT WAS MORE OF A 'TRIPLE-BLIND' TEST. THE PATIENTS DIDN'T KNOW WHICH ONES WERE GETTING THE REAL DRUG, THE DOCTORS DIDN'T KNOW, AND, I'M AFRAID, NOBODY KNEW."

This is taking a bit too far the principle that it is best to be blind to as many aspects of the study as possible to avoid expectancy effects.

person who tested the participants should do the scoring. In this study, the researchers who test participants should ideally be blind to the hypothesis, even if they cannot be blind to group membership. A general rule of thumb is to *test participants and score data as blindly as possible to avoid experimenter biases.*

Automation

Reducing experimenter–participant contact often reduces potential biases. One way to accomplish this is to standardize and **automate** instructions to participants and procedures for obtaining and recording participants' responses. Instructions to participants can be recorded, and the timing of instructions and recording of participants' responses can be automated with electronic equipment. The use of computers to present controlled stimuli in experiments has become standard procedure in many laboratories.

Using Objective Measures

Using **objective measures** of dependent variables is critical. A measure is objective when it is based on empirically observable and clearly specified events about which two or more people can easily agree. In contrast, subjective measures involve the impressions of the observers, which are often based on poorly specified and/or unobserved events. An example of a subjective measure is an observer's feeling that a person is anxious in a public-speaking situation. It is subjective because the observer does not specify what events were observed. Thus, it would be difficult for another observer to make the same observations and come to the same conclusions about the anxiety level of the speaker. In contrast, good objective measures precisely define the behaviors to be observed and require minimal judgments on the part of the observer. Consequently, objective measures are less prone to experimenter biases. Such measures usually produce impressive levels of interrater agreement and make replication by other researchers easier. For example, public-speaking anxiety can be operationally defined in terms of observable behavior, such as sweating, stammering, rapid speech, face flushing, and hands shaking. With objective measures, researchers know what a score means; with subjective measures, they are never sure.

Multiple Observers

In any research, especially when there might be questions about objectivity in making observations, a common control is to employ several observers to record participants' behavior. Data obtained by multiple observers are compared for agreement using interrater reliability coefficients or an index of **percent agreement.** Suppose, for example, that two raters are simultaneously observing a videotape of a group of chimpanzees. At random intervals, the observers are signaled to rate the behavior occurring at that moment as either aggressive or not aggressive. The observers are separated in booths, but are watching the same video monitor. Thus, the observers are independently rating exactly the same behaviors. Ten signals are given, and each observer rates ten instances of behavior as aggressive or not aggressive. The two observers' ratings can then be compared, as shown in Table 9.1, and a percent agreement computed. A more sophisticated index of agreement is **Kappa,** which takes into account the base rates. The **base rate** is the relative frequency of the behavior being rated. For example, if 20% of the behavior being rated is aggressive, the base rate for aggression is 20%. It is generally easier to get high percent agreement between raters when one behavior occurs almost all the time. The Kappa takes this into account. Using Kappa is beyond the scope of this textbook, but the interested student should consult Cohen (1960) and Raulin and Lilienfeld (1999) for more detail. Computational procedures for Kappa are included on the *Student Resource CD.*

Using Deception

The most common control for subject effects is to obscure the true hypothesis of the study. The researcher can deliberately misinform participants about the study or withhold

TABLE 9.1 *Computing Percent Agreement*

This hypothetical example illustrates the computation of percent agreement, or the percentage of times two raters agree on an observation.

Interval	Rater 1	Rater 2	Agree?
1	Aggressive	Aggressive	Yes
2	Aggressive	Aggressive	Yes
3	Not Aggressive	Aggressive	No
4	Not Aggressive	Not Aggressive	Yes
5	Not Aggressive	Not Aggressive	Yes
6	Not Aggressive	Not Aggressive	Yes
7	Aggressive	Aggressive	Yes
8	Aggressive	Not Aggressive	No
9	Not Aggressive	Not Aggressive	Yes
10	Aggressive	Aggressive	Yes

$$\text{Percent agreement} = \frac{\text{no. of agreements}}{\text{no. of observations}} \times 100 = \frac{8}{10} \times 100 = 80\%$$

information that might reveal the hypothesis. This control, called **deception,** is usually minor, but deception can become quite elaborate. The ethical standards for research assume that the use of deception places the participants at risk. Therefore, plans to include deception must be justified, and the researcher must provide a complete debriefing at the end of the study.

A procedure known as the **balanced placebo design** uses deception to study the effects of alcohol on behavior. Participants are asked to drink a beverage that contains either tonic only or vodka and tonic (Marlatt, Demming, & Reid, 1973; Rohsenow & Marlatt, 1981). However, what participants drink and what they are told they are drinking are not necessarily the same thing. Suppose that the study included 100 participants; 50 participants are given vodka and tonic, and 50 are given tonic. Of the 50 participants who drink tonic, half (25) are told that they are drinking tonic, and the other half (25) are told that they are drinking vodka and tonic. Similarly, half (25) of the 50 participants who drink vodka and tonic are led to believe that they are drinking tonic, and the remaining participants (25) are told that they are drinking vodka and tonic. These conditions are illustrated in Table 9.2. Because vodka is tasteless, it is almost impossible to distinguish it by taste alone as long as the drink is not too strong. To reinforce the deception that participants are drinking a vodka-tonic mixture instead of only tonic, the drinks are mixed in front of participants. Vodka (actually water in the no-alcohol condition) is carefully measured from what appears to be a new, unopened vodka bottle, with tonic added from a separate labeled bottle. This design is interesting in many respects. First, several ethical issues are raised by the deception. Therefore,

TABLE 9.2 *Balanced Placebo Design*

This table illustrates the four cells of the balanced placebo design. This design separates the pharmacological effects of alcohol from the expectancy effects.

		People Led to Believe	
		Drinking alcohol	Not drinking alcohol
Actual Situation:	Drinking alcohol		
	Not drinking alcohol		

appropriate safeguards must be included in the study. Second, it is equally desirable to have the experimenter blind to participant condition. To accomplish this, a cleverly hidden coding system is used on the bottles. The experimenter knows which bottle(s) to pour the drinks from, but does not know what each bottle contains.

The balanced placebo design has been used to separate the pharmacological effects of alcohol from the expectations of the drinker. In several studies (cf. Lang & Sibrel, 1989), the behavior of the participants was affected more strongly by whether they thought they were drinking alcohol than whether they actually were drinking alcohol. In other words, expectation effects were more potent than the pharmacological effects of alcohol. What makes the balanced placebo design work is that the participants *can* be deceived. As long as the drinks are not too strong or the participants do not drink too much alcohol, the taste and physiological cues are not strong enough to be detected. Identifying the parameters that make a deception like this work requires careful pilot testing. In some cases, a balance placebo or similar deception is possible with some participants but not with others. For example, 10-year-old children with attention-deficit/hyperactivity disorder (ADHD) apparently cannot tell whether they are taking stimulant medication or a placebo, despite the dramatic effects the medication has on their behavior. In contrast, 15-year-old children with ADHD can easily discriminate placebo and stimulant medication (Pelham et al., 1992; Pelham, 1994). In this case, a placebo deception is possible for the 10-year-olds, but not for the 15-year-olds.

Quick-Check Review 2: Control over Subject and Experimenter Effects

2.1. Name and describe the five types of controls for subject and experimenter effects.

2.2. How do single- and double-blind procedures differ?

2.3. How is deception used for control?

Control through Participant Selection and Assignment

The manner in which participants are selected and assigned to groups can affect both the internal and external validity of a study.

Participant Selection

Participant selection refers to the identification of people to participate in a study. The term *sampling* is synonymous with participant selection. Appropriate participant selection enhances external validity, allowing researchers to generalize their results. In nearly all psychological research, the investigator's interest is not limited to specific participants, but rather is focused on the larger, more general group—the population. For example, suppose that a poll is taken on Americans' attitudes toward (1) the animal rights movement, (2) hunting and trapping, and (3) gun ownership. The results of this hypothetical poll indicate that Americans are heavily opposed to animal rights (87%), highly supportive of hunting and trapping (98%), and strong opponents of gun control legislation (97%). A closer examination reveals that the poll was administered to licensed hunters in rural Montana. Obviously, there is a major problem of sampling and of external validity. From this sample of active hunters living in a western state, it is unreasonable to draw conclusions about Americans in general. Because the sample was not selected to represent all Americans, the findings of the study cannot be generalized to all Americans.

To understand participant selection, you must distinguish among (1) populations and samples, (2) general populations, target populations, and accessible populations, and (3) representative samples, random samples, stratified random samples, and ad hoc samples. The *population* is the larger group of all events of interest (people, laboratory animals, and so on) from which a sample is selected. The *sample* is a smaller number of events selected from the population and used in a study as if the sample adequately represented the population.

The **general population** is the large group of all persons, events, and so on. The **target population** is the subset in which the researcher is ultimately interested. It is usually a naturally occurring subpopulation, such as all grammar school children, all adult females, all registered voters, and so on. Target populations are typically not easily available. For example, suppose that you are interested in the level of understanding of basic science concepts in college freshmen. You cannot readily sample from all the college freshmen in the world. You do, however, have access to the 400 freshman in two local colleges. The 400 freshmen become the **accessible population** from which you will select the sample. Generalizations from your study can be made confidently to the accessible population, but you must be cautious about generalizing to the target population. Because nearly all psychological research is carried out by sampling accessible populations, such as introductory psychology students at a particular university, *we must always be cautious about generalizations made to the target population.* Replication can strengthen confidence in broader generalizations. Each replication can be carried out on different accessible populations. If the results replicate in each accessible population, your confidence in the generalizability of the findings is increased.

Researchers almost never study populations directly. Instead, they select a sample from an accessible population. They must be careful to select a **representative sample,** that is, a sample that adequately reflects population characteristics, if they want to generalize their findings. The basic idea of representativeness is simple. If the sample is representative, then the characteristics found in the population, such as sex distribution, age, intelligence, socioeconomic class, ethnicity, attitudes, political affiliations, and religious beliefs, will be found in the sample in the same proportions as in the target population. Although the concept is simple, actually obtaining a representative sample can be challenging. Furthermore, small samples often do not adequately represent populations (see Box 9.1). In general, the larger the sample is, the more likely that the sample will adequately represent the population, because larger samples tend to reduce the effects of sampling error. Another issue is that most psychological research is conducted with samples drawn from accessible populations that are not necessarily representative of the target population. The relationship among the general population, the target population, the accessible population, and the sample is illustrated in Figure 9.1.

Sampling of participants is a critical issue in social science research. Many methods have been developed to solve the problems of obtaining representative samples.

BOX 9.1 • *Small Samples Cannot Easily Represent Populations*

Why do small samples often fail to represent populations adequately? Suppose that you are sampling from a population of 1000 marbles in a large box. Fifty percent of the marbles are red, 25% are blue, and 25% are green. In this case, you know exactly what the population looks like; rarely will that be the case in real life. How big a sample do you need to represent the population adequately? Clearly, no sample of one marble could represent the population. If you select just one marble, it will be red, blue, or green. The only generalization you could make from that sample of one marble is that all the marbles in the population are the same color as the one sampled. A similar argument could be made for a sample of two marbles, which at best could represent only two of the three colors in the population. A three-marble sample might represent the three colors, but could not represent the three colors plus the fact that red is twice as common as either blue or green. Furthermore, if you compute the probability of every possible sample of three marbles, you will find that less than 20% of the possible samples contain one red, one blue, and one green marble. The minimum sample that could accurately represent the population is four marbles (two red, one blue, and one green); but if you set up a box of marbles as described and try taking samples of four marbles, you will be shocked at how rarely that particular combination comes up. Even in this simple example (a population varying on a single characteristic with only three different values), you would need samples of 30 or more marbles before the sample gave a reasonably accurate representation of the composition of the population most of the time.[1] In the far more complicated real world, in which participants vary on hundreds of variables, small samples almost never adequately represent the population.

[1]The mathematics of this computation is beyond the scope of this text. The interested student is referred to any introductory text on mathematical probability.

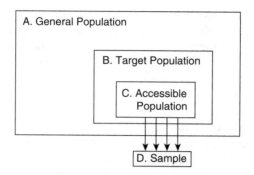

General population: All events, persons, animals, etc. (e.g., all children).

Target population: All events, persons, etc., of a particular class of interest to the researcher. This is the population to which we want to generalize our findings (e.g., all elementary school children).

Accessible population: The subset of a target population that is available to the research (e.g., elementary school children in the local school district).

Sample: The subset of an accessible population on which measures are taken. Note that occasionally a sample is drawn directly from a target population, such as in national polls of voter preferences.

FIGURE 9.1   *Relationship of the General Population to the Target Population, the Accessible Population, and the Sample*

Although some of the methods are beyond the scope of this text, we will consider three solutions to the problem of selecting a representative sample: (1) random sampling, (2) stratified random sampling, and (3) ad hoc samples.

Random Sampling.   **Random sampling** from a population means drawing the sample so that (1) every member of the population has an equal chance of being selected for the sample and (2) the selections do not affect each other, that is, the selections are independent. With random sampling, no systematic biases lead some members of the population to have a greater chance than others of being selected. If the selection of participants is truly random, then characteristics of the population, such as age, ethnicity, and intelligence, will likely be distributed in the sample in roughly the same proportion as in the population.

The best way to draw an unbiased sample from a population is to draw a random sample. This is rather like picking numbers out of a hat. In actual practice, numbers are usually drawn, not from a hat, but from a **table of random numbers** (see Appendix D) or a **random-number generator** (a computer program for generating random numbers). Both random-number tables and random-number generators meet two criteria: (1) each number has the same chance of being selected and (2) each number is independent of the others. Suppose that you want to draw a sample of 60 participants from the accessible population of 400 freshman in local colleges. You would list all 400 freshmen and assign each a number from 1 to 400. You then use the table of random numbers or a random-number generator to get random numbers from 1 to 400 until you have a total of 60 nonduplicated numbers.

Random numbers are useful for making any decision based on the principle of randomness. For example, later in this chapter you will learn about using random numbers for assigning participants to experimental conditions.

Stratified Random Sampling.   In **stratified random sampling,** separate random samples are drawn from each of several subpopulations. The subpopulations are defined in advance on the basis of one or more critical organismic variables that are likely to influence scores on the dependent measures. Small variations in the distribution of these variables in a sample can have a large effect on the results. For example, you might suspect that age is strongly correlated with the dependent measure of political preference. Therefore, the sample should closely approximate the distribution of age in the population studied. Rather than rely on random sampling, you divide the population into subpopulations on the basis of age. You then create a total sample by selecting the appropriate proportion of participants from each subpopulation. If 16% of the population is between the ages of 20 and 25, you select randomly, from that subpopulation, the number of participants it would take to make up 16% of the total sample. If the sample is 200 participants, 32 participants would be selected from the 20 to 25 age range. Stratified random samples are used extensively in sophisticated political polling operations. With this technique, samples as small as 1000 people can so closely represent the population that the outcome of elections involving several million voters can be accurately predicted. Other variables that can be stratified include, for example, socioeconomic level, education, sex, and ethnic identification.

Although random sampling is a major control for threats to external validity, psychological research rarely employs random sampling from a target population. Target populations are often difficult to access. For any large population, target or accessible, listing and numbering every individual to prepare for random selection is a sizable task. Random and stratified random samplings from a target population are important in some research, such as in political surveys, but most psychological research does not employ random selection. Rather, participants are obtained from an accessible population, such as introductory psychology students, children from local schools, and so on. Furthermore, participants are almost always volunteers. Those who do not volunteer are not included, and thus any resulting sample may be biased. The ethical demand that participants be volunteers makes it difficult for researchers to obtain a random sample of any population.

To obtain participants, researchers sometimes advertise in newspapers and college bulletin boards, offering a payment for each volunteer. Such financial incentives can increase participation rates by 50% or more (Lynn, 2001).

Ad Hoc Samples.   How can results be generalized from samples that are not randomly selected from a target population? The answer is twofold: first, you should generalize cautiously and conservatively; second, you should generalize only to other people (or to laboratory animals or events or places) having characteristics similar to those of the sample. That is, *researchers must be careful not to generalize beyond the limits of the sample.* In the examples given earlier, researchers can generalize their results only to people who are like those in their studies. In other words, the population to which you can safely generalize is defined by the characteristics of the sample. This type of sample is called an **ad hoc sample,** which is used in most psychological research. For example, a great deal of psychological research is carried out with introductory psychology students as participants. To generalize beyond ad hoc samples and yet maintain external validity, we must know the characteristics of the participants and keep the generalizations within the limits of these characteristics. Thus, when using ad hoc sampling, researchers need to obtain such descriptive data as participants' age, physical and psychological characteristics, and family socioeconomic data. The more completely the sample is described, the more secure we can be in establishing the limits of generalization and the more confidence we can have in making generalizations. When possible, it is valuable to obtain descriptive information on participants who are invited, but decline to participate, and participants who drop out before the study is completed. Comparing these participants with the participants who agree to and complete the study helps to pinpoint potential biases in participant selection and attrition that would limit generalization.

Thus, the researcher is advised to draw a random sample whenever it is feasible. In most instances, it will not be feasible, and an ad hoc sample will be used. Here the researcher should obtain sufficient descriptive information about the participants to establish the limits for generalization. The process of sampling research participants is illustrated in examples on the *Student Resource CD.*

Participant Assignment

Once participants are selected, the researcher must assign them to experimental conditions. Unbiased **participant assignment** is critical in experiments. For example, suppose that you want to test the effectiveness of teaching statistics to college students using a new computerized teaching program. In the experimental condition, students will have statistics lessons and assignments presented on the computer. In the control condition, other students will have statistics lessons and assignments presented by the instructor, using classroom lectures and demonstrations. There are two levels of the independent variable: computer presentation and teacher presentation. Suppose that 120 students have been selected as participants and that we want to assign 60 to each condition. We want to avoid, for example, assigning all female participants to one condition and all male participants to the other, or assigning the best math students to the same condition. Take another example: In a study of office working conditions, six groups of typists are compared on their typing speed (number of words per minute) and accuracy (number of errors) under six different room temperatures: 55°, 60°, 65°, 70°, 75°, and 80°. A sample of 48 typists is selected and randomly assigned to the six groups (eight participants per group). Random assignment makes it unlikely that all the best typists would be in one group. Therefore, it satisfies a very important basic principle, the **principle of initial equivalence,** which holds that all groups to be compared in an experiment must be equivalent at the start of the experiment. Of course, the groups are never *exactly* equivalent. Rather, group differences are no more than would be expected from sampling error. Random assignment automatically meets this requirement.

The ideal experiment would include (1) random selection of participants from a known population and (2) random assignment of participants to conditions. The ideal, however, is seldom achieved. As noted earlier, random selection is rare in psychological research. Therefore, caution is needed when generalizing results. *Of far greater importance in an experiment is random assignment of participants to conditions.* Random assignment is a powerful control procedure that helps to reduce many known and unknown threats to internal validity, the central issue in experiments. Researchers distinguish between free random assignment and matched random assignment.

Free Random Assignment.   **Free random assignment** of participants to conditions involves using a table of random numbers or a random-number generator. For example, in the experiment on typing speed and working conditions, the 48 participants can be randomly assigned to six conditions, eight participants per condition. The researcher numbers the participants from 01 to 48, consults the table of random numbers or a random-number generator, and assigns the first participant number encountered to the first condition, the next participant number to the second condition, and so on. The seventh participant is assigned to the first condition, eighth to the second, and so forth. The researcher continues in this way until all 48 participants are assigned to the six conditions. The same random assignment procedure would be used to assign 60 participants to the two conditions in the study of teaching arithmetic to third graders.

Randomization is a control method used in participant selection and assignment. *Randomization is the most basic and single most important control procedure,* having several major advantages: (1) it can be used to control threats to internal and external validity; (2) it can control for many variables simultaneously; and (3) it is the only control procedure that can control for unknown factors. When participants are randomly assigned to groups or conditions, potential confounding variables are distributed without biases, even if the variables have not been specifically identified. Other control methods are effective with known extraneous variables that threaten the study's validity, but randomization is effective in reducing the bias of unknown variables. This is an extremely important point. No researcher can identify all the variables that might affect the dependent measures. However, by randomly assigning participants to conditions, the researcher can distribute even the unknown factors more evenly among conditions. Note that random assignment controls for subject variables, such as age and IQ. It does not control for environmental or setting variables, such as time of day, room temperature, or background noise. For these variables, other methods, such as the general control procedures discussed earlier, are used. However, a good general rule for the researcher is *whenever possible, randomize.*

Matched Random Assignment.   **Matched random assignment** of participants to conditions is often used in small-sample research. It involves matching participants on a relevant variable and then randomly assigning the matched participants to groups, with one matched participant to each group. Many psychological studies are carried out with small numbers of participants, and researchers are often faced with the task of assigning 20 to 30 participants to two or three conditions.

Free random assignment works best with large samples, but with a small sample of participants, randomized groups can be unequal on important variables. For example, suppose that you are interested in investigating the effects of a motor-skills training program on high-tech assembly workers in an electronic equipment factory, but you have the time and resources to study only 12 workers. Your research hypothesis is that those who receive the motor-skills training (the experimental group) will improve their work performance; that is, they will show greater productivity, fewer errors, and an increase in job satisfaction compared with those who do not receive the training (the control group). Free random assignment of so small a number might result in unequal groups on important variables. You might find, for example, that most of the females or the workers with the most years of work experience have been assigned to the same group. Thus, the experimental and control groups would not have been equivalent on potentially important variables at the start of the study, and results might be due to the original differences between the groups, rather than to the effects of the independent variable, motor-skills training. That is, the independent variable might be confounded by one or more extraneous variables.

To solve the problems of working with small numbers of participants, you could use matched random assignment. To do this, you must first decide what variables are the most important potential confounding factors. Suppose that you decide that the sex of the worker is not likely to be a confounding variable. However, you suspect that the number of years worked might confound the results because more experienced workers are likely to be more proficient than less experienced workers. To carry out the matching, you would first obtain the needed information for each participant, that is, how many years each has worked. Then you list the workers ordered by years of experience, as shown in Table 9.3 and match them on this variable by taking the workers in pairs, successively, down the list. Smith, the most experienced, is matched with the next, Jones. Franks is matched with Ordell, and so on. You can now assign the participants to two groups by using a table of random numbers or by tossing a coin. Using the random-number table, the first participant of each pair is assigned to Group 1 if the number is odd or to Group 2 if the number is even. If a coin toss is used, heads or tails determine group assignment. Whichever method is used, the second participant in each pair is assigned to the other group. This procedure might result in the assignment of participants shown in Table 9.4.

TABLE 9.3   *Preparing for Matched Random Assignment*

In this example, the people available for a study are ordered based on their number of years of work experience and then paired. At the assignment stage, one member of each pair will be randomly selected and assigned to the first group, and the other member will be assigned to the second group.

Name	Sex	Number of Years Worked	Name	Sex	Number of Years Worked
Smith	F	15.7	Spero	M	9.5
Jones	M	13.8	Kling	F	9.3
Franks	M	12.2	Ruiz	F	9.0
Ordell	M	11.4	Barker	M	8.6
Samuels	F	11.0	Stanton	M	4.3
Collucci	F	10.6	Harringer	M	2.4

As is seen in Table 9.4, the mean number of years of work experience for the two groups (9.86 years and 9.60 years) are close. Because the groups are comparable on years worked, this variable cannot confound the results. Note that the groups do not have equal numbers of males and females. However, the differences are small, and sex was not considered to be a potential confounding variable in the study. This expectation, of course, might be incorrect, but given the state of knowledge at the time of the study, it is a reasonable expectation.

Matching helps to make small-group research more sensitive to the effects of the independent variable by distributing potential confounding variables equally in the groups. You can even match on more than one variable. However, it is generally not feasible to match on several variables simultaneously, because the task becomes so cumbersome and difficult that it is more efficient to test more participants and assign them to groups randomly.

Matching requires that researchers identify the variables to be matched and obtain measures of the variables for each participant. Participants can be matched on any variable. How does a researcher determine which variables are most important to match? Think about it. The variables to be matched are those, other than the independent variable, that will have the largest effect on the dependent variable. This is precisely why they need to be controlled. This issue will be addressed in more detail in Chapter 11.

Other Matching Procedures.   Other matching procedures are available. An alternative to participant-by-participant matching is to match characteristics of groups (see Chapman & Chapman, 1973). This procedure is more commonly used in differential research, but it can be useful in some experimental situations. In such situations, the researcher first identifies the variables on which the groups are to be matched and

TABLE 9.4   *Workers Matched on Experience*

The matched participants from Table 9.3 were randomly assigned to produce the groups shown here. Note how closely the groups are matched on years of work experience.

	Group 1			*Group 2*	
Name	*Sex*	*Years Worked*	*Name*	*Sex*	*Years Worked*
Jones	M	13.8	Smith	F	15.7
Franks	M	12.2	Ordell	M	11.4
Collucci	F	10.6	Samuels	F	11.0
Kling	F	9.3	Spero	M	9.5
Ruiz	F	9.0	Barker	M	8.6
Stanton	M	4.3	Harringer	M	2.4
% Females	3/6 = 50%				2/6 = 33%
Mean No. Yr Worked	9.86				9.60

measures these variables for each potential participant. Using a randomization procedure, the researcher assigns participants to one of the two groups and calculates this
group's mean and standard deviation on each variable to be matched. The researcher
then selects the second group of participants so that it has a comparable mean and
standard deviation on the variables. The result is that the two groups are equivalent on
the matching variables, but individuals in one group are not matched with individuals
in the other group. Because the groups are comparable on the matching variables, potential confounding is avoided.

A variation of matching is to equate groups by holding the variable constant. For
example, if you want to match on age, you could use only participants of approximately the same age. If there is little or no variability on this factor between the experimental and control groups, this factor cannot be a source of confounding. However, a
disadvantage to matching by holding the variable constant is that it reduces external
validity; that is, it reduces the ability to generalize the results of the study to the larger
population. For example, if you used only adult participants, you would be unable to
generalize with confidence to adolescents.

Matching by building the variable into the study is another control method. It
creates what is known as a *factorial design,* which will be discussed in Chapter 12.
Suppose that you want to evaluate how the manner of dress affects social class ratings
among high school students. High school students are asked to rate social class for a
dozen students that they have never met and about whom their only information is a 2-
minute video sequence of a hallway conversation with friends. The independent variable is the manner of dress of the students to be rated. The dependent variable is the
social class rating made by the participants. However, you are concerned about confounding due to differences in age and social development; that is, freshman might
view the concept of social class differently from seniors. To control for this, you make
the academic class variable (freshman, sophomore, junior, senior) a part of the study.
Therefore, participants in each group are of similar age, and you are able to determine
the influence of the age variable.

Several exercises on the *Student Resource CD* illustrate the process of assignment of participants to conditions.

Quick-Check Review 3: Control through Participant Selection and Assignment

3.1. Define the general population, target population, accessible population, and sample.

3.2. Why is it important that samples be drawn carefully from a population?

3.3. Define each type of sampling discussed in this section.

3.4. Why is unbiased assignment of participants to conditions so important in experiments?

3.5. What does matching participants control?

Control through Experimental Design

Protecting internal validity is critical in experiments because it bears on the very essence of experimentation: the predicted causal relationship between the independent and dependent variables. Experimental methods are the best procedures for protecting internal validity. **Experimental design** refers to the careful arrangement of all parts of the experiment so as to (1) test the effects of the independent variable on the dependent variable and (2) protect against threats to internal validity.

Several experimental designs are available. The basic experimental designs are discussed in Chapter 10, and variations on those designs are discussed in Chapters 11 and 12. Here we will introduce the concept of experimental design by first discussing a nonexperimental design: the pretest–posttest design illustrated in Figure 9.2. Suppose that a psychologist is studying children with attention-deficit/hyperactivity disorder (ADHD). A central problem of these children is an inability to stay focused on a task. Therefore, they often have difficulty learning to read. The psychologist develops a cognitive self-control training program geared specifically to reading tasks. Once trained in a six-step cognitive procedure, the children silently rehearse the steps just before approaching any reading task in school. The researcher tests the effectiveness of the training by using a pretest–posttest design. She first took pretraining measures of reading ability of five children with ADHD, then trained them in the six-step cognitive self-control procedures, and then again tested them for reading ability.

Suppose that the researcher found a statistically significant difference between the pretest and posttest measures. This finding might seem sufficient to conclude that the training improved reading, but it is not. Such a conclusion cannot be drawn because of possible confounding. To avoid confounding variables (in this case, due to maturation and history), the researcher would have to anticipate them and build suitable controls into the research design. In this instance, a good control would be a no-treatment **control group,** that is, an equivalent group of ADHD children who do not receive cognitive self-control training. Suppose that there are 20 ADHD children in the program. The researcher could randomly assign 10 of the children to the **experimental group** that receives the treatment and 10 to the control group that does not. All the children would remain in the general program and receive the same general treatment. However, only the experimental group would receive the cognitive self-control training. This is the pretest–posttest, control-group design illustrated in Table 9.5.

FIGURE 9.2 *Simple Pretest–Posttest Design*

TABLE 9.5   *Pretest–Posttest, Control-Group Design*

A. Experimental group	Pretest for reading ability	Self-control training	Posttest for reading ability
B. Control group	Pretest for reading ability	No self-control training	Posttest for reading ability

The question is whether the experimental group shows significantly greater reading performance than the control group at the posttest. Suppose that this is exactly what the researcher finds. Then the researcher can have considerably more confidence in concluding that self-control training is responsible for the difference, because the confounding variables of maturation and history have been controlled. Maturation is controlled because, if the experimental and control groups are equivalent at the start of the experiment, the researcher can expect maturation to occur equally in the two groups. Confounding due to history is controlled because both groups receive all other treatments in the general program. Thus, if some program factor other than self-control training affects reading performance, it would affect both groups equally.

For the control-group design to be effective, it is *essential that the experimental and control groups be comparable at the start of the experiment.* If the experimental group has more of the most capable, older, or better-adjusted children, then confounding due to selection is present. Confounding due to selection is controlled by assigning the participants to the two groups in an unbiased manner. Thus, in this example, random assignment of participants controlled for confounding due to selection, and the inclusion of a no-treatment control group controlled for confounding due to maturation and history. Routinely including these two basic control procedures in designs of this sort, (1) unbiased assignment of participants to conditions and (2) inclusion of appropriate control groups or conditions, controls most potential confounding.

In the ADHD study, the independent variable of cognitive self-control training is presented at two levels: all or none. The independent variable must vary in experiments; it must be actively manipulated so that it varies from one condition to another. There can be more than two levels; the hypothetical study of typists' productivity at different room temperatures described earlier included six levels of the independent variable. This design does not have one control group, but six levels of the independent variable, each of which operates as a control for all other levels.

Scientific research generally is characterized by attention to details, such as developing carefully reasoned and clearly stated concepts, well-developed operational definitions, use of inductive–deductive logic, careful measurement of the observed variables, and use of appropriate statistical methods to analyze data. Experiments share these characteristics, but also have the following five characteristics:

1. A clearly stated research hypothesis concerning predicted causal effects of one variable on another
2. At least two levels of the independent variable
3. Unbiased assignment of participants to conditions

4. Specific and systematic procedures for empirically testing the hypothesized causal relationships
5. Specific controls to reduce threats to internal validity

The task in experiments is to answer questions about causality and to control for threats to validity. To do so, the researcher must arrange the experiment in such a way as to answer this research question: Does the hypothesized causal relationship between the independent and dependent variables exist? The task of arranging the components of the experiment is what is meant by experimental design. In essence, experimental design provides a detailed plan for the conduct of the experiment. Once the design is formalized, the researcher proceeds through it step by step as planned. Remember that at the high-constraint level of experimentation, there is no flexibility to alter any part of the design once the study begins. Chapters 10 through 12 discuss a variety of experimental designs.

Quick-Check Review 4: Control through Experimental Design

4.1. What does unbiased assignment of participants to groups accomplish?

4.2. What are the five characteristics of any experimental design?

Chapter Summary

Four major groups of control procedures were defined: (1) general control procedures, (2) control of subject and experimenter effects, (3) control through participant selection and assignment, and (4) control through experimental design.

General control procedures include careful preparation of the research setting, specification of measurement instruments, and replication. Subject and experimenter effects are controlled by keeping the researcher and participants blind to both the hypotheses and the condition under which each participant is tested and by using automated procedures, objective measures, multiple observers, and deception when necessary. Appropriate participant selection, such as random sampling, helps to control for threats to external validity, whereas random assignment of participants to conditions helps to control for threats to internal validity.

Experiments test hypothesized causal relationships between at least two variables in a way that rules out alternative explanations of the results. Procedures to control for threats to validity are at the center of experimental design. The development of controls to their highest degree is a major factor that distinguishes experimentation from other levels of constraint in research.

Most threats to validity can be controlled by routinely including three basic control procedures: (1) unbiased participant selection or careful description of an ad hoc sample, (2) unbiased assignment of participants to conditions, and (3) inclusion of appropriate control groups.

Key Terms

Define the following key terms. Be sure that you understand them. They are discussed in the chapter and defined in the glossary.

control	Kappa	random-number generator
exact replication	base rate	stratified random sampling
systematic replication	deception	ad hoc sample
conceptual replication	balanced placebo design	participant assignment
blind	participant selection	principle of initial
single-blind procedure	general population	equivalence
double-blind procedure	target population	free random assignment
placebo	accessible population	matched random assignment
automation	representative sample	experimental design
objective measure	random sampling	control group
percent agreement	table of random numbers	experimental group

10

Control of Variance through Experimental Design

Single-Variable, Independent-Groups Designs

Observation is a passive science; experimentation is an active science.

—Claude Bernard, *Introduction á l'Etude de la Medecine Experimental,* 1865

CD Resource Material _____

Web Resource Material _____

215

This chapter introduces basic experimental designs and their supporting concepts. It begins by outlining key points in experimental design and then discusses a concept that was first introduced in Chapter 5, variance. Experimental design involves the measurement and control of sources of variance. The chapter reviews nonexperimental designs to illustrate how they fail to provide adequate control before discussing experimental designs. The statistical procedures used to evaluate basic experimental designs are then discussed. The chapter ends by outlining other experimental designs that are covered in Chapters 11 and 12.

Scientific research uses highly evolved procedures to find answers to questions. It is at the experimental level of constraint that the design process is most completely developed. Experiments share five specific characteristics. The experiment:

1. States one or more hypotheses about predicted causal effects of the independent variable(s) on the dependent variable(s).
2. Includes at least two levels of the independent variable.
3. Assigns participants to conditions in an unbiased manner, such as through random assignment.
4. Includes specific procedures for testing hypotheses.
5. Includes controls for major threats to internal validity.

Planning is critical in experimental research. The researcher (1) develops a problem statement, (2) identifies and defines important theoretical constructs, (3) identifies and operationally defines independent and dependent variables, (4) formulates research hypotheses, (5) identifies a population, (6) deals with all ethical considerations, (7) selects and assigns participants to conditions, (8) specifies the details of observational procedures, (9) anticipates threats to validity, (10) creates controls, and (11) specifies the procedures for data analysis. All this planning is carried out before observing a single participant. Experimental design refers to both the activity involved in the planning of the experiment and the product—the plan itself. A well-developed experimental design provides a blueprint for the experimenter to follow. We cannot emphasize enough the importance of developing a clear experimental design *before beginning observations.* Careful planning can build in the controls necessary to have confidence in our conclusions. Therefore, *plan the experiment carefully and carry it out exactly as planned.*

Variance

We previously discussed several concepts that we will bring together in this section, including variance (Chapter 5), internal validity (Chapter 8), and control (Chapter 9). Much of the following material is a summary of those earlier discussions.

Variation is necessary in experiments. Without variation there would be no differences to test. In experiments, the independent variables are manipulated in order to cause variation between experimental and control conditions. However, extraneous variation, that is, variation not associated with the independent variable manipulation, is a problem. It can threaten the validity of a study by allowing alternative explanations of results;

this reduces confidence in drawing causal inferences. Experimental design is a blueprint for controlling extraneous variation. It has two basic purposes: (1) to provide answers to questions by testing causal hypotheses and (2) to control variance in order to increase internal validity (Kerlinger, 1992). Note that several concepts—levels of constraint, reducing threats to validity, control of variance—are related, all referring to issues of control. Variance is the major underlying concept in experimental research.

Sources of Variance

There are two relevant sources of variance in experimental design: (1) systematic between-groups variance and (2) nonsystematic within-groups variance, which is also called error variance.

Systematic Between-Groups Variance.   An experiment tests the effects of an independent variable on the dependent variable(s). This is done by setting up at least two levels of the independent variable and measuring participants' responses on the dependent variable(s). The researcher predicts that the dependent measures will differ significantly among the groups defined by the independent variable; that is, there will be significant variability among the group means. Significant variability means that the variability among the means will be larger than expected on the basis of sampling error alone. Recall from Chapter 5 that sampling error refers to the natural variation among samples drawn from the same population. Researchers predict a *significantly high variance between the groups* in an experiment. If there is little between-groups variance, that is, if the groups are essentially the same on the dependent measures, then the independent variable had no effect.

Suppose, for example, that a researcher wants to test the hypothesis that a recorded laugh track in television comedies increases viewers' enjoyment of the show. One hundred people have been randomly assigned to two groups, 50 in each group. The experimental group views the show with a laugh track, and the control group views the same show minus the laugh track. Then all participants rate their enjoyment of the show. Because participants have been randomly assigned, the researcher can assume that there is no significant difference between the groups prior to the manipulation. The prediction is that the group with the laugh track will rate the show as more enjoyable than will the control group; that is, we expect to find a significant between-groups variance at the completion of viewing.

Finding a significant difference between the groups, that is, finding that the **systematic between-groups variance** is high, does not mean that the independent variable is responsible for the difference. The significant difference may be due to either (1) the effect of the independent variable (**experimental variance**), (2) the effects of uncontrolled confounding variables (**extraneous variance**), or (3) a combination of the two. That is, the between-groups variance is a function of both experimental effects and confounding variables. Furthermore, the natural variability due to sampling error adds a small amount of group variability. The systematic between-groups variance in the experiment might be statistically significant, thus tempting the researcher to conclude that there is a causal relationship between the independent variable and dependent variable.

But suppose that the between-groups variance is high only because of systematic influence of confounding variables and not because of the independent variable; that is, suppose that the observed differences were due to the extraneous variance and not to the experimental variance. Statistical tests determine only whether there is a significant difference between the groups, not whether the observed difference is due to experimental or extraneous variance. If there is any possibility that the group differences are due to extraneous factors, then we cannot draw a causal inference. It is for this reason that confounding must be anticipated and procedures selected to control it. *Therefore, you want to maximize the experimental variance (due to the independent variable) and control the extraneous variance (due to confounding variables).*

Nonsystematic Within-Groups Variance.   The term **error variance** denotes the **nonsystematic within-groups variability.** Error variance is due to random factors that affect some participants more than others within a group, whereas systematic variance reflects influences on all members of each group. Error variance may be increased by unstable factors, such as some participants feeling ill or upset when tested. Error variance may also be increased by stable factors, such as individual differences in motor coordination, personality, interest, and motivation. Error variance is also increased by experimenter or equipment variations that cause measurement errors for some participants but not for others in the same group. Because no two participants are exactly alike and no procedure is perfect, there will always be some error variance.

Nonsystematic within-groups influences are largely random. There should be just as much chance that random influences will occur in one direction as in another and will have as much chance of affecting any one participant in the group as any other. Thus, if random influences cause some participants to score lower than they ordinarily would, other random influences will cause other participants to score higher than they ordinarily would. That is, within-groups random influences tend to cancel each other. Although some participants score too high, others score too low, but the mean of the group as a whole is not affected, although the variance is affected. In contrast, systematic between-groups factors influence all participants in a group in one direction. The effects are not random; they do not cancel each other. As a result, the mean of the group is moved up or down by systematic between-group factors depending on the direction of their influence.

In summary, we make the distinction between

1. Systematic between-groups variance, which includes
   a. Experimental variance (due to independent variables) and
   b. Extraneous variance (due to confounding variables)
2. Nonsystematic within-groups error variance (due to chance factors).

It is important to repeat that the between-groups variance is a function not only of the systematic between-groups variance (experimental and extraneous variance), but also of the nonsystematic effects that are due to sampling error. Even when there is absolutely no systematic between-groups variance, there will still be small differences between groups due to sampling error. Systematic between-groups variance increases the between-groups variance beyond the variability due to sampling error. The way data are analyzed is to compare the between-groups variation and within-groups variation. As you will see later, the ratio of these two measures defines the *F*-test:

$$F = \frac{\text{measure based on between-groups variation}}{\text{measure based on within-groups variation}} \qquad (10.1)$$

Without statistical detail, let us consider the principles involved in evaluating the relationship of the between-groups variation and the within-groups variation. The measure based on the between-groups variation (the numerator) is due to both the systematic effects (experimental variance plus extraneous variance) and the effects of sampling error (error variance). The measure based on within-groups error variation (the denominator) is due only to error variance. These terms are computed in such a way that the error variance is the same value in both the numerator and the denominator of the formula. Therefore, the preceding equation can be written as

$$F = \frac{\text{sytematic effects} + \text{error variance}}{\text{error variance}} \qquad (10.2)$$

Suppose that there are no systematic effects. In this case, both the numerator and the denominator represent error variance only, and the ratio would be 1.00. Whenever the *F*-ratio is near 1.00, it means that no systematic effects are present. In other words, the between-groups variation is no larger than we would expect by chance alone. On the other hand, suppose that the measure based on the between-groups variation is substantially greater than the measure based on the within-groups error variation. This would suggest that there are systematic effects. In this case, the researcher would conclude that the groups do differ. This is the basic idea behind the *F*-test.

Controlling Variance in Research

To show a causal effect of the independent variable on the dependent variable, the experimental variance must be high and not distorted by excessive extraneous variance or masked by error variance. The greater the extraneous and/or error variance, the more difficult it becomes to show the causal effects of an independent variable on a dependent variable. This idea leads to a general but important rule: *In experimentation, each study is designed so as to maximize experimental variance, control extraneous variance, and minimize error variance.*

Maximizing Experimental Variance.   Experimental variance is due to the effects of the independent variable(s) on the dependent variable(s). There must be at least two levels of the independent variable in an experiment. In fact, it is advisable to include more than two levels of the independent variable, because more information can then be gained about the relationship between the independent and dependent variable(s). To demonstrate an effect, the researcher must be sure that the independent variable really varies; that is, the experimental conditions truly differ from one another.

It is often useful to include a **manipulation check** in a study to evaluate whether the manipulation actually had its intended effect on participants. Suppose that in a study of the effects of anxiety on performance the researcher plans to manipulate anxiety by changing the feedback given to participants during a training period, reasoning that participants who think that they are doing poorly will be more anxious than participants who think that they are doing well. Therefore, the researcher sets up two conditions. In one, the participants are told that they did well during training and should have no problems during the actual testing (the low-anxiety group). A second group is told that they did badly during the training and that they must try harder if they want to avoid making themselves look foolish (the high-anxiety group). How do you know if this manipulation actually affected the anxiety level of participants? One way is to ask participants to rate their anxiety and see if the experimental group was more anxious than the controls. This procedure of checking on the effectiveness of an experimental manipulation is called a *manipulation check*. If the groups did not differ on anxiety, then the manipulation of anxiety was ineffective. Consequently, the study provides no basis to evaluate the effect of anxiety on the dependent measure.

The importance of a manipulation check is illustrated in the results of the hypothetical study that is graphed in Figure 10.1. This study looked at differences in the level of hostile expression among men and women in response to an anger provocation. It was hypothesized that males typically externalized anger and therefore reacted with hostility when angered. In contrast, it was hypothesized that women internalized anger, thus not acting hostile when angered. The rationale for a study like this comes from the psychodynamic explanation of depression, which is conceptualized as "anger turned inward." Because women are twice as likely to develop depression as men, this study looked at a possible mechanism for this sex difference, specifically, that women are more likely to internalize anger, thus increasing their risk for depression.

Anger was manipulated by having the researcher mess up several things in a row during the study, thus forcing participants to repeat parts of the study. The results of this hypothetical study are illustrated in Figure 10.1(a), and the results clearly seem to be consistent with the hypothesis. However, two manipulation checks were included in the study, which are shown in Figures 10.1(b) and (c). These checks looked at the reported level of anger and the level of physiological arousal, respectively. If the anger provocation was effective, these variables should show it. Even if women turned anger inward and therefore did not report experiencing increased anger, the physiological measures should be elevated. However, in this hypothetical study, both the reported levels of anger and the levels of physiological arousal show the same pattern in men and women as the expressed hostility-dependent measure.

How do we interpret such findings? The most parsimonious interpretation is that the anger manipulation worked for males but not for females. Perhaps females were more empathetic to the problems that the researcher was experiencing? What is clear is that it would not be wise to say that this study shows that women internalize anger more than men because they expressed less hostility. Perhaps another anger provocation procedure, such as insulting comments about a person's appearance or attitudes, would have angered both men and women and shown a different pattern of results. What the manipulation check shows is that caution is necessary because it is not clear that anger was actually produced in both the men and women. If the manipulation check had shown that both men and women reported equivalent levels of increased anger and showed equivalent levels of increased arousal, then it would be more clear that men express hostility more than women when angered.

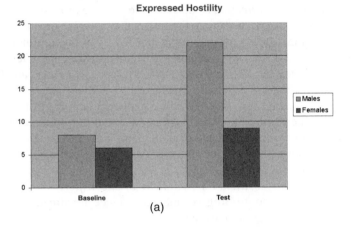

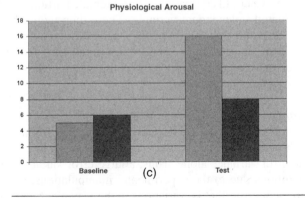

FIGURE 10.1 *Importance of Including Manipulation Checks* This hypothetical data set illustrates how manipulation checks can clarify the meaning of data. The hostility data suggest that males do react with more hostility when angered than females, but the manipulation checks suggest that the reason for this pattern is that the anger provocation only worked for the males.

Controlling Extraneous Variance.   As discussed earlier, extraneous variables are those between-group variables, other than the independent variables, that have effects on whole groups and may thus confound the results. Most of the common sources of extraneous variance were discussed in Chapter 8. To demonstrate the effects of an experimental manipulation, it is necessary to control extraneous variables and keep them from differentially affecting the groups. In this regard, two important ideas are basic in experimentation: We must be sure that (1) the experimental and control groups are as similar as possible at the start of the experiment and (2) that they are treated in exactly the same way except for the independent-variable manipulation. These were discussed in Chapter 9 and are summarized here. The general concept to remember in controlling extraneous variance is to *make sure that the independent-variable manipulation is the only difference in the researcher's treatment of the experimental and control groups.* Several methods for controlling extraneous variance are aimed at ensuring that the groups are equal at the beginning of the study.

1. The best method of controlling for extraneous variance is random assignment to groups, which decreases the probability that the groups will differ on extraneous variables. Thus, *whenever possible, randomly assign participants to conditions.*
2. If a factor, such as age, ethnic identification, social class, intelligence, or sex, is a potential confounding variable, we can control it by selecting participants who are as homogeneous as possible on this variable. For example, we could select only males or only females or select participants who are within a few IQ points of each other. The cost of using this as a control is that it limits generalizability. By using only males or females, for example, conclusions are limited to only one sex.
3. A potential confounding variable also can be controlled by *building it into the experiment as an additional independent variable.* Thus, if sex is a potentially confounding variable, we could compare male and female participants by adding sex as a nonmanipulated independent variable. There then would be two independent variables in the study, a design known as a factorial design (see Chapter 12). Note that sex is not manipulated because it is a preexisting factor.
4. Extraneous variance can be controlled by matching participants or by using a within-subjects design (see Chapter 11).

Minimizing Error Variance.   Error variance is within-groups variance that is due to chance factors and individual differences. There is always some error variation. Remember that a statistically significant difference between conditions is one that is greater than is expected based on the error variance alone. Thus, a large error variance can obscure differences between conditions due to the experimental manipulations. One source of error variance is measurement error, that is, variations in the way a participant responds from trial to trial due to such factors as unreliability of the measurement instruments. To minimize these sources of error variance, we must *maintain carefully controlled conditions of measurement and be sure that the measuring instruments are reliable.*

Another major source of error variance is individual differences. Within-subjects or matched-subjects designs, which are covered in Chapter 11, minimize this source of error variance. There are problems in using within-subjects designs, such as sequence effects, but the within-subjects design does reduce error variance by eliminating the individual differences component.

This brief discussion of maximizing experimental variance, controlling extraneous variance, and minimizing error variance is a summary of the earlier discussions of control. That is, control in research is **control of variance.** The general control procedures discussed in Chapter 9 deal with the control of error variance. Other control procedures help to control both error variance and extraneous variance. The most powerful control for extraneous variance is a properly selected experimental design in which participants are randomly assigned to conditions.

Quick-Check Review 1: Variance

1.1. What is systematic, between-groups variance?

1.2. Define experimental variance and extraneous variance.

1.3. What is error variance?

1.4. What is the *F*-test? What is it used for?

1.5. What are the ways of controlling extraneous variance?

1.6. How do we minimize error variance?

Nonexperimental Approaches

To appreciate the advantages of experimental designs, you need to understand the limitations of nonexperimental approaches. We will discuss several such approaches, including these:

1. Ex post facto studies
2. Single-group, posttest-only studies
3. Single-group, pretest–posttest studies
4. Pretest–posttest, natural control-group studies

In this and the next section, we will consider examples of research, beginning with nonexperimental approaches and progressing to experimental designs. As we progress along this continuum, notice that each successive design controls for more sources of extraneous variance. We will borrow heavily in the following discussion from the classic book of Campbell and Stanley (1966).

Ex Post Facto Studies

In the **ex post facto study** ("after the fact"; illustrated in Table 10.1), the researcher observes current behavior and attempts to relate it to earlier experiences. A therapist might observe some difficulty in a client and conclude that the problem was caused by

TABLE 10.1 *Ex Post Facto Approach*

Group A	(Naturally occurring events) (No direct manipulation)	Measurement

This design cannot eliminate rival hypotheses because none of the potentially confounding factors are controlled.

earlier life events that the therapist never directly observed or manipulated. For example, many people have concluded that abused children become abusive parents based on the observation that a large proportion of abusive parents report that they were abused as children. This conclusion is arrived at in an ex post facto manner. As reasonable as the conclusion seems, we can have little confidence in its validity because there were no controls for confounding factors. If we cannot control for confounding, then rival hypotheses cannot be eliminated. The simple observation above does not rule out the possibility that abusive parents are no more likely to have been abused as children than nonabusive parents. Thus, a causal relationship between the independent and dependent variables cannot be inferred.

Let's look at another example. Suppose that a researcher suspects that such food additives as artificial colors, flavors, and preservatives stimulate hyperactive behavior in some children. Obtaining a sample of 30 hyperactive children, the researcher finds that 28 of them (93%) eat foods containing these additives every day. The number seems high to the researcher, and the findings are consistent with the researcher's suspicion that there may be a relationship between food additives and hyperactivity. The researcher can even formulate the hypothesis for future testing that food additives stimulate hyperactivity. However, because the researcher followed an ex post facto procedure, a valid conclusion that a causal relationship exists between food additives and hyperactive behavior cannot be made.

An ex post facto study can generate hypotheses to test with higher-constraint studies, but is not itself capable of testing causal hypotheses. Because no independent variable is manipulated in ex post facto studies, controls to guard against confounding cannot be applied. Consequently, the researcher cannot know which variable(s) may have affected the results and therefore *cannot eliminate rival hypotheses.* That is, any of several confounding variables may have been responsible. For example, the hyperactivity might be due to parental behavior, genetic factors, or the influences of other children, none of which were evaluated. Consequently, results from ex post facto studies should be interpreted with great caution.

Single-Group, Posttest-Only Studies

The **single-group, posttest-only study,** illustrated in Table 10.2, is at a somewhat higher level of constraint than ex post facto procedures. Here the independent variable is manipulated with a single group and the group is then measured.

Suppose, for example, that a clinician wants to determine whether eliminating foods containing the additives thought to increase hyperactivity will help hyperactive

TABLE 10.2   *Single-Group, Posttest-Only Study*

Group A	Treatment	Posttest

The term ***treatment*** as used in these tables refers to any kind of manipulation of the independent variable. This design fails to control the confounding factors of placebo effects, maturation, history, and regression to the mean.

children. She asks parents of 20 children diagnosed as hyperactive to eliminate the foods from their children's diets for 4 weeks. At the end of the period, the children are tested for hyperactivity, and 12 out of the 20 children are found to be hyperactive. Here there has been an actual manipulation in the form of the dietary change, as well as measurement of posttreatment hyperactivity levels. But there are problems in this approach that prevent the researcher from drawing causal inferences about the treatment's effect on hyperactivity.

There are several confounding factors. Perhaps the children did not change at all, but because there was no pretreatment measurement, there was no way of knowing this. Perhaps there was a change, but it was a placebo effect, a change produced only by the expectation of improvement. Perhaps the children did improve, but the improvement was due to some other uncontrolled factor, such as another program in which the children were involved. Perhaps the children matured over the 4 weeks of treatment, and their low hyperactivity was actually due to their natural maturation. Perhaps they did become less active during the program but it was only a natural return to their normal activity level. It may have been a temporary peak in their activity level that prompted parents to bring their children in for treatment. In other words, the single-group, posttest-only study does not control for the confounding variables of placebo effects, history, maturation, or regression to the mean. The researcher cannot even be sure if there was any change in activity level.

Single-Group, Pretest–Posttest Studies

Single-group, pretest–posttest studies, illustrated in Table 10.3, are an improvement over the posttest-only approach because they include a pretreatment evaluation. The researcher studying hyperactivity, for example, might select a sample of hyperactive children and (1) observe them for rates of hyperactive behavior, (2) impose the 4-week dietary restrictions, and (3) observe them again for hyperactivity at the end of the 4 weeks. Suppose that the posttest measurement of hyperactivity is significantly less than the pretest measurement; the children clearly improved from pretest to posttest. Now we know that there was improvement, but the single-group, pretest–posttest study still fails to control for placebo effects, maturation, history, and regression to the mean. That is, the measured improvement might have occurred only because the children and parents expected improvement (placebo effect), because the children matured during the treatment period (maturation), because of some other factor in the program that was operating but was uncontrolled (history), or because the pretest measures of hyperactivity were at an abnormally high peak and they naturally returned in

TABLE 10.3   *Single-Group, Pretest–Posttest Study*

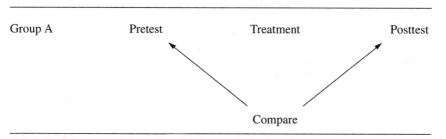

Group A   Pretest   Treatment   Posttest

Compare

This design fails to control the confounding factors of placebo effects, maturation, history, and regression to the mean.

time to about their mean level (regression). To avoid these confounding variables, an additional control is necessary, as you will see shortly.

In the preceding discussion, we noted that the single-group, pretest–posttest study fails to control for the confounding variable of maturation. In some research, however, maturation is not considered a confounding variable; rather, it is the phenomenon under study. Developmental psychologists focus much of their research on the process of maturation. They often use designs similar to the pretest–posttest design described here, but without the manipulation. This is called a longitudinal design, in which the same participants are followed over time. Typically, multiple measures are taken over the course of a developmental study. This multiple-measures design is called a **time-series design.** In a developmentally focused longitudinal study, maturation is elevated from the status of a confounding variable to the phenomenon of interest. Thus, the "treatment" shown in Table 10.3 is actually the passage of time. However, it is important to realize that such variables as history can confound the study of maturation unless appropriate controls are included. We will discuss this in more detail in the section on time-series designs in Chapter 13.

Pretest–Posttest, Natural Control-Group Studies

A good control to add to the preceding studies is a no-treatment control group. In the **pretest–posttest, natural control-group study,** which is illustrated in Table 10.4, naturally occurring groups are used, only one of which receives the treatment. Participants are not randomly assigned to groups as they would be in an experimental design.

TABLE 10.4   *Pretest–Posttest, Natural Control-Group Study*

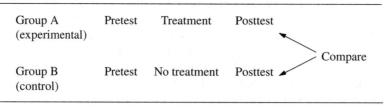

Group A (experimental)	Pretest	Treatment	Posttest	
				Compare
Group B (control)	Pretest	No treatment	Posttest	

This design fails to control for selection, but provides control for history and maturation.

For example, two intact classrooms might be used, with students from one classroom assigned to the first group and students from the other classroom assigned to the second group. Addition of this control group significantly strengthens the design.

The natural control-group approach is very close to an experimental design. However, this approach still has a weakness in that there is no procedure, such as random assignment, to ensure that the two groups are statistically equivalent at the start of the study; that is, the only difference between the groups is due to sampling error. For example, suppose that in forming the experimental and control groups the researcher asked parents if they were willing to try the 4-week dietary restrictions. The children of those parents who were willing to expend the effort were put in the experimental group, and those who were not were put in the control group. The serious confounding in this procedure is that the experimental and the control groups are different in terms of parents' willingness to try the dietary restrictions. In other words, the dietary restriction treatment is confounded with parents' willingness to cooperate. We might assume that parents who are willing to do everything necessary to change their child's diet in hope of decreasing their child's hyperactivity may be more motivated to help their child to change. Any posttreatment differences between the groups on measures of hyperactivity might be due to either factor: dietary restriction or parental willingness to cooperate. The children in the two groups may even have been different on the level of hyperactivity before the experiment began. It may be that parents with the most hyperactive children are the most desperate and are therefore the most likely to try *any kind* of treatment. The pretest in the design would allow a researcher to check this possibility.

When you compare groups of participants at different levels of the independent variable, it is essential that the groups be equivalent on the dependent measures at the start of the study. Random assignment of participants to conditions is one way of increasing your confidence that the groups are equivalent at the start of the study. Random assignment to conditions is one of the hallmarks of experimental design, which is the topic of the next section.

Quick-Check Review 2: Nonexperimental Approaches

2.1. Identify four nonexperimental approaches. Define each and discuss its limitations.

2.2. Of these four approaches, which is the weakest? Why?

2.3. When is maturation not considered a confounding variable? What type of design is typically used to study maturational processes?

Experimental Designs

Two critical factors distinguish **experimental designs** from most nonexperimental designs. They are *control groups* (or conditions) and *randomization*. These two factors will control most threats to internal validity. The addition of one or more control groups to nonexperimental designs can improve them considerably. Including proper control groups helps to control history, maturation, and regression to the mean. The experimental designs discussed here all include at least one control group. To make the control groups effective, participants must be randomly assigned to conditions. Also, the random selection of participants from a population is a valuable control that helps to protect external validity. Randomization is a powerful tool. A good general rule to follow in designing research is to *randomize whenever possible.*

Because there are so many different experimental designs, we will divide our discussion into several sections. In this chapter, we will discuss designs appropriate for evaluating a single independent variable using independent groups of participants. Chapter 11 focuses on designs for testing a single independent variable using correlated groups of participants. Chapter 12 focuses on designs used for testing more than one independent variable in a single experiment. Chapter 13 focuses on designs that test causal hypotheses in natural environments.

Although many variations of experimental designs are possible, four basic designs are used to test a single independent variable using independent groups of participants. These **single-variable, between-subjects designs** include the following:

1. Randomized, posttest-only, control-group design
2. Randomized, pretest–posttest, control-group design
3. Multilevel, completely randomized, between-subjects design
4. Solomon's four-group design

Randomized, Posttest-Only, Control-Group Design

Suppose that you want to evaluate the effects of an experimental treatment for disruptive behavior,[1] a special tutorial program for reading skills, visual stimulus complexity on target detection, or food additives on hyperactivity. In each case, you wish to manipulate a variable and measure the effects, but you want to do it in such a way that unwanted variance is controlled and validity is protected. The best approach by far is an experiment.

The most basic experimental design is the **randomized, posttest-only, control-group design,** which includes randomization and a control group. You first randomly select participants from a general or accessible population or carefully define an ad hoc sample. Your participants are then randomly assigned to the experimental (treatment) and control (no-treatment) conditions. The resulting design, using the letter R to indicate random assignment to groups, is illustrated in Table 10.5. The arrows denote the critical comparison to be made to test the hypothesis that the independent variable significantly affected the dependent measures. The critical comparison is between the two levels of the independent variable (experimental and control groups) on the dependent variable at posttest. It is critical for this comparison that the two groups be equivalent at the beginning of the study. If they are not, then you cannot know if differences at the posttest are due to the independent variable or to preexisting differences

---

[1]Note that the terms *treatment* and *manipulation* are used interchangeably.

TABLE 10.5   *Randomized, Posttest-Only, Control-Group Design*

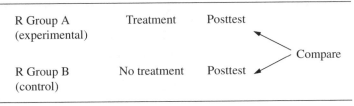

The R in front of the group label means that participants are randomly assigned to groups.

between the groups. Random assignment of participants to groups increases the probability that the groups are equivalent at the beginning of the study. Furthermore, when participants are randomly assigned to groups, the small probability that the groups might not be equal due to sampling error is automatically factored into the statistical analysis. When participants have been randomly assigned to groups, the groups are said to be **statistically equal,** because the small differences that do exist are the results of sampling error.

Several threats to validity are controlled by the randomized, posttest-only, control-group design. Random selection or ad hoc sample definition protects external validity. Threats to internal validity from regression to the mean and from attrition are reduced by random assignment of participants. Regression to the mean is controlled because, even if the participants were selected because they were extreme, the random assignment assures that both groups will have roughly the same number of extreme participants, and thus both should experience the same level of regression. The random assignment also assures that groups are statistically equal on all variables, because there is no bias in the selection process for the groups. Threats to internal validity from instrumentation, history, and maturation are reduced by the inclusion of the no-treatment control group. These threats are controlled by the inclusion of a control group because these effects should be equal in the groups.

An experimental design is effective only if the appropriate general control procedures are routinely applied. These procedures were covered in Chapter 9. Carefully preparing a setting, using reliable dependent measures, or applying single-blind or double-blind procedures when appropriate will control extraneous variance and minimize error variance. An experimental design alone, without using these general control procedures, is not sufficient for ruling out confounding variables. For example, failing to keep the person who actually tests participants blind to group assignment will allow the possibility of confounding due to experimenter effects. The control imposed by the experimental design is forfeited by the failure to include the necessary general control procedures. In the food additive study, a double-blind procedure should be used because both placebo and experimenter effects are anticipated. The no-treatment control group must be indistinguishable from the treatment group for the participants. This could be accomplished by having the researcher provide specially packaged foods to all participants in both groups. The only difference would be that the food given to the experimental participants would not contain the additives thought to increase hyperactivity. Ideally, you would want identical packaging and food that looks and tastes the same in each condition.

Randomized, Pretest–Posttest, Control-Group Design

Recall that the pretest–posttest, natural control-group design discussed earlier in the chapter is not an experiment, because it does not include random assignment to groups to ensure that the groups are comparable at the beginning of the study. In the **randomized, pretest–posttest, control-group design,** which is illustrated in Table 10.6, participants are randomly assigned to experimental and control groups. All participants are pretested on the dependent variable, the experimental group is administered the treatment, and both groups are then posttested on the dependent variable. The critical comparison is between the experimental and control groups on the posttreatment measure.

The randomized, pretest–posttest, control-group design improves on the randomized posttest-only, control-group design by adding a pretreatment measurement of the dependent variable. Random assignment of participants to groups ensures that the groups are statistically equal. The pretest provides a way to check if they are actually equivalent on the dependent variable at the start of the experiment, thus adding another level of confidence to the results. Adding a pretest also permits calculation of a pre-posttest difference or change score. Adding a pretest has advantages, but it also carries disadvantages, which are discussed later in the chapter.

Multilevel, Completely Randomized, Between-Subjects Design

The designs discussed so far have had only two levels of the independent variable. The **multilevel, completely randomized, between-subjects design** is a simple extension of the previously discussed designs. Instead of participants being randomly assigned to two conditions, they are randomly assigned to three or more conditions, as shown in Table 10.7. Pretests may or may not be included, depending on the questions that the investigator wants to answer. Because this design is only an extension of earlier designs, it controls for the same confounding variables as the simple two-group designs.

Recall the description in Chapter 9 of a study in which room temperature was varied to test its effects on the speed and accuracy of typing. This study used a multi-

TABLE 10.6   *Randomized, Pretest–Posttest, Control-Group Design*

| R Group A (experimental) | Pretest | Treatment | Posttest | |
| R Group B (control) | Pretest | No treatment | Posttest | Compare |

TABLE 10.7   *Multilevel, Completely Randomized, Between-Subjects Design*

R Group 1	Pretest	Treatment 1	Posttest	
R Group 2	Pretest	Treatment 1	Posttest	
.	.	.	.	
.	.	.	.	Compare
.	.	.	.	
R Group *N*	Pretest	Treatment 1	Posttest	

This design may or may not include a pretest.

level, completely randomized, between-subjects design in which 48 typists were randomly assigned to six groups of 8 typists each. Each group of typists was tested at a different room temperature (the independent variable), and their typing speed and accuracy were measured (the dependent variable).

"*Everything's been so completely randomized out there that we seem to have lost our research assistants among the subjects!*"

It may be possible to carry randomization too far, but researchers generally want to use randomization whenever possible.

Solomon's Four-Group Design

The addition of a pretest improves control in experimental design, but it also creates a new problem: the possibility that the pretest will affect participants' responses to the treatment or to the posttest. We might expect such pretesting effects to be the same in the experimental and control groups, but it is also possible that the pretest might interact with the experimental manipulation, producing confounding **interaction effects.** That is, the effect of the pretest might not be constant for the groups, but will vary depending on the level of the independent variable. For example, suppose that a researcher is interested in testing whether adolescents' attitudes toward cigarette smoking can be changed by presenting them with a videotape about the health hazards of tobacco use. One hundred high school students are randomly selected, given a pretest measuring their attitudes toward the use of tobacco, and then are randomly assigned to experimental and control groups. The pretest shows that the two groups are statistically equivalent on attitudes toward tobacco use at the start of the study. The experimental group is then shown the videotape and the control group is not. Both groups are then retested on their attitudes toward tobacco use, and the experimental and control groups' posttest measures are compared.

As well designed as this study appears, it is possible that the pretest of attitudes might sensitize the participants to what the research is about. When the videotape is presented to the experimental group, this sensitization may interact with this new information and change the way that participants respond. The experimenter might erroneously conclude that the observed difference is due only to the videotape, when it may actually be due to the interaction of the pretest and the videotape. If no pretest had been given, the videotape may have been less effective.

In an attempt to control such effects, Richard Solomon (1949) developed an extension of control group design. **Solomon's four-group design,** which is illustrated in Table 10.8, combines the randomized, pretest–posttest, control-group design and the posttest-only, control-group design. Groups A and B in Table 10.8 constitute the pretest–posttest, control-group design component, and Groups C and D constitute the posttest-only design component. Groups A and B are the experimental and control groups, respectively, and they provide the basic comparison needed to test the hypothesis. Groups C and D represent a replication of this basic comparison, but without the pretest. The critical comparison is between the posttest measures of Groups A and B. The random assignment of participants to conditions ensures that the groups are statistically equivalent at the start of the study, and the pretest provides a way to test their

TABLE 10.8   *Solomon's Four-Group Design*

R Group A	Pretest	Treatment	Posttest
R Group B	Pretest		Posttest
R Group C		Treatment	Posttest
R Group D			Posttest

equivalence. Random assignment also controls for potential confounding due to statistical regression. The potential confounding due to history and maturation are controlled by the inclusion of the control group (Group B). Group C, which includes the treatment and posttest, but no pretest, controls for the possible interaction effects of the pretest. Comparing the posttest measures of Groups C and A provides a basis for determining whether the pretest in Group A had an interactive effect. The final control, Group D, includes only the posttest and provides further control for the effects of maturation. The posttest measures for Group D should be similar to those of Group B and different from Groups A and C.

Solomon's four-group design is a powerful design that provides excellent control. However, because it requires the resources of two experiments, it is not recommended for routine use. Rather, it is best used for experiments in research areas in which the basic hypotheses have already been tested and supported using simpler designs, and a test of greater rigor is desired. It is also used when an interaction between the treatment and the pretest is expected.

Each of the four experimental designs discussed in this section uses randomization to assign participants to conditions. Actually, what is required is the *unbiased assignment of participants to conditions,* which is achieved through free random assignment or matched random assignment (see Chapter 9). Thus, we can utilize matching procedures and still maintain an experimental design. Designs employing matching procedures are discussed in the next chapter. Examples from the literature of the four research designs discussed here are included on the *Student Resource CD.*

Quick-Check Review 3: Experimental Designs

3.1. What is the most basic experimental design?

3.2. Name and describe each of the other three experimental designs discussed in this section.

3.3. How does random assignment of participants to groups and the inclusion of a control group control confounding?

3.4. What problem does the Solomon four-group design address?

3.5. Why is it important to be sure that the groups are equivalent at the start of an experiment?

Statistical Analyses

The level of measurement of the dependent variable determines the appropriate statistical procedure (see Chapters 4 and 5). For example, a chi-square test is typically used with nominal data; the Mann–Whitney *U*-test is typically used with ordered data; a *t*-test or an analysis of variance is typically used with score data. Most dependent variables at the experimental level generate score data.

t-*Test*

The *t*-test evaluates the size of the difference between the means of the two groups. The difference between the means is divided by an **error term,** which is a function of the variance of scores within each group and the size of the samples. The *t*-test is easily applied, commonly used, and useful when we want to test the difference between two groups. Its disadvantage is that it can compare only two groups at a time.

Analysis of Variance

Many studies are multilevel designs in which more than two groups are used. For these studies, an analysis of variance (ANOVA) is required. In the typists study described earlier, there are six levels of the independent variable room temperature. Because there are six groups, a one-way ANOVA is used to test whether any of the six groups is statistically different from any of the other groups. The qualifier *one-way* simply means that there is only one independent variable in the study.

To introduce ANOVA, it is necessary to review some of the earlier discussion of variance. Variance is a relatively simple concept, but it can seem confusing in the context of ANOVAs, because it is calculated more than once based on different combinations of the same data. ANOVA uses both the within-groups variance and the between-groups variance. **Within-groups variance** is a measure of nonsystematic variation within a group. It is error or chance variation among individual participants within a group and is due to factors such as individual differences and measurement errors. It represents the average variability within the groups. The between-groups variance represents how variable the group means are. It is a measure both of the systematic factors that affect the groups differently and of the variation due to sampling error. The systematic factors include (1) experimental variance, which is due to the effects of the independent variables, and (2) extraneous variance, which is due to confounding variables. Even if there are no systematic effects, the group means are likely to be slightly different from one another due to sampling error. The **between-groups variance** represents how variable the group means are. If all groups have approximately the same mean, the between-groups variance will be small; if the group means are very different from one another, the between-groups variance will be large.

The variance is based on the sum of squares, which is the sum of squared deviations from the mean. In an analysis of variance, there is a sum of squares on which the between-groups variance is based, a sum of squares on which the within-groups variance is based, and a total sum of squares. In the ANOVA procedure, the sum of squares is calculated for each of these; that is, the total sum of squares is **partitioned** into the between-groups sum of squares and the within-groups sum of squares:

$$\begin{pmatrix} \text{Total sum} \\ \text{of squares} \end{pmatrix} = \begin{pmatrix} \text{Between-groups} \\ \text{sum of squares} \end{pmatrix} + \begin{pmatrix} \text{Within-groups} \\ \text{sum of squares} \end{pmatrix} \tag{10.3}$$

These principles can be illustrated by using the example described earlier, the study of the effects of room temperature on typing speed, in which 48 typists are randomly assigned to six conditions defined by the temperature of the room in which their typing speed was tested. Table 10.9 shows the data for this study. The first step in doing an ANOVA is to compute each of the sums of squares: the sum of squares between groups, the sum of squares within groups, and the total sum of squares. (See the *Student Resource CD* for the computational procedures.) The next step is to compute between-groups and within-groups variances, which are called **mean squares.** The mean squares are computed by dividing each of the sums of squares by the appropriate degrees of freedom (df). The between-groups sum of squares is divided by the number of groups minus 1 (in this case, 6 – 1 = 5). The within-groups sum of squares is divided by the total number of participants minus the number of groups (in this case, 48 – 6 = 42). The between-groups and within-groups mean squares are then compared by dividing the between-groups mean square by the within-groups mean square. The result is the *F*-ratio, which will be interpreted shortly. The results of these computations are summarized in an **ANOVA summary table** as shown in Table 10.10. The ANOVA summary table shows the sources of variation in column 1, the degrees of freedom associated with each source of variation in column 2, the sum of squares in column 3, the mean squares in column 4, the value of *F* in column 5, and the probability value in column 6.

TABLE 10.9 *Typing Speeds for 48 Typists Who Were Randomly Assigned to One of Six Room Temperature Conditions*

Listed below are the typing speeds

	55°	60°	65°	70°	75°	80°
	49	71	64	63	60	48
	59	54	73	72	71	53
	61	62	60	56	49	64
	52	58	55	59	54	53
	50	64	72	64	63	59
	58	68	81	70	55	61
	63	57	79	63	59	54
	54	61	76	65	62	60
Mean:	55.75	61.88	70.00	64.00	59.13	56.50

TABLE 10.10 *ANOVA Summary Table for the Study of the Effects of Room Temperature on Typing Speed*

Source	df	SS	MS	F	p
Between groups	5	1134.67	226.93	5.51	.0006
Within groups	42	1731.25	41.22		
Total	47	2865.92			

The statistical significance of the ANOVA is based on the **F-test** (named after its originator, Sir Ronald Fisher). Fisher's *F*-test involves the ratio of the between-groups mean square to the within-groups mean square:

$$F = \frac{\text{mean square between groups}}{\text{mean square within groups}} \qquad (10.4)$$

Consider some of the possibilities that might be found in this ratio. If there were no *systematic* between-groups differences, there would still be some *chance* differences between the groups. These chance differences are due to sampling error. If there were no systematic between-groups differences, both the mean square between groups (based on between-groups variability) and the mean square within groups (based on within-groups variability) would estimate the same quantity, the error variance. In this case, the *F*-ratio should have a value of approximately 1.00. If there are systematic between-groups differences, the *F*-ratio will be greater than 1.00. Any factors that increase the size of the numerator relative to the denominator will make the ratio larger. Furthermore, any factors that decrease the size of the denominator relative to the numerator will also make the ratio larger. Thus, the ratio is increased by either increasing the between-groups mean square or by decreasing the within-groups mean square. The between-groups mean square is increased by maximizing the differences between the groups. The within-groups mean square is minimized by controlling as many potential sources of random error as possible. In other words, it is desirable to *maximize experimental variance and minimize error variance.* This theme should be sounding familiar by now.

The larger the *F*-ratio is, the greater the variance between groups relative to the variance within groups. A large *F* indicates that the experimental manipulations may have had an effect. In practice, if there are no systematic differences between groups, the *F*-ratio will sometimes be larger than 1.00 by chance alone. Therefore, we do not reject the hypothesis that there are no systematic differences unless the *F*-ratio is larger than we would expect by chance alone. Statistical analysis programs routinely compute both the *F*-ratio and the *p*-value associated with it. If the *p*-value is less than the alpha level chosen, the null hypothesis is rejected, and the researcher concludes that at least one of the groups is significantly different from at least one other group.

Specific Means Comparisons in ANOVA

Note that the *F*-test in the analysis of variance indicates whether significant group differences exist, but not which group or groups are significantly different from the others. This is not a problem when only two groups are compared, because the significant *F*-ratio indicates that the two groups differ. By inspecting their means, it can be seen whether the difference is in the predicted direction. But when there are three or more groups to compare, an additional step is needed; the researcher must **probe** to determine where the significant difference(s) occurred. Probing is done by statistically testing the differences between the group means. Specific comparisons are best carried out as a planned part of the research, that is, as a **planned comparison,** which is sometimes called an **a priori comparison** or a **contrast.** Here the experimenter makes predictions before data are collected about which groups will differ and in what directions based on theoretical concepts that underlie the experiment.

Occasionally, an a priori prediction cannot be made, and an ANOVA is carried out to answer the question of whether there are any differences. Under these conditions, if a significant *F* is found, the pattern of means is evaluated using a **post hoc comparison,** which is also called an **a posteriori comparison** or **incidental comparison.** The scientific rigor and informational value are generally greater for the planned comparisons than for the post hoc comparisons.

Several statistical procedures can be used for the specific comparisons depending on whether they are planned or post hoc. It should be noted that a *t*-test is not an appropriate procedure for doing a post hoc comparison of means. The *t*-test used as a post hoc probe may indicate that significant differences exist when in fact they do not. Appropriate post hoc tests, such as the Tukey, Newman–Keuls, or Sheffe, have built-in procedures designed to deal with problems with the Type I error level. These problems are too complex to discuss adequately here. The interested student can consult Shavelson (1996) for computational procedures and the rationale. The basics of these procedures are also covered on the *Student Resource CD.*

Interpreting results is a process of making sense out of complicated findings, and a useful first step in the interpretation process is to look at the pattern of means. The means for the typing-speed example are listed in Table 10.9 and organized into a graph in Figure 10.2. Graphs are usually easier to read than tables and are particularly helpful when there is more than one independent variable.

The basic experimental designs have served researchers well, but several other experimental designs are also available. Researchers make two distinctions in experimental research designs. One distinction is between independent-groups designs (also called between-subjects designs) and correlated-groups designs (either within-subjects designs or matched-subjects designs). In **independent-groups designs,** different participants

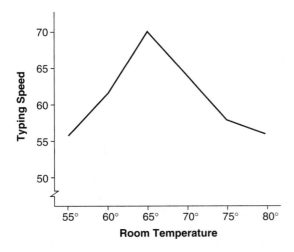

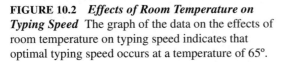

FIGURE 10.2 *Effects of Room Temperature on Typing Speed* The graph of the data on the effects of room temperature on typing speed indicates that optimal typing speed occurs at a temperature of 65°.

appear in each group. In **correlated-groups designs,** the same or closely matched participants appear in each group. The second distinction is between **single-variable designs** (also called **univariate designs**) and **multivariable designs** (also called **factorial designs**). Single-variable designs have only one independent variable, whereas factorial designs have two or more independent variables in a single study. This chapter covered single-variable, independent-groups designs. Chapter 11 will cover correlated-groups designs, and Chapter 12 will cover factorial designs.

Quick-Check Review 4: Statistical Analysis

4.1. At what measurement levels are chi-square and Mann–Whitney *U*-tests used?

4.2. Under what conditions is the *t*-test most likely used? The ANOVA?

4.3. What information is typically found in the ANOVA summary table?

4.4. In ANOVA, what does it mean if the *F*-ratio is significantly greater than 1?

4.5. What are planned comparisons and post hoc tests?

Chapter Summary

Experimental design focuses on controlling unwanted variance and thus reducing threats to validity. Variance includes systematic between-groups variance and nonsystematic within-groups error variance. Between-groups variance is a function of both experimental variance (due to the independent variable) and extraneous variance (due to confounding variables). A major principle in experimentation is to design the study in order to maximize experimental variance, control extraneous variance, and minimize error variance.

There are many experimental designs. We have organized them by making two distinctions: (1) single-variable designs versus factorial designs and (2) correlated-groups versus independent-groups designs. This chapter focuses on independent-groups, single-variable designs. Later chapters will cover correlated-groups designs, factorial designs, and several specialized experimental designs used in field settings.

Key Terms

Define the following key terms. Be sure that you understand them. They are discussed in the chapter and defined in the glossary.

systematic between-groups variance	control of variance	pretest–posttest, natural control-group study
experimental variance	ex post facto study	experimental designs
extraneous variance	single-group, posttest-only study	single-variable, between-subjects designs
nonsystematic within-groups variance, or error variance	singled-group, pretest–posttest study	randomized, posttest-only, control-group design
manipulation check	time-series design	

statistically equal
randomized, pretest–posttest,
    control-group design
multilevel, completely
    randomized, between-
    subjects design
interaction effects
Solomon's four-group design
error term
within-groups variance

between-groups variance
partitioned
mean squares
ANOVA summary table
F-test
probe
planned comparison, or a
    priori comparison, or
    contrast

post hoc comparison, or a
    posteriori comparison, or
    incidental comparison
independent-groups designs
correlated-groups designs
single-variable design, or
    univariate designs
multivariable design, or
    factorial design

11

Control of Variance through Experimental Design

Correlated-Groups and Single-Subject Designs

The real problem is not whether machines think, but whether men do.

—B. F. Skinner, 1969, *Contingencies of Reinforcement*

CD Resource Material

- Computational Procedures for Repeated-Measures ANOVA
- Examples of Repeated-Measures ANOVA
- Examples of Within-Subjects Designs
- Examples of Matched-Subjects Designs
- Examples of Single-Subject Designs
- Study Guide/Laboratory Manual

Web Resource Material _____

- Research Design
- Single-Subject Designs

Random assignment to conditions, a cornerstone of experimental design, assures statistical equivalence of groups at the beginning of the study. However, slight differences between groups still exist due to sampling error. The designs featured in this chapter take another approach to assuring group equivalence at the start of the study. **Correlated-groups designs** assure group equivalence by either using the same participants in all groups or participants that have been closely matched. They are called correlated groups designs because this assignment strategy assures that the participants in one group are correlated with the participants in the other groups. Some researchers do not consider correlated-groups designs to be experiments because they do not use free random assignment; others believe that they are experiments because they meet the requirements of equivalence of groups and because other controls can be applied to eliminate rival hypotheses. Correlated-groups designs have the advantages of being generally more sensitive than between-subjects designs to the effects of the independent variable.

Two correlated-groups designs are covered in this chapter. **Within-subjects designs** (also called **repeated-measures designs**) test each participant under each condition. **Matched-subjects designs** match participants on relevant variables prior to the study and then randomly assign the matched sets of participants, one member of each set to each group. In addition to these designs, the chapter covers single-subject designs, which are extensions of within-subject designs.

Within-Subjects Design

In within-subjects designs, all participants are exposed to all experimental conditions, thereby making the conditions correlated. *In essence, each participant serves as his or her own control.* This section discusses how to use and analyze within-subjects designs, as well as the strengths and weaknesses of these designs.

Using Within-Subject Designs

Suppose that in a target-detection experiment we want to test whether participants can identify a target faster if there are fewer distracter items. The target is either T or F. The participant's task is to find the single target in each letter array and push either the T or F response button. Each person is tested under three conditions: 10, 15, and 20 distracter items. There are 10 trials at each of the three levels of distraction, and the 10 trials are summed to give the total search time for the distraction level. The hypothesis is that finding the target will take longer if there are more distracters. The design of this study is illustrated in Table 11.1. The characteristics of within-subjects designs are these:

1. Each participant is tested under each experimental condition.
2. Therefore, the scores in each condition are correlated with the scores in the other conditions.
3. The critical comparison is the difference between correlated groups on the dependent variable.

In within-subjects designs, participants are sampled from a target or accessible population, and each participant is exposed to all conditions of the experiment. This design is similar to a single-group, pretest–posttest design except that, in the single-group, pretest–posttest design, each participant responds to the pretest and the posttest in that order. In contrast, in within-subjects designs, each participant responds in two or more conditions, and the order of presentation of conditions is not necessarily fixed as it must be in a pretest–posttest study.

Because it is similar to the single-group, pretest–posttest design, a within-subjects design has many of the same weaknesses. For example, because the same participants appear in all conditions, the experience in one condition might affect how participants respond in subsequent conditions. Thus, differences between the conditions might be due not to the independent variable, but to the confounding effects of one condition on later conditions. This potential confounding, called sequence effects, is controlled by varying the order of presentation of conditions. A major control for sequence effects is **counterbalancing,** in which the order of presentation of conditions to participants is systematically varied. In **complete counterbalancing,** all possible orders of conditions occur an equal number of times. The result is that (1) each participant is exposed to all conditions of the experiment, (2) each condition is presented an equal number of times, (3) each condition is presented an equal number of times in each position, and

TABLE 11.1 *An Example of a Within-Subjects Design*

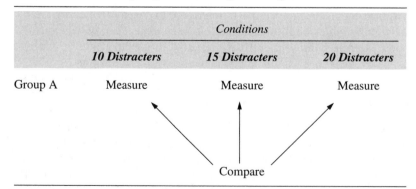

	Conditions		
	10 Distracters	*15 Distracters*	*20 Distracters*
Group A	Measure	Measure	Measure

Compare

The order of presentation of conditions varies from participant to participant, as shown in Table 11.2.

(4) each condition precedes and follows each other condition an equal number of times. Sequence effects and their controls are discussed more extensively later in the chapter.

Table 11.2 shows the various orders of conditions for the hypothetical target-search study. Note that the four conditions outlined in the previous paragraph are met with this set of orders. Hypothetical data for the experiment are also given in Table 11.2. The data are the total time (in seconds) to find the targets in the three levels of distraction. The first column lists the six participants, the second column shows the order of presentation of the stimulus conditions to each participant, and the last three columns show the search times for each of the three experimental conditions.

Analyzing Within-Subjects Designs

The first step in analyzing the results of within-subjects designs is to organize and summarize the data, as shown in Table 11.2. In this hypothetical study, the search times are longest on average for the 20-distracter condition, next for the 15-distracter condition, and shortest for the 10-distracter condition. These results suggest that the hypothesis might be supported. But are the differences between conditions large enough to state with confidence that similar differences exist in the populations? In other words, are the differences statistically significant?

The most commonly used statistical analysis for the single-variable, within-subjects experiment is an ANOVA similar to the one discussed in Chapter 10. However, because the conditions are correlated in a within-subjects design, the ANOVA is modified to take this correlation into account. The appropriate ANOVA for a within-subjects design is called a **repeated-measures ANOVA.**

The major advantage of a within-subjects design is that it effectively equates the conditions prior to the experiment by using the same participants in each condition. Therefore, the single largest contributing factor to error variance—individual differences—has been removed. What effect would this have on the F-ratio? Because

TABLE 11.2 *Hypothetical Data for the Target-Search Study*

Participants	Order of Presentation	Condition (time estimation in seconds)		
		A (10)	*B* (15)	*C* (20)
1	ABC	18.33	22.39	24.97
2	ACB	15.96	20.72	21.79
3	BAC	19.02	22.78	25.46
4	BCA	25.36	27.48	27.91
5	CAB	19.52	24.64	26.75
6	CBA	23.27	24.96	25.49
	Mean scores	20.24	23.83	25.40

the individual difference portion of the error term has been removed, the denominator in the F-ratio is smaller and therefore the F is larger. This means that the procedure will be more sensitive to small group differences.

In a repeated-measures ANOVA, the total sum of squares is computed in the same way as in a one-way ANOVA. What is called a between-groups sum of squares in a one-way ANOVA is called a between-conditions or simply a between sum of squares in a repeated-measures ANOVA. Terminology is changed in the repeated-measures ANOVA because there is only one group of participants. The within-groups sum of squares in the repeated-measures ANOVA is split into two terms, subjects and error. The **subjects term** is the individual differences component of the within-groups variability. The **error term** is what is left when the individual differences component is removed. The repeated-measures ANOVA tests the null hypothesis that there are no differences between conditions by dividing the mean square between by the mean square error. As in the independent-groups ANOVA, the ratio of mean squares is an F-ratio. Both computational and computer analysis procedures for a repeated-measures ANOVA are presented on the *Student Resource CD*. The results of the analysis of the data in Table 11.2 are presented in Table 11.3.

A significant F-ratio in the ANOVA indicates that at least one of the condition means is significantly different from at least one other condition mean. Additional tests must be conducted to determine which means are significantly different from which other means. Computational procedures for these tests can be found in most advanced statistics textbooks (e.g., Keppel, 1991; Myers & Well, 1995). Most computerized statistical analysis packages include these tests as an option.

Strengths and Weaknesses of Within-Subjects Designs

When properly used, within-subjects designs have important advantages. First, because the same participants are in each condition, there are no group differences due to sampling error. This guarantees that participants in each condition are equivalent at the start of the study, thus eliminating the possible confounding due to group differences at the beginning of the study.

Another important advantage of within-subjects designs is that they are more sensitive than between-subjects designs to the effects of the independent variable. Why is the sensitivity greater for within-subjects designs? Remember the design principle that researchers should try to maximize experimental variance (variance due to the effects of the independent variable), control extraneous variance (variance due to confounding), and minimize error variance (variance due to individual differences and

TABLE 11.3 *Summary Table: Repeated-Measures ANOVA*

Source	df	SS	MS	F	p
Between	2	83.69	41.85	32.25	<.001
Subjects	5	95.85	19.17		
Error	10	12.97	1.30		

chance factors). A within-subjects design not only minimizes but *actually eliminates the variance due to individual differences, thereby reducing error variance.* The larger the individual differences in a population, the greater the benefit derived from using a within-subjects design. This greater sensitivity to the effects of the independent variable leads many researchers to prefer within-subjects designs to between-subjects designs when given the choice.

Another advantage of a within-subjects design is that fewer participants are needed. For example, an independent-groups design with 20 participants in each of three conditions will require 60 participants. Using a within-subjects design with 20 participants per condition will require only 20 participants. In addition, because of its greater sensitivity, the within-subjects design might require even fewer participants per condition. For example, 14 participants in a within-subjects design might provide the same statistical power as 20 participants per condition in a between-subjects design. Reducing the sample size normally reduces statistical power, but the greater sensitivity of the within-subjects design will balance the loss of statistical power from using fewer participants.

There is yet another advantage of within-subjects designs, one that further increases efficiency. Because the same participants are tested under several conditions, instructions can be given once instead of at the beginning of each condition, or the instructions may require only slight modifications for each condition. For example, the participants in the target-search study have the same task in each condition, so there is no need to repeat the instructions. If instructions are complicated or if a practice period is part of the instructions, the time savings can be considerable.

Although within-subjects designs have many advantages, they also have important disadvantages. The disadvantages all stem from the fact that each participant is exposed to each condition. Therefore, participants' experience in one condition may affect their responses to the conditions that follow, known as sequence effects. If not controlled, sequence effects could confound the results, thus preventing the researcher from confidently drawing a causal inference about the effects of the independent variable. Sequence effects are strongest when a treatment has a permanent or long-lasting effect on participants. Examples can be found in animal experimentation, when chemical or surgical changes are implemented, or in human experiments, when knowledge or attitudes are changed. A within-subjects design should not be used when the effects are permanent or long-lasting. Even if the effects are temporary, there is still the risk of sequence effects.

The two most important sequence effects are practice and carry-over effects. **Practice effects** are due to the growing experience with procedures over successive conditions, rather than to influences of any particular condition on other conditions. If there are five conditions, for example, many participants will perform better in the last two or three conditions because of practice effects. This enhancement of performance on later conditions constitutes a **positive practice effect.** On the other hand, if the procedure is lengthy or demanding, participants might become fatigued, and their performance will decline in later conditions. This is called a **negative practice effect.** Both practice effects can confound a study if not controlled. Practice effects depend on participants' experience as they move sequentially through the conditions, so they occur regardless of the particular sequence of conditions.

Carry-over effects are due to the influence of a particular condition or combination of conditions on responses to later condition(s). Carry-over effects may be greater for one condition than for the others. For example, there may be some aspect of a particular condition (for example, condition A) that produces an effect on any condition that follows it. Thus, wherever condition A appears in a sequence, the next condition will be influenced. Suppose that in the target-detection study described earlier the conditions are always presented in the order 10-distracter, 15-distracter, and 20 distracter conditions. Furthermore, suppose that participants are capable of finding the target in the 10-distracter condition by focusing on all 11 items at once (called parallel search), but the 15- and 20- distracter conditions have too many items for this strategy to work. Therefore, the optimal strategy for the search when there are many distracters is to look systematically at each letter until the target is found (called serial search). If the 10-distracter list always appears first, the participants will learn to try a parallel search, which will hamper target detection in the 15- and 20-distracter conditions, thus distorting the data. If, on the other hand, the 20-distracter list always appears first, the participants will learn to try the serial search first, thus distorting the data for the 10-distracter condition. Note that carry-over effects of one condition may be the same on all subsequent conditions, or they might affect only some of the subsequent conditions; that is, carry-over effects may be differential. In either case, carry-over effects constitute an extraneous variable and must be controlled.

There are two ways of controlling sequence effects: (1) holding the extraneous variable constant and (2) varying the order of presentation of conditions. Positive practice effects can be controlled by holding the practice variable constant. Specifically, all the participants would be trained to the same criterion of performance before the first condition begins. Thus, all participants would be familiar with the procedures before they respond to any of the experimental conditions. A control for fatigue (negative practice effects) could be the inclusion of a rest period between the conditions, allowing fatigue that was building up to dissipate before going on to the next condition. These procedures minimize practice effects, but control is best achieved by varying the order of presentation of conditions.

Varying the order of presentation of conditions is the *only* way to control carry-over effects. It can be accomplished by using either a random or counterbalanced order of presentation. The logic of both procedures is to control sequence effects by having these effects contribute equally to all conditions. The **random order of presentation** randomly assigns a different order of the conditions for each participant. In this way, practice effects are not systematically maximized in one condition, and carry-over effects should occur as much to any one condition as to any other.

Counterbalancing involves systematically arranging the order of conditions so that all possible orders are represented the same number of times. Counterbalancing can be complete or partial. To calculate how many conditions are needed for **complete counterbalancing,** calculate $X!$ (read, "X factorial"), in which X is the number of conditions. A factorial is calculated by multiplying the number by all integers smaller than the number. Thus, for the target-detection study, which has three conditions, there are six possible orders, as follows:

$$X! = 3 \times 2 \times 1 = 6$$

The six possible orders are shown in Table 11.2. Participants are assigned to orders of presentation, with an equal number of participants assigned to each order. If there are 30 participants, 5 will be assigned to each of the 6 orders. Counterbalancing is best used with a small number of conditions because it becomes complicated when there are many conditions. With two conditions, A and B, there are only two orders of presentation ($X! = 2 \times 1 = 2$). These are AB and BA. With three conditions, there are six orders of presentation. But with four conditions, there are 24 orders ($X! = 4 \times 3 \times 2 \times 1 = 24$), and if the experiment has five conditions there are 120 orders ($X! = 5 \times 4 \times 3 \times 2 \times 1 = 120$). Suppose that the experiment has seven conditions. Go ahead and calculate how many orders of presentation would be needed for complete counterbalancing.

As the number of conditions increases, the use of complete counterbalancing becomes more unwieldy. Complete counterbalancing is not feasible for more than three or four conditions. If there are more conditions, **partial counterbalancing** may be the best solution. For example, to meet the counterbalancing criteria for four conditions, one would need at least 24 participants. But suppose that you have only 10 participants and four conditions and you still want to use a within-subjects design and control for sequence effects? In this case, you could (1) randomize the order of presentation for each participant, (2) randomly select 10 of the 24 possible orders and randomly assign participants to these orders, or (3) use a more formalized partial counterbalancing procedure known as a **Latin square design.** Latin squares are counterbalanced arrangements named after an ancient Roman puzzle that required arranging letters in rows and columns so that each letter occurs only once in each row and once in each column. The result is that each letter appears an equal number of times as each other letter, appears in each position in the sequence an equal number of times as any other letter, and follows each other letter an equal number of times. This provides a partially counterbalanced presentation of treatments. (More complete discussions of Latin square designs are provided in Edwards, 1985, Keppel, 1991, and Myer and Well, 1995.)

There is another approach to reducing sequencing effects, but it is possible only in some situations. In the target-detection example, each condition consisted of 10 trials. The earlier presentation suggested that all 10 trials would be completed together, but often that is unnecessary. If, instead, the researcher took the 30 trials (10 in each of the 3 conditions) and randomly ordered them, sequencing would be reasonably controlled. If the researcher does not want to completely trust randomization, the trials could be **randomized within blocks.** This involves taking a block of one trial from each condition and randomizing their order before going on to the next block.

If strong carry-over effects are expected, the within-subjects design is not recommended, even if the preceding controls are included. Carry-over effects tend to add error variance to scores, which can offset any increased sensitivity normally expected from a within-subjects design. If strong carry-over effects are expected, it is best to use either a between-subjects design or a matched-subjects design.

The ability to control sequence effects is the reason that the within-subjects design is considered to be an experimental design and the single-group, pretest–posttest design introduced in Chapter 10 is considered to be a nonexperimental design. The order of presentation cannot be counterbalanced because the pretest must always precede the treatment and the posttest must always follow the treatment. The pretest–posttest design requires a separate control group to control confounding.

In summary, the within-subjects design is a type of correlated-groups design in which each participant is tested under each condition of the experiment. The major strength of the within-subjects design is that it *equates* groups prior to the experimental manipulation and is therefore more sensitive to the effects of the independent variable. Using the same participants in each condition eliminates the single largest contributing factor to error variance—individual differences. The greater sensitivity of the within-subjects design leads many to prefer it to between-subjects designs. The major disadvantage of within-subjects designs is sequence effects. Sequence effects are usually controlled by varying the order of presentation of conditions. Examples of the use of the within-subjects design from the research literature are presented on the *Student Resource CD*.

Quick-Check Review 1: Within-Subjects Designs

1.1. What are correlated-groups designs?

1.2. What is the major potential confounding factor in within-subjects designs, and how can it be controlled?

1.3. How do within-subjects designs reduce error variance?

1.4. What are the strengths and weaknesses of within-subjects designs?

1.5. What is meant by complete counterbalancing?

Matched-Subjects Design

Matched-subjects designs have many of the strengths of within-subjects designs as well as some advantages of their own. Instead of using each participant as his or her own control by testing each participant under all conditions, the matched-subjects design uses different participants in each condition, but closely matches participants before they are assigned to conditions. This process of matching before assignment to conditions is referred to as matched random assignment (see Chapter 9). The characteristics of matched-subjects designs are these:

1. Each participant is exposed to only one level of the independent variable.
2. Each participant has a matched participant in each of the other conditions so that the groups are correlated.
3. The analysis takes into account which participants were matched with which other participants.
4. The critical comparison is the difference between the correlated groups, in which the correlation is created by the matching procedure.

Although matched-subjects designs are not used often, they are valuable. They are most likely to be used when the cost of the study per participant is very high, thus limiting the sample that can be studied. In such a case, matching increases the sensitivity and statistical power of the study without adding extensively to the cost.

Using Matched-Subjects Designs

This section begins with a discussion of when and how to use the matched-subjects design. It then discusses the statistical procedures for analyzing data from matched-subject studies. It concludes with a discussion of the strengths and weaknesses of the design. Matched-subjects designs are used when researchers want to take advantage of the greater sensitivity of within-subjects designs, but cannot, or prefer not to, use a within-subjects design. Matched-subjects designs are most often used when exposure to one condition causes long-term changes in participants, making it impossible for participants to appear in the other conditions. For example, when surgical procedures are used in physiological studies, the procedures permanently alter the animal, making it impossible to use the animal in another condition that requires nonaltered participants. When participants learn a content area or behavior under one condition, they are no longer suitable participants for testing under other conditions. For example, suppose that the Air Force wanted to compare two methods of teaching map reading to its navigation students. If one group of participants was successfully taught map reading using method A, then these participants could not be used for testing the effectiveness of method B. A separate group of participants would have to be trained using method B, and then the two groups would be compared. These are examples of extreme forms of carry-over effects. As you learned earlier, it is best to avoid within-subjects designs if large carry-over effects are anticipated.

There are other situations in which a researcher might avoid a within-subjects design. One situation is when the demands on participants' time in each condition is excessive so that it is unreasonable to ask participants to be tested under all conditions. Researchers may also choose to avoid a within-subjects design if they are concerned that participants who are tested under all conditions might discern the hypothesis of the study and thus influence the results through expectancy effects and/or demand characteristics (see Chapter 8).

To avoid the problems of within-subjects designs, researchers can choose an independent-groups design and randomly assign participants to each of the various experimental conditions. However, an independent-groups design relies on chance to equate the groups. Therefore, it is not as sensitive to small effects of the independent variable as is a correlated-groups design because statistical tests must take into account the possibility that independent groups of participants may not be equal on the dependent measure before the study begins. Matched-subjects designs provide a solution to this problem; they make it more likely that the groups are equivalent at the beginning of the study by explicitly matching on relevant variables.

How do you match participants for a matched-subjects design? You want to match participants on relevant variables, but what does this mean? Which variables are relevant? In the within-subjects design, these questions were irrelevant because each participant served as his or her own control. Therefore, participants were matched on all variables, whether relevant or not, because they were the same participants in each condition. However, many factors that differentiate one person from another may be irrelevant for a particular study. For example, eye color may be a relevant variable if you are studying ways of increasing attractiveness, but is probably irrelevant if you are studying visual acuity. *A variable is relevant if it is likely to have an effect on the dependent variable in a study.* Participants' eye color may influence the ratings of their attractiveness, but should not influence their level of visual acuity. The more powerful the effect of a variable on the dependent variable, the more important it is to match participants on this variable to assure comparable groups. To use a matched-subjects design effectively, you must identify the relevant variables and match the groups participant for participant on these variables.

The procedure for matching participants on a given variable and assigning them to groups was described in Chapter 9 (see matched random assignment). In that example, we matched participants on age by ordering them by age, then dividing them into pairs by selecting the two oldest, then the next two oldest, and so on. Finally, we randomly assigned one member of each pair to one of the two groups and automatically assigned his or her partner to the other group. The result is two groups of participants matched on the variable of age. It is legitimate during the pairing process to exclude participants for whom a close age-mate is not available. One participant may be older than the rest of the children, with no other participants of a comparable age. This participant would not be paired with any other participant and so would not be assigned to any condition. We could have extended this process to three or more conditions by matching in sets of three or more participants. We would then randomly assign one member from the matched set to the first condition, randomly assign one of the remaining members to the second condition, and so on, until there is only one member left in the matched set and only one condition for this person. Of course, as we increase the number of experimental conditions to which we want to assign matched participants, we also increase the likelihood that participants will have to be excluded because close matches cannot be found for them.

One can extend the matching procedure to matching on more than one variable. Matching on age and sex of the participants, for example, is only slightly more complicated because one of the matching variables (sex) has only two levels. We could pair participants on age, except that we would pair the males only with other males and the females only with other females. This way, participants in each pair will be similar to each other on both matching variables: they will be the same sex and approximately the same age. We might lose a few more participants than before from the potential sample because appropriate matches could not be found, but the loss should not be too great.

However, if we match on two variables in which both variables are continuous, participant loss can be large, because an appropriate match for each participant may be hard to find. For example, if we match on age and IQ, we would first want to order all the participants on one of the variables, such as age. We would then divide the participants into small subgroups defined by having all the participants in each group within a narrow age range. Then within each of these subgroups, we would order on the second variable, in this case IQ. Within each group, we would pair as many participants as possible using as the criteria that each member of the pair must have similar IQs. We would probably find several people in each age group with no close IQ match, and these people would be excluded from the potential sample. If the study required three conditions, we would match in triplets, which would make it even more likely that participants would be excluded because appropriate matches could not be found. A general rule of thumb is that matching on more than one continuous variable is difficult to accomplish and will usually result in significant participant loss.

If matching is used as a research strategy, it is best to match on only one or two of the most important and significant variables. Again, *match on variables that are strongly related to performance on the dependent measure(s).* If age makes little difference in how participants perform on the dependent measure, it makes little sense to match participants on age. Because age does not affect the dependent measure, it cannot confound the results. If we have several variables that could have strong effects on the dependent measure, matching on all of them simultaneously is unworkable. Instead, we should match on those variables that show the greatest natural variability (variance) in the population. Characteristics that are more variable in the population are more likely to show large mean differences by chance in randomly selected groups if an explicit matching procedure is not employed. Therefore, they should be given the highest priority when deciding on which variables to match in a matched-subjects design. For example, with college students as participants, age is probably not an important variable on which to match, because there is little variability in age among college students and a difference of one or two years makes little difference in students' behavior. However, when doing research with young children, age can be an extremely important variable. An age difference in children of even a few months can have major effects on their behavior. Therefore, matching on age may be an important control in many research studies with children.

Although it can be difficult to identify the critical variables on which to match, in most cases the needed information is already available in published studies. These studies often report observed correlations of many potential confounding variables with their dependent measures. If you are using similar dependent measures, these correlations will help you to decide on which variables to match in your study. Therefore, you should familiarize yourself with past research and with the population that you are studying in order to make good design decisions. This is true regardless of the design being contemplated, but is particularly true in matched-subjects designs. However, even with the information from past research, you are unlikely to identify all confounding variables for matching. Therefore, it is necessary to randomly assign participants in a matched set to conditions. Random assignment within sets controls for unidentified confounding variables.

Analyzing Matched-Subjects Designs

Analyzing data from a matched-subjects design is no more complicated than analyzing data from a within-subjects design. The key is to maintain the ordering of data, from the matching of participants at the beginning of the study through the analysis of data at the end. In the within-subjects design, the scores from each condition for a given participant are put on the same line, as shown in Table 11.2. In the matched-subjects design, the scores on a given line represent the scores of different participants tested under different conditions, but all the participants in a given line are specifically matched with the other participants on that line prior to the beginning of the study.

Once the data are organized, we analyze them as if all the scores on a given line came from the same participant, instead of from matched participants. The repeated-measures ANOVA is used to determine whether the observed mean differences between groups is large enough to assert that real differences exist in the populations: that is, are the differences statistically significant? If participants are carefully matched on relevant variable(s), then their scores on the dependent measures in each condition should be correlated with one another. This design would have the same high statistical power to detect small differences between conditions as the within-subjects design has, but without some of the problems of the latter, such as carry-over or practice effects.

Strengths and Weaknesses of Matched-Subjects Designs

The matched-subjects design has similar strengths to the within-subjects design, but different weaknesses. Both designs have greater sensitivity to small differences between conditions than do between-subjects designs. Whereas between-subjects designs rely on chance to equate groups, correlated-groups designs use selection and assignment procedures that almost guarantee that groups are equivalent. If the groups are equivalent before the study begins, they do not have to show large differences after the manipulation to convince us that treatment had an effect.

Because matched- and within-subjects designs have greater sensitivity, the researcher can use a smaller number of participants and still be confident about detecting population differences if differences exist. For example, for three conditions with 20 participants in each condition, a between-subjects design will require 60 participants. However, because of the greater sensitivity of the matched-subjects design, we may need only 16 matched participants in each condition to test the null hypothesis with the same confidence that we would have using 20 participants in each condition in the between-subjects design. This is a direct consequence of the increased statistical power or sensitivity of the designs. We can safely reduce the sample size because the design provides a balancing increase in sensitivity.

An advantage of the matched-subjects design over the within-subjects design is that there are no problems of practice and carry-over effects. Therefore, control procedures such as counterbalancing are not needed. But there are disadvantages to the matched-subjects design. One is that it requires extra work. The researcher must decide on what variable(s) to match and must obtain measures of this variable from all potential participants. The matching process is tedious, especially when matching on more than one variable. Finally, the requirement of matching participants in sets can eliminate many potential participants because suitable matches cannot be found for them. We may need to pretest a large sample of participants on the matching variables to obtain a modest sample of matched participants. It may be more efficient to use large sample sizes in a between-subjects design.

In summary, matched-subjects designs have many of the advantages of within-subjects designs while avoiding the problems of sequence effects. In the simplest situation (two conditions), participants are matched in pairs on one or more relevant variables. Then one member of the pair is randomly assigned to one condition and the other member is automatically assigned to the other condition, a process known as matched random assignment. In a situation with three conditions, participants are matched in triplets and each member of the triplet is randomly assigned to one of three conditions. The matched-subjects design is used when increased sensitivity is needed and when a within-subjects design is inappropriate because large carry-over effects are expected. Examples of research using matched-subjects designs are included on the *Student Resource CD*.

Quick-Check Review 2: Matched-Subjects Designs

2.1. What major confounding factor found in within-subjects designs is avoided by using matched-subjects designs?

2.2. What are the characteristics of matched-subjects designs?

2.3. Under what conditions would we use matched-subjects designs?

2.4. What are the disadvantages of using matched-subjects designs?

Single-Subject Experimental Designs

Single-subject (or *N*-of-one) **experimental designs** are extensions of within-subject designs in that each participant appears in each condition of the experiment. They are also variations on time-series designs (discussed in Chapter 13), in which repeated measurements are taken over time and manipulations are performed at different points along the time sequence. Single-subject experimental designs have become highly developed alternatives to more traditional group designs. For example, they are used routinely in research in behavior modification to evaluate treatment effects.

Single-subject *experimental* designs should not be confused with the single-case studies discussed in Chapter 6. Those approaches are used in clinical research for in-depth clinical *descriptions* of single individuals and *to generate, but not test, hypotheses.* The ex post facto, single-case study is weak, not because it has only one participant, but because the researcher does not control the independent variable(s). This is the critical difference. Because the independent variables are not manipulated in the single-case study, *alternative hypotheses cannot be ruled out.* However, with single-subject, experimental designs, independent variables are manipulated and their effects on dependent variables are observed. The power of these designs is in the control of independent variables, which reduces potential confounding and enhances internal validity. Thus, single-subject designs are inherently experimental in nature and can test causal hypotheses.

There are two situations in which single-subject experimental designs are preferable to group comparisons: (1) evaluating change in a single participant and (2) obtaining information that might otherwise be lost in a group comparison. Obviously, such designs are appropriate when there is only one participant, such as evaluating the effectiveness of a clinical treatment for a particular client or determining whether a school program improves a particular child's academic performance. A single-subject experiment might be weak in external validity, although not necessarily so, but it protects internal validity and provides valid and reliable information about a single individual.

Traditional group-comparison designs summarize a group's performance and, in the process, might lose important information about each individual's performance. For example, suppose that 20 phobic participants are pretested on the intensity of their fears and then randomly assigned to treatment and control conditions. After treatment, the treated group has a significantly lower mean fear score than the control group. Because this experimental design does an excellent job of controlling confounding, the researcher can conclude that the treatment was effective. However, on closer examination it is apparent that, although the treated group reported less fear on average than the control group, there is considerable variability within each of the two groups. Some of the treated participants still have fear scores that are higher than those of the untreated participants. Furthermore, additional inspection might well show that, while most of the control participants did not improve, some did and, although most of the treated participants improved, some did not and others became worse. In other words, individuals responded differently to the same treatment. Although the treatment may be effective on average, it might not be effective for some participants.

In the 1950s and 1960s, clinical research failed to support the effectiveness of traditional psychotherapy. However, on closer inspection it was clear that some clients improved, some remained the same, and some became worse. When taken as a group, the changes tended to cancel out each other. Obscured by group-comparison designs was the improvement of *some* clients following psychotherapy. Sidman (1960) and Bergin and Strupp (1970) suggested studying these improved individuals in order to (1) determine whether the improvements were due to systematic effects of the treatment or to chance variation and (2) identify factors that made psychotherapy effective for some people but not for others. Recognizing the problems of group designs, they argued for the development of experimental methods to study single individuals.

Historically, the intensive experimental study of individuals had a prominent place in psychology for half a century, until the late 1930s, when psychologists began adopting new group comparison research designs and statistical procedures (Morgan & Morgan, 2001). Sir Ronald Fisher's book, *The Design of Experiments* (1935), introduced multisubject, group-comparison designs and statistical procedures, and researchers soon followed Fisher's lead. However, B. F. Skinner[1] (1904–1990) was an influential exception. Skinner and others continued to develop single-subject experimental designs for the **experimental analysis of behavior**—methods for the intensive, systematic, and controlled study of individual participants. New journals appeared (*Journal of the Experimental Analysis of Behavior,* 1958; *Behavior Research and Therapy,* 1963; *Journal of Applied Behavior Analysis,* 1968; *Journal of Behavior Therapy and Experimental Psychiatry,* 1969; *Behavior Therapy,* 1970; *Behavior Modification,* 1974). The experimental analysis of single individuals became particularly important in clinical psychology, which is now heavily reliant on behavioral treatment methods.

---

[1]Read the quotation at the beginning of this chapter. Do you understand what Skinner was referring to?

In single-subject experiments, there is no control group. To demonstrate causality, a controlled manipulation of the independent variable is needed. The comparison is made between the participant's initial pretreatment behavior and his or her postintervention behavior. The logic of single-subject experiments is fairly simple, and their strength is in the precision with which they are carried out. *A causal inference can be made with confidence if (1) the person's behavior changes consistently in the predicted direction when the treatment is presented and (2) confounding factors can be ruled out.* Several factors are critical in this evaluation, including operationally defining appropriate target behaviors, obtaining baseline measures, applying the treatment manipulation, and monitoring changes in behavior.

The first step is to operationally define the target behavior. For example, a smoking-cessation treatment program might target the number of cigarettes smoked and the intensity of the person's craving for a cigarette. The first might be defined as the number of cigarettes smoked in each 24-hour period and the latter as the person's daily ratings, on a 10-point scale, of his or her cravings. Note that the target behavior is the dependent variable.

After operationally defining target behaviors, a **baseline period** is selected. The baseline period is the time from initial monitoring until the onset of the treatment manipulation. The duration of the baseline varies with the nature of the target behavior. Usually, several days or a week is long enough to establish that the target behavior is consistent and representative for the individual. The researcher wants to avoid a nonrepresentative baseline period, when the behavior is momentarily elevated or depressed. During the baseline, the person records each cigarette smoked and rates his or her need to smoke at various points during each day. With other targeted behavior or with children, the researcher usually carries out the baseline observations. With these baseline data established, the actual treatment can begin.

During the treatment phase, the targeted behaviors are carefully monitored, observed, and recorded. The treatment, of course, will be specific to the nature of the targeted behavior. The treatment is the independent variable, and it, too, must be clearly operationally defined. This sequence of a no-treatment baseline, followed by a treatment period, and then by posttreatment measures is the basic manipulation in single-subject experiments. The critical comparison is between the single participant's pretreatment and posttreatment scores on the target behavior. This basic paradigm is illustrated in Figure 11.1. This is a within-subjects, time-series process in which target behaviors (the dependent variable) of a single participant are measured before, during, and after treatment (the manipulation of the independent variable). The baseline measurement of target behaviors serves the same purpose that a control

BASELINE	TREATMENT	POSTTREATMENT
PHASE	PHASE	PHASE

FIGURE 11.1 *Single-Subject Experimental Designs* Single-subject experimental designs always include, at a minimum, a baseline, treatment phase, and posttreatment assessment.

group serves in between-groups designs. There are three major variants of the basic paradigm: ABA reversal designs, multiple baseline designs, and time-series designs. (See Kratochwill, 1978, and Barlow and Hersen, 1984, for detailed discussions of single-subject designs.)

ABA Reversal Designs

In **ABA reversal designs,** the effects of an independent variable on a dependent variable are demonstrated by measuring the dependent variable over several time periods, during which the treatment is applied and then removed. At a minimum, there is a no-treatment baseline period, during which the target behavior is observed, a treatment period in which the manipulation is carried out, and a return or reversal to the no-treatment condition (ABA). In nearly all instances, the sequence ends with another B condition (ABAB). The effects of the independent variable (the treatment) on the dependent variable (the behavior to be changed) are demonstrated if the behavior changes in the predicted direction whenever the conditions are reversed. There are numerous published reports of ABAB reversal procedures. The following hypothetical study concerns self-stimulatory behavior that is often engaged in by children who have mental retardation, autism, or brain injury. It includes head banging, self-biting, gouging, screaming, violent head shaking, and so on. This behavior interferes with treatment programs. Such behavior may be maintained, at least in part, by the responses of staff members. For some children, being ignored seems to help to maintain the self-stimulatory behavior; for others, the staff's attention to the episodes may help to maintain it.

Betty, a child with mental retardation, displays a complex self-stimulatory behavior that consists of loud shrieks, facial grimacing, and rapid arm flapping. The three behaviors occur together many times each day and are maintained for as long as 25 minutes. This interferes with Betty's learning and disrupts the progress of the other children. After observing the child, a psychologist hypothesizes that the teacher's attention reinforces and maintains the behavior; when not paid attention to, Betty begins self-stimulation. The teacher then attends to the child to soothe and comfort her, not realizing that it may be her efforts to help Betty to control the behavior that are actually helping to maintain it.

To test the hypothesis, the psychologist sets up an ABA reversal design, in which condition *A*, the baseline, involves the teacher's usual approach of attending to Betty whenever she displays the behavior. Condition *B* is the treatment period, during which a differential reinforcement procedure is used with the teacher providing attention and support for Betty whenever she refrains from the self-stimulatory behavior, but withdrawing attention whenever Betty engages is disruptive behavior. Observations of Betty's disruptive behavior are carried out for 1 hour at the same time each day. Figure 11.2 shows the behavioral changes as the *A* and *B* conditions are sequentially reversed. These data suggest that there may be a causal relationship between teacher attention and Betty's self-stimulatory behavior. Note in Figure 11.2 that another reversal was added at the end. The ABA sequence is sufficient to suggest causality. Why did the psychologist add that extra reversal, back to the B condition? (Think about this. We will return to it shortly.)

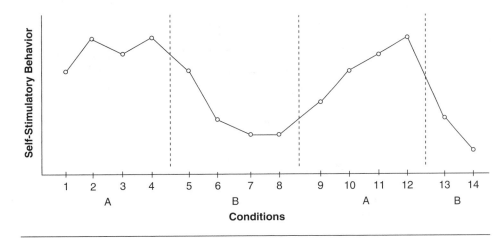

FIGURE 11.2 *Example of an ABA Reversal Design* An ABA reversal design in which the level of attention is manipulated contingent on self-stimulation by a single child. Note that, because the level of self-stimulation is lower in the B condition, the researcher has done the ethical thing in returning the child to this condition at the end of the study.

Reversal designs test causal relationships between an independent variable and a dependent variable. In this case, the independent variable is the teacher's attention. It is presented at two levels, baseline (*A*), in which teacher's attention is given when the self-stimulation occurs, and the intervention (*B*), in which teacher's attention is withdrawn when self-stimulation occurs. The experimental manipulation is the sequential reversal of levels *A* and *B*. The dependent variable is Betty's self-stimulatory behavior and is operationally defined in terms of the number of minutes of self-stimulation behavior during the 1-hour observation period each day. The question being asked is one of causality: Does the teacher's attention affect self-stimulation for Betty? If the behavior changes in the predicted direction, increasing or decreasing each time that the reversal occurs, that this is a compelling demonstration that the independent variable, and not some confounding variable, has affected the dependent variable.

In this hypothetical example, an intervention was tested for reducing undesirable behavior. But the same ABAB reversal design can be used to test the effectiveness of interventions to increase the strength of positive behaviors. This could include improving academic achievement, acquiring self-control skills, increasing positive interactions with peers, and so on. These are common goals in programs for children with developmental disabilities, emotional disorders, or learning problems. For example, DeLeon, Iwata, and Roscoe (1997) studied the responses of 14 children with mental retardation. Although most of the children showed preference for food rewards, 2 children preferred other rewards, specifically, leisure-time activity. The researchers used a reversal design to show improvements in adaptive behavior through a training program that used leisure time as the positive reinforcement for these 2 children. The children's adaptive responses were observed in a baseline period in which there was no leisure-time reward and were then observed in a treatment condition in which leisure time was used as a reward. Baseline and treatment reversals were carried out again. As seen in Figure 11.3, the adaptive behavior of both children increased from baseline to treatment at each reversal. Again, why is the last treatment condition included? In this case and the example presented earlier of Betty, the behavior under the *B* condition was preferable to the behavior under the *A* condition. Once the effect of the independent variable on the dependent variable have been demonstrated, the researcher has an ethical obligation to use that effect to return participants to the best possible position, that is, to reinstate condition *B*.

Multiple-Baseline Design

Although the ABA reversal design is a powerful demonstration of the effects of one variable on another, there are situations in which reversal procedures are not feasible or

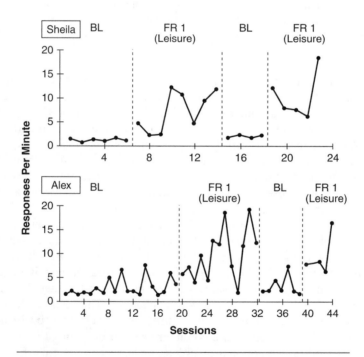

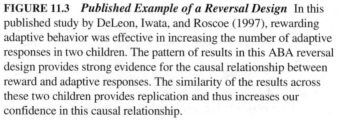

FIGURE 11.3 *Published Example of a Reversal Design* In this published study by DeLeon, Iwata, and Roscoe (1997), rewarding adaptive behavior was effective in increasing the number of adaptive responses in two children. The pattern of results in this ABA reversal design provides strong evidence for the causal relationship between reward and adaptive responses. The similarity of the results across these two children provides replication and thus increases our confidence in this causal relationship.

ethical. For example, suppose that the baseline behavior of a child is injurious or that the researcher succeeds in improving the academic performance of a child in school. In both cases, it is unreasonable to reverse conditions once we achieved improved functioning. For the first child, a return to baseline could risk injury; for the second, it could disrupt academic performance. Thus, the reversal design used in the last example might be unacceptable. But a multiple-baseline design would be acceptable.

In the **multiple-baseline design,** the effects of the treatment are demonstrated on different behaviors successively. To illustrate, suppose that a fifth-grade boy is doing poorly in math and reading, although he appears to have the ability to achieve at a high level. He is also disruptive, continually interrupting and generally failing to attend to the academic work. A psychologist observes the class and sees that whenever the boy acts up the teacher scolds, corrects, and lectures him in front of the class in an effort to embarrass him. The boy seems to accept the attention with a good deal of pleasure. However, on the rare occasions when he does his academic work, the teacher ignores him. "When he is working, I leave well enough alone," the teacher says. "I don't want to risk stirring him up."

Based on these observed contingencies, the psychologist hypothesizes that the teacher's attention to the boy's disruptive behavior may be a major factor in maintaining this behavior, whereas the teacher's failure to attend to the boy's good academic work may help to account for its low occurrence. The psychologist sets up a multiple-baseline design to test the hypothesis about the importance of teacher attention on both disruptive and academic behavior. The independent variable is teacher attention and the dependent variables are the child's (1) disruptive behavior, (2) math performance, and (3) reading performance. The independent variable is presented at two levels: presence of contingent teacher attention and absence of contingent teacher attention. Figure 11.4 shows the sequence of phases of the hypothetical study. During baseline, all three dependent variables are measured while the teacher continues the usual procedure of trying to punish the disruption and ignore academic behavior. Disruptive behavior is high, and math and reading performance are low in this phase. In the second phase, the teacher's attention to disruptive behavior (punishment) is withdrawn and disruptive behavior is ignored. In this phase, the teacher focuses on rewarding math performance while both disruptive behavior and reading continue to be ignored. In the third phase, both reading and math performance receive the teacher's rewarding attention, while disruption continues to be ignored. The changes in the dependent variables associated with the independent-variable manipulations provide evidence for the hypothesis that contingent teacher attention is an important controlling factor in the child's behavior.

There are three major variations of the multiple-baseline design (Barlow & Hersen, 1984):

- *Across behaviors:* In this variation, different behaviors of the same individual are compared, as in the example above.
- *Across individuals:* In this variation, participants who are matched on relevant variables are compared. The same behavior is measured for each individual, and the same treatment manipulations are applied to test whether the treatment procedure is effective for different individuals.

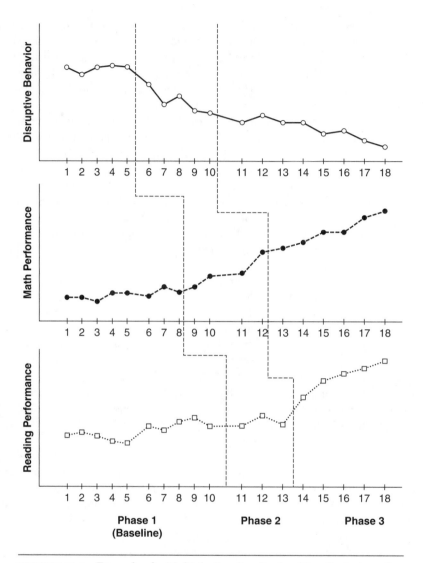

FIGURE 11.4 *Example of a Multiple-Baseline Design* Hypothetical results of a multiple-baseline design study in which contingent teacher attention is shown to decrease disruptive behavior and improve math performance and reading performance for a single child. The dashed line indicates when teacher attention was manipulated for each of the target behaviors.

- *Across settings and time:* In this variation, a treatment is applied to a behavior for one individual in different settings or time periods. For example, we might want to know if a treatment that is effective in the classroom is also effective at home or in other settings.

Single-Subject, Randomized, Time-Series Design

A **single-subject, randomized, time-series design** is a time-series design for a single participant with one additional element: the point at which the treatment begins is determined randomly. Time-series designs, which will be discussed in more detail in Chapter 13, involve measuring a dependent measure several times over a long period with an experimental intervention occurring at a selected point during the observations. To illustrate the single-subject, randomized, time-series design, suppose that Joey, a child in a special class, does not complete his daily work. During the 15-minute lesson periods in which he is supposed to be responding to a workbook lesson and marking answers on the page, Joey looks around the room or just closes his eyes and does no work. Frequent reminders by the teacher rouse him briefly, but not enough for him to complete the lessons. The teacher is convinced that Joey has the skills to do the academic work, but how can the teacher help him?

An effective motivational intervention with children is a token reinforcement system in which tokens are given for desired behaviors. The child accumulates tokens

"*Hey, Dad! Who sez you guys could play with* _my_ *tokens!*"

One of the problems with using a token economy system with your kids. However, token economies are often effective in improving behavior in both children and adults.

and can spend them for desirable items and privileges. The tokens are reinforcements that strengthen the rewarded behavior. If a single-subject, randomized, time-series design is employed, the child's arithmetic achievement might be monitored for 6 weeks (30 school days), which would yield a time graph of 30 measurements. A minimum number of days, perhaps the first 5 and the last 5 (1–5 and 26–30), are devoted to pretreatment and posttreatment measures of arithmetic achievement. This ensures adequate pretreatment and posttreatment measures. The researcher then selects randomly one of the middle 20 days as the point for introducing the manipulation, the use of token reinforcement for arithmetic achievement. A table of random numbers is used to select the starting day, and the ninth day is selected for introducing the token reinforcement. The beginning of the manipulation is preceded by 8 days of arithmetic achievement measured under the usual nontoken condition followed by 22 days of measurements of the dependent variable under the token reinforcement condition. A marked improvement in arithmetic achievement coincident with the randomly selected ninth measurement, as shown in Figure 11.5, provides convincing evidence of the effects of the token system. It is unlikely that such marked improvement would occur by chance at exactly the point at which the *randomly* introduced treatment occurs. It is also unlikely that this particular time-series pattern would have occurred because of maturation or history.

Replication in Single-Subject Designs

As you have learned, replication of research findings is important. If findings cannot be replicated, then their validity is in doubt. There are several questions concerning replication in single-subject experiments. First, if we repeat the treatment with the same person, will the results be replicated, that is, will they generalize over time for that person? A second question concerns whether the treatment will be effective with

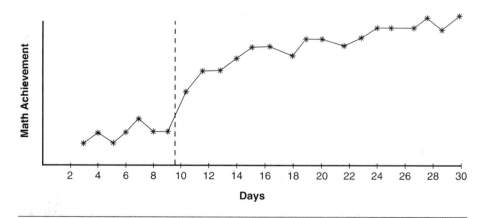

FIGURE 11.5 *Example of a Randomized, Time-Series Design* Hypothetical results of a single-subject, randomized, time-series design in which a token economy was effective in improving math performance for this child.

other people who have the same problem, that is, will the treatment generalize to other persons? A final question concerns whether the treatment will be effective under other conditions. For example, will it work with a different therapist or in another setting, and will it work for psychological problems other than the one on which it was originally tested? These are issues of generalization across time, persons, conditions, and target behaviors. The issue of generalization is one of replication. That is, across time, persons, conditions, and behaviors, can the treatment's effectiveness be replicated? Sidman (1960) discussed two ways of achieving replication: direct replication and systematic replication. Barlow and Hersen (1984) added another way, clinical replication.

Single-subject direct replication means repeating the experiment with the same participant or a series of participants who present the same behavioral issue. For example, in an ABA procedure, each time that a reversal to baseline occurs, followed by the treatment condition, a replication has been carried out. Theoretically, at least, there is no limit to the number of replications that can be carried out. Direct replication provides information on a given individual's responses over time and thus establishes the reliability of the procedure—that is, is it effective each time that it is applied?

Having established its effectiveness with one or more persons with the same behavioral issues, we now want to expand the replication. Carrying out a series of single-subject experiments with different people in different settings and with new target behaviors does this. These experiments constitute **single-subject systematic replication,** the carefully planned and executed testing for generalization after direct replication has established the effectiveness and reliability of the procedure for one person or a series of persons with the same target behavior.

Direct and systematic replication in single-subject experiments typically test the effectiveness of one treatment at a time on a specific target behavior. However, in the applied world of clinical treatment, therapists create and test complex treatment packages that address multiple problem behaviors. To accomplish this, Barlow and Hersen (1984) discuss a third form of replication, **single-subject clinical replication.** This more complex approach is used primarily in clinical treatment settings. It typically involves an integrated treatment package of two or more procedures that are applied to a succession of participants. The target is usually a set of problematic behaviors of a clinical disorder. For example, the participants might be adults with depression, and the targeted behaviors might be negative mood expression, low level of physical activity, and social isolation. The treatment package might consist of medication, cognitive therapy, increased physical activity, and graduated desensitization to social activity.

Although the research is more complex, the basic single-subject procedures are employed in clinical replication. To accommodate the complex treatment packages and multiple target behaviors, variations of multiple-baseline designs are typically used. Barlow and Hersen discuss clinical replication as the next step in replication, building on earlier replication as follows:

1. Direct replication establishes the reliability and effectiveness of a single treatment for a single target behavior in a succession of participants.
2. With that established, systematic replication then establishes the reliability and effectiveness of the treatment with other persons, in other settings, and for other

target behaviors (and/or other clinical problems). When several different treatments have been developed and tested, two or more are combined into a treatment package.

3. Finally, clinical replication tests the reliability and effectiveness of the combined treatment package for multiple related behaviors, for a succession of clients, and across different settings. (For a more complete discussion, see Barlow and Hersen, 1984.)

These designs are applicable to single participants. However, replication can be achieved by having two or more participants in each experiment. These, strictly speaking, would be small-*n* experiments. The procedures would be virtually the same as in single-subject experiments.

To summarize, single-subject designs are extensions of within-subjects designs. These designs are usually variations on time-series designs in which repeated measurements are taken over time and manipulations are performed at different points. Single-subject designs represent alternatives to some of the more traditional designs. They are especially useful in the evaluation of treatments and are used often in research on behavior modification.

Quick-Check Review 3: Single-Subject Experimental Designs

3.1. What are single-subject designs? For what are they used?

3.2. How do single-subject experiments differ from the single-case studies introduced in Chapter 6?

3.3. How is internal validity protected in single-subject experiments?

3.4. Describe reversal, multiple-baseline, and randomized time-series designs.

3.5. What are the major strengths and weaknesses of single-subject designs?

3.6. Why is external validity weak in a single-subject design?

3.7. What are the major ways of replicating single-subject designs?

3.8. Explain how causality is determined in single-subject designs.

Chapter Summary

Correlated-groups designs include within-subjects designs, matched-subjects designs, and single-subject designs. In within-subjects and single-subjects designs, the correlation is the result of having the same participants appear in all conditions. In matched-subject designs, the correlation is created by matching participants on one or more relevant variables. Regardless of the method used, the result is the same—greater confidence in the comparability of groups before the start of the study, thus increasing sensitivity when testing for differences between conditions.

Correlated-groups designs raise new issues not found in other designs. For example, each participant is exposed to all conditions in within-subjects designs. This raises the possibility that the exposure to one or more of the conditions may affect the performance in later conditions (sequence effects). Matching participants and randomly assigning one member of each matched set of participants to each condition eliminates these problems, but raises new issues. The most important issue in matched-subjects designs is the selection of the variable(s) on which to match. Even when this question is answered, the actual matching can be difficult and tedious. Still, both within- and matched-subjects designs provide powerful ways to answer causal questions.

Single-subject designs are extensions of within-subjects designs. They are particularly useful in the evaluation of clinical and educational intervention for individuals. The most commonly used single-subject designs are the reversal design, the multiple-baseline design, and the single-subject, randomized, time-series design.

Key Terms

Define the following key terms. Be sure that you understand them. They are discussed in the chapter and defined in the glossary.

correlated-groups design
within-subjects design, or
    repeated-measures design
matched-subjects design
counterbalancing
repeated-measures ANOVA
subjects term
error term
practice effects
positive practice effect
negative practice effect

carry-over effects
random order of presentation
complete counterbalancing
partial counterbalancing
Latin square design
randomized within blocks
single-subject experimental
    designs, or *N*-of-one
    design
experimental analysis of
    behavior

baseline period
ABA reversal designs
multiple-baseline design
single-subject, randomized,
    time-series design
single-subject direct
    replication
single-subject systematic
    replication
single-subject clinical
    replication

12

Control of Variance through Experimental Design

Factorial Designs

In the discovery of secret things and in the investigation of hidden causes, stronger reasons are obtained from sure experiments and demonstrated arguments than from probable conjectures and the opinions of philosophical speculators of the common sort.

—William Gilbert, *De Magnete,* 1600

CD Resource Material

- Statistical Analysis of Factorial Designs
- Examples of Factorial Designs

- Study Guide/Laboratory Manual

Web Resource Material

- Childhood Fears
- Research Design
- Factorial Designs

- Analysis of Variance (ANOVA)
- Analysis of Covariance (ANCOVA)
- Mulitvariate Analysis of Variance (MANOVA)

The designs discussed in Chapters 10 and 11 have only one independent variable. However, many designs include multiple independent variables in the same experiment. These are called **factorial designs.** Factorial designs allow researchers to study both individual and interactive effects of the independent variables on the dependent variable. This chapter begins by discussing basic factorial design terminology, procedures, and analyses. It then discusses variations of factorial designs and concludes with an advanced discussion of ANOVA.

Factorial Designs

Suppose that you are responsible for developing an effective treatment program for children who are afraid of the dark. By interviewing children and parents, you determine that the children's fears vary considerably from one night to another. On some nights, they do not seem afraid, but on most nights they are fearful. When fearful, the children have difficulty sleeping and they disrupt the entire family. Thus, it appears that, although the children's fears are related to darkness, other variables are operating. In further interviews, you find that many of the children report vivid and frightening images of monsters, ghosts, vampires, burglars, and so on, when they are put to bed and left alone in the dark. Can it be that darkness is a necessary but not sufficient condition for the fear reaction? Might the children's fears be triggered by a combination of being in the dark and having fearful images? That is, darkness alone or fearful images alone may not be sufficient to trigger the fear, but the combination of the two triggers fear.

The question about the two variables having effects when they are in combination is a question about their **interaction.** Behavior is rarely determined by single variables; rather, it is usually determined by several factors that interact. An interactive effect between two variables is an effect that is greater than summing the effects of the two variables; a true interaction is not simply additive—it is an enhancement.

In our hypothetical fear-of-the-dark research, a factorial design can be used to study two independent variables and their interaction (illumination and frightening images). The independent variables in a factorial design are called **factors.** In this experiment, the dependent variable, the children's fear, can be measured by heart rate, which has been shown in previous research to reflect fear arousal. Measured electronically,

TABLE 12.1 *A 2 × 2 Factorial*

	Factor A (illumination)	
	Level A_1 (*lighted condition*)	*Level A_2* (*dark condition*)
Factor *B* (images)		
Level B_1 (feared)	A_1B_1	A_2B_1
Level B_2 (neutral)	A_1B_2	A_2B_2

heart rate can be taken under two conditions of illumination (lighted condition and dark condition) and two conditions of visual images (fear and neutral images). That is, factor *A* (illumination) is presented at two levels and factor *B* (images) is presented at two levels. The two independent variables, each presented at two levels, produce four treatment combinations called a **matrix of cells.** The result is a 2 × 2 (read "two-by-two") factorial design, as shown in Table 12.1. Although an important study, subjecting children to potentially fearful situations raises ethical concerns, as discussed in Box 12.1

The **design notation** for factorial studies (e.g., 2 × 2, 3 × 3 × 2) shows how many independent variables and how many levels of each variable are included. Each number

---

BOX 12.1 • *Ethical Considerations in the Dark-Fears Study*

In the hypothetical study of children who fear darkness, the children are exposed to conditions that may frighten them: darkness and fearful images. What are the major ethical concerns? First, the participants are children. As such, they are presumed to be unable to understand the implications of the research and therefore are unable to give informed consent. Ethical guidelines assume that children, by virtue of being under the age of consent, are automatically participants at risk in any research. Therefore, steps must be taken by the researcher to reduce risks. One obvious safeguard is to obtain the informed consent of the children's parents, who presumably will be able to understand the situation and make a reasonable decision.

Another issue is whether the children want to participate. Because they are minors, children cannot legally give their informed consent. However, even if informed consent is properly obtained from a responsible adult, the child may still refuse to participate, that is, not agree (assent) to it. Thus, the ethical researcher obtains the children's assent to participate by explaining the procedure and asking whether they want to take part. If a child says no or shows reluctance, the researcher must interpret that as a lack of assent. Furthermore, in obtaining consent and assent, the researcher should give a full account of the procedures, provide ample opportunity for questions, and answer all questions. Parents and children should also have the opportunity to ask more questions and to seek explanations after the conclusion of the experiment.

The researcher must also consider other possible risks to participants, such as psychological distress from participation. For example, the children should be assured that they may stop the procedure whenever they wish. Also, researchers and assistants should be sufficiently experienced with children to observe whether a child is becoming unduly upset so that they can (1) soothe and reassure the child and/or (2) discontinue the procedure for the child. All children should be carefully debriefed to minimize discomfort. Researchers should design the procedures to minimize distress, and only those procedures essential for the study should be used.

Finally, there is an ethical issue that bears directly on the adequacy of the experimental design itself: *It is the responsibility of the researcher to assure that the study is competently designed and carried out so that there can be a high degree of confidence in results and conclusions.* Why is this an ethical issue and not just a design issue? Because it is the researcher's responsibility to ensure that participants' time, effort, and risk taking, however minimal, are given in an effort that will likely yield knowledge. The researcher must ensure that participants do not make contributions to a research project that is poorly designed and from which little knowledge can be gained. Participants' contributions must not be trivialized and wasted by an incompetent design. Can you see other potential risks for the participants in our experiment? If so, how would you reduce them?

in the notation represents one independent variable and denotes the number of levels of that variable. Thus, the notation 3×3 indicates that the design has two independent variables with three levels of each variable. The $2 \times 3 \times 2$ notation indicates that the design has three independent variables with two levels of factor A, three levels of factor B, and two levels of factor C. Notice that, in standard usage, factors are labeled with capital letters, A, B, C, and so on, as shown in the tables. As the designs become more complex, more cells are produced, more participants are required, and the results become increasingly difficult to interpret. Thus, although any number of factors and levels can be combined in factorial designs, there are practical limits to the complexity of the designs. They can become unwieldy and difficult to carry out and interpret. Table 12.2 diagrams several factorial designs.

Main Effects and Interactions

Factorial designs are used to test hypotheses involving more than one independent variable. Two different kinds of hypotheses are tested in a factorial design: the impact of each independent variable on the dependent variable (called **main effects**) and the effect of any combination of two or more independent variables on the dependent variable (called *interactions*). Box 12.2 provides a more extensive description of effects.

Factorial designs, like single-variable designs, can be set up as between- or within-subjects designs. We will consider first the between-subjects factorial designs in which a different group of participants is assigned to each cell. Each of these independent groups includes the scores of participants on the dependent variable, and a mean of the scores is calculated for each group. Table 12.3 shows the 2×2 matrix for our hypothetical children's dark-fears study and includes a mean heart rate for the participants in each cell, as well as the row and column means for each variable. Note that the matrix is, in a sense, two separate studies that are combined. Figure 12.1(a) shows that the column means (factor A) can be compared, just as if one were the experimental and the other the control group in a single-variable design. This comparison can answer this question: Is there a significant difference in fear, as measured by heart rate, between the darkness and the lighted conditions? That is, are heart rates different for children tested under darkness conditions than for children tested under lighted conditions? Comparing the two levels of factor B (images), as shown in Figure 12.1(b), is also a comparison of two independent groups. The question answered here is whether there is a significant difference in heart rates between participants in the fear-image and neutral-image conditions.

The comparisons illustrated in Figures 12.1(a) and (b) are the tests of the main effects of the independent variables on the dependent variable. In the dark-fears study, we can test whether heart rates differ under lighted and dark conditions (main effect of illumination) and whether they differ under fearful and neutral images (main effect of fear imagery). The factorial design is efficient in that it is two studies in one. These questions about main effects could be answered by conducting two separate, single-variable studies, but questions about an interaction of the two variables can be answered only when the independent variables are combined into a single study. When we combine the two separate designs by crossing them, as shown in Figure 12.1(c), the 2×2 matrix is formed, with four cells within which are the data for testing interactions. This allows us to investigate not only main effects, but also to address a more complex question:

TABLE 12.2   *Examples of Factorial Designs*

(a) 2 × 2 Design with Two Factors and Two Levels of Each Factor

	Factor A	
	A_1	A_2
Factor *B*		
B_1	A_1B_1	A_2B_1
B_2	A_1B_2	A_2B_2

(b) 3 × 2 Design with Two Factors; Three Levels of *A*, Two Levels of *B*

	Factor A		
	A_1	A_2	A_3
Factor *B*			
B_1	A_1B_1	A_2B_1	A_3B_1
B_2	A_1B_2	A_2B_2	A_3B_2

(c) 3 × 3 Design with Two Factors and Three Levels of Each Factor

	Factor A		
	A_1	A_2	A_3
Factor *B*			
B_1	A_1B_1	A_2B_1	A_3B_1
B_2	A_1B_2	A_2B_2	A_3B_2
B_3	A_1B_3	A_2B_3	A_3B_3

**(d) 2 × 3 × 2 Design with Three Factors and Two levels of *A*,
Three Levels of *B*, and Two Levels of *C***

	Factor C			
	C_1		C_2	
	Factor A		*Factor* A	
	A_1	A_2	A_1	A_2
Factor *B*				
B_1	$A_1B_1C_1$	$A_2B_1C_1$	$A_1B_1C_2$	$A_2B_1C_2$
B_2	$A_1B_2C_1$	$A_2B_2C_1$	$A_1B_2C_2$	$A_2B_2C_2$
B_3	$A_1B_3C_1$	$A_2B_3C_1$	$A_1B_3C_2$	$A_2B_3C_2$

BOX 12.2 • *What Is an Interaction?*

The concept of an interaction is the single most important issue in factorial research. This concept is best explained with a simple example. Accident researchers know that driving faster increases the risk of an accident. The speed at which people drive (the independent variable) has a predictable effect on the accident rate (the dependent variable). In the language of factorial designs, we would say that there is a main effect for speed on accident frequency. Researchers also find that the more slippery the road, the higher the accident rate. Here there is a main effect for slickness of the roads on accident rates. Of course, if people drive fast on slippery roads, an even higher rate of accidents would be expected because both risk factors are present. But this is not necessarily an interaction. We say there is an interaction effect only if the increase in the accident rate is more than would be expected if the independent effects of the two risk factors were simply added together. For example, if driving 20 miles per hour faster doubles the risk of accidents and driving on a slick road triples the rate of accidents, then the additive effects of these two variables might suggest a sixfold increase in accident rates (doubled for driving fast and then that increased rate is tripled for driving on slick surfaces). If, however, we find that driving 20 miles per hour faster and on a slick surface increases the accident rate 15-fold, we clearly are getting more than just the additive effects of these two risk factors. We have a clear interaction, in which the effect of faster driving is greater on slick roads than on dry roads. Driving speed probably interacts with other variables, such as bumpiness of the roads, degree of traffic, and the amount of alcohol that the driver has consumed. In each case, the effect of increased driving speed differs depending on whether one of these other variables is present.

Are the effects of one variable different depending on the level of the other variable? This interaction is the major question in our hypothetical dark-fears study. In fact, in most factorial studies the primary focus is on the interaction.

Conducting the factorial experiment is similar to, but more complex than, conducting single-variable studies. The 2 × 2 factorial, because it is essentially two

TABLE 12.3 *Hypothetical 2 × 2 Factorial Design*

This hypothetical study includes two factors believed to affect children's night fears. Factor A is the level of illumination, and factor B is the type of images.

	Factor A *(illumination)*		
	Level A_1 *(lighted)*	*Level* A_2 *(dark)*	*Row Means*
Factor B (images)			
Level B_1 (feared)	A_1B_1 (98.3)	A_2B_1 (114.1)	106.2
Level B_2 (neutral)	A_1B_2 (98.1)	A_2B_2 (99.9)	99.0
Column Means	98.2	107.0	

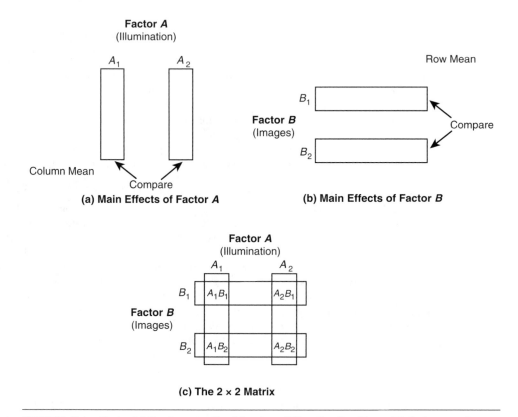

FIGURE 12.1 *Factorial Design as a Combination of Two Studies* Factorial designs can be thought of as combining two or more studies into a single study. Looking at each factor individually provides a test of the main effects. Combining the factors provides a test of the interaction of the factors.

designs combined into a single study, contains more than one null hypothesis. There are three null hypotheses for each dependent measure: (1) there is no difference between the levels of factor *A* (no main effect for factor *A*), (2) there is no difference between the levels of factor *B* (no main effect for factor *B*), and (3) there is no significant interaction of factors *A* and *B*. In factorial designs with more than two factors, there will be even more null hypotheses to test. These null hypotheses are usually tested with an analysis of variance.

Because of the increased complexity of factorial designs compared to single-variable designs, the potential threats to internal validity are more complex. Suppose that one or more of the null hypotheses are rejected. As in single-variable designs, the next step is to check for possible confounding so as to rule out alternative explanations of the findings. If satisfied that confounding variables are adequately controlled, we can conclude that the data support the hypothesis that there is at least one causal relationship involving the independent and dependent variables.

The hypothesis-testing procedure in factorial designs is similar to the procedure used in single-variable designs. The reasoning is exactly the same. The major difference is that, because there are more independent variables in the factorial design, there are several null hypotheses to test, rather than only one, and therefore there is more chance for confounding to occur. Furthermore, the interpretation of interactions is more complex than the interpretation of differences in a single-variable study.

Possible Outcomes of Factorial Designs

There are many possible outcomes of a factorial design. There may be main effects for one or more factors, but no interaction; there may be interactions, but no main effects; there may be both interactions and main effects; and there may be neither main effects nor interactions. Figure 12.2 illustrates several 2 × 2 and 2 × 3 factorial designs. The mean score for each cell is shown, and the **row means** and **column means** for each level of each factor are also indicated. Row means are the means for all the people in a row, and column means are the means for each column. For purposes of this discussion, we will assume that (1) the observed differences are sufficiently large to be statistically significant and (2) there are an equal number of participants in each cell. The data are shown in graphic form. If you follow along with Figure 12.2, the following discussion will make much more sense.

Figure 12.2(a) illustrates a 3 × 2 factorial design with both a 3 × 2 matrix and a graph. Around the margins of the 3 × 2 table are the means for each level of each variable (i.e., for levels A_1, A_2, A_3, and levels B_1 and B_2). Within each of the six cells is the mean score for the group in that condition (A_1B_1, A_1B_2, A_2B_1, A_2B_2, A_3B_1, A_3B_2). In this hypothetical experiment, the means are equal, and there are obviously no significant differences anywhere in the matrix. Thus, there are no significant main effects for factors A or B and no significant interactions. On the graph, the levels of variable A (A_1, A_2, A_3) are shown on the abscissa (the horizontal or *x*-axis), and the values of the dependent variable are shown on the ordinate (the vertical or *y*-axis). Means for cells A_1B_1, A_2B_1, and A_3B_1 are all located at the value 50 and are identified with small circles. The points are connected to show graphically the overall effect of A on the dependent measure at the B_1 level of B, and this line is labeled B_1. Clearly, there is no effect of A on the dependent measure at level B_1 because all values are the same. The effects of A at level B_2 are plotted in the same way. They fall on the same points along the same line, all at the value 50. They are marked with stars. Again, there is no effect of A at the B_2 level. By inspecting either the table or the graph, we can see that there are no main effects and no interaction.

Figure 12.2(b) illustrates a 2 × 2 factorial in which there is a significant main effect for factor A, no significant main effect for factor B, and no interaction. The B_1 and B_2 lines in the graph are identical, indicating that B has had no effect. But the mean of A_2 is greater than the mean of A_1, indicating an effect for factor A. The 2 × 2 matrix shows the same results, with the mean for levels B_1 and B_2 equal (at 45) and the means for levels A_1 and A_2 different (30 and 60). Interactions are most easily seen in the graph of the cell means. When there is an interaction, the lines are not parallel. In this example, both lines show the same upward swing from left to right, so there is no interaction effect. Thus, there is a main effect for A, no main effect for B, and no interaction.

	A_1	A_2	A_3	Mean
B_1	50	50	50	50
B_2	50	50	50	50
Mean	50	50	50	

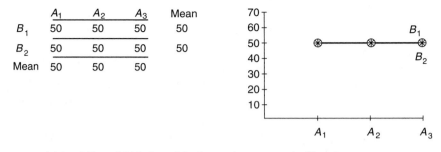

(a) 3 × 2 Factorial (*A*, *B*, and the interaction are not significant)

	A_1	A_2	Mean
B_1	30	60	45
B_2	30	60	45
Mean	30	60	

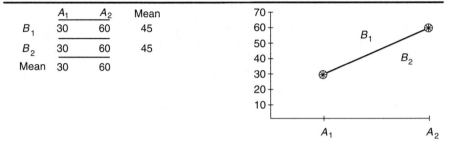

(b) 2 × 2 Factorial (*A* is significant; *B* and the interaction are not significant)

	A_1	A_2	Mean
B_1	70	70	70
B_2	40	40	40
Mean	55	55	

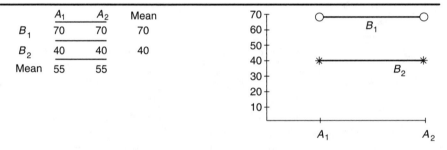

(c) 2 × 2 Factorial (*B* is significant; *A* and the interaction are not significant)

	A_1	A_2	A_3	Mean
B_1	10	30	80	40
B_2	30	50	100	60
Mean	20	40	90	

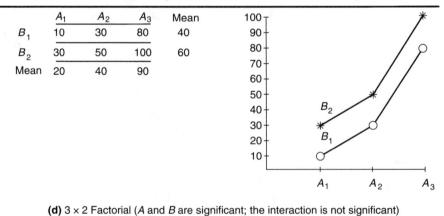

(d) 3 × 2 Factorial (*A* and *B* are significant; the interaction is not significant)

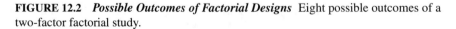

FIGURE 12.2 *Possible Outcomes of Factorial Designs* Eight possible outcomes of a two-factor factorial study.

	A_1	A_2	A_3	Mean
B_1	40	50	60	50
B_2	60	50	40	50
Mean	50	50	50	

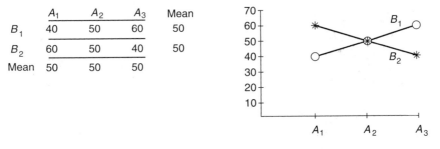

(e) 3 × 2 Factorial (the interaction is significant: *A* and *B* are not significant)

	A_1	A_2	A_3	Mean
B_1	30	40	50	40
B_2	40	40	40	40
Mean	35	40	45	

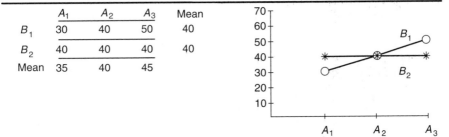

(f) 3 × 2 Factorial (*A* and the interaction are significant; *B* is not significant)

	A_1	A_2	A_3	Mean
B_1	30	40	50	40
B_2	70	60	50	60
Mean	50	50	50	

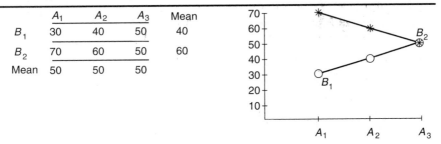

(g) 3 × 2 Factorial (*B* and the interaction are significant; *A* is not significant)

	A_1	A_2	Mean
B_1	40	40	40
B_2	40	60	50
Mean	40	50	

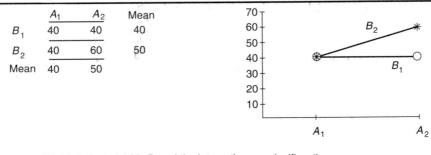

(h) 2 × 2 Factorial (*A*, *B*, and the interaction are significant)

FIGURE 12.2   Continued

Figure 12.2(c) illustrates a 2 × 2 factorial design in which there is a main effect for factor B, no main effect for factor A, and no interaction. The means for levels A_1 and A_2 are the same, whereas the means for levels B_1 and B_2 are different. In the graph, the B_1 and B_2 lines are separated, showing that there is a difference between the levels. Because the lines are parallel, there is no interaction between A and B.

Figure 12.2(d) shows a 3 × 2 factorial in which there is a main effect for both factor A and factor B, but no interaction. The means are different at each of the three levels of factor A and each of the two levels of factor B. As in Figure 12.2(c), the parallel lines indicate that there is no interaction.

Figure 12.2(e) illustrates a 3 × 2 factorial with a significant $A \times B$ interaction, but no significant main effects. Note that the column means for the three levels of factor A are the same, indicating that there is no main effect for factor A. The same is true for factor B. Thus, there is no significant main effect for A or B. But when plotted on the graph, the two lines cross, indicating an $A \times B$ interaction. Indeed, one value of drawing a graph is that interactions become readily apparent. Factor A has a different effect on the dependent measure when paired with B_1 than when paired with B_2. This is a classic interaction, in which the effect of one variable is systematically influenced by a second variable. Note also that the column means and row means in Figures 12.2(a) and (e) are identical. However, in Figure 12.2(a) the pattern of means within the cells indicates no interaction, whereas the pattern of means in Figure 12.2(e) does indicate an interaction. This illustrates that the column and row means provide an indication of main effects only, and we must inspect the individual cells on the graph to see an interaction.

Figure 12.2(f) shows a main effect for A and an $A \times B$ interaction. When both a main effect and an interaction occur, we always interpret the interaction first. The remaining examples can be read in similar fashion. We also have included a number of exercises in the lab manual on the *Student Resource CD* to provide additional practice with these challenging concepts and procedures.

An Example: Children's Dark-Fears Study

Let us return to our hypothetical children's dark-fears study. Suppose that the participants for this experiment include 40 children (20 boys and 20 girls), all afraid of the dark. Participants are randomly assigned to the four conditions of the 2 × 2 matrix (10 children per condition). Random assignment helps to ensure the equivalence of the four conditions at the outset of the study.

There are two independent variables. Variable A (illumination) is presented at two levels: a lighted and a darkened condition. Variable B (images) is presented at two levels: fear and neutral images. The dependent variable is the children's fear as measured by their heart rates. The research hypotheses are that there will be higher heart rates under dark conditions than under lighted conditions and higher heart rates under the fear-images condition than under the neutral-images condition and that the greatest effects on heart rates will occur when darkness and fear-images conditions are combined. That is, there will be a main effect for factor A, a main effect for factor B, and a significant $A \times B$ interaction. Participants are tested individually while seated comfortably facing a projection screen. A small sensor is placed on a finger to monitor heart rate. Participants are told that they will be shown 10 slides and will be asked questions about them later. Each slide is shown for 15 seconds with a 5-second pause between slides. Cell A_1B_1 represents the lighted-plus-fear-images condition. The lights are kept on in the room and the fear-image slides are presented (e.g., ghostly images, such commonly feared animals as snakes, a burglar entering a house, and so on). Cell A_2B_1 represents the dark-plus-fear-images condition. The lights in the room are turned off and the participants are presented the fear images. Cell A_1B_2 represents the neutral-images-lighted condition, and cell A_2B_2 represents the neutral-images-dark condition. The general procedures in these two conditions are the same as described before except that the slide images presented are neutral, such as landscapes and buildings. The heart rate of each participant is monitored during the testing period. Thus, we have heart rate for 40 participants—10 participants in each of four different conditions.

Table 12.4 shows hypothetical data for the 10 participants in each of the four conditions of the study. The row mean of 106.2 is the mean for fear images; the row mean of 99.0 is the mean for neutral images; 98.2 and 107.0 are the column means for light and dark conditions, respectively. The individual cell means are shown in parentheses.

TABLE 12.4 *Heart Rates for 40 Dark-Fears Children*

| Factor B (images) | Factor A (illumination) | | Row Mean |
	Level A_1 (lighted)	Level A_2 (dark)	
	112	131	
	106	125	
	102	121	
	101	116	
	99	113	
B_1 (fear)	99	112	
	97	111	
	95	110	
	92	103	
	80	99	
	(98.3)	(114.1)	106.2
	115	119	
	110	112	
	105	107	
	103	102	
	100	95	
B_2 (neutral)	98	95	
	97	95	
	90	92	
	83	91	
	80	90	
	(98.1)	(99.9)	99.0
Column Mean	98.2	107.0	

To test for main effects, we compare the means of the two levels of each factor. The means of the two levels of *A* (98.2 and 107.0) are compared to determine whether there is a main effect for illumination [Figure 12.3(a)]. To determine whether there is a main effect for *B*, we compare the means for the fear and neutral images (106.2 and 99.0) [Figure 12.3(b)]. To determine whether there is an interaction, we compare means of the four cells to see whether the effects of one independent variable on the dependent variable are different depending on the level of the other independent variable. The interaction is most easily seen in the graph shown in Figure 12.4. It is helpful to graph the cell means, because it will help you to see whether an interaction might exist and whether the mean differences suggest the presence of main effects.

Looking at the data in Table 12.4 and the graph in Figure 12.4, we see that participants in the dark condition have a higher mean heart rate (107.0) than the participants in the lighted condition (98.2), suggesting that there may be a main effect for illumination. The fear-images condition has a higher mean heart rate (106.2) than the neutral-images condition (99.0), suggesting that there may be a significant main effect for image type. The two lines in Figure 12.4 are not parallel, suggesting the possibility of an $A \times B$ interaction. The B_1 line slopes upward, moving from a mean of 98.3 to a

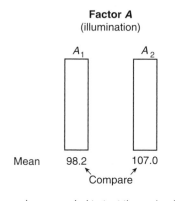

(a) Comparisons needed to test the main effects for Factor *A*

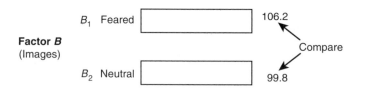

(b) Comparison needed to test the main effects for Factor *B*

FIGURE 12.3   *Testing for Main Effects*   Main effects are tested by comparing the means for each factor while ignoring the grouping on other factors.

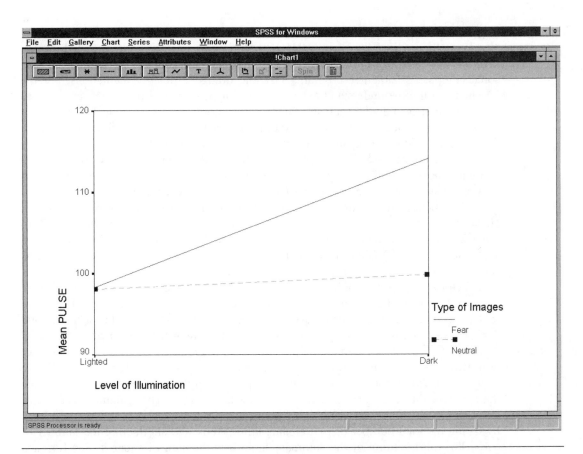

FIGURE 12.4 *Graph of the Children's Dark-Fears Study* The fact that the lines in this graph of the children's dark-fears data are not parallel suggests the possibility of an interaction. When both main effects and interactions are found, the main effects should be interpreted in light of the interaction.

mean of 114.1. The slope of this line appears to be due to the elevation of the A_2B_1 cell, in which the dark condition and the fear images are combined. The mean of this cell is elevated compared with the other three cells. Fear images produce high heart rates, but only in the presence of the dark condition. The B_2 line is nearly flat; that is, the amount of light has little effect when neutral images are used. This seems clearly to be an interaction. Thus, we may have an $A \times B$ interaction, a main effect for A, and a main effect for B.

Analysis of Variance in Factorial Designs

The appropriate statistical analysis for factorial designs is analysis of variance (ANOVA). The calculations for ANOVA are usually carried out by use of **computer-analysis**

programs, such as the *Statistical Package for the Social Sciences (SPSS), SPSS for Windows, Biomedical Programs (BMDP), Statistical Analysis System (SAS), Statistica, Statview,* and *Minitab.* Many of these programs are available to run on your personal computer. Computer programs take the drudgery out of calculations, but the researcher still must understand experimental design, statistical principles, and how to use the computer to do the analysis. Knowledge of computer use is critical for researchers, but this knowledge is not a substitute for understanding the principles of research design and statistical analysis. Remember our admonition in Chapter 1: a laboratory technician is not necessarily a scientist; it is not the technician's manipulation of laboratory equipment, including computers, that defines science. Science is defined by the *process of systematic thinking* that guides the use of laboratory techniques.

Statistical computations for complex ANOVAs are beyond the scope of this text. However, we do cover statistical analysis procedures on the *Student Resource CD.* In this section, we will focus on understanding an ANOVA and interpreting the results. The results of an ANOVA are typically presented in an ANOVA summary table, as shown in Table 12.5. The first column of the summary table lists the sources of variation: factor *A* (illumination), factor *B* (images), the *A* × *B* interaction, the within-groups variance (error), and the total variance. In the second column, the degrees of freedom (df) associated with each source have been entered. Note that associated with the total variance there are 39 degrees of freedom, 1 less than the total number of participants. The total degrees of freedom are then apportioned to factors *A* and *B* and their interaction [two levels of *A,* thus $df_a = (2 - 1) = 1$; two levels of *B,* thus $df_b = (2 - 1) = 1$; the degrees of freedom for the interaction is the product of the degrees of freedom for the main effects, thus $df_{a \times b} = df_a \times df_b = (2 - 1) \times (2 - 1) = 1$]. The remaining degrees of freedom (36) are associated with the within-groups or error variance and are calculated by taking the total number of participants in the study and subtracting the number of cells. The third column of the summary table lists the sum of squares (SS) for each source. Note that the total sum of squares is, in fact, the total; that is, the sum of all component sums of squares will equal the total sum of squares. In the fourth column, each sum of squares has been divided by its associated degrees of freedom to yield the mean square (MS), which is the variance as it is calculated by the ANOVA procedure. In the fifth column, the mean squares have been divided by the within-groups mean square (the error term). This between-groups variance divided by the within-groups variance is

TABLE 12.5   *ANOVA Summary Table*

The ANOVA summary table organizes the statistical analysis. This is the summary table for the data shown in Table 12.4.

Source	df	SS	MS	F	p
Factor *A* (illumination)	1	765.62	765.62	7.88	.008
Factor *B* (image type)	1	525.62	525.62	5.41	.026
AB interaction	1	497.02	497.02	5.12	.030
Error	36	3497.50	97.15		
Total	39	5285.78	135.53		

the *F*-ratio. Thus, *F*-ratios for each factor and the interaction are calculated and recorded in the summary table. The probability (*p*) of each *F*-ratio is shown in column 6 of the summary table. If the *p*-value is less than the chosen alpha level, the null hypothesis is rejected and we conclude that there is an effect.

In our ANOVA, there is a significant interaction ($p = .03$, alpha = .05). That is, fear, as measured by heart rate, is highest when darkness and fear images are presented together. The summary table also shows significant main effects for both illumination level and image type, but they can be understood only in terms of the interaction. That is, under the neutral-images condition the light or dark condition does not make a difference; likewise, under lighted conditions, the fear images do not cause more fear than do the neutral images. The main effects are due to the interaction—to the condition A_2B_1 in which the fear images and darkness occur together. When we interpret results that include both an interaction and a main effect, *we always begin the interpretation with the interaction.* The main conclusion that can be drawn from this hypothetical study is that neither fear images alone nor darkness alone appears to be sufficient to stimulate children's night fears, but the two together are a sufficient condition for children's night fears. To accept the finding of a main effect for *A* without interpreting it in terms of the interaction could lead us to an erroneous conclusion that the darkness itself causes increased fear.

The *Student Resource CD* describes several published studies that use factorial designs.

Quick-Check Review 1: Factorial Designs

1.1. What are factorial designs?

1.2. Explain: A factorial study tests at least three null hypotheses for each dependent measure.

1.3. What is meant by an interaction? A main effect?

1.4. Under what conditions would a factorial, rather than a single-variable design, be used?

1.5. In terms of main effects and interactions, what outcomes are possible in a factorial?

1.6. What are the limitations to the number of factors that can be included in a factorial design?

1.7. Why is it best to interpret the interaction first if both a main effect and an interaction are significant?

Variations of Basic Factorial Design

Factorial designs are used with increasing frequency in psychology, not only because of their efficiency in testing several causal hypotheses in a single design, but also because they are better at representing the complex nature of behavior in natural environments.

Many factorial designs are either within-subjects factorials, in which each participant is tested under all conditions, or mixed designs, that blend different types of factors into a single factorial study. Both of these designs are discussed in this section.

Within-Subjects or Repeated-Measures Factorial

We have already discussed randomized, between-subjects factorial designs in which participants are randomly assigned to conditions and each participant appears in only one cell. This basic factorial design was illustrated in the children's dark-fears study. An alternative factorial design is the **repeated-measures** or **within-subjects factorial.** If we had employed it in the dark-fears factorial study, each participant would have been tested under each of the four conditions. The ANOVA carried out to test for statistical significance is a **repeated-measures factorial ANOVA,** which takes into account the correlated groups.

Recall from Chapter 11 that using a within-subjects design involves disadvantages that stem from the fact that each participant is exposed to each condition. This means that sequence effects (practice and carry-over effects) may confound the results. Potential sequence effects may be so strong that a within-subjects design is not appropriate. However, when not precluded by such strong sequence effects, a within-subjects design has decided advantages over a between-subjects design. As with the single-variable design, use of a within-subjects design in a factorial experiment can (1) provide greater sensitivity to the effects of the independent variable by reducing the individual-differences component of the error term, (2) assure equivalence of groups at the start of the experiment because the participants in each condition are identical, (3) require fewer participants, and, related to the third point, (4) be more efficient. In the dark-fears study, for example, if we want 10 participants in each of the four conditions, then only 10 participants are needed for a repeated-measures design, but 40 participants are needed for a between-subjects design. This could be a major advantage when participants are difficult to obtain or when considerable preparation is required for each participant. Many researchers prefer a repeated-measures design over a between-subjects design because fewer participants are required. This is true for both single-variable and factorial experiments.

Mixed Designs

When there is more than one factor, it is possible that the factors will be of different types. For example, one factor may be a within-subjects factor, whereas the other may be a between-subjects factor. Participants would respond to all levels of the within-subjects factor, but be randomly assigned to only one level of the between-subjects factor. This is one type of mixed design.

The term **mixed design** is used in two different ways, which can lead to considerable confusion. In one meaning, mixed design refers to a factorial that includes a between-subjects factor and a within-subjects factor. In the other meaning, mixed design refers to a factorial that includes a manipulated factor and a nonmanipulated factor. It is important to distinguish between the two types of mixed designs.

Between-Subjects and Within-Subjects Factors. In this meaning of the term mixed design, in which both **between-subjects factors** and **within-subjects factors** exist in the same study, the critical issue is a statistical one. For example, suppose that a study has "level of distraction" as the within-subjects factor and the "amount of potential reward for success" as the between-subjects factor, as shown in Table 12.6. Each participant is assigned to one of the potential reward conditions (the between-subjects factor) and tested under all levels of distraction (the within-subjects factor). Of course, for the within-subjects factor, the order of presentation of conditions is counterbalanced to control sequence effects. In this mixed design, the ANOVA formulas will differ depending on which factors are within-subjects factors and which are between-subjects factors. Recall that in analyzing within-subjects designs the statistical procedures must take into account the correlated nature of the data. Computation of ANOVAs for mixed designs is beyond the scope of this text. In most cases, data from such designs are analyzed using statistical computer programs.

Manipulated and Nonmanipulated Factors. In this meaning of the term mixed design, in which both **manipulated factors** and **nonmanipulated factors** are included, the essential issue is one of interpretation of results, rather than statistical procedures. In a mixed design in which one factor is a nonmanipulated variable and one factor is a manipulated variable, participants are randomly assigned to conditions of the manipulated variable, but are assigned to levels of the nonmanipulated variable based on their preexisting characteristics. For example, if a researcher is studying the effects of crowding on aggression, participants could be randomly assigned to one of three conditions: alone, slightly crowded, and crowded. The level of aggression of participants in each of these conditions would then be observed. The researcher actively manipulates the variable of crowding.

Suppose that the researcher is also interested in sex differences in response to crowding, suspecting that there is an interaction between sex of participant and level of crowding on the dependent measure of aggression. Sex is a nonmanipulated variable; the researcher places participants in the male or female group based on their sex. This design is shown in Table 12.7. The formulas for the statistical analyses are not affected by whether the variables are manipulated or nonmanipulated, as they are when we are dealing with between- and within-subjects factors. The importance of whether a factor is manipulated or nonmanipulated comes into play when we *interpret* the statistical analysis.

TABLE 12.6 *One-Between, One-Within Factorial Design*

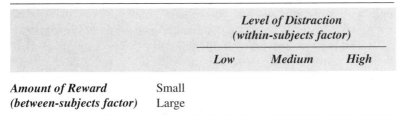

	Level of Distraction (within-subjects factor)		
	Low	*Medium*	*High*
Amount of Reward Small ***(between-subjects factor)*** Large			

In this design, participants are randomly assigned to either the small-reward or the large-reward condition and then are tested under all three levels of distraction.

TABLE 12.7 *One-Manipulated Variable, One-Nonmanipulated Variable Mixed Design*

	Level of Crowding (manipulated factor)		
	No Crowding	*Slightly Crowded*	*Very Crowded*
Sex of Participant Male			
(nonmanipulated factor) Female			

In this design, male and female participants are randomly assigned to one of the three levels of crowding. Both factors are between-subjects factors. Participants are randomly assigned to the level of crowding (manipulated variable) and assigned to male or female based on their sex (nonmanipulated variable).

Research designs using manipulated factors are experiments that control confounding variables. We can therefore safely draw causal inferences based on analysis of the main effects of the variables. Research designs using nonmanipulated factors are not experiments. Instead, they represent differential research. Remember that in differential research participants are not randomly assigned to groups and therefore groups may differ on variables other than the independent variable. These potential differences may cause confounding; unless we can rule out all potential confounding, we cannot draw causal inferences with confidence. Therefore, interpreting the main effects of nonmanipulated factors must be done cautiously and with attention to likely confounding variables. In our example, we must be cautious in drawing the inference that sex caused any observed differences in aggression. Furthermore, the same caution used in the interpretation of main effects for nonmanipulated factors should be used in the interpretation of any interaction involving a nonmanipulated factor. The interaction between sex and level of crowding on aggression should be interpreted as cautiously as the main effect of sex.

Mixed in Both Ways. Finally, it is possible to have a mixed design that is mixed in both of the ways just described. Table 12.8 presents such a situation. In this example, the researcher wants to compare accuracy of recognition of neutral and emotionally charged words in people with schizophrenia and control participants. The researcher arranges a factorial design in which both neutral and charged words are presented to the people with schizophrenia and controls for short intervals using a tachistoscope. Note that this is a factorial with one nonmanipulated variable (diagnosis) and one manipulated variable (type of words). Although participants could be randomly assigned to the levels of factor *A* (type of words), the researcher cannot randomly assign participants to factor *B* (diagnosis). In addition to being a mixed design in the preceding sense, this example is also a mixed design in that one factor (diagnosis) is a between-subjects variable, whereas the other factor (types of words) is a within-subjects variable. The researcher first classifies each factor on the dimension of between-subjects versus within-subjects factors in order to select the appropriate ANOVA for statistical analysis. Then each factor is classified on the dimension of manipulated versus non-

TABLE 12.8 *Design That Is Mixed in Both a Statistical Sense (One-Between, One-Within) and in an Experimental Sense (One-Manipulated, One-Nonmanipulated)*

		Type of Words *(within-subjects factor)*	
		Neutral	*Emotional*
Diagnosis *(between-subjects factor)*	Schizophrenic Normal		

In this design, diagnosis is a between-subjects factor, whereas type of words is a within-subjects factor. This will affect the ANOVA formulas used. In addition, diagnosis is a non-manipulated factor, whereas the type of words is a manipulated factor. This will affect the confidence of our causal inference.

manipulated factors to interpret the results of the statistical analysis. Again, the researcher must be especially cautious in drawing conclusions based on observed main effects and interactions with nonmanipulated factors.

Quick-Check Review 2: Variations of Basic Factorial Designs

2.1. What is the major advantage of a repeated measures factorial?

2.2. What are the two meanings of mixed design?

2.3. Explain the implications of mixed designs for (a) interpretation of results and (b) statistical analyses.

ANOVA: A Postscript

Analysis of variance (ANOVA) is one of the most flexible statistical tools available for the evaluation of data. ANOVA compares the variability of the means against a standard based on the variability of scores within each group. If the means are more variable than expected, the researcher concludes that the independent variable had an effect. The concept of comparing the variability between groups to the variability within groups is constant in every ANOVA, no matter how complicated it becomes.

In an ANOVA with three or more groups, if F is statistically significant, specific means comparisons must be made to find which groups differ significantly from the others. The specific means comparisons are carried out as a priori or as post hoc comparisons (see Chapter 10). In a repeated-measures ANOVA, participants are tested under each condition. The repeated-measures ANOVA takes this fact into account in computing the within-subjects variance.

With factorial designs the analysis of variance is extended still further. Here the effects of each independent variable and the interactive effects of combinations of independent variables are examined. For example, with two factors (A and B), there are three

"He wouldn't listen to me when he was designing the study — so now he has to interpret a five-way interaction."

Interpreting complex interactions can be extremely difficult.

possible effects: the *A* main effect, the *B* main effect, and the interaction between *A* and *B*. With three factors, there are three main effects (*A*, *B*, and *C*), three two-way interactions (*AB*, *AC*, and *BC*), and one three-way interaction (*ABC*) for a total of seven different effects. Four factors produce the following possible effects: *A, B, C, D, AB, AC, AD, BC, BD, CD, ABC, ABD, ACD, BCD,* and *ABCD*. Finally, the factorial ANOVAs can take into account which factors are within-subjects factors and which are between-subjects factors.

Although it can become complicated as factors are added to a study, extending the logic and the computational formulas of the analysis of variance to factorial designs is not difficult. The formulas themselves can become quite complex, but for the most part, researchers rely on computers to perform the actual computation. Because there are many different effects, there are many different *F*-ratios; but each *F*-ratio represents a comparison of between-groups variability to within-groups variability. Furthermore, the *F*-ratio in these complex designs is interpreted in exactly the same way as in simpler designs; if the probability of obtaining the *F* or a larger *F* is less than the alpha level, the null hypothesis that there are no group differences is rejected. The problem is not in the computation of complex ANOVAs, but in the interpretation stage, in which the researcher must visualize and explain complex interactions (see the cartoon). The combination of consistency in how the ANOVA is used and the flexibility of the procedure to analyze data from so many different designs makes analysis of variance the most widely used statistical technique in psychology.

Given the diversity of ANOVA procedures, it is perhaps not surprising that ANOVA procedures been extended into still other designs. These advanced procedures are generally beyond the scope of this book and are described here only briefly.

Analysis of Covariance

Another widely used technique is **analysis of covariance** (**ANCOVA**). Unfortunately, ANCOVA is easily misused by those who do not understand its nuances (Lord, 1967). Analysis of covariance is used in the same way as analysis of variance with one addition. As part of the analysis, the effects of a theoretically unimportant, but nonetheless powerful, variable are removed from the dependent variable scores. For example, if you want to study the effects of reinforcement strategies on learning in young children, you could set up a study with two or three levels of the independent variable. You could then randomly assign the sample of children to each condition and measure how well they perform on the measure of learning (the dependent variable). Of course, the age of the children will affect how quickly they learn material. However, you are not interested in the variable of age in this study. You could hold age constant by using only participants who are in a narrow age range. You could also use a matching procedure to make sure that the groups are equivalent on age at the beginning of the study. On the other hand, you could randomly assign participants to groups and use analysis of covariance to remove statistically the effects of age from the dependent measure. Analysis of covariance delivers a more sensitive test of the hypothesis because unwanted variability is statistically removed as part of the analysis. We must caution, however, that ANCOVA is a complicated procedure, with many potential pitfalls. For a detailed discussion of ANCOVA, consult Keppel (1991).

Multivariate Analysis of Variance

Another extension of analysis of variance, which is becoming much more popular as sophisticated computer analysis packages become available, is **multivariate analysis of variance (MANOVA).** The difference between an ANOVA and a MANOVA is in the dependent variable. An ANOVA has only one dependent variable, whereas a MANOVA has multiple dependent variables. Conceptually, it is similar to the extension from one-way ANOVAs to factorial ANOVAs, except that MANOVAs have multiple dependent variables. The full power of MANOVA procedures is still being discovered. Just as in analysis of covariance, using MANOVA procedures correctly and interpreting the results appropriately require an extensive understanding of the technique.

Clearly, analysis of variance techniques are flexible and powerful procedures for analyzing data from almost any design. With the aid of the computer, the computations can be done quickly and easily. However, the researcher still has to understand research design to set up the computer analyses correctly. Even more critical, the researcher must understand when ANOVA procedures are appropriate to use and how to use them. Even for professionals who conduct little research, knowing these concepts is important in understanding and evaluating the research reported by others. For this reason, doctoral and master's programs in psychology include extensive course work in statistics. Finally, performing the appropriate statistical analysis is only the first step in the evaluation of data. The next step is interpreting the meaning of the results. Interpreting meaning requires evaluating the entire study on such issues as potential confounding and the adequacy of control procedures. Statistical procedures, even such clever and useful ones as ANOVA, do not impart meaning to data. Only the researcher, well trained in science, can take this last important step.

> ### Quick-Check Review 3: ANOVA: A Postscript
>
> **3.1.** What does an analysis of covariance do?
> **3.2.** How does a MANOVA differ from an ANOVA?

Chapter Summary

Factorial designs include more than one independent variable. They are efficient and flexible designs that combine information from the equivalent of two or more single-variable studies. Their greatest advantage is that they yield information about the interactive effects of the independent variables.

Factorial designs can be of several types, in which the factors are (1) between-subjects variables or within-subjects variables, (2) manipulated variables or nonmanipulated variables, or (3) mixed factorials. A factorial with a within-subjects component must be analyzed with statistical procedures that take into account the correlated nature of the data. A factorial with a nonmanipulated component must be interpreted cautiously, because causality cannot be properly inferred from nonmanipulated independent variables.

ANOVAs are used to analyze factorial designs. It is helpful to graph cell means and, by inspection of the graph, to note whether significant interactions and/or main effects seem likely. When the analysis indicates that both main effects and an interaction are significant, the main effects should always be interpreted in terms of interaction.

Key Terms

Define the following key terms. Be sure that you understand them. They are discussed in the chapter and defined in the glossary.

factorial designs
interaction
factors
matrix of cells
design notation
main effects
row means
column means
computer analysis programs
Statistical Package for the Social Sciences (SPSS)

SPSS for Windows
Biomedical Programs (BMDP)
Statistical Analysis System (SAS)
Statistica
Statview
Minitab
repeated-measures factorial, or within-subjects factorial

repeated-measures factorial ANOVA
mixed design
between-subjects factors
within-subjects factors
manipulated factors
nonmanipulated factors
analysis of covariance (ANCOVA)
multivariate analysis of variance (MANOVA)

13

A Second Look at Field Research

II. Field Experiments, Program Evaluation, and Survey Research

People don't usually do research the way people who write books about research say that people do research.

—A. J. Bachrach, 1981

CD Resource Material _____

- Examples of Field Research
- Student Study Guide/Laboratory Manual

Web Resource Material _____

- Flashbulb Memories
- Managed Care
- Quasi-experimental Designs

R esearch in natural settings was introduced in Chapter 6, where the focus was on low-constraint field research (naturalistic observation, case studies, and archival research). These methods are useful in gathering facts, observing contingencies, becoming familiar with phenomena, developing hypotheses for later high-constraint research, and testing correlational hypotheses. But research in natural settings is not limited to low-constraint methods. This chapter covers higher-constraint field research, including field experiments, program evaluation, and survey research.

Conducting Field Research

It is increasingly common for psychological research to be carried out in field settings. For example, there are demands to evaluate the effectiveness of education and public health programs, to assess the effects of such large-scale events as disasters and economic recessions, and to determine employee reactions to changed work conditions or consumers' reactions to new products. These are questions about causality, which cannot readily be answered by low-constraint research because it does not rule out alternative hypotheses. Conducting experimental research in natural settings is difficult because of the limitations imposed by the settings. For example, there might not be enough participants to create experimental and control groups, random assignment of participants to groups and precise measures of dependent variables may be impossible in the field, and manipulation of independent variables is difficult. In some studies, such as a study of the psychological effects of a natural disaster, manipulating the independent variable is impossible. Finally, it is often difficult to maintain projects in the field because key decision makers may cancel or curtail ongoing projects.

Reasons for Doing Field Research

There are three major reasons for conducting experiments in field settings:

1. To test the external validity of causal conclusions arrived at in the laboratory
2. To determine the effects of events that occur in the field
3. To improve generalization across settings

Experimental laboratory research tests causal hypotheses under controlled conditions designed to maximize internal validity. However, the cost for this improvement in internal validity may be a reduction in external validity. That is, the more precise and constrained the laboratory, the less natural the procedures and findings. As a consequence, laboratory research might not always generalize to the natural environment.

> The advantages of experimental control for inferring causation have to be weighed against the disadvantages that arise because we do not always want to learn about causation in controlled settings. Instead, for many purposes, we would like to be able to generalize to causal relationships in complex field settings, and we cannot easily assume that findings from the laboratory will hold in the field. (Cook & Campbell, 1979, p. 7)

For example, suppose that a controlled experiment is conducted in a university laboratory school and a new teaching method is found to be superior to the standard procedures used in schools throughout the state. No matter how much confidence the researcher has in the internal validity of the experimental results, it would be unwise to assume that when the new teaching method is adopted in schools across the state, operating under a variety of conditions, the method will be just as effective. Why? Because the field situations may be very different from the laboratory. The researcher should test the new instructional procedures in field situations to increase confidence in the generalizability of the results. This is particularly important in applied research, in which the goal is not only to understand phenomena, but also to use the new understanding in practical ways.

The second reason for doing field research is to meet growing demands for testing the effectiveness of such social programs as special education, public health campaigns, crackdowns on drunk drivers, and programs that give tax incentives to corporations. Each of these programs has an implicit assumption: the educational program will improve literacy; the public health program will reduce drug addiction; the drunk-driving crackdown will reduce highway fatalities; the tax incentives will increase economic growth. Unfortunately, such assumptions are seldom tested. Social programs, as well meaning as they may be, are often created for political ends. Seldom are supporters committed to testing program effectiveness. Politically, it may be better not to subject programs to testing than to find that one's costly and fine-sounding pet project does not work. Donald Campbell (1969) argued that developed countries should carry out social reforms as controlled social experiments, and the fate of each program should depend on the objective data. Such evaluations of new programs are not yet routinely carried out.

The third reason for conducting field research is to increase generalizability. To understand this, we must distinguish three types of generalization:

1. Generalization of results from the participants in the study to the larger population
2. Generalization of the results of the study over time
3. Generalization of results from settings of the study to other settings

The third type of generalization may be enhanced when the research is conducted in naturalistic settings.

Consider the example given earlier in which the effectiveness of a new teaching program was tested in a university laboratory school. The high-constraint laboratory setting, high in internal validity, is not necessarily strong in external validity. However, if the new program is found to be superior to other teaching methods in regular schools, the researcher can have greater confidence in inferring that the results can be generalized to other, similar classroom settings.

Neisser and Harsch (1992) conducted a clever field study to verify the external validity of a phenomenon that had been well established in the laboratory. Elizabeth Loftus and others had shown that memory is fragile and subject to significant distortion and that people are often unaware of the distortions (e.g., Loftus & Hoffman, 1989). In 1986, the day after the *Challenger* space shuttle exploded, killing the crew, Neisser and Harsch (1992) asked 44 college students to write down how they heard about the explosion and what they did. They asked them again 30 months later. None of these participants was entirely accurate in recall at 30 months, and over one-third gave dramatically different accounts the day after and 30 months later of how they found out about the *Challenger* disaster. More striking is that participants were certain that their memories 2.5 years after the accident were accurate, often describing the memories as exceptionally vivid. Many were astonished, even flabbergasted, when confronted with their own handwritten accounts made the day after the disaster. Participants could not believe that memories that seemed so vivid and accurate could be so distorted over time and that they would have no realization that the memories were distorted. This field study of memory enhances confidence in the external validity of the laboratory studies of the malleability of memory. It also suggests that these laboratory findings are relevant in real-world situations, such as eye-witness testimony in courts (Loftus & Ketcham, 1991).

Difficulties in Field Research

Ideally, field experiments should be conducted so as to be able to draw causal inferences. However, doing so can be difficult. In many field situations, we cannot apply laboratory controls or assign participants to groups. This is frequently the case in natural settings, such as schools, or when natural events affect a large number of people. For example, suppose that you want to know how much a natural disaster, such as a hurricane, affected residents' physical health. The natural event is the independent variable and the residents' health is the dependent variable. Note that the researcher has no control over the independent variable. How then does the researcher measure the reactions and draw causal inferences? To take another example, suppose that in studying children a researcher cannot randomly assign participants to different groups for treatment because participants are all part of a single class following a common program. That is, they are always together, and whatever is applied to one child is applied to all others. Assigning the children to different groups for purposes of the study will seriously interfere with the ongoing program, and the program director will not allow it. We want to conduct research with as much control as possible in order to draw causal inferences, and yet we know that random assignment or, for that matter, any unbiased assignment of participants to conditions is impossible. Under these restrictions, how can a new treatment be tested? The question here is this: How can questions about causality in natural settings be answered when many of the usual manipulation and laboratory control procedures are unavailable?

This chapter discusses two solutions to this question: quasi-experimental designs and program evaluation. Quasi-experimental designs are research designs that have been developed to answer causal questions in natural settings. Program evaluation is not a particular design, but is an increasingly important research area that includes many designs and strategies for assessing field settings. Single-subject experiments (covered in Chapter 11) can also test causal questions in field settings.

Flexibility in Research

We now want to bring up something that all scientists know, but that is not normally discussed in methods courses. Take a look at the Bachrach quote that opened this chapter. Is Bachrach correct? Well, yes and no. What does his statement mean? Bachrach was talking about flexibility and creativity in research—much as we did in Chapter 1 in our discussion of serendipity. Researchers use their hunches, flashes of insight, flights of creativity, and alertness to interesting, unanticipated events that can crop up. Such alertness can open new directions to be explored, helping to frame old questions in new ways or to formulate new ways of studying things. Creativity and flexibility are especially needed in field research, in which the controlled laboratory is not there to help keep everything organized and systematic.

Bachrach did not mean to imply that real research is unsystematic. Rather, he points out that there is an important place in the process to engage in the freer flights of research thinking. These free flights have their usefulness precisely because they exist in a total research context that includes the organization, structure, and precision of science. This systematic structure makes it possible to engage in the hunches and intellectual leaps without bringing the whole enterprise down to a chaotic jumble. When scientists are engaged in hypothesis testing, particularly of causal hypotheses, it is the systematic structure and precision that are needed. But, within that structure, opportunities for unanticipated discoveries may appear, and the good researcher does not ignore them.

So why do we bring this up now, so late in this text? We think it is important for the student to have learned the fundamentals of research before taking such free-flight leaps. It is like abstract artists, who need first to learn how to draw and paint before they can be completely free to create new and less constrained art forms. With such background, the researcher can be more flexible, which is often necessary in quasi-experimental designs and field research.

Quick-Check Review 1: Conducting Field Research

1.1. What is field research?

1.2. List three reasons for conducting field research.

1.3. What are the major difficulties in conducting field research?

1.4. What three types of generalization were discussed in this section?

1.5. Why is flexibility in field research important?

Quasi-experimental Designs

The highest degree of control is obtained with experiments. However, in some situations an experiment is impossible, but a quasi-experimental design is feasible. *Quasi* means approximately. Thus, a **quasi-experiment** is almost an experiment, but not quite equal to it. Quasi-experiments have the essential form of experiments, including a causal hypothesis and some type of manipulation to compare two or more conditions. They do control for some confounding, but do not have as much control as experiments. Thus, we must be cautious in drawing causal inferences from quasi-experiments. Donald Campbell (1969) argued that quasi-experimental designs should be used whenever experiments cannot be carried out. In many field situations, quasi-experiments *will still provide considerably more useful information than not experimenting at all.* Keep in mind that quasi-experimental designs are different from low-constraint methods in that they have many of the experimental control procedures.

Quasi-experimental designs include a comparison of at least two levels of an independent variable, but the actual manipulation is not always under the experimenter's control. For example, if a researcher compares health before and after a natural disaster, the disaster obviously cannot be manipulated, but the researcher can compare the health records from local hospitals before and after the disaster. Likewise, in many field situations, participants cannot be randomly assigned to groups; indeed, the researcher often cannot assign participants at all, but rather must accept the natural groups as they exist. Thus, in quasi-experimental designs:

1. We state causal hypotheses.
2. We include at least two levels of the independent variable, but cannot always manipulate the independent variable.
3. We usually cannot assign participants to groups, but must accept existing groups.
4. We include specific procedures for testing hypotheses.
5. We include some controls for threats to validity.

Compare these characteristics with the characteristics of an experiment in Chapter 10.

This chapter focuses on two quasi-experimental designs: the nonequivalent control-group design and the interrupted time-series design. Students who wish information about other quasi-experimental designs can consult Cook and Campbell (1979).

Nonequivalent Control-Group Design

The best way to test causal hypotheses with confidence is to compare groups that are created by the researcher through random assignment. This makes it likely that the groups are equivalent at the beginning of the study. The initial equivalence of groups is crucial in experimental design. However, in some situations participants are not assigned randomly and, therefore, the groups may not be equivalent at the beginning of the study. There are several designs in this category, all of which attempt to solve the problem of comparing two groups that we suspect are not equivalent at the beginning of the study. We introduced one design in this category in Chapter 10 (the pretest–posttest, natural control-group design).

Researchers frequently have no choice in field research but to use already existing groups; thus, participants are not randomly assigned. Even though the groups appear to be similar, it cannot be assumed that they are equivalent at the start of the study. The groups may differ on both the dependent variable and other potential confounding variables.

Campbell and Stanley (1966) popularized the **nonequivalent control-group design,** in which the groups to be compared already exist in the natural environment and therefore may not be truly equivalent at the start of the study. However, Campbell and Stanley suggested that already existing groups may often be similar to one another on most relevant variables. The more similar that natural groups are to one another, the closer the design approximates an experiment. Cook and Campbell (1979) extended these principles to situations in which naturally occurring groups are clearly not equivalent on potential confounding variables. Even in this extreme situation, it is sometimes possible to draw strong conclusions if the researcher carefully evaluates all potential threats to validity. The ideal is an experiment in which participants are randomly assigned to groups. If this is not possible, the best alternative is to use nonequivalent control groups in which the groups give every indication of being similar on most of the relevant variables. But even when this requirement cannot be met, careful analysis of the design and the results can sometimes allow the researcher to draw useful conclusions from what appears to be a weak research design (Cook & Campbell, 1979). Table 13.1 lists examples of research using a nonequivalent control-group design.

There are two major problems with nonequivalent groups: (1) the groups may differ on the dependent measure(s) at the start of the study, and (2) there may be other differences between the groups. The basic strategy to address the first issue is to measure the experimental and control group on the dependent measure both before and after the manipulation. The pretest allows us to determine how similar the groups are

---

TABLE 13.1   *Field Situations with Nonequivalent Groups*

---

1. Researchers want to evaluate the effectiveness of an antismoking campaign using two different schools. They suspect that one school has a higher rate of smoking than the other.
2. A company wants to test how new work rules might affect their employees' attitudes toward work. One department is selected as an experimental group and another as the control group. However, there is evidence that the first department has more positive work attitudes than the second.
3. A psychology professor wants to compare examination results in a research methods course based on two different textbooks. The professor teaches one section of the course at 8:00 A.M. on Monday, Wednesday, and Friday and the other at 4:00 P.M. on Tuesday and Thursday. The professor suspects that students who chose the early section may be different from those who chose the later section.
4. A new treatment approach for hyperactivity is to be tested in a special school using three existing classes. The classes, however, are at different levels of hyperactivity.

---

on the dependent variable(s) at the beginning of the study. This similarity is important: the more similar the groups are, the closer the design is to an experiment.

The researcher addresses the issue that groups may differ on variables other than the dependent variable (confounding due to selection) by ruling out each potential confounding variable. This is accomplished by identifying potential confounding variables, measuring them, and verifying that the groups do not differ on them. This is the strategy we outlined in Chapter 7 when we discussed selecting control groups in differential research. In differential research, groups potentially differ on several variables besides the variable that defined the groups. If we select the right control group(s), however, we can minimize confounding and thus move this nonequivalent control-group design closer to an experimental design. A typical nonequivalent control-group design is shown in Table 13.2.

Causality is inferred when the results show that the control group remains essentially the same from pretreatment to posttreatment, but the experimental group changes markedly. Although the nonequivalent control-group design controls for many potential sources of confounding, some confounding variables may be uncontrolled. The confounding that can affect the outcome will vary from study to study. A complete discussion of the principles for identifying confounding variables and interpreting their likely effects on a nonequivalent control-group study is beyond the scope of this book. The interested reader is referred to Cook and Campbell (1979) for a more complete discussion.

Figure 13.1 shows six possible outcomes of a nonequivalent control-group design. In Figures 13.1(a) and (b), the experimental and control groups are equivalent on the dependent measure at the beginning of the study. Of course, the groups may differ on other important variables, in which case the researcher must rule out confounding due to selection. In Figures 13.1(c) through (f), the groups differ on the dependent measure at pretest. In these instances, the researcher must rule out confounding due to selection and regression to the mean. For purposes of illustration, it is assumed that all changes shown are in the predicted direction.

In Figure 13.1(a), both the experimental and control groups show an increase on the dependent measure from pretest to posttest. The groups are equivalent at the beginning and show equivalent change over time. Thus, there appears to be no effect of the

TABLE 13.2 *Nonequivalent Control-Group Design*

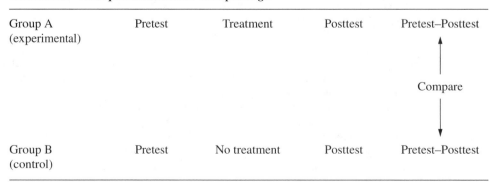

Group A (experimental)	Pretest	Treatment	Posttest	Pretest–Posttest
				↑
				Compare
				↓
Group B (control)	Pretest	No treatment	Posttest	Pretest–Posttest

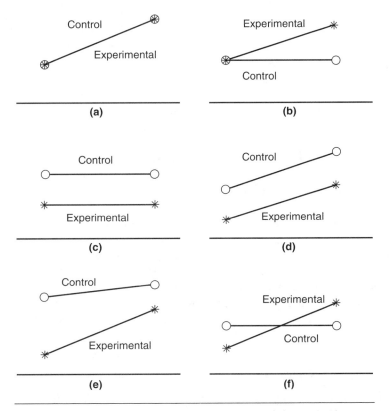

FIGURE 13.1 *Interpreting Nonequivalent Control-Group Designs*
Some possible outcomes of nonequivalent control-group designs are
illustrated graphically. Some outcomes are relatively easy to interpret,
whereas others are difficult or impossible to interpret.

independent variable. In Figure 13.1(b), the groups are equivalent on the dependent
measures at the beginning of the study. The experimental group shows a large change,
whereas the control group does not change from pretest to posttest. There does appear
to be an effect of the independent variable. However, before drawing this conclusion the
researcher must still rule out possible confounding due to selection. In Figure 13.1(c),
neither group changes from pretest to posttest. The obvious interpretation is that the
manipulation had no effect on the dependent variable. Figure 13.1(d) shows a similar
change in both groups from pretest to posttest. However, because both groups changed
in the same manner, we cannot attribute the change to the independent variable. It appears more likely that some maturation process or historical event common to both
groups may be responsible for the change in scores. Figure 13.1(e) shows a slight
change in the control group, but a marked change in the experimental group. Such results suggest an effect of the independent variable. However, there is still the potential
for regression to the mean, which limits confidence in this interpretation. Recall from

Chapter 8 that regression is a potential source of confounding whenever we begin an experiment with extreme scores. In Figure 13.1(e), the marked pretest difference between groups might represent extreme scores for the experimental group, which then regressed toward the mean level represented by the control group. Thus, the change in the experimental group may not be due to the independent variable. In Figure 13.1(f), the control group does not change, but the experimental group changes in the predicted direction, even going beyond the level of the control group. This is called a **crossover effect.** Such results provide considerable confidence in a causal inference. Maturation is an unlikely alternative hypothesis, because the control group presumably matured, but did not change. If maturation were responsible, it is unlikely that the effect would be so different in the two groups. Regression to the mean is also unlikely because the experimental group increased, not only to the mean of the control group, but beyond it.

The preceding examples represent reasonably interpretable data from nonequivalent control–group studies. Other situations can be more difficult, and sometimes impossible, to interpret. Using nonequivalent control-group designs and correctly interpreting data from them require considerable expertise and they are not recommended to beginning students. As we said before, an experiment is the best approach. When an experiment is not possible, a quasi-experiment in which groups are apparently equivalent is the best compromise. Only if neither of these alternatives is feasible should the researcher consider using a quasi-experimental design with nonequivalent groups.

Interrupted Time-Series Design

In an **interrupted time-series design,** a single group of participants is measured several times both before and after some event or manipulation (Orwin, 1997). Time-series designs are variations of within-subjects designs in which the same participants are measured in different conditions. The time-series design is similar to a simple pretest–posttest design except that multiple pretest and posttest measures are taken. That is, a series of measures is taken over time, "interrupted" by the manipulation, after which another series of measures is taken.

The simple pretest–posttest design is weak, leaving so many potential confounding factors uncontrolled that, even if a statistically significant difference is found, we cannot draw causal inferences (see Chapter 10). For example, recall the study of the use of relaxation to reduce the disruptive behavior of autistic children. A major potential confounding factor in this simple pretest–posttest study is regression to the mean. The disruptive behavior may naturally fluctuate over time, displaying considerable variability. The intervention might be applied only at a high point in this natural variation, just before the disruptive behavior decreased again. Thus, the observed improvement might not be due to the treatment, but only to the natural variability of behavior; the reduction would have occurred about that time without the treatment. Multiple measures give several points of comparison over time, thus allowing the researcher to recognize regression to the mean effects.

To apply the interrupted time-series design in the study of autistic children, we (1) measure disruption several times during a baseline observation period, (2) apply the treatment, and (3) measure disruptive behavior several more times after the intervention. This is exactly what Graziano (1974) did. Disruptive behavior of four autistic children was measured and recorded for a full year as a normal part of the monitoring carried out in the program. The treatment (relaxation training) was applied, and the behavioral measures were again taken for more than a year following the treatment. Figure 13.2 shows the results. Inspection of the graph shows considerable variation during the 1-year pretreatment baseline. Following treatment, there was a marked decrease in disruptive behavior,[1] reaching zero and remaining there. The results suggest that the decrease following treatment was not due to normal fluctuation or regression to the mean. It also seems unlikely to be due to maturation of all participants during the same period of time. Although a good demonstration of the effects of relaxation training, there is still a major confounding factor remaining. Can you identify it? (We will return to this point soon.)

Interrupted time-series designs are useful in settings in which the effects of some event—naturally occurring or manipulated—may be assessed by taking multiple measurements both before and after the event. These designs can take advantage of data already gathered over a long period of time. They can also be used in studies in which the presumed causal event occurs to all members of a population. For example, suppose that a state government wants to reduce traffic collisions by reducing the speed limit from 65 to 55 mph. Because the new speed limit applies to every driver in the state, there cannot be an experimental group of state drivers for whom the new limit applies and a control

---

[1]Note the peak of disruptive behavior immediately after training began. This peak is a common clinical phenomenon called a *frustration effect,* which occurs when new procedures are initiated with autistic children. Frustration effects are generally temporary. Note, too, that the disruption dropped dramatically following this short burst.

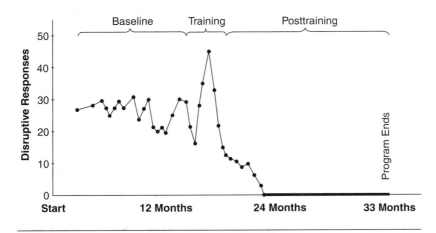

FIGURE 13.2 *Relaxation Treatment for Disruptive Behavior* A time-series design using four children with autism demonstrates that relaxation training decreases the frequency of disruptive behavior.

group for which it does not. This is an ideal situation for the interrupted time-series design. Figure 13.3 is a hypothetical graph of such a time-series study. The graph shows variation in the number of serious accidents during the preintervention phase, with an overall slight increase throughout the year. Following the new speed limit, there is a sharp reduction that eventually stabilizes at a new, lower level of accidents for the remainder of that year and into the next. Are these results sufficient to draw a reasonably confident conclusion that the reduced speed limit is effective in reducing the number of serious accidents? Let us consider the major potential confounding factors.

Selection is not at issue because this is essentially a within-subjects design and the two groups being compared, the state's drivers before and after the decreased speed limit, were thus equivalent at the start of the study. Testing effects are not critical because the measures taken are unobtrusive; that is, all measures are taken from traffic records and not directly from participants. Maturation is not an issue because it is unlikely that all of the state's drivers suddenly became better drivers at the same time that the speed limit changed. Regression to the mean is not an issue. Note that the postintervention decrease in accidents is much sharper, lasts longer, and reaches a lower mean level than the preintervention fluctuations. Primarily because of its multiple measures at pre- and posttreatment, the interrupted time-series design controls for most potential confounding. It is a far stronger design than the simple pre-post design in which only one measure is taken at each phase.

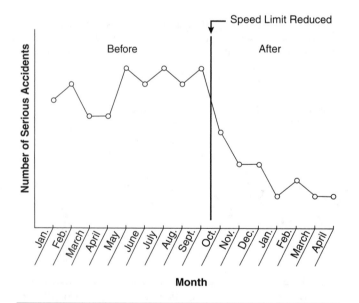

FIGURE 13.3 *Interrupted Time-Series Design* Using an interrupted time-series design, this hypothetical study illustrates the effects of a reduction in the state speed limit on the number of serious accidents.

With time-series designs, however, two potentially confounding factors remain: history and instrumentation. History can confound results in any procedure that requires a fairly long period of time, because any number of other events might account for changes in the dependent variable. For example, in our hypothetical speed-limit study, the state might have also sharply increased the number of patrol cars, the number of speeding tickets, and the severity of penalties for speeding and for drunk driving. Any of these actions may have contributed to the decrease in accidents. Thus, when using the interrupted time-series design, the experimenter must be careful to identify potential confounding due to history and rule it out. In this example, we must be sure that the state did not initiate these actions at the same time that it decreased the speed limit. (Recall a few paragraphs earlier when you were asked to identify the remaining major confounding factor in the time-series design for the relaxation training study. If you identified it as history, you were correct.)

Instrumentation is also a potential threat to validity in time-series designs. When people initiate new approaches or programs, there might also be accompanying changes in recording procedures. For example, if the state government was more systematic about collecting accident statistics after the speed limit change, any observed changes could be due to either the change in speed limit or the way the data were gathered. Such confounding due to instrumentation must be ruled out.

In a time-series study, the change must be sharp to be interpreted as anything other than a normal fluctuation. Any postintervention change that is slight or gradual is difficult to interpret as being due to the causal effects of the intervention. It should also occur immediately after the intervention unless there is a theoretical reason to expect a delay. For example, if an intervention by the government is expected to change consumer spending, but only after it has affected other economic variables, the change in consumer spending may be delayed and still indicate an effect of the intervention.

Note two important points about the interrupted time-series design. First, it is a flexible design that can be used in many situations. It can evaluate events that are large- or small-scale, that have already occurred, and that are either manipulated (such as the decreased speed limit) or not manipulated (such as a natural disaster). Think about this. How might you use this design to evaluate, for example, a large-scale natural disaster that has already occurred? Second, the time-series design can use existing data, such as data on auto accidents. This is one reason why this design is often used by government agencies to track the effects of new programs.

The interrupted time-series design is powerful and useful in many naturalistic situations. However, it can be improved by adding one or more comparison groups. In our hypothetical study of the effects of a change in speed limit on the number of accidents, we could use similar data from a neighboring state that did not reduce the speed limit as a comparison. This helps to control such confounding variables as history and maturation. For example, Guerin and MacKinnon (1985) studied the effects of a California law that required children under age 4 to be in federally approved child car seats while riding in cars. Using an interrupted time-series design, the authors examined the effects of the new law on child auto injuries. The number of injuries for children under age 4 was obtained from state records for a period covering 48 months prior to the start of the new law and for 12 months following its initiation. As a comparison, the researchers recorded auto injury data for children between 4 and 7 years of age, who were not covered by the law. They predicted that there would be a decrease for the younger group, but not for the older group of children. As shown in Figure 13.4, after the law went into effect, there was a drop in injuries in the younger group, but not in the older group, and the differences persisted over the next 12 months. In addition, the younger group was compared with a group of young children from Texas, where no child car seat law existed. The children in Texas did not show a decrease during the same period. Adding these two comparison groups increased confidence that the new law, and not other factors, accounted for the reduction in children's injuries.

Interrupted time-series designs can be used to test causal hypotheses in field settings in which the usual laboratory controls cannot be applied. Table 13.3 gives examples of published studies that used interrupted time-series designs. The studies are listed in the references at the end of this book so that the interested student can read the original reports.

Graphing the results of interrupted time-series studies provides considerable information, but simply inspecting the graph does not address whether the observed differences are statistically significant. Testing for statistical significance in time-series

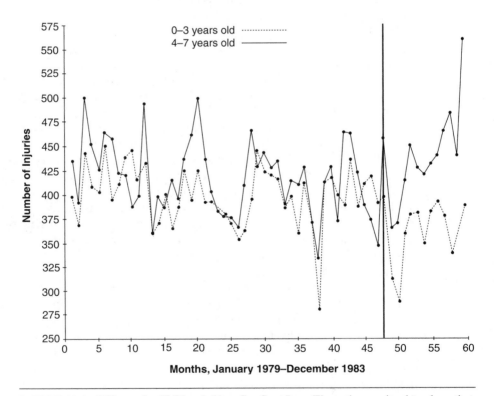

Months, January 1979–December 1983

FIGURE 13.4   *Effects of a Children's New Car Seat Law*   These time-series data show that a new car seat law reduced the number of injuries in 0 to 3-year-old children in comparison with 4 to 7-year-old children, who were not covered by the law.

Source: Guerin and MacKinnon, 1985.

TABLE 13.3 *Research Using Interrupted Time-Series Design*

1. Phillips (1983) used time-series designs to investigate the effects of televised violence on homicide rates. Using broadcasts of heavyweight boxing matches as the independent variable and homicide rates as the dependent variable, Phillips found a 12.4% increase in homicide rates following telecasts of the boxing matches.
2. Hilton (1984) used a time-series design to investigate the impact on highway fatalities of several measures to counteract drunk driving in California.
3. O'Carroll et al. (1991) studied the impact on homicide rates of a Detroit law that mandated jail sentences for illegally carrying a firearm. They found that the new law reduced street homicides, but not homicides in the home.
4. Two sports psychologists (Brewer & Shillinglaw, 1992) investigated the effectiveness of a four-session psychological skills training workshop in improving the competitiveness of intercollegiate lacrosse players.
5. Catalano and Serxner (1992) used an interrupted time-series design to investigate the relationship between employment security and birth weight of children. They found that during periods of employment uncertainty, such as when companies are laying off people, male babies average lower birth weight than during periods when employment is more secure.
6. Stolzenberg and D'Alessio (1997) used an interrupted time-series design to assess the impact of California's "3 strikes and you're out" law on the rate of serious crimes. As a control, they studied petty theft, which was not covered by the law.
7. McKay, Todaro, Neziroglu, and Yaryura-Tobias (1996) used an interrupted time-series approach to study the effectiveness of a treatment procedure for obsessive–compulsive disorder.

designs requires sophisticated procedures that are beyond the scope of this book. The interested student is referred to Glass, Wilson, and Gottman (1975) or Kazdin (1998) for a more detailed discussion.

Quick-Check Review 2: Quasi-Experimental Designs

2.1. Define quasi-experimental designs.

2.2. What is their value? What are their limitations?

2.3. When are nonequivalent control-group designs most effective in testing causal hypotheses?

2.4. How are interrupted time-series designs a variation on within-subjects designs?

2.5. What are the two major confounding factors with time-series designs?

Program Evaluation

The task in **program evaluation research** is to evaluate how successfully a program meets its goals. For example, researchers may need to evaluate a food-stamp program, a state highway speed-control program, or the effectiveness of rehabilitation programs for criminal offenders. In these days of tight budgets, a key word is accountability. The goal of program evaluation is to provide evidence on whether the money spent on the program is accomplishing the goals intended.

Program evaluation is not a set of research designs distinct from the designs discussed earlier in the text. Instead, these designs are modified to meet the constraints of the situation. The best possible research design, the design that permits the strongest conclusions, should always be used. However, program realities frequently restrict our choice of design.

Practical Problems in Program Evaluation Research

Unique practical considerations are inherent in program evaluation research. In lower-constraint research, participants are observed in natural settings even though it is difficult to impose effective controls in such settings. Program evaluators normally are restricted to observing public behavior. For example, an unobtrusive study of the sexual behavior of married couples would be unethical, not to mention illegal. Higher-constraint research brings participants into the laboratory, allowing considerable control. In contrast, program evaluation research evaluates the effectiveness of programs that operate in complex and often uncontrolled natural settings. Furthermore, program evaluators are often interested in how effective the program is in meeting the needs of clients—often a private and personal matter for each client. Finally, in most cases, the participants in the program have not volunteered for a research study. Rather, they became involved in the program because they had needs addressed by the program. Therefore, the program evaluator is faced with difficult practical and ethical considerations that few other researchers face.

Ethical constraints are common in program evaluation. Often the program is designed to meet an urgent need that cannot be ignored. The most valid research design would randomly assign participants to one of two conditions, the program group and the no-program group. But is it ethical to deny food stamps to some randomly selected individuals to see whether they really suffer malnutrition more than individuals who are given food stamps? Is it ethical to deny some children access to a special education program designed to overcome learning disabilities so that the program can be evaluated? Sometimes, more than ethical concerns restrict the researcher. In a learning disabilities program, for example, we could argue that the program is experimental and might not work. In fact, it might do more harm than good. Therefore, denying some participants access to the program to allow a cleaner evaluation of its effectiveness is ethical. However, it may not be acceptable from a political perspective. Depending on the perceived value of the program, the school board may believe that it is politically impossible to deny some students access. Any of these issues can prevent the use of an experimental design in the evaluation.

Another ethical issue affecting program evaluation research is informed consent. Voluntary consent to participate in research is the cornerstone of most ethical guidelines. But people being served by a particular program may feel obligated to participate even if they do not wish to. They may fear that the benefits that they receive from the program will be withdrawn if they do not cooperate. The program evaluator must be careful to minimize this kind of subtle coercion.

There are also practical issues that make program evaluations challenging. Unlike controlled studies in the laboratory, the program is in a natural setting and usually not under the control of the evaluator. Staff members are interested in doing the best job they can in running the program, and evaluating it is often secondary. A good program evaluator needs excellent political skills to convince staff to cooperate in the evaluation and to maintain their cooperation throughout. Often, when staff are involved in an evaluation, they resent the time that is taken away from their important work of providing services. If the evaluator is not sensitive to these realities, the relationship between the evaluator and staff in a program can become hostile. The program evaluator must be aware of potentially biasing factors in the data being gathered. A staff is generally interested in showing the program in its best possible light, not only because it is theirs, but because a program that appears to be ineffective might not get continued funding. Clients may have a vested interest in the program if they believe that it has been helpful, and they may therefore inflate their ratings of its effectiveness. On the other hand, some clients may believe that better programs could be implemented; therefore, they deflate their ratings of effectiveness. Such potential biases make it especially important that the evaluator rely on many data sources, at least some of which are objective measures.

Issues of Control

Control in program evaluation research is as important as in any research. Because of the naturalistic nature of the program evaluation setting, it is often difficult to apply controls. However, many controls can be applied, three of which are discussed here.

Selecting Appropriate Dependent Measures.   Most programs are developed with several goals in mind. Therefore, the program evaluator needs to use several dependent measures to evaluate the effectiveness of the program in meeting each intended goal. Some measures will focus on actual change in the individuals served by the program, and some will focus on changes outside the program, such as enhanced economic activity in the community. It is useful to include satisfaction measures from both the people served by the program and from the community in general. Although satisfaction measures do not indicate the program's effectiveness, they may influence future effectiveness. An effective but unpopular program will need to work to address this issue or continued funding will be jeopardized.

Minimizing Bias in Dependent Measures.   In any research, it is essential to minimize measurement bias. This is particularly important in program evaluation research, where the possibility of bias is high because data are often collected by the same people who run the program. Program evaluators try to minimize such bias by using objective rather than subjective measures and by using people who are not involved in the administration of the program to gather data. Many broad-based programs are intended to have communitywide effects that can be monitored using routinely available data, such as census data. No technique for minimizing bias will be completely effective in all situations. One of the better approaches is to use several dependent measures. If each is a valid measure and they all point to the same general conclusion, the evaluator can be confident of the results.

Control through Research Design in Program Evaluation.   As with any research project, the major controls are incorporated into the research design. The strongest program evaluation design is an experiment with random assignment of participants. When this cannot be done, the strongest alternative design should be used.

Typical Program Evaluation Designs

Dozens of research designs have been used for program evaluations, but three or four designs account for most of this research.

Randomized Control-Group Design.   The ideal program evaluation design is a control-group design with random assignment of participants to conditions. This design provides maximum control. The control group may be either a no-treatment control, a wait-list control, or some alternative treatment. Ethical considerations often dictate the nature of the control group. For example, under some conditions it might not be ethical to assign participants to a no-treatment control group. Instead, the best treatment currently available is used as a control against which the experimental procedure is compared.

Nonequivalent Control-Group Design.   If a randomized control-group design is impossible, the best alternative is a nonequivalent control-group design. It is often possible to identify a natural control group that is likely to be similar to the group you are evaluating. Our earlier example of evaluating the California child passenger restraint law used this design with time-series data. The researchers (Guerin & MacKinnon, 1985) selected two control groups: (1) children in the same age range from another state and (2) slightly older children (4 to 7 years old) from California. Children were not randomly assigned to these groups, but there was no reason to believe that the groups were different on variables likely to affect risk of death or injury from automobile accidents. So, even though this was not an experiment, it came very close to an experiment in its ability to rule out confounding variables.

Single-Group, Time-Series Design.   If a control group is not possible, the best alternative strategy is a time-series design. Repeated measures on the dependent variables before, during, and after the program can control many threats to internal validity. Depending on the funding source, pretest measures may be difficult to obtain because there is often pressure to begin services as soon as funds are released. Still, this design is flexible and useful in many situations. In fact, even when a control group is possible, using a time-series strategy will increase confidence in the evaluation of the program's effectiveness.

Pretest–Posttest Design.   The pretest–posttest design is weak. Unfortunately, it is used much too often in program evaluation research. With only two measures and no control group, most of the threats to internal validity are not controlled. The simple pretest–posttest design is not recommended.

Program Evaluation: An Example

Managed care is a concept that has quickly become a part of health insurance coverage in this country. With managed care, the insurance company or an organization hired by the insurance company attempts to control health care costs by monitoring health care and authorizing each procedure according to the principle of whether it is "medically necessary." The promise is that managed care will provide quality health care at lower cost by reducing waste and eliminating unnecessary procedures. Critics charge that managed care reduces costs by denying necessary treatment. In a debate of this magnitude, it is surprising that almost no data exist on the effectiveness of managed care programs in meeting their stated goals.

Raulin and his colleagues (Raulin, Brenner, deBeaumont, & Vetter, 1995; Raulin, deBeaumont, Brenner, & Vetter, 1995) used a nonequivalent control-group design to evaluate the effectiveness of a program to manage mental health benefits. Stratified random samples were selected from two insurance plans operated by the same insurance carrier; one included management of mental health benefits and one represented the standard insurance policy. The samples were stratified on age, sex, and severity of diagnosis, factors that are known to affect the outcome and cost of psychological treatment. Participants were selected from health insurance plans that were matched on their total mental health coverage. Although participants were not randomly assigned to groups, the selection procedure produced groups from the same geographical area that were closely matched on key demographic variables and had equivalent health care insurance coverage.

Participants selected by these procedures were recruited by letter to participate. To increase the likelihood of participation, participants were offered a financial incentive for participation. As is often the case in program evaluation studies, initial procedures had to be modified because they did not work well. Face-to-face interviews were replaced with a phone interview to make it more convenient for participants, and an initial $25 per hour reimbursement rate was raised to $40 per hour. Of course, not all participants that were contacted by letter chose to participate. It would be unethical to insist that everyone participate. Therefore, the sample may not have been representative of the population because of self-selection biases for participants. Approximately one-fourth of the participants selected for the study did agree to participate, and there were no differences between the participants who agreed to participate and those who refused on key demographic variables.

The managed care program evaluated in this study was designed to accomplish several things. Therefore, several dependent measures were needed in the evaluation to evaluate adequately how well the program was functioning. People in treatment were evaluated on (1) symptom level, using several well-validated symptom measures; (2) mood, also using measures with established validity; and (3) satisfaction with their care and their insurance coverage. In addition, cost data were obtained from the insurance carrier for both mental health coverage and for other medical care. Previous research had suggested that skimping on mental health coverage increases general medical costs because the people will take their concerns to their family physician.

The data suggest that the management of mental health benefits did not decrease the quality of care as measured by the standardized symptom and mood scales and the satisfaction measures used in the study. The mental health care costs were reduced by approximately 50% in the managed care group, and there were no differences between the groups on medical costs.

This was not a perfect study; no program evaluation ever is. Compromises have to be made when testing programs because of ethical and practical constraints. But this study did provide useful data on the effectiveness of a particular program relative to an alternative program. Caution is necessary in generalizing from this study to managed care programs in general. This study involved only the management of mental health benefits and therefore indicated little about whether managing general medical benefits would work as well. The managed care firm evaluated was relatively small, operated locally, and run by an unusually well qualified clinical director. It is not clear that one could generalize the findings of this study to other managed care operations, which now are almost all large national operations. But even with these limitations, this study provides useful data for making critical policy decisions on how to spend our health care dollars.

In summary, program evaluation research faces the major problem of attempting high-constraint research in low-constraint naturalistic settings. However, by carefully selecting dependent measures and using the strongest research design possible, the evaluation can get useful information about the effectiveness of programs in meeting their stated goals. Program evaluation is a valuable tool in the management of limited resources, because ineffective programs consume dollars that might have been spent on effective programs. Program evaluation is both a science and an art; we need good research, political, and communication skills to do it well. More than any other kind of research project, program evaluation depends on the ability of the researcher to gain the cooperation of people who are not necessarily committed to the cause of maximizing internal and external validity. It is a rapidly growing area of research, and the challenges of evaluating field programs are unique and require specific research skills (Posavac & Carey, 1997).

Quick-Check Review 3: Program Evaluation

3.1. What is the major purpose of program evaluation research? What is its importance?

3.2. What is the major difficulty in conducting program evaluation?

3.3. How can internal validity be maximized in program evaluation research?

3.4. What research designs are used most frequently in program evaluation?

3.5. How is program evaluation research both a science and an art?

Surveys

Surveys gather information by specifically asking participants about their experiences, attitudes, or knowledge. This section describes how surveys are used, the types of surveys, the steps in survey research, and how to select and construct an appropriate survey instrument. Survey research is not a single research design (Schuman & Kalton, 1985). Rather, it utilizes several basic research procedures to obtain information from people in their natural environments. Surveys can be relatively simple, with just a few questions that can be asked over the telephone. They can also be complicated and sophisticated instruments that test hypothesized relationships among variables and that require lengthy, face-to-face interviews. Because surveys impose constraints on respondents by posing specific questions, they are a variation of case-study research. Surveys also can be used to test relationships among variables, which is a variation of correlational research. In fact, survey instruments can be used in virtually any type of research, from case studies through experimental studies.

Types of Surveys

We will discuss two types of surveys: status surveys and survey research.

Status Survey.   A **status survey** is used to describe current characteristics of a population. For example, surveys to determine voter preferences or teachers' satisfaction with their professions are status surveys. These are commonly used in public health research to determine rates of illness and health-related behaviors. A recent example is the status survey of frequency of food consumption in the United States (Longnecker, Harper, & Kim, 1997). Status surveys were in use as long ago as the 1830s in England, when the working conditions in mines and factories during the Industrial Revolution were first investigated.

Survey Research.   **Survey research** was developed in the 20th century. It seeks not only the current status of population characteristics, but also tries to discover relationships among variables. Lepine, Gastpar, Mendlewicz, and Tylee (1997) carried out the first large-scale pan-European survey of adults with depression. They surveyed nearly 80,000 adults in six countries, finding more than 13,000 persons who suffered from depression (a prevalence of 17%). Their survey determined the rates of major depression (10% of all people), and they found that 43% had never sought help for their depression and that only 35% of those with depression had received any treatment at all. Only 25% of those who had been treated received antidepressant medication, one of the major treatments for depression. Much of this was a status survey, but the researchers were also interested in relationships between, for example, depression and work productivity. They found that individuals with major depression lost four times as many workdays as those without the disorder. This survey provided important information on a serious health problem and its treatment in Europe.

Steps in Survey Research

Surveys are the most familiar and ubiquitous form of research in the social sciences. Surveys can be carried out by anyone who wants to find out what people are thinking or feeling about specific issues or events. At first glance, it may appear an easy task to conduct surveys; after all, a survey is simply asking people what they are thinking. But, as we will see, detailed planning is necessary if surveys are to be successful.

The major goal of a survey is to learn about the ideas, knowledge, feeling, opinions, attitudes, and self-reported behavior of a defined population. To carry out a survey, the researcher must identify the content area, construct the survey instrument, define the population, draw a representative sample, administer the survey instrument, analyze and interpret the data, and communicate the results. These steps are overlapping, and each step demands careful work (see Table 13.4).

Among the first tasks of the researcher is to determine the informational area to be studied, the population to be surveyed, and how the survey instrument is to be administered. These decisions guide the construction and administration of the survey instrument, which might be an interview schedule for surveys done in person or by telephone or a questionnaire for self-administered surveys. For example, Milbrath, Hausbeck, and Enright (1991) wanted to determine the knowledge and attitudes of New York State high school students (the population) about environmental problems (the area of information) using a group-administered questionnaire (the form of the survey).

Types of Survey Instruments

The survey instrument may be a **questionnaire** or an interview schedule. In a self-administered questionnaire, the respondents read the instructions and write or mark their answers to the questions. In group-administered questionnaires, such as might be carried out in a classroom, the researcher might read and clarify the instructions to the respondents. In telephone or in-person interviews, the instrument is called an **interview schedule,** and the researcher reads the questions to the respondent and records the answers. The survey instrument lists the questions in the order in which they are to be answered and provides instructions and means for answering them. If it is a self-administered questionnaire, it must be a clear guide for the respondent. If it is to be administered by a

---

TABLE 13.4   *Steps in Survey Research*

1. Determine what area of information is to be sought.
2. Define the population to be studied.
3. Decide how the survey is to be administered.
4. Construct the first draft of the survey instrument; edit and refine the draft.
5. Pretest the survey with a subsample; refine it further.
6. Develop a sampling frame and draw a representative sample.
7. Administer the final form of the instrument to the sample.
8. Analyze, interpret, and communicate the results.

researcher, it must be a clear guide for the interviewer. In either event, the questions are listed in a fixed order for all respondents. The language must be clear and concise and must be appropriate for the population being studied. Overall, a questionnaire should have an uncluttered and orderly appearance and must be well within the reading and comprehension abilities of the respondents.

Questionnaires and interviews begin with an introduction, which explains the purpose of the survey and gives instructions to the respondent. The questions then fall into two main categories: demographic and content questions. The demographic questions seek information about the respondents, such as age, sex, occupation, marital status, and so on. These are **factual items,** and they can be verified independently. Most of the items are content items, dealing with the participant being surveyed. **Content items** ask about the respondents' opinions, attitudes, knowledge, and behavior. People's opinions and attitudes are subjective, vary among individuals, and are not evaluated as right or wrong. Questions about what people think of particular political parties or where they stand on such issues as animal rights, abortion, or environmental issues ask about opinions.

Frequently, surveys ask about the respondents' knowledge, such as high school students' knowledge of geography, history, or science. Questions that ask, "What is the capital of Afghanistan?" or "What percentage of paper products in the United States is made of recycled paper?" are tests of knowledge. Answers to these questions can be evaluated independently and objectively as right or wrong.

Content items can also focus on the overt behavior of the respondent. For example, the question "What proportion of your newspapers have you recycled in the past year?" asks about the person's behavior. Theoretically, behavior-focused items can be objectively verified. However, the information in surveys is the self-report of people and, although relatively convenient to obtain, there are obvious concerns over the reliability and validity of self-reports.

Surveys typically include all types of items—demographic, attitude, opinion, knowledge, and behavior items. In the Milbrath et al. (1991) survey of eleventh graders, for example, the content focused on the respondents' knowledge, attitudes, opinions, and behavior with reference to environmental issues. By also including demographic items, these investigators were able to identify potential relationships between the knowledge and attitudes of the students and demographic characteristics.

Developing the Survey Instrument

The survey instrument is developed in several steps. The researcher must determine exactly what questions are to be asked, in what form, and in what order. The instrument must be constructed so that it adequately covers the area of information sought and is appropriate for the targeted population. Construction of the survey instrument also depends on the procedure that is going to be used to administer it. A face-to-face interview generally requires a much more detailed survey instrument than is typical for a telephone survey, which usually includes a few simple items in a 1- or 2-minute conversation. In contrast, personal interview surveys can include many questions, many opportunities for the interviewer to probe for more information, and may require several hours to complete.

Surveys can be administered by mail, telephone, or personal interview. The most information and generally the best results are obtained when the survey is administered in a face-to-face interview, although such interviews are time consuming and expensive. The personal interview is effective, but also time consuming and expensive.

Construction of the survey instrument is one of the most time-consuming steps in the survey research process. The researcher must have a clear understanding of the nature of the information desired, and the questionnaire should be kept focused on that area. Sometimes researchers try to cover too many areas or they attempt a "shotgun" approach, in which clear reasons for the questions are lacking. These approaches make the questionnaire hard for the respondent to answer and difficult to analyze and understand later. A basic rule in survey research is that the instrument should have a clear focus and should be guided by hypotheses held by the researcher. This means that survey research is not well suited to early exploratory research, because it requires some orderly expectations by the researcher.

Let us suppose that we want to survey local schoolteachers (the population) on their views about using corporal punishment to discipline children (the area of information). We decide to use a self-administered, mailed questionnaire (the form of administration). Having determined the general area of inquiry, the population to be surveyed, and the form of administration, the next step is to develop the instrument.

The researcher writes items that cover the area of information desired (use of corporal punishment) and are in language appropriate for the population (teachers). The items should be clearly written, unambiguous, and concise and should be preceded by clear instructions. After the items are written, they are edited for clarity and meaning and are pretested, usually on a small sample from the population to be surveyed. Based on the pretesting, the items may be refined, and the final form of the instrument is prepared.

The items in the questionnaire or interview schedule can take several forms: **open-ended items, multiple-choice items,** and **Likert-scale items.** In our hypothetical questionnaire, we might ask the following open-ended question:

What do you think of using corporal punishment in disciplining children?

If this were a questionnaire, we would leave sufficient space for the respondents to write their answers. In an interview, we would tape-record their answers for later coding and scoring. An example of a multiple-choice question is:

What proportion of parents use corporal punishment to discipline their children?

a. 10%   b. 25%   c. 50%   d. 75%   e. 100%

In Likert scales, the items are arranged on a continuum, with extreme positions at the endpoints. Respondents are typically asked to indicate the degree to which they agree with a statement, such as:

Corporal punishment is necessary in raising children.

Strongly Agree   Agree   Uncertain   Disagree   Strongly Disagree

This item could be scored from 1 to 5. The respondent would answer all the items on the questionnaire, and the overall score would be the total of the scores on each item.[2] A single questionnaire might include items in each format (open ended, multiple choice, and Likert). If so, it is good procedure to keep those of the same format together. Additional details on survey construction techniques are included on the *Student Resource CD.*

Sampling Participants

Obtaining an adequate sample is one of the most important factors in conducting surveys. When the population about which we seek information is large and diverse, it is impossible to question every member of this population. The U.S. census is an example of such an attempt. Taking the census is expensive and time consuming. Instead, in most surveys, we draw a sample of the population and then generalize the findings from our sample to the population.

The population in a survey is the larger group about whom we wish to obtain information. Some examples of survey populations are eligible voters for a presidential election, high school teachers in California, readers of the *National Review,* middle school children in Milwaukee, students at the University of Texas, Chevrolet owners, and so on. In our example, we have taken the first step by tentatively identifying the population as local schoolteachers. Now we must be more precise by specifying a geographic area or specific school systems and other characteristics of the population, such as the grade levels of the teachers or their areas of teaching expertise (science, social studies, English, etc.). The survey might include all schoolteachers or be limited to grammar school or full-time teachers. We must decide whether to include teachers in private schools or limit the population of study to public school teachers. Suppose that we decide to study all full-time, state-certified, public school teachers in a four-county area (grades 1 through 12) whose primary task is classroom teaching. Note the variability among the population: Some will be male and some female; some will be special-education teachers; others will have specialized areas such as music and shop; their ages will vary considerably from the early 20s to the late 60s; their experiences and abilities as teachers will also vary greatly.

Sampling Considerations. Having constructed and tested the survey instrument and identified the population to be studied, the researcher must also specify the sampling procedures. We will draw a sample of people from a known population and administer the survey to each participant in the sample. Survey information is obtained from a sample, but the goal is to learn about the population from which the sample is drawn. Using the terminology developed earlier in the text, whenever we use a sample as a basis for generalizing to a population, we are engaging in a process of inductive inference (from the specific sample to the general population). Inductive reasoning is the

---

[2]Other scaling methods such as the Thurstone, Guttman, and Semantic Differential Scales could be used, but a detailed discussion of all the scaling formats is beyond the scope of this text. See Dawis (1987) and Kerlinger (1992) for more details.

general process involved in the use of inferential statistics. To have confidence in inductive inferences from sample to population, the sample must be carefully drawn to *represent adequately the population to which we want to infer.* The heart of survey research is the selection of representative samples. Without it, the results will tell us only about the sample and are useless in learning about a larger population.

Sampling Procedures.   Sampling procedures fall into two major categories: (1) nonprobability sampling and (2) probability sampling. **Nonprobability sampling** methods include, for example, carrying out a survey by interviewing the first 50 people you meet on the street or as many people as you can interview who are coming out of a polling place at election time. Newspaper, television, and radio surveys are often carried out in this way to obtain a quick public response to an issue while it is still a current news item. The advantage of nonprobability sampling is the ease with which it can be carried out. Its weakness is that the first 50 people, or whatever other nonprobability sample is obtained, might not be a representative sample of the population, and the survey results might therefore be biased.

Probability sampling procedures give us greater confidence that the sample adequately represents the population. In probability sampling, each person has some known probability of being included in the sample. The two major probability sampling methods are simple random sampling and stratified random sampling.

In **simple random sampling** every member of the identified population has an equal chance of being selected. There is no bias in simple random sampling that can lead to persons with certain characteristics having a higher probability of being selected than persons without these characteristics. Simple random sampling, however, requires that we have a list of all members of the population. Clearly, this would be difficult to obtain if the population is large, such as all people living in the United States or all children and youth enrolled in primary and secondary schools. With such large populations, we cannot use simple random sampling. If the population is more limited, such as all children in a specific school or all psychologists in private practice in a certain city, an initial list (called a **sampling frame**) is more feasible. We could randomly select from such sampling frames without much difficulty. Thus, simple random sampling is used for survey research in which population size allows a workable sampling frame from which individuals can be randomly selected. For example, suppose that we want to survey 50 of the 317 local families who have children with mental retardation in school. The sampling frame would consist of the names of all 317 families. Each would be assigned a number from 1 to 317, and we would use a table of random numbers to select randomly the sample of 50 families. However, as careful as we may be to obtain an accurate sampling frame, it may be incomplete. Changes might occur between the time we obtain the list and begin selecting the sample. Families may move into or away from the town; people may become ill or die. Thus, a sampling frame is almost always incomplete and is an approximation of the true population.

Stratified random sampling procedures are used when it is important to ensure that subgroups within a population are adequately represented in the sample. In essence, the researcher divides the population into subgroups or **strata,** and a random sample is taken from each stratum. Suppose that we want to conduct a survey on 100 of the 1737 students in McKinley High School. We would not want to bias the results by over- or underrepresenting any groups (e.g., freshmen, sophomores, juniors, seniors, minority students, males, females, and so on). A stratified random sample, drawing randomly from each strata, would be used. The number drawn from each stratum would be based on the proportion of students in this stratum in the population. In this way, we can have confidence that the sample accurately represents the population, at least on the dimensions on which we stratified the sample.

Sample Size and Confidence Intervals.   Having developed the survey instrument and determined the sampling procedure, the researcher must also determine the size of the sample that will be needed. In general, larger samples represent populations better than smaller samples. But exactly how large the sample should be must be determined for each project. Costs and time are important considerations in determining how large a sample can be handled in a project. But, more importantly, the size of the sample needed to represent a population adequately depends on the degree of *homogeneity* in the population. A **homogeneous** population is one in which the members are similar to one another. In general, if the population is homogeneous, then smaller sample sizes are possible. On the other hand, the more **heterogeneous** the population, the more diversity there is that must be represented in the sample. Therefore, the sample must be larger to represent the diversity accurately. Thus, in determining how large a sample must be to represent the population, we must make an estimate of the variability of the characteristics of the population; that is, we estimate the size of the standard deviation of the population for the characteristic that we want to measure. With this, we can then determine the confidence limits for estimating population characteristics based on the measured sample characteristics. For example, if we computed a sample mean of 10.50, we expect the population mean to be close to this figure. How confident we are that our sample mean is close to the population mean depends on the sample size. The larger the sample size, the more confidence we have. We express our confidence with something called a **confidence interval.** For example, we could compute that we are "95 percent confident that the population mean is between 9.75 and 11.25" (our confidence interval). Methods for calculating required sample size and confidence intervals are beyond the scope of this text. Interested students are referred to Rossi, Wright, and Anderson (1985).

Survey Research Design

Having developed and tested the survey instrument, identified the population of interest, and drawn the sample, the researcher must also determine the research plan or design to be used in gathering the survey data. Two basic designs are used in survey research: (1) the cross-sectional design and (2) the longitudinal or panel design.

Cross-sectional Design.   A **cross-sectional design** involves administering the survey once to a sample, yielding data on the measured characteristics as they exist at the time of the survey. The information can be completely descriptive, such as a status survey, or can involve testing relationships among population characteristics. A variation of the cross-sectional design allows comparisons to be made of population characteristics at different points in time, such as surveying the occurrence of depression in 1985, 1990, 1995, 2000, and 2005 to determine changes over time. Another variation is to sample subgroups defined by age, such as 20–30, 30–40, 40–50, and so on. Businesses are often interested in such surveys to help them to determine the best ways to market products. If the successive surveys use independent samples of respondents, the design is cross sectional.

Longitudinal Design.   The **longitudinal** or **panel design** is a within-subjects survey research design in which the same group or panel of participants is surveyed successively at different times. Longitudinal surveys make it possible to assess changes within individuals over time. It is often difficult, however, to obtain participants who are willing to be surveyed several times, and often large numbers of participants drop out of the study before it is completed.

Quick-Check Review 4: Surveys

4.1. Distinguish between status surveys and survey research.

4.2. What are the major goal in surveys?

4.3. Describe two forms of survey instruments.

4.4. What are the types of items that can be used in surveys?

4.5. What is stratified random sampling?

4.6. What are confidence limits?

4.7. Define cross-sectional and longitudinal designs.

Chapter Summary

Low-constraint research enables researchers to observe the natural flow of behavior in natural settings, try out new procedures, initiate research in new areas of inquiry, negate general propositions and, most important, observe contingencies and develop hypotheses that can be tested at higher-constraint levels. However, low-constraint methods cannot rule out alternative hypotheses and therefore cannot test causal hypotheses. This chapter returned to a discussion of research in naturalistic settings that was first presented in Chapter 6. Here, however, higher-constraint research was covered, including experimental research in naturalistic settings. Three major topics were discussed: quasi-experimental designs, program evaluation, and surveys.

Two quasi-experimental designs, the nonequivalent control-group design and the interrupted time-series design, were discussed, including their strengths and weaknesses. Program evaluation involves the use of many of the designs covered in this text to evaluate the practical effectiveness of programs carried out in naturalistic settings. Although program evaluation is difficult because of the many constraints imposed by the natural setting on the researcher, it has become a major area of applied research in the social sciences.

Surveying is a large and growing area of research in the natural environment. Researchers ask questions of participants concerning virtually any issue. Questions may include everything from basic demographic information, to knowledge questions, to questions about attitudes and experiences. The heart of the survey is the sampling methods used to ensure a representative sample. Surveys can be carried out as longitudinal or cross-sectional studies.

Additional examples of field research are provided on the *Student Resource CD.*

Key Terms

Define the following key terms. Be sure that you understand them. They are discussed in the chapter and defined in the glossary.

quasi-experiments
nonequivalent control-group
    design
crossover effect
interrupted time-series
    design
program evaluation research
survey
status survey
survey research

interview schedule
questionnaire
factual items
content items
open-ended items
multiple-choice items
Likert-scale items
nonprobability sampling
probability sampling
simple random sampling

sampling frame
stratified random sampling
strata
homogeneous
heterogeneous
confidence interval
cross-sectional design
longitudinal (panel) design

14

Final Preparations before Data Collection

Ignorance never settles a question.

—Benjamin Disraeli, 1866, Speech given in the House of Commons.

Selecting Appropriate Statistical Procedures
An Initial Example
A Decision-Tree Model
   Decision-Tree Flowcharts
   Identify Research Variables
   Describe the Study
   Identify the Study's Major Characteristics
   Select the Appropriate Statistics
Secondary Analyses
   Post Hoc Analyses
   Secondary Analyses to Help to Explain
     the Results
   Data Snooping
Caveats and Disclaimers

Pre-data Check
  I. Initial Problem Definition
 II. Clarity of the Research Hypotheses
III. Statistical Analysis Procedures
IV. Theoretical Basis and Operational
     Definitions

  V. Adequacy of the Independent Variable
     Manipulation
 VI. Adequacy of Dependent Measures
VII. Are All Controls in Place?
VIII. Participants
   Participant Selection
   Sample Size
   Participant Assignment
   Participant Availability
   Research Ethics Considerations
 IX. Preparation of the Setting
   Space and Equipment
   Personnel
  X. Adequacy of Participant Preparation, Instruction, and Procedures

Chapter Summary

Key Terms

CD Resource Material

- The Decision-Tree Flowcharts
- Examples Using the Decision-Tree Flowcharts
- Exercises Using the Decision-Tree Flowcharts

- Functional Decision-Tree Flowchart
- The Pre-data Checklist Tutorial
- Study Guide/Laboratory Manual

Web Resource Material

- Statistics on the World Wide Web
- Statistics Resources: Books and Publishers
- Statistics Resources Worthy of Interest
- Other Beginning Statistics Resources around the WWW

- Probability and Statistics
- Introductory Statistics Demonstrations

This chapter covers two important ideas: selecting appropriate statistical procedures and checking every aspect of the research design before data collection. Both discussions summarize material presented earlier, but the ideas are important enough to justify an entire chapter.

Selecting Appropriate Statistical Procedures

Research is a systematic process of inquiry proceeding from initial ideas to final communication. At each phase, the researcher makes important decisions. One decision made in the design phase—before data collection—is determining what statistical procedures to use in analyzing the results. This demand is relaxed somewhat at the more flexible naturalistic level, but becomes increasingly important at higher levels of constraint. We select statistical tests that are appropriate for the data that we plan to collect and for the questions that we are asking.

Choosing appropriate statistical procedures is often difficult for students. The large array of research designs and statistical procedures can be overwhelming and can make it difficult to know where to focus. But, like everything else in research, systematic procedures simplify the decisions and bring the process under control. Chapters 5, 10, 11, and 12 set the groundwork for this systematic approach by describing several research designs and illustrating appropriate statistical procedures.

An Initial Example

The characteristics of the research, such as the number of independent variables, type of question, and level of measurement for each dependent variable, determine the appropriate statistical procedures. Let us take an example of a relatively simple study and determine how to analyze it statistically. Remember, the first step is to identify the important characteristics of the study.

Incidental Learning in Rats

An experimenter has hypothesized that laboratory rats can learn incidentally without specific rewards. Twenty rats are first exposed to several different mazes for 2 hours. After the exposure, none of the animals shows any signs of stress when placed in new mazes. The 20 maze-adapted animals are randomly assigned to two conditions—10 animals per condition. The experimental group is allowed to explore the test maze for 1 hour without any rewards. The control group does not explore the test maze. All animals are then given learning trials in the test maze, and each successful trial is reinforced with food reward. The experimental and control groups are compared on the number of learning trials needed to reach a criterion of five successive correct trials. The research hypothesis is that the experimental group, having explored the test maze prior to their reinforced learning trials, needs significantly fewer learning trials to reach criterion than the control group.

Our task is to determine the appropriate statistical procedure to use in the research on learning in rats. The preceding description provides all the information that we need. Remember that the characteristics of the research determine what statistical procedures to use. Thus, we need to refer to the description and ask questions that will identify the characteristics of the research.

1. *What is the level of constraint for the research?*   Experimental.
2. *What are the independent variables?*   There is one independent variable, the amount of exploration of the maze prior to learning trials.
3. *What are the levels of the independent variable?*   There are two levels, prior exploration and no prior exploration.
4. *What type of design is the research, that is, independent groups, correlated groups, mixed, and so on?*   Independent-groups design.
5. *What are the dependent variables?*   There is one dependent variable, maze learning.
6. *What is (are) the dependent measure(s); [that is, how is (are) the dependent variable(s) measured]?*   There is one dependent measure, the number of maze-running trials needed to reach criterion.
7. *What is the level of measurement of each dependent measure?*   Ratio.
8. *What type of data is generated for the dependent measure?*   Score data.
9. *What is (are) the research hypothesis (hypotheses)?*   There is one research hypothesis: the experimental group will require fewer learning trials than the control group to reach criterion.
10. *What kind of test is needed, a test of relationship, a test of differences, etc.?*   A test of differences—specifically, a test of the null hypothesis of no differences between the experimental and control groups.

We have now determined that our example study is an independent-groups experimental design in which a hypothesized difference between two groups is tested. There is only one dependent variable, maze learning, and measuring it yields score data. The appropriate statistical procedure is one that can test differences between independent groups with score data. You may recall from earlier discussions that the *t*-test for independent groups or the one-way ANOVA is appropriate. We also routinely include descriptive statistics to summarize data and help us to interpret the results.

In this simple example, the decision about what statistical procedure to use is easily made. In more complex research, where there may be several research hypotheses and several dependent measures, we may need a number of statistical procedures, perhaps a different one for each hypothesis. In such complex research, the decisions are not so readily apparent, but the procedure to arrive at them is essentially the same. First we describe the research. Then we ask a number of questions to identify its important characteristics. Finally, we use the characteristics identified and proceed to make decisions to arrive at the appropriate statistical procedures. We have incorporated this sequence of steps into a decision-tree model.

A Decision-Tree Model

The remainder of this section describes a decision-making model for determining the appropriate statistical procedure(s) for research designs. We use a **decision tree,** in which we follow a line of thinking, reach a decision point, make the decision, and then branch off in appropriate directions based on the decision. These lines of thinking and the branching-off process are organized in five decision-tree flowcharts, which are shown in Figures 14.1 through 14.5. The flowcharts are also provided on the *Student Resource CD*. The researcher begins by describing the research and identifying the major characteristics of the research and then proceeds through the flowcharts until the appropriate statistical procedures are determined. The questions to be answered in the decision tree were discussed in earlier chapters. There are no new concepts in this chapter; rather, this chapter makes the decision process more formal and systematic.

Decision-Tree Flowcharts.   The **decision-tree flowcharts** organize the decision-making process. Because the procedures discussed may not be clear after a first reading, we recommend that you reread them and complete the exercises on the *Student Resource CD* until you thoroughly understand them. In the next section, we present an

Flowcharts can simplify almost any complex decision. (Reprinted by permission of Sidney Harris.)

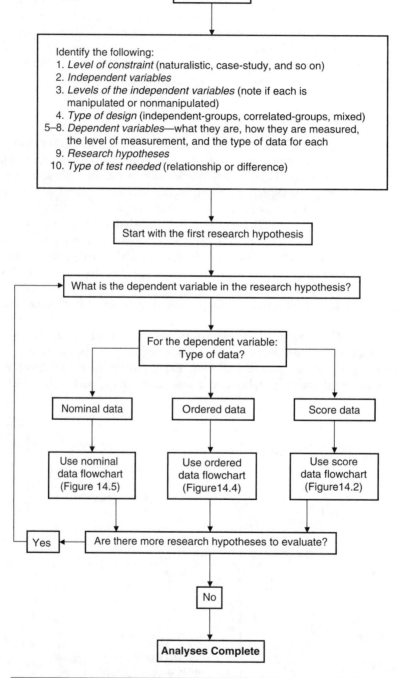

FIGURE 14.1 *Initial Flowchart*

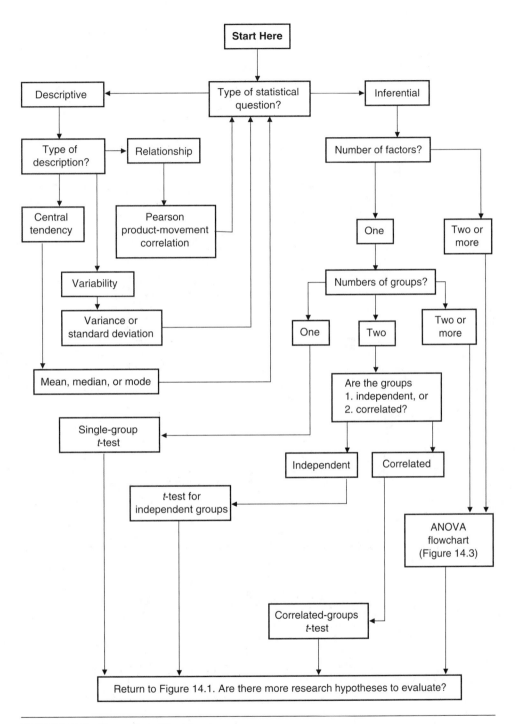

FIGURE 14.2 *Score Data Flowchart*

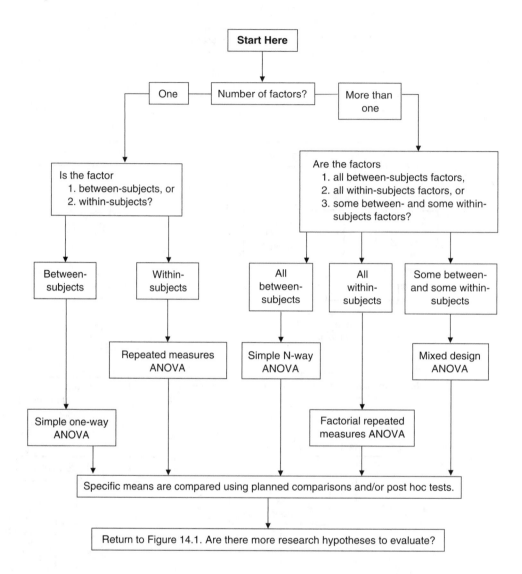

FIGURE 14.3 *ANOVA Flowchart*

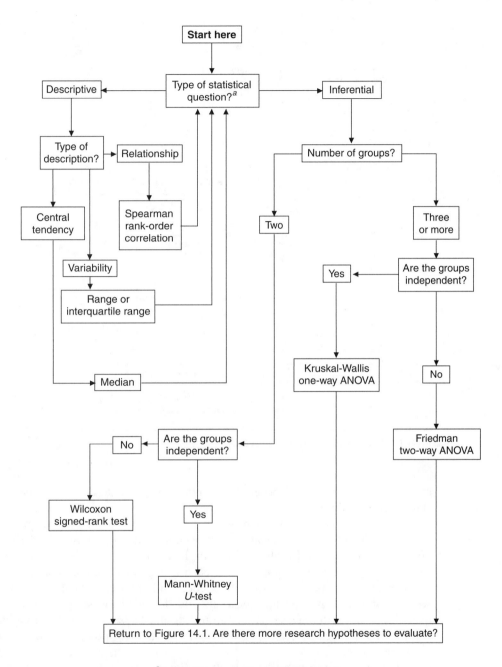

^a It is best to start with descriptive statistics.

Note: Computational formulas for the statistical procedures described here can be found in Siegel (1956).

FIGURE 14.4   *Ordered Data Flowchart*

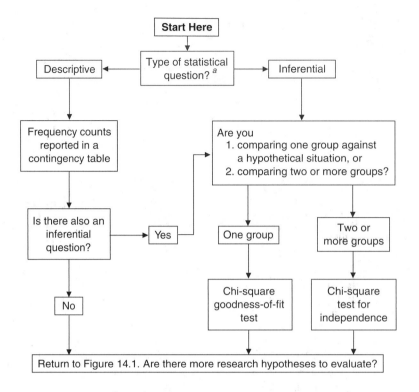

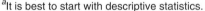

[a]It is best to start with descriptive statistics.

FIGURE 14.5   *Nominal Data Flowchart*

example of research and proceed through the flowcharts to determine the appropriate statistical procedures.

Most studies test several research hypotheses and include several dependent measures. Therefore, several statistical procedures may be required. Descriptive statistics are first computed for all variables in the study. If there are separate groups, the descriptive statistics are computed for each group. In lower-constraint research, descriptive statistics may be all that are needed. In higher-constraint research, however, we typically have refined the questions and designed the study to answer specific questions about differences between groups. In most cases, we cycle through the flowcharts several times to determine appropriate statistical procedures before all questions are answered.

Figures 14.1 through 14.5 present the flowcharts for determining the appropriate statistical procedure. Figure 14.1 shows the overall structure of the decision tree; it is the initial flowchart. Figures 14.2 through Figure 14.5 present specific sections of the overall flowchart given in Figure 14.1. Although the flowcharts may look imposing, they are easy to follow.

Identify Research Variables. We begin by identifying key aspects of the research design. This process is illustrated with a hypothetical study of social problem solving in sixth-grade boys and girls. This study is more complex than the animal-learning study presented earlier because several research hypotheses are being tested. Thus, we need to determine several statistical analyses. No matter how complex the study may be, the procedures for determining an appropriate statistical analysis are the same.

1. Describe the study.
2. Identify its major characteristics.
3. Make systematic decisions using the flowcharts.

Describe the Study. Here is a brief description of the study.

Sex Differences in Children's Social Problem-Solving Skills

The study compares sixth-grade boys and girls on their problem-solving skills in social situations. From the sixth grade of a local grammar school, 20 boys and 20 girls are randomly selected and evaluated on three different measures. In the first measure, participants are tested individually. Ten social situations are described to each participant. Each situation involves a social problem or conflict (e.g., another student pushes ahead in line). Three ways to solve the conflict are described for each situation, and the participant is asked to choose one of the three solutions (i.e., a multiple-choice test). For each problem, one solution is clearly the most socially appropriate and therefore is considered to be the correct answer. The score is the number of correct choices for the ten social situations. The task is presented to the children on videotape to standardize the presentation and to maximize the children's attention. The second dependent measure is the teacher's ranking of the children on social competence. The ranking is based on observations of the children's behavior in three settings: the structured classroom, an unstructured social activity within the classroom, and recess. For the third dependent measure, an independent rater classifies each of the children as either "above average in social competence" or "below average in social competence" based on standardized information provided by the teachers.

The research focuses on sex differences in problem-solving skills. The statement of the problem is this: Do sixth-grade boys and girls differ on problem-solving skills? The problem statement combined with operational definitions leads to three research hypotheses.

Identify the Study's Major Characteristics. Having described the study, the next step is to identify its major characteristics.

1. *Level of constraint?* Differential (i.e., differences between two preexisting groups).
2. *Independent variables?* There is one independent variable, the sex of participants. It is a nonmanipulated independent variable.
3. *Levels of the independent variable?* There are two levels of the independent variable, boys and girls.
4. *Type of design?* Independent-groups, differential design.

5–8. *Dependent variable(s)?* There are three dependent variables (5). Their measures are listed in the table that follows (6), along with the level of measurement for each (7), and the type of data generated by each measure (8).

Dependent Measure	Level of Measurement	Type of Data
Score on the social-skills multiple-choice test	Ratio	Score
Ranking of participants on social competence	Ordinal	Ordered
Independent classification of social competence	Nominal	Nominal

9. *Research hypotheses?* There are three research hypotheses:
  a. Sixth-grade boys and girls differ in the identification of the correct social response in a multiple-choice task.
  b. Sixth-grade boys and girls differ in their ranking on social competence based on observations in three behavior settings.
  c. Sixth-grade boys and girls differ in the proportion classified as either "above average on social competence" or "below average on social competence."
10. *What kind of test is needed?* For each hypothesis, a test of differences between independent groups is needed.

This study is a differential, independent-groups design with two levels of the nonmanipulated independent variable. The dependent measures generate three different levels of data. Therefore, different statistical procedures will be used to analyze data from each dependent measure. We are interested in testing for group differences.

Select the Appropriate Statistics. After the major characteristics of the study are identified, the next step is to determine the appropriate procedures for descriptive statistics and inferential statistics for each of the three hypotheses. It is useful to begin with descriptive statistics.

The first hypothesis uses a multiple-choice test as the dependent measure. We start by calculating descriptive statistics and do so separately for each of the two groups (boys and girls). The flowcharts help us to select the appropriate statistics. We have already accomplished the first task outlined in the initial flowchart (Figure 14.1), identifying the major characteristics of the study. Therefore, we move down the flowchart and begin with the first research hypothesis. The first hypothesis is this: Sixth-grade boys and girls differ in the identification of the correct social response in a multiple-choice task. The dependent variable for the hypothesis is the social skills multiple-choice test. We follow Figure 14.1 to the point where the flowchart inquires, "For the dependent variable: Type of data?" As we have already determined, this dependent variable produces score data. Therefore, following the flowchart, we are directed to use the score data flowchart (Figure 14.2).

We are interested in descriptive statistics at this point, so we move to the left branch of Figure 14.2. Here we are asked, "Type of description?" Normally, for score data we want both a measure of central tendency and a measure of variability. The flowchart tells us that the mean, median, and mode are appropriate measures of central tendency and the variance and standard deviation are appropriate measures of variability for score data.

Now that we have determined the appropriate descriptive statistics for the first hypothesis, we turn to inferential statistics for the first hypothesis. The score data flowchart (Figure 14.2) directs us back to the box asking, "Type of statistical question?" We are interested in an inferential question, so we branch to the right in Figure 14.2, where it asks for the number of factors. Because we have one factor (sex), we follow that branch to where it asks for the number of groups. Because we have two groups (boys and girls), we can go in either of two directions. The rightmost branch takes us to a one-way analysis of variance (see Figure 14.3). The middle branch leads to a *t*-test (for independent groups). Both are correct procedures and will lead to the same conclusions about differences between the groups. Having selected an inferential statistical procedure for the first research hypothesis, we return to Figure 14.1. Thus, we determine that for hypothesis 1 we calculate means, medians, modes, variances, and standard deviations as descriptive statistics and use an independent-groups *t*-test or a one-way ANOVA for the inferential statistic.

As we move down the initial flowchart (Figure 14.1), we are asked whether there are more research hypotheses to evaluate. Because there are, we look to the middle portion of the flowchart where it asks, "What is the dependent variable in the research hypothesis?" We identify the variable and move down to where it asks what type of data it represents. For the second research hypothesis, the dependent measure is the teacher's rankings of the children's social competence (ordered data). The flowchart tells us to consult Figure 14.4, the ordered data flowchart. We are interested in descriptive statistics, so we branch to the left and are informed that the median is an appropriate measure of central tendency and the range or the interquartile range is the appropriate measure of variability for ordered data. Having determined the appropriate descriptive statistics for the second research hypothesis, we now turn to the inferential statistics. We follow the flowchart back to the box asking, "Type of statistical question?" We branch right to find an appropriate inferential statistical procedure. If we follow the flowchart correctly (for two independent groups), it will suggest a Mann–Whitney *U*-test.

The third research hypothesis uses a dependent variable that is measured on a nominal scale, and we are therefore directed by the initial flowchart to use Figure 14.5, the nominal data flowchart. If we follow the flowchart correctly, we determine that frequency counts in a contingency table are an appropriate descriptive statistic. Likewise, an appropriate inferential procedure is a chi-square test for independence.

If our study were a larger one with more research hypotheses, we would continue this process of using the flowcharts to find the correct descriptive and inferential statistics and compute the statistics for all remaining dependent measures in the study. The example illustrates the need to be well organized during the work because of the many different decisions to be made. Carefully labeling the results will minimize errors during later analyses and report writing. Most research studies employ more than one measure and test more than one research hypothesis. Although computers can simplify the task of computation, the researcher still needs to decide what statistics to compute and to label and organize the computer output carefully to avoid later confusion.

We recommend that you use these flowcharts with other research examples. With practice, you will become familiar with the rules in the flowcharts and eventually will not need to refer to them. Indeed, that is a goal. But initially, when learning to make decisions, the flowcharts provide a convenient way to organize information when selecting a statistical procedure. We have included exercises on the *Student Resource CD,* which also has a functional version of these flowcharts that links to both the appropriate manual and computerized data analysis tutorials.

Secondary Analyses

After completing descriptive and inferential analyses, we often carry out secondary analyses. **Secondary analyses** typically fall into three categories: (1) post hoc analyses or planned comparisons to look at specific mean differences after conducting an overall ANOVA, (2) analyses designed to help to explain the pattern of results, or (3) unplanned exploratory analyses (sometimes referred to as data snooping).

Post Hoc Analyses. When doing an ANOVA with more than two groups, specific mean comparisons are the logical next step in the interpretation of significant *F*-ratios. The significant *F* in a one-way ANOVA, for example, tells us only that at least one of the means is significantly different from at least one other mean. It does not tell us which means are different from which other means. Most often, the interpretation requires this more specific information, which can be provided by a variety of post hoc tests or planned comparisons.

Secondary Analyses to Help to Explain Results. Another set of secondary analyses involves looking at variables that may help to explain the observed set of results. Suppose that differences are found, but that they are difficult to interpret because we cannot be sure that some confounding variable was adequately controlled. This problem is minimized in experimental research, because the high level of control reduces confounding. In lower-constraint research, particularly in differential research, these issues can be real problems, and secondary analyses are often essential to interpret data adequately.

A set of secondary analyses that should be included in the report of any research project regardless of its level of constraint is descriptive statistics on the demographic characteristics of the sample, such as age, social class, and level of education. Such information allows researchers to compare the samples from different studies. The samples also provide the information needed to determine the limits of generalizability of the findings.

These are only some of the uses of secondary statistical analyses to help to interpret findings of a primary analysis. Some of the analyses in this category are very sophisticated and beyond the scope of this text. It is important to realize, however, that in many lower-constraint research studies the secondary analyses may outnumber the primary analyses and be critical in the interpretation of the results.

Data Snooping. The third set of secondary analyses is what we have called **data snooping.** Here researchers can play their hunches and see whether, for example, there are relationships, differences, or interactions that were not predicted. Data snooping is useful in lower-constraint studies, in which clues to many potential relationships among variables may be buried in the data. Good data snooping is as much an art as a science. However, it is important to note that we must be cautious in interpreting relationships discovered in such a post hoc treasure hunt. If we are appropriately cautious, data snooping can be a rich source of hypotheses for later research, and it should not be overlooked. At least one high-level text is devoted entirely to this art (Tukey, 1977).

Caveats and Disclaimers

The flowchart system outlined in this chapter is designed as a teaching device—a way to organize and formalize what is often a difficult task for students. The inferential statistics portion of this system focuses on the kinds of questions asked most often in psychological hypotheses—specifically, are there mean differences between groups on the dependent measure? Other kinds of questions, such as "Are there differences in the variability between the groups?" are not covered by the set of flowcharts. For such questions, other reference sources need to be consulted (Keppel, 1991; Myers & Well, 1995). However, for most questions investigated in psychological research, the flowcharts identify an appropriate statistical procedure to use.

The statistical procedures suggested by the flowcharts are not the only appropriate procedures for answering a specific question. In almost all cases, there are alternative data-analysis procedures. The statistical procedures given in the flowcharts are the ones most commonly used in these situations, but other procedures may also be appropriate. Therefore, the flowcharts are more helpful in finding a statistical procedure to

BOX 14.1 • *The Robust Nature of Parametric Statistics*

At several points in the text, we note that statistical tests make assumptions about the data. For example, an implicit assumption of the *t*-test and ANOVA procedures is that data are on at least an interval level of measurement (score data). But these tests make other assumptions about data that are not highlighted in the text because they are not critical. Sometimes an assumption on which an inferential statistical procedure is based can be violated without threatening the validity of the conclusion drawn from the statistical test. In such a case, we say that the statistical procedure is **robust** to violations of the assumption. For example, many statistical tests assume that scores in the population are distributed normally (i.e., they form a symmetric bell-shaped distribution). If the population of scores is actually skewed, we have violated an assumption of the statistical test. If that statistical procedure is not robust to this assumption, the violation distorts the procedure, making conclusions drawn from the statistical analysis suspect. Fortunately, most statistics are robust to violations of assumptions about population distributions. Therefore, we can use them confidently regardless of the shape of the distributions.

As it turns out, most statistics are robust to violations of almost all assumptions on which they are based if the sample size in each of the groups is approximately equal. This conclusion is based on a series of computer simulation studies known as **Monte Carlo studies** (named after the famous gambling resort). In a Monte Carlo study, the computer is used to simulate sampling of participants from populations with known characteristics. In this way, the researcher can see what effect violations of assumptions have on the accuracy of decisions. The approach has been used to investigate the effects of violations of single assumptions or violations of more than one assumption at the same time (Levy, 1980). Monte Carlo studies continue to show the remarkable robustness of most statistics to assumption violations when sample sizes are equal. Consequently, these assumptions are not emphasized in the text and are not built into the decision rules of the flowcharts.

Note the emphasis before on equal sample sizes. Unless sample sizes of groups are approximately equal, violations of assumptions may affect the validity of statistical procedures. Hence, from a design perspective, particularly for the novice researcher, it is beneficial to try to have approximately equal sample sizes.

use in a study than in evaluating whether a particular statistical approach used by another researcher is appropriate (see Box 14.1).

<hr>

Quick-Check Review 1: Selecting Appropriate Statistical Procedures

1.1. What is the first step in selecting appropriate statistical procedures?
1.2. How do the flowcharts help us to select appropriate statistical procedures?
1.3. Can the flowcharts be used to decide if a research study used the appropriate statistical procedures?

<hr>

Pre-data Check

At some point, the researcher is ready to make the observations, which involve recording participants' responses that will later be analyzed, interpreted, and communicated. Research plans are complex; if not constructed properly, then all the work of collecting data might be wasted. Thus, the researcher must be sure that all planning has been completed before beginning to gather data. Much like a pilot who makes a preflight check to ensure that the plane is functioning properly before takeoff, the researcher should carry out a **pre-data check** to see if the research is "ready to fly." The steps in the pre-data check are discussed in what follows and summarized in Table 14.1 and on the *Student Resource CD*.

I. Initial Problem Definition

Each study begins with a literature review based on your initial ideas. In that process you refined your statement of the problem and identified the major variables. Now you must check to see that those variables have been operationally defined appropriately.

1. Has a literature review of initial ideas been completed?
2. Has the problem statement been clearly developed?
3. Are variables identified and operationally defined?

II. Clarity of the Research Hypotheses

Next we check the research hypotheses. Research hypotheses predict a specific relationship between variables, which may be differential, correlational, or causal. The research hypotheses should indicate the type and, if appropriate, the direction of the relationship.

4. Do the research hypotheses clearly state the type and direction of the relationship among the variables?

TABLE 14.1   *Summary of Pre-data Checklist*

I. Initial Problem Definition
   1. Literature review completed?
   2. Problem statement developed?
   3. Variables identified and operationally defined?

II. Research Hypothesis
   4. Research hypothesis clearly states expected relationship among the variables?

III. Statistical Analysis
   5. Descriptive statistics planned?
   6. Inferential statistics planned?
   7. Post hoc or secondary analyses planned?

IV. Theoretical Basis
   8. Theoretical base for study clear?
   9. Do hypotheses and procedures address the issues?

V. Independent Variable Manipulation (experimental research)
   10. Independent variable manipulations planned?
   11. Manipulations pretested?
   12. Manipulation check planned?

VI. Dependent Measures
   13. Dependent measures operationally defined?
   14. Dependent measures piloted?
   15. Reliability and validity data available?
   16. Did you include procedures to measure reliability?

VII. Controls
   17. Controls for threats to internal validity in place?
   18. Controls for threats to external validity in place?

VIII. Participants
Participant Selection
   19. Sample adequately represents target population?
   20. Demographic variables measured?

Sample Size
   21. Sample sufficiently large?

Participant Assignment
   22. Participants properly assigned to conditions (experimental research)?
   23. Groups carefully defined (differential research)?
   24. Information on the matching preserved for analysis (matched-subjects design)?

Participant Availability
   25. Participants available?
   26. Participants scheduled?
   27. Participant-fee procedures ready?

(continued)

TABLE 14.1   Continued

Research Ethics

28. IRB approval obtained (human research)?

29. Informed consent forms available (human research)?

30. Debriefing and/or feedback procedures ready (human research)?

31. Ethical guidelines checked and research approved (animal research)?

IX. Preparation of the Setting

Space and Equipment

32. Adequate space available?

33. Free of distractions?

34. Equipment checked?

Personnel

35. Sufficient research staff?

36. Assistants adequately trained for emergencies?

37. Assistants adequately trained in procedures?

38. Blind procedures in place?

X. Adequacy of Participant Preparation, Instruction, Procedures

39. Instructions to participants clear?

40. Instructions and procedures piloted?

If all check out, then you are "ready to fly."

III. Statistical Analysis Procedures

Statistical procedures are selected before the data are gathered. Select the descriptive and inferential statistical procedures appropriate for each research hypothesis. (Here you can use the flowcharts presented in Figures 14.1 through 14.5.)

5. Are all descriptive statistical procedures planned?

6. For each hypothesis, are inferential statistical procedures planned?

7. Are you planning post hoc or secondary analyses? If so, what are they?

IV. Theoretical Basis and Operational Definitions

After you have obtained and analyzed your data, you will have the all-important task of interpreting and communicating the results. These rational processes provide meaning to your research and its discoveries and implications for theory. Your work may stimulate further research and influence practical applications. Thus, it is critical that you have a clear understanding of the theoretical bases for your research. Make sure that your hypotheses and your procedures address the issues that you raised initially so that your results can be related to those issues.

8. Is the theoretical base for your study clear?

9. Do your hypotheses and procedures address the issues?

V. Adequacy of the Independent Variable Manipulation

Experimental manipulations must be carefully selected and carried out.

10. Have the independent variable manipulations been carefully planned (experimental and control groups clearly operationally defined)?
11. Have the manipulations been pretested? Are changes needed?
12. Has a manipulation check been planned?

VI. Adequacy of the Dependent Measures

Dependent measures must be clearly defined, both conceptually and operationally. They should be pretested for feasibility, and you should evaluate reliability and validity data if available. If these are new measures, they should have been pretested and reliability and validity data obtained. In either event, be sure that you have included procedures to measure their reliability in your current research. Know how the responses are to be recorded and scored. Piloting helps you to estimate how long the tasks will take and what problems might arise. Problems with the procedures should all be solved before you test a single participant. Be sure that you know the level of measurement and type of data for each dependent measure. These measures will constitute your data—be careful and precise in obtaining them.

13. Are all dependent measures operationally defined?
14. Have they been pretested or piloted?
15. Do you have prior reliability and validity data?
16. Did you include procedures to measure reliability?

VII. Are All Controls in Place?

Check to see that all your controls are in place to protect internal and external validity. You do not want to complete your data collection only to find that some uncontrolled factor provides an alternative explanation of your results.

17. Are controls for threats to internal validity in place?
18. Are controls for external validity in place?

VIII. Participants

Participant Selection. Do the participants adequately represent the target population? You should know the type of sample that you have (a random sample, a stratified random sample, an ad hoc sample). Adequate demographic measures must be included to define the sample, especially if this is an ad hoc sample. Measures of age, sex, socioeconomic class, and so on, are necessary if (1) generalizations are to be made beyond the research sample and (2) replication is anticipated.

19. Will the sampling procedures select a sample that adequately represents the target population?

20. Have demographic measures been included to describe the sample and evaluate how well it represents the population?

Sample Size. There must be enough participants to meet all the conditions of the study (i.e., to fill all cells of the design and to provide enough data to meet the needs of the statistical analyses).

21. Is the sample sufficiently large?[1]

Participant Assignment. If the research involves group comparison and an experimental manipulation, participants must be assigned to conditions. Participant assignments should be carried out according to the research design.

22. Have participants been assigned to conditions according to the research design?
23. If it is a differential design, have the groups been carefully defined?
24. If it is a matched-subjects design, has the information on the matching been preserved to allow its use in the analysis?

Participant Availability. Procedures should be in place for contacting and scheduling participants, getting their consent, and paying them if funds are available.

25. Are participants available?
26. Have participants been scheduled or a procedure for scheduling them set up?
27. Are participant payment procedures, if required, in place?

Research Ethics Considerations. Ethical issues should be anticipated and handled, and participant safeguards should be in place.

28. Has IRB ethics approval been obtained?
29. For human research, are the informed consent forms available?
30. Are debriefing and/or feedback procedures ready?
31. For animal research, have all the ethical guidelines been checked and followed?

IX. *Preparation of the Setting*

Space and Equipment. The research space should be prepared appropriately for the research, and all needed equipment should be in place and functioning correctly.

32. Is adequate space available?
33. Is it free of distracting conditions?
34. Has all equipment been checked out?

---

[1]This is a complex question having to do with statistical power. The mathematical procedures for defining "sufficiently large" are beyond the scope of this text. The interested student is referred to Cohen (1988).

Personnel (e.g., Research Assistants).   Proper training of research assistants is critical to ensure that the data will be collected properly.

35. Is there a sufficient number of research assistants?
36. Are the assistants adequately trained for emergencies?
37. Are the assistants adequately trained in the research procedures?
38. Are single- or double-blind procedures necessary and in place?

X. Adequacy of Participant Preparation, Instruction, and Procedures

Instructions, procedures, and tests should be prepared and piloted. There should be no surprises for the experimenter; you do not want to "waste" a single participant.

39. Are all instructions to participants clear?
40. Have the instructions and procedures been piloted?

Quick-Check Review 2: Pre-data Check

2.1. Why is it important to run a pre-data check before we begin to collect data?
2.2. If the pre-data check finds problems, what should the researcher do?

Chapter Summary

Selecting an appropriate statistical procedure can be confusing for beginning students. A flowchart system is presented that organizes the process of selecting statistical procedures. This system starts with a description of the major characteristics of the research study and then proceeds through a series of questions that lead students step by step toward the selection of appropriate statistical procedures.

We also present in the chapter a pre-data checklist similar to the preflight checklist used by pilots. After the study is designed, the procedures are determined, and everything is set to go, the pre-data check provides a final verification that you are ready to collect the data.

Key Terms

Define the following key terms. Be sure that you understand them. They are discussed in the chapter and defined in the glossary.

decision tree   data snooping   Monte Carlo study
decision-tree flowcharts   robust   pre-data check
secondary analyses

15

Research Methodology

An Evolving Discipline

The questions we do not yet even have the wit to ask will be a growing preoccupation of science in the next 50 years.

—Sir John Maddox. The unexpected science to come. *Scientific American*, 1999.

CD Resource Material

Web Resource Material

This chapter opens with a brief overview of concepts that were discussed in earlier chapters. It then discusses new developments in psychology and psychological research. As you will see, contemporary scientific methods are being influenced by several factors, including the development of new statistical methods, the cross-stimulation among different disciplines, the trend toward expanding research from the laboratory to natural settings, the burgeoning developments in computer technology, and continuing societal demands for solutions to problems. Many of the developments briefly introduced here will likely be found in research methods textbooks of the future. This chapter closes with a reminder that the essential nature of science is its integration of rationalism and empiricism. But, first, let's review some critical concepts from the text.

Research is an active process of asking and answering questions, in which there is a constant interplay between inductive and deductive thinking. The methods selected to answer a research question depend on many factors, including practical and ethical constraints and the desire to obtain the most valid answers possible. This text described the traditional methods of research used in biological and social sciences, highlighting such concepts as validity, threats to validity, and control.

The research strategies discussed in this text are by no means all-inclusive, and other strategies continue to be used in answering questions about behavior. There is no best way of answering all questions in science. Selecting the most effective approaches depends on the kinds of questions asked. However, regardless of the kinds of questions asked or the procedures used, there are defined phases in every research project. Research begins with a general idea that is carefully refined into a specific question or problem. Procedures are selected, modified, and adapted to answer the question(s). Observations are made, data are analyzed, results are interpreted, and the research is communicated to other professionals and to the public.

Another idea emphasized throughout the text is that good research can be conducted at different levels of constraint. In this respect, we differ from some of our colleagues who maintain that experiments are always the best ways of answering research questions. We agree that experimental research is the appropriate level for answering causal questions. However, experimental research is often impossible to carry out. For example, under some conditions, manipulating variables may be outside the practical control of the experimenter or may be ethically unacceptable. But these questions are no less worthwhile. Therefore, a portion of this text has been devoted to alternative procedures: low-constraint research procedures that can test questions of feasibility, discover contingencies, and generate hypotheses that can be tested at higher constraint levels. The sections that follow will go beyond these basic concepts to suggest how research questions in psychology are changing and how the research methods are evolving.

New Directions in Research Methodology

Science is continually evolving with new questions being raised and new methodologies being developed. This section touches on a few of these changes in psychology.

The Evolution of Research Questions and Methods

The methods used in a research area change as original questions are answered and new questions are formulated. An example is the historical sequence of the study of genetic influences on schizophrenia (Gottesman, 1991). The initial question was whether genetic factors contributed to schizophrenia. Schizophrenia was known to run in families, but genetic and environmental influences were confounded. That is, the higher frequency of schizophrenia in the families of people with schizophrenia might have been caused by genetic influences, environmental conditions, or both. Research methods were needed to separate the influences of genetics and environment. One of the ways developed was to study people who had been adopted as infants and who later developed schizophrenia. These people had a set of relatives who shared their genetic heritage (their biological relatives) and a set of relatives who shared their environment (their adoptive relatives). The rates of schizophrenia in each of these sets of relatives indicated the contributions of genetics and environment to the development of schizophrenia. These studies showed that schizophrenia is more likely in the biological relatives than in the adoptive relatives of people with schizophrenia who had been adopted at birth, indicating that genetic factors play an important role in the development of schizophrenia.

With that question answered, new questions were raised: How do genes increase risk of schizophrenia? and How does schizophrenia develop? These new questions were addressed by examining the developmental histories of people with schizophrenia for clues. This, however, is an ex post facto approach, and it does not allow us to test causal hypotheses. A better method was needed. Because it was known that genes influenced risk for schizophrenia, Mednick and Schulsinger (1968) suggested studying individuals who are genetically related to people with schizophrenia—the offspring of mothers with schizophrenia. The approach was called *high-risk research* because the participants identified for study had a much higher risk of developing schizophrenia than an unselected sample. However, 95% of all people with schizophrenia do not have a parent with schizophrenia. Therefore, this research approach produced a biased sample of people at risk for schizophrenia. A behavioral high-risk approach was proposed, which identified people at risk for schizophrenia on the basis of personality characteristics (Chapman, Chapman, Raulin, & Edell, 1978). The current functioning of these participants could be studied (e.g., Lubow & De la Casa, 2002; Meyer & Hartzinger, 2001; Silverstein, Raulin, Pristach, & Pomerantz, 1992), and the participants could be followed over time to determine their risk for schizophrenia and other disorders (Chapman, Chapman, Kwapil, Eckblad, & Zinser, 1994; Kwapil, 1998).

Researchers intensified their efforts to identify biological mechanisms responsible for the disorder. In the search for such mechanisms they measured performance known to be related to specific brain functioning (Gooding, Kwapil, & Tallent, 1999; Nunn & Peters, 2001). They looked at the brain structures of people with schizophrenia and compared them with controls (e.g., DeLisi et al., 1997). They also looked at general brain functioning (e.g., Freedman, et al., 2002; Gruzelier, 1994; Stevens, 1997). They constructed computer simulations of brain functioning for various hypothesized schizophrenic brain dysfunctions to see if the models would create the symptoms seen in people with schizophrenia (Cohen & Servan-Schreiber, 1992; Siekmeier & Hoffman, 2002). The study of key participants, such as identical twins in which one has schizophrenia while the other does not, has helped to identify environmental factors contributing to the disorder (Cantor-Graae et al., 1994; Torrey et al., 1994; Walker, Bonsall, & Walder, 2002). The nature of the risk factors has been probed with mathematical procedures developed for this specific purpose by Meehl and his colleagues (e.g., Waller & Meehl, 1998). Several investigators using these techniques have found evidence for a taxonic category of risk, that is, for a risk factor that is all or nothing (Blanchard et al., 2000; Korfine & Lenzenweger, 1995). The information gained from all these lines of research and a dozen other research approaches has fueled a renewed attack on this devastating emotional disorder.

This example illustrates how questions help to shape research designs. Studies designed to answer one question often raise other questions in the process. The new questions sometimes require new research approaches, which often are created by scientists as a by-product of a "need to find the answer." We cannot predict what the next major research approach in the study of schizophrenia will be. It will be selected and/ or created as the need develops, and the need to do so will be shaped by answers to current questions. However, the principles behind any new research approach will be the same ones underlying the designs discussed in this text.

New Statistical Methods

Statistical procedures are tools, and like all tools they are designed to do certain jobs. But new tools open up new possibilities. There are now hundreds of statistical procedures in regular use by research scientists. Some have been around for decades; others for only a few years; still others are in the developmental stage. We will briefly describe several statistical techniques that have had, or promise to have, major impact on the field of psychology.

Analysis of Variance.   We have discussed analysis of variance extensively throughout the text. No statistical procedure has had more impact on research design in psychology than ANOVA. The publication of R. A. Fisher's book *The Design of Experiments* (1935) dramatically changed the way in which research in psychology was conducted. Prior to publication of this book, psychological research involved the careful analysis of behavior from single participants. After Fisher's book, research with groups of participants became the norm. Most of the research methods covered in this text rely on ANOVA procedures for data analysis. In fact, the classic graduate-level statistics texts in psychology (e.g., Myers, 1972; Winer, 1971) have titles suggesting that they are about experimental design. Experimental designs and the statistical procedures to analyze data from these designs are closely connected.

Multidimensional Scaling.   **Multidimensional scaling** techniques refer to a group of statistical procedures that seek to identify underlying structures in nature (Carroll & Arabie, 1998). For example, if you identify all the words in the dictionary that refer to personality traits, you will be shocked to find that there are thousands. Could nature really be that complex and, if so, might there be a way of organizing these traits in a more simplified manner? McCrae and Costa (1987, 1999) identified five underlying factors that account for all these individual personality traits using a variation of multidimensional scaling called factor analysis. Their model, called the five-factor model of personality, suggests that every personality trait is a unique combination of various amounts of five underlying personality dimensions. These dimensions are agreeableness, conscientiousness, openness to experience, extroversion (positive emotionality), and neuroticism (negative emotionality).

Multidimensional scaling techniques seek to identify underlying factors that account for complex patterns of scores. It is presumed that such underlying factors correspond to real variables in life. For example, could there be a brain mechanism that modulates the degree of positive emotionality—how good a person feels? Several mechanisms have been suggested. If such brain mechanisms are identified and if their functioning correlates highly with personality variables, they might be very important in personality development.

It was once believed that the mathematical wizardry of multidimensional scaling procedures would help us to make sense of a vast and complex world (Kruskal & Wish, 1978). This proved to be an unrealistic expectation. Nevertheless, these procedures have led to a much greater understanding of our psychological world (e.g., Katsikitis, 1997; Samson, Zatorre, & Ramsey, 1997) and have stimulated even newer and more promising techniques, such as path analysis and taxometric search procedures.

Path Analysis.   **Path analysis** is a relatively new procedure for interpreting correlational data. It is one of several regression procedures in a general class known as latent-variable models. Latent-variable models assume that the observed data are due to a specified set of latent (or unobserved) variables. Path analysis tests the viability of a hypothesized causal model of the relationship between observed variables. For example, suppose that we hypothesize that three variables (A, B, and C) are causally related to another variable (E). For our hypothetical example, we will assume that variable E is risky sex behavior, which is operationally defined as engaging in unprotected sex with a partner whose HIV status is unknown. Understanding why people engage in risky sex may provide insights into how to reduce such dangerous behavior. Suppose that we hypothesize that three factors affect risky sex behavior: a feeling of invulnerability (variable A), the availability of information on AIDS transmission (variable B), and the strength of the belief that AIDS is a disease that only gay men and IV drug users get (variable C). Furthermore, we believe that variables B and C have their effect on risky sex behavior by influencing the likelihood that someone will bother to learn about what is risky behavior when the information is available to them (variable D). This model is illustrated in Figure 15.1 using the traditional notation of path analysis. The straight lines with arrows represent hypothesized causal connections. Curved lines with bidirectional arrows acknowledge possible correlations between the initial variables. Variables D and E also have short arrows, called residuals, which represent variation that is unexplained by the model. The model can be made more complex by adding additional variables. For example, we might hypothesize that drinking might increase risky sex behavior and knowing someone with AIDS might

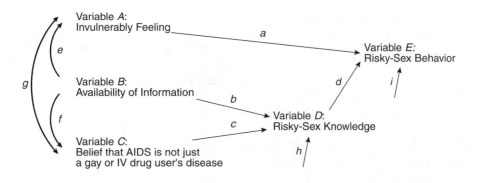

FIGURE 15.1 *Model of Risky Sex Behavior* Latent variable model of several factors thought to contribute to risky sex behavior.

decrease the feeling of invulnerability, thus decreasing risky sex behavior. But, for our example, we will focus on only the variables shown in Figure 15.1. Each line or path in the model is represented by a lowercase letter, which represents the path coefficient. These path coefficients are calculated from the intercorrelation matrix of the variables in the model. The computational procedures are well beyond this text, but the interested student can consult Loehlin (1992). If the path coefficients are large and the residuals are small, the model is considered feasible. You may want to consult the research literature to see how path analysis is used and interpreted. A good example is Dermen, Cooper, and Agocha (1998), who describe an analysis of risky sex behavior and its relationship to alcohol use.

Taxonomic Search Procedures.   A **taxon** is a group that is different in kind from another group. For example, males are a taxon that is qualitatively different from the taxon of females. In contrast, anxious people are probably different from less anxious people only in the fact that they are higher on the dimension of anxiety (i.e., a quantitative difference). It is often valuable to know whether there is a taxonic difference or a dimensional difference separating one group from another. It is easy to tell that some phenomena, such as sex, are taxonic. Other phenomena are obviously dimensional, such as intelligence, with people distributed continuously across a dimension. But what about phenomena like schizophrenia? Is schizophrenia a category distinctly different from a nonschizophrenic state or is it a dimension in which extreme individuals qualify for a diagnosis? Knowing the answer to this question can help to focus the search for the causes for schizophrenia. If schizophrenia is taxonic, it is more likely that a single primary gene is involved in the disorder.

   Taxometric search procedures are designed to address such questions. These procedures are applied when we suspect that there might be a taxonomy, but the only indicators that we have show a continuous distribution. This is best illustrated with an example that we already know represents a taxonomy. Suppose that we hypothesize that there are two types of people (males and females), but that there are no obvious distinguishing characteristics, such as sex organs, to classify people. Unlike sex, most taxonomies in nature do not have obvious ways to identify the categories. We note that some people are taller and heavier and that body shape tends to be different in tall versus short people. We may also notice more muscular development and more body hair on average in the taller individuals and slightly more sociability in shorter individuals. Yet when we measure any one of these characteristics, we find that they show a continuous distribution. Still we suspect that each of the distributions is really the sum of two distinct distributions, as illustrated in Figure 15.2, which shows the distribution of height for a large group of people, with the dashed lines representing the hypothesized distributions for females and males. Remember, in this hypothetical example, we do not know if these subgroup distributions (male versus female) really exist.

Taxometric search procedures look for mathematical relationships between variables that should exist *only* if the data are taxonic. If these relationships exist, there are likely to be two distinct categories. If they do not exist, there is likely to be a dimension on which participants are distributed. A variety of taxometric procedures have been developed. The details of these procedures are well beyond what we could cover in this text. The interested reader is referred to Waller and Meehl (1998) for specifics.

Statistical Analysis of Neuroimages.   When we talk about statistics in psychological research, we usually think of statistical tests. But statistics have contributed in other ways. Modern imaging techniques, such as CAT scans or MRIs, rely heavily on statistics to work. CAT scans pass x-rays through the brain from several angles and record the images. MRIs use magnetic fields to form brain images from several angles. Once these images are available, statistical procedures, which are conceptually similar to multidimensional scaling, determine what the three-dimensional brain must look like in order to produce all these images. These statistical procedures were so clever that

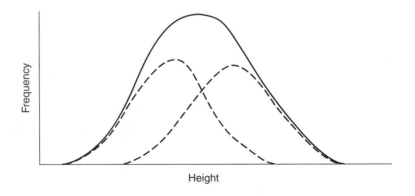

FIGURE 15.2 *Distribution of Two Underlying Taxonomies* Example of how a distribution from two distinct taxons can give no obvious evidence that an underlying taxonomy exists. However, taxometric search procedures can detect subtle mathematical properties that are indicative of an underlying taxonomy.

their developers received the Nobel Prize for their work. The imaging techniques that rely on these statistical procedures have expanded our ability to study the brain and understand its functioning (e.g., DeLisi et al., 1997).

Meta-analysis and Cumulative Knowledge

Meta-analysis helps to objectify an important process that has long been a central part of science. As discussed in Chapter 2, scientists typically begin their research by examining previous research. They review previous studies on the topic and summarize their conclusions in review papers. They might compute a box score in these reviews that lists how many of the studies support a given hypothesis and how many do not. The reviewer judges the quality of each study, which indicates how seriously each study should be taken. For example, one well-designed study may carry much more weight than three or four poorly designed studies. If all the studies have the same outcome, drawing conclusions is easy. But it is common to have some studies showing one effect, whereas others show a different effect or no effect at all.

Meta-analysis is a procedure for statistically combining the results of multiple studies on the same topic (e.g., Abramowitz, 1998; Rosenthal, 1998; Johnson & Eagly, 2000). For example, if there are 16 published studies that employ a cognitive therapy for treating depression, a meta-analysis of these studies would compute an index from each study of how effective the treatment was compared with the control procedure. These indexes are measures of effect size (i.e., the difference between experimental and control conditions expressed in standard deviation units). For example, an effect size of .5 means that the experimental and control conditions showed a mean difference that was one-half of their average standard deviation. These effect sizes are then averaged across studies. The averages are usually weighted by the sample size of each study and sometimes by the quality of the study. So a study with 50 participants would be given more weight in the meta-analysis than a study with 10 participants. A study with strong control procedures and careful measurement could be given more weight than a study with fewer controls and, therefore, more chance of confounding. The overall effect size computed in a meta-analysis indicates numerically how strongly the independent variable affected the dependent variable. Like any statistical analysis, the value of the analysis depends on the quality of the data. In this case, the data represent several studies, and the quality of the designs and execution of the studies determine how confident we can be in the results of the meta-analysis. Some recent examples of meta-analytic studies are summarized in Box 15.1. Many writers have commented on the drawbacks of significance testing in empirical research and the value of meta-analyses in overcoming them (e.g., Schmidt, 1992; Cohen, 1992, Wilson, 2000). The following discussion reviews these arguments.

Literature Reviews.   Psychology, like other sciences, routinely assesses the status of research areas. Typically, this is done through formal literature reviews in which previous research is critically examined, findings and ideas from many studies are abstracted and integrated, and conclusions are drawn about the state of that area. These literature reviews are important summary statements, but several researchers have

BOX 15.1 • *Some Examples of Meta-analytic Research*

Contrary to the general belief from earlier reviews that virtually no treatments are effective for criminal offenders, this meta-analysis shows that treatment does produce improvement. [Hollin, C. R. (1999). Treatment programs for offenders: Meta-analysis, "what works," and beyond. *International Journal of Law and Psychiatry, 22,* 361–372.]

Preventing relapse in persons who were successfully treated for substance abuse is important. Cognitive–behavioral methods for relapse prevention are frequently included in drug-treatment programs. Do these methods work? This meta-analysis examined 26 studies, with 70 hypotheses and a combined sample of 9504 participants. The results indicated that relapse prevention is generally effective, particularly for alcohol problems. [Irvin, J., Bowers, C., Dunn, M., & Wang, M. C. (1999). Efficacy of relapse prevention: A meta-analytic review. Journal of Consulting and Clinical Psychology, 67, 563–570.]

Concerns have been raised that such frequently used psychological tests as the MMPI (Minnesota Multiphasic Personality Inventory) may be biased against minorities, making them look more pathological than they really are. This meta-analysis examined 50 empirical studies, with a combined sample of 8633 participants, that compared African Americans, European Americans, and Latino Americans on their MMPI scores. The results showed that the groups do not differ from each other statistically or clinically. The main conclusion is that the tests do not unfairly portray African Americans or Latinos as pathological. [Hall, G. C., Bansal, A., & Lopez, I. R. (1999). Ethnicity and psychopathology: A meta-analytic review of 31 years of comparative MMPI/MMPI-2 research. *Psychological Assessment, 11,* 186–197.]

argued that these traditional reviews are flawed and less useful than had been thought (Light & Pillemer, 1984; Hunt, 1997).

Alpha Levels and Knowledge.   Most research information is based on statistical procedures that use arbitrary alpha levels in testing the null hypothesis (typically .01 or .05). Thus, when a well-designed study produces statistically significant results, the findings are accepted as valid new knowledge. If the analysis fails to show statistical significance, then it is typically concluded that no new knowledge has been discovered. Indeed, studies that fail to find statistical significance are rarely published and therefore are not easily available to the research community. Thus, the accumulated knowledge of a field, such as that presented in traditional literature reviews, is heavily weighted with information that is based on statistically significant findings.

What about the research results that do not reach statistical significance? Might there be useful information there that is being ignored? Many writers argue that is exactly what is happening; the accumulated scientific knowledge in psychology does not include the information that may reside in studies that were ignored because they failed to reach statistical significance. Consequently, the accumulated knowledge might be drastically limited, hindering the field's progress.

Beta Levels and Knowledge.   Recall from Chapter 5, setting a stringent alpha (.05 or .01) guards against Type I errors, the tendency to conclude that there is an effect of one variable on another when there is none. But minimizing Type I errors increases the probability of Type II errors, that is, the probability of concluding that there is no effect when there is. It is the collective judgment of scientists that Type I errors are more serious than Type II errors because they claim an effect that does not exist. Type II errors *result in the loss of information,* but they do not assert a nonexistent effect. Thus, alpha is set low to minimize the more serious Type I errors.

People often interpret significance tests in an either–or fashion: that is, if the results are statistically significant, then *there is an effect of one variable on another,* and if the results are not statistically significant, then there is *no effect of one variable on another* (Oakes, 1986; Schmidt, 1992). In actuality, there might have been effects that were not strong enough to reach statistical significance. Such might occur, for example, if the sample is small or participant selection or assignment is biased. Effects lie along a continuum, with some effects being small and not reaching significance and others large and statistically significant. By ignoring the small effects, information on relationships among variables is being discarded. That is, the field may be committing a Type II error—failing to recognize real effects. Furthermore, consistently making such Type II errors would significantly truncate the cumulative knowledge in the field (Hunter & Schmidt, 1990). How can science deal with this problem?

Meta-analysis and the Problem of Type II Errors. Meta-analysis deals with the Type II error problem by calculating effect sizes of studies and weighting these effect sizes for qualitative factors, such as the number of subjects and the inclusion of controls. This analysis goes beyond the simple statement of statistical significance and the categorical acceptance or rejection of the null hypothesis. It quantifies the strength of the effect. For example, studies with large sample sizes may be statistically significant at the .05 level but, nevertheless, have small effect sizes. Conversely, studies with modest sample sizes may fall short of statistical significance and yet have moderate effect sizes.

Literature reviews are critical in science. Reviews based on meta-analyses can mine what we might call the Type II error area to unearth important information previously ignored. Meta-analytic techniques are fairly new, but they have the potential to significantly influence the direction of research. Indeed, the important breakthroughs in science of the future might not come from individual research reports of single studies, but from the careful meta-analysis of large groups of research (Schmidt, 1992). This possible future for science would include primary and theoretical scientists, with primary scientists conducting individual studies and providing the data and theoretical scientists applying sophisticated meta-analyses to the accumulated studies to "make the scientific discoveries" (Schmidt, 1992, p. 1180). Meta-analysis provides technology for combining results across diverse samples and different measures of outcome. Although imperfect, meta-analysis is probably better than the traditional totally verbal methods of summarizing studies in literature reviews. Several informative books are available for students who want additional understanding of meta-analysis, such as Light and Pillemer (1984), Hunt (1997), and Cooper (1998).

The Impact of Other Disciplines

Developments in related disciplines can have a significant impact on the discipline of psychology. One of the best examples is the study of neurological influences on human behavior. Developments in the field of biochemistry, which permitted much finer analyses of organic chemicals, made possible the discovery that there are many more neurotransmitters involved in the functioning of the central nervous system than previously believed. This increase in the number of known chemical transmission agents required scientists to rethink the role of neurotransmitters. The concept of specific transmitter influences in precise locations within the brain and other parts of the nervous system became a much more intellectually appealing theory. But how do we study specific influences of specific neurotransmitters in specific locations in the brain? Much of the previous research on neurotransmitters operated under the assumption that there are general levels of these chemicals in the system, and the procedures used for measuring the chemicals were usually nonspecific with respect to the location of the action of each neurotransmitter. There was a need to develop techniques to sample from specific locations. Because brain-functioning processes are part of the living organism and not only a matter of the organism's structure, it was necessary to accomplish the sampling without damaging the organism. A sampling of brain tissue at autopsy provides little useful information. It would also be enormously helpful to be able to experimentally manipulate specific neurotransmitters at specific locations. A procedure known as **micro-iontophoresis** (Curtis & Crawford, 1969) was developed, which allowed researchers to inject chemicals into the synapses of neurons while the animal was awake and functioning. This allowed experimental manipulation of neurotransmitters at specific locations of the brain to gauge their effect on behavior.

The research of Elaine Hull and her students illustrates some of these techniques as well as even newer technologies. Dr. Hull has been studying neuromechanisms that control sexual behavior in rats. Presumably, similar mechanisms control the sexual behavior of humans. She and her students have refined techniques to implant surgically **microcannulae** (tiny tubes) into specific locations of a rat's brain. With these implants the animal is able to function normally without discomfort, but the researcher can manipulate neurotransmitter activity by injecting specific **neurotransmitter agonists** (substances that enhance or mimic the action of specific neurotransmitters) or **antagonists** (substances that block the action of specific neurotransmitters). This technique must not cause pain, because even a rat is less likely to engage in sex if it has a headache. Her research systematically identified the brain mechanisms that control sexual motivation, motor behavior related to sexual activity, and sexual reflexes (e.g., Hull et al., 1999; Markowski et al., 1994; Moses et al., 1995; Putnam et al., 2001).

Hull's laboratory work is now using a new, even more amazing technique. It is useful to observe the normal functioning of a system in addition to experimentally manipulating the system. Earlier, less refined methods sampled specific brain activity by removing a section of the brain and measuring the content of neurotransmitters and their metabolites. An alternative is to sample the chemical composition in an alert and active animal using a technique called **microdialysis,** which involves implanting a cannula that has a tube within a tube, with the outer tube having a chemically porous tip. Neurotransmitters diffuse across this tip into the fluid that is pumped slowly through the outer tube into a collection vial. The levels of neurotransmitters in the fluid can then be measured. This technique can identify the temporal sequence of brain actions involved in sexual activity. Drugs can also be dissolved in the fluid, from which they can diffuse into the brain. As is always the case in science, these new techniques are providing answers to important questions and, in the process, raising more questions that demand still newer techniques. Hull and her colleagues have confirmed through a series of studies an earlier theory that a specific brain region (the medial preoptic area) seems to control sexual motivation, as well as the ability to copulate (Hull, Du, Lorrain, & Matuszewich, 1995). Here the developments in other scientific disciplines—biochemistry and neuroscience—have affected research in another science, psychology.

As another example, consider the use of noninvasive MRI in surgery. This computer-controlled imaging technology constructs and displays three-dimensional images (i.e., virtual reality constructions) as life-sized models of such internal body structures as the brain. With these realistic images, surgeons have virtually "x-ray vision." With the patient on the operating table and a monitor displaying the patient's brain, the surgeon can see inside the skull and can observe and monitor the surgical procedures. Brain surgery, such as the removal of tumors, that could not have been carried out just a few years ago for fear of damaging adjacent brain areas invisible to the surgeon has been successfully carried out using the new imaging techniques (Grimson, Kikinis, Lolesz, & McL. Black, 1999). Psychological research often uses imaging techniques like the MRI. Noninvasive comparative observations of the brains of persons with Alzheimer's disease, autism, brain damage, or schizophrenia are now routinely used (Raulin, 2003). Learning and memory research with animals, monitoring brain activity as the animal responds to controlled stimuli, can be carried out using functional MRIs. There seems little doubt that behavioral research will utilize such advanced MRI scanning techniques.

Interdisciplinary Research

As a science grows, there is increasing specialization. Such specialization focuses researcher's efforts on specific problems and allows the development of sophisticated approaches to problems. But a disadvantage of increasing specialization is that researchers can lose sight of the broader picture. Today it is common to find researchers from different disciplines coming together to pool their knowledge in interdisciplinary research projects, which provides a broader perspective despite modern specialization.

Behavioral medicine is an excellent example of this interdisciplinary approach. The field has brought together physicians and researchers in neurology, physiology, and several areas of psychology. Another example is the interdisciplinary integration of sociology, law, and psychology (Levine & Howe, 1985; Levine & Wallach, 2002). Still another example is the rapidly growing field of artificial intelligence. In this interdisciplinary field, mathematicians, psychologists, and computer scientists developed models of thinking that can be programmed on computers. Such interdisciplinary fields as neuroscience and cognitive science are growing rapidly as the value of these interdisciplinary partnerships becomes more apparent. Interdisciplinary research will continue to increase, providing greater integration in the understanding of human functioning.

Moving Research out of the Laboratory

Many psychologists are rediscovering old methods as a result of their concern for external or ecological validity. Naturalistic and case-study research is becoming more common in areas that previously relied almost exclusively on higher-constraint research. For example, many researchers argue that understanding the development of a person requires that we take a historical perspective, noting the developmental influences that color his or her current perspective on life. This more individualized approach to developmental psychology is different from what has been the tradition over the last few decades. It reinforces the point made throughout the text: lower-constraint research is a legitimate way of examining certain research questions and sometimes may even be the best way to study a phenomenon.

Research in natural settings need not give up the controls of the laboratory. Well-controlled experiments can be carried out in natural settings. For example, the work of Ramey and his colleagues with severely disadvantaged children in real-world settings demonstrated that early interventions can have powerful and permanent effects on a child's development (e.g., Campbell et al., 2002; Ramey, 1995). In response to demands for such real-world information, researchers have increased their research efforts in natural settings. Conducting research in natural settings is difficult and challenging, but the reward of good generalization of results to other real-world settings makes the effort worthwhile.

One weakness of laboratory research is the possibility of low external validity. Campbell and Stanley (1966) cautioned that "we cannot easily assume that findings from the laboratory will hold in the field" (p. 7). This issue is one of **ecological validity,** the accurate generalization of laboratory findings to real-world settings, and it has caused some controversy in the field. The argument is that laboratory experimentation may be so constrained that its findings do not represent external reality. In a word, they may be trivial. But other scientists argue that research in natural environments may be so uncontrolled that internal validity is sacrificed. This argument is likely to continue, given the complexity of human behavior. But this controversy may be overstated. Anderson, Lindsay, and Bushman (1999) argue that the notions of the poor ecological validity of laboratory research and the poor internal validity of field research are unsupported beliefs, rather than empirical facts. These researchers calculated the effect sizes of 38 pairs of laboratory studies and comparable field studies. They found a significant positive correlation (.728) between the effect sizes of the laboratory studies and the field studies, which are illustrated in the scatter plot in Figure 15.3. They concluded that the laboratory–field correspondence is high and that laboratory research appears to be discovering real phenomena and not mere trivial findings. The strong correlation between the results of laboratory and field studies also suggests that the internal validity of the field studies is also strong. Well-designed studies, whether in laboratory or field settings, can support valid, generalizable conclusions.

The Impact of Computers

The monumental growth of computer technology has had a major impact on research. Not since the Industrial Revolution has so much changed so quickly. Much of the radical improvement is due to the development of the microprocessor, that tiny silicon sliver that now drives notebook computers, fax machines, wristwatches, kitchen appliances, factories, automobiles, airplanes, and boats. Today's typical notebook computer

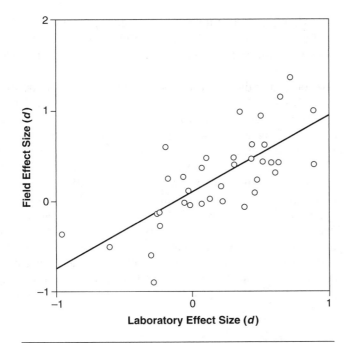

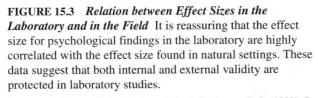

FIGURE 15.3 *Relation between Effect Sizes in the Laboratory and in the Field* It is reassuring that the effect size for psychological findings in the laboratory are highly correlated with the effect size found in natural settings. These data suggest that both internal and external validity are protected in laboratory studies.

Source: Anderson, C. A., Lindsay, J. J., & Bushman, B. J. (1999). Research in the psychological laboratory: Truth or triviality. *Current Directions in Psychological Science, 8,* 3–9. Reprinted with permission.

is far more powerful than a 1960s computer that had to be housed in several floors of a large building and does the work far more rapidly and more reliably. Since the introduction of personal computers in the late 1970s, the power of these machines has doubled every 18 months (Patterson, 1995; Rupley & Clyman, 1995). Today you can buy a PC that is about 50,000 times more powerful than the original PC for less than half the cost (in inflation-corrected dollars). If microprocessors continue to develop at this or a similar rate, then the computers of 2025 will be able to utilize astounding new software that will manage tasks that we can now barely imagine. This computer technology will certainly help scientists to pursue the now unknown scientific questions that are hinted at in the quotation at the beginning of this chapter.

Consider the impact of computers on communication. Today more than 100 million computers around the world are interconnected, but this represents only about 2% of the world's population (Dertouzos, 1999). Imagine the impact on global communication and the potential effects on human institutions, cross-cultural interactions, and scientific communication if 5% or—can we imagine it?—50% or more of the world's population were interconnected through hundreds of millions of vastly more powerful computers than we have today.

Computers have dramatically increased the efficiency of the laboratory. Tasks that once took an enormous amount of time can now be done in seconds. The most obvious benefactor of this improved efficiency is the data-analysis phase. Students who have worked through something as complex as a two-way ANOVA on a pocket calculator can appreciate the time savings of computer analyses. The computer can run a million analyses in less time than it takes most people to compute a simple mean from their data. The increased efficiency has allowed the development of complex and labor-intensive analysis procedures, such as multivariate ANOVAs and multidimensional scaling. This has created an explosion in the number and sophistication of analysis procedures. We may be reaching the limit of this growth in data analysis, however, not because computers cannot do the computations, but because humans may not be able to comprehend the results. For example, the computer can easily analyze a factorial study with a dozen or more factors. The mathematical formulas for computation

After years of working on the project, Professor Gronski discovers there are practical limits to miniaturization.

Not every technological development is desirable.

are easily generalized to more complex designs, and computers can perform the computations quickly. But few people can actually visualize and understand the meaning of, for example, a five-way interaction—five different factors combining in a unique way to affect the dependent variable.

Such developments in computerized data analysis may also have created problems. Perhaps data analysis has become too easy, and some of the care previously exercised on the design and execution of studies may have been lost. One of our colleagues worked her way through graduate school in the early 1950s by conducting factor analyses. The analyses were carried out using the most modern calculating instruments of the time—mechanical calculators. To complete a typical analysis required 9 months of working 20 hours per week. Today, a computer performs the same analysis in less than a second. A knowledgeable student can set up the analysis in a few minutes. When an analysis takes 9 months to complete and costs thousands of dollars, we make sure that the data being analyzed are as precise and accurate as possible and that the analysis is appropriate for the data available and the question(s) being asked. It is not clear that the same care goes into these aspects of the research now that the analyses are so easy and inexpensive to accomplish.

The computer improves the efficiency and quality of psychological research in other ways. Researchers use computers to interact with and to gather data from participants, reducing the number of mistakes that result in lost or distorted data. The computer carries out complex procedures flawlessly for one participant after another. This also minimizes experimenter bias. Computers can take and record measures in a completely objective manner, presenting stimuli in exactly the same way to each participant and performing all these tasks in a perfectly replicated manner in study after study. The software to run studies or carry out analyses can be shared with other researchers, increasing the precision in the replication of laboratory procedures.

Some laboratory paradigms would be impossible without computers. The computer is not limited to presenting stimuli in a single predetermined sequence. Rather, it is capable of recording responses, evaluating them, and choosing the next step based on participants' responses. This permits scientists to test more complex hypotheses than are possible with a static presentation of a given set of stimuli. Of course, mechanical equipment that is responsive to participants has been available for years. The Skinner box is the best-known example. What the computer adds is an expansion of the range and level of complexity of response. It also dramatically simplifies the task of modifying procedures to test new hypotheses. With the old mechanical equipment, modifying procedures often meant physically changing the equipment or designing and building new equipment. With computer-controlled studies, only software changes are required. In many computer-controlled laboratories, new studies can be up and running in a few hours instead of weeks or months.

The computer also offers us new ways of understanding phenomena. An example of such an approach is the computer modeling of cognitive processes (Weitzenfeld, Arbib, & Alexander, 2002). **Computer modeling** is an idea that is borrowed and adapted from the artificial intelligence field. In **artificial intelligence,** computers are programmed to behave intelligently, to solve problems, and to react to stimuli. Artificial intelligence systems are not necessarily designed to duplicate human functioning, but computer models of cognitive functions do attempt to duplicate human functions. Instead of developing complex abstract models of cognitive processes and designing factorial studies that are too complicated to understand, researchers create a computer model of functioning that they can manipulate to observe the effects.

A class of computer models that has received considerable attention is called **parallel distributed processing (PDP)** or **connectionist models** (Stein & Ludick, 1998). These models simulate mathematically the interconnection of networks of neurons. Neurons in the brain are heavily interconnected, and the brain uses parallel processing to accomplish its remarkable feats in very little time. In contrast, computers process material serially, one task after another, using very fast electronic circuits. PDP models have been developed to mimic several human processes, including perception, learning, language use, and memory retrieval. The models are intriguing for many reasons. First, they learn to function correctly, not by being programmed with a set of rules, but rather by being exposed to input and output information and by adjusting the strength of the mathematical parameters to give more accurate responses. In other words, these models learn from experience. In theory, these PDP models can learn extremely complex behavior with sufficient exposure to relevant situations. PDP computer chips are now being produced for research purposes and are now being used in robotic devices to test their limits. This research area not only promises a new perspective on brain functioning, but also has the potential for major technological breakthroughs.

PDP models are psychologically interesting because they often perform like humans. When learning to respond correctly, these models make the same mistakes that humans make. For example, a model designed to learn how to form plural nouns from singular nouns seems to learn quickly that many nouns add an "s" (e.g., toy–toys), but that there are exceptions (e.g., mouse–mice). During the learning process, the model is apt to produce *mices* as the plural of *mouse,* much as children do. These models seem to produce behavior that is rule based, but no rules were ever given to the program (Oaksford & Chater, 1998). Human behavior often appears to be rule based, but theorists have often wondered how people acquired the rules.

In the second edition of this text, we introduced parallel distributed processing models as one of the cutting-edge areas of psychology. At the time, there were only a handful of books and just over 100 published papers. In the 10 years since that edition, over 9000 articles, chapters, and books have been published on the topic, an explosion of research and theory almost unmatched in psychology. These models have provided new perspectives on such cognitive functions as reasoning (e.g., Kasabov & Shishkov, 1993; Shastri, 1999), learning (e.g., Dennett, 1993), language processing (e.g., Collier, 1994; Farkas & Li, 2001), and visual processing (Weitzenfeld et al., 2002), to name but a few. In addition, a variety of pathological conditions have been modeled with PDP procedures, including obsessive–compulsive disorder (e.g., Stein & Hollander, 1994), dyslexia (e.g., Plaut & Shallice, 1993; Seidenberg, 1993; Snowling, Hulme, & Goulandris, 1994), aphasia (e.g., Harley, 1993), and schizophrenia (e.g., Cohen & Servan-Schreiber, 1992; Siekmeier & Hoffman, 2002). PDP models have challenged dozens of psychological theories.

The goal in computer modeling is to find a model that can reproduce human behavior accurately. The idea is analogous to using scale models of airplanes and testing them in wind tunnels. Theories and formulas predict how certain factors will affect the aerodynamics of an airplane. However, so many factors come into play in real-life situations that scientists can make only educated guesses about what would happen to a real airplane. But with a model and the wind tunnel to simulate flight conditions, scientists can actually test their guesses and fine-tune a system that has become so complex that it strains the limits of human understanding. Researchers may soon be able to accomplish similar goals with computer models of cognitive functioning.

Computers have even had an impact on the way scientists collaborate. Electronic mail (e-mail) has made it possible for researchers at distant universities to collaborate easily, passing messages and information back and forth in seconds, all at little or no cost. Computer technology is now being used to enhance even more direct collaboration regardless of the distance between researchers (Crawford, Hurd, & Weller, 1996; Schrage, 1991). With modern software, researchers in different cities can be working on the same document at the same time, sharing ideas as if they were gathered around a table writing a draft of an article. This new computer technology allows collaborators to be spread all over the world and still be able to work closely together. The explosion in this technology was discussed in Chapter 2 (see Box 2.1).

The impact of computers on psychological research is only beginning to be felt. The directions for the future will be shaped by the inventiveness of today's scientists. Computers are becoming so inexpensive that every active laboratory in the country will have computing power. Many believe that computers will offer whole new ways of looking at questions and will permit new research paradigms that will answer questions yet to be imagined. It is an exciting period for science, but we must not forget that it is the scientist's imagination and not the silicon of the computer chips that fuels this explosion. The computer is a powerful resource, but human thought and creativity harness this resource. Basic science is unlikely to be changed by the computer. The computer will add efficiency, but the scientist will still ask the questions, decide the best ways to search for the answers, set up the studies, and evaluate the results.

Scientific Research and Society

Most students reading this book today will, in 50 years, be about 70 to 75 years old. Will you have retired from work at that time? Perhaps science will have made it more likely that you will continue to work for many more years. Perhaps society will have changed to the degree that retirement will no longer be an appropriate concept, with current practices of work and careers dramatically changed in a world too remote from us to imagine. It is tempting to be enthralled by scientific and technological advances and then try to extrapolate to the future and ask, "What will science be discovering in another half-century? What will life be like?"

The momentous scientific discoveries of the 19th century laid the groundwork for a future that people in the 1890s thought that they could foretell. In a thought-provoking essay, Maddox (1999) reviewed the major scientific discoveries of the 19th century that helped to change the world (see Table 15.1), but these discoveries proved to be well short of the final answers that many people wanted. Much of what then seemed certain was later changed, reconceptualized, or discarded as unimportant. Science in the 20th century developed concepts and procedures that the earlier scientists and the general public had never envisioned. The directions of the 20th century's scientific

TABLE 15.1 *Major Scientific Discoveries of the 19th Century*

- John Dalton's confirmation that matter is made of atoms (1808)
- Sadi Carnot's surmise that converting one form of energy to another is inherently limited (about 1830)
- James P. Joule's demonstration of the conservation of energy (1851)
- Charles Darwin's and Alfred Russel Wallace's discovery of natural selection and the eventual Darwinian theory of evolution (1859)
- James Maxwell's mathematical unification of electricity and magnetism (about 1880)

Source: Adapted from Maddox, 1999.

developments were very different from what had been anticipated. One lesson that Maddox draws is that we need to be realistic about our infatuation with our own scientific discoveries. The direction of science is unpredictable because it is driven by new discoveries. The discoveries that will be made in this 21st century are as unpredictable by us now as the 20th century's developments were to those in the 1890s. Maddox believes that we cannot imagine the scientific discoveries that await us over the next half-century (see the quotation at the start of this chapter).

For example, consider the current research on the human genome (Collins & Jegalian, 1999). The mapping and sequencing was recently completed, several years ahead of schedule. Where will that information lead? Will it tell us about evolution, when and how we diverged from the great apes? Will it explain how and when the human brain and human skills, such as language and art, developed? Will it be the basis for technology that will allow programmatic development of future human brains? How these and other scientific discoveries will affect the future is unclear, but that they will affect the future is unquestioned.

Scientific advances of such magnitude as the human genome project lead us into a complex many-dimensioned universe of ideas and technologies, with uncountable turns, twists, knots, ascents, descents, and dead ends and even forays through time. This intertwined mass, like tangled roots in a tropical jungle pool, presents us with a seemingly impenetrable confusion of possible futures. How can we read it from here and predict the direction of each tendril of discovery? Simply, we cannot.

Quick-Check Review 1: New Directions in Research Methodology

1.1. How does meta-analysis improve the process of reviewing and synthesizing several studies of the same question?

1.2. What is path analysis, and how is it used?

1.3. How do micro-iontophoresis and microdialysis improve the study of brain functioning?

1.4. How have computers changed psychological research?

Science: An Interaction between Empiricism and Rationalism

It is important to restate a point made in Chapter 1: new laboratory technologies do not define a science. Rather, a scientific discipline is defined by its subject matter and by the processes used to answer questions of interest to that discipline.

Science combines empiricism and rationalism. By requiring that scientific theories conform to both logical restrictions and the realities of the world, we demand more of scientific theories than of any other system of knowing. Few scientific theories stand up to this kind of double scrutiny. Theories are constantly being rejected because they are either logically inconsistent (a rational criterion) and/or they do not accurately predict data (an empirical criterion). Science progresses by rejecting inadequate theories and proposing and testing new theories that will stand up better to the rigorous demands of rationalism and empiricism. Initially, students may find this process to be negativistic: researchers always try to criticize and reject theories, rather than prove them. However, it is not negativism but rather *skepticism* that characterizes science. Scientists use theories, but they never fully accept them. They constantly question a theory's validity. Good scientists expect that all theories eventually will be replaced by better theories. In science, little is accepted on faith except for the method of science.

Science has become a major enterprise in today's world. Millions of people work in and around scientific laboratories. Scientific disciplines have become more specialized as their knowledge base grows. As disciplines develop, research techniques evolve to handle the specific questions of each discipline. Therefore, different scientific disciplines appear to be using different research methods. This text covered many of the most commonly used research techniques in the discipline of psychology. Although the techniques covered differ somewhat from those used in other sciences, they are more surface differences than conceptual differences. A research biologist would have no trouble conceptually understanding the research methodology of chemistry or psychology, and vice versa. In this text, we presented concepts and built specific research techniques on them. If you understand the concepts that underlie techniques, it will be relatively easy to understand new research techniques, whether they are from the discipline of psychology or some other science.

New research techniques are an almost inevitable result of a developing science. New scientific disciplines are also inevitable as the knowledge base of science builds and increased specialization is required. What was once philosophy is now a dozen different basic sciences. What was once physics is now physics, astronomy, and chemistry. Specialization is necessary, given the incredible complexity of many disciplines, but it tends to isolate disciplines from the ideas and discoveries of other sciences. Organizations such as the American Association for the Advancement of Science (AAAS) strive to unite the many subdisciplines of science and maintain a healthy level of communication among disciplines. Support for this effort comes from the belief that the method of science (empiricism coupled with rationalism) is a strong bond between apparently diverse areas. It is hoped that students gain from this text an understanding of research approaches in psychology and an understanding of science and scientific thought in general. The specific research approaches in psychology are applications of basic scientific processes to a particular subject matter—the behavior of organisms.

Quick-Check Review 2: Science: An Interaction between Empiricism and Rationalism

2.1. What processes define science?

2.2. How does science progress?

The Essence of Science: A Reminder

It is appropriate to end this book by repeating an idea that we have stressed throughout: The essence of science is its *way of thinking*. The important tools of scientists are their skills in systematically combining rational thinking and empirical findings to ask and answer questions about nature. The scientist's enthusiasm, skepticism, curiosity, hunches, and creativity, coupled with a little serendipity, are essential components in the process of scientific thinking, as are the technologies of each discipline. But, mostly, it is the *thinking process that constitutes the essence of science*. To emphasize this point, recall the imagery used in Chapter 1: A scientist can operate very scientifically while sitting under a tree in the woods, thinking through a problem, and using apparatus no more technical than a pad and pencil.

Quick-Check Review 3: The Essence of Science

3.1. What is the essence of science?

3.2. Explain how a scientist can conduct science while sitting under a tree.

Key Terms

Define the following key terms. Be sure that you understand them. They are discussed in the chapter and defined in the glossary.

multidimensional scaling
path analysis
taxon
taxometric search procedures
meta-analysis
micro-iontophoresis

microcannulae
neurotransmitter agonists
neurotransmitter antagonists
microdialysis
behavioral medicine
computer modeling

artificial intelligence
ecological validity
parallel distributed
    processing (PDP)
connectionist models

Appendix A

Using the Student Resource CD *and Web Site*

This text includes the most comprehensive set of supplementary resources available in any research methods text. These resources are available through the CD included with the text and through a constantly updated Web site for the text. This appendix will describe what is available and how to access it.

Resources Available

The *Student Resource CD* provides the vast majority of supplementary material, and the Web site provides more time-critical material. The Web site is updated about twice a year to provide students with the most up-to-date and comprehensive information available.

CD

The CD includes (1) an interactive *Student Study Guide/Laboratory Manual*, (2) tutorials on library research, statistical computation, computerized statistical analysis, and writing reports in APA style, (3) an extensive guide to APA publication format, and (4) numerous exercises and handouts, all keyed to specific chapters. All the material can be accessed using an ordinary web browser (Netscape or Internet Explorer) and will work on both Windows and Macintosh systems.

Web Site

The Web site provides additional material, which is periodically updated. Any new resources developed for the text are immediately added to the Web site. Corrections or updates to the text itself are also included. Finally, an extensive list of links to sites that cover topics or people covered in the text is available. This list is updated and expanded approximately twice a year. Its address is **www.ablongman.com/graziano.**[1]

Accessing the CD Material

We have structured the CD to make it easy to use. You can access anything on the CD from the main menu (start.htm) and can move easily from one section to another. The Table of Contents for the CD is always visible on the top of the screen.

Using a Web Browser

The material on both the CD and the Web site has been formatted as web pages to simplify access. We recommend using newer versions of one of the graphical web browsers, such as Netscape Navigator® or Internet Explorer®, although we have designed the CD and Web site so that older versions of web browsers should work fine. Both of these programs are readily available either free or for a very nominal cost. Check with your computing center on campus if you do not have one of these programs. If you have a computer with Windows® operating system, you probably already have a copy of Internet Explorer.

Modern web browsers are easy and intuitive to use. They all operate pretty much the same way. Figure A.1 shows the interface for Netscape Navigator, and Figure A.2 shows the interface for Internet Explorer. We have included a tutorial on each of these browsers on the *Student Resource CD*. Of course, you need to know the basics of web browsers to access the CD, so this section will provide those. Only a few elements are critical to know to access the text's CD or Web site, and these elements are virtually the same for both Netscape and Internet Explorer.

You move within a web-based document by pointing and clicking. You can click on the buttons of the program or the pull-down menus to accomplish such tasks as printing the page that you are viewing. This process is identical to how you operate

---

[1]The complete address for the Web site is **http://www.ablongman.com/graziano/index.htm.** Most web browsers allow you to drop the "http://" part, and the "/index.htm" is the default file that will be accessed and so need not be specified.

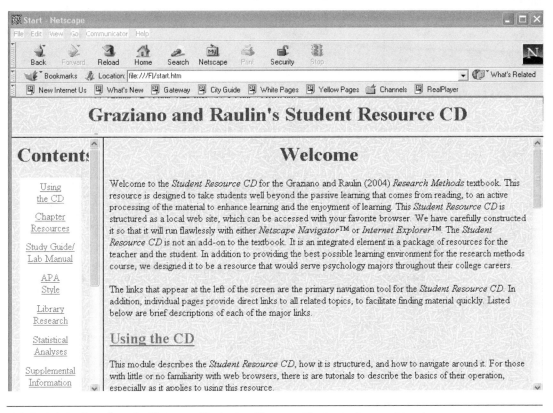

FIGURE A.1 *Interface for Netscape Navigator* Netscape Navigator is one of two browsers that are widely used to navigate the Web.

other computer programs, so most people with even a little computer experience quickly adapt to using web browsers. You can also click on a **hyperlink** in the document that you are viewing to navigate within and between documents. A hyperlink contains the address for other linked documents. It can be attached to either an image or text. If it is attached to text, the text will usually be printed in a different color from the rest of the text and will be underlined. When you move the arrow to the link, the arrow will change to a hand and the address of the link will be displayed at the bottom of the screen. Clicking the left mouse button will take you to that linked document. You can return to the original document by clicking the back arrow button at the top of the screen. In both the *Student Resource CD* and the Web site, the menu is always available on the left of the screen to help you to navigate.

You open a web-based document by clicking in the white address space at the top of the web browser and entering the address for the Web site you want to visit. This space is labeled *Location* in Netscape and *Address* in Internet Explorer. This process is

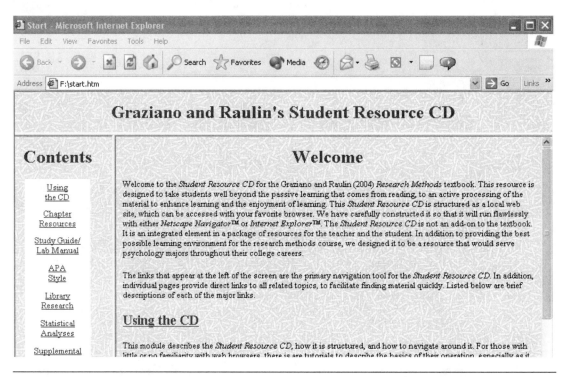

FIGURE A.2   *Interface for Internet Explorer*   Internet Explorer is one of two browsers that are widely used to navigate the Web.

FIGURE A.3   *Opening the Graziano and Raulin Web Site*   To open a Web site, type the address of the Web site into the Address box of Internet Explorer or the Location box of Netscape Navigator. It is convenient to save this address to avoid having to retype it each time. You save it to your Favorites in Internet Explorer or to Bookmarks in Netscape Navigator.

shown in Figure A.3. The address for the Web site for this text is www.ablongman.com/ graziano. Both Netscape and Internet Explorer allow you to save the addresses of places that you visit often. Just click on *Bookmarks* in Netscape or *Favorites* in Internet Explorer to save the address. Once saved, you can pick the address out of a list of saved addresses by clicking on these same buttons.

The *Student Resource CD* should start automatically whenever you insert it in your CD drive. If it does not start automatically, select the *File Menu* and the *Open Page* option from Netscape or the *File Menu* and *Open* option from Internet Explorer and enter the filename. The filename to open the *Student Resource CD* is X:\start.htm, in which the letter that designates the CD drive for your computer replaces X. For example, if the letter D designates your CD drive, you would enter D:\start.htm as the filename. You can also search for the file by using the *Choose File* option in Netscape or the *Browse* option in Internet Explorer. Both of these operate like any other program that is searching for a file to open. Another alternative is to use the Windows Explorer to find the start file on the CD, as shown in Figure A.4. Clicking on the start.htm file will open the file. Once you open the *Student Resource CD,* you will get the screen that is shown in Figure A.5.[2] Click on *Start* and the opening screen will appear. You can add this location to your bookmarks in Netscape or your list of favorites in Internet Explorer, which will make it easier to quickly open the *Student Resource CD* later. Just remember that the address that you are recording assumes that the *Student Resource CD* is in your CD drive.

[2]For the remainder of this appendix, we will use the Internet Explorer Browser to display pages from the text Web site and CD.

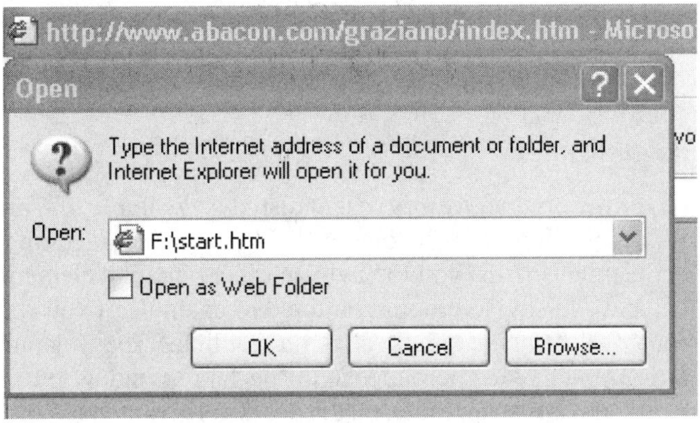

FIGURE A.4 *Opening the* **Student Resource CD** To open the *Student Resource CD,* use the browse button to find the file labeled start.htm on the CD, click on it to put it in the Open box, and then click on OK to start the CD.

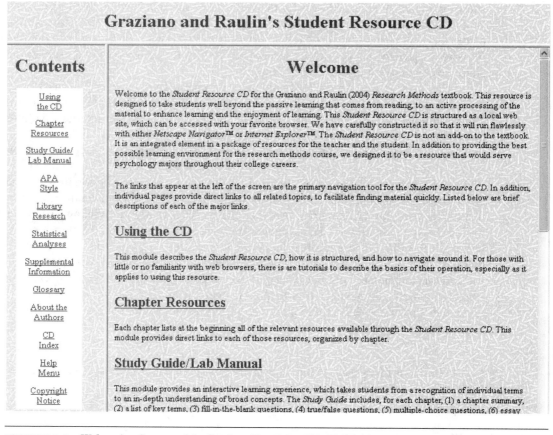

FIGURE A.5   *Welcoming Screen of the* **Student Resource CD**   This is the opening screen for the *Student Resource CD.*

Table of Contents and Index

The opening screen for the *Student Resource CD* displays the Table of Contents on the left of the screen. A description of each content entry is also included on this opening screen. The Table of Contents helps you to navigate quickly to any element on the CD. Just point at the item and click the left mouse button. For example, if you want to use the electronic *Study Guide/Lab Manual,* simply click on that link.[3] The welcoming page for the *Study Guide/Lab Manual* will then appear in the large window on the screen as shown in Figure A.6. There is also an index that is accessible from the Table of Contents that provides direct links to every feature of the *Student Resource CD.* Clicking on the index entry in the Table of Contents will provide the screen shown in Figure A.7.

------

[3]From now on, when we say click on an item we mean move the arrow to that item and click on the left mouse button.

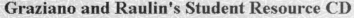

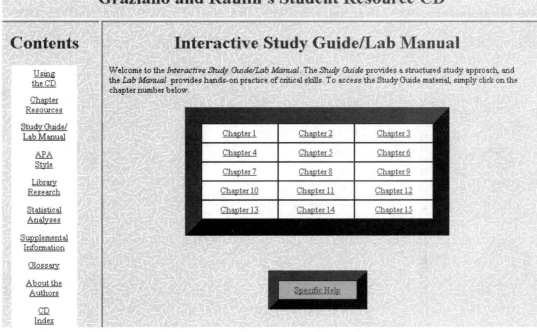

FIGURE A.6 **Study Guide/Lab Manual** The *Study Guide/Lab Manual* can be easily accessed by clicking on the link to it in the Table of Contents on the top of the page. You then access the chapter that you want by clicking on its link in the box.

Accessing Material Referenced in the Text

At the beginning of each chapter is a list of CD resources for that chapter. You can access any of these items by clicking on the *Chapter Resources* entry in the Table of Contents, which will give you the screen shown in Figure A.8. This screen provides direct links to each of these resources.

Using the Study Guide/Lab Manual

The electronic *Study Guide/Lab Manual* provides an excellent review of material in a structured and organized way. Each chapter has eight sections: (1) a chapter summary, (2) a list of key terms, (3) fill-in-the-blank questions, (4) true–false questions, (5) multiple-choice questions, (6) essay questions, (7) laboratory exercises, and (8) a suggested reading list. Clicking on the *Study Guide/Lab Manual* entry in the Table of Contents presents the welcoming screen shown in Figure A.6. In addition, individual chapters of the *Study Guide/Lab Manual* can be accessed from the *Chapter Resources* page.

The electronic *Study Guide* is interactive. For example, clicking on any of the key terms will immediately send you to the glossary, where the term is defined. Clicking the

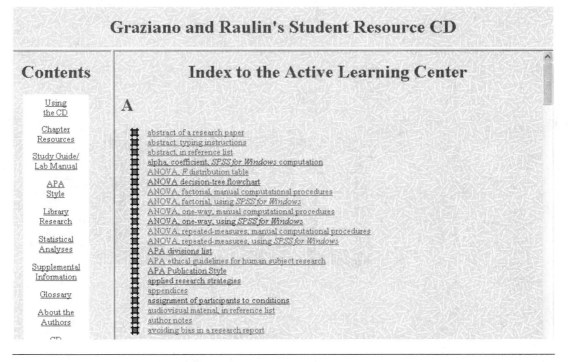

FIGURE A.7   **Student Resource CD *Index***   The index provides a direct link to every resource available on the CD. Many resources have multiple listings in the index to facilitate the search for a specific item.

back arrow key of the web browser will bring you back to the list. Clicking on any of the blanks in the fill-in-the-blanks questions will give you the missing words. Clicking on any answer in the true–false or multiple-choice questions will give you immediate feedback on your accuracy.

We have designed the *Study Guide* to give you a thorough review of the material in each chapter. The chapter summary gives you an overview. The key terms list, with its direct access to the glossary, gives you the new terms introduced in that chapter. The fill-in-the-blanks questions familiarize you with the use of these terms. The true–false, multiple-choice, and essay questions move you from recognizing correct and incorrect statements, to recognizing correct answers in an array of incorrect answers, to being able to generate correct answers on your own. The laboratory exercise section gives you hands-on experience with the concepts covered in the chapter, and the suggested reading list provides additional resources for students who want to learn more about the material. If you use the *Study Guide/Lab Manual* diligently, you should have a solid understanding of the material in the text.

Using SPSS for Windows

A second CD can accompany this text at the instructor's discretion. This second CD contains the student version of *SPSS for Windows*. You will need to copy this program

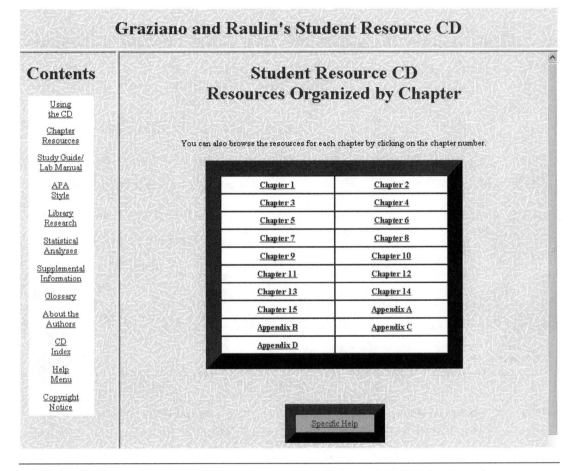

FIGURE A.8   *Chapter Resources*   All the resources listed at the beginning of the chapter can be accessed by clicking on the Chapter Resources link in the table of contents.

onto your hard drive as part of a setup procedure in order to operate the program. The SPSS program disk starts automatically when you put it in the CD drive, producing the startup screen shown in Figure A.9. The *Student Resource CD* includes extensive explanations of each procedure mentioned in the text and how to accomplish these procedures using *SPSS for Windows.* Click on the *Statistical Analyses* entry in the Table of Contents for an *SPSS* tutorial.

Accessing the Web Material

We will assume that your computer has access to the Web and that you know how to activate the access. Some connections are direct and therefore always operate. For example, many dorm rooms now come equipped with Ethernet connections to the

FIGURE A.9 SPSS for Windows The *SPSS for Windows* opening screen provides several options. To run the program, you must first install in on your computer.

university's mainframe computer, which also serves as the access point to the Internet. If you use your computer from home, you likely connect to the Internet through a modem (a device to send computer signals over phone or cable lines) and an Internet service provider (a company that provides Internet access for a fee). If none of this sounds familiar to you, we recommend that you check with the support people at the university's computing center. Most universities provide free consultation on how to access computing resources, including the Internet, to students, faculty, and staff.

The instructions for accessing the text's Web site were detailed earlier in the Using a Web Browser section. Enter **www.ablongman.com/graziano** as the address or location in the white box at the top of the browser and hit the Enter key. The program will then access the welcoming page of the Graziano and Raulin Web site, as shown in Figure A.10.

The Web site operates in a manner similar to the *Student Resource CD*. There is a Table of Contents on the left to give you quick access to any element of the site. There are several sections to the Web site. The Overview entry in the Table of Con-

Welcome to the Graziano and Raulin Web Site

Research Methods

A Process of Inquiry

Click Here to View the Site in Frames

(recommended if your browser allows frames)

Click Here to View the Site Without Frames

FIGURE A.10   *Graziano and Raulin Web Site*   The Graziano and Raulin Web site is designed to complement the text, providing updated material and access to other useful Web resources.

tents describes each available resource on the Web site. The major Web site resources are links to relevant sites organized by chapter, new material and errata for the text, practice quizzes, resources for instructors, and a feedback form. We encourage your feedback—both positive and negative. We have found student feedback very helpful in improving the text in the next edition.

Appendix Summary

This text includes at no additional cost a *Student Resource CD* and a regularly updated Web site. Both are accessed from a standard graphical web browser, such as Netscape or Internet Explorer. The *Student Resource CD* and Web site provide the student with resources designed to enhance the research methods course and serve as useful resources through your undergraduate and even your graduate education.

Appendix B

Writing a Research Report
APA Publication Style

Publication is a critical part of the research process. Literally, publication means "to make public." Making science a public discipline serves two purposes. First, it facilitates building on current knowledge by making it accessible to everyone. Second, publication brings each finding to the scrutiny of many scientists who can independently review the logic, procedures, results, and conclusions.

There is much to communicate in a research report, yet space restrictions demand that a report be concise. Thus, guidelines are necessary to aid communication while minimizing the journal space used. The publication manual prepared by the American Psychological Association (2001) is used as a guide by most psychology journals and journals in several other disciplines. Psychology majors, particularly those planning to attend graduate school, may wish to purchase a copy of the manual.[1] The *Student Resource CD* outlines most key elements of APA publication style, going

---

[1]The Publication Manual of the American Psychological Association can be purchased directly from the American Psychological Association at nominal cost [*www.apa.org*]. The American Psychological Association publishes a workbook to help students to learn APA style (Gelfand & Walker, 1994), and other inexpensive texts are available (e.g., Rosnow & Rosnow, 1998) that focus exclusively on writing reports in APA style.

well beyond the basic coverage of this appendix. The *Student Resource CD* can provide a useful reference for years to come.

Structure of a Research Article

Organization is one key to a good research article. The American Psychological Association recommends that the body of a research article be organized into four parts: introduction, method, results, and discussion. In addition, the report should have a title page and a short (100 to 120 word) abstract, a reference section, and, if necessary, figures and tables. The abstract briefly describes the study and its findings, permitting readers to determine if the article is of interest to them and should be read more thoroughly. The abstract is also published in one or more journals (e.g., *Psychological Abstracts*) or computer databases (e.g., *PsycINFO*) that specialize in abstracts. These journals or databases are cross-referenced to make it easier for a researcher to identify relevant research. The reference section provides details on where the reports of previous research can be found. There are specific standards on how to record this information so that it can be presented in a concise and complete manner. Occasionally, additional attachments are included at the end of an article in the form of appendices. These may contain extended information, materials, or scales that are not readily available elsewhere. The major sections of a journal article are shown in Table B.1.

Writing the Research Report

This section covers the preparation of each section of a research report. Clarity and precision in the presentation of research results are important. Where appropriate, specific information on APA publication style is given.

TABLE B.1 *Major Sections and Subsections of a Manuscript*

1. Title page
2. Abstract
3. Introduction
4. Method
   a. Participants
   b. Apparatus
   c. Procedure
5. Results
6. Discussion
7. References
8. Appendices
9. Footnotes and Author Note
10. Tables
11. Figure Captions
12. Figures

Using Levels of Headings to Organize

An outline is one of the best ways to organize any report. The familiar indentation pattern of the outline makes it easy to see the overall structure of the report. A well-written article follows the organization of an outline. In the article, however, different levels of headings are used instead of indentation to indicate the outline organization. Table B.2 presents examples of five different levels of headings that can be used in a research report.

Sections of a Research Report

Title Page.   The title page includes the title of the article, the list of authors, the institutional affiliations of the authors, and a running head. The title should be concise while still describing the focus of the study. Phrases such as "a report on" or "a study of" add little information and should be avoided. A running head is placed at the top of the title page. It is an abbreviated title with no more than 50 characters and spaces. When the article is printed in a journal, the running head will appear at the top of each page. Note that page numbering begins with the title page (page number 1) and continues serially for all the pages except the artwork (i.e., figures).

Abstract.   The abstract summarizes the research paper in no more than 120 words. It must include all elements of the research report. Enough information should be given so that people who read the research study after reading the abstract will not be surprised by what they find in the article. Even though the abstract appears first, it is usually written last because it essentially summarizes the work. Although the abstract is one of the shortest sections of the study, it is often the most difficult to write because so much must be said in limited space. The abstract is published by abstracting services such as *Psychological Abstracts* or *PsycINFO*.

TABLE B.2   *Five Levels of Headings*

THIS IS A CENTERED UPPERCASE HEADING (LEVEL 5)

This is a Centered Upper- and Lowercase Heading (Level 1)

This is a Centered, Italicized Underlined, Uppercase and Lowercase Heading (Level 2)

This is an Italicized Uppercase and Lowercase Side Heading (Level 3)

    This is a paragraph heading (Level 4). The paragraph heading is in indented, lowercase, and italicized and should end with a period as shown.

Note: If only one level of heading is needed in a report, use level 1; if two levels are needed, use levels 1 and 3; if three levels are needed, use levels 1, 3, and 4; if four levels are needed, use levels 1, 2, 3, and 4; if 5 levels are needed, use all of the above with the level 5 heading subordinating the other four levels as shown above. Traditionally, the Method, Results, and Discussion headings are at Level 1.

Introduction.   The introduction states the research problem and discusses prior research. It begins with a broad or general statement of the research problem and proceeds to narrow the focus to the specific research being reported. A good introduction need not be long, but it must be well organized. You should focus only on those prior research studies directly relevant to the current research study and should not attempt to review all the research in a broad area. The introduction usually ends with a specific statement of the research hypotheses to be investigated. A good rule of thumb is that, if the hypotheses seem to follow naturally from everything that precedes them, the introduction is well organized and well structured. If, on the other hand, a reader finds some or all of the hypotheses to be surprising in light of what was stated previously, then the introduction is not well focused and fails to provide the rationale for the current study.

In the introduction, you reference other research by naming the researcher(s) and the date when the research was published. With this information, the reader can turn to the reference list and find where the work was published. There are two standard forms for referring to published work, as shown in the following examples:

> In previous research, most participants found the situation to be realistic (Johnson & Hall, 1999).

> Johnson and Hall (1999) reported that most participants found the procedure to be realistic.

For citing several studies, we can use the following format:

> Several investigators have found this situation to be realistic for their subjects (Johnson & Hall, 1997, 1999a, 1999b; Kelley, 1986; Michaels, Johnson, & Smith, 1996; Smith & Rodick, 1994).

These conventions tell the reader what was found, which researchers made the observation, and when. APA referencing conventions were used throughout this text. Each reference that appears in a research article must appear in the reference section, and all references that appear in the reference list must appear in the paper.

Method.   The purpose of the method section is to describe how the research was carried out. Participants and how they were selected, the apparatus, equipment and/or materials, and the procedures used are all described. These are typically discussed in separate subsections.

The participants subsection describes how participants were selected and their demographic characteristics (such as age, education, and sex), from where participants were obtained (a college course, a psychiatric hospital, or a shopping mall), and what inducements were used to obtain their cooperation (e.g., money or experimental credit for students). In addition, the researcher should describe how participants were assigned to groups. If it is a differential research study, the procedures used to classify participants for group assignment should be described. If participants drop out of the experiment or decline to participate, the number of such participants and the groups that they were in should be reported. There should be enough information to allow a researcher to compare the sample with samples from similar research projects.

The next subsection will depend on the study. It might be called the apparatus or equipment subsection; materials, instruments, or measures subsection; or some combination of these terms. In this subsection, all physical aspects of the research study are described. If the study involves equipment, the type of equipment used and the settings of the equipment should be reported. If psychological tests are used, the tests should be described with information on how to obtain them. If the tests are unique or custom-made for the study, they should either be included as an appendix or made available to any reader on request. The goal of the apparatus or equipment subsection is to provide readers with sufficient information to allow them to replicate the study.

The procedure subsection describes how the study was carried out. If additional manipulation of data was carried out, it should be described in the procedure section. For example, if particular scoring procedures were used, they should be described. If specific instructions were given to participants, they should be included. In other words, the procedure subsection should tell the reader everything that the participants and the researcher did during the course of the study.

Results. The results section tells the reader what was found. A statistical description of the results is usually needed, as well as appropriate statistical tests. Reporting statistical findings in a concise yet understandable way requires that the writer follow certain conventions. The usual convention is to present both descriptive and inferential statistics. When reporting inferential statistics, you should report what statistic was used, the number of degrees of freedom, the computed value of the statistic, and the probability of obtaining the computed value of the statistic by chance. Each of these is organized in a precise order (see Table B.3). All non-Greek, single-letter terms used in reporting statistical results (e.g., *F*, *t*, *p*) should be italicized in the manuscript. With this format, readers can easily interpret the significance of results even if they are not familiar with the statistical procedure used, because the probability value is interpreted in the same way for all the tests. Anytime *p* is less than .05 (a traditional value of alpha), we conclude that the findings are unusual enough that it is unlikely that they could have occurred as a result of chance.

Although it is important to express the statistical significance of comparisons made in the study, it is equally important to give the reader the information needed to

---

TABLE B.3 *Reporting Statistics in a Research Report*

Reporting *t*-tests
Boys were found to be significantly more aggressive than girls in the playground situation, $t(28) = 2.33$, $p < .05$.

Reporting ANOVAs
There was a significant difference in performance between the three distraction conditions, $F(2, 27) = 3.69$, $p < .05$.

Reporting chi squares
Psychology majors were significantly more likely to classify themselves as "humanistic" than were engineering majors, $\chi^2(1, N = 60) = 4.47$, $p < .05$.

interpret the results, such as the means or frequencies. Often the most effective way of doing this is to organize it in a table or figure. Tables and figures should be carefully labeled for the reader. Tables should give the reader enough information so that they can be interpreted without information from the text. Each table should be numbered using Arabic numerals starting with number 1. The first line of the table should read "Table" and the number. The next line of the table should be a brief title. An example of a typical table title might be "Mean Reaction Times for Distracted and Nondistracted Participants." The table title should be italicized. If the title is more than one line long, it should be double-spaced. The actual values in the table will be arranged in columns and rows, with the columns and rows clearly labeled. The columns should be labeled at the top of each column and the rows at the far left-hand side of the table. If additional information is necessary to interpret the table, it should be included at the bottom in the form of a footnote. An example of a typical table format is in Table B.4.

Figures should also be self-explanatory. Both the *x*- and the *y*-axis should be labeled, and each figure should have a title. Figures should be numbered sequentially starting with number 1 and should be numbered independently of tables. When submitting a paper for publication, each figure should be professionally drawn and submitted as a glossy print. The figures are numbered on the back of the print, and the figure numbers and titles appear on a separate sheet. Figure B.1 presents an example.

In preparing a manuscript for publication, tables and figures are assembled and placed at the end of the manuscript. Each table or figure should be referred to in the manuscript.

There is no one correct way of presenting the results of a study. It is often useful for the researcher to try to organize results in various ways by testing both tables and figures to determine which method is most effective.

Discussion. The author interprets and evaluates the results in the discussion section. It is helpful to begin the discussion section by briefly summarizing the results in nontechnical language. Then the reader should be told what you believe that the results

TABLE B.4   *Typical Table in a Research Report*

Table 1
Posttreatment Measures for the Three Treatment Approaches

	Type of Therapy		
Measures	*Behavioral*	*Cognitive*	*Analytic*
Number of activities[a]	4.6	3.8	2.1
Beck scores[b]	16.7	15.3	17.5
Insight ratings[c]	2.0	3.1	3.7

[a]The mean number of recreational activities in a one-week period.
[b]Mean Beck Depression Inventory scores; higher scores indicate greater depression.
[c]Rating based on an independent interview; ratings range from 1 (no insight) to 5 (maximum insight).

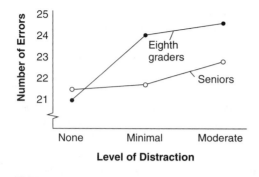

FIGURE B.1 *Example of a Line Graph*

mean. The interpretation of the results should follow logically from the actual data obtained in the study. It is useful in the discussion section to focus on the future directions that research might take. If there are weaknesses in the current study, the author should describe ways that they may be overcome in future studies. If the study suggests new hypotheses, the author should suggest ways in which the hypotheses might be adequately tested. The goal of any research project is to find answers to questions, but the outcome of most good research projects is to suggest new and important questions that still need to be answered. Suggesting directions for future research is a natural part of any well-designed, well-executed research project.

References. The reference list provides the reader with the information needed to seek out the original source of information. Each study discussed in the paper is listed in alphabetical order by the last name of the author(s). Works by the same author are arranged chronologically according to publication date. In addition to the author(s) and the title of the research study, a complete reference to the research report is included. The most common reference is to an article in a research journal. The format for such a reference is to list (1) the author(s), last name first, (2) the year the paper was published listed in parentheses, (3) the title of the article, (4) the journal title, (5) the volume of the journal, and (6) the pages of the article. The journal title and the volume number are italicized. Here are two examples of references to journal articles:

Collier, R. (1994). An historical overview of natural language processing systems that learn. *Artificial Intelligence Review, 8,* 17–54.

Benson, D. F., & Stuss, D. T. (1990). Frontal lobe influences on delusions: A clinical perspective. *Schizophrenia Bulletin, 16,* 403–411.

A similar format is used to reference a book. Again, we list (1) the author(s), (2) the year the book was published in parentheses, (3) the title of the book in italics, (4) the city in which the book was published, and (5) the publisher. Here are examples:

Kazdin, A. E. (1998). *Research design in clinical psychology* (3rd ed.). New York: Macmillan.

Loftus, E. F., & Ketcham, K. (1994). *The myth of repressed memory: False memories and allegations of sexual abuse.* New York: St. Martin's Press.

The reference section of this text provides many other examples of references.

Writing Style

Good writing is important whether you are writing a journal article or a letter home. It is one of the most difficult things to teach, and it can be learned only through practice. However, there are different kinds of writing. Writing a journal article requires technical writing. Precision, conciseness, and organization are important in technical writing. Flowery adjectives and a poetic style are best left to the creative writer.

The primary purpose of writing a research report is communication, and anything that obscures communication should be avoided. Pronouns should be used sparingly and should never be ambiguous. Abbreviations should also be used sparingly and should always be explained to the reader. Using active voice and simple sentence structure can help a writer to avoid numerous communication pitfalls. Traditionally, the research report is written in the past tense and primarily in the third person (e.g., "The experimenter assigned each participant..."), although there is a current trend to use more first person in research reports. A good way to improve a research report is to have someone who was not involved in the research review the report. Anything that is unclear to this reviewer will probably also be unclear to other readers. Writing manuals such as Strunk, White, and Angell's (1999) *The Elements of Style* or Zinsser's (1998) *On Writing Well* are valuable resources for any writer. The *Student Resource CD* supplement includes a brief list of the most common writing problems and how to correct them.

Although some researchers find the writing phase to be challenging and rewarding, many find writing a research report to be a demanding task. It is made somewhat easier if the research is carefully planned and well organized. For most researchers, however, telling people about something that they have discovered is exciting.

Appendix Summary

The final stage of any research project is the communication of the results. Appendix A lists some of the basic features of the APA writing style for research reports. A journal article is a carefully organized presentation of the research and its findings. The body of the article is divided into introduction, method, results, and discussion sections, which help to organize the entire paper. In addition, the article should have an abstract that summarizes the study and a complete list of references.

Appendix C

Conducting Library Research

Using the Library

Researchers always want to relate their ideas and research findings to those of other researchers. University libraries accumulate these findings to facilitate the research of the university faculty and students. This appendix briefly outlines strategies for library research. The *Student Resource CD* provides additional details and several examples of library searches.

Library Resources

Research ideas and findings are found in books, journals, technical reports, and a variety of other media. A small college library often will have 250,000 or more books and journals. A major university library may have 5,000,000 or more books and subscribe to more than 10,000 journals, each journal publishing 100 or more articles per year. In addition, almost any university library will have electronic and mail access to the collections of virtually all other libraries through interlibrary loan. When you enter the modern university library, you are in touch with nearly all the information that has ever been published! (You should be impressed by this thought and properly respectful of the library and of the professionals who operate it.) Fortunately, you will need only a small fraction of this information for your own research. This appendix describes how to find what you need.

The Reference Librarian

The reference librarian is one of the researcher's best friends—a professional who knows the smoothest routes through the maze of reference information. A good reference librarian can help you to track down almost anything. Whether you need to find a particular book or to learn how to use the library's computer search resources, the reference librarian is a valuable consultant. Most university libraries also have courses or documentation to help you to master the library's resources. Although we will be outlining in this appendix many of the basic sources and strategies for library research, we cannot stress enough the importance of utilizing the expertise available in your own library. A university library is much more than just a collection of books.

How Research Materials Are Organized

We make a distinction between primary and secondary sources in the research literature. Primary sources publish the details of research studies. Research journals and dissertations are the main primary sources. Secondary sources publish integrative reviews of broad areas of research. Some journals specialize in such reviews. Other secondary sources include books and chapters in edited books. This section describes each of these sources of information.

Primary Sources

Journal Articles.   Journals provide both primary and secondary sources of information, although the majority of journals are primary sources that report results of original research studies. Research reports include a brief literature review, a statement of the problem, the hypotheses to be tested, a detailed account of the procedures, the results and statistical analyses, and a discussion of how the researchers interpret the results. In the discussions of their findings, researchers relate their results to prevailing models or theories, thus helping to integrate new information and add to the base on which further research and theory development will rest.

Dissertations.   Dissertations are research studies conducted by advanced graduate students as part of the requirements for a Ph.D. Many of these studies are eventually published in journals, but they are also available in their original form to researchers interested in the same or similar questions. Universities will include the dissertations conducted at their own institutions as part of their library collection, but a copy of virtually any dissertation can be obtained in a few days through an organization called University Microfilms, which maintains copies of each dissertation from hundreds of universities.

Secondary Sources

Secondary sources provide reviews of entire areas of research by organizing and discussing many research reports. However, they are not intended to provide the detail that you will find in the original journal articles. Furthermore, the newest research discussed in a secondary source is at least a year old because of the normal publication lag. You will still have to search current journals to find the most recent research. These secondary sources provide important information; they summarize, organize, critique, and integrate research areas and identify further directions for research and theory development. They also list the critical studies in the area in their reference sections. They are an invaluable source in your literature review and are particularly useful when you need a broad, integrated view of your topic.

Review Articles.   Although most journals report the results of original research studies, other journals specialize in review articles. Several journals in psychology are devoted completely to reviews, for example, *Psychological Bulletin, Psychological Review, Behavioral Science,* and *Clinical Psychology Reviews.*

Books and Chapters in Books.   Reviews of research areas are also published in books and chapters in books. In fact, edited books are becoming a major secondary source of information in psychology. Fortunately, *Psychological Abstracts* and *PsycINFO* now include both books and book chapters in their databases.

Annual Reviews.   This series, published by Annual Review, Inc., provides an annual volume in each of many scientific disciplines, including psychology and neuroscience. The *Annual Review of Psychology,* for example, contains comprehensive review articles of psychological research in defined areas. You should check recent volumes to see if there is a review of your topic. If there is, you will find a wealth of information about research in your field and many references to other work.

Finding the Relevant Research

You can find relevant research by using abstracting services, keyword searches, and citation indexes.

Abstracting Services

Abstracting services provide abstracts of articles, often from hundreds of different journals, organized by title, author, and keywords. Most of these services are now computerized to provide quick and easy access to the material.

Psychological Abstracts. *Psychological Abstracts,* updated and published monthly by the American Psychological Association (APA), provides abstracts and source information (i.e., journals, books) for virtually everything relevant to the field of psychology. *Psychological Abstracts* is organized by keywords, which are summarized in a separate publication, the *Thesaurus of Psychological Index Terms* (described later). The APA also publishes a series of journals called *PsycSCAN,* which is quarterly compilations of references organized under several topics (e.g., clinical, applied, developmental).

In addition to the bound volumes of *Psychological Abstracts,* the APA also has several computer search programs (*PsycINFO, PsycLIT, PsycFILE,* and *PASAR*). *PsycINFO* is the most commonly used and probably the most convenient for students. It covers virtually the same material as the bound volumes of *Psychological Abstracts.* All the literature search programs published by the APA (bound volumes and computerized) are subsumed under the general heading *PsycINFO Services.*

ERIC (Educational Resource Information Center). *ERIC* indexes and abstracts research in education and related areas. If your topic is related to educational research, you should consult *ERIC* as well as *Psychological Abstracts.*

Subject or Keyword Services

A number of sources reference materials by title, author, and keywords, but do not include the abstract. Even without the abstract, these indexes can be a valuable source for identifying relevant materials. Several examples are given next.

Library Catalogs. The most familiar index to most students is the library card catalog. This is actually a misnomer, because most card catalogs have been replaced by computerized versions of the same index, which can be accessed through terminals in the library or elsewhere on campus or even from your own computer at home. The library catalog lists all the books in the library's collection. You can search by author, title, or subject. In computerized libraries, you may even be able to see if the book is available to be checked out.

Books in Print. *Books in Print* is a quarterly publication listing all books that are currently in print. Most libraries have hard-cover volumes of *Books in Print,* with books indexed by author, subject, and title. Many libraries now have this index available through computer searches.

Index Medicus. Just as *Psychological Abstracts* provides a citation index for literature of interest to psychologists, *Index Medicus* provides an index to biomedical literature. It does not, however, provide abstracts of the literature, but does include full references (author, title, date, source). When your topic has biomedical aspects, you should also consult *Index Medicus.* The computerized version of *Index Medicus* is called *Medline,* which now includes abstracts.

Readers' Guide to Periodical Literature. This general index covers a wide area of popular literature and provides citations, but not abstracts.

Literature Citation Indexes

The abstract and keyword services above are helpful in finding material by topic or author. There are times when you want to find literature through another means—the citations to previous work that publications make. Certain lines of research are so indebted to one or two early publications that you can find virtually every article on the topic by identifying the articles that cite these early publications. Several important indexes permit citation searches. The *Science Citation Index* and the *Social Science Citation Index* are two examples of this kind of reference. These indexes publish citation information in physical sciences (e.g., biology, chemistry, physics) and in the social sciences (e.g., sociology, psychology, economics), respectively. You can find references to work in psychology in both indexes.

Table C.1 lists the major indexes for psychological research.

Search Strategies

There is a variety of methods for locating relevant research on a topic. Each will be briefly outlined in this section.

Searching by Topic

Identifying Key Terms.   How do you search through the mass of information in the various indexes to find what you need for your project? Like all research, library re-

---

TABLE C.1   *Library Resources for Psychological Research*

---

1. Review Articles and Chapters
   Annual Review of Psychology
   Psychological Bulletin
   Psychological Review
   Behavioral Science
   Clinical Psychology Reviews

2. Abstract Services and Citation Indexes (both bound and computer formats)
   Psychological Abstracts (bound volumes)
   PsycINFO (psychological abstracts on computer)
   ERIC (Educational Resource Information Center)
   Books in Print (bound volumes and computer format)
   Index Medicus and *Medline* (computer index)
   Social Science Citation Index
   Science Citation Index

3. Other Important Information Sources
   Thesaurus of Psychological Index Terms
   Library catalog
   Readers' Guide to Periodical Literature

---

search needs a clear problem statement. Before you begin, be sure you know what you are looking for. You will need both a clear statement of the problem and a list of the key terms that identify relevant research papers. The right key terms will help you to find exactly what you need. The *Thesaurus of Psychological Index Terms,* published by the American Psychological Association, can be very helpful. It not only lists the index terms that are used in *Psychological Abstracts,* but also lists the cross-referenced terms that might also identify relevant literature on a topic. Find your topic in the *Thesaurus,* and it will list the index terms under which you will find appropriate references. Use these as your key terms to conduct your library search. Similar publications listing index terms are available for other abstract services.

Computer Searches.   Fortunately, many libraries now have extensive facilities for computer searches, saving a great deal of time and making your search more complete and systematic. *PsycINFO, Books in Print, ERIC, Medline,* and dozens of other indexes can be accessed through computer terminals in the library and elsewhere. Consult your reference librarian to learn how to use these systems. The procedures for doing computer searches vary from one system to another, but most systems operate under the same general principles. All systems have records (containing all the information about a publication) and fields within each record. Each field contains specific information about a publication (e.g., title, author, journal, keywords, and abstract). You can search a specific field or all fields to find information. For example, if you know that relevant research was published by "John Smith," you can search the author field for this name.

There are many strategies for computer searches, but most people start by searching for keywords. Most indexes will have a keyword field in which a small number of descriptive terms summarize the main content of the paper. Searching this field for certain topics is adequate for many searches. But computers are so fast that it is easy to search everything (title, keywords, abstract, etc.) to find potentially relevant papers.

Entering keywords to narrow a search is an art that requires considerable logic and some practice. In most systems, entering the term "child" will identify any article that has the terms child, childhood, children, and child's.[1] Similarly, entering the term "schizophren" will identify articles that have the terms schizophrenia or schizophrenic. A term like "schizo" will identify the same articles, but will also include articles that have terms like schizotypal, schizotaxia, or schizotype.

Some keywords identify several thousand potential articles, while others identify few articles. If the list is too large, you will have to reduce it to make it manageable. You might refine the list by limiting it to only those papers published in a given time period, perhaps the last 5 or 10 years. But you probably want to also narrow the list by further restricting the topic. To do this you must understand two Boolean operators, AND and OR. If you are interested in childhood fears, you could use the term "childhood fears" in your search. However, such a search would miss articles that did not use that specific phrase (perhaps using a phrase like "fears common in childhood" instead). Using the Boolean operator AND to search for "fear AND child" would likely

---

[1]All these have the root "child" in them.

give you a more complete search. Any article that had both the term "fear" and the term "child" in its record would be identified.[2] The operator AND will narrow a search by requiring that two conditions be met. In contrast, the operator OR will broaden a search by identifying articles that meet one of several specified conditions. For example, searching for "frontal OR parietal OR occipital OR temporal" would identify any article that mentions one of these lobes of the brain.

Once you have identified a set of records that seem relevant, you can enter commands to display the records (titles, authors, sources, and abstracts). By reading the titles and/or abstracts you can select those that appear to be most appropriate for your topic and eliminate the rest. At this point you will have a screen display of a fairly refined list of appropriate articles. Using the print command will give you a printout of your selected references and their abstracts.

Now the real work begins. Your list of references is just that—a list. What remains is locating each paper, book, and chapter, reading them, integrating the information, and writing your paper or research proposal. As you proceed, you will eliminate more of the cited work as not appropriate or useful and you will also find more references in the various reference sections of each paper that you read. Discussed next are two useful strategies for identifying other relevant papers.

Searching Backward

Every article, chapter, or book reviews relevant research and gives you the references for those studies. This is an invaluable source of relevant material. Of course, not every paper referenced in articles will be relevant to your topic, but some will be. Recently published articles and review articles are especially useful with this strategy. Inspecting the reference list from relevant articles will help to identify other investigators doing work on your topic. Searching the author field for the names of these investigators is often a useful supplementary strategy. These strategies are not a substitute for the topic search described above, but can be valuable in identifying additional relevant papers.[3]

Searching Forward

The searching forward strategy is possible because of the existence of citation indexes. If virtually all articles on a topic cite one or more classic articles, then you can identify these later articles by using an appropriate citation index. Again, this strategy is not a substitute for searching by topic, but can be a useful supplement.

Table C.2 summarizes the literature search process.

---

[2]Each computer index has its own rules for specifying searches with Boolean operators. Be sure to check the documentation or talk with a reference librarian for details of the system that you are using.

[3]A note of caution is warranted here. It is bad form to cite a paper that you have not read based on information that you obtained from another researcher's citation of that source. It is entirely possible that the other researcher misunderstood the paper and therefore cited the material incorrectly.

TABLE C.2 *The Literature Search Process*

---

1. Have a clear statement of the literature search problem.
2. From this problem statement, identify the key terms for your topic. Use the *Thesaurus of Psychological Index Terms* to help to determine your key terms.
3. Consult with your reference librarian and determine which citation indexes are most likely to include the information that you seek.
4. Search the citation indexes using your key terms. *PsycINFO* is probably the most useful for you. Look for secondary as well as primary sources. Read the titles and abstracts of the papers and chapters; narrow your list by deleting those that seem least relevant.
5. Print out the list of remaining references; find the original articles, books, and chapters; read them.
6. As you gain information from your reading, you will refine your ideas, gain new ideas, and will further refine your problem statement.
7. Consult other citation indexes (*ERIC, Social Science Citation Index, Readers' Guide*, etc.).
8. You can consult your reference librarian at any point in this search!

Appendix Summary

The importance of library research cannot be overestimated. Without library resources, each investigator would effectively be "reinventing the wheel" with every research study. Fortunately, the modern university library not only has the relevant past research, but also has the complex indexing necessary to find the material that you need. This appendix summarized the library resources available to students and described some of the strategies you might use to find background material for a study. Our discussion was very brief, however, and only touched the surface of this topic. The *Student Resource CD* gives more details and several examples. We also strongly encourage you to use the services of the reference librarian to learn more about the specific resources available at your institution. Reed and Baxter (1992) outline in more detail the resources and strategies covered in this appendix.

Appendix D

Random Numbers

To use the table of random numbers, select any starting point and any direction (up, down, left, or right). For example, if you want to assign participants randomly to each of five groups, you might start at the beginning of row 85 and move left to right. You number the groups 1 through 5. You assign the first participant to the group designated by the first digit between 1 and 5 that you encounter; the second participant is assigned to the group designated by the next suitable digit encountered, and so on. By this method, the first 10 participants are randomly assigned to the following groups: 1, 3, 1, 1, 2, 2, 4, 2, 1, 3.

It is also possible to randomize within blocks so that the same number of participants is in each condition. For example, if you want to assign the first five participants—one to each of the five groups—and you use the same starting point (beginning of row 85), you get the following assignment: 1, 3, 2, 4, 5. Your second block of five participants is assigned to the following groups: 3, 2, 5, 4, 1. Variations of these procedures can be used for random selection of participants from an accessible population and assignment of groups to conditions.

In addition to the table of random numbers in this appendix, we have included a random number generator program on the *Student Resource CD* to automate the task of randomly selecting participants or randomly assigning them to groups.

Row Number										
00000	10097	32533	76520	13586	34673	54876	80959	09117	39292	74945
00001	37542	04805	64894	74296	24805	24037	20636	10402	00822	91665
00002	08422	68953	19645	09303	23209	02560	15953	34764	35080	33606
00003	99019	02529	09376	70715	38311	31165	88676	74397	04436	27659
00004	12807	99970	80157	36147	64032	36653	98951	16877	12171	76833
00005	66065	74717	34072	76850	36697	36170	65813	39885	11199	29170
00006	31060	10805	45571	82406	35303	42614	86799	07439	23403	09732
00007	85269	77602	02051	65692	68665	74818	73053	85247	18623	88579

Row Number									
00008	63573	32135	05325	47048	90553	57548	28468	28709	83491	25624
00009	73796	45753	03529	64778	35808	34282	60935	20344	35273	88435
00010	98520	17767	14905	68607	22109	40558	60970	93433	50500	73998
00011	11805	05431	39808	27732	50725	68248	29405	24201	52775	67851
00012	83452	99634	06288	98033	13746	70078	18475	40610	68711	77817
00013	88685	40200	86507	58401	36766	67951	90364	76493	29609	11062
00014	99594	67348	87517	64969	91826	08928	93785	61368	23478	34113
00015	65481	17674	17468	50950	58047	76974	73039	57186	40218	16544
00016	80124	35635	17727	08015	45318	22374	21115	78253	14385	53763
00017	74350	99817	77402	77214	43236	00210	45521	64237	96286	02655
00018	69916	26803	66252	29148	36936	87203	76621	13990	94400	56418
00019	09893	20505	14225	68514	46427	56788	96297	78822	54382	14598
00020	91499	14523	68479	27686	46162	83554	94750	89923	37089	20048
00021	80336	94598	26940	36858	70297	34135	53140	33340	42050	82341
00022	44104	81949	85157	47954	32979	26575	57600	40881	22222	06413
00023	12550	73742	11100	02040	12860	74697	96644	89439	28707	25815
00024	63606	49329	16505	34484	40219	52563	43651	77082	07207	31790
00025	61196	90446	26457	47774	51924	33729	65394	59593	42582	60527
00026	15474	45266	95270	79953	59367	83848	82396	10118	33211	59466
00027	94557	28573	67897	54387	54622	44431	91190	42592	92927	45973
00028	42481	16213	97344	08721	16868	48767	03071	12059	25701	46670
00029	23523	78317	73208	89837	68935	91416	26252	29663	05522	82562
00030	04493	52494	75246	33824	45862	51025	61962	79335	65337	12472
00031	00549	97654	64051	88159	96119	63896	54692	82391	23287	29529
00032	35963	15307	26898	09354	33351	35462	77974	50024	90103	39333
00033	59808	08391	45427	26842	83609	49700	13021	24892	78565	20106
00034	46058	85236	01390	92286	77281	44077	93910	83647	70617	42941
00035	32179	00597	87379	25241	05567	07007	86743	17157	85394	11838
00036	69234	61406	20117	45204	15956	60000	18743	92423	97118	96338
00037	19565	41430	01758	75379	40419	21585	66674	36806	84962	85207
00038	45155	14938	19476	07246	43667	94543	59047	90033	20826	69541
00039	94864	31994	36168	10851	34888	81553	01540	35456	05014	51176
00040	98086	24826	45240	28404	44999	08896	39094	73407	35441	31880
00041	33185	16232	41941	50949	89435	48581	88695	41994	37548	73043
00042	80951	00406	96382	70774	20151	23387	25016	25298	94624	61171
00043	79752	49140	71961	28296	69861	02591	74852	20539	00387	59579
00044	18633	32537	98145	06571	31010	24674	05455	61427	77938	91936
00045	74029	43902	77557	32270	97790	17119	52527	58021	80814	51748
00046	54178	45611	80993	37143	05335	12969	56127	19255	36040	90324
00047	11664	49883	52079	84827	59381	71539	09973	33440	88461	23356
00048	48324	77928	31249	64710	02295	36870	32307	57546	15020	09994
00049	69074	94138	87637	91976	35584	04401	10518	21615	01848	76938
00050	09188	20097	32825	39527	04220	86304	83389	87374	64278	58044
00051	90045	85497	51981	50654	94938	81997	91870	76150	68476	64659

Row Number									
00052	73189	50207	47677	26269	62290	64464	27124	67018	41361	82760
00053	75768	76490	20971	87749	90429	12272	95375	05871	93823	43178
00054	54016	44056	66281	31003	00682	27398	20714	53295	07706	17813
00055	08358	69910	78542	42785	13661	58873	04618	97553	31223	08420
00056	28306	03264	81333	10591	40510	07893	32604	60475	94119	01840
00057	53840	86233	81594	13628	51215	90290	28466	68795	77762	20791
00058	91757	53741	61613	62669	50263	90212	55781	76514	83483	47055
00059	89415	92694	00397	58391	12607	17646	48949	72306	94541	37408
00060	77513	03820	86864	29901	68414	82774	51908	13980	72893	55507
00061	19502	37174	69979	20288	55210	29773	74287	75251	65344	67415
00062	21818	59313	93278	81757	05686	73156	07082	85046	31853	38452
00063	51474	66499	68107	23621	94049	91345	42836	09191	08007	45449
00064	99559	68331	62535	24170	69777	12830	74819	78142	43860	72834
00065	33713	48007	93584	72869	51926	64721	58303	29822	93174	93972
00066	85274	86893	11303	22970	28834	34137	73515	90400	71148	43643
00067	84133	89640	44035	52166	73852	70091	61222	60561	62327	18423
00068	56732	16234	17395	96131	10123	91622	85496	57560	81604	18880
00069	65138	56806	87648	85261	34313	65861	45875	21069	85644	47277
00070	38001	02176	81719	11711	71602	92937	74219	64049	65584	49698
00071	37402	96397	01304	77586	56271	10086	47324	62605	40030	37438
00072	97125	40348	87083	31417	21815	39250	75237	62047	15501	29578
00073	21826	41134	47143	34072	64638	85902	49139	06441	03856	54552
00074	73135	42742	95719	09035	85794	74296	08789	88156	64691	19202
00075	07638	77929	03061	18072	96207	44156	23821	99538	04713	66994
00076	60528	83441	07954	19814	59175	20695	05533	52139	61212	06455
00077	83596	35655	06958	92983	05128	09719	77433	53783	92301	50498
00078	10850	62746	99599	10507	13499	06319	53075	71839	06410	19362
00079	39820	98952	43622	63147	64421	80814	43800	09351	31024	73167
00080	59580	06478	75569	78800	88835	54486	23768	06156	04111	08408
00081	38508	07341	23793	48763	90822	97022	17719	04207	95954	49953
00082	30692	70668	94688	16127	56196	80091	82067	63400	05462	69200
00083	65443	95659	18238	27437	49632	24041	08337	65676	96299	90836
00084	27267	50264	13192	72294	07477	44606	17985	48911	97341	30358
00085	91307	06991	19072	24210	36699	53728	28825	35793	28976	66252
00086	68434	94688	84473	13622	62126	98408	12843	82590	09815	93146
00087	48908	15877	54745	24591	35700	04754	83824	52692	54130	55160
00088	06913	45197	42672	78601	11883	09528	63011	98901	14974	40344
00089	10455	16019	14210	33712	91342	37821	88325	80851	43667	70883
00090	12883	97343	65027	61184	04285	01392	17974	15077	90712	26769
00091	21778	30976	38807	36961	31649	42096	63281	02023	08816	47449
00092	19523	59515	65122	59659	86283	68258	69572	13798	16435	91529
00093	67245	52670	35583	16563	79246	86686	76463	34222	26655	90802
00094	60584	47377	07500	37992	45134	26529	26760	83637	41326	44344
00095	53853	41377	36066	94850	58838	73859	49364	73331	96240	43642

Row Number									
00096	24637	38736	74384	89342	52623	07992	12369	18601	03742	83873
00097	83080	12451	38992	22815	07759	51777	97377	27585	51972	37867
00098	16444	24334	36151	99073	27493	70939	85130	32552	54846	54759
00099	60790	18157	57178	65762	11161	78576	45819	52979	65130	04860
00100	03991	10461	93716	16894	66083	24653	84609	58232	88618	19161
00101	38555	95554	32886	59780	08355	60860	29735	47762	71299	23853
00102	17546	73704	92052	46215	55121	29281	59076	07936	27954	58909
00103	32643	52861	95819	06831	00911	98936	76355	93779	80863	00514
00104	69572	68777	39510	35905	14060	40619	29549	69616	33564	60780
00105	24122	66591	27699	06494	14845	46672	61958	77100	90899	75754
00106	61196	30231	92962	61773	41839	55382	17267	70943	78038	70267
00107	30532	21704	10274	12202	39685	23309	10061	68829	55986	66485
00108	03788	97599	75867	20717	74416	53166	35208	33374	87539	08823
00109	48228	63379	85783	47619	53152	67433	35663	52972	16818	60311
00110	60365	94653	35075	33949	42614	29297	01918	28316	98953	73231
00111	83799	42402	56623	34442	34994	41374	70071	14736	09958	18065
00112	32960	07405	36409	83232	99385	41600	11133	07586	15917	06253
00113	19322	53845	57620	52606	66497	68646	78138	66559	19640	99413
00114	11220	94747	07399	37408	48509	23929	27482	45476	85244	35159
00115	31751	57260	68980	05339	15470	48355	88651	22596	03152	19121
00116	88492	99382	14454	04504	20094	98977	74843	93413	22109	78508
00117	30934	47744	07481	83828	73788	06533	28597	20405	94205	20380
00118	22888	48893	27499	98748	60530	45128	74022	84617	82037	10268
00119	78212	16993	35902	91386	44372	15486	65741	14014	87481	37220
00120	41849	84547	46850	52326	34677	58300	74910	64345	19325	81549
00121	46352	33049	69248	93460	45305	07521	61318	31855	14413	70951
00122	11087	96294	14013	31792	59747	67277	76503	34513	39663	77544
00123	52701	08337	56303	87315	16520	69676	11654	99893	02181	68161
00124	57275	36898	81304	48585	68652	27376	92852	55866	88448	03584
00125	20857	73156	70284	24326	79375	95220	01159	63267	10622	48391
00126	15633	84924	90415	93614	33521	26665	55823	47641	86225	31704
00127	92694	48297	39904	02115	59589	49067	66821	41575	49767	04037
00128	77613	19019	88152	00080	20554	91409	96277	48257	50816	97616
00129	38688	32486	45134	63545	59404	72059	43947	51680	43852	59693
00130	25163	01889	70014	15021	41290	67312	71857	15957	68971	11403
00131	65251	07629	37239	33295	05870	01119	92784	26340	18477	65622
00132	36815	43625	18637	37509	82444	99005	04921	73701	14707	93997
00133	64397	11692	05327	82162	20247	81759	45197	25332	83745	22567
00134	04515	25624	95096	67946	48460	85558	15191	18782	16930	33361
00135	83761	60873	43253	84145	60833	25983	01291	41349	20368	07126
00136	14387	06345	80854	09279	43529	06318	38384	74761	41196	37480
00137	51321	92246	80088	77074	88722	56736	66164	49431	66919	31678
00138	72472	00008	80890	18002	94813	31900	54155	83436	35352	54131
00139	05466	55306	93128	18464	74457	90561	72848	11834	79982	68416

Row Number									
00140	39528	72484	82474	25593	48545	35247	18619	13674	18611	19241
00141	81616	18711	53342	44276	75122	11724	74627	73707	58319	15997
00142	07586	16120	82641	22820	92904	13141	32392	19763	61199	67940
00143	90767	04235	13574	17200	69902	63742	78464	22501	18627	90872
00144	40188	28193	29593	88627	94972	11598	62095	36787	00441	58997
00145	34414	82157	86887	55087	19152	00023	12302	80783	32624	68691
00146	63439	75363	44989	16822	36024	00867	76378	41605	65961	73488
00147	67049	09070	93399	45547	94458	74284	05041	49807	20288	34060
00148	79495	04146	52162	90286	54158	34243	46978	35482	59362	95938
00149	91704	30552	04737	21031	75051	93029	47665	64382	99782	93478
00150	94015	46874	32444	48277	59820	96163	64654	25843	41145	42820
00151	74108	88222	88570	74015	25704	91035	01755	14750	48968	38603
00152	62880	87873	95160	59221	22304	90314	72877	17334	39283	04149
00153	11748	12102	80580	41867	17710	59621	06554	07850	73950	79552
00154	17944	05600	60478	03343	25852	58905	57216	39618	49856	99326
00155	66067	42792	95043	52680	46780	56487	09971	59481	37006	22186
00156	54244	91030	45547	70818	59849	96169	61459	21647	87417	17198
00157	30945	57589	31732	57260	47670	07654	46376	25366	94746	49580
00158	69170	37403	86995	90307	94304	71803	26825	05511	12459	91314
00159	08345	88975	35841	85771	08105	59987	87112	21476	14713	71181
00160	27767	43584	85301	88977	29490	69714	73035	41207	74699	09310
00161	13025	14338	54066	15243	47724	66733	47431	43905	31048	56699
00162	80217	36292	98525	24335	24432	24896	43277	58874	11466	16082
00163	10875	62004	90391	61105	57411	06368	53856	30743	08670	84741
00164	54127	57326	26629	19087	24472	88779	30540	27886	61732	75454
00165	60311	42824	37301	42678	45990	43242	17374	52003	70707	70214
00166	49739	71484	92003	98086	76668	73209	59202	11973	02902	33250
00167	78626	51594	16453	94614	39014	97066	83012	09832	25571	77628
00168	66692	13986	99837	00582	81232	44987	09504	96412	90193	79568
00169	44071	28091	07362	97703	76447	42537	98524	97831	65704	09514
00170	41468	85149	49554	17994	14924	39650	95294	00556	70481	06905
00171	94559	37559	49678	53119	70312	05682	66986	34099	74474	20740
00172	41615	70360	64114	58660	90850	64618	80620	51790	11436	38072
00173	50273	93113	41794	86861	24781	89683	55411	85667	77535	99892
00174	41396	80504	90670	08289	40902	05069	95083	06783	28102	57816
00175	25807	24260	71529	78920	72682	07385	90726	57166	98884	08583
00176	06170	97965	88302	98041	21443	41808	68984	83620	89747	98882
00177	60808	54444	74412	81105	01176	28838	36421	16489	18059	51061
00178	80940	44893	10408	36222	80582	71944	92638	40333	67054	16067
00179	19516	90120	46759	71643	13177	55292	21036	82808	77501	97427
00180	49386	54480	23604	23554	21785	41101	91178	10174	29420	90438
00181	06312	88940	15995	69321	47458	64809	98189	81851	29651	84215
00182	60942	00307	11897	92674	40405	68032	96717	54244	10701	41393
00183	92329	98932	78284	46347	71209	92061	39448	93136	25722	08564

Row Number									
00184	77936	63574	31384	51924	85561	29671	58137	17820	22751	36518
00185	38101	77756	11657	13897	95889	57067	47648	13885	70669	93406
00186	39641	69457	91339	22502	92613	89719	11947	56203	19324	20504
00187	84054	40455	99396	63680	67667	60631	69181	96845	38525	11600
00188	47468	03577	57649	63266	24700	71594	14004	23153	69249	05747
00189	43321	31370	28977	23896	76479	68562	62342	07589	08899	05985
00190	64281	61826	18555	64937	13173	33365	78851	16499	87064	13075
00191	66847	70495	32350	02985	86716	38746	26313	77463	55387	72681
00192	72461	33230	21529	53424	92581	02262	78438	66276	18396	73538
00193	21032	91050	13058	16218	12470	56500	15292	76139	59526	52113
00194	95362	67011	06651	16136	01016	00857	55018	56374	35824	71708
00195	49712	97380	10404	55452	34030	60726	75211	10271	36633	68424
00196	58275	61764	97586	54716	50259	46345	87195	46092	26787	60939
00197	89514	11788	68224	23417	73959	76145	30342	40277	11049	72049
00198	15472	50669	48139	36732	46874	37088	63465	09819	58869	35220
00199	12120	86124	51247	44302	60883	52109	21437	36786	49226	77837

Appendix E

Answers to Quick-Check Review Questions

Listed in this appendix are brief answers to the Quick-Check Review questions.

Chapter 1

1.1 The essence of science is its way of thinking, which combines rationalism and empiricism.

1.2 Because science represents a way of thinking, it is possible to think scientifically in any situation.

1.3 A prepared mind refers to the ability to recognize and react to unexpected findings because the person has a sufficient background in and understanding of the phenomena under study.

1.4 Scientists are pervasive skeptics who challenge accepted wisdom, are intellectually excited by searching for answers to questions, and are willing to tolerate uncertainty.

1.5 Scientists and artists share curiosity, creativity, skepticism, tolerance for ambiguity, commitment to hard work, and systematic thinking.

2.1 The common methods of acquiring knowledge are tenacity, intuition, authority, rationalism, empiricism, and science.

2.2 Science combines empiricism and rationalism.

2.3 Naïve empiricism insists on experiencing evidence directly through the senses. In contrast, sophisticated empiricism allows indirect evidence of phenomena, such as the effects of gravity on falling objects.

2.4 The limitation of rationalism is that the premises must be correct as determined by other information for the conclusions to be correct. The limitation of empiricism is that, by itself, it does little more than collect facts; it needs rational processes to organize these facts.

2.5 Science provides for both the organization of facts, the collection of new facts, and the determination of what new facts would be more interesting to find.

3.1 The early practical skills illustrated the advantage of abstract information in solving everyday problems, thus justifying the kind of scientific study that seeks to systematically develop such information.

3.2 Thales is considered the father of science. He rejected mysticism and studied a variety of natural phenomena using a combination of empirical observation and rational processes.

3.3 During the Middle Ages, science was used only to illustrate and support theological ideas.

3.4 Modern technology is the outgrowth of scientific discoveries, whereas modern science is a way of thinking and studying phenomena. Although technology and science are often associated with one another, they are not the same thing.

3.5 The orderliness belief is the implicit belief that the universe operates in an orderly, lawful manner. Without this belief, it would make no sense to engage in scientific investigation because there would be no general principles to discover.

4.1 Some of the more influential schools of psychology were structuralism, functionalism, psychoanalysis, Gestalt psychology, behaviorism, humanistic psychology, and cognitive psychology.

4.2 Modern psychology tends to be integrative in that its theories and ideas cut across several perspectives.

4.3 Psychology needs to be scientific and objective because the subjective impressions of people about psychological events tend to be inaccurate.

4.4 Although psychology is considered a social science, its roots clearly are in the natural sciences, such as biology and physics.

Chapter 2

1.1 Data are the observations of behavior on which the science of psychology is built.

1.2 Facts can be directly observed. In contrast, constructs are inferences by the investigator to explain observations by assuming some unseen mechanism. Some examples of facts are scores on a test, speed of action by participants, and the choice made by participants. Some examples of constructs are intelligence, attitudes, and feelings.

1.3 Reification of a construct means that the person has started to believe that the construct is a fact.

1.4 Constructs are based on facts and are used to predict new facts.

1.5 The assumptions on which science is built are (1) a true, physical universe exists; (2) while there may be randomness and thus unpredictability in the universe, it is primarily an orderly system; (3) the principles of this orderly universe can be discovered, particularly through scientific research; (4) knowledge of the universe is always incomplete. New knowledge can, and should, alter current ideas and theories. Therefore, all knowledge and theories are tentative.

1.6 Going from empirical observations to constructs is inductive reasoning; going from constructs to make predictions about new observations is deductive reasoning.

2.1 A theory is a formalized set of concepts that summarizes and organizes observations and inferences, provides tentative explanations for phenomena, and provides the bases for making predictions.

2.2 Inductive theories depend heavily on empirical observations and tend to stray little from empirical observations. In contrast, deductive theories go well beyond the existing database and emphasize testing new predictions from theories.

2.3 A model is a miniature representation of reality. It describes some, but not all, of the characteristics of reality. Models are useful in research because constructing and examining models can provide insights into natural phenomena.

2.4 Observations are the facts of research, whereas inferences are inductive leaps beyond the observations.

2.5 Many technically incorrect theories nevertheless make accurate predictions in many situations and therefore are useful in these situations.

2.6 For a theory to be scientific, there must be some predictions that, if found, would lead to a rejection of the theory.

3.1 The two dimensions in our model of research are levels of constraint and phases of research.

3.2 The phases of research are (1) idea generating, (2) problem definition, (3) procedures design, (4) observation, (5) data analysis, (6) interpretation, and (7) communication.

3.3 Levels of constraint refer to a continuum of demands on the adequacy of information, which is defined by the level of control available during the observation phase.

3.4 The groups in differential research are naturally occurring, whereas the groups in experimental research are formed through random assignment.

Chapter 3

1.1 The two main sources of research questions are your own interests and the research of other investigators.

1.2 Applied research is designed to solve practical problems. In contrast, basic research is interested in finding new knowledge without any specific application in mind.

1.3 A variable is any set of events that may have different values.

1.4 Basic research often provides the understanding of natural phenomena that can later be used to address a variety of practical problems.

2.1 Behavioral variables are observable responses of the organism. Stimulus variables are those aspects of the environment that could potentially affect behavior. Organismic variables are characteristics of the participants. Independent variables are manipulated by the research to see what effect they might have on other variables (the dependent variables). Finally, extraneous variables are unplanned and uncontrolled factors that can arise in an experiment and affect the outcome.

2.2 The researcher manipulates independent variables to see what effect they might have on dependent variables. Manipulating independent variables allows researchers to identify the causal impact of independent variables.

2.3 Manipulated independent variables are actively controlled by the researcher. In contrast, nonmanipulated independent variables are defined by preexisting characteristics of participants.

2.4 Holding a variable constant involves preventing the variable from varying. For example, the researcher can hold the variable of age constant by testing only those participants who are at a particular age.

3.1 Extraneous variables are unplanned and uncontrolled factors that can arise in an experiment and affect the outcome.

3.2 Extraneous variables must be controlled in research because, without such control, we cannot have confidence in the research results.

3.3 Validity refers to how well a study, a procedure, or a measure does what it is supposed to do.

3.4 Controls reduce the effects of extraneous variables and thus increase our confidence in the validity of the research findings.

4.1 The moral dilemma in research is that society demands new information, but obtaining that information may violate the rights of individuals. This dilemma is addressed by allowing individuals to decide for themselves whether they will participate in a given study.

4.2 Informed consent involves a person agreeing to participate in a study after being fully informed about the study and its risks. It is obtained in writing. It is important because it addresses the moral issues around possible violation of a person's rights when the decision to participate is not in the hands of the research participants.

4.3 Institutional Review Boards are groups set up at universities, hospitals, and research centers to screen each research proposal for risks and approve only those studies that have sufficient ethical safeguards.

4.4 The major ethical concerns in animal research are that animals cannot give informed consent and the nature of the research carried out on animals is generally more invasive than that carried out on humans. The major focus is on providing animals with humane care and minimizing discomfort and pain.

4.5 Diversity issues in research refer to the need to include a broad representation of people in research projects so that the results can be generalized to as many people as possible.

Chapter 4

1.1 Measuring a variable is assigning numbers that represent the levels of the variable.

1.2 Without accurate measurement, we cannot be confident of the accuracy of the data and therefore cannot be confident of the accuracy of the conclusions based on the data.

1.3 The important characteristics of the abstract number system are identity, magnitude, equal intervals, and a true zero.

1.4 The more closely a measure matches the properties of the abstract number system, the more mathematical operations that are permissible. Among other things, this allows the use of more powerful statistical procedures.

2.1 Nominal scales are naming scales. Ordinal scales order phenomena based on their magnitude. Interval scales convey information about both order and the distance between values. Finally, ratio scales provide the best match to the number system.

2.2 Nominal scales produce nominal or categorical data. Ordinal scales produce ordered data. Interval and ratio scales produce score data.

2.3 Nominal scales have the property of identity; ordinal scales have the properties of identity and magnitude; interval scales have the properties of identity, magnitude, and equal intervals; ratio scales have the properties of identity, magnitude, equal intervals, and a true zero.

2.4 A true zero means that zero on the scale represents none of the property being measured. For example, someone who is zero years old has yet to be born. When a scale has a true zero, taking the ratio of two measures on the scale provides a meaningful number. For example, someone who made \$100 made twice as much as someone who made \$50.

3.1 The best way to minimize measurement error is to develop well-thought-out operational definitions and follow them exactly.

3.2 Operational definitions transform theoretical variables into concrete events by stating precisely how these variables are to be measured.

3.3 Social desirability is the tendency to respond in what participants believe to be the most socially acceptable manner. Such response tendencies distort measures and therefore threaten the validity of research.

3.4 Convergent validity involves multiple lines of research converging on the same conclusions. Such convergence gives researchers confidence that the phenomenon under study is well understood.

4.1 Reliability refers to the constancy of a measure. The types of reliability are inter-rater reliability, test–retest reliability, and internal consistency reliability.

4.2 A measure can be reliable without being valid, but cannot be valid without being reliable.

4.3 If the effective range of a scale is inadequate for the population under study, the data will be distorted.

4.4 Floor effects occur when there is too little lower range and the scores bunch up at the bottom of the scale. In contrast, ceiling effects occur when scores bunch up near the top of the scale.

4.5 Having too limited a range attenuates the variability of scores and distorts those scores that cannot be adequately represented by the range available.

4.6 Reliability refers to the consistency of a measure, whereas validity refers to its accuracy.

Chapter 5

1.1 The differences among people are called individual differences.

1.2 Descriptive statistics are used to describe and simplify data, whereas inferential statistics help the researcher to draw conclusions from the data.

2.1 Frequency distributions show the number of participants with each possible score. Frequency distributions can be used with any kind of data.

2.2 Cross-tabulation involves simultaneously categorizing participants on more than one variable.

2.3 Frequency distributions give the frequency for each possible score, whereas grouped frequency distributions provide the frequency for ranges of scores in which the ranges are of equal size.

2.4 Continuous distributions require grouped frequency distributions because there are theoretically an infinite number of scores in a continuous distribution.

2.5 The most common distribution shapes are symmetric, negatively skewed, and positively skewed. The most common symmetric distribution is the normal distribution.

3.1 The three measures of central tendency are the mean, median, and mode.

3.2 The chief measures of variability are the range, variance, and standard deviation.

3.3 Correlations quantify the strength and direction of a relationship between variables. Regression uses the relationship between variables to predict one variable from knowing the value of the other variable.

3.4 A standard score indicates how far a score is above or below the mean measured in standard deviation units. It is computed by subtracting the mean from the score and dividing the difference by the standard deviation.

3.5 The variance takes into account all the scores in a distribution, whereas the range only uses the highest and lowest scores.

3.6 The mean takes into account all the scores in a distribution and is therefore not affected much by the change in one or two scores. In contrast, the mode can be very unstable, with a shifting of one or two scores moving the mode considerably.

3.7 A correlation, unlike other descriptive statistics, describes the relationship among two or more variables.

4.1 A population is the larger group of all the people of interest, whereas the sample is a subset that is drawn from the population.

4.2 Sampling error is the variation among different samples drawn from the same population.

4.3 A population parameter is a characteristic of the population, such as the mean, that is computed by testing everyone in the population. A sample statistic is the same characteristic computed from a sample drawn from that population.

4.4 Alpha level refers to the somewhat arbitrary cutoff point that is used for making the decision to reject the null hypothesis. Type I error is rejecting the null hypothesis when it is true. Type II error is failing to reject the null hypothesis when it is false.

4.5 Inferential statistics are used to draw conclusions about populations based on samples, whereas descriptive statistics merely describe the data.

5.1 The tests that are traditionally used for testing for mean differences are the *t*-test and ANOVA. The *t*-test should be used when there are two groups, and the ANOVA can be used with two or more groups. Note that the appropriate *t*-test or ANOVA depends on whether the groups are independent or correlated.

5.2 A power analysis involves determining how large the sample size should be to detect a group difference if this difference exists. It is important because it assures that the researcher has sufficient power before the study is started.

5.3 Statistical significance refers to whether the observed group difference is large enough to conclude that a group difference exists in the population. Practical significance refers to whether the size of the group difference is large enough to be personally meaningful to people.

5.4 Meta-analysis statistically averages the results from independent studies of the same phenomenon.

Chapter 6

1.1 Both Darwin and Goodall studied natural phenomena in natural environments without doing anything to influence these phenomena.

1.2 All these investigators worked extensively with individuals, observing their behavior, but also asking questions or testing them under various conditions.

1.3 Naturalistic research involves observing phenomena in natural settings. In contrast, case-study research involves modifying the settings somewhat to see how the modifications affect the performance of participants.

2.1 Naturalistic research should be used whenever we are interested in the natural flow of behavior in natural settings. Case studies are used when we are interested in single individuals. Both can be used to test the generalizability of findings from the laboratory.

2.2 A contingency is a probabilistic relationship between variables ("If X occurs, Y is likely to occur."). It does not necessarily imply a causal connection. Such contingencies can be used to generate causal hypotheses for higher-constraint research.

2.3 Laboratory research must simplify and constrain real-life settings to have the control needed. Such changes may threaten generalizability. In contrast, naturalistic research has less problem with generalizability because it is conducted in natural settings.

2.4 Naturalistic research can negate a general proposition by finding a single counter-example. It cannot establish one because it does not adequately sample from the population and thus does not represent the population well.

3.1 Problem statements in low-constraint research are often general because there may be no basis for generating more specific questions.

3.2 The two types of observers in low-constraint research are unobtrusive observers and participant observers.

3.3 Unobtrusive measures are measures of behavior that are not obvious to the person being observed and, consequently, are less likely to influence the person's behavior.

3.4 Archival records are measures that provide information about phenomena that have already occurred. They are usually collected routinely, such as course grades or census data.

3.5 The goal in sampling is to obtain a representative sample. However, in low-constraint research, the samples are often not representative.

3.6 Sampling situations broadly permits the researcher to see if behavior differs across settings.

3.7 Measurement reactivity refers to the phenomenon of participants behaving differently than they might normally because they know that they are being observed.

4.1 Low-constraint research often studies available samples, which are often not representative of the population.

4.2 Low-constraint research is flexible and allows the researcher to follow interesting leads. Unfortunately, this also means that it is difficult to describe and is therefore difficult for others to replicate.

4.3 The ex post facto fallacy is drawing unwarranted causal conclusions from the observation of a contingent relationship.

4.4 Experimenter reactivity is any action by researchers that tends to influence the response of participants. Experimenter bias is any effect that the researcher's expectations might have on the observations or recording of these observations.

Chapter 7

1.1 Correlational research assesses the strength of a relationship between two or more variables.

1.2 A correlation quantifies the strength and direction of the relationship between the two measures. Such information can be used for predicting one variable from the other variable.

1.3 Correlational research cannot determine causality.

1.4 Correlational research cannot prove a theory, but it can negate one.

2.1 Differential research compares two or more groups that are differentiated on the basis of some preexisting variable.

2.2 Differential research uses a nonmanipulated independent variable.

2.3 Artifacts are apparent effects of independent variables that are actually the effects of other variables not properly controlled. They confound the research and therefore prevent the researcher from drawing strong conclusions.

2.4 Differential research is structurally similar to experimental research in that two or more groups are being compared on the dependent measure. It is conceptually similar to correlational research in that all variables are measured and none are manipulated.

3.1 Both correlational and differential research quantify the degree of relationship between two or more variables and are unable to identify causal relationships.

3.2 Differential research is considered higher constraint than correlational research because additional control procedures are available in differential research, which can increase the confidence of the conclusions drawn from studies.

3.3 Differential research designs are used in situations in which the manipulation of an independent variable is impractical, impossible, or unethical.

4.1 Experimenter expectancy is the tendency of investigators to see what they expect to see, and experimenter reactivity is the tendency of investigators to influence the behavior of participants.

4.2 Moderator variables modify the relationship between other variables. Sex is a common moderator variable.

4.3 The two most commonly used correlations are the Pearson product–moment correlation and the Spearman rank–order correlation. If both variables are measured on at least an interval scale, then a Pearson product–moment correlation coefficient should be computed. If one variable is measured on an ordinal scale and the other variable is at least ordinal, then the appropriate coefficient is a Spearman rank–order correlation.

4.4 The coefficient of determination is the square of the correlation, and it indicates the proportion of variability in one measure that can be predicted by knowing the other measure.

5.1 Differential research is used whenever we want to know whether groups that are formed based on a preexisting variable are different from one another.

5.2 Unless groups in differential research differ on only a single variable, it is impossible to determine which variable may have accounted for any observed group differences. In other words, we have confounding.

5.3 A nonmanipulated independent variable is a variable that existed prior to the study and is used to assign participants to groups in differential research.

5.4 Careful selection of control groups in differential research can minimize confounding by forming groups that differ on only a single variable.

6.1 Neither correlational nor differential research is capable of determining that a causal relationship between variables exists.

6.2 Causal relationships cannot be determined, because both of these approaches measure but do not manipulate variables.

6.3 Two variables are said to be confounded when they vary together. Because they vary together, any observed relationships with other variables might be caused by either of the variables or both of them, thus limiting conclusions.

Chapter 8

1.1 Initial ideas are converted into problem statements, which state the hypothesized nature of the relationship among variables. Problem statements are converted into research hypotheses by operationally defining each variable.

1.2 The research hypothesis is a combination of the statement of the problem and the operational definitions of the variables.

1.3 The research hypothesis is a specific, testable hypothesis that can be evaluated with data.

1.4 The research hypothesis includes the statistical hypothesis, the confounding-variable hypothesis, and the causal hypothesis.

1.5 Until all confounding-variable hypotheses are ruled out, we cannot accept the causal hypothesis.

1.6 Problem statements can be worded in different ways that imply different research designs. Furthermore, the variables can be operationally defined in different ways, each creating a different research hypothesis.

2.1 Validity has several meanings, the most basic of which refers to methodological soundness or appropriateness. That is, a valid test measures what it is supposed to measure; a valid research design tests what it is supposed to test.

2.2 Statistical validity addresses the question of whether statistical conclusions are reasonable. Construct validity refers to how well the study's results support the theory behind the research. External validity refers to the degree to which generalization of the results of a study to other participants, conditions, times, and places is possible. Internal validity concerns this question: Was the independent variable responsible for the observed changes in the dependent variable?

2.3 Internal validity is concerned about the accuracy of the conclusions about the relationship between independent and dependent variables.

3.1 Maturation refers to the normal and expected changes that occur over time and that may affect the outcome in studies that take a while to complete for each participant. History refers to the external events that can occur during the evaluation of participants and that may affect performance.

3.2 Based on regression to the mean, the winner of this year's World Series is unlikely to win the World Series next year.

3.3 In this case, the confounding variable of attrition is operating.

3.4 Sequence effects are found only in within-subjects designs.

4.1 Subject effects are any changes in the behavior of participants that are due to being in the study, rather than to the variables under study.

4.2 Demand characteristics are unintentional cues given to participants on how they are expected to behave. Participants often react to these cues and therefore behave differently than they ordinarily would.

4.3 Experimenter expectancies might cause researchers to bias results in several ways, thus creating experimenter effects that confound the study.

Chapter 9

1.1 Careful preparation of the setting can reduce the presence of potential confounding variables, thus increasing internal validity. External validity can be enhanced by making the laboratory situation as natural and lifelike as possible.

1.2 All measures used in research should be both reliable and valid.

1.3 Exact replication is repeating the experiment as nearly as possible in the way it was carried out originally, whereas systematic replication is repeating the study with some systematic theoretical or procedural modification of the original work.

2.1 Blind procedures keep either the participants, researchers, or both unaware of to what condition each participant is assigned. Automation standardizes instructions and/or data collection, thus decreasing opportunities for experimenter effects. Objective measures take the subjective component out of the measuring process. Multiple observers allow an assessment of the reliability of the measures. Finally, deception prevents participants from seeing the purpose of the study and thus reduces potential subject effects.

2.2 In a single-blind procedure, the researcher gathering the data is blind to group assignment, whereas in the double-blind procedure, both the researcher and the participants are unaware of group assignment.

2.3 Deception reduces subject effects by preventing participants from recognizing what is being studied.

3.1 The general population is the large group of all persons, whereas the target population is the subset in which the researcher is ultimately interested. The accessible population is the population available to the researcher, and the sample is a group drawn from the accessible population.

3.2 Unless samples are drawn carefully, they are unlikely to be representative of the population, thus restricting generalizability.

3.3 Random sampling involves drawing the sample so that every member of the population has an equal chance of being selected and the selections do not affect each other. Stratified random sampling involves drawing separate random samples from each of several subpopulations. Ad hoc samples are drawn from accessible populations.

3.4 Without unbiased assignment of participants to conditions, it is possible that the groups will differ on variables other than the independent variable that defines the groups, thus introducing confounding.

3.5 Matched random assignment controls for individual differences by having participants in each group matched with participants in the other groups.

4.1 Unbiased assignment to groups makes it unlikely that the groups will differ on any variable other than the independent variable.

4.2 The five characteristics of an experimental design are (1) a clearly stated research hypothesis concerning predicted causal effects of one variable on another, (2) at least two levels of the independent variable, (3) unbiased assignment of participants to conditions, (4) specific and systematic procedures for empirically testing the hypothesized causal relationships, and (5) specific controls to reduce threats to internal validity.

Chapter 10

1.1 Systematic between-groups variance reflects consistent group differences due to the independent variable, uncontrolled confounding variables, or both.

1.2 Experimental variance is due to the effect of the independent variable, whereas extraneous variance is due to the effects of uncontrolled confounding variables.

1.3 Error variance is the nonsystematic within-groups variability that is due to random factors that affect some participants more than others.

1.4 The *F*-test is an inferential statistical procedure that tests for mean differences among groups.

1.5 Extraneous variance is controlled by making sure that experimental and control groups are as similar as possible at the start of the experiment and treating all participants exactly the same way, except for the independent variable manipulation. Ways to assure that the groups are similar at the start of the study include (1) randomly assigning participants to groups, (2) selecting participants who are as homogeneous as possible, (3) building potential confounding variables into the experiment as an additional independent variable, and (4) matching participants or using a within-subjects design.

1.6 Error variance can be minimized through careful measurement and/or using a correlated-groups design to control individual differences.

2.1 Four nonexperimental approaches are (1) ex post facto studies, (2) single-group, posttest-only studies, (3) single-group, pretest-posttest studies, and (4) pretest–posttest, natural control-group studies. Ex post facto studies attempt to relate observed phenomena to earlier experiences that were not directly observed or manipulated. In the single-group, posttest-only study, the independent variable is manipulated with a single group and the group is then measured. In the single-group, pretest–posttest studies, a single group of participants is measured both before and after a manipulation. Finally, in the pretest–posttest, natural control-group design, naturally occurring groups are used, only one of which receives the treatment. None of these designs adequately controls confounding variables, although the natural control-group design comes close if the groups are reasonably similar at the start of the study.

2.2 The weakest design of those covered in this section is the ex post facto design, which controls virtually none of the potential confounding variables.

2.3 Maturation is not considered a confounding variable in studies of development. Developmental studies typically employ time-series designs.

3.1 The most basic experimental design is the randomized, posttest-only, control-group design.

3.2 In the randomized, pretest–posttest, control-group design, participants are randomly assigned to experimental and control groups, all participants are pretested on the dependent variable, the experimental group is administered the treatment, and both groups are then posttested on the dependent variable. In the multilevel, completely randomized, between-subjects design, participants are randomly assigned to three or more conditions. Pretests may or may not be included. Finally, the Solomon four-group design combines the randomized, pretest–posttest, control-group design and posttest-only, control-group designs.

3.3 Control groups control for history, maturation, and regression to the mean. To make control groups effective, participants must be randomly assigned to conditions to assure that the groups are comparable at the beginning of the study.

3.4 The Solomon four-group design controls for the possible interaction of the pretest and treatment.

3.5 If groups are not equivalent at the beginning of the study, any observed differences could be due to the manipulation, the initial differences, or both.

4.1 Chi-square tests are used with nominal data, and Mann–Whitney *U*-tests are used with ordinal data.

4.2 The *t*-test is used when two groups are being compared on a dependent measure that produces score data. ANOVAs are used when two or more groups are compared on a dependent measure that produces score data.

4.3 ANOVA summary tables show the sources of variation, the degrees of freedom associated with each source of variation, the sums of squares, the mean squares, the *F*-ratios, and the probability values for each *F*.

4.4 If the *F* is significantly greater than 1, at least one mean is significantly different from at least one other mean.

4.5 Planned comparisons and post hoc tests are specific means comparisons that are either planned before the research is conducted or performed without such preplanning, respectively.

Chapter 11

1.1 Correlated-groups designs are designs that assure group equivalence by either using the same participants in all groups or participants that have been closely matched.

1.2 The major confounding factor in within-subjects designs is sequence effects, which are controlled by counterbalancing.

1.3 Within-subjects designs reduce error variance by removing the individual differences component.

1.4 The strengths include greater sensitivity, reduction in the number of participants needed, and a general increase in efficiency. The primary weakness is confounding due to sequence effects.

1.5 Complete counterbalancing means that an equal number of participants is assigned to every possible order of conditions.

2.1 There are no sequence effects to worry about in matched-subjects designs.

2.2 The characteristics of matched-subjects designs are that (1) each participant is exposed to only one level of the independent variable, (2) each participant has a matched participant in each of the other conditions so that the groups are correlated, (3) the analysis takes into account which participants were matched with which other participants, and (4) the critical comparison is the difference between the correlated groups, in which the correlation is created by the matching procedure.

2.3 Matched-subjects designs are used when researchers want to take advantage of the greater sensitivity of within-subjects designs, but cannot, or prefer not to, use a within-subjects design. Matched-subjects designs are most often used when exposure to one condition causes long-term changes in participants, making it impossible for participants to appear in the other conditions.

2.4 The disadvantages of using a matched-subject design include the extra work in identifying the variables to match on, the actual matching, and the loss of participants because no suitable match could be found.

3.1 Single-subject designs are extensions of within-subjects designs in which a single individual is tested under multiple conditions. They are used most often in evaluating a treatment program for a single client.

3.2 The single-case study is used to describe clients, rather than to evaluate whether a treatment has been effective. In contrast, single-subject experimental designs manipulate independent variables in a manner that permits causal conclusions.

3.3 Single-subject experimental designs control internal validity by controlling when the independent variable manipulations are carried out. To demonstrate a causal connection, the dependent variable response must be consistently related to when the independent variable was manipulated.

3.4 In ABA reversal designs, the effects of an independent variable on a dependent variable are demonstrated by measuring the dependent variable over several time periods, during which the treatment is applied and then removed. In the multiple-baseline design, the effects of the treatment are demonstrated on different behaviors successively. Finally, a single-subject, randomized, time-series design inserts a treatment at some randomly determined point in a series of measures of the dependent variable.

3.5 The strength of single-subject experimental designs is that they allow researchers to make causal inferences. The weakness is that the data provide little information about the generalizability of the findings unless systematic replication studies are run.

3.6 External validity is weak because a single participant will never adequately represent the diversity in the general population.

3.7 Single-subject direct replication involves repeating the study with the same participant or a series of participants with the same behavioral issue. Single-subject systematic replication involves carrying out a series with different people in different settings and with new target behaviors. Single-subject clinical replication involves using an integrated treatment package of two or more procedures that are applied to a succession of participants.

3.8 In single-subject experimental procedures, causality is inferred when each manipulation of the independent variable results in a predictable change in the dependent variable.

Chapter 12

1.1 Factorial designs are research designs with more than one independent variable.

1.2 A factorial design will test a minimum of three null hypotheses. With two factors, there will be the main effects of each factor and the interaction of the two factors. With more factors, there will be more null hypotheses to test.

1.3 An interaction involves two variables that have a different effect when combined than they have when not combined. Main effects refer to the individual effects of each factor on the dependent variable.

1.4 Factorial designs are used when the researcher is interested in the interactive effects of two or more independent variables.

1.5 Any combination of main effects and factorials is possible in a factorial study.

1.6 The only limitations to the number of factors that can be included in a study is that the number of participants needed increases rapidly as more factors are added and researchers are often unable to interpret the complex interactions that might be found in a factorial study with several independent variables.

1.7 We should always interpret the main effects in light of the interaction because the main effects may be present only when some specific combination of the factors is present. The dark-fears study illustrates this point.

2.1 The major advantages of a repeated measures factorial are that fewer participants are needed and there is a greater sensitivity to the effects of the independent variables on the dependent variable.

2.2 Designs can be mixed by having factors that include (1) at least one within-subjects factor and at least one between-subjects factor, (2) at least one manipulated factor and at least one nonmanipulated factor, or (3) mixed factors in both of these ways simultaneously.

2.3 Designs that are mixed in terms of within- and between-subjects factors must take into account which factors are between-subjects and which are within-subjects in setting up the data analysis. Designs that are mixed in terms of manipulated and nonmanipulated factors must take into account which factors are manipulated and which are nonmanipulated in the interpretation.

3.1 Analysis of covariance removes the effects of a theoretically unimportant, but nonetheless powerful, variable from the dependent variable scores as part of the analysis of the effects of the independent variable on the dependent variable.

3.2 A MANOVA includes more than one dependent variable, whereas an ANOVA includes only a single dependent variable in the analysis.

Chapter 13

1.1 Field research is any research study that is carried out in the natural environment, regardless of the level of constraint of the study.

1.2 Field research is conducted (1) to test the external validity of causal conclusions arrived at in the laboratory, (2) to determine the effects of events that occur in the field, and (3) to improve generalization across settings.

1.3 The major difficulties in field research are that many of the normal laboratory controls may be unavailable and some independent variables are beyond the control of the researcher.

1.4 The three types of generalization are (1) generalization of results from the participants in the study to the larger population, (2) generalization of the results of the study over time, and (3) generalization of results from settings of the study to other settings.

1.5 In the field it is not uncommon to see things that may indicate something significant about how variables relate. Flexible and observant researchers will be able to recognize the potential importance of such observations and thus plan and carry out further research that will provide more definitive information about the phenomenon.

2.1 A quasi-experiment is almost an experiment, but not quite equal to it.

2.2 Quasi-experiments can be used to test causal hypotheses in natural settings with reasonable control of extraneous variables. Their weakness is that they rarely control for all possible sources of confounding and, therefore, researchers must be careful in drawing causal inferences.

2.3 Nonequivalent control-group designs are most effective when the naturally occurring groups are very similar, perhaps because they were formed by some random process, such as living in counties that either did or did not experience a flood.

2.4 Interrupted time-series designs are a variation on within-subjects designs because the participants are tested under all conditions.

2.5 The variables most likely to confound the results of an interrupted time-series study are history and instrumentation.

3.1 The major purpose of program evaluation is to determine the effectiveness of a given program in meeting its goals. This is critical, because money spent on ineffective programs could be used on more worthwhile projects.

3.2 The major difficulty in program evaluation is that the evaluator often has to rely on the cooperation of those implementing the program and, therefore, excellent political skills are required.

3.3 Internal validity in program evaluations can be enhanced by (1) selecting appropriate dependent measures, (2) minimizing potential bias in these measures, and (3) selecting the strongest research design possible.

3.4 The most widely used designs in program evaluation are the randomized control-group design, the nonequivalent control-group design, and the single-group, time-series design. Although the pretest–posttest design is used in some program evaluations, it is a weak design that should be avoided.

3.5 Program evaluation research is a science in that the issues of internal and external validity must be addressed. It is an art in that it takes cleverness and political skill to structure the assessment so as to maximize validity and cooperation from those involved with the program.

4.1 Status surveys describe the current characteristics of a population, whereas survey research tries to discover relationships among variables.

4.2 The major goal of a survey is to learn about the ideas, knowledge, feeling, opinions, attitudes, and self-reported behavior of a defined population.

4.3 The survey instrument may be a questionnaire or an interview schedule. Participants respond to a questionnaire themselves, usually in writing. Interview schedules are used by survey interviewers, who record the answers and follow up on ambiguous answers with additional questioning.

4.4 Factual items ask about information that can be verified independently. Content items ask about the respondents' opinions, attitudes, knowledge, and behavior.

4.5 Stratified random sampling involves dividing the population into subgroups or strata and randomly sampling from each stratum.

4.6 Confidence limits are the upper and lower bound of an interval in which we have a specified level of confidence that the population value lies within that interval.

4.7 A cross-sectional design involves administering the survey once to a sample, yielding data on the measured characteristics as they exist at the time of the survey. The longitudinal design is a within-subjects survey research design in which the same group of participants is surveyed at different times.

Chapter 14

1.1 The first step in selecting appropriate statistical procedures is to describe the characteristics of the study and the questions being asked.

1.2 Flowcharts organize the decision process by walking the person through the process, using the information about the nature of the study to answer a series of questions.

1.3 Flowcharts can help you to select an appropriate statistical procedure. However, they do not list all appropriate procedures and therefore cannot be used to determine if a statistical procedure used by another investigator is appropriate.

2.1 A thorough check of procedures before beginning a research study makes sure that every detail has been properly addressed in the design stage.

2.2 If the pre-data check uncovers problems, they should be addressed and solved before the study is begun.

Chapter 15

1.1 Meta-analysis provides a mathematical way of objectively combining studies to arrive at a general conclusion about the effects of one variable on another. It allows studies that normally would not have sufficient power to test a null hypothesis to, nevertheless, contribute information.

1.2 Path analysis tests the viability of a hypothesized causal model of the relationship among observed variables using only the correlations among these variables as input.

1.3 Micro-iontophoresis and microdialysis allow researchers to measure and/or manipulate neurotransmitters at specific locations in the brain of a functioning animal to see how these neurotransmitters affect behavior.

1.4 Computers have affected research in several ways, including, but not limited to, (1) making data analysis and data management easier, (2) carrying out the procedures for studies, thus reducing experimenter biases, (3) making possible complex procedures that would be impossible without computers, (4) modeling complex processes that might otherwise be beyond the conceptual ability of researchers, and (5) improving communication among researchers.

2.1 Science is defined by the processes of empiricism and rationalism.

2.2 Science progresses by rejecting inadequate theories and proposing and testing new theories that will stand up better to the rigorous demands of rationalism and empiricism.

3.1 The essence of science is its way of thinking.

3.2 Because the essence of science is its way of thinking, it is entirely possible to be thinking scientifically about a question in any setting. The technology of science makes research easier, but does not define the process of science.

Glossary

a posteriori comparison   See *post hoc test.*

a priori comparison   See *planned comparison.*

ABA reversal design   See *reversal design.*

abscissa   The *x*-axis on a graph.

abstract   A brief description of a research study that appears at the beginning of the research paper and is included in abstract journals such as *Psychological Abstracts*. The length of an abstract is restricted to a specified number of characters because abstracts are now routinely transferred to computerized databases.

abstract number system   The commonly used number system with its well-defined rules and characteristics, including identity, magnitude, equal intervals, and true zero.

accessible population   The subset of a target population that is available to the researcher and from which the sample is drawn.

ad hoc sample   Sample of participants drawn from an accessible population. Characteristics of the ad hoc sample must be described to define the limits of generalizability.

all-or-none bias   The tendency to see statements as either true or false when they are actually probabilistic. Virtually all scientific theories are probabilistic in that they correctly predict what will happen a percentage of the time.

alpha level   Level of Type I error (the probability of rejecting the null hypothesis when the null hypothesis is true).

analysis of covariance (ANCOVA)   Statistical procedure similar to analysis of variance; used to evaluate whether two or more groups have different population means. Analysis of covariance statistically removes the effects of extraneous variables on the dependent variable and hence increases the power of the statistical test.

analysis of variance (ANOVA)   Statistical procedure used to analyze for mean differences between two or more groups. ANOVAs compare the variability between groups with the variability within groups. Many variations of analysis of variance are possible, including repeated measures ANOVAs and factorial ANOVAs.

ANOVA summary table   Table that organizes the results of an analysis of variance computation. For each source of variation, the appropriate degrees of freedom, sums of squares, mean squares, and *F*-ratios are listed. (Examples are given in Chapters 10 through 12.)

apparatus subsection   The section of a research report in which the physical aspects of the study (apparatus, measuring instruments, etc.) are described.

applied psychology   Any use of psychological principles, theories, or technologies to deal with existing problems or concerns. Applied psychology refers to research that is specifically aimed at understanding and correcting problems faced by people.

applied research   Research to provide solutions to practical problems. Applied research is contrasted with basic research.

archival records   Any source of data (such as census data) for events that have already occurred.

artifact   Any apparent effect of a major conceptual variable that is actually the result of an uncontrolled confounding variable. Artifacts threaten the validity of research.

artificial intelligence   Machines that are designed to evaluate and respond to situations. Most artificial intelligence machines are computer based, and many of them have achieved remarkable levels of performance in specific areas.

association   Relationship or correlation.

assumptions of science   Basic tenets that form the bases for more complex scientific theory and research.

attrition   Potential confounding variable in research. Attrition is the loss of participants before or during the research. The participants who remain may not be representative of the population. Hence, conclusions might not generalize to the entire population.

authority A way of acquiring knowledge. New ideas are accepted as valid because some respected authority has declared the idea to be true.

automation Use of equipment to conduct most or all aspects of presenting stimuli and recording participants' responses. Automation reduces the work, increases precision in data gathering, and minimizes experimenter bias.

average deviation The sum of the deviations from the mean divided by the number of scores.

balanced placebo design A 2 × 2 research design developed in alcohol research in which the factors are (1) what participants actually consume (alcohol or no alcohol) and (2) what participants are told that they are consuming (alcohol or no alcohol). This design permits the separation of the pharmacological from the expectation effects of alcohol. See *deception.*

Barnum statement Any statement that appears to be insightful, but is actually true only because it is true for almost all issues, situations, or people. For example, telling someone that he or she has difficulties at times maintaining a focus on long-term goals is a Barnum statement.

baseline period In ABA and time-series designs, this is the time from initial monitoring of target behavior until the start of the treatment or manipulation.

base rate Naturally occurring frequency of events (i.e., before any manipulations to alter the rates have been carried out).

basic research Fundamental or pure research. Basic research is carried out to add to knowledge, but without applied or practical goals. Basic research is often contrasted with applied research.

batch mode Processing a computer task by telling the computer all the steps that you want and then letting the computer follow these instructions to completion. This contrasts with the interactive approach more common with personal computers, in which the computer does one step, provides output, and then waits for your next command.

behavior Any observable act from an organism. Behavior is the subject matter of psychology.

behavior modification A set of teaching or therapeutic procedures, used primarily in education and clinical practice, that is based on laboratory-derived principles of learning. Also known as behavior therapy.

behavioral medicine See *health psychology.*

behavioral neuroscience A field of study that relates the behavior of an organism to the brain mechanisms contributing to the behavior.

behavioral variable Variable representing an organism's behavior.

behaviorism A philosophical perspective in psychology that argues that a scientific psychology should base its theories on observable events only. This perspective challenged the introspective methodologies that dominated early psychology.

beta The probability of making a *Type II error.*

between-groups variance Index of the variability among group means.

between-subjects design Research design using two or more groups in which each participant appears in only one of the groups.

between-subjects factors Independent variables in factorial designs in which participants are assigned to conditions so that each participant appears in only one condition.

bimodal A distribution of scores that has two modes.

Biomedical Programs (BMDP) Computer package for statistical analyses.

blind When the researcher and/or participant is not aware of information that would, if available, increase the likelihood of biasing the experimental results. See *single-blind procedure* and *double-blind procedure.*

canonical correlation A correlation between two sets of variables. The first canonical correlation is derived by computing the linear combination of each set of variables that will give the highest possible correlation. Additional canonical correlations can be computed using different linear combinations of the variables in each set. This technique helps scientists to understand complex relationships between constructs that cannot be easily tapped by a single measure.

carry-over effects These effects result from a participant's involvement in one condition affecting his or her performance in all subsequent conditions. Carryover effects occur only in within-subjects designs.

case study See *case-study level of constraint.*

case-study level of constraint Research in which minimal constraints are placed on participants' behavior. Case-study research usually focuses on the behavior of a single participant.

categorical data Synonymous with *nominal data.*

categorical variable Synonymous with *discrete variable.* A categorical variable can have only a finite number of values.

causal hypothesis Usual form of the research hypothesis in experimental research. It states that the independent variable has a causal relationship to the dependent variable. To accept this hypothesis, we must reject the null hypothesis and all confounding-variable hypotheses.

causal inference   Conclusion that the change in the independent variable resulted in a change in the dependent variable. It may be drawn only if all potential confounding variables are controlled.

causally related   Two variables are causally related if a change in one variable results in a predictable change in the other variable and the change occurs as a direct result of the action of the first variable.

ceiling effects   See *scale attenuation effects.*

central tendency   Average or typical score in a distribution. Three measures of central tendency are the mean, median, and mode.

chi-square   A statistical distribution that forms the basis for inferential statistics used with nominal data.

classification variables   Organismic or participant variables used to classify participants into discrete groups. Classification variables are used for assigning participants to groups in differential research.

coding data   Process by which scores are assigned to behaviors. The coded data are usually in a form that can be more easily analyzed.

coefficient alpha   An index of internal consistency reliability.

coefficient of determination   The square of the Pearson product–moment correlation. It represents the proportion of variability in one variable that can be predicted on the basis of information about the other variable.

cognitive psychology   The subdiscipline of psychology that studies perceptual processing and basic thought processes.

cognitive science   A broad field that encompasses several disciplines, including behavioral neuroscience, neurophysiology, computer science, and linguistics, all of which are interested in modeling and understanding basic brain processes.

cohort effect   The concept that people of a given chronological age in a given culture may behave similarly throughout their lives and differ from people of other ages because of shared life experiences.

column means   In factorial designs, one factor is usually illustrated as separate columns of data, in which each column represents a different level of the factor. A second factor might be illustrated as rows of data, in which the different rows represent levels of the second factor. Column means are computed by taking the mean of all participants who appear in a given column regardless of their level on the second factor.

communication phase of research   Research phase in which the rationale, hypotheses, methods, results, and interpretations of the study are presented in oral or written form to other researchers.

complete counterbalancing   See *counterbalancing.*

computer-analysis programs   Sophisticated computer programs for statistical analyses. Some examples are *Biomedical Programs (BMDP), Statistical Package for the Social Sciences (SPSS), Minitab, Statistica, and Statistical Analysis System (SAS).*

computer file   A set of information stored digitally and made available to computers for processing. A computer file can include a program, data, or output.

computer modeling   Using a computer to simulate a psychological process as close as possible to the way in which it is actually performed by people.

conceptual replication   Repeating a study using different operational definitions for the variables.

confidence interval   An interval in which we predict the population parameter to fall with a specified level of confidence. For example, a 95% confidence interval will contain the population parameter 95% of the time.

confidentiality   An ethical requirement in most research; sensitive and personal information provided by participants should be protected and made unavailable to anyone other than the researchers.

confounded   Two variables are said to be confounded if they vary simultaneously so that it is impossible to determine which variable was responsible for the observed change in the dependent variable.

confounding variable   Any uncontrolled variable that might affect the outcome of a study. A variable can confound a study only if (1) there is a mean difference between the groups on the variable and (2) there is a correlation between the variable and the dependent measure.

confounding variable hypothesis   Actually, a set of hypotheses. Each confounding variable hypothesis states that a particular confounding variable is responsible for the observed changes in the dependent measure. Each hypothesis must be rejected before we can safely infer a causal relationship between the independent and dependent variables.

connectionist models   A computer modeling approach in which the computer model is based on heavily interconnected sets of cells in which the action of any one cell affects the actions of many other cells. Connectionist models are designed to function in a manner similar to the way that we believe the brain functions. Also know as parallel distributed processing (PDP) models.

constants Variables that are prevented from varying (i.e., held constant).

constraints Restrictions placed on the researcher in an effort to increase the precision of the research and enhance the validity of conclusions.

construct An idea constructed by the researcher to explain observed events. Constructs are not direct representations of reality; they are not facts. They are explanatory fictions because, in most cases, we do not know the real reason for a particular event. Once formulated, constructs are used as if they are true (i.e., analogically) to predict relationships between variables in new situations.

construct validity Validity of a theory. Most theories in science present broad conceptual explanation of relationships among variables and make many predictions. Construct validity is established by verifying the accuracy of each possible prediction that might be made from the theory. Because the number of predictions is usually infinite, construct validity can never be fully established. However, the more independent predictions from the theory verified as accurate, the stronger the construct validity of the theory.

content items In questionnaires and interviews, content items focus on respondents' opinions, attitudes, and knowledge, rather than on *factual items* that can be independently verified.

contingency A relationship between two or more variables in which the first event is highly predictive of the occurrence of the second event. The relationship between the variables is probabilistic and does not necessarily imply a causal connection.

continuous variable Any variable that can theoretically take on an infinite number of values. Continuous variables are often contrasted with discrete or categorical variables.

contrast See *planned comparison.*

control See *control in research.*

control group A group of participants used in either differential or experimental research that serves as a basis of comparisons for other groups. The ideal control group is similar to the experimental group on all variables except the independent variable that defines the group.

control in research Any procedure that is designed to reduce confounding.

control of variance Control in research is essentially, control of error variance and extraneous variance in order to detect more effectively systematic between-groups variance.

controlled research Research that employs adequate controls to rule out competing hypotheses and thus to draw causal conclusions.

convergent operations A term for the agreement or similarity among findings from different studies that were carried out with different operational definitions of the same concepts.

convergent validity Occurs when different studies, using different operational definitions, produce similar findings.

correlated-groups design Research design in which participants in each of the groups are related to participants in the other groups. Two correlated-groups designs are (1) within-subjects design and (2) matched-subjects design. These designs provide more powerful tests of the hypotheses because they control for individual differences. They are contrasted with independent-groups design.

correlated-subjects design See *correlated-groups design.*

correlated *t*-test Statistical procedure used to test for mean differences between two groups in a within-subjects or matched-subjects design.

correlation Degree of relationship between two or more variables.

correlation coefficient An index of the degree of relationship between variables.

correlational level of constraint Research designed to quantify the relationship between two or more variables. There is no manipulation of variables and no attempt to draw causal inferences.

correlational research Research that seeks to measure the relationship between variables without trying to determine causality. The term is sometimes used broadly to include any nonexperimental research design, such as differential research and quasi-experimental designs.

counterbalancing Control procedure used in within-subjects designs to control for sequence effects. It is most practical when there is a small number of conditions in the study. With complete counterbalancing, all possible arrangements of conditions are included; with incomplete counterbalancing only some of the possible arrangements are included.

criterion The variable that we are attempting to predict in regression.

criterion measure   The variable that we want to predict in regression.

crossover effect   In quasi-experimental research, a finding in which two nonequivalent groups show one pattern of scores before the manipulation and the reverse pattern of scores after the manipulation. The name derives from the crossing of the lines when such a result is graphed.

cross-sectional design   A design that compares the performance, attitudes, or histories of people of different ages or at different times in history. The groups are defined by the age range of the people in the groups or the historical time in which participants were tested. In a cross-sectional study, participants appear in only one group. This design is often contrasted with longitudinal designs.

cross-sectional research   Research in which a cross-sectional research design is used.

cross-tabulation   Procedure for organizing frequency data that displays the relationship between two or more nominal variables. A cross-tabulation table contains individual cells, with the number in each cell representing the frequency of participants who show that particular combination of characteristics.

cursor   The symbol on the screen of a personal computer that indicates where action will take place. The cursor is moved around the screen using a *mouse* or other pointing device.

data   Plural noun that refers to information gathered in research. Conclusions are drawn on the basis of an evaluation of the data.

data-analysis phase of research   Research phase in which data gathered from observing participants are statistically analyzed.

data snooping   Type of secondary analysis of data to help to generate hypotheses for further study.

debriefing   A procedure to help safeguard the rights of participants. At the completion of a study that uses deception, the full nature of the study is disclosed and participants' questions are answered.

deception   Procedures used in research to hide from the participant the true nature of the study. Many studies require deception to prevent participant expectancy effects, but the use of deception raises ethical issues. Ethical use of deception requires complete debriefing of the participants at the end of the study.

decision tree   An organized pathway leading to a defined goal, in which at various points a decision is made about which of two or more branches to follow to the next decision point.

decision-tree flowcharts   Flowchart model in which answers to specific questions lead to branching to a new set of questions or procedures. Chapter 14 presents a decision-tree model for selecting appropriate statistical tests.

deductive reasoning   Reasoning from the general to the particular. In deductive reasoning, specific predictions are made about future events based on theories.

deductive theory   A theory that emphasizes constructs and the relationship between constructs and seeks to make predictions from the theory that can be tested with empirical research. Often contrasted with *inductive theory* and *functional theory*.

degrees of freedom (df)   A statistical concept. One degree of freedom is lost each time that a population parameter is estimated on the basis of a sample. The distribution of most statistics are tabled by degrees of freedom (df).

demand characteristics   Any aspect of the situation created by the researcher that suggests to the participant what behavior is expected.

demographic variables   Data that describe the participants in a study (e.g., their age, gender, or education). This information should be routinely collected and reported in research.

dependent variable   Variable that is hypothesized to have a relationship with the independent variable.

descriptive statistics   Statistics or statistical procedures that summarize and/or describe the characteristics of a sample of scores.

design notation   A way of indicating the number of factors and how many levels of each factor. For example, a $2 \times 4 \times 3$ design has three factors, with the first factor having two levels, the second four levels, and the third three levels.

difference score   Difference between scores on the dependent measure at two points in time.

differential level of constraint   Research in which two or more groups defined on the basis of a preexisting variable are compared on a dependent measure.

differential research   Research that involves comparing two or more existing groups on a dependent variable.

diffusion of treatment   Potential confounding variable that occurs when participants in one condition communicate information to participants in another condition. This can be a particular problem in research settings in which participants are in close communication with one another, such as in a school or hospital or in the undergraduate psychology participant pool of a university.

direct differences *t*-test   See *correlated t-test.*

discrete variable   A variable that can take on only a finite number of values. Often contrasted with *continuous variable.*

discussion section   The final section of a research report, in which the researcher interprets the findings in light of other research and theory.

dispersion   How spread out the scores are in a sample.

double-blind procedure   Research procedure in which neither the researcher nor the participant knows to which condition the participant was assigned. The purpose is to minimize the possibility of experimenter bias and participant expectancies.

ecological validity   Experiments achieve ecological validity when they reproduce accurately real-life situations, thus allowing easy generalization of their findings. See *external validity.*

effect size   An index of the size of the statistical difference between groups that is expressed in standard deviation units.

effective range   Characteristic of any dependent measure; the range over which the dependent measure accurately reflects the level of the dependent variable.

electronic mail   A mechanism for sending messages via the Internet to anyone who has an electronic mail address.

e-mail   See *electronic mail.*

empirical   Based on observed data. For example, a relationship between variables is empirically established if it has been observed to occur.

empiricism   System of knowing that is based solely on observation of the events.

enumerative data   Synonymous with *nominal data.*

equal intervals   A characteristic of the abstract number in which the difference between units are the same anywhere on the scale.

equipment subsection   See *apparatus subsection.*

error term   Generic term used in many different statistics; it provides a basis for comparing observed differences between groups. The error term is usually based on a measure of the variability of scores within each group.

error variance   Variability within a group that is caused by chance factors that affect some participants and not others. Also called within-group variance and nonsystematic within-group variance. Error variance should be minimized in research.

ethical checks   A series of questions that a researcher must ask about the research and the specific procedures included to safeguard participants.

evaluative biases of language   Language has a tendency to blend description and evaluation, which can distort the perceptions of objective behavior.

ex post facto design   Nonexperimental research design in which the current situation of the participant is observed and related to previous events. Because there are no manipulations of variables, confounding variables cannot be controlled and alternative hypotheses cannot be ruled out. Therefore, it is a weak design and causal inferences cannot be drawn from it.

ex post facto fallacy   Error in reasoning in which we assume that the observed relationship between current events and some historical events represents a causal relationship.

ex post facto study   See *ex post facto design.*

exact replication   Repeating a study by using exactly the same procedure used in the original study. See also *replication.*

experiment   High-constraint research procedure in which participants are randomly assigned to two or more conditions and compared on a dependent measure. Experimental designs provide adequate control over virtually all possible confounding variables.

experimental analysis of behavior   Procedures for the controlled study of single individuals or small groups, which are based on B. F. Skinner's operant conditioning concepts.

experimental design   In experimental design, participants are assigned to groups or conditions without bias, such as with random assignment, and all appropriate control procedures are used.

experimental group   Group of participants assigned to one or more conditions defined by a specified level of the independent variable. Contrasted with a *control group.*

experimental level of constraint   Research in which participants are assigned to two or more groups or conditions without bias and are compared on at least one dependent measure. At the experimental level of constraint, the research provides adequate controls for most confounding variables and therefore allows researchers to draw causal inferences.

experimental research   See *experimental level of constraint.*

experimental variance   The variability between groups that is brought about by an experimental manipulation.

experimenter bias   The potential problem in research of the interfering effects of the researcher's attitudes and biases if they are not controlled.

experimenter effects   Any uncontrolled effects on research due to the experimenter's biases, attitudes, reactivity to the research or participants, and expectations for results that will support the hypothesis.

experimenter expectancy   An experimenter's unintentional biasing of results due to expectations for desired results that will support the hypothesis. See also *experimenter bias* and *experimenter effects*.

experimenter reactivity   See *experimenter bias*.

exploratory research   Low-constraint research conducted early in the study of a aresearch area that is designed to investigate feasibility and to generate rather than test hypotheses.

extraneous variables   Any factors not controlled by the experimenter that may affect the outcome of the study.

extraneous variance   Variability in scores on the dependent measure that can be accounted for by the effects of extraneous variables.

factorial ANOVA   Analysis of variance procedure for evaluating factorial designs.

factorial designs   Research designs employing more than one independent variable simultaneously. The major advantage of a factorial design is that it can measure the interactive effects of two or more independent variables.

factors   Each independent variable in a factorial design.

facts   Empirically observed events.

factual items   In questionnaires and interviews, those questions that can be independently verified, such as the respondent's age, gender, and occupation. In contrast, *content items* cannot be factually verified.

field research   Research conducted outside the laboratory. Field research might include low-constraint research, such as naturalistic or case-study research, or may include higher-constraint procedures conducted in natural settings. An advantage of field research is that results are more easily generalized because observations are made in a real-world setting.

fields (in computer files)   In data files, the field represents a variable, which has a score for each participant. Normally, the fields are shown as columns in a data matrix, and the rows represent *records*.

filler items   Questions included in the dependent measure but not scored as part of the dependent measure. Their purpose is to distract participants from the purpose of the study.

floor effects   See *scale attenuation effects*.

flowcharts   Organizational device that allows us to reach a decision by following a path defined by answers to particular questions. Chapter 14 illustrates the use of flowcharts to select the appropriate statistical test for any given research procedure.

F-ratio   A test statistic computed by taking the ratio of two variances. *F*-ratios are used most often in analysis of variance in which the two variance estimates are based on (1) the difference between group means and (2) the difference among participants within groups.

F-test   See *F-ratio*.

free random assignment   Assignment of participants to groups so that the assignment of any given participant has no effect on the assignment of any other participant.

frequencies   The number of objects or participants that fall into a specified category. Frequencies represent *nominal data*.

frequency data   Synonymous with *nominal data*.

frequency distribution   Organizational device used to simplify large data sets.

frequency polygon   Graph that illustrates a frequency distribution. It is constructed by putting a dot above each possible score (which is listed on the *x*-axis) at a height that indicates the appropriate frequency of that score (which is indicated on the *y*-axis). The dots are then connected to form a graph of the frequency distribution.

functional theory   Functional theories tend to emphasize equally the inductive and deductive aspects of theory building. Often contrasted with *inductive theory* and *deductive theory*.

functionalism   A philosophical perspective that stresses the need to study how the mind functions. Often contrasted with *structuralism*.

fundamental research   Another term for *basic research*.

general control procedures   Control achieved through preparation of settings, careful response measurement, and replication.

general population   See *population*.

generalizability   Extent to which the findings from a research study are applicable to the outside world.

generalization   The process of assuming that the findings from one's study will also apply to other situations, places, or times. See *generalize*.

generalize   To assume that the findings of a particular research study will be found for other participants or in other settings.

Gestalt psychology   A philosophical perspective in the field of perception that rests on the concept that the whole is greater than the sum of its parts. Gestalt psychologists seek to find broad principles describing how people process complex sensory input.

graphs   A means of presenting data visually. Some examples of graphs are histograms and frequency polygons.

graphs of factorial data   Graphs that provide a visual illustration of main effects and interactions in factorial studies.

grouped frequency distribution   Frequency distribution that provides the frequency of scores in intervals of equal size. Grouped frequency distributions are used with *continuous data* or in situations in which there is a large range of possible scores.

health psychology   A relatively new applied discipline in psychology that focuses on understanding and modifying behavior that affects a person's physical health.

heterogeneous   A group is said to be heterogeneous if there is considerable variability within the group.

heuristic influence   The nonsystematic impact of research or theory in stimulating new research.

histogram   A bar graph in which the frequency of any given score or the mean for any given group is represented by the height of the bar. Histograms allow us to see the shape of a distribution or compare the performance of participants tested under various conditions.

history   Potential confounding variable. History represents any change in the dependent variable over the course of a research study that is a function of events other than the manipulation of the independent variable.

homogeneity   See *homogenous*.

homogeneous   A population is said to be homogeneous if the participants in the population are similar to one another.

humanistic psychology   A philosophical perspective that emphasizes subjective experience and the distinctively human qualities of choice and self-realization.

hyperlink   A link between Web documents that allows a user to transfer to the linked document by clicking on the link.

icon   Small pictures on a computer screen that represent a program, action, or data set. Clicking on the icon will usually start a program or action.

idea-generating phase of research   First step in any research project during which the researcher selects a topic to study.

identity   A characteristic of the abstract number system in which each number has a specific meaning or identity.

incidental comparison   See *post hoc test*.

incidental learning   Learning that occurs without specific reinforcement, usually while learning a different task.

incomplete counterbalancing   See *counterbalancing*.

independent-groups design   See *between-subjects design*.

independent samples   Samples that include different participants in each group and in which the selection of participants for one sample does not influence the selection of participants for any other sample.

independent variable   Any variable in research that defines separate groups of participants. Participants may be assigned to these groups on the basis of either (1) some preexisting characteristics (*differential research*) or (2) some form of random assignment (*experimental research*).

individual differences   Natural differences between people. Individual differences tend to obscure the effects of an independent variable on the dependent measure(s).

inductive reasoning   Reasoning from the particular to the general. Used to generate theories or models based on observations or ideas.

inductive theory   Inductive theories are built on a strong empirical base and tend to stray little from that empirical base. Often contrasted with *deductive theory* and *functional theory*.

inference   Any conclusion drawn on the basis of some set of information. We draw inferences on the basis of the empirical data that we collect and the ideas that we construct.

inferential statistics   Statistical procedures that compute the probability of obtaining the pattern of data if all participants were actually drawn from the same population. If the probability of obtaining such a pattern of scores is low, we reject the hypothesis that all participants were drawn from the same population (*null hypothesis*) and conclude that there were meaningful differences between groups or conditions.

informed consent   Critical principle in the ethical treatment of participants. Participants have the right to know exactly what they are getting into and to refuse to participate.

informed consent form   A form signed by each human participant prior to the beginning of the study. The informed consent form must present enough detail about the study and its risks to permit participants to make informed decisions about their participation. The consent form should be reviewed and approved by the Institutional Review Board as part of its evaluation of the research proposal.

initial equivalence (principle of)   The groups to be compared in an experiment must be equivalent at the start of the experiment.

Institutional Review Board (IRB)   Formal body that operates in most institutions that conduct research. The IRB reviews all research proposals to determine if they meet ethical guidelines.

instrumentation   Potential confounding variable involving changes in the measuring instrument over time that causes the instrument to give different readings when no change has occurred in participants.

instruments subsection   See *apparatus subsection.*

interaction affects   Combined effect of two or more independent variables on the dependent variable that is more than the sum of the individual effects. Interactions can be measured only in factorial designs.

internal consistency reliability   Index of the homogeneity of the items of a measure. Items that are homogeneous correlate strongly with one another, suggesting that they all measure the same characteristic.

internal validity   Accuracy of a research study in determining the relationship between the independent and dependent variables. Internal validity can be assured only if all confounding variables have been controlled.

interpretation phase of research   Research phase in which the results of statistical analyses of data are interpreted in light of (1) the adequacy of control procedures, (2) previous research, and (3) existing theories about the behavior under study.

interrater reliability   Index of the consistency of ratings between separate raters. It is indexed by the correlation between the ratings of two raters.

interrater reliability coefficient   A correlation coefficient expressing the degree of agreement of observations made by two or more raters. See *reliability.*

interrupted time-series design   Type of research design suitable for either individuals or groups in which multiple measures of the dependent variable are taken before and after an experimental manipulation. Time-series designs provide some control for history and maturation, even without the inclusion of a control group.

interval scale   Scale of measurement in which the distance between any two adjacent scores is the same as the distance between any other two adjacent scores, but zero is not a true zero. An example of an interval scale is temperature measured in either Celsius or Fahrenheit.

interview schedule   A standardized interview, with each question spelled out for the interviewer. Interview schedules provide consistency in interviews.

introduction   The first substantive section of a research paper in which the authors review previous research and theory to provide a framework and rationale for the study.

intuition   A way of acquiring knowledge. In intuition, ideas come to people supposedly without intellectual effort or sensory processes.

invasion of privacy   Ethical issue in research. Researchers should make every effort to protect participants' privacy by maintaining confidentiality of records.

Kappa   An index of interrater agreement that factors into the index the probability of chance agreement. As a consequence, Kappa coefficients are comparable across a wide range of base rates and conditions.

knowledge   Any information about the world. Knowledge may be achieved in different ways.

Laboratory Animal Care Committee   A formalized committee that reviews every research proposal that involves animals for ethical issues. Every research center that conducts animal research must have such a local committee.

Latin-square design   A procedure used to provide a measure of counterbalancing in a within-subjects design. Instead of using all possible orders of presentation, as in complete counterbalancing, a Latin-square design uses a set of orders that ensures that every experimental condition appears equally often in every position.

levels of constraint   Degree of systematic control applied in research. The labels assigned to these levels of constraint are *naturalistic, case study, correlational, differential,* and *experimental.*

levels of headings   The mechanism used in published research articles for organizing the report. Levels of headings are similar to an outline, with the various sections and subsections of the report representing different levels of the outline.

Likert-scale items   In Likert scales, each item is rated on a continuum. For example, the scale may range from "strongly agree" to "strongly disagree."

linear relationship   Relationship between variables that, when plotted in a standard coordinate system, cluster around a straight line. Most correlation coefficients are sensitive only to linear relationships between variables.

list server   A mechanism that permits continuous electronic conversations between people who may be spread all over the world. Electronic mail messages sent to a list server are distributed to everyone on a distribution list, allowing the easy exchange of ideas among large groups of people.

logic   Set of operations that can be applied to statements and conclusions drawn from these statements to determine the internal accuracy of the conclusions.

longitudinal (panel) design   A research design frequently used in developmental psychology in which a group of participants is followed over time, with the dependent measures repeated during follow-up testings. This design is often contrasted with *cross-sectional designs.*

longitudinal research   Research that uses a longitudinal research design.

magnitude   A characteristic of the abstract number system in which the numbers have an inherent order.

main effects   In a factorial design, main effects refer to the individual effects of the independent variables. In contrast, interaction effects are the combined effects of two or more independent variables on the dependent variable.

mainframe computer   A large computer designed to serve the needs of multiple users at the same time. Universities typically provide mainframe computing resources for a variety of computing needs, including serving as a gateway to the Internet and e-mail. Mainframe computers are usually accessed through dedicated terminals on campus or through a personal computer.

mainstream psychology   Contemporary psychology, which is largely an integration of many of the earlier schools of psychology and their theoretical models.

manipulated factors   Independent variables in a factorial design in which the levels of the factors are determined by active manipulation by the experimenter.

manipulated independent variable   Type of independent variable found in an experimental research study. When manipulated independent variables are used, participants are randomly assigned to groups or conditions.

manipulation   The explicit control of the independent variable by the researcher.

manipulation check   Procedure designed to verify that the independent variable varied in the different groups or conditions. A manipulation check is independent of any evaluation of the effect of the independent variable on the dependent variable.

Mann–Whitney *U*-test   A nonparametric inferential statistic used to test the difference between two groups when the dependent measure produces ordinal data.

matched-pairs *t*-test   See *correlated t-test.*

matched random assignment   Experimental procedure used to help to ensure that groups are equivalent at the beginning of the study. In matched random assignment, participants are matched in small groups (size is determined by the number of conditions in the study) on relevant variables, and each member of the group is randomly assigned to one of the conditions of the study until all members have been assigned to one condition. Matched random assignment is an alternative to a within-subjects design and should be considered whenever significant sequence effects are expected in a within-subjects design.

matched-subjects design   Research design in which participants are matched on a variable that is highly correlated with the dependent measure. Once matched, each participant is randomly assigned to each group defined by the independent variable. The design helps to control for individual differences without introducing the sequence problems inherent in a within-subjects design.

materials subsection   See *apparatus subsection.*

matrix of cells   Structure of cells in a factorial design.

maturation   Potential confounding factor involving changes in participants during the course of the study that results from normal growth processes.

mean   Arithmetic average of scores. The mean is the most commonly used measure of central tendency, but should be computed only for score data.

mean square   In analysis of variance (ANOVA), the mean square is a variance estimate. Several mean squares are computed in any ANOVA. The ratio of mean squares is the *F*-test.

measurement error   Any inaccuracy found in the measurement of a variable. Although it is impossible to determine the precise degree and direction of measurement error for a given participant, it is possible to specify the average error associated with a particular measure.

measurement reactivity   Any effect on the participant's behavior that results from the participant being aware that he or she is being observed. Measurement reactivity can be reduced by using *unobtrusive measures.*

measures of central tendency   Statistics that indicate the typical score, including the *mean, median,* and *mode.*

measures subsection   See *apparatus subsection.*

median   Middle score in a distribution.

meta-analysis   A procedure that allows the statistical averaging of results from independent studies of the same phenomena. Meta-analyses essentially combine studies on the same topic into a single large study, thus providing an index of how strongly the independent variable affected the dependent variable in the set of studies.

method section   The section of the research report that details the nature of the sample and the procedures used in the study.

microcannulae   Tiny tubes that can be surgically implanted in the brains of animals. These tubes allow the animal to function normally, with no pain or discomfort, while allowing researchers to study brain functioning by delivering specific chemicals to specific regions of the animal's brain to see their impact on functioning.

microdialysis   A procedure similar to *micro-iontophoresis,* except that the tiny tubes are actually one tube inside another with a porous tip to the outer tube. This permits the researcher to pump substances through the tube, allowing the natural chemicals of the brain to be sampled through the porous end of the tube. This process permits researchers to see what chemicals are produced and active in specific brain regions while the animal is performing specific tasks and thus helps researchers to understand potential biological mechanisms behind specific behavior.

micro-iontophoresis   A procedure involving the implantation of tiny tubes or *microcannulae* into specific regions of the brains of animals. This process can be done without causing pain to the organism. It allows the researcher to deliver specific chemical substances to specific regions of the brain in order to see what impact the chemicals have on the functioning of the animal.

Minitab   Computer package for statistical analysis of data.

mixed designs (between- and within-subjects variables)   Factorial design in which at least one of the factors is a between-subjects factor and at least one of the factors is a within-subjects factor. The pattern of between- and within-subjects factors affects the selection of the statistical analysis.

mixed designs (manipulated and nonmanipulated variables)   Factorial design in which at least one of the factors represents a nonmanipulated independent variable and at least one of the factors represents a manipulated independent variable. The distinction between manipulated and nonmanipulated variables affects the interpretation of results, because we must take into account the fact that at least some of the factors are nonmanipulated factors and therefore represent differential research.

mode   Most frequent score in a distribution.

model   A representation of the complex reality of the real world.

moderator variable   Any variable that has an effect on the observed relationship between two or more other variables. When a moderator variable is operating, it is best to measure the relationship between variables separately in subgroups defined by the moderator variable.

Monte Carlo studies   A procedure that evaluates the effectiveness of statistical tests by simulating with a computer the repeated sampling of participants from a population with known parameters. The characteristics of the populations can be systematically varied to see what effect these variations have on the accuracy of the statistical decision. This process allows us to determine empirically the probability of Type I and Type II errors and thus to see the strength of the impact of violations of the assumptions of statistical procedures.

mouse   A device for moving the cursor on the screen of a personal computer. Sliding the mouse on a table moves the cursor and clicking the buttons on the mouse performs various tasks.

multidimensional scaling   A group of statistical methods that is used to simplify data by finding a small number of dimensions or factors that collectively account for most of the variability in a group of scores.

multilevel, completely randomized, between-subjects design   A research design using more than two groups, in which participants are randomly assigned to groups and each participant appears in only one group.

multiple-baseline design   Research design often used with single participants when we want to infer a causal relationship between the independent and dependent variables. Baselines on several different behaviors are taken, and treatments are applied at different points in time for each behavior being monitored.

multiple-choice items   In a questionnaire, each question or item is presented with several answers from which the respondent chooses one.

multiple correlation   A correlation in which a criterion is correlated with a set of variables. The correlation is computed by finding the linear combination of the set that will provide the highest possible correlation with the criterion.

multiple observers   Control used to evaluate the accuracy of observations made by two or more independent observers.

multivariable designs   See *factorial designs.*

multivariate analysis of variance (MANOVA)   Extension of analysis of variance in which two or more dependent measures are simultaneously evaluated.

multivariate correlational designs   Correlational designs that include more than two variables.

multivariate techniques   Advanced statistical procedures used to evaluate complex relationships among several variables.

naïve empiricism Extreme dependence on personal experience in order to accept events as facts. An example: "If I don't see it, then it does not exist."

naturalistic level of constraint Research carried out in natural settings in which the researcher makes no attempt to manipulate the environment as part of the research.

naturalistic observation Observing the natural flow of behavior of participants in their natural environment without imposing any experimental manipulations.

negative correlation Relationship between two variables in which an increase in one variable predicts a decrease in the other.

negative practice effect A decrement of performance that results from previous exposure of the participant to the measurement procedures.

negatively skewed A distribution in which scores are concentrated near the top of the curve, thinning out as the curve approaches the bottom, giving the characteristic tail that points to the bottom or negative end of the distribution.

neuronetworks *Connectionist models* are sometimes referred to as neuronetworks because they are designed to resemble the massive interconnections between units that are typical of brain neurons. However, most theorists argue that the connectionist models now in use are dramatic oversimplifications of neural processes and, therefore, we should be cautious in using terms such as neuronetworks to describe them.

neurotransmitter agonists A chemical that enhances the action of a neurotransmitter.

neurotransmitter antagonists A chemical that blocks the action of a neurotransmitter.

nominal data Data produced when a nominal scale of measurement is used. Nominal data are frequencies of participants in each of the specific categories.

nominal fallacy The tendency to confuse a label for a behavior as the explanation for the behavior. For example, labeling people as kind because they do many kind things for other people is reasonable, but it is circular to then say that they do these kind things because they are kind people.

nominal scale Scale of measurement in which only categories are produced as scores. Examples are diagnostic classification, sex of the participant, and political affiliation.

nonequivalent control-group design Quasi-experimental design in which two or more groups that may not be equivalent at the beginning of the study are compared on the dependent measure.

nonexperimental designs Any research design that fails to provide adequate controls for confounding.

nonlinear relationship Any relationship between two or more variables that is characterized by a scatter plot in which the points cluster around a curved instead of a straight line. Most correlation coefficients are insensitive to nonlinear relationships.

nonmanipulated factors Independent variables in a factorial design in which participants are assigned to groups on the basis of some preexisting factor. See *differential research.*

nonmanipulated independent variable The preexisting variable that determines group membership in a differential research study.

nonparametric statistics Inferential statistical procedures that do not rely on estimating such population parameters as the mean and variance.

nonprobability sampling Any sampling procedure in which some participants have a higher probability of being selected than other participants or the selection of a given participant changes the probability of selecting other participants. Often contrasted with *probability sampling.*

nonreactive measure Any dependent measure that provides consistent scores regardless of whether the participant is aware of being measured.

nonsytematic within-groups variance Variance due to random factors that affect some participants more than others. Nonsystematic within-groups variance should be minimized in research. Also called error variance.

normal distribution Distribution of scores that is characterized by a bell-shaped curve in which the probability of a score drops off rapidly from the midpoint to the tails of the distribution. A true normal curve is defined by a mathematical equation and is a function of two variables (the mean and variance of the distribution). Normal distributions are useful in psychology, because psychological variables tend to show distributions that are close to normal.

null hypothesis States that the participants from each group are drawn from populations with identical population parameters. The null hypothesis is tested by *inferential statistics.*

objective measure Any measure that requires little or no judgment on the part of the person making the measurement. Objective measures are more resistant to experimenter biases than *subjective measures.*

observation Empirical process in which data about a phenomenon are gathered and reported. Observation is the central task in all research.

observation phase of research Research phase in which the data are gathered.

observational variable Any variable that is observed and not manipulated in research. The term is usually used in low-constraint research, in which the independent and dependent variable distinction does not apply.

observed organismic variable Any characteristic of the participant that can be measured and used for classification.

one-way ANOVA Statistical procedure that evaluates differences in mean scores of two or more groups in which the groups are defined by a single independent variable.

open-ended items Items or questions on a questionnaire that the participant answers in his or her own words.

operational definition Detailed set of procedures used to measure or manipulate a variable.

ordered data Data produced by ordinal scales of measurement.

orderliness belief Belief dating from ancient artisans that events in nature are predictable.

ordinal scale Scale of measurement in which the scores can be rank ordered, but the distance between any two adjacent scores will not necessarily be the same as the distance between any other two adjacent scores.

ordinate The *y*-axis on a graph.

organismic variable Any characteristic of the participant that can be used for classification. An organismic variable may be either directly observed (*observed organismic variable*) or inferred on the basis of the responses of the participant (*response-inferred organismic variable*).

outline The essential features or main aspects of ideas, organized under headings and subheadings.

panel design See *longitudinal design.*

parallel distributed processing (PDP) See *connectionist models.*

parametric statistics Inferential statistical procedures that rely on sample statistics to draw inferences about such population parameters as the mean and variance.

parsimony The guiding principle in science that a simple theory is preferred over a more complex theory if both theories explain the data equally well.

partial correlation A correlation between two variables in which the effects of a third variable are statistically removed from one of the two original variables before computing the correlation.

partial counterbalancing Control procedure used in within-subjects designs to control for sequence effects. Partial counterbalancing is used when there are too many conditions to make complete counterbalancing feasible.

participant assignment Procedure of assigning participants to groups or conditions. Participant assignment may be made randomly (*experimental research*) or on the basis of preexisting variables (*differential research*).

participant effects See *subject effects.*

participant observer Any researcher gathering data in a setting in which the researcher is an active part. Participant observation is less obtrusive than other observational procedures, but the possibility for experimenter reactivity is high.

participant selection The procedures by which potential participants for a research study are identified. Participant selection affects *external validity.* Participant selection may include *random sampling, stratified random sampling,* or designation of an *ad hoc sample.*

participant variable Synonymous with *organismic variable.*

participants at risk Participants involved in a research project that poses potential risk to them. When participants are at risk, the researcher is responsible for informing them of the risks and minimizing the risks.

participants' rights Guarantees of proper treatment that participants can justly expect in research.

participants subsection That section of a research report in which the participants and the methods of participant selection are described.

partitioned In an ANOVA calculation, the total sum of squares is separated (partitioned) into the between-groups sum of squares and the within-groups sum of squares.

path analysis A procedure that seeks to unravel causal links between variables from correlational data by hypothesizing detailed causal models and factoring the correlation matrix to see how closely the pattern of observed relationships fits the hypothesized causal model.

Pearson product–moment correlation Index of the degree of linear relationship between two variables in which each variable represents *score data.*

percent agreement A measure of interrater reliability in which the percentage of times that the raters agree is computed.

percentile Normative score that converts the raw score earned by a participant into a number from 0 to 100 that reflects the percentage of participants who score lower.

percentile rank See *percentile.*

perfect correlation Correlation of a +1.00 or a −1.00. When two variables are perfectly correlated, knowing the score on one variable permits perfect prediction of the other. In a scatter plot, a perfect correlation is shown by all points falling on a straight line (but not a horizontal or vertical line).

personal computer A self-contained computer dedicated to serving the needs of a single user. Most personal computers are either desktop models, with a keyboard, screen, and a box housing the computer and accessories, or notebook models, in which all critical elements are built into a small, portable package. Personal computers are often contrasted with *mainframe computers.*

phase of research The stages of a research project. These phases are idea generating, problem definition, procedures design, observation, data analysis, interpretation, and communication.

placebo An inert or innocuous control treatment or medication that appears to participants to be identical to the experimental treatment.

placebo effect Any observed improvement due to a sham treatment. Placebo effects are probably the result of participants' expectations for treatment effectiveness.

planned comparison Sometimes called a *contrast;* a specific comparison of mean performance between groups in a research study. Planned comparisons must be planned before data collection and should be based on theoretical considerations.

population Any clearly defined set of objects or events (people, occurrences, animals, etc.). Populations usually represent all events in a particular class.

population parameters Any summary statistic computed on the entire population.

positive correlation Relationship between two variables in which one variable increases as the other variable increases.

positive practice effect Enhancement of performance on a dependent measure that results from previous exposure to the measurement procedure.

positively skewed A distribution in which scores are concentrated near the bottom of the curve, thinning out as the curve approaches the top, giving the characteristic tail that points to the top or positive end of the distribution.

post hoc comparison Also called a posteriori comparison or incidental comparison. See *post hoc test.*

post hoc test Secondary analysis that evaluates relationships between variables that were not specifically hypothesized by the researcher prior to the study.

power See *power of a statistical test.*

power analysis Procedures that determine the power of a statistical test or research procedure to detect group differences if these differences exist.

power of a statistical test Ability of an inferential statistical procedure to detect differences between groups when such differences actually exist.

practical significance Often contrasted with *statistical significance.* Practical significance refers to whether the observed difference between groups or conditions is large enough to have a meaningful impact on the participant.

practice effects Any change in performance that results from previous exposure to the measurement procedure.

precision versus relevance problem The concern that higher-constraint, laboratory research may be less relevant than lower-constraint naturalistic research and, conversely, that lower-constraint research may be unacceptably imprecise.

pre-data check An assessment of each point in a research design prior to data collection.

predictor See *predictor measure.*

predictor measure The variable used to predict the *criterion measure.* For example, a test score (the predictor measure) might be used to predict future performance in a job.

preexisting variable Any characteristic of participants that existed prior to the research study. If preexisting variables are not controlled, they can confound the results of a study. Preexisting variables are particularly problematic in differential research.

pretest–posttest design Set of research designs in which participants are tested at two points in time, that is, before and after the administration of the independent variable.

pretest–posttest, natural control-group design Nonexperimental research design in which preexisting groups are measured before and after the manipulation of an independent variable. These naturally occurring groups are assigned to different levels of the independent variable.

principle of initial equivalence The necessity in an experiment of having comparison groups equal on the dependent measure at the beginning of the experiment before any manipulation occurs.

probability The ratio of specific events to the total number of possible events. For example, the probability of rolling a five on each roll of a die is 1/6.

probability sampling A sampling procedure in which all participants have an equal probability of being selected and the selection of any participant does not change the probability of selecting any other participant. Often contrasted with *nonprobability sampling.*

probe Refers to the process of comparing the mean performance among groups of participants in a research study to see which groups are statistically different from one another.

problem-definition phase of research Research phase in which research ideas are converted into precise questions to be studied.

procedure subsection The section of a research report that describes how the study was carried out.

procedures-design phase of research Research phase in which the specific procedures to be used in the gathering and analyzing of data are developed.

process of inquiry The perspective taken by this text that views research as a dynamic process focused on formulating questions and systematically answering these questions through research.

program evaluation research Specific area of field research for evaluating the effectiveness of a program in meeting its stated goals.

properties of the abstract number system See *abstract number system.*

pseudoscience Popular distortions of scientific knowledge and procedures that appear on the surface to be scientific, but lack critical scientific procedures. Some fields, such as astrology, extrasensory perception, the study of alien abductions, and medical quackery, have traditionally relied on pseudoscience to appear legitimate.

psychoanalysis The psychological treatment approach based on the psychodynamic theories of Freud and his followers.

psychology Scientific study of the behavior of organisms.

psychophysics One of the earliest approaches to the study of behavior. Psychophysics involves the presentation of precise stimuli to participants under controlled conditions and the recording of the participants' responses.

pure research Another term for basic or fundamental research. See *basic research.*

***p*-value** The probability of obtaining the statistic (e.g., *t* or *F*) or a larger statistic by chance if the null hypothesis is true. Statistical analysis programs routinely compute *p*-values in addition to the test statistic.

qualitative research method A research approach that seeks to understand psychological operations by observing the broad, interconnected pattern of variables, rather than the strength of the statistical relationship of variables.

quasi-experimental design Research designs that approximate experimental designs, providing experimentlike controls to minimize threats to internal validity.

questionnaire A psychological instrument that lists questions to be asked of participants.

random-number generator A computer function that generates an endless sequence of random numbers.

random order of presentation A way of controlling for carry-over effects in within-subjects designs. Each participant is tested under all conditions, but the order of the conditions is randomly determined for each participant.

random sampling Procedure for selecting participants in which each participant has an equal chance of being selected and the selection of any one participant does not affect the probability of selecting any other participant. In most research, random sampling from the population is not feasible. Instead, researchers rely on sampling from an *accessible population.*

randomization Any procedure that assigns a value in an unpredictable or random way, such as by use of tables of random numbers. Randomization procedures may be used for selecting participants, assigning participants to groups or conditions, or assigning the order in which participants experience successive conditions.

randomize within blocks A control procedure to reduce sequence effects that involves using a block of one trial from each condition in the experiment and randomizing their order before going on to the next block.

randomized, posttest-only, control-group design Experimental design in which participants are randomly assigned to two groups, and each group is tested on the dependent variable after the independent-variable manipulation.

randomized, pretest–posttest, control-group design Experimental design in which participants are randomly assigned to two groups and each participant is tested on the dependent variable both before and after manipulation of the independent variable.

range Distance between the lowest score and the highest score.

ratio scale Scale of measurement in which the intervals between scores are equal and the zero point on the scale represents none of the quality being measured (a true zero). Examples of ratio scales are height, weight, and frequency of an event.

rationalism   A way of knowing about the universe that relies on systematic logic and a set of premises from which logical inferences are made.

reactive measure   Any measurement procedure that produces different scores depending on whether participants are aware that they are being measured.

records (in computer files)   Each record typically represents the data for a single subject or a group of matched subjects.

reference list   The listing of sources of information (e.g., research article, book, or chapter) that contributed to a research paper. The *APA Publication Manual* specifies how to list a reference so that others can quickly find it.

reference section   The section of a research report that follows the substantive sections of the report and lists each paper and article that contributed to the ideas and procedures of the study.

regression   A mathematical procedure that produces an equation for predicting a variable (the criterion) from one or more other variables (the predictors). The procedures for determining the regression equation are designed to maximize the accuracy of the prediction. Linear regression equations are usually used, although it is possible to develop nonlinear regression equations.

regression equation   The mathematical equation that predicts the value of one variable from one or more other variables.

regression to the mean   Potential confounding variable that occurs whenever participants are selected because of extreme scores (either very high or very low). When retested on the same or a similar variable, the original extreme sample tends to be less extreme on average.

reification of a construct   Incorrectly accepting a construct as a fact.

relationship   Any connection between two or more variables. There are many types of relationships, from contingencies to causal relationships.

relative score   See *standard score.*

reliability   Index of the consistency of a measuring instrument in repeatedly providing the same score for a given participant. There are many different types of reliability, each referring to a different aspect of consistency, including *interrater reliability, test–retest reliability,* and *internal consistency reliability.*

repeated-measures ANOVA   Statistical procedure to evaluate the mean differences between two or more conditions in which participants are tested under each condition. The repeated-measures ANOVA takes into account the fact that the same participants appear in all conditions.

repeated-measures design   Any research design in which participants are tested more than once. Examples of such designs are pretest–posttest designs, within-subjects designs, and time-series designs.

repeated-measures factorials   Factorial design in which all factors are within-subjects factors. Each participant is tested under every possible combination of conditions in the design.

replication   To repeat a study with no changes in the procedure (*exact replication*), small-theory-driven changes (*systematic replication*), or changes in the operational definitions of variables (*conceptual replication*).

representative sample   Sample of participants that adequately reflects the characteristics of the population from which the sample was drawn.

representativeness   Degree to which a sample is representative of the population from which the sample was drawn.

research data   See *data.*

research ethics   Set of guidelines designed to protect human and nonhuman participants from the risks of participating in research.

research hypothesis   Precise and formal statement of a research question. The research hypothesis is constructed by adding operational definitions for each variable to the statement of the problem.

research setting   Any characteristics of the situation and/or surroundings in which a research project is carried out. Settings may vary from natural, real-world settings to highly constrained and carefully controlled laboratory settings.

response-inferred organismic variable   A hypothesized internal attribute of an organism that cannot be directly observed but, instead, is inferred on the basis of observed behavior. Examples are intelligence, anxiety, and love.

response-set biases   Any tendency for a participant to distort responses to a dependent measure. Response-set biases create measurement errors.

results section   The section of a research report that describes the findings and reports on the statistical analyses of the data.

reversal (ABA) design   Research design often used with single participants, in which the effects of an independent variable on a dependent variable are inferred from observations made first without the independent variable present, then with the independent variable present, and again without the independent variable present. If an effect is noticed both when the independent variable is added and when it is later removed, it is likely that the independent variable is causally related to the dependent measure.

rival hypothesis   Any feasible alternative hypothesis to the causal hypothesis.

robust   A statistical test is said to be robust to violations of the assumptions on which the test is based if the test consistently leads to accurate conclusions despite the assumption violations.

row means   In factorial designs, one factor is usually illustrated as separate rows of data in which each row represents a different level of the factor. A second factor is illustrated as columns of data in which the columns represent various levels of the second factor. Row means are computed by taking the mean of all participants who appear in a given row regardless of their level on the second factor.

sample   Any subset drawn from a population. Researchers work with samples of participants and draw inferences about the larger population.

sample statistic   Descriptive index of some characteristic of the sample of participants. *Population parameters* are estimated on the basis of sample statistics.

sampling   Process of drawing a sample from a population. Many sampling techniques are available, including *random sampling, stratified random sampling,* and various nonrandom sampling techniques.

sampling error   Chance variation among different samples drawn from the same population.

sampling frame   In survey research, a sampling frame is a list of all participants from an available population. The sampling frame is a subset of a larger population from which a representative sample is drawn.

scale attenuation effects   Any aspect of the measuring instrument that limits the ability of the instrument to make discriminations at the top of the scale (*ceiling effects*) or the bottom of the scale (*floor effects*).

scales of measurement   Characteristics of the scores produced by a measurement instrument. Scales of measurement vary on how closely scores match the real number system. There are four generally recognized scales of measurement: *nominal, ordinal, interval,* and *ratio scales.*

scatter plot   Graphic technique that illustrates the relationship between two or more variables. In a two-variable situation, we construct a scatter plot by labeling the *x*-axis with one variable and the *y*-axis with the other variable and plotting each participant's pair of scores in the *xy* coordinate system. Scatter plots illustrate the type, direction, and strength of relationships.

science   Way of knowing that combines rationalism and empiricism to form a system that places great demands on procedures, data, and theories.

scientific research   Systematic research that is based on the combination of rationalism and empiricism, that is, based on science.

Scientific Revolution   Period of time (15th through 17th centuries) in which scientific methods and applications became independent from theology and developed rapidly into a generally recognized way of understanding nature.

scientist   Anyone who utilizes the methods of science to study phenomena.

scientist–practitioner model   A model for the training of clinical psychologists that teaches both research and clinical skills in an integrated manner. The rationale is that clinical psychology is an emerging discipline in which practitioners need to learn from new research and contribute to the knowledge base by conducting their own research. This approach is also known as the Boulder model, named after the conference held in Boulder, Colorado, at which these principles were endorsed.

score data   Data produced by interval or ratio scales of measurement.

secondary analyses   Analyses that look at questions that are not directly stated in the original research hypothesis but may be relevant to understanding the primary analyses.

selection   A potential confounding variable that involves any process that may create groups not equivalent at the beginning of the study.

sequence effects   The confounding effects on performance in later conditions due to having experienced previous conditions.

serendipity   Unanticipated, seemingly "lucky" scientific discoveries. Alert scientists seize on and develop unanticipated observations that others might have ignored.

similarity–uniqueness paradox   The tendency to simplify comparisons between objects by seeing them as either similar to one another or different from one another, when in reality they are probably both.

simple random sampling   See *random sampling.*

single-blind procedure   Research procedure in which the researcher is unaware of the condition to which each participant is assigned. The purpose of the single-blind procedure is to minimize measurement biases.

single-group, posttest-only study   Nonexperimental research design in which the researcher manipulates the independent variable and then takes a postmanipulation measure on the dependent variable. The difference between this design and an ex post facto design is the manipulation of the independent variable.

single-group, pretest–posttest study   Nonexperimental design in which a group of participants is measured on a dependent variable, the independent variable is manipulated, and a second measure on the dependent variable is taken. The design allows comparison between pretest and posttest scores, but, because no control group exists, confounding variables are not adequately controlled.

single-subject clinical replication   A specialized form of replication for single-subject designs used primarily in clinical settings.

single-subject direct replication   Repeating a single-subject experiment with the same participant or other participants with the same target behavior in order to establish the effectiveness and reliability of the procedure. Direct replication does not establish its generalization to other persons, conditions, or target behaviors. For that, *single-subject systematic replication is needed.*

single-subject experimental designs   Research designs that seek information sufficient to draw causal inferences. Single-subject designs have some form of built-in control to compensate for the fact that no control group exists. Typical examples of single-subject designs include the *reversal design; single-subject, randomized time-series design;* and *multiple-baseline design.*

single-subject, randomized, time-series design   Design frequently used in naturalistic settings in which multiple measures on the dependent variable are taken both before and after manipulation of an independent variable. This design provides partial control of confounding variables by allowing the researcher to see patterns in the movement of the dependent measure over time and specific changes in the dependent measure that appear to be a function of the manipulation of the independent measure.

single-subject systematic replication   The carefully planned and executed testing for generalization of a procedure to other conditions, persons, and target behaviors after direct replication has established the effectiveness and reliability of the procedure for one or more participants with the same target behavior.

single-variable, between-subjects design   Research designs that include only one independent variable and in which participants are randomly assigned to groups.

single-variable designs   Research designs that include just one independent variable.

skeptic   A person who characteristically applies skepticism—the unwillingness to accept information as valid without documentation to confirm it.

skepticism   Unwillingness to accept information as valid without documentation to confirm it. Skepticism is one of the strongest tools available to scientists.

skewed distribution   Any distribution of scores in which scores bunch up at the end of the distribution. Skewed distribution is often contrasted with *symmetric distribution.*

skewed negatively   Distribution in which scores are concentrated near the top of the scale, with few scores near the lower end of the scale.

skewed positively   Distribution in which scores are concentrated near the bottom of the scale, with few scores near the top of the scale.

social desirability   Response set in which participants tend to say what they believe is expected of them (i.e., they present themselves in a socially desirable light).

Solomon's four-group design   Sophisticated experimental design that combines the *randomized, posttest-only, control-group design* and the *randomized, pretest–posttest, control-group design.*

sophisticated empiricism   Indirect observation of facts through mediational constructs and procedures. Sophisticated empiricism does not limit us to our own personal senses. For example, we cannot directly see or measure gravity, but we can infer it from observing falling bodies.

Spearman rank–order correlation   Correlation coefficient that indexes the degree of relationship between two variables, each of which is measured on an ordinal scale.

specific means comparison   The process of evaluating differences in group performance in a research study with more than two groups to see which groups are statistically different from which other groups. Specific means comparisons can be carried out as either *planned comparison* or *post hoc tests.*

spread   Synonymous with *variability.*

spreadsheet   A mechanism for organizing data in rows and columns. Typically, a data spreadsheet is organized so that each row represents the data for one participant and each column represents the scores on one variable.

SPSS for Windows A computer package (*Statistical Package for the Social Sciences*) for statistical data analysis on a Windows-based computer.

standard deviation An index of variability that is the square root of variance.

standard error of the differences between means The denominator in a *t*-test.

standard score A score that gives the relative standing in a distribution. It is computed by subtracting the distribution mean from the score and dividing that difference by the standard deviation of the distribution.

statement of the problem First major refinement of initial research ideas in which a clear statement of the expected relationship between variables is made. The statement of the problem is refined into one or more research hypotheses by specifying the operational definitions of each variable.

Statistica Computer package for statistical data analysis.

Statistical Analysis System (SAS) Computer package for statistical data analysis.

statistical hypothesis Synonymous with *null hypothesis*.

Statistical Package for the Social Sciences (SPSS) Computer package for statistical data analysis.

statistical power See *power of a statistical test*.

statistical significance A finding is said to achieve statistical significance if it is unlikely that such a finding would have occurred by chance alone. See *statistically significant differences*.

statistical symbols Conventional shorthand used to denote statistical terms. For example, α is the statistical symbol for the level of Type I error.

statistical validity Accuracy of conclusions drawn from a statistical test. To enhance statistical validity, we must meet the critical assumptions of a statistical procedure.

statistically equal When participants have been randomly assigned to groups, the groups are said to be statistically equal because the small differences that do exist are the result of sampling error.

statistically significant correlation A correlation large enough that we would conclude that there is a non-zero relationship between the variables.

statistically significant differences A large enough difference between two or more means that it is unlikely to be a chance occurrence.

statistics Mathematical procedures used to evaluate the results of a research study. Some statistical proce-

dures describe data (*descriptive statistics*); others help to draw conclusions from the data (*inferential statistics*).

status survey A simple survey designed to provide a description of the current status of some population characteristic.

Statview A statistical analysis package for Macintosh computers.

stimulus variable Any part of the environment to which an organism reacts. A stimulus variable may be a natural part of the environment and observed by the researcher or may be actively manipulated by the researcher.

strata Subpopulations within populations from which we draw samples. See *stratified random sampling*.

stratified random sampling Variation of random sampling in which a population is divided into narrow strata along some critical dimension. Participants are then selected randomly from each strata in the same proportion that the strata are represented in the population. Stratified random sampling increases the representativeness of samples and is used extensively in sophisticated survey research.

structuralism A philosophical perspective in which scientists seek to identify the structure of the underlying mechanisms that control behavior. This approach was popularized by Wundt. Often contrasted with *functionalism*.

subject assignment See *participant assignment*.

subject effects Any response by participants that does not represent the way that they would normally behave if not under study. Two powerful subject effects are the *placebo effect* and a participant's response to *demand characteristics*.

subject selection See *participant selection*.

subject variables See *oranismic variables*.

subjective measures Measures based primarily on participants' uncorroborated opinions, feelings, biases, or judgments. Subjective measures, as contrasted with *objective measures,* are more prone to distortions due to *experimenter effects*.

subjects at risk See *participants at risk*.

subjects' rights See *participants' rights*.

subjects subsection See *participants subsection*.

subjects term In a repeated-measures ANOVA, the subjects term is the individual differences component of the within-groups variability.

sum of squares Sum of the squared differences from the mean. The sum of squares is the numerator in the variance formula.

summary statistics Descriptive statistics that provide, in a single number, some general characteristic of the sample. Typical summary statistics are the mean, median, variance, and standard deviation.

survey A set of questions posed to a group of participants about their attitudes, beliefs, plans, life-styles, or any other variable of interest.

survey research Research that seeks to use survey procedures to identify relationships among the variables being surveyed.

symmetric distribution Graphical representation of any distribution in which the right half of the distribution is a mirror image of the left half. Symmetric distributions are often contrasted with *skewed distributions*.

systematic between-groups variance The variability between groups that is brought about by either the experimental manipulation or by some uncontrolled confounding variable.

systematic influence The stimulating effects of previous research and theories in providing testable propositions for further study.

systematic replication Repeating a study with small, theory-based changes in procedures. Systematic replication is more common than exact replication because it verifies original findings while also expanding knowledge of the phenomena.

table Organizational device in which information is summarized and organized.

table of random numbers A table containing a long list of randomly generated numbers. Such tables are used for random selection and assignment of participants.

target population Population to which we hope to generalize the findings of a research study. The researcher rarely has access to more than a portion of the target population.

taxometric search procedures A set of mathematical procedures that seeks to identify taxometric categories. If the sample includes individuals from more than one taxon, predictable mathematical relationships should exist between traits, and these mathematical relationships should be different from those expected if there are no underlying taxometric categories.

taxon A subgroup that is different in kind and not just degree from other subgroups. For example, males and females represent different taxa (plural of taxon) because they are genetically different from each other.

technology Physical instruments or tools used by researchers. Technology does not define science; it merely provides tools for scientists.

tenacity Way of knowing based on accepting an idea as true because it has been accepted as true for a long period of time.

testing Potential confounding variable that represents any change in a participant's score on a dependent measure due to the participant having been tested previously.

test–retest reliability Index of the consistency in scores over time. Test–retest reliability is computed by calculating the Pearson's product–moment correlation between scores from two testings separated by some specified time interval.

theology The philosophical tenets and/or study of religion.

theoretical concept Abstraction (thought or idea) that defines the relationship between two or more variables.

theory The collection of ideas about how and why variables are related to one another. It is built on empirical observations and is validated by making predictions deduced from the theory, which are then empirically tested.

time-series design See *interrupted time-series design*.

title page The first page of a research report manuscript that lists the authors and their affiliations, the title of the paper, and a running head (a brief title that will appear at the top of each page in the published paper).

treatment See *manipulation*.

trimodal A distribution that has three modes (most frequently occurring score).

true experiment See *experiment*.

true zero Characteristic of a measurement scale in which zero represents none of the concept being measured.

t-test Statistical procedure designed to test for mean differences between two groups of participants.

t-test for independent groups Statistical procedure designed to test for mean differences between two groups of participants in which all participants appear in one and only one group.

two-group posttest-only design A design in which two groups of participants are compared after some manipulation of the independent variable.

two-way ANOVA Statistical procedure for the analysis of a factorial design with two independent variables.

Type I error Probability of rejecting the *null hypothesis* when the null hypothesis is true.

Type II error Probability of not rejecting the *null hypothesis* when the null hypothesis is false.

univariate Having to do with one variable. For example, a univariate distribution would provide the distribution for a single variable.

univariate designs   See *single-variable designs.*

unobtrusive measure   Any measure that can be taken on participants without their being aware that they are being measured.

unobtrusive observer   Anyone who is able to observe the behavior of participants without the participants' being aware that they are being observed.

validity   Major concept in research that has several meanings (*internal validity, external validity, construct validity, statistical validity*). In a general sense, validity refers to the methodological and/or conceptual soundness of research (e.g., "Does this experiment really test what it is supposed to test?").

variability   Differences among participants on any given variable.

variable   Any characteristic that can take on different values.

variance   Summary statistic that indicates the degree of variability among participants. The variance is es-

sentially the average squared deviation from the mean and is the square of the standard deviation.

within-groups variance   Variability among participants within a group or condition. It provides a basis for comparing mean differences between groups in most statistical procedures.

within-subjects design   Research design in which individual differences are controlled by having the same participants tested under all conditions.

within-subjects factorial   A factorial design in which each participant appears in each condition.

within-subjects factors   Independent variables in factorial designs in which each participant is tested under all conditions.

x-axis (abscissa)   The horizontal axis in a graph.

y-axis (ordinate)   The vertical axis in a graph.

Z-score   See *standard score.*

References

Abondanza, M. (2000). *Report of the Membership Committee Chair:* Ottawa: Canadian Psychological Association.

Abramowitz, J. S. (1998). Does cognitive–behavioral therapy cure obsessive–compulsive disorder? A meta-analytic evaluation of clinical significance. *Behavior Therapy, 29,* 339–355.

Abramson, L. Y., Seligman, M. E. P., & Teasdale, J. D. (1978). Learned helplessness in humans: Critique and reformulation. *Journal of Abnormal Psychology, 87,* 49–74.

American College of Surgeons. (1991). The use of animals in research. *Bulletin of the American College of Surgeons, 76,* 18.

American Psychological Association. (1986). *Guidelines for ethical conduct in the care and use of animals.* Washington, DC: Author.

American Psychological Association. (1996). *Guidelines for ethical conduct in the care and use of animals.* Available at either **www.apa.org/science/anguide.html** or American Psychological Association, Science Directorate, 750 First Street, Washington D.C. 20002-4242.

American Psychological Association. (1998). Ethics of research with human participants. Draft report being circulated for comment. Available at **www.apa.org.**

American Psychological Association. (2000). *Membership of the APA.* Available at **www.apa.org.**

American Psychological Association. (2001). *Publication manual of the American Psychological Association* (5th ed.). Washington, DC: Author.

Anastasi, A., & Urbina, S. (1997). *Psychological testing* (7th ed.). Upper Saddle River, NJ: Prentice Hall.

Anderson, C. A., Lindsay, J. J., & Bushman, B. J. (1999). Research in the psychological laboratory: Truth or triviality? *Current Directions in Psychological Science, 8,* 3–9.

Auge, I. I., Wayne, K., & Auge, S. M. (1999). Naturalistic observation of athletic drug-use patterns and behavior in professional-caliber bodybuilders. *Substance Use and Misuse, 34,* 217–249.

Bachrach, A. J. (1981). *Psychological research: An introduction.* New York: Random House.

Baker, L. A., Mack, W., Moffitt, T. E., & Mednick, S. (1989). Sex differences in property crime in a Danish adoption cohort. *Behavior Genetics, 19,* 355–370.

Bandura, A. I. (1969). *Principles of behavior modification.* New York: Holt, Rinehart and Winston.

Barber, T. X., & Silver, M. J. (1968). Fact, fiction and the experimenter bias effect. *Psychological Bulletin Monograph Supplement, 70,* 1–29.

Barlow, D. H. (Ed.). (2001). *Clinical handbook of psychological disorders* (3rd ed.). New York: Guilford.

Barlow, D. H., & Hersen, M. (1984). *Single case experimental designs: Strategies for studying behavior change* (2nd ed.). New York: Pergamon.

Bartlett, J. (1980). *Bartlett's familiar quotations.* (15th ed.). Boston: Little, Brown.

Bass, E., & Davis, L. (1988). *The courage to heal: A guide for women survivors of sexual abuse.* New York: Harper & Row.

Bass, E., & Davis, L. (1994). *The courage to heal: A guide for women survivors of sexual abuse: featuring "Honoring the truth: A response to the backlash"* (3rd ed. Rev). New York: HarperPerennial.

Benjafield, J. G. (1996). *A history of psychology.* Boston: Allyn & Bacon.

Benjamin, L. J. (Ed.). (1997). *A history of psychology* (2nd ed.). New York: McGraw-Hill.

Bergin, A. E., & Strupp, H. H. (1970). New directions in psychotherapy research. *Journal of Abnormal Psychology, 76,* 13–26.

Blanchard, J. J., Gangestad, S. W., Brown, S. A., & Horan, W. P. (2000). Hedonic capacity and schizotypy revisited: A taxometric analysis of social anhedonia. *Journal of Abnormal Psychology, 109,* 87–95.

Blanchard, J. J., Horan, W. P., & Brown, S. A. (2001). Diagnostic differences in social anhedonia: A longitudinal study of schizophrenia and major depressive disorder. *Journal of Abnormal Psychology, 110,* 363–371.

Bleuler, E. (1950). The fundamental symptoms. In E. Bleuler (Ed.), *Dementia praecox; or the group of schizophrenias* (J. Ziskin, trans.) (pp. 14–54). New York: International University Press. (Original work published in 1911.)

Boesch, C., & Boesch-Acherman, H. (1991). Dim forest, bright chimps. *Natural History,* September, 50–56.

Bornas, X., Tortella-Feliu, M., Llabres, J., & Fullana, M. A. (2001). Computer-assisted exposure treatment for flight phobia: A controlled study. *Psychotherapy Research, 11,* 259–273.

Botting, J. H., & Morrison, A. R. (1997). Animal research is vital to medicine. *Scientific American, 276*(2), 83–85.

Bower, B. (1998). Psychology's tangled web. *Science News, 153*(25), 394–395.

Brewer, B. W., & Shillinglaw, R. (1992). Evaluation of a psychological skills training workshop for male intercollegiate lacrosse players. *Sport Psychologist, 6,* 139–147.

Briem, V., & Hedman, L. R. (2001). Behavioural effects of mobile telephone use during simulated driving. *Ergonomics, 38,* 2536–2562.

Brotemarkle, R. A. (1966). Fifty years of clinical psychology: Clinical psychology, 1896–1946. In I. N. Mensh (Ed.), *Clinical psychology: Science and profession* (pp. 63–68). New York: Macmillan.

Busch, L. (1991). Science under wraps in Prince William Sound. *Science, 252,* 772–773.

Campbell, D. T. (1969). Reforms as experiments. *American Psychologist, 24,* 409–429.

Campbell, D. T., & Stanley, J. C. (1966). *Experimental and quasi-experimental designs for research on teaching.* Chicago: Rand McNally.

Campbell, F. A., Ramey, C. T., Pungello, E., Sparling, J., & Miller-Johnson, S. (2002). Early childhood education: Young adult outcomes from the Abecedarian Project. *Applied Developmental Science, 6,* 42–57.

Canadian Council on Animal Care. (1993). *Guide to the care and use of experimental animals.* Ottawa: Author.

Cantor-Graae, E., McNeil, T. F., Torrey, E. F., Quinn, P., Bowler, A., Sjöström, K., & Rawlings, R. (1994). Are neurological abnormalities in well discordant monozygotic co-twins of schizophrenic subjects the result of perinatal trauma? *American Journal of Psychiatry, 151,* 1194–1199.

Carroll, J. D., & Arabie, P. (1998). Multidimension scaling. In M. H. Birnbaum (Ed.), *Measurement, judgment, and decision making: Handbook of perception and cognition* (2nd ed.) (pp. 179–250). San Diego, CA: Academic Press.

Carroll, M. E., & Overmier, J. B. (Eds.) (2001). *Animal research and human health: Advancing human welfare through behavioral science.* Washington, DC: American Psychological Association.

Catalano, R., & Serxner, S. (1992). The effect of ambient threats to employment on low birthweight. *Journal of Health and Social Behavior, 33,* 363–377.

Chambless, D. L., & Ollendick, T. H. (2001). Empirically supported psychological interventions: Controversies and evidence. *Annual Review of Psychology, 52,* 635–716.

Chapman, L. J., & Chapman, J. P. (1969). Illusory correlation as an obstacle to the use of valid psychodiagnostic signs. *Journal of Abnormal Psychology, 74,* 271–287.

Chapman, L. J., & Chapman, J. P. (1973). *Disordered thought in schizophrenia.* Upper Saddle River, NJ: Prentice Hall.

Chapman, L. J., Chapman, J. P., & Raulin, M. L. (1976). Scales for physical and social anhedonia. *Journal of Abnormal Psychology, 85,* 374–382.

Chapman, L. J., Chapman, J. P., Kwapil, T. R., Eckblad, M., & Zinser, M. C. (1994). Putatively psychosis-prone subjects 10 years later. *Journal of Abnormal Psychology, 103,* 171–183.

Chapman, L. J., Chapman, J. P., Raulin, M. L., & Edell, W. S. (1978). Schizotypy and thought disorder as a high risk approach to schizophrenia. In G. Serban (Ed.), *Cognitive defects in the development of mental illness* (pp. 351–360). New York: Brunner-Mazel.

Cialdini, R. B. (1993). *Influence: The psychology of persuasion* (2nd ed.). New York: William Morrow.

Clagett, M. (1948). The medieval heritage: Religious, philosophic, scientific. In J. L. Blau, J. Buchler, & G. T. Matthews (Eds.), *Chapters in western civilization* (Vol. 1, pp. 74–122). New York: Columbia University Press.

Cohen, J. A. (1960). A coefficient of agreement for nominal scales. *Educational and Psychological Measurement, 20,* 37–46.

Cohen, J. A. (1988). *Statistical power analyses for the behavioral sciences* (2nd ed.). Mahwah, NJ: Erlbaum.

Cohen, J. A. (1992). A power primer. *Psychological Bulletin, 112,* 155–159.

Cohen, J., & Cohen P. (1983). *Applied multiple regression/correlation analysis for the behavioral sciences* (2nd ed.). Mahwah, NJ: Erlbaum.

Cohen, J. D., & Servan-Schreiber, D. (1992). Context, cortex, and dopamine: A connectionist approach to behavior and biology in schizophrenia. *Psychological Review, 99,* 34–77.

Collier, R. (1994). An historical overview of natural language processing systems that learn. *Artificial Intelligence Review, 8,* 17–54.

Collins, F. S., & Jegalien, K. G. (1999). Deciphering the code of life. *Scientific American, 281,* 6, 86–93.

Columbo, J. (2001). The development of visual attention in infants. *Annual Review of Psychology, 52,* 337–367.

Cook, T. D., & Campbell, D. T. (1979). *Quasi-experimentation: Design and analysis issues for field studies.* Chicago: Rand McNally.

Coombs, C. H., Raiffa, H., & Thrall, R. M. (1954). Some views on mathematical models and measurement theory. *Psychological Review, 61,* 132–144.

Cooper, H. M. (1998). *Synthesizing research: A guide for literature reviews.* Thousand Oaks, CA: Sage.

Cooper, H. M., & Lindsay, J. J. (1998). Research synthesis and meta-analysis. In L. Bickman & D. J. Rog (Eds.), *Handbook of applied research methods* (pp. 315–337). Thousand Oaks, CA: Sage.

Copi, I. M., & Cohen, C. (2002). *Introduction to logic* (11th ed.). Upper Saddle River, NJ: Prentice Hall.

Crawford, S. Y., Hurd, J. M., & Weller, A. C. (1996). *From print to electronic: The transformation of scientific communication.* Medford, NJ: American Society for Information Science by Information Today.

Curtis, D. R., & Crawford, J. M. (1969). Central synaptic transmission—microelectrophoretic studies. *Annual Review of Pharmocology, 9,* 209–240.

Danitz, T. (1997). Making up memories? *Insight on the News,* Dec. 15, 1997, *13*(46), 14–15.

Darley, J. M., & Latane, B. (1968). Bystander intervention in emergencies: Diffusion of responsibility. *Journal of Personality and Social Psychology, 8,* 377–383.

Darwin, C. (1859). *On the origin of species by means of natural selection, or the preservation of favored races in the struggle for life.* London: John Murray (New York: Modern Library, 1967).

Darwin, C. (1877). A biographical sketch of an infant. *Mind, 2,* 285–294.

Davis, P. W. (1997, July). *Naturalistic observations of 250 children hit in public settings.* Paper presented at the fifth International Family Violence Research Conference, Durham, NH.

Dawis, R. (1987). Scale construction. *Journal of Counseling Psychology, 39,* 481–489.

DeLeon, I. G., Iwata, B. A., & Roscoe, E. M. (1997). Displacement of leisure reinforcers by food during preference assessments. *Journal of Applied Behavior Analysis, 30,* 475–484.

DeLisi, L. E., Sakuma, M., Kushner, M., Finer, D. L., Hoff, A. L., & Crow, T. J. (1997). Anomalous cerebral asymmetry and language processing in schizophrenia. *Schizophrenia Bulletin, 23,* 255–271.

Dennett, D. C. (1993). Learning and labeling. *Mind and Language, 8,* 540–548.

Dermen, K. H., Cooper, M. L., & Agocha, V. B. (1998). Sex-related alcohol expectancies as moderators of the relationship between alcohol use and risky sex in adolescents. *Journal of Studies on Alcohol, 59,* 71–77.

Dertouzos, M. (1999). The future of computing. *Scientific American, 281*(2), 52–55.

Dollard, J., & Miller, N. E. (1950). *Personality and psychotherapy.* New York: McGraw-Hill.

Dunbar, K. (1994). How scientists really reason: Scientific reasoning in real-world laboratories. In R. J. Sternberg & J. Davidson (Eds.), *The nature of insight* (pp. 365–395). Cambridge, MA: MIT Press.

Eckblad, M. L., Chapman, L. J., Chapman, J. P., & Mishlove, M. (1982). *The revised social anhedonia scale.* Unpublished test, University of Wisconsin–Madison.

Edwards, A. L. (1985). *Experimental design in psychological research.* New York: Harper & Row.

Egeth, H. E., & Yantis, S. (1997). Visual attention: Control, representation, and time course. *Annual Review of Psychology, 48,* 269–297.

Everitt, B. J., & Robins, T. W. (1997). Central cholinergic systems and cognition. *Annual Review of Psychology, 48,* 649–684.

Fancher, R. E. (2000). Snapshots of Freud in America 1899–1999. *American Psychologist, 55,* 1025–1028.

Farkas, I., & Li, P. (2001), A self-organizing neural network model of the acquisition of word meaning. In E. M. Altmann, A. Cleeremans, C. D. Schunn, & W. D. Gray (Eds.), *Proceedings of the 2001 Fourth International Conference on Cognitive Modeling* (pp. 67–72). Mahwah, NJ: Erlbaum.

Farrington, B. (1949a). *Greek science: 1. Thales to Aristotle.* Harmondsworth: Pelican Books.

Farrington, B. (1949b). *Greek science: 2. Theophrastus to Galen.* Harmondsworth: Pelican Books.

Feng, A. S., & Ratnam, R. (2000). Neural basis of hearing in real-world situations. *Annual Review of Psychology, 51,* 699–725.

Ferraro, F. R., Szigeti, E., Dawes, K. J., & Pan, S. (1999). A survey regarding the University of North Dakota Institutional Review Board: Data, attitudes, and perceptions. *Journal of Psychology, 133,* 272–280.

Festinger, L. (1957). *A theory of cognitive dissonance.* Stanford, CA: Stanford University Press.

Fisher, R. A. (1935). *The design of experiments.* London: Oliver & Boyd.

Freedman, R., Adler, L. E., Olincy, A., Waldo, M. C., Ross, R. G., Stevens, K. E., & Leonard, S. (2002). Input dysfunction, schizotypy, and genetic models of schizophrenia. *Schizophrenia Research, 54,* 25–32.

Freud, S. (1938a). The interpretation of dreams. In A. A. Brill (Ed. & Trans.), *The basic writings of Sigmund Freud* (pp. 179–549). New York: Random House (originally published in 1900).

Freud, S. (1938b). The psychopathology of everyday life. In A. A. Brill (Ed. & Trans.), *The basic writings of Sigmund Freud* (pp. 33–178). New York: Random House (originally published 1901).

Gabrieli, J. D. E. (1998). Cognitive neuroscience of human memory. *Annual Review of Psychology, 49,* 87–115.

Gaito, J. (1980). Measurement scales and statistics: Resurgence of an old misconception. *Psychological Bulletin, 87,* 564–567.

Gelfand, H., & Walker, C. J. (1994). *Mastering APA style: Student's workbook and training guide* (2nd ed.). Washington, DC: American Psychological Association.

Gilbert, W. (1600). *De magnete, magnetisque, corporibus, et de magno magnete, tellure physiologia nova.* London.

Gillam, C. (1999). Kansas takes evolution out of curriculum. *Buffalo News,* Aug. 12, 1999 (p. A-5).

Ginsburg, H. P., Inoue, N., Seo, K. (1999). Young children doing mathematics: Observations of everyday activities. In J. V. Copley (Ed.), *Mathematics in the early years* (pp. 88–99). Washington, DC: National Association for the Education of Young Children.

Glanz, J. (2000). State insecurity: The trials of secret science. *New York Times,* June 18, 2000 (p. 4–4).

Glass, G. V., Wilson, V. L., & Gottman, J. M. (1975). *Design and analysis of time series.* Boulder, CO: Laboratory of Educational Research Press.

Gleick, J. (1987). *Chaos: Making a new science.* New York: Penguin Books.

Goodall, J. (1971). *In the shadow of man.* Boston: Houghton Mifflin.

Goodall, J. (1978). Chimp killings: Is it the man in them? *Science News, 113,* 276.

Goodall, J. (1986). *The chimpanzees of Gombe.* Cambridge, MA: Belknap Press/Harvard University Press.

Gooding, D. C., Kwapil, T. R., & Tallent, K. A. (1999). Wisconsin Card Sorting Test deficits in schizotypic individuals. *Schizophrenia Research, 40,* 201–209.

Goodwin, C. J. (1999). *A history of modern psychology.* New York: Wiley.

Gottesman, I. I. (1991). *Schizophrenia genesis: The origins of madness.* New York: Freeman.

Gould, S. J. (1997, May). Leonardo's living earth. *Natural History, 106,* 18.

Graham, K., & Wells, S. (2001). Aggression among young adults in the social context of the bar. *Addiction Research and Theory, 9,* 193–219.

Graziano, A. M. (1974). *Child without tomorrow.* Elmsford, NY: Pergamon Press.

Graziano, A. M. (1992). Why we should study sub-abuse violence against children. *Child, Youth, and Family Services Quarterly, 15*(4), 8–9.

Graziano, A. M. (2001). *Developmental disabilities: Introduction to a diverse field.* Boston: Allyn & Bacon.

Graziano, A. M., & Kean, J. (1968). Programmed relaxation and reciprocal inhibition with psychotic children. *Behaviour Research and Therapy, 6,* 433–437.

Graziano, A. M., & Mooney, K. C. (1982). Behavioral treatment of "nightfears:" A 2 to 3 year follow-up.

Journal of Consulting and Clinical Psychology, 50, 598–599.

Graziano, M. S. A., Cooke, D. F., & Taylor, S. R. (2000). Coding the location of the arm by sight. *Science, 290,* 1782–1786.

Graziano, M. S. A., & Gross, C. (1993). A bimodal map of space: Somatosensory receptive fields in the macaque putamen with corresponding visual receptive fields. *Experimental Brain Research, 97,* 96–109.

Graziano, M. S. A., & Gross, C. (1998). Spatial maps for the control of movement. *Current Opinion in Neurobiology, 8,* 195–201.

Grimson, W. E. L., Kikinis, R., Lolesz, F. A., & McL. Black, P. (1999). Image guided surgery. *Scientific American,* June, *280*(6), 62–69.

Gross, C. G. (1997). Leonardo da Vinci on the brain and eye. *History of Neuroscience, 3,* 347–354.

Gruzelier, J. H. (1994). Syndromes of schizophrenia and schizotypy, hemispheric imbalance and sex differences: Implications for developmental psychopathology. *International Journal of Psychophysiology, 18,* 167–178.

Gryta, M. (1998). Two drivers indicted in alleged "road rage" incident on Thruway. *Buffalo News,* August 21, B-5.

Guerin, D., & MacKinnon, D. P. (1985). An assessment of the California Child Passenger Restraint Requirement. *American Journal of Public Health, 75,* 142–144.

Hall, G. C., Bansal, A., & Lopez, I. R. (1999). Ethnicity and psychopathology: A meta-analytic review of 31 years of comparative MMPI/MMPI-2 research. *Psychological Assessment, 11,* 186–197.

Harley, T. A. (1993). Connectionist approaches to language disorders. *Aphasiology, 7,* 221–249.

Helmstadter, G. C. (1970). *Research concepts in human behavior.* New York: Appleton-Century-Crofts.

Hergenhahn, B. R. (1997). *An introduction to the history of psychology* (3rd ed.). Pacific Grove, CA: Brooks/Cole.

Hilton, M. E. (1984). The impact of recent changes in California's drinking and driving laws on fatal accident levels during the first postintervention year: An interrupted time series analysis. *Law and Society Review, 18,* 605–627.

Holden, C. (1995). Etheric archives. *Science, 267,* 1764.

Hollin, C. R. (1999). Treatment programs for offenders: Meta-analysis, "what works," and beyond. *International Journal of Law and Psychiatry, 22,* 361–372.

Hull, C. L. (1943). *Principles of behavior.* New York: Appleton-Century-Crofts.

Hull, E. M., Du, J., Lorrain, D. S., & Matuszewich, L. (1995). Extracellular dopamine in the medial preoptic area: Implications for sexual motivation and hormonal control of copulation. *Journal of Neuroscience, 15,* 7465–7471.

Hull, E. M., Lorrain, D. S., Du, J., Matuszewich, L., Lumley, L. A., Putnam, S. K., & Moses, J. (1999). Hormone–neurotransmitter interactions in the control of sexual behavior. *Behavioural Brain Research, 105,* 105–116.

Hunt, M. M. (1997). *How science takes stock: The story of meta-analysis.* New York: Russell Sage Foundation.

Hunter, J. E., & Schmidt, F. L. (1990). *Methods of meta–analysis: Correcting error and bias in research findings.* Newbury Park, CA: Sage.

Hyman, R. (1964). *The nature of psychological inquiry.* Upper Saddle River, NJ: Prentice Hall.

Irvin, J., Bowers, C., Dunn, M., & Wang, M. C. (1999). Efficacy of relapse prevention: A meta-analytic review. *Journal of Consulting and Clinical Psychology, 67,* 563–570.

Jacob, T., Tennenbaum, D., Seilhamer, R. A., & Bargrel, K. (1994). Reactivity effects during naturalistic observation of distressed and non-distressed families. *Journal of Family Psychology, 8,* 354–363.

Jacobson, J. W., Mulick, J. A., & Schwartz, A. A. (1995). A history of facilitated communication: Science, pseudoscience, and antiscience science working group on facilitated communication. *American Psychologist, 50,* 750–765.

Johnson, B., & Eagly, A. (2000). Quantitative synthesis of social psychological research. In H. Weiss & C. Judd (Eds.), *Handbook of research methods in social and personality psychology* (pp. 496–528). New York: Cambridge University Press.

Kasabov, N. K., & Shishkov, S. I. (1993). A connectionist production system with partial match and its use for approximate reasoning. Special issue: Architectures for integrating neural and symbolic processes. Connection science. *Journal of Neural Computing, Artificial Intelligence, and Cognitive Research, 5,* 275–305.

Katsikitis, M. (1997). The classification of facial expressions of emotion: A multidimensional scaling approach. *Perception, 26,* 613–626.

Kazdin, A. E. (1998). *Research design in clinical psychology* (3rd ed.). Boston: Allyn & Bacon.

Keith, A. (1954). Darwin and the "Origin of Species." In H. Shapley, S. Rapport, & H. Wright (Eds.), *A treasury of science* (pp. 437–446). New York: Harper & Brothers.

Kendler, H. H. (1993). Psychology and the ethics of social policy. *American Psychologist, 48,* 1046–1053.

Keppel, G. (1991). *Design and analysis: A research handbook.* Upper Saddle River, NJ: Prentice Hall.

Kerlinger, F. N. (1992). *Foundations of behavioral research* (3rd ed.). Fort Worth, TX: Harcourt Brace.

Kety, S. S., Rosenthal, D., Wender, P. H., & Schulsinger, F. (1968). The types and prevalence of mental illness in the biological and adoptive families of adopted schizophrenics. In D. Rosenthal & S. S. Kety (Eds.), *The transmission of schizophrenia* (pp. 345–362). Oxford: Pergamon.

Klahr, D., & Simon, H. A. (2001). What have psychologists (and others) discovered about the process of scientific discovery? *Current Directions in Psychological Science, 10,* 75–79.

Koegel, R. L., & Koegel, L. K. (1995). *Teaching children with autism: Strategies for initiating positive interactions and improving learning opportunities.* Baltimore, MD: Paul H. Brookes.

Korfine, L., & Lenzenweger, M. F. (1995). The taxonicity of schizotypy: A replication. *Journal of Abnormal Psychology, 104,* 26–31.

Korn, J. H. (1997). *Illusions of reality: A history of deception in social psychology.* New York: State University of New York Press.

Kratochwill, T. R. (Ed.). (1978). *Single-subject research: Strategies for evaluating change.* New York: Academic Press.

Kruskal, J. B., & Wish, M. (1978). *Multidimensional scaling.* Beverly Hills, CA: Sage.

Kwapil, T. R. (1998). Social anhedonia as a predictor of the development of schizophrenia-spectrum disorders. *Journal of Abnormal Psychology, 107,* 558–565.

Lang, A. R., & Sibrel, P. A. (1989). Psychological perspectives on alcohol consumption and interpersonal aggression: The potential role of individual differences in alcohol-related criminal violence. *Criminal Justice and Behavior, 16,* 299–324.

Lavie, P. (2001). Sleep–wake as a biological rhythm. *Annual Review of Psychology, 52,* 277–303.

Lepine, J. P., Gastpar, M., Mendlewicz, J., & Tylee, A. (1997). Depression in the community: The first pan-European study DEPRES (Depression Research in European Society). *International Clinical Psychopharmacology, 12,* 19–29.

Levine, A. G. (1982). *The Love Canal: Science, politics and people.* Lexington, MA: D. C. Heath.

Levine, M., & Howe, B. (1985). The penetration of social science into legal culture. *Law and Policy, 7,* 173–198.

Levine, M., & Wallach, L. (2002). *Psychological problems, social issues, and law.* Boston: Allyn & Bacon.

Levy, K. (1980). A Monte Carlo study of analysis of covariance under violations of the assumptions of normality and equal regression slopes. *Educational and Psychological Measurement, 40,* 835–840.

Light, R. J., & Pillemer, D. B. (1984). *Summing up: The science of reviewing research.* Cambridge, MA: Harvard University Press.

Lilienfeld, S. O. (1998). Pseudoscience in contemporary clinical psychology: What it is and what we can do about it. *Clinical Psychologist, 51*(4), 3–9.

Loehlin, J. C. (1992). *Latent variable models: An introduction to factor, path, and structural analyses* (2nd ed.). Mahwah, NJ: Erlbaum.

Loftus, E. F., & Hoffman, H. G. (1989). Misinformation and memory: The creation of new memories. *Journal of Experimental Psychology: General, 118,* 100–104.

Loftus, E. F., & Ketcham, K. (1991). *Witness for the defense: The accused, the eye witness, and the expert who puts memory on trial.* New York: St. Martin's Press.

Loftus, E. F., & Ketcham, K. (1994). *The myth of repressed memory: False memories and allegations of sexual abuse.* New York: St. Martin's Press.

Loftus, E. F., & Polage, D. C. (1999). Repressed memories: When are they real? How are they false? *Psychiatric Clinics of North America, 22,* 61–70.

Longnecker, M. P., Harper, J. M., & Kim, S. (1997). Eating frequency in the nationwide food consumption survey (U.S.A) 1987–1988. *Appetite, 29,* 55–59.

Lord, F. M. (1967). A paradox in the interpretation of group differences. *Psychological Bulletin, 68,* 304–305.

Lovaas, O. I. (1973). *Behavioral treatment of autistic children.* Morristown, NJ: General Learning Press.

Lovaas, O. I. (1996). The UCLA young autism model of service delivery. In C. Maurice (Ed.), *Behavioral intervention for young children with autism* (pp. 241–250). Austin, TX: Pro–Ed.

Lubinski, D., & Benbow, C. P. (1992). Gender differences in abilities and preferences among the gifted: Implications for the math–science pipeline. *Current Directions in Psychological Science, 1,* 61–66.

Lubow, R. E., & De la Casa, G. (2002). Latent inhibition as a function of schizotypality and gender: implications for schizophrenia. *Biological Psychology, 59,* 69–86.

Lynn, P. (2001). The impact of incentives on response rates to personal interview surveys: Role and perceptions of interviewers. *International Journal of Public Opinion Research, 13,* 326–336.

Maddox, J. (1999). The unexpected science to come. *Scientific American. 281,* 6, 62–67.

Markowski, V. P., Eaton, R. C., Lumley, L. A., Moses, J., & Hull, E. M. (1994). AD_1 agonist in the MPOA facilitates copulation in male rats. *Pharmacology Biochemistry and Behavior, 47,* 483–486.

Marlatt, G. A., Demming, B., & Reid, J. B. (1973). Loss of control drinking in alcoholics: An experimental analogue. *Journal of Abnormal Psychology, 81,* 233–241.

Martin, P. R., & Bateson, P. P. G. (1993). *Measuring behavior: An introductory guide* (2nd ed.). Cambridge: Cambridge University Press.

Maxwell, J. A. (1996). *Qualitative research design: An interactive approach.* Thousand Oaks, CA: Sage.

McCrae, R. R., & Costa, P. T., Jr. (1987). Validation of the five-factor model of personality across instruments and observers. *Journal of Personality and Social Psychology, 52,* 81–90.

McCrae, R. R., & Costa, P. T., Jr. (1999). A five-factor theory of personality. In L. A. Pervin & O. P. John (Eds.), *Handbook of personality: Theory and research* (pp. 139–153). New York: Guilford.

McGrew, W. C. (1992). *Chimpanzee material culture.* Cambridge: Cambridge University Press.

McGuire, W. J. (1997). Creative hypothesis generating in psychology: Some useful heuristics. *Annual Review of Psychology, 48,* 1–30.

McKay, D., Todaro, J. F., Neziroglu, F., & Yaryura-Tobias, J. A. (1996). Evaluation of a naturalistic maintenance program in the treatment of obsessive-compulsive disorder: A preliminary investigation. *Journal of Anxiety Disorders, 10,* 211–217.

McKoon, G., & Ratcliff, R. (1998). Memory-based language processing: Psycholinguistic research in the 1990s. *Annual Review of Psychology, 49,* 25–42.

Meacham, J. A. (1994). Discussions by e-mail: Experiences from a large class on multiculturalism. *Liberal Education, 80,* 36–39.

Meacham, J. A. (1995). E-mail discussions in a large class. *Interface* (UB Computing and Information Technology Newsletter), *26* (6, January/February). Accessible through e-mail by sending the following message to *listserv@uvbm.cc.buffalo.edu:* Get meacham.v26i0al Interface.

Mednick, S. A., & Schulsinger, F. (1968). Some powerful characteristics related to breakdown in children with schizophrenic mothers. In D. Rosenthal & S. S. Kety (Eds.), *The transmission of schizophrenia* (pp. 267–291). Oxford: Pergamon.

Meehl, P. E. (1990). Toward an integrated theory of schizotaxia, schizotypy, and schizophrenia. *Journal of Personality Disorders, 4,* 1–99.

Meredith, R. (1996). Man is guilty of murder in death after bridge dispute. *New York Times,* April 30, Sect. A, p. 16.

Messer, S. C., & Gross, A. M. (1995). Childhood depression and family interaction: A naturalistic observation study. *Journal of Clinical Child Psychology, 24,* 77–88.

Meyer, T. D., & Hautzinger, M. (2001). Hypomanic personality, social anhedonia and impulsive nonconformity: Evidence for familial aggregation? *Journal of Personality Disorders, 15,* 281–299.

Michell, J. (1986). Measurement scales and statistics: A clash of paradigms. *Psychological Bulletin, 87,* 564–567.

Milbrath, L. W., Hausbeck, K. M., & Enright, S. M. (1991). *An inquiry into environmental education: Levels of knowledge, awareness and concern among New York State high school students.* Unpublished technical report. Buffalo: State University of New York.

Miller, G., & Dingwall, R. (Eds.). (1997). *Context and method in qualitative research.* Thousand Oaks, CA: Sage.

Miller, N. E. (1971). *Neal E. Miller: Selected papers.* Chicago: Aldine Atherton.

Miller, N. E. (1985). The value of behavioral research with animals. *American Psychologist, 40,* 423–440.

Milton, J., & Wiseman, R. (1999). Does Psi exist? Lack of replication of an anomalous process of information transfer. *Psychological Bulletin, 125,* 387–391.

Morgan, D. L., & Morgan, R. K. (2001). Single-participant research design: Bringing science to managed care. *American Psychologist, 56,* 119–127.

Morrison, A. R. (2001). A scientist's perspective on the ethics of using animals in behavioral research. In M. E. Carroll & J. B. Overmier (Eds.), *Animal research and human health: Advancing human welfare through behavioral science* (pp. 341–356). Washington, DC: American Psychological Association.

Moses, J., Loucks, J. A., Watson, H. L., Matuszewich, L., and Hull, E. M. (1995). Dopaminergic drugs in the medial preoptic area and nucleus accumbens: Effects on motor activity, sexual motivation, and sexual performance. *Pharmacology, Biochemistry, and Behavior, 51,* 681–686.

Mukerjee, M. (1997). Trends in animal research. *Scientific American, 276*(2), 86–93.

Murray, T. A. (1996). *The worth of a child.* Berkeley, CA: University of California Press.

Myers, J. L. (1972). *Fundamentals of experimental design* (2nd ed.). Boston: Allyn & Bacon.

Myers, J. L., & Well, A. D. (1995). *Research design and statistical analysis.* Mahwah, NJ: Erlbaum.

Nagel, E. (1948). The development of modern science. In J. L. Blau, J. Buchler, & G. T. Matthews (Eds.), *Chapters in western civilization* (Vol. 1, pp. 241–284). New York: Columbia University Press.

National Institutes of Health. (1994). *Preparation and maintenance of higher mammals during neuroscience experiments.* NIH Publication No. 91–3207. Bethesda, MD: National Eye Institute.

National Institutes of Health. (1995). *Guidelines for the conduct of research involving human subjects.* Bethesda, MD: Author.

National Institutes of Health. (1996). *O.P.R.R. Public Health Service Policy on Humane Care and Use of Laboratory Animals.* Rockville, MD: NIH Office for Protection from Research Risks.

National Institutes of Health. (1998). *Policies and Guidelines on the inclusion of children as participants in research involving human subjects.* Bethesda, MD: Author.

Neisser, U. (1976). *Cognition and reality.* San Francisco: W. H. Freeman.

Neisser, U., & Harsch, N. (1992). Phantom flashbulbs: False recollection of hearing the news about *Challenger.* In E. Winograd & U. Neisser (Eds.), *Affect and accuracy in recall: Studies of "flashbulb" memories* (pp. 9–31). New York: Cambridge University Press.

Nelson, G. (1970). [Interview.] In S. Rosner & I. E. Abt (Eds.), *The creative experience* (pp. 251–268). New York: Grossman.

Nunn, J., & Peters, E. (2001). Schizotypy and patterns of lateral asymmetry on hemisphere-specific language tasks. *Psychiatry Research, 103,* 179–192.

Nunnally, J. C., & Bernstein, I. H. (1993). *Psychometric theory* (3rd ed.). New York: McGraw-Hill.

Oakes, M. (1986). *Statistical inference: A commentary for the social and behavioral sciences.* New York: Wiley.

Oaksford, M., & Chater, N. (Eds.) (1998). *Rational models of cognition.* New York: Oxford University Press.

O'Carroll, P. W., Loftin, C., Waller, J. B., McDowall, D., et al. (1991). Preventing homicide: An evaluation of the efficacy of a Detroit gun ordinance. *American Journal of Public Health, 81,* 576–581.

Oppel, F. (Ed.). (1987). *Early flight: From balloons to biplanes.* Secaucus, NJ: Castle.

Oppenheimer, J. R. (1956). Analogy in science. *American Psychologist, 11,* 127–135.

Orne, M. T. (1962). On the social psychology of the psychological experiment: With particular reference to demand characteristics and their implications. *American Psychologist, 17,* 776–783.

Orwin, R. G. (1997). Twenty-one years old and counting: The interrupted time series comes of age. In E. Chelimsky & W. R. Shadish (Eds.), *Evaluation for the 21st century: A handbook* (pp. 443–465). Thousand Oaks, CA: Sage.

Osberg, T. M., & Raulin, M. L. (1989). Networking as a tool for career advancement among academic psychologists. *Teaching of Psychology, 16,* 26–28.

Park, R. L. (1999). *The road from foolishness to fraud.* New York: Oxford University Press.

Parker, A. J., & Newsome, W. T. (1998). Sense and the single neuron: Probing the physiology of perception. *Annual Review of Neuroscience, 21,* 227–278.

Patterson, D. A. (1995). Microprocessors in 2020. *Scientific American. 273* (3):62, Sept.

Pauling, L. (1981). Cited in A. J. Bachrach, *Psychological research: An introduction* (4th ed., p. 3). New York: Random House.

Pearce, J. M., & Bouton, M. E. (2001). Theories of associative learning in animals. *Annual Review of Psychology, 52,* 111–139.

Pelham, W. E. (1994). *Attention deficit hyperactivity disorder.* Colloquium presented at the State University of New York at Buffalo (November 3).

Pelham, W. E., Murphy, D. A., Vannatta, K., Milich, R., Licht, B. G., Gnagy, E. M., Greenslade, K. E., Greiner, A. R., & Vodde-Hamilton, M. (1992). Methylphenidate and attributions in boys with attention-deficit hyperactivity disorder. *Journal of Consulting and Clinical Psychology, 60,* 282–292.

Penrose, L. S., & Penrose, P. R. (1958). Impossible objects: A special type of visual. The British Psychological Society. *British Journal of Psychology, 49,* 31–33.

Phillips, D. P. (1983). The impact of mass media violence on U.S. homicides. *American Sociological Review, 48,* 560–568.

Phillips, K. A. (1996). *The broken mirror: Understanding and treating body dysmorphic disorder.* New York: Oxford University Press.

Pierce, K., & Schriebman, L. (1997). Multiple peer use of pivotal response training social behaviors of classmates with autism: Results from trained and untrained peers. *Journal of Applied Behavior Analysis, 30,* 157–160,

Plaut, D. C., & Shallice, T. (1993). Deep dyslexia: A case study of connectionist neuropsychology. *Cognitive Neuropsychology, 10,* 377–500.

Popper, K. R. (1959). *The logic of scientific discovery.* New York: Basic Books.

Posavac, E. J., & Carey, R. G. (1997). *Program evaluation: Methods and case studies* (5th ed.). Upper Saddle River, NJ: Prentice Hall.

Prilleltensky, I. (1994). Psychology and social ethics. *American Psychologist, 49,* 966–967.

Pruitt, D. G., Parker, J. C., & Mikolic, J. M. (1997). Escalation as a reaction to persistent annoyance. *International Journal of Conflict Management, 8,* 252–270.

Putnam, S. K., Du, J., Sato, S., & Hull, E. M. (2001). Testosterone restoration of copulatory behavior correlates with medial preoptic dopamine release in castrated male rats. *Hormones and Behavior, 39,* 216–224.

Ramey, C. T. (1995, June). *Biology and experience codetermine intellectual development: Beyond additive models.* Part of the Presidential Symposium entitled "Beyond the Bell Curve: Genes, Intelligence and Achievement in Perspective" presented at the Annual Convention of the American Psychological Society, New York.

RAND Corporation. (1955). *A million random digits.* Glencoe, IL: Free Press of Glencoe.

Raulin, M. L. (1998, February). *Making a party of 400 seem intimate: Using an e-mail discussion network in Introductory Psychology.* Paper presented at the Eastern Psychological Association Convention, Boston.

Raulin, M. L. (2003). *Abnormal psychology.* Boston: Allyn & Bacon.

Raulin, M. L., deBeaumont, S. M., Brenner, V., & Vetter, C. J. (1995, June). *Comparing outcome of psychological/psychiatric intervention in managed care and traditional health insurance environments.* Poster presented at the Annual Convention of the Association of Applied and Preventive Psychology, whose Convention is held jointly with the American Psychological Society, New York.

Raulin, M. L., Brenner, V., deBeaumont, S. M., & Vetter, C. J. (1995, November). *The impact of managed care on treatment outcome: Initial findings.* Poster presented at the annual convention of the Association for the Advancement of Behavior Therapy, Washington, DC.

Raulin, M. L., & Graziano, A. M. (1995). Quasi-experiments and correlational studies. In A. M. Coleman (Ed.), *Psychological research methods and statistics* (pp. 1122–1141). London: Longman.

Raulin, M. L., & Lilienfeld, S. O. (1999). Research strategies for studying psychopathology. In T. Millon, P. H. Blaney, & R. D. Davis (Eds.), *Oxford textbook of psychopathology* (pp. 49–78). New York: Oxford University Press.

Reed, J. G., & Baxter, P. M. (1992). *Library use: A handbook of psychology* (2nd ed.). Washington DC: American Psychological Association.

Reese, W. L. (1996). *Dictionary of philosophy and religion: Eastern and Western thought.* Atlantic Highlands, NJ: Humanities Press.

Reynolds, C. F., III, Degenholtz, H., Parker, L. S., Schulberg, H. C., Mulsant, B. H., Post, E., & Rollman, B. (2001). Treatment as usual (TAU) control practices in the PROSPECT study: Managing the interaction and tension between research design and ethics. *International Journal of Geriatric Psychiatry, 16,* 602–608.

Roberts, F. S. (1979). *Measurement theory with applications to decision-making utility and the social sciences.* Reading, MA: Addison-Wesley.

Roberts, R. M. (1989). *Serendipity: Accidental discoveries in science.* New York: Wiley.

Rohsenow, D. J., & Marlatt, G. A. (1981). The balanced placebo design: Methodological considerations. *Addictive Behavior, 6,* 107–122.

Rosenhan, D. L. (1973). On being sane in insane places. *Science, 179,* 250–258.

Rosenthal, R. (1976). *Experimenter effects in behavioral research.* New York: Halsted Press.

Rosenthal, R. (1994). Science and ethics in conducting, analyzing, and reporting psychological research. *Psychological Science, 5,* 127–134.

Rosenthal, R. (1998). Meta-analysis: Concepts, corollaries, and controversies. In J. Adair & D. Belanger (Eds.), *Advances in psychological science, Vol. I: Social, personal, and cultural aspects* (pp. 371–384). Hove, England: Psychology Press/Erlbaum.

Rosenthal, R., & Fode, K. L. (1963a). The effect of experimenter bias on the performance of the albino rat. *Behavioral Science, 8,* 183–189.

Rosenthal, R., & Fode, K. L. (1963b). Three experiments in experimenter bias. *Psychological Reports, 12,* 491–511.

Rosnow, R. L., & Rosnow, M. (1998). *Writing papers in psychology: A study guide* (4th ed.). Pacific Grove, CA: Brooks/Cole.

Rossi, P. H., Wright, J. D., & Anderson, A. B. (1985). *Handbook of survey research.* New York: Academic Press.

Rubin, J. Z., Pruitt, D. G., & Kim, S. (1994). *Social conflict, escalation, stalemate, and settlement.* New York: McGraw-Hill.

Rupley, S., & Clyman, J. (1995, September 12). P6: The next step. *PC Magazine, 14*(15), 102–118.

Samson, S., Zatorre, R. J., & Ramsey, J. O. (1997). Multidimensional scaling of synthetic musical timbre: Perception of spectral and temporal characteristics. *Canadian Journal of Experimental Psychology, 51,* 307–315.

Schmidt, F. L. (1992). What do data really mean? Research findings, meta-analysis, and cumulative knowledge in psychology. *American Psychologist, 47,* 1173–1181.

Schrage, M. (1991). Computer tools for thinking in tandem. *Science, 253,* 505–507.

Schulz, D. P., & Schulz, S. E. (2000). *A history of modern psychology* (7th ed.). Fort Worth, TX: Harcourt Brace.

Schuman, H., & Kalton, G. (1985). Survey methods. In G. Lindzey & E. Aronson (Eds.), *The handbook of social psychology* (3rd ed., Vol. 1, pp. 635–698). New York: Random House.

Seidenberg, M. S. (1993). A connectionist modeling approach to word recognition and dyslexia. *Psychological Science, 4,* 299–304.

Seligman, M. E. P. (1974). Depression and learned helplessness. In R. J. Friedman & M. J. Katz (Eds.), *The psychology of depression: Contemporary theory and research.* Washington, DC: Winston-Wiley.

Shastri, L. (1999). Advances in SHRUTI—a neurally motivated model of relational knowledge representation and rapid inference using temporal synchrony. *Applied Intelligence, 11,* 78–108.

Shavelson, R. J. (1996). *Statistical reasoning for the behavioral sciences* (3rd ed.). Boston: Allyn & Bacon.

Sidman, M. (1960). *Tactics of scientific research: Evaluating scientific data in psychology.* New York: Basic Books.

Siekmeier, P. J., & Hoffman, R. E. (2002). Enhanced semantic priming in schizophrenia: a computer model based on excessive pruning of local connections in association cortex. *British Journal of Psychiatry, 180,* 345–350.

Silverstein, S. M., Raulin, M. L., Pristach, E. A., & Pomerantz, J. R. (1992). Perceptual organization and schizotypy. *Journal of Abnormal Psychology, 101,* 265–270.

Simonsen, E., & Parnas, J. (1993). Personality research in Denmark. *Journal of Personality Disorders, 7,* 187–195.

Skinner, B. F. (1938). *The behavior of organisms.* New York: Appleton-Century-Crofts.

Skinner, B. F. (1956). A case history in scientific method. *American Psychologist, 11,* 221–233.

Skinner, B. F. (1969). *Contingencies of reinforcement: A theoretical analysis.* New York: Appleton-Century-Crofts.

Skinner, B. F. (1972). *Cumulative record: A selection of papers* (3rd ed.). New York: Appleton-Century-Crofts.

Skinner, B. F. (1990, August). *Skinner's keynote address: Lifetime scientific contribution remarks.* Presentation at the annual convention of the American Psychological Association, Boston. (Available on audio- or videocassette from the American Psychological Association Continuing Education Section.)

Snowling, M., Hulme, C., & Goulandris, N. (1994). Word recognition in developmental dyslexia: A connectionist interpretation. *Quarterly Journal of Experimental Psychology: Human Experimental Psychology, 47,* 895–916.

Society for Neuroscience. (1991). *Handbook of the use of animals in research.* Washington, DC: Author.

Society for Neuroscience. (1995). *Membership directory.* Washington, DC: Author.

Solomon, R. L. (1949). An extension of control group design. *Psychological Bulletin, 46,* 137–150.

Spearman, C. E. (1904). "General intelligence" objectively determined and measured. *American Journal of Psychology, 15,* 200–292.

Spitzer, R. L. (1975). On pseudoscience in science, logic in remission, and psychiatric diagnoses: A critique of Rosenhan's "On being sane in insane places." *Journal of Abnormal Psychology, 84,* 442–452.

Stein, D. J., & Hollander, E. (1994). A neural network approach to obsessive–compulsive disorder. *Journal of Mind and Behavior, 15,* 223–237.

Stein, D. J., & Ludik, J. (Eds.) (1998). *Neural networks and psychopathology: Connectionist models in practice and research.* Cambridge, England: Cambridge University Press.

Sternberg, R. I., & Lubart, T. I. (1992). Buy low and sell high: An investment approach to creativity. *Current Directions in Psychological Science, 1,* 1–15.

Stevens, J. R. (1997). Anatomy of schizophrenia revisited. *Schizophrenia Bulletin, 23,* 373–383.

Stevens, S. S. (1946). On the theory of scales of measurement. *Science, 103,* 677–680.

Stevens, S. S. (1957). On the psychophysical law. *Psychological Review, 64,* 153–181.

Stolzenberg, L., & D'Alessio, S. J. (1997). "Three strikes and you're out": The impact of California's new mandatory sentencing law on serious crime rates. *Crime and Delinquency, 43,* 457–469.

Strayer, D. L., & Johnson, W. A. (2000). Driven to distraction: Dual-task studies of simulated driving and conversing on a cellular telephone. *Psychological Science, 12,* 462–466.

Strunk, W., Jr., White, E. B., & Angell, R. (1999). *The elements of style* (3rd ed.). Upper Saddle River, NJ: Prentice Hall.

Sussman, S., Hahn, G., Dent, C. W., Clyde, W., & Stacy, A. (1993). Naturalistic observation of adolescent tobacco use. *International Journal of the Addictions, 28,* 803–811.

Sutton, S. K., & Davidson, R. J. (1997). Prefrontal brain asymmetry: A biological substrate of the behavioral approach and inhibition systems. *Psychological Science, 8,* 204–210.

Thagard, P. (1998). Ulcers and bacteria: Discovery and acceptance. *Studies in the History and Philosophy of biology and biomedical science, 9,* 107–136.

Tinbergen, N. (1951). *The study of instinct.* London: Oxford University Press.

Tinbergen, N. (1963). *The herring gull's world.* London: Collins.

Tomlinson, T. (1990). *Case study: conceiving children to use for tissue transplantation.* East Lansing, MI: Medical Humanities Report, Michigan State University, Spring Center for Ethics and Humanities in the Life Sciences.

Toomey, J., & Adams, L. A. (1995). Naturalistic observation of children with autism: Evidence for intersubjectivity. In L. L. Sperry & P. A. Smiley (Eds.), *Exploring young children's concepts of self and other through conversation. New directions in child development, No. 69* (pp. 75–89). San Francisco: Jossey-Bass.

Torrey, E. F., Taylor, E. H., Bracha, H. S., Bowler, A. E., McNeil, T. F., Rawlings, R. R., Quinn, P. O., Bigelow, L. B., Rickler, K., Sjöström, K., Higgins, E. S., & Gottesman, I. I. (1994). Prenatal origin of schizophrenia in a subgroup of discordant monozygotic twins. *Schizophrenia Bulletin, 20,* 423–432.

Tufte, E. R. (1997). *Visual explanations: images and quantities, evidence and narrative.* Cheshire, CT: Graphics Press.

Tukey, J. W. (1977). *Exploratory data analysis.* Reading, MA: Addison-Wesley.

Ulrich, R. E. (1991). Animal rights, animal wrongs and the question of balance. *Psychological Science, 2,* 197–201.

VandenBos, G. R. (1997, September). Electronic journals database coming soon. *APA Monitor,* available online at **www.apa.org.**

Walker, E. F., Bonsall, R., & Walder, D. J. (2002). Plasma hormones and catecholamine metabolites in monozygotic twins discordant for psychosis. *Neuropsychiatry, Neuropsychology, and Behavioral Neurology, 15,* 10–17.

Waller, N. G., & Meehl, P. E. (1998). *Multivariate taxometric procedures: Distinguishing types from continua.* Thousand Oaks, CA: Sage.

Webb, E. J., Campbell, D. T., Schwartz, R. D., & Sechrest, L. (1966). *Unobtrusive measures: Nonreactive research in the social sciences.* Chicago: Rand McNally.

Weiner, B. (1975). "On being sane in insane places": A process (attributional) analysis and critique. *Journal of Abnormal Psychology, 84,* 433–441.

Weis, L., & Fine, M. (2000). *Speed bumps: A student-friendly guide to qualitative research.* New York: Teachers' College Press.

Weitzenfeld, A., Arbib, M., & Alexander, A. (2002). *The neural simulation language: A system for brain modeling.* Cambridge, MA: MIT Press.

Wender, P. H., Kety, S. S., Rosenthal, D., Schulsinger, F., Ortmann, J., & Lunde, I. (1986). Psychiatric disorder in the biological and adoptive families of adopted individuals with affective disorders. *Archives of General Psychiatry, 43,* 923–929.

Whitehead, A. B. (1925). *Science and the modern world.* New York: Macmillan.

Whiten, A., & Boesch, C. (2001). The cultures of chimpanzees. *Scientific American, 284*(1), 60–67.

Wilson, D. (2000). Meta-analysis in alcohol and other drug abuse treatment research. *Addiction, 95* (Suppl. 3), S419–S438.

Winer, B. J. (1971). *Statistical principles in experimental design* (2nd ed.). New York: McGraw-Hill.

Wolpe, J. (1958). *Psychotherapy by reciprocal inhibition.* Stanford, CA: Stanford University Press.

Wolpe, J. (1990). *The practice of behavior therapy* (4th ed.). New York: Pergamon Press.

Woods, S. C., Schwartz, M. W., Baskin, D. G., & Seeley, R. J. (2000). Food intake and the regulation of body weight. *Annual Review of Psychology, 51,* 255–277.

Wright, A. A. (1998). Auditory list memory in rhesus monkeys. *Psychological Science, 9,* 91–98.

Zinsser, W. (1998). *On writing well* (6th ed). New York: HarperCollins.

Author Index

442

Subject Index

Note: **Boldface** pages locate figures; *Italic* pages locate tables.